War, Peace, and Human Nature

War, Peace, and Human Nature

The Convergence of Evolutionary and Cultural Views

EDITED BY

Douglas P. Fry

OXFORD
UNIVERSITY PRESS

OXFORD
UNIVERSITY PRESS

Oxford University Press is a department of the University of Oxford.
It furthers the University's objective of excellence in research, scholarship,
and education by publishing worldwide.

Oxford   New York
Auckland   Cape Town   Dar es Salaam   Hong Kong   Karachi
Kuala Lumpur   Madrid   Melbourne   Mexico City   Nairobi
New Delhi   Shanghai   Taipei   Toronto

With offices in
Argentina   Austria   Brazil   Chile   Czech Republic   France   Greece
Guatemala   Hungary   Italy   Japan   Poland   Portugal   Singapore
South Korea   Switzerland   Thailand   Turkey   Ukraine   Vietnam

Oxford is a registered trademark of Oxford University Press
in the UK and in certain other countries.

Published in the United States of America by
Oxford University Press
198 Madison Avenue, New York, NY 10016

© Oxford University Press 2013

Library of Congress Cataloging-in-Publication Data
War, peace, and human nature : the convergence of evolutionary and
cultural views / Douglas P. Fry, editor.
p. cm.
ISBN 978-0-19-985899-6 (hardcover : alk. paper)
1. War and society.   2. Peace—Social aspects.   3. Human behavior.   4. Human evolution.
5. Social evolution.   I. Fry, Douglas P., 1953–
GN497.W285 2013
303.6'6—dc23
2012016714

ISBN 978-0-19-985899-6

1 3 5 7 9 8 6 4 2
Printed in the United States of America
on acid-free paper

To Bonoboess

Contents

Foreword

FRANS B. M. DE WAAL

Not so long ago, every discussion about human evolution revolved around aggression. As if aggressive tendencies were all we had, and as if other animals had few other things to do than fight. It is perhaps not surprising that following the devastations of World War II, humans were depicted as xenophobic "killer apes"—in contrast to real apes, which were regarded as pacifists. Humans had behaved badly and science felt it needed an explanation. Popular books by Konrad Lorenz, the Austrian ethologist, and Robert Ardrey, an American journalist, made the evolutionary connections, partly based on a single puncture wound in the fossilized skull of an ancestral infant, known as the Taung Child. Its discoverer had concluded that our ancestors must have been carnivorous cannibals, an idea repackaged by Ardrey in *African Genesis* by saying that we are risen apes rather than fallen angels (Ardrey, 1961). It was only much later that others suggested that the Taung Child might have been preyed upon by a leopard or eagle.

The idea of humans as killer apes was rather curious given how little pleasure we take in lethal combat. Species-typical tendencies normally include built-in rewards. Nature has ensured that we find fulfillment in eating, sex, and nursing, all of which are required for survival and reproduction. If warfare were truly in our DNA, we should happily engage in it. Yet, soldiers report a deep revulsion to killing, and only shoot at the enemy under pressure. They end up with haunting memories. Far from being a recent phenomenon, combat trauma was already known to the ancient Greeks, such as Sophocles, who described the "divine madness" now known as Post Traumatic Stress Disorder (PTSD).

A most illuminating book in this regard is *On Killing* by Dave Grossman (1995; Hughbank & Grossman, chapter 25), who describes the elimination of others as something that does not come naturally to our species. Grossman follows in the footsteps of Leo Tolstoy, who gave us *War & Peace,* saying that he was more interested in how and why soldiers kill, and what they feel while doing so, than in how generals arrange their armies on the battlefield. The majority of soldiers, although well-armed, never kills. During World War II, only one out of every five American soldiers actually fired at the enemy. Similarly, it has been calculated that during the Vietnam War, American soldiers fired over 50,000 bullets for every enemy soldier killed. Most bullets ended up in the air.

As amply documented in Parts II and III of this volume, the evidence that we have always waged war is rather thin. During most of our prehistory, we were nomadic hunter-gatherers, which today are not particularly known for warfare. Although archeological signs of individual murder go back hundreds of thousands of years, similar evidence for warfare is lacking from before the Agricultural Revolution of about 12,000 years ago. If we go back further in time, we end up with *Ardipithecus ramidus*, a 4.4. million-year-old hominin that has been described as relatively peaceful (owing to its reduced canine teeth) compared to the chimpanzee (Lovejoy, 2009). Chimpanzees can be lethally violent, especially during territorial encounters between communities (Wilson, chapter 18). But instead of concluding from Ardipithecus' dentition that our ancestors were less war-prone than apes, the comparison should perhaps have included that other close relative of ours, the bonobo, which also has relatively small canines. Bonobos have never been reported to kill each other, neither in captivity nor in the field. They sometimes mingle across territorial borders, and are known as "make love—not war" primates for solving power issues through sexual activity (de Waal, 1997; White, Waller, & Boose, chapter 19).

Inasmuch as bonobos are genetically exactly equally similar to us as chimpanzees (Prüfer et al., 2012), there is a need to rewrite the traditional blood-soaked evolutionary scenarios of our lineage. An even more massive revision is underway in relation to cooperative tendencies. Developments in psychology, neuroscience, economics, and animal behavior have begun to question the view, dominant until a decade ago, that animal life, and by extension human nature, turns around unmitigated competition. In primatology, the counter movement started with research into conflict resolution and the value of friendships (de Waal & van Roosmalen, 1979; Smuts, 1985).

Since I was part of these early developments, let me describe how conflict resolution was first recognized in the large chimpanzee colony at the Arnhem Zoo, in the Netherlands. It happened one day when the colony was locked indoors in one of its winter halls. In the course of a charging display, the highest-ranking male fiercely attacked a female. This caused great commotion as other apes came to her defense. After the group had calmed down, an unusual silence followed, as if the apes were waiting for something to happen. This took a couple of minutes. Suddenly the entire colony burst out hooting, and one male produced rhythmic noise on metal drums stacked up in the corner of the hall. In the midst of this pandemonium, two chimpanzees kissed and embraced.

I, the observer, reflected on this sequence for hours before the term "reconciliation" came to mind. This occurred when I realized that the two embracing individuals had been the same male and female of the original fight. The very first documentation of the concept, expressed in the Dutch term "verzoening," is found in an entry of November 19th,

1975, in my handwritten Arnhem diaries. In the same month, another entry introduced the Dutch equivalent of "consolation," for reassuring body contact provided by bystanders to victims of aggression. Once recognized, both interaction patterns were seen on a daily basis. It became indeed hard to imagine that they had gone unnoticed for so long.

Numerous studies have documented postconflict reunions in monkeys and apes. The main thrust of these studies has been that primates are attracted to each other following a fight, seeking friendly contact especially with individuals with whom they enjoy a mutually beneficial relationship (de Waal, 2000). The behavioral expression of reconciliation varies per species, but in most cases its effect is restoration of the relationship to previous levels of tolerance and affiliation. Such results have been reported for a variety of macaque species as well as gorillas, bonobos, golden monkeys, mangabeys, capuchins, and so on. Most of these studies were conducted in captivity, but reconciliation has also been demonstrated in the field. Similar evidence exists for nonprimates, such as wolves, dolphins, hyenas, and elephants. Reconciliation is a common mechanism of relationship repair that, it bears noting, would be superfluous if animal social life were entirely ruled by dominance and competition (Part V of this volume).

Qualitative descriptions of spontaneous assistance among primates are abundant, ranging from bringing a mouthful of water to an incapacitated individual to slowing down travel for injured companions. Similar descriptions exist for elephants and cetaceans. The help provided can be quite costly. For example, a female chimpanzee may react to the screams of her closest associate by defending her against an aggressive male, thus taking great risk on her behalf. Such coalitions are among the best documented forms of cooperation in primatology (Harcourt & de Waal, 1992). The level of cooperation among nonhuman primates tends to be underappreciated, however, such as when it is attributed to kinship in an attempt to set it apart from human cooperation with non-relatives. According to DNA data from the field, however, most cooperative partnerships among male chimpanzees concern unrelated individuals (Langergraber, Mitani, & Vigilant, 2007). Bonobos show the same pattern. Female bonobos maintain a close social network that allows them to collectively dominate most males despite the fact that females are the migratory sex, hence largely unrelated within each community (de Waal, 1997). Our closest relatives are marked, therefore, by high levels of cooperation among non-relatives.

Expressions of empathy are common and resemble those of our own species (de Waal, 2008). In child research, for example, a family member is typically instructed to feign distress or pain, upon which touching, stroking, and close-up eye-contact by the child is interpreted as a sign of sympathetic concern. In chimpanzees, bystanders to a fight may go over to the loser and put an arm around his or her shoulders or provide calming contact. Such acts of consolation visibly reduce stress in the recipient, and show the same sex difference in children and chimpanzees, with females engaging more in it than males (Romero, Castellos, & de Waal, 2010).

We do know from studies on mice, humans, and apes that empathy is biased toward the in-group. For example, while watching videotaped yawns of members of their own species, chimpanzees join the yawns of their own group members, but not those of unfamiliar chimpanzees (Campbell & de Waal, 2011). This in-group bias makes perfect sense from an evolutionary perspective, since it is with the members of one's own group that one tends to cooperate. At the same time, however, it poses a profound challenge for the modern human world, which seeks to integrate various groups, ethnicities, and nations.

Nevertheless, empathy may be our only hope. The mechanism can be activated by individuals outside the in-group, even outside our own species, such as when we empathize with a stranded whale. This is definitely not the sort of situation for which empathy evolved in our species, yet once in existence, the application of many capacities emancipates from its original context. We might not have the problem of PTSD, nor the reluctance of military men to kill, if it weren't for empathy with all life forms, including enemy lives. So, while empathy has trouble reaching beyond the in-group, it resists political indoctrination and does not allow itself to be fully suppressed.

The present volume helps readers put human nature in perspective amidst all the pessimism we have seen over the last few decades. Not that concern about human aggression is unjustified, but it needs to be balanced with that other potential that we have, which is to make peace, get along, and develop societies based on cooperation. The idea that this is not part of human nature, that it is merely a thin moral veneer over an otherwise nasty biology, is massively contradicted by the contributions assembled here.

References

Ardrey, R. (1961). *African genesis: A personal investigation into the animal origins and nature of man*. New York: Simon & Schuster.

Campbell, M. W., and de Waal, F. B. M. (2011). Ingroup-outgroup bias in contagious yawning by chimpanzees supports link to empathy. *PLoS-ONE, 5*: e18283.

de Waal, F. B. M. (1997). *Bonobo: The forgotten ape*. Berkeley, CA: University of California Press.

de Waal, F. B. M. (2000). Primates: A natural heritage of conflict resolution. *Science, 289*, 586–590.

de Waal, F. B. M. (2008). Putting the altruism back into altruism: The evolution of empathy. *Annual Review of Psychology, 59*, 279–300.

de Waal, F. B. M., & van Roosmalen, A. (1979). Reconciliation and consolation among chimpanzees. *Behavioral Ecology & Sociobiology, 5*, 55–66.

Grossman, D. (1995). *On killing: The psychological cost of learning to kill in war and society*. New York: Back Bay Books.

Harcourt, A. H., & de Waal, F. B. M. (1992). *Coalitions and alliances in humans and other animals*. Oxford University Press, Oxford.

Langergraber, K. E., Mitani, J. C. & Vigilant, L. 2007. The limited impact of kinship on cooperation in wild chimpanzees. *Proceedings of the National Academy of Sciences, USA, 104*, 7786–7790.

Lovejoy, C. O. (2009). Reexamining human origins in light of *Ardipithecus ramidus*. *Science, 326*, 74e1–74e8.

Prüfer, K., Munch, K., Hellmann, I., Akagi, K., Miller, J. R., et al. (2012). The bonobo genome compared with the chimpanzee and human genomes. *Nature, 486* (7404), 527–531.

Romero, M. T., Castellanos, M. A., & de Waal, F. B. M. (2010). Consolation as possible expression of sympathetic concern among chimpanzees. *Proceedings of the National Academy of Sciences, USA, 107*: 12110 –12115.

Smuts, B. B. (1999 [orig. 1985]). *Sex and friendship in baboons*. Cambridge: Harvard University Press.

Acknowledgments

I am very grateful to James Cook, Editor at Oxford University Press, for his enthusiastic support of this project from its inception and for guidance of various sorts from start to finish. I also would like to thank Rebecca Clark for her friendly efficiency and help with many aspects of this project, Susie Hara for excellent copy editing, and Jashnie Jabson for steering the book smoothly through production. I am most grateful to my colleagues who have participated in this book project by providing stimulating chapters and also for putting up with my reminders and requests as delivered in my role as editor. At Åbo Akademi University, I would like to thank Ingrida Grigaitytë for her efficient and good natured help with editorial tasks. Anna Szala kindly assisted with library research pertaining to several chapters. Thanks also go out to colleagues Klas Backholm, Kaj Björkqvist, Joám Evans Pim, R. Brian Ferguson, Ingrida Grigaitytë, Sarah B. Hrdy, Sabine Mickelsson, Patrik Söderberg, Anna Szala, Peter Verbeek, Jim Welch, and Karin Österman for providing suggestions and advice of various sorts, facilitating the editing process, or for offering useful comments on one or more draft chapters. Financial backing and logistical support from the Wenner Gren Foundation for Anthropological Research, the U.S. National Science Foundation (0313670), the Lorentz Center at the University of Leiden, and Åbo Akademi University are gratefully acknowledged. The cooperation and support of Mieke Schutte, Henriette Jensenius, Martje Kruk-de Bruin, and Pauline Vincentin, all of the Lorentz Center, made a workshop on Aggression and Peacemaking co-organized with Johan van der Dennen in 2010 possible, an event that facilitated the fruitful and dynamic exchange of ideas among some of the contributors. Finally, I would like to express deep appreciation to Frans de Waal for his pivotal role in opening up the topics of conflict resolution, reconciliation, peacemaking, and empathy as areas of scientific inquiry. I am very pleased that peace themes, not only war themes, are well-represented across these chapters.

List of Contributors

David P. Barash, Department of Psychology, University of Washington.

Christopher Boehm, Departments of Biological Sciences & Anthropology, University of Southern California.

Klaree J. Boose, Department of Anthropology, University of Oregon.

Sarah F. Brosnan, Georgia State University, Department of Psychology.

Marina L. Butovskaya, Russian Academy of Sciences, Institute of Ethnology & Anthropology.

Bram Orobio de Castro, Department of Developmental Psychology, Utrecht University.

Frans B. M. de Waal, Living Links, Yerkes National Primate Research Center & Psychology Department, Emory University.

David H. Dye, Department of Earth Sciences, University of Memphis.

Kirk Endicott, Department of Anthropology, Dartmouth College.

Joám Evans Pim, Center for Global Nonkilling, Baixo A—Rianxo—Corunha—Galiza, Spain.

R. Brian Ferguson, Department of Sociology & Anthropology, Rutgers University—Newark.

Douglas P. Fry, Peace, Mediation & Conflict Research, Department of Social Sciences, Åbo Akademi University in Vasa and Bureau of Applied Research in Anthropology, University of Arizona, Tucson.

Agustín Fuentes, Department of Anthropology, University of Notre Dame.

Peter M. Gardner, Department of Anthropology, University of Missouri.

Dave Grossman, USA (ret. Lt. Col.), Director, Killology Research Group.

Jonathan Haas, The Field Museum, Chicago, IL.

Richard J. Hughbank, USA (ret. Major), CMAS, CHS-IV, Graduate Homeland Security Studies, Northwestern State University of Louisiana.

Robert L. Kelly, Department of Anthropology, University of Wyoming.

Maaike Kempes, Department of Developmental Psychology, Utrecht University.

Hanna Kokko, Centre of Excellence in Biological Interactions, Division of Evolution Ecology and Genetics, Research School of Biology, Australian National University.

Darcia Narvaez, Department of Psychology, University of Notre Dame.

Matthew Piscitelli, Department of Anthropology, University of Illinois at Chicago.

Paul Roscoe, Department of Anthropology, University of Maine.

Robert M. Sapolsky, Departments of Biological Sciences, Neurology and Neurological Sciences, and Neurosurgery, Stanford University and Institute of Primate Research, National Museums of Kenya, Nairobi, Kenya.

Liesbeth Sterck, Behavioural Biology, Utrecht University.

Robert W. Sussman, Department of Anthropology, Washington University.

Anna Szala, Psychology Department, Kazimierz Wielki University, Poland.

Robert Tonkinson, Anthropology & Sociology, School of Social & Cultural Studies, The University of Western Australia.

Peter Verbeek, Miyazaki International College, Japan.

Michel T. Waller, Department of Anthropology, University of Oregon.

Frances J. White, Department of Anthropology, University of Oregon.

Michael L. Wilson, Department of Anthropology & Department of Ecology, Evolution and Behavior, University of Minnesota.

War, Peace, and Human Nature

1

War, Peace, and Human Nature

The Challenge of Achieving Scientific Objectivity

Douglas P. Fry

In this chapter, I will highlight some of the salient points in each of the book's five topical sections. More than that, some philosophy of science necessarily enters the picture. When the central topic involves human nature, how could it be otherwise? I hope to demonstrate with concrete recent examples that cultural bias significantly distorts the study of peace and war. Rather than relax the striving for objectivity and adherence to the canons of science, the way to address this serious problem, I suggest, is to develop a greater awareness of the powerful grasp that cultural beliefs have on research related to peace and war, strive for self-awareness of one's own beliefs and biases regarding this topic, and apply the rigors of well-practiced science to one's own research and to the assessment of the findings of others.

Since most people grow up in one particular cultural setting, it is all too easy to assume that what is true for us is also applicable elsewhere. Herein lies one aspect of the cultural bias trap: over-generalizing from one culture onto humanity before gathering comparative data. Edwin Burrows (1963, p. 421) expresses this idea nicely when he writes "We generally assume that we know . . . what is universally human. But a little scrutiny will show that such conclusions are based only on experience with one culture, our own. We assume that what is familiar, unless obviously shaped by special conditions, is universal." To take Burrows (1963) seriously, understanding human nature must lead us beyond our own cultural traditions, practices, and beliefs that too often are just taken as given truths immune from scrutiny.

Specifically, when it comes to human nature, war, and peace, Burrows' warning should be written in red ink, perhaps surrounded with a few flashing lights, because Western cultural tradition has been broadcasting a most dubious answer to questions of war, peace, and human nature for two millennia. In *The Western Illusion of Human Nature*, Sahlins (2008) documents a violent and misanthropic theme, from Hesiod and Thucydides of ancient

Greece, to St. Augustine and St. Thomas, Machiavelli and his contemporaries, Hobbes himself of course, on through to the views of the US Founding Fathers as reflected in the *Federalist Papers* and in more recent years in evolutionary psychology with its insistence that war is millions of years old, murderers live next door, and killers-have-more-kids (see Miklikowska & Fry 2012). Sahlins (2008:52) notes that through the strapping of this view to religious dogma, "Original Sin pretty much sealed the deal. . . . Endless desires for the flesh would lead to endless war: within men, between men, and with Nature." This view of human nature is not based on scientific research, rather, it is part of a cultural belief system passed down over generations, integrated into religious and historical narratives, reinforced in daily conversations, recounted in drama and literature, expressed in political discourse, bolstered by cultural symbols and cherished values, and reproduced as it is learned and absorbed by the young (chapter 6). As such, this Western view of human nature resides at the level of assumptions and presumptions in people's minds as something they just "know" to be true (chapter 27). How could the practice of science remain immune from such a threat to objectivity in the study of war and peace?

When we talk of human nature, some consistency is implied in the "personality" or "character" of the species overall, some foundational elements of humanness that we would expect to find across cultural circumstances. As behavioral traits that more or less arise naturally regardless of whether one is raised in New York City, comes of age in Samoa, or grows up in New Guinea, we might infer that such features, whatever they might be, would reflect evolved predispositions that have served survival and reproductive functions in the evolutionary past—that they reflect adaptive behavioral traits, in other words. However, before assuming adaptive functions, we must keep in mind that the widespread distribution of a trait across cultures—reliance on agriculture, for example, or the practice of war—could be due to culture contact and diffusion rather than evolutionary function.

How do we tell if a behavioral trait reflects human nature? I suggest we employ a hierarchy of evaluation. First, remembering Burrows (1963), we should ask: is the behavior truly universal? If so, then second, does it reflect culture contact and diffusion, as for example the contemporary spread of cell phone usage around the planet? Third, if diffusion seems unlikely, does the behavior make sense in relation to the conditions under which the species has evolved? Here we also need to consider if we are really talking about behavioral traits of individuals that therefore could have been susceptible to the forces of natural selection and not a social institution per se such as slavery or agriculture. Once focused on the behaviors of individuals, we can consider the design of the behavior in relationship to possible fitness consequences under environmental conditions similar to those in which the species evolved (chapter 20)—that is, in the Environment of Evolutionary Adaptiveness (EEA). In other words, before we dash off to proclaim a widespread trait to reflect human nature, it would be sensible to consider whether a reasonable argument can be made that the behavioral trait in question seems designed to contribute to survival and reproduction in the context of the ancestral evolutionary environment, the EEA, of the species (chapter 20).

How do we make inferences about the EEA? There are at least three ways: the findings of archaeology itself, ethnographic analogy or the studying of extant cultures to glean insights about social life in prehistory, and primate analogy or the studying of nonhuman primates to gain an understanding about human behavior via phylogenetic comparisons (chapter 20). For example, a comparative evolutionary perspective suggests that the strong close ties apparent among unrelated female bonobos and their practice of mating often with multiple males may have evolved to counter acts of male infanticide (chapter 19; de Waal 1997, pp. 118–123). Turning to humans, a tendency to engage in reciprocal food sharing beyond the immediate family can be proposed as an evolved adaptive behavior. First, it is widespread across cultures and would seem to be independent of cultural diffusion. Second, the fact that meat sharing is ubiquitous in the ancestral social type, nomadic band society, suggests a similar practice in the EEA. Third, the reciprocal exchange of food, especially meat, in a nomadic forager economy can have survival and reproductive fitness benefits over a nonsharing strategy as analyzed through both direct and indirect reciprocity and social network models (Apicella, Marlowe, Fowler, & Christakis, 2012; chapter 5; Nowak, 2011; Trivers, 1971). Returning to war, it is insufficient to make a case that participating in warfare is an evolved adaptation solely on the basis of warfare being widespread ethnographically and during the recent Holocene timeframe without also demonstrating how *within a plausible reconstruction of the human EEA* fitness benefits in terms of survival and reproduction would have accrued to individuals who engaged in life-threatening warring behavior in comparison to those who did not.

Following upon a discussion in Part I of ecological and evolutionary models, Part II of the book examines what archaeology shows about war, peace, and human nature. Part III facilitates the use of a specialized type of ethnographic analogy, nomadic forager analogy, to glean insights about violence, war, conflict management, and peace in the past and thus also about human nature. Part IV takes a comparative view and offers some insights on human nature based on primate studies. Finally, Part V takes a new direction in the investigation of war, peace, and human nature by zooming in on a long neglected topic: The ubiquitous exercising of restraint against killing and other forms of serious violence.

As we go along, I will point out some major issues related to each of the book sections, but more than this, I wish to highlight how a great deal of contemporary thinking about war, peace, and human nature falls markedly short of objective science. In the halls of academia, unfortunately, bias is alive and well. As scientists and scholars, we could use more self-reflection and vigilance. Are deeply ingrained cultural beliefs about human nature currently affecting our research on peace and war? Disturbing as it may be, I suggest that the answer is "yes."

Part One: Ecological and Evolutionary Models

The chapters in this section help to set the context for much that follows. Several themes can be mentioned. David Barash (chapter 2), Peter Verbeek (chapter 4), and Agustín Fuentes (chapter 5) mention the key concepts of ultimate and proximate causality. Ultimate causes relate to evolution and genetics in comparison to more situational proximate causes. A key point is that different kinds of explanations need not be placed in opposition with others. These different types of explanations are addressing different types of questions.

Both David Barash (chapter 2) and Hanna Kokko (chapter 3) discuss the level of selection issue and briefly review individual selection, kin selection, and group selection models. Hanna Kokko presents background on the group selection controversy. One implication is that restrained or limited patterns in animal fighting need not be viewed as altruistic behavior. As both Barash and Kokko point out, game theory shows that altruism and cooperation can evolve via individual selection. These authors consider some of the implications of game theory for understanding human aggression and cooperation as does Sarah Brosnan (chapter 20) later in the book.

As Darwin observed, variation exists in nature, and as David Barash points out, generally speaking, the most extreme traits tend to be maladaptive. Peter Verbeek introduces the idea of species-typical versus species-atypical aggression; whereas most individuals will display species-typical patterns of aggression because they have been favored by natural selection over past generations, nonetheless, occasional species-atypical behavior is to be expected as well, which generally-speaking will not be adaptive. An obvious illustration is that if a rhesus monkey is raised under conditions of peer deprivation, as reported by Maaike Kempes and her colleagues (chapter 22), the resulting intense aggression is species-atypical. The exceptionally rare killing that might occur between rivals of the same species in nature should not be assumed to represent species-typical behavior. As Agustín Fuentes (chapter 5) notes, "Groups of monkeys may fight over food sources, ant colonies fight over space, and many other types of animal groups engage in conflicts, but none of them are planned, organized, and lethal with regularity."

Part Two: Lessons from Prehistory:
War and Peace in the Past

A central issue is how old is war? If war is an evolutionary adaptation and therefore in the registry of human nature traits, then it must have an evolutionary history. On the other hand, if warfare is a more recent development, then evidence for it would be absent in the depths of prehistory, in the human EEA. Additionally, if war was lacking in the EEA, we should also be able to find evidence for its *origins* in the comparatively recent archaeological record. The chapters in this section provide data relevant to answering this central question about the birth of war. David Dye (chapter 8) covers eastern North America, Robert Kelly (chapter 9) considers violence for several areas in western North America, R. Brian Ferguson (chapter 11) reviews the record for Europe and the Near East, and Jonathan Haas and Matthew Piscitelli (chapter 10) look at world prehistory. The answer to the central question is that *warfare is not ancient* (chapter 23). This is a very timely and important answer for two interconnected reasons.

First, the great antiquity of war continues to be assumed and asserted on the basis of indirect indicators such as widespread war in the ethnographic record or in the archaeological record only *within the last 10,000 years* (see Ferguson, chapter 7), while simultaneously the evidence from older periods and the knowledge available on extant nomadic forager societies are ignored, dismissed, or distorted.

The second reason that the objective assessment of the evidence on the antiquity of war is very important is that erroneous assertions that war is as old as or even older than humanity itself can serve to justify the waging of war today, exaggerate threats, and propagate fear. A view, erroneous though it may be that war is ancient and presumably thus reflects some natural feature of humankind or human social life, feeds a suspicious and hostile view toward other peoples and countries, making the preparation for war and the practice of war that much easier. The reasoning, or in many cases "gut reaction," seems to be: if war is in human nature, then we'd better be prepared to fight and perhaps strike first. This implicit assumption, in great part simultaneously stemming from and reinforcing of the violent view of human nature, can be seen as contributing to arms races, preemptive strikes, excessive spending on weapons, hostility toward others, and inordinate fear of other nations or groups, who are by this thinking, naturally inclined to attack. I am suggesting, in other words, that in widespread assertions that war is ancient, we are seeing a cultural belief with very important real world ramifications. Such a view may be in the short-term self-interests of a minority (e.g., arms dealers), but it is not in the long-term interests of humanity overall. As I discuss in the book's concluding chapter, in the ever-more interdependent world community, global cooperation to successfully address climate change and other shared challenges to human survival is critically needed, and holding an erroneous warlike image of human nature only hinders the process of working together on the scale that is necessary.

There is more of interest in Part II. In correspondence with Sahlins' (2008, p. 1) thesis that, "time and again for more than two millennia the people we call 'Western' have been haunted by the specter of their own inner being: An apparition of human nature so avaricious and contentious that, unless it is somehow governed, it will reduce society to anarchy," Robert Sussman (chapter 6) discusses how Hobbesian perspectives saturate writings on the human past and on human nature, noting the litany of reincarnations of these less-than-original sin-based views such as Killer Apes, Man the Hunter, Demonic Males, and more. Pinker's (2011) *The Better Angels of Our Nature* could be added to Sussman's string of examples that reiterate the same Occidental storyline. Ferguson (chapter 7) grabs this figurative baton from Sussman to run through, case-by-case, how Pinker (2011) is exaggerating war in prehistory. The evidence presented by David Dye, Robert Kelly, and Jonathan Haas and Matthew Piscitelli complements Ferguson's critique: Pinker's thesis that chronic war stretches back over the far-reaching millennia before the agricultural revolution is not substantiated by the actual data. Only one archaeological site worldwide, Jebel Sahaba, may reflect warfare older than 10,000 years ago if the early date for the site can be substantiated.

The chapters in Part II indicate that whereas homicide has occurred periodically over the enduring stretches of Pleistocene millennia, warfare is young, that is, arising within the timeframe of the agricultural revolution. Both Robert Kelly and R. Brian Ferguson point out that evidence of trauma on one or several skeletal remains is not enough to document warfare as opposed to homicide; there must be other archaeological indicators such as fortifications and settlements situated in defendable locations. David Dye provides sequences for eastern North America that show the origins of feuding and warfare as well as an overall trend of war's profusion and intensification concomitant with increasing social complexity. But that is only part of the picture. Dye also shows the peacemaking potential across time and the development of peacemaking institutions. He concludes that the societies of eastern North America developed ritual, political, and social institutions and behaviors "that ameliorated conflict, promoted cooperation, and achieved restraint" (chapter 8). Finally, R. Brian Ferguson (chapter 11) gives us a remarkable *peace surprise* from the Southern Levant, but I won't give away the specifics.

Part Three: Nomadic Foragers: Insights About Human Nature

Nomadic forager societies are especially important. For over 99 percent of the time that the genus *Homo* has existed on the planet, about two million years, nomadic huntingand-gathering has been the sole type of lifestyle. Hence the most suitable type of extant society to study for insights about the past and human nature is nomadic forager society. As Bicchieri (1972, pp. iii, iv-v, emphasis added) expresses:

> For more than 99 percent of the approximately two million years since the emergence of a recognizable human animal, man has been a hunter and gatherer. . . . Questions concerning territorialism, the handling of aggression, social control, property, leadership, the use of space, and many other dimensions are particularly significant in these contexts. To evaluate any of these focal aspects of human behavior without taking into consideration the socioeconomic adaptation that has characterized most of the span of human life on this planet will eventually *bias conclusions and generalizations.*

The first several chapters in this section provide case study data on particular nomadic forager societies: Kirk Endicott (chapter 12) on the Batek of Malaysia, Robert Tonkinson (chapter 13) on the Mardu of Australia, Marina Butovskaya (chapter 14) on the Hadza of Tanzania, and Peter Gardner (chapter 15) on six South Indian forager societies. None of these cultures engage in war or feuding. Virtually no homicides occur among the South Indians foragers or the Batek, two homicides were reported for the Hadza in a 30-year period (Marlowe, 2010), and the number of homicides for the Mardu remains undetermined but killings do occur on occasion. None of these societies place a positive value on aggressive behavior. The ideal Mardu should "know shame/embarrassment," be self-effacing, respectful, compassionate, generous, and agreeable. The South Indian societies value tolerance, respect, equality, and self-restraint; Hadza will divorce a spouse who is aggressive and Marina Butovskaya characterizes the Hadza as "relatively peaceful." The Batek have an ethic of nonviolence and in practice are highly successful at living nonviolently. Physical fighting is very rare among the Batek and the South Indian foragers but occurs more often among the Hadza and especially the Mardu.

What do Part III authors report as the typical reasons for conflict? The Hadza get angry due to sexual jealousy or theft of honey or meat from a kill; jealousy also is mentioned for the South Indian tribes; the infrequent disputes among the Batek stem from "adultery, broken promises, insults, envy, and hoarding of food," and typical Mardu disputes stem from running off with someone else's spouse, accusations of sorcery killings, and failure to reciprocate or fulfill one's obligations. Notice, by the way, what is missing: these nomadic foragers are not fighting over land, for political power, or material wealth, and they are not raiding to abduct women from other groups or attempting to kill cultural outsiders should opportune situations for killing present themselves.

In terms of how disputes are handled, avoidance is used in all four case studies, verbal expression of grievances or discussion is mentioned for three case study societies, mediation/conciliation is described for three societies, the distraction or separation of disputants by friendly peacemakers is mentioned for two societies (but may well occur in the others), and periodic physical fighting is told to occur in two societies (Hadza and Mardu) and is very rare in the other two cases. Additionally, the South Indian foragers have a belief that crimes will be punished by forest deities, and they exhibit a high degree of tolerance and self-restraint; the Hadza may negotiate a settlement as to how to divide contested meat or honey, perhaps after a physical altercation has taken place. In sum, there is no shortage of nonlethal ways to deal with conflict, some exercised by individuals acting on their own and some facilitated by third parties.

Christopher Boehm (chapter 16) focuses on how conflicts are managed between *different* groups for a sample of 49 nomadic forager societies. Again, pertaining only to inter-group conflict, which can involve very personal disputes between families or individual members of different groups or more general group-versus-group hostilities, Boehm finds negotiations to be used in 59 percent of the sample, avoidance in 35 percent, truces in 27 percent, and formal peacemaking meetings in 16 percent. Taken together, the case study chapters and Boehm's comparative research show nomadic foragers to engage in a plethora of conflict management and conflict resolution strategies within and between groups.

Darcia Narvaez (chapter 17) closes Part III by discussing the substantial mismatch between our contemporary society and the conditions under which the genus *Homo* has evolved. She hopes that we might learn from nomadic foragers to create a more caring, less violent world. She also points out over the course of her chapter how Hobbesian views within evolutionary psychology impose a set of biases from twenty-first century US culture, or Western culture more generally, unto humanity over all.

Before moving on to the next section, I must alert readers to some issues regarding foragers and forager analogy. To begin with, there are several types of foragers, aka hunter-gatherers (two terms I use interchangeably but prefer foragers). First, there are nomadic, egalitarian bands. Second, there are horse-dependent bands. Third, there are hierarchical (nonegalitarian) semi-sedentary or sedentary hunter-gatherers, sometimes referred to as complex hunter-gatherers, that often occupy areas with rich aquatic resources. On the evolutionary time line we are considering, the latter two types are very recent compared to nomadic forager band societies. Specifically the sedentary/hierarchical societies date, with very few exceptions, within the last 12–13,000 years, many originating only in the last couple of millennia, and equestrian-dependent forager bands originated only within the last several hundred years in the New World, adopting the horse from the Spanish.

Here comes a semantic muddle. Some researchers use the term hunter-gatherers to refer to nomadic forager bands only: Bicchieri (1972) quoted above is an example as he talks about living as hunter-gatherers for the 99 percent of the time the human animal has been on the planet. Bicchieri does not mean to imply that for the last two million years our ancestors were riding horses or owning slaves (a practice in some sedentary/hierarchical hunter-gatherer societies).

Other writers, however, use the term hunter-gatherers more generally to refer to all three groups together. In this book, when Robert Kelly (chapter 9) examines population pressure in relation to internal conflict, he uses the term hunter-gatherers in an inclusive manner, although noting the subtypes. Specifically, Kelly's Table 9.1 lists homicide rates among hunter-gatherers in this inclusive meaning and thus includes three cases that are not nomadic forager societies (the Yurok, Modoc, and Piegan, aka Blackfoot). Likewise Kelly's Table 9.3 and Figure 9.1a, which report on the relationship between population pressure and internal conflict, are not related exclusively to nomadic forager band societies, but again reflect the inclusive use of the term hunter-gatherers. In Kelly's Table 9.3, 8 out of the 21 societies listed are sedentary/hierarchical or equestrian hunter-gatherer societies. Kelly's goal is to look for relationships between population pressure and violent conflict across the hunter-gatherer subsistence mode, and he finds a relationship, but his findings that include warlike sedentary and equestrian foragers should not be misconstrued to apply only to a sample of nomadic forager band societies. Kelly himself notes in his chapter that, as the overall pattern, "egalitarian [i.e., nomadic] foragers do not go to war as much as sedentary, nonegalitarian foragers" (see also Fry, 2006; Kelly, 1995). Christopher Boehm refers to sedentary foragers and equestrian foragers as "exceptionally bellicose."

If the goal is to gain insights about the evolutionary past of the Pleistocene—that is, in the EEA—through ethnographic analogy, then clearly we would want to select only nomadic foragers as a frame of reference. This is the point that Bicchieri is making, as quoted above. I agree as does Christopher Boehm. Whereas there is general agreement that the focus should be on nomadic forager societies when the goal is to gain insights about the more distant past (e.g., beyond the origin of agriculture), differences of opinion arise about exactly how to sample the nomadic forager subgroup to be able to draw the most valid inferences about the past.

For example, Christopher Boehm assembles a sample of nomadic foragers that he calls Late Pleistocene Appropriate (LPA), which reflects minimal contact with outside influences at the time of description, but one result is that his sample heavily represents the Arctic region (24 out of 49 societies). On this particular issue, Marlowe (2005, 2010) takes the exact opposite stand and excludes Arctic foragers "if we are interested in the period before 30,000 years ago" (Marlowe, 2005). An existing cross-cultural sample called the Standard Cross-Cultural Sample (SCCS) represents 186 cultural provinces worldwide and has been assembled to address Galton's problem of non-independent sampling. I have derived from the SCCS a nomadic forager subsample with 21 cases for use in my studies of war and peace (Fry, 2006, 2011; Ekholm Fry & Fry, 2010). Boehm, Marlowe, and I agree that equestrian foragers also should be thrown out when the goal is to draw inferences about the past; Boehm and I, with relatively small samples, also avoid the sedentary/ hierarchical societies, but sedentary foragers constitute a minority of Marlowe's warm climate, non-equestrian sample of about two hundred cases. I have specified for inclusion in my subsample of the 186 SCCS societies only those that are nomadic or semi-nomadic and that depend for subsistence needs on *5 percent or less* on agriculture or animal husbandry. To determine these parameters, I have used the published codes by Murdock so as to select societies from the SCCS on the basis of precisely defined criteria (Fry, 2006; Murdock, 1967, 1981; Murdock & White, 1969). This methodology resulted in the sample of 21 nomadic forager societies. Marlowe (2005, 2010) is not quite as limiting, stating that *almost* all of the societies in his sample rely on domesticated food for *less than 10 percent* of their diet as the cutoff mark for inclusion.

These sampling issues will not be resolved within this brief discussion, but I would like to offer several reflections based on my experience working with the forager ethnographic data over the last decade or so. First, since the problematic practice of including data from equestrian foragers, sedentary-hierarchical foragers, sedentary horticulturalists, or other recent kinds of societies to draw inferences about the Pleistocene is a recurring one, although mostly by non-anthropologists (e.g., Bowles, 2009; Bowles & Gintis, 2011; Ember, 1978; Goldstein, 2001; Pinker, 2011), it bears emphasis that when the goal is to reconstruct past lifeways and gain insights about what sort of conflicts arose and how they may have been handled by the ancestors of modern humans over the last 50,000 to 100,000 years or more, then *we do want to focus on nomadic forager societies as analogs—not any other type of society*. On this point, Boehm, Marlowe, and I totally agree. We certainly don't want mixed samples that include mounted foragers, sedentary/hierarchical foragers, tribal peoples, horticulturalists, pastoralists, city-dwellers, and so on. Murdock (1968, p. 15) also was on top of this issue back in 1968 when he specified: "I omit all groups which I would categorize as mounted hunters, sedentary fishermen, or incipient tillers." Bowles (2009, Table 2; see also Bowles & Gintis, 2011, Table 6.4), however, assembles a tiny sample of eight societies for estimating "adult mortality due to warfare" as far back as 100,000 or even 1.6 million years ago (Bowles & Gintis, 2011, p. 17). The tiny sample includes the Modoc as non-egalitarian foragers and a group of Ayoreo as horticulturalists/hunters. Hence 25 percent of the sample are not nomadic forager societies, but nonetheless Bowles includes them to estimate war mortality over the long-reaching span of the Pleistocene. I will return to the Bowles (2009) article a little later because in addition to this problem all is not what it seems.

A second realization gleaned from my experience with nomadic forager studies is that whereas no sample is going to present a perfect picture of ancestral societies, nonetheless, *using a sample selected on the basis of explicit clear criteria is far better than self-selecting ethnographic examples* (or archaeological sites, as discussed in chapter 7 by R. Brian Ferguson) to bolster a particular argument. Self-selection is ripe for bias. In contrast to self-selecting cases, it is advisable either to use *all* available cases if this is feasible (chapter 11) or else employ clear-cut sampling criteria to reduce sampling bias and to make it clear on what foundation conclusions and interpretations rest. Sampling bias may result from conscious intention or unconscious factors, or some combination of the two. (An example of selection bias that presents the exceptions as if they showed the rule is provided in Fry, 2006, p. 282, note 37.)

Third, on the basis of studying ethnographic accounts on nomadic forager societies from around the globe, some on very isolated groups and others on societies that have had contact with outsiders and some on societies that do some trading and others that do not, I am struck by consistencies across nomadic forager societies despite all the variations in geography, history, degree of contact, and habitat. Patterns do exist. This leads me to think that, ultimately, *some central features may be very robust across nomadic forager societies*. For example, whether in the Arctic or elsewhere, and whether subjected to little or more-than-a-little external contact, nomadic foragers practice *avoidance* as a very typical response to a conflict. This preference for avoidance seems ubiquitous among nomadic foragers; the number of ethnographic reports that mention it is a mile long (see for data and additional citations chapters 12, 13, 14, 15, & 16; Fry, 2006, 2011; Marlowe, 2010).

Similarly, across nomadic band societies, "the usual story" behind an initial homicide is that two men want the same woman (e.g., Fry, 2006, 2011; Hill, Hurtado, & Walker, 2007; Lee, 1979; Marlowe, 2010). Then, if it occurs, "the usual story" for a second homicide is revenge for a first with the payback aimed directly at the murderer and perpetrated by family members of the original victim. And, for nomadic foragers, typically the story stops there, an outcome that restores the balance tit-for-tat (Fry, 2011; Fry et al., 2010; Kelly, 2000). Hence, revenge was mentioned as a motive in 15 out of the 21 nomadic forager societies in the SCCS (Fry, 2011; see also chapter 12). And the nature of disputes at the nomadic band level of social organization, regardless of sampling subtlety, reflects very personal issues. It seems to me that these overall patterns of nomadic band life are robustly expressed across geographical regions, degree of involvement with trade, and so forth, as long as the groups in question retain their nomadic foraging lifeways.

There is another recurrent pattern that should be taken into account by anyone interested in violence and conflict management: as alcohol becomes available to nomadic forager societies violence goes up. Often the traditional mechanisms of social control and conflict management are not effective in dealing with drunken aggression. Increased aggression due to intoxication has been noted for the Hadza (chapter 14), Casiguran Agta (Headland, 1989; Griffin, 2000), Slave (Helm, 1961), Micmac (Le Clercque, 1910), Mardu (chapter 13), among others, and the fact that the nonviolent Paliyan of South India purposefully shun alcohol to avoid its negative effects on self-restraint makes the same point (chapter 15). Needless to say, alcohol was not available in the EEA. One implication is that the presence or absence of alcohol must be taken into consideration before extrapolating onto the past the homicide rates of nomadic foragers following alcohol-exposure.

A final observation to highlight about nomadic band societies is that since most lethal disputes are personal, then so-called raiding is a misnomer to the degree that the term raiding implies group-versus-group community conflict, that is, warfare. *The often-espoused idea that members of one nomadic band regularly raid other bands to steal women, gain territory, or simply to kill as many people as possible is for the most part a misconception not substantiated by a visit to the facts.* Recall Burrows' (1963) warning not to assume that what exists in one's own cultural tradition applies elsewhere. In most situations involving nomadic forager societies, so-called raiding is directed at the particular person who has committed an offense such as fleeing to another band with someone else's wife. Long ago, Service (1966, p. 60) surveyed nomadic band societies and emphasized the personal causes of conflict as "an elopement, or an illegal love affair of some kind, or simply an insult." The targets of homicide attempts are rarely randomly chosen members of other groups. They are offenders who have committed specific misdeeds or acts of abuse. Griffin (2000, p. 103) tallies the reasons for 13 cases of homicide among the Casiguran Agta: "Eight cases involved estranged love, marital problems, and competition for a woman's attention. Three cases involved insults and heated arguments. One killing involved death in the forest under ambiguous circumstances." Hill et al. (2007, p. 451–452) write of the Hiwi: "Most of the adult killings were due either to competition over women, reprisals by jealous husbands (on both their wives and their wives' lovers), or reprisals for past killings." Descriptions such as these from copious ethnographic sources do reveal the personal nature, motivations, and causes of most lethal aggression among nomadic foragers. Those persons interested in evolutionary questions regarding lethal aggression would most profitably follow the data. Oddly in this case, the data on who kills whom and for what reasons continue to be ignored in favor of near data-free assertions that nomadic forager life is rife with war (e.g., Bowles, 2009; Bowles & Gintis, 2011; Ember, 1978; Pinker, 2011). Recognizing the personal nature of most lethal disputes in nomadic forager society is important when it comes to the evolutionary questions of war, peace, and human nature. Homicides are reported among a majority of nomadic forager societies but at the same time the majority of such societies do not engage in warfare (Fry, 2006, 2011; Kelly, 1995). Therefore, it is not justified to simply assume that so-called raids among nomadic foragers *typically* occurred in the context of warfare. It is time to reconsider lethal aggression in nomadic band society at the level of the individual players.

Part Four: The Primatological Context of Human Nature

There are a couple of main points that I'll highlight for this section. First, the chapters herein serve to illustrate behavioral flexibility as a characteristic not only of our species but also of the Order Primates more generally. Within the Order, baboons have the highest rate of agonistic behavior, much of it stemming from the males (Sussman & Garber, 2007). Robert Sapolsky (chapter 21) shows the importance of "culture" in affecting the peacefulness of a wild baboon troop, and Maaike Kempes, Liesbeth Sterck, and Bram Orobio de Castro (chapter 22) similarly provide documentation of the importance of learning within a social group of peers regarding the restraint of aggression among rhesus monkeys. In baboons, subadult males transfer troops, which has the effect of preventing matings between them and their close female relatives who remain in the natal group. The typical pattern is for these young male transfers to find their places over time within an existing male dominance hierarchy. In the troop studied by Robert Sapolsky, the dominant males met with a tragic end, and one result was the development of a much more peaceful troop of baboons. The intriguing observation is that as young males arrived as transfers from other troops where the typical pattern of male aggression reigned, they adjusted to the peaceful group by grooming more and aggressing less. I cannot help but mention the parallel to the Moriori described by Kirk Endicott (chapter 12) who also became more peaceful once they became separated from their Maori culture of origin. Peace and war are not static states and people can choose peace over war.

Back in Part I, Peter Verbeek introduced the terms species-typical aggression and species-atypical aggression. This distinction seems applicable to the findings of Maaike Kempes and her colleagues. Rhesus monkeys, when raised in the more natural situation of having contact with peers, develop restrained patterns of agonism in comparison to socially deprived monkeys that more often severely attack other macaques. Social interaction with peers plays a role in the learning of species-typical aggression. In Part V, Anna Szala and I (chapter 23) have more to say on this topic.

Sarah Brosnan (chapter 20) begins with an overall observation: social interactions in animals are "remarkably peaceful." Brosnan focuses on understanding the factors that are important for the evolution of cooperation. One interesting finding is that species that regularly cooperate are more sensitive to inequality than are species that cooperate less or not at all. Experiments demonstrate that monkeys who need help to get food share more with their helpful companion. Thus, interdependence leads to behavior that maintains a positive relationship. And monkeys, like humans, cooperate when they reap a benefit (chapter 27). Brosnan concludes that in cooperative species strong selection pressures have resulted in behaviors that minimize conflict so as to allow for maximal cooperation.

Bonobos and chimpanzees are the closest living relatives to *Homo sapiens*. These two species are very different when it comes to the peacefulness-aggressiveness continuum as Michael L. Wilson (chapter 18) and Frances J. White, Michel T. Waller, and Klaree J. Boose (chapter 19) make clear. Unlike chimpanzees, bonobos never have been observed to engage in lethal aggression. One critical difference between the two species is that female bonobos form strong social bonds and effectively cooperate to keep male aggression in check.

Human females also play peacemaking and protective roles. Among the nomadic forager societies in the SCCS, accounts of friendly peacemaking by women were found in 12 out of 21 cases. As an example among the Ju/'hoansi (formerly called the !Kung), "Two of /Ti/kay's half-sisters, who were present, threw themselves on him, pulled him away, and sat down beside him, holding his arms" (Marshall, 1959, p. 362; see also chapter 13). The methods attempted by nomadic forager women to squelch a fight included physical restraint (reported in 8 of 21 societies), creating a distraction (in 3 societies), verbal persuasion (in 2 societies), and removing men's weapons (in 3 societies) (Ekholm Fry & Fry, 2010).

Christopher Boehm (chapter 16) considers what the common ancestral species to bonobos, chimpanzees, and humans might have been like. He adopts the conservative approach that for a feature to be considered present in the last common ancestor (LCA), then the feature must be present in all three living species. Humans and chimpanzees engage in lethal aggression but bonobos do not, so by Boehm's reasoning, lethal aggression is a behavior that developed subsequent to the LCA. Michael L. Wilson (chapter 18), however, entertains the possibility that since warlike behavior occurs in both humans and chimpanzees, it could date back in time to the LCA. Alternatively, notes Wilson, warring behavior in the two species could have evolved independently for similar reasons. As already discussed, both the archaeological evidence and nomadic forager analogy suggest that intergroup killings were not prevalent in the human past, and additionally, as also discussed earlier, it still needs to be established that war is an evolved adaptation and not simply a capacity. We will return to these topics shortly.

I would like to echo a point made by Peter Verbeek (chapter 4) that, following one of the founders of ethology, Niko Tinbergen, each species should be studied in its own right. So, to understand peace and war in humans, we should look toward the human data directly, and to understand intergroup and intragroup killing in chimpanzees, we should study chimpanzees directly. This said, it also is valuable to adopt a broad-spectrum basis of comparison for gaining an understanding of evolutionary trends and principles (chapter 20; chapter 23; Fry et al., 2010).

The next question is whether the lethal aggression observed in humans or in chimpanzees could be considered species-typical aggression or species atypical aggression. Regarding chimpanzees, Michael L. Wilson (chapter 18) and Robert W. Sussman (chapter 6) hold different points of view. Regarding humans, Anna Szala and I (chapter 23) make a case that killing in humans may be species atypical and that nonlethal, restrained patterns of agonism are species-typical in humans, just as they are in virtually all mammals. As members of twenty-first century Western society, we are so accustomed to thinking about human violence and war as part and parcel of human nature that this proposal that killing could be considered species-atypical goes against common presumptions.

Part Five: Taking Restraint Against Killing Seriously

Ironically, restraint in human agonism, although vitally important and regularly occurring, has remained invisible. We are so accustomed to acting with restraint, and expecting restraint from others, that we just take this potent feature of typical social interaction for granted. When I walk to work, arrive at the university, or enter a classroom to teach, I do not expect that I will be physically attacked by strangers, colleagues, or students—nor does it come to mind that I would strangle a reckless bicyclist on my walk to work, knife a secretary who reminds me about overdue paperwork, or even just slap a student for arriving late to class. I point out with tongue in cheek that the prevalent human restraint against homicide can be demonstrated by asking any assembled group "Have any of you ever been murdered?" A less whimsical question, that is only slightly less likely to receive a unanimous "no" response from the group is, "Have you ever murdered someone?" Again, the restraint against killing is invisible, just taken for granted by the vast majority of us as we go about our lives not expecting to kill any one and not expecting the hundreds or thousands of people we see in a single day to kill us. Obviously, homicides do occur. But my point is that, first, they are rare and unusual events given the number of social interactions, including disputes and arguments, that occur without any killing taking place, and second, the restraint against taking another life is species-typical, whereas the rare exceptions that do occur are species-atypical. In this section, Anna Szala and I (chapter 23) discuss this perspective on restraint from a species-comparative evolutionary perspective.

The other three chapters in Part V serve to provide more evidence that restraint is a powerful and ubiquitous force that would merit a great deal more attention. Richard J. Hughbank and Dave Grossman (chapter 25) take up the discussion in the military context to argue that soldiers have a natural reluctance to take human life, even on the battlefield, where it is their obligation to do so, and this resistance to killing must be overcome by extensive training that even then is not always successful.

Joám Evans Pim (chapter 26) explores a particular example of human restraint against physical aggression: the song duel. Evans Pim finds copious evidence for this nonviolent format for competition cross-culturally and fills his chapter with intriguing examples. He begins by considering Galizan song duels in some detail and then branches out from there to other cultures. The context and rules of song duels allow potentially dangerous conflicts to be dealt with in a playful way that helps to prevent physical aggression including, at an extreme, lethal aggression.

Paul Roscoe (chapter 24) takes us to Papua New Guinea and the Yangoru Boiken culture to illustrate how symbols and ceremonies reflect restraint at both individual and group levels. As an example, pigs came to symbolize the weapons of war—spears—and hence there is no longer a need to fight it out with real spears when one could "attack" with a gift of pigs. "Pig-exchange, in sum, was a symbolic form of war: symbolic 'enemies' threw symbolic 'spears' that symbolically 'killed' one another."

Finally, reference to restraint in diverse contexts also can be found sprinkled across other chapters in this volume. Hanna Kokko (chapter 3) points out that "lethal fighting is not really the norm in the animal kingdom." Correspondingly, David Barash (chapter 2) writes that selection "sets the limit on excessive aggressiveness." Peter M. Gardner (chapter 15) discusses how restraint serves a role in the control of aggression among south Indian foragers, and David H. Dye (chapter 8) mentions patterns of restraint in ethnohistorical and archaeological contexts.

Cultural Bias Scuttles Scientific Objectivity

In *The Better Angels of Our Nature*, Pinker (2011, p. xxiv) argues that levels of violence and warfare have been decreasing from a very Hobbesian past, plagued by "chronic raiding and feuding that characterized life in a state of nature." Pinker (2011, p. xxi) asserts: "Violence has declined over long stretches of time, and today we may be living in the most peaceable era in our species' existence." Physical violence may have been decreasing over *recent* millennia, but this trend does not represent humanity's entire evolutionary drama. Pinker constructs his account of steadily more peaceful human existence starting not at the raising of the curtain, and not even in the middle of the play, but only in the final act. Contra Pinker, the incidence of warfare and violent mayhem over the last 10 millennia actually follows an *n*-shaped curve, rather than merely the steep drop-off in recent times that Pinker highlights. The worldwide archaeological evidence shows that war was simply absent over the vast majority of human existence—the time period beginning far to the left side of the *n* curve. But with a gradual worldwide population increase (see chapter 10, Figure 10.1), the shift from universal nomadic foraging to settled communities, the development of agriculture, a transition from egalitarianism to hierarchical societies— and, very significantly, the rise of state-level civilization five thousand to six thousand years ago—the archaeological record is clear and unambiguous: war developed, despots arose, violence proliferated, slavery flourished, and the social position of women deteriorated. This comparatively recent explosion in pre-state and then state-based violence is represented on the rising left side of the letter *n* in the curve, but taking place within the last 10,000 years.

In making the claim that the story of the entire human past "is a shockingly violent one," Pinker (2011, p. 1) presents estimates of what he interchangeably calls the "percentage of all deaths that are caused by violence" (p. 48) and "percentage of deaths in warfare" (p. 49), although violent deaths and warfare deaths are not really synonyms. A consideration of the percentages of war deaths that Pinker presents in his Figure 2.2 bar chart is critical because *this information is the linchpin upon which his entire argument for a "shockingly violent" past depends.* If the data shown in Pinker's bar chart are unreliable or inaccurate, then Pinker's thesis that violence today is at an all time low also crumbles. I agree with Pinker about the ability of a state to squelch violence within its domain and in fact have pointed out this phenomenon myself (Fry, 2006; chapter 27). However, the archaeological and "hunter-gatherer" data presented by Pinker in support of his thesis are seriously flawed.

Looking at the prehistoric cases of so-called war deaths, the oldest site that Pinker includes, Gobero, Niger, is dated to 16,000 years ago. This is not very old in relation to the existence of our species or to the genus *Homo*, but it is older than the beginning of the agricultural revolution. However, there were *no war deaths* from Gobero. Absolutely none. So the Gobero site is older than agriculture, but with a war death rate of zero, and obviously it provides no support for Pinker's contention that chronic raiding and feuding would have existed 16,000 years before the present. If anything, the total lack of war deaths at Gobero is one of many pieces of data that contradict such a presumption (chapter 10; chapter 11).

One important observation about Pinker's archaeological war death cases is that with the possible exception of Jebel Sahaba, they all come from the most recent period of prehistory, the Holocene. Showing warfare in this recent time period is simply not relevant to Pinker's claim about shocking levels of violence over the entire existence of our species. R. Brian Ferguson (chapter 7) addresses the myriad issues with the archaeological cases that Pinker selects, and dubs this group Pinker's List. Therefore, I will focus on the societies that Pinker labels "hunter-gatherers," and the reason for putting quotation marks around this term will soon become apparent.

Pinker (2011, p. 50) explains that his subsample of "hunter-gatherers" comes "from eight contemporary or recent societies that make their living primarily from hunting and gathering. They come from the Americas, the Philippines, and Australia. The average rate of death by warfare is within a whisker of the average estimated from the bones: 14%, with a range from 4% to 30%."

The story of Pinker's "hunter-gatherers" is about to take some bizarre twists. Pinker took his eight cases directly from the article by Bowles (2009; see also Bowles & Gintis, 2011) mentioned earlier in this chapter. First, the eight "hunter-gatherer" cases are far from representative. It can easily be imagined that war deaths would be overrepresented if one goes looking for ethnographic cases from which to calculate percentages of war deaths. Later I will demonstrate statistically that this is almost certainly the case. Second, a sample of eight cases is tiny. Third, as noted earlier in this chapter not all of the cases are nomadic forager societies.

Recently I was asked to write a book review essay on several books including *A Cooperative Species* by Bowles and Gintis (2011), which republishes Bowles's (2009) eight cases. The high "war mortalities" for some of the foraging societies caught my attention—as seemingly extreme—and so I sought out several of the original ethnographic sources used by Bowles (2009) and thus inherited by Pinker (2011).

For two of Pinker's cases, the Ache of Paraguay and the Hiwi of Venezuela/ Colombia, *all of the so-called war deaths involved frontiersmen ranchers killing the indigenous people*, a tragic situation that has nothing to do with levels of warfare death in nomadic hunter-gatherers during the Pleistocene. Here are quotations from the original source. Hill and Hurtado (1996, p. 48), explain that "the Ache were relentlessly pursued by slave traders and attacked by Paraguayan frontiersmen from the time of the conquest right up until peaceful contact." Hill and Hurtado (1996, p. 52) also state, "Most mention that the frequent hostile encounters with Paraguayans in the forest had driven them to desire a peaceful relationship with their more powerful neighbors." And the original source also tells: "Although the reservations had problems, no Ache who lived there was ever shot by a Paraguayan in the types of skirmishes that had been common throughout the past several hundred years on the Paraguayan forest frontier" (Hill & Hurtado, 1996, p. 53). *All* 46 deaths used by Bowles (2009) to calculate so-called warfare mortality among the Ache are listed as "shot by Paraguayan" by Hill and Hurtado (1996, Table 5.1, pages 171–173). Remember that Pinker's (2011) purpose is to estimate hunter-gatherer war mortality in "a state of nature," not to tally the killings of indigenous people by Paraguayan nationals. Hill and Hurtado (1996, p. 54) mention that a German anthropologist was evicted from Paraguay after he published reports of "genocide" inflicted on the Ache. This case surely presents an inappropriate model for "a state of nature" before the development of the state or before the agricultural revolution.

The Hiwi case parallels that of the Ache, as local *criollo* ranchers massacred Hiwi in attempts to usurp their land (Hill et al., 2007, pp. 451, 452). Hill et al. (2007, p. 444) note that ranchers had been invading Hiwi territory throughout the twentieth century, and, for example, explain that "members of the study population described here were victims of the 'Rubiera Massacre' carried out on a Columbian ranch on Christmas Day, 1968, which resulted in the deaths of 16 men, women, and children (and left only two survivors who were interviewed as part of this demographic study)." To be absolutely clear, *the only so-called war deaths* reported are those where indigenous people were murdered or massacred by Venezuelans. *All* of these killings have been counted as so-called war deaths, as if they have relevance to estimating war-related deaths in the Pleistocene (Bowles, 2009, using the data in Hill et al., 2007, Table 4, p. 450; Pinker, 2011, Figure 2.2).

Moving on, the Casiguran Agta case also is problematic. One reason is an error in arithmetic. Headland (1989, p. 69), the original source cited by Bowles (2009; Bowles & Gintis, 2011), provides a tally of four raids between 1936 and 1950 in which Casiguran Agta were killed: 1950 raid, 1 death; 1947 raid, 5 deaths; 1938 raid, 1 death; "shortly after World War II" raid, 2 deaths, or a total of *9 Casiguran Agta deaths*. Bowles (2009; Bowles & Gintis, 2011) used *10 deaths* in his calculations, *not* 9. Also of relevance to Pinker's fundamental purpose of getting at "life in a state of nature," Headland [1989, p. 61] reports "an influx of immigrant colonists into the area, and the resulting cutting back of the forest and decline of game and fish," food resources upon which the Agta depend. Two of the nine war deaths were actually inflicted on the Casiguran Agta by immigrant Ilokano farmers, raising the question: Shouldn't these two killings be discounted since the explicit goal of Bowles/Pinker is to estimate war deaths over the evolution of the species during the pre-agricultural Pleistocene? It seems possible that loss of their land to immigrant farmers also might be contributing to intra-Agta killing (see Kelly, chapter 9), and thus this raises the broader issue as to whether the Casiguran Agta case is suitable for estimating prehistoric war deaths at all.

What is left of the eight cases used by Pinker? The first and third highest percentages of so-called war deaths (Ache and Hiwi, respectively) do not remotely resemble the original model used by Bowles (2009; Bowles & Gintis, 2011) of nomadic forager groups warring with each other across the vast prehistoric period beginning about 12,000 years ago and extending back to at least 100,000 or even 1.6 million years ago. In the Ache and Hiwi cases, we don't even see in the mortality numbers indigenous peoples warring with other indigenous societies. Instead, the Ache and Hiwi so-called war deaths are actually indigenous people being gunned down by local ranchers (and in other cases enslaved) as their lands are progressively taken from them. The proposal that this scenario can be used to provide reasonable estimates of war deaths for nomadic forager "life in a state of nature" doesn't cut muster. The 30 percent of deaths attributed to "war" for the Ache and the 17 percent attributed to the Hiwi are inappropriate to use in estimating mortality costs of warfare in the Pleistocene.

By the way, Bowles also miscalculates the Hiwi percentage of war deaths by using 76 total adult deaths instead of the 86 adult deaths that are represented in the original source, a mistake which if corrected, results in 15 percent, down 2 percent from the percentage published by Bowles then Pinker (2011; see Bowles, 2009, supporting online material Table S2 for the 76 figure that Bowles uses in his calculating and compare this with the 86 adult deaths from Hill et al., 2007, Table 4, the row labeled "Total deaths," by adding 31 + 24 + 23 + 8 = 86, not 76, total adult deaths for the so-called "precontact" period). I put "precontact" in quotes because in my opinion 100 years, at least, of being murdered and massacred by encroaching outsiders does not jibe with the pristine implications of the word precontact.

The rate of 5 percent war deaths for the Agta is also slightly inflated due to a miscount of victims, 10 instead of 9 (or 7 if the 2 killings of Agta by immigrant farmers are excluded). Furthermore, the Ayoreo group of forager/horticulturalists probably should not have been included in a sample of "hunter-gatherers" to begin with as horticulture was not practiced in the Pleistocene. I have not yet looked into the Ayoreo case to see if the reported deaths actually reflect Ayoreo warfare or constitute another case of outsiders slaughtering indigenous peoples (in consideration of this possibility, see Survival International, 2012, on the Ayoreo). Additionally, I suggest, as discussed previously in this chapter, that the Modoc, as semi-settled/hierarchical hunter-gatherers, also should be dropped from the sample.

If we redo the estimation of war deaths for this sample of eight but now use zero war deaths for both the Ache and Hiwi instead of 30 percent and 17 percent, respectively, since the body counts have nothing to do with nomadic foragers killing each other, the average overall percentage for the Bowles/Pinker's eight cases is reduced to 9 percent, down from

14 percent. And if we remove the Ayoreo and the Modoc, as societal types inappropriate for estimating war deaths in the Pleistocene, then the average for a sample of size six becomes 7 percent. This assumes, of course, that the remaining four cases reflect legitimate instances of nomadic forager war deaths and correct calculations. Furthermore, this recalculation entails correcting only the Ache and the Hiwi percentages and does not attempt to correct for the counting error for the Casiguran Agta or any other possible mistakes.

We have a frame of reference to consider in thinking about war deaths among nomadic forager societies. If we compare the original Bowles/Pinker sample to the SCCS sample where only 8 out of 21 nomadic forager societies practice war, there certainly is a major incongruity that 100 percent, 8 out of 8, of the Bowles/Pinker sample supposedly engage in war (Fry, 2006, 2011). By contrast, using the SCCS nomadic subsample as a yardstick, we might expect war and therefore war deaths in about 38 percent (8 out of 21) of a sample of nomadic forager societies, not in 100 percent of such a sample. As a statistical frame of reference, relaxing the sample size requirements, a difference of proportions test comparing 38 percent with 100 percent for these two samples is highly significant ($Z = 3.01$, two tailed $p = .003$), suggesting that these two samples were not drawn from the same parental population. Given the foregoing discussion about the type of Ache and Hiwi killings that have been mislabeled as war deaths, the counting and calculating errors for the Hiwi and Casiguran Agta cases, and the tiny, self-selected nature of the Bowles/Pinker sample to begin with, it is obvious that there are some serious problems here. Moreover, if this sample is held up against the comparative standard provided by the SCCS nomadic forager subsample (which, recall, was assembled on the basis of precise criteria from a larger worldwide ethnographic sample), then the bias toward war and war deaths in the Bowles/Pinker sample is unmistakable. By the way, it also can be noted that for 7 out of the 21 SCCS nomadic band societies, the prevalence of *homicide* is very low, reported as: rare, very rare, never mentioned to occur, none known, and unknown (Fry, 2011, p. 235). Therefore, not only is 62 percent of the SCCS nomadic forager subsample nonwarring, but 29 percent (6 out of 21) of the SCCS subsample is *both low homicide and nonwarring*. Given the vast amount of knowledge that has been accumulated on nomadic forager peoples from around the world that show them, as a social type, *not* to be particularly warlike and in some cases also to have very low rates of homicide, then any suggestion that the Bowles/Pinker sample corresponds with reality lacks credence. The assertion that this Bowles/Pinker sample could provide anything close to a valid estimate of war deaths for the entire existence of the species in a state of nature is absurd.

In the broader picture, what is going on here? Without providing a single citation, Pinker asserts: "Foraging peoples can invade to gain territory, such as hunting grounds, watering holes, the banks or mouths of rivers, and sources of valued minerals like flint, obsidian, salt, or ochre. They may raid livestock or caches of stored food. And very often they fight over women. Men may raid a neighboring village for the express purpose of kidnapping women, whom they gang-rape and distribute as wives. They may raid for some other reason and take the women as a bonus. Or they may raid to claim women who had been promised to them in marriage but were not delivered at the agreed-upon time. And sometimes young men attack for trophies, coups, and other signs of aggressive prowess, especially in societies where they are a prerequisite to attaining adult status." (Pinker, 2011, p. 46). Some such behaviors and practices do occur in the worldwide ethnographic record that includes various types of societies, but rarely do the traits in Pinker's litany of mayhem apply to nomadic forager societies, our best analogs for the Pleistocene past. And then we have the Bowles/Pinker team telling us that across the entire existence of the human species, as shown by Pinker's List of prehistoric sites and Pinker's "hunter-gatherers," life in nature consisted of chronic raiding and feuding with 14 or 15 percent of all deaths attributable to warfare. And the "hunter-gatherer" evidence (e.g., on the Ache or Hiwi) used to draw this conclusion is truly remarkable, but not in a good way. The degree of disconnect between what the archaeological and nomadic forager data actually show, on the one hand (for example, see Parts II & III of this book), and what Bowles and Pinker assert on the other is monumental.

Bar charts and numeric tables depicting percentages of war deaths for "hunter-gatherers" convey an air of scientific objectivity and validity. But in this case it is all an illusion. This war-saturated view of humanity simply mirrors longstanding perceptions of human nature in the West. From one angle it is shocking how publications—replete with sampling issues, counting errors, omissions of relevant contextual information, and various types of dubious assumptions—make it onto the printed pages of the respected journal *Science* and major presses, passing by peer reviewers, editors, and publishers. But from a philosophy of science angle that takes into consideration the biasing potential of cultural belief systems on science, this occurrence is comprehensible. Scientists and scholars, editors and publishers, reviewers and readers, already "know" all about warlike human nature and have digested the myth of a warlike past—such "knowledge," in other words, is an aspect of their shared Occidental belief system. Such "knowledge" is not born of objective science. On this human nature issue, it is time to stop assuming that the world is flat and instead carefully reexamine the actual data. In the words of Carl Sagan, "At the heart of science is an essential balance between two seemingly contradictory attitudes—an openness to new ideas, no matter how bizarre or counterintuitive, and the most ruthlessly skeptical scrutiny of *all* ideas, old and new" (Clark, 2002, p. 50).

Acknowledgments

I extend my grateful thanks to Joám Evans Pim, R. Brian Ferguson, and Sarah B. Hrdy for their useful comments on a draft of this chapter.

References

Apicella, C., Marlowe, F., Fowler, J., & Christakis, N. (2012). Social networks and cooperation in hunter-gatherers. *Nature, 481*, 497–502.

Bicchieri, M. (Ed.) (1972). *Hunters and gatherers today*. Prospect Heights, IL: Waveland.

Bowles, S. (2009). Did warfare among ancestral hunter-gatherers affect the evolution of human social behaviors? *Science, 324,* 1293–1298.

Bowles, S., & Gintis, H. (2011). *A cooperative species: Human reciprocity and its evolution.* Princeton: Princeton University Press.

Burrows, E. (1963). *Flower in my ear: Arts and ethos Ifaluk Atoll.* Seattle: University of Washington Press.

Clark, G. A. (2002). Neandertal archaeology—Implications for our origins. *American Anthropologist, 104,* 50–67.

de Waal, F. (1989). *Bonobo: The forgotten ape.* Berkeley: University of California Press.

Ekholm Fry, N., & Fry, D. P. (2010). *Aggression and conflict resolution among females in nomadic band societies* (pp. 345–355). New York: Peter Lang.

Ember, C. (1978). Myths about hunter-gatherers. *Ethnology, 17,* 439–448.

Fry, D. P. (2006). *The human potential for peace: An anthropological challenge to assumptions about war and violence.* New York: Oxford University Press.

Fry, D. P. (2011). Human nature: The nomadic forager model. In R. W. Sussman & C. R. Cloninger (Eds.), *Origins of altruism and cooperation* (pp. 227–247). New York: Springer.

Fry, D. P., Schober, G., & Björkqvist, K. (2010). Nonkilling as an evolutionary adaptation. In J. Evans Pim (Ed.), *Nonkilling societies* (pp. 101–128). Honolulu: Center for Global Nonkilling.

Griffin, M. (2000). Homicide and aggression among the Agta of Eastern Luzon, the Philippines, 1910–1985. In P. Schweitzer, M. Biesele, & R. Hitchcock (Eds.), *Hunters and gatherers in the modern world* (pp. 94–109). New York: Berghahn.

Headland, T. (1989). Population decline in a Philippine Negrito hunter-gatherer society. *American Journal of Human Biology, 1,* 59–72.

Helm, J. (1961). *The Lynx Point people: The dynamics of a Northern Athabaskan band.* Ottawa: National Museum of Canada, Bulletin Number 176, Anthropology Series Number 53.

Hill, K., & Hurtado, A. M. (1996). *Ache life history: The ecology and demography of a foraging people.* New York: Aldine de Gruyter.

Hill, K., Hurtado, A. M., & Walker, R. S. (2007). High adult mortality among Hiwi hunter-gatherers: Implications for human evolution. *Journal of Human Evolution, 52,* 443–454.

Kelly, R. C. (2000). *Warless societies and the origin of war.* Ann Arbor: University of Michigan Press.

Kelly, R. L. (1995). *The foraging spectrum: Diversity in hunter-gatherer lifeways.* Washington, DC: Smithsonian.

Le Clercq, C. (1910). New relations of Gaspesia. In W. Ganong (Trans. & Ed.), *Publications of the Champlain Society, volume 5* (pp. 1–452). Toronto: The Champlain Society.

Lee, R. B. (1979). *The !Kung San: Men, women, and work in a foraging community.* Cambridge: Cambridge University Press.

Marlowe, F. (2005). Hunter-gatherers and human evolution. *Evolutionary Anthropology, 14,* 54–67.

Marlowe, F. (2010). *The Hadza hunter-gatherers of Tanzania.* Berkeley: University of California Press.

Marshall, L. (1959). Marriage among !Kung Bushmen. *Africa, 29,* 335–364.

Miklikowska, M., & Fry, D. P. (2012). Natural born nonkillers: A critique of the killers have more kids idea. In D. Christie & J. Evans Pin (Eds.), *Nonkilling psychology* (pp. 43–70). Honolulu: Center for Global Nonkilling.

Murdock, G. P. (1967). Ethnographic atlas: A summary. *Ethnology, 6,* 109–236.

Murdock, G. P. (1968). The current status of the world's hunting and gathering peoples. In R. B. Lee & I. DeVore (Eds.), *Man the hunter* (pp. 13–20). Chicago: Aldine.

Murdock, G. P. (1981). *Atlas of world cultures.* Pittsburgh: University of Pittsburgh Press.

Murdock, G. P., & White, D. (1969). Standard cross-cultural sample." *Ethnology, 8,* 329–369.

Nowak, M. A. (2011). *SuperCooperators: Altruism, evolution, and why we need each other to succeed* (with R. Highfield). New York: Free Press.

Pinker, Steven (2011). *The better angels of our nature.* New York: Viking.

Sahlins, M. (2008). *The Western illusion of human nature.* Chicago: Prickly Paradigm Press.

Service, E. R. (1966). *The hunters.* Englewood Cliffs, NJ: Prentice-Hall.

Survival International (2012). http://www.survivalinternational.org/tribes/ayoreo. Accessed April 14, 2012.

Sussman, R. W., & Garber, P. (2007). Cooperation and competition in primate social interaction. In Campbell, C., Fuentes, A., MacKinnon, K. C., Panger, M., & Bearder, S. (Eds.), *Primates in perspective* (pp. 636–651). New York: Oxford University Press.

Trivers, R. (1971). The evolution of reciprocal altruism. *Quarterly Review of Biology, 46,* 35–57.

PART ONE

Ecological and Evolutionary Models

2

Evolution and Peace

A Janus Connection

David P. Barash

To some people, evolution and peace seem to be at odds. Tennyson's image of "nature, red in tooth and claw" combined with Herbert Spencer's phrase "survival of the fittest" have generated an unrealistic presumption that the evolutionary process is necessarily bloody and aggressive, rewarding violence and—by extension—war, while rendering peace not only undesirable but essentially impossible (Smith, 2009). On the other hand, there is just enough truth to this caricature to make it difficult to shake it off altogether, although the Tennyson/Spencer perspective contains more than enough misrepresentation to warrant its refutation.

At the same time, there are others—perhaps fewer—who proclaim the opposite: that evolution by natural selection predisposes us toward kindness, benevolence, cooperation, and peace. They emphasize that war, in particular, is a social phenomenon and a cultural invention, something that somehow goes against our biological nature and entraps us only occasionally and despite the better angels of that nature (Fry, 2007).

When it comes to the conjunction of evolution and peace, reality is complex, nuanced, and uncertain. The most appropriate image may well come from neither of these extremes, neither from Ares—the Greek god of war—nor from Irene, the lesser-known Greek goddess of peace, but rather, from ancient Roman religion and mythology: the god Janus, typically pictured with two faces, each one looking in a different direction (Figure 2.1). Evolution is, in fact, somewhat consistent with peace; equally, it is somewhat consistent with war. Like Janus, it has two faces, neither of which is predominant.

Let's start with some definitions, which suggest key convergences as well as divergences between evolution and peace. Peace is typically thought to be a situation of calm, and—at the minimum—an absence of organized violence. Evolution refers to change, specifically in the gene frequencies of a population over time. (Note that individuals do not evolve; populations, lineages, and species do.) Peace is widely supposed to be static;

FIGURE 2.1 The most appropriate human nature image may well come from neither extreme, neither from Ares—the Greek god of war—nor from Irene, the lesser-known Greek goddess of peace, but rather, from ancient Roman religion and mythology: the god Janus, typically pictured with two faces, each one looking in a different direction (Photo Credit: Public Domain, Wikipedia).

evolution, dynamic. Peace is ostensibly cooperative; evolution, competitive. Peace is something toward which we are expected to strive; evolution—especially our evolutionary past, and thus our "innate" inclinations—is something with which we are stuck. Furthermore, we are ostensibly stuck with inclinations that hinder our striving.

There is some truth to this conclusion. Evolution indeed occurs via the competitive replacement of genes by alternative alleles. Which ones? Those that are more successful in getting their bodies to engage in behavior that results in greater success for themselves (actually, identical copies of themselves) in other bodies are the ones that succeed at the expense of others whose combined impact is, on the whole, less salutary. Competitive? Yes. Violent? Not necessarily.

The most widespread popular interpretations of "nature, red in tooth and claw" and of "survival of the fittest" involve bloody images of wolves pulling down a moose or perhaps a cheetah outrunning an impala: vivid, but misleading. Thus, the key evolutionary competition is not between wolves and moose, or cheetah and impala (i.e., between predator and prey), but rather, among wolves or among cheetahs. And here, again, the most common inference would be wolves fighting it out against other wolves, cheetahs against cheetahs, and so forth. Once more, there is some truth to this caricature, too, but overwhelmingly, the essential competition among wolves—albeit intraspecific—plays itself out not in head-to-head, fang-to-fang, claw-to-claw ferocity but in effectiveness in turning moose meat into wolf bodies, and thus, wolf genes. Moreover, the behavioral patterns employed during intraspecific aggression are typically quite different from those used during interspecific predation, just as the neuroanatomic and neurophysiologic substrates underlying these behaviors are distinct.

Although some proportion of this intraspecific, evolutionary competition is a function of wolfish predatory violence, a far larger contribution is made by other aspects of wolf phenotypes, such as success in attracting and keeping a mate, in provisioning one's offspring, in establishing oneself within the pack, in resisting disease, drought, parasites, and in balancing the needs of one's body against the pressure to contribute to the success of copies of one's genes in *other* bodies—namely, offspring and other relatives.

Here we encounter one of the most important insights of modern evolutionary biology, a realization that has been misinterpreted by the public nearly as much as it has been path-breaking and insight-generating for biologists: the Janus-faced paradox of altruism. Natural selection is without question the primary driving force of evolution, and insofar as it operates via the unsentimental replacement of genes, it seems to offer little prospect of peaceful cooperation. This, in turn, meant that the numerous examples of animal (and human) altruism presented a daunting biological challenge: how can evolution by natural selection explain the persistence of behaviors that enhance the fitness of someone else— the recipient—at the expense of the benefactor? The rigid, amoral calculus of natural selection would seem to preclude any genetic underpinnings for behavior that is essentially self-defeating. Another way to put it: How can evolution generate seemingly altruistic acts which—by definition—*decrease* the frequency of any predisposing genes?

And yet, altruism abounds in nature, among animals as among *Homo sapiens*. A prairie dog who spots a coyote, for example, is likely to give an alarm call, which alerts other prairie dogs to the predator but at the same time informs the coyote of the location of the alarm-caller. Why be an alarm-caller when you can quietly and safely enter your burrow, letting others suffer the consequence of their inattention? Silence would seem to be not only evolutionarily self-serving, but more consistent with a strictly competitive strategy. By the same token, evolutionists had been troubled—not ethically, mind you, but scientifically—by the fact that among many animal species, individuals give "food calls" when they locate a good meal, although this typically means less nutrition for themselves. Among other puzzling cases, the most challenging was the ultimate example of self-sacrificial altruism: worker bees, wasps, and ants, among which individuals forego reproduction altogether and labor instead for the breeding success of someone else, namely the queen.

This scientific dilemma was largely solved by recognition of what is currently known as "inclusive fitness" theory, which points out that natural selection acts at the level of genes rather than individual bodies. Accordingly, when an individual behaves altruistically (e.g., a prairie dog giving an alarm call) what is actually taking place is that genes for alarm calling within the body of the "alarmist" are in fact conveying a fitness benefit to identical copies of the same genes, residing within the bodies of the beneficiaries, those who hear the call and take appropriate action. As a result, even though the alarm-calling individual may reduce his or her fitness via this behavior, alarm-calling genes are in fact enhancing *their own* evolutionary success—that is, their fitness (Dawkins, 1989).

This basic pattern operates across numerous species, encompassing a wide range of behavior. It effectively solves the evolutionary paradox of altruistic behavior by introducing yet another paradox: actions that appear altruistic (and thus, inconsistent with our understanding of how natural selection works) at the level of individual bodies turn out to be consistent after all, essentially because at the level of individual genes, they aren't altruistic but rather selfish. Of course, this does not imply conscious self-serving intent on the part of the genes in question. Rather, it simply emphasizes our best understanding of how natural selection works, by genes maximizing the long-term success of identical copies of themselves, regardless of where (i.e., in whom) they are lodged.

The story thus far may well be familiar to many readers, including non-biologists who have followed recent advances in sociobiology, evolutionary psychology, evolutionary biology, or whatever moniker one prefers. My reason for exploring it in the context of a book on war, peace, and human nature is that the popularity of the word "selfish" applied to genes (largely due to the justly influential book, *The Selfish Gene*, by Richard Dawkins, 1989) has, for many, generated a regrettable misunderstanding. Thus, even as evolutionary biologists have developed a highly plausible explanation for dramatically cooperative, prosocial behaviors—i.e., those labeled "altruistic"—this significant advance has been widely taken to provide yet more evidence that evolution leads overwhelmingly to violent, nasty, competitive behaviors . . . those that are irredeemably "selfish."

The result has been an upsurge in the assumption that the impact of evolution by natural selection must lead irretrievably to pessimism about the biological prospects for peace. Equally misleading, it has also led commentators who should know better to caricature Darwinism as cynically denying the possibility of peace and peacemaking. The former can lead to unnecessary despair about the human future, while the latter simply creates a straw man which can then be disputed along with a great show of pro-humanistic optimism. My point is that when it comes to "selfish genery," reality is more nuanced. Evolution is indeed selfish (for the genes in question), but to a large extent it achieves this end by generating behavior (by individuals) that is altruistic and prosocial (Krebs, 2011).

It must be noted that some of the fine tuning of inclusive fitness theory is under dispute, as behooves any vibrant science. (This is especially true when it comes to the impact of "kin selection" upon the evolution of sterile worker castes in the highly social Hymenopteran insects.) Also disputed is the matter of "levels of selection," the extent to which natural selection operates among genes as opposed to individuals, or even groups. Although the great majority of biologists—including myself—agree that natural selection is more potent in proportion as its level is fine-grained (e.g., more effective among individuals than among groups, and more so among genes than among individuals), in some quarters there has been an increase in the perceived legitimacy of so-called group selection, especially in the case of human beings (Sober & Wilson, 1999).

On the one hand, arguments against group selection remain cogent, especially for cases in which individual, selfish benefit is likely to swamp any pro-group, "altruistic" inclinations, a tendency that is particularly predisposed by the fact that for them to persist, group-level adaptations would have to result in a selection differential among groups that more than compensates for fitness differences between selfish and altruistic individuals within such groups. Moreover, mathematical models suggest that gene flow between groups would further facilitate the spread of any selfishness-predisposing alleles by introducing them into groups composed of other-oriented altruists who are necessarily vulnerable to such invasion. Current data for extant nomadic foragers indicates that in fact this pattern may well have been predominant among ancestral human populations as well.

On the other hand, it is at least possible that despite its acknowledged rarity in the natural world, selection at the level of groups might have been somewhat influential in human evolution, if only because human beings seem likely to have been especially effective in policing "defectors" from prosocial group norms, thereby possibly ameliorating the tendency for selection to favor selfish individualists over group-oriented cooperators. The scientific jury is currently out with respect to this question, especially in the case of *Homo sapiens* (Barash, 2012).

This issue is entirely relevant for our purposes, since group selection—although so unlikely as to be virtually impossible among most living things—may yet turn out to have been somewhat influential in the case of our own species. If so, it would provide yet another potential avenue whereby prosocial, altruistic cooperation could have evolved. (As we'll soon see, however, group selection itself—like altruism and selfishness—is a two-edged sword when it comes to the question of human warlike versus peaceful tendencies.) In theory, altruism could evolve at the level of groups if benevolent altruists conveyed sufficient benefit to the group as a whole that such a group, including its constituent altruist genes, prospered at the expense of other groups that lacked comparable altruists. If so, then prosocial, altruistic traits could evolve even if they were not preferentially directed toward genetic relatives—that is, even if they were not the outcome of "selfish genes."

There are, however, a couple of significant hurdles that must be overcome in order for group selection to emerge as a significant evolutionary force. In particular, the fitness benefit conveyed to entire groups must be sufficient to compensate for the fitness loss necessarily borne by altruists within their groups. For most living things, this appears to be an insuperable obstacle, given that the differential reproductive success of groups would have to exceed the differential success of individuals, which is to say that groups would have to wink in and out of existence with lifespans that are shorter than that of their constituent individuals, a situation that is highly unlikely. In addition, unless altruistic beneficence is preferentially directed toward genetic relatives (in which case it is indistinguishable from kin selection) group selection for altruism seems doomed to fall victim to "free riders" within groups who take advantage of the altruism of others without having to pay the cost of being altruistic themselves.

Even though the pendulum of scientific opinion continues to swing strongly against group selection as a robust driver of evolution among most species, it might have operated among *Homo sapiens*—perhaps uniquely among organisms. This is because human beings may also be unique among living things in their ability to establish and enforce group norms, thereby protecting against excessive payoffs to free-riders. It is accordingly possible that some of the traits that uniquely characterize human beings—notably, religion—which impose a cost on participants and are otherwise difficult to explain in evolutionary terms, might have evolved in response to a selective push operating at the level of groups. It has plausibly been suggested, for example, that the adaptive payoff of religion may derive from advantages in coordination and social solidarity experienced by groups as a result of the religious affiliation of their individual members.

Lest peace advocates celebrate prematurely, however, I need to point, first, to the fact that kin selection and reciprocity may well prove sufficient to explain human adaptations otherwise attributed to group selection. Moreover, even if group selection is eventually found to be fundamental to human evolution, it is yet another example of that two-edged sword mentioned earlier. Thus, among those group-level benefits that could have accrued to our ancestors, it is entirely possible (perhaps even likely) that success in competition with other groups would have loomed large. Included among the significant threats experienced by our early prehuman and human ancestors, other prehuman and human groups could have loomed large. Groups sharing the same religion, within which individuals are more likely to sacrifice for the benefit of others, and that displayed greater social cohesion as consequence, might very well have profited via these characteristics by greater success when it came to warfare against other groups. Insofar as group selection was instrumental in sculpting the human species, the result was therefore as likely to predispose *Homo sapiens* toward competitive war as toward cooperative peace.

At the same time, a strong case can and has been made that nomadic forager social systems in particular predispose against violent intergroup competition, for several reasons. For one, population structure of extant groups suggests that individuals often have close genetic relatives in neighboring groups, which would mitigate against violent conflict. For another, conflicts when they do arise typically are interpersonal—between two men, for example, over a woman—rather than among groups. In addition, it is common for competition over variable and limited resources to result in reciprocal sharing and cooperation rather than prototypical warfare. It should also be pointed out that the primary threat to ancestral human beings may have been posed by nonhuman animal predators rather than other human beings. The greatest likelihood is that proto-, pre-, and early humans faced numerous challenges: from other organisms, other human beings, as well as numerous and complex environment-based challenges, with no single one having been clearly determinative.

President Harry Truman is reputed to have lamented the absence of one-armed economists, as follows: when he asked his economic advisers for the likely outcome of a particular government policy, he would be given a possible scenario, after which he would be told, "But on the other hand. . . ." Something similar results when attempting to evaluate the impact of human evolution acting upon early group structure (whether via group or individual selection). Thus, studies of pretechnological "war" among horticulturalists such as the Yanomamö and Mundurucu suggest relatively high levels of interindividual as well as intergroup violence and mortality. Once again, the situation seems more complicated, bifurcated, and perhaps genuinely ambiguous than partisans on either side of the "primitive peace/primitive war" divide would prefer.

Janus Would Understand

Let's turn next to the question of stability versus change. Although evolution is defined as change in a population's genetic makeup over time, the reality is that much (perhaps most) of natural selection involves what is known as "stabilizing" or "normalizing selection," which is to say, selection against the extremes. Picture a normal curve in which both tails are selected against. The result is continuance of the original distribution. A classic and instructive example comes from the foundational research of H. C. Bumpus, an ornithologist at Brown University, who collected 136 house sparrows that had been stunned during an intense storm. Roughly one-half of the animals died and one-half survived. Bumpus (1899) found that those who died were those whose physical measurements (body weight, wing length, etc.) were extreme, whereas the survivors were those in the middle of the distribution. Rather than promoting change, natural selection kept things as they had been.

Similar results have been found for a wide range of characteristics, from the birth-weight of human infants to the aggressive inclinations of free-living bull elk. Evolutionary change, of course, does not equate to war, nor does stasis imply peace, but it is worth noting that neither one is necessarily more "natural."

By the same token, one of the most significant developments in evolutionary biology has had a profound influence on our understanding of those two great, complementary yet opposed processes: competition and stasis. I am referring to game theory, specifically (but not limited to) the concept of Evolutionarily Stable Strategies. This is a complex story, which for our purposes, and at the risk of some oversimplification, can usefully be seen through the lens of natural selection. Evolutionarily Stable Strategies were identified and studied as a means of better understanding situations in which multiple behavioral strategies are maintained in a population, at equilibrium, over time. Thus, a naïve but nonetheless defensible expectation is that evolution would necessarily favor one trait, allele, or gene-based phenotype (the one that is more fit) over its alternatives. The reality, however, is that not uncommonly, we observe the more or less peaceful coexistence of more than one such "morph" at the same time.

This is made possible, by—among other things—variations on "frequency dependent selection," in which above a certain frequency, a behavior that does well when rare reaches a point at which its success diminishes as its numbers increase. In such cases, fitness is high when frequency is low, but with fitness diminishing as its numbers grow, stability can be reached at which two or more forms may exist, stably, over time (Barash, 2003).

A notable example of this is the "Hawk/Dove Game," in which violent actors (Hawks) initially do well against a population of nonviolent ones (Doves), essentially because Hawks "defeat" Doves in one-to-one confrontations, thereby increasing in numbers . . . only to find themselves at an eventual disadvantage because as a result of their increasing numbers, there is increasing likelihood that Hawks will begin to encounter other Hawks, as a result of which Hawks lose fitness. More precisely, Hawks can profit when rare, so long as they do better against Doves than Doves do against Hawks, and better than Doves do against other Doves. However, as the frequency of Hawks becomes so high that Hawks are liable to meet other Hawks, and if Hawks—who, by definition, escalate violence when confronting anyone else—do sufficient damage to each other relative to the value of the resource over which they are competing, then Doves are likely to enjoy a higher fitness and, accordingly, will increase in frequency. Depending on the cost of fighting and the value of the resource(s) in question, the result can be an Evolutionarily Stable Strategy in which Doves and Hawks experience equal fitness at a particular frequency in the population.

For our purposes, it is notable that evolution can thus promote a situation in which Hawks do not drive Doves to extinction. Score one, perhaps, for "peace." But at the same time—and once again depending critically on the payoffs involved—such an equilibrium also involves continued maintenance of the Hawk phenotype. Score one, accordingly, for "war." Insofar as Evolutionarily Stable Strategies are prominent in nature (and increasingly, we are finding that they are), they accordingly operate both to promote prosocial stability and peace, as well as the continued existence of inclinations toward antisocial confrontation and war.

The situation is equally Janus-like when it comes to another type of evolutionary game, the renowned Prisoner's Dilemma. For succinctness, I shall assume that most readers are familiar with the details and proceed to the "bottom line." When two players are mutually engaged and each has a choice between "cooperation" or "being nice," and "defection" or "being nasty," a Prisoner's Dilemma results if the highest payoff (called T, the Temptation to defect) results when one is nasty at the same time that the other is nice, the next highest is obtained when both cooperate (called R, the Reward of mutual cooperation), followed by the number three payoff (P, the Punishment of mutual defection) and last of all, S (the Sucker's payoff, which comes from being nice when the other player is nasty).

Extensive analyses of Prisoner's Dilemma, both in theory and empirically, once again yield a Janus-faced result. On the one hand, it is devilishly difficult to avoid the Evolutionarily Stable Strategy of mutual defection, a condition analogous to unrelenting violence and thus, war. This is because under conditions of a Prisoner's Dilemma, each player is driven to defect, for two reasons: first, out of fear that if she cooperates, she will be Suckered by the other, who would be tempted to defect, and second, owing to her own Temptation to defect, in hopes of receiving the highest payoff while consigning the other player to the lowest. The result is a dilemma because when both defect, each receives P—the Punishment of mutual defection—which is distinctly lower than the R that would have been available if they had only figured out a way of peacefully cooperating. Chalk one up for war.

But not so fast! It turns out that there are strategies available that promise an escape from the Prisoner's Dilemma. The best-known such strategy is so-called tit-for-tat, achieved when players follow the deceptively simple rule of beginning with cooperation and then doing on each subsequent play precisely what the other player did on the previous round. Such a strategy is "forgiving," in that it doesn't hold a grudge against a defecting opponent who shows contrition by returning to cooperation; in addition, it isn't greedy, in that it doesn't attempt to take advantage of the other player. In fact, tit-for-tat never wins; rather, it prospers by peacefully but assertively avoiding a serious loss (Axelrod, 2006).

Although much heralded as a means of evolving cooperation, tit-for-tat is itself somewhat more punitive—and thus fitness-reducing—than certain alternatives, that are yet more forgiving. Once again, the take-home message for our purposes is that game theory applied to the option of mutual cooperation (peace) versus mutual defection (war), yields a multi-faceted outcome: favoring defection under certain circumstances (in cases of Prisoner's Dilemma, and especially when such games are played only once), but various strategies of cooperation under others (especially when the games are iterated and such strategies as tit-for-tat are available).

Another important source of error in assessing the impact of evolution upon tendencies for peace and war concerns the public understanding of "fitness," once again captured—erroneously—by Herbert Spencer's regrettable phrase "survival of the fittest." (Darwin deserves some of the blame here as well, since he unwisely adopted the usage in subsequent editions of *The Origin of Species*.) There are a couple of problems here. First, although simple survival is obviously a prerequisite for evolutionary success, it counts only insofar as it contributes to that success: that is, to the ability of genes to catapult themselves into future generations. Rather than a simplistic case of eat-or-be-eaten, for example, evolution's demand is more like: replicate yourself (you genes) or be eventually replaced by those that do. *How* you do this, on the other hand, is a different and much more complex question.

This leads us to the second problem with "survival of the fittest," namely the assumption that in promoting fitness, evolution necessarily favors genetic variants (and their phenotypic expressions) that are physically imposing and maximally inclined toward violence. Sometimes physical fitness is indeed associated with evolutionary fitness, for obvious reasons. Similarly, violent inclinations are sometimes associated with evolutionary fitness, again for obvious reasons—especially, for example, in the case of a polygynous (harem-forming) species, in which males have a high variance in reproductive success and, as a result, are more fit in proportion as they succeed in intimidating or literally defeating their rivals and therefore obtain multiple matings and thus, a high fitness payoff.

But it is also true that just as selection often acts against the extremes (recall those storm-tossed sparrows!), it sets a limit on excessive aggressiveness. For example, bull elk (called "red deer" in the United Kingdom, where the relevant research was conducted) who spend too much time threatening and fighting with other bulls lose fitness because of other, less aggressively inclined bulls who sneak into the harem and copulate with the cows (Clutton-Brock, Guinness, & Albon, 1982). Similar examples of "aggressive neglect" have been reported for birds as well, leading to the safe generalization that many roads lead to evolutionary fitness, of which violence and its concomitants are merely one . . . and sometimes, too much violence is selected *against*.

So far, so good for the peace-seeking side of evolution. The widespread error of conflating fitness with violence and competition cannot be debunked too often. At the same time, however, there remains a powerful sense in which fitness maximization points the Janus face of evolution toward competition as well. (Just consider the fact that bull elk are in fact much more aggressive than cows, due to the adaptive reality that harem formation conveys fitness payoffs upon males who are aggressive enough to have displaced other males.) Natural selection operates essentially via fitness differentials rather than absolute numbers; *relative fitness,* not simple abundance, is key. And thereby hangs a tale.

Fitness is essentially a ratio, with the numerator reflecting the success of genes in projecting copies of themselves into the future and the denominator, the success of alternative genes. Since a gene (or an individual, a population, even—in theory—a species) maximizes its success by producing the largest such ratio, it can do so either by reducing the denominator or increasing the numerator. Most creatures, most of the time, find it easier to do the latter than the former, which is why living things generally are more concerned with feathering their nests than de-feathering those of others.

But natural selection is not ethically driven. It smiles upon any tactics that promote the underlying strategic goal of fitness maximization, hence it is not limited to amplifying the numerator (simple success, however achieved), but is equally inclined toward anything that effectively reduces the denominator: that is, anything that on balance reduces the success of competitors. Not surprisingly, therefore, biologists have discovered infanticide in numerous species, including lions and many nonhuman primates such as langur monkeys and chimpanzees. The basic pattern is that when a dominant male is overthrown, his replacement often systematically kills the nursing infants (unrelated to himself), thereby inducing the lactating mothers to resume their sexual cycling, whereupon they mate with their infant's murderer (Hausfater & Hrdy, 2008). It is truly awful, such that even hard-eyed biologists had a difficult time accepting its ubiquity, and even—until recently—its "naturalness." But natural it is, and a readily understood consequence of natural selection as a mindless, automatic, and value-free process, whose driving principle is if anything not just amoral but—by any decent human standard—downright immoral.

Add cases of animal rape, deception, nepotism, siblicide, matricide, and cannibalism, in addition to well-documented cases of lethal intergroup violence among chimpanzees, and it should be clear that natural selection has blindly, mechanically, yet effectively favored self-betterment and genetic self-promotion, often—although not exclusively—achieved by means of violent competition. If the outcome in certain cases is less reprehensible than outright slaughter, it is only because natural selection only sometimes works to reduce the denominator of the "fitness ratio." Most of the time, it increases the numerator. But all the time, the only outcome assessed by natural selection is whether a given tactic works—whether it enhances fitness by increasing the fitness ratio—not whether it is good, right, just, admirable, or in any sense moral or affirming of peace.

Much as the human mind is drawn toward simple either/or statements (either up or down, black or white, good or bad, "with us or with the terrorists"), reality is more nuanced, complex, and Janus-faced. This applies particularly to the seemingly simple question of whether or not human beings are "naturally" or "instinctively" aggressive or violent. Popular treatments of human beings as "killer apes" have clearly been misguided in their single-mindedness; ditto for others purporting to demonstrate that we are unilaterally cooperative and peaceful. In 1986, a group of scientists met in Spain and authored what came to be known as the "Seville Statement on Violence," a document that was subsequently endorsed by UNESCO. In summary, this brief but influential manifesto described as "scientifically incorrect" the following notions: "we have inherited a tendency to make war from our animal ancestors," "war or any other violent behavior is genetically programmed into our human nature," "in the course of human evolution there has been a selection for aggressive behavior more than for other kinds of behavior," "humans have a 'violent brain,'" and that "war is caused by 'instinct' or any single motivation." The Seville Statement was well-meaning in that it was intended to counter the claim that war is in our genes and hence, is inevitable, a perspective that is quite dangerous in that it could become a self-fulfilling prophecy, promoting the myth that since both war and violence are biologically mandated, it is useless to struggle against them.

Yet, the Seville Statement is not, strictly speaking, scientifically correct. Just as there is danger in accepting an overly bleak, neo-Hobbesian view that evolution has condemned humanity to unavoidable violence and war, there is danger in an unrealistically optimistic, neo-Rousseauian perspective that minimizes our risks by seeing *Homo sapiens* through rose-tinted glasses. The reality is that to some extent and under certain circumstances, we *have* in fact inherited—if not a tendency then a capacity—to make war from our animal ancestors, violent behavior *is* genetically programmed into our human nature, selection *has* favored aggressive behavior, we *have* a violent brain, and so forth. Note, however, my qualifying preamble "to some extent and under certain circumstances." Moreover, a *capacity* to do something, depending upon environmental circumstances, is different from a rigid necessity, or even a general tendency, come what may. We have inherited not just an ability but also a capacity to make peace, *under certain conditions*. Violent behavior is genetically programmed into our human nature to the extent that we are capable of behaving violently (moreover, inclined to do so) but again, only *under certain conditions*. A more accurate "statement" than the one from Seville would be that because of natural selection, human beings have a capacity to be peaceful and warlike, cooperative and competitive, loving and violent . . . depending upon conditions. Those conditions include but are not limited to the amount and nature of resources available (such as food, mates, living and breeding space), the nature of social expectation, cultural traditions and indoctrination, degree of embed-dedness among kin and other reciprocating individuals, and so forth.

Like the proverbial cartoon in which both an angel and a devil perch upon each person's shoulder, whispering in her ears and vying for attention, our evolutionary heritage offers different routes for future behavior, without necessarily predisposing us in any one direction (Barash & Webel, 2009).

Among the uniquely defining physical traits of *Homo sapiens* is our species' exceptionally large and complex brain, and, no less consequential, our predisposition toward rational thought. It therefore can (and has) been argued that human beings are uniquely capable of rebelling against our darker biologically-influenced inclination, thereby predisposing us toward peace and away from war. Indeed, we may well be unique in the natural world in being able to say no to most of our more complicated and subtle genetically-given inclinations. (It is much more difficult, on the other hand, to rebel against the simpler and more fundamental biological demands such as those causing us to eat when hungry, sleep when tired, exchange gases in our lungs or chemicals in our kidneys.)

But once again, the situation is multi-facetted, such that we simply cannot count on humanity's cognitive capacities to avoid or terminate wars; after all, the Manhattan Project and the ensuing design and construction of nuclear weapons represent a pinnacle of highly refined rational thought. For all the intense emotions it arouses, the conduct of war itself requires elaborate planning and a very high level of rational calculation . . . not to mention, ironically, peaceful cooperation among war-makers on each side.

Nonetheless, I am fully in accord with this concluding statement from Seville: "Just as wars begin in the minds of men, peace also begins in our minds. The same species who invented war is capable of inventing peace. The responsibility lies with each of us."

So, are we doomed by our evolutionary past—more precisely, by its imprint upon the present—to a future of unending and eternal war? The answer, clearly, is no. Our genes whisper within us, they do not shout. When it comes to violence, whether organized or individual, *Homo sapiens* are subject to genetic influences, not determinism. Does this mean, therefore, that we can take comfort in being innately peace-loving and pacifist? Once again, the answer is clearly no. Insofar as we are subject to genetic influences, not determinism, it is equally certain that just as these influences don't mandate violence, neither do they mandate nonviolence. We have within us the biologically generated, Janus-like capacity to face in either direction (or, more confusingly, in both at the same time!), combined with a biologically mandated obligation to neither one.

At this point, readers looking to evolution for guidance can be forgiven if they feel confused, even frustrated by the not-so-simple fact that our biological heritage is so ambiguous, or—if you prefer—ambivalent. Either way, although it is definitely worthwhile to interrogate our evolutionary background for indications as to our predilections, the answer leads us to Jean-Paul Sartre's famous formulation that human beings are "condemned to be free." Whether devotees of peace choose to be relieved to learn that we are not biologically obliged to war, or to be distraught that by the same token, we are not unilaterally predisposed, through our biology, to peace, we are all stuck with an obligation (if not necessarily a predisposition) to respond to Sartre's simple, daunting, existentialist challenge: "You are free. Choose."

I have heard the following story, said to be of Native American origin (ostensibly Cherokee), but have been unable to confirm it. Whether "true" or not—in the sense of being a genuine folktale—it is certifiably true for our purposes, as a statement of our species-wide situation. A young child was greatly frightened by her dream, in which two wolves fought viciously, growling and snapping their jaws. Hoping for solace, she described this dream to her grandfather, a wise and highly respected elder. The grandfather explained that her dream was indeed true: "There are two wolves within each of us, one of them benevolent and peace-loving, the other malevolent and violent. They fight constantly for our souls."

At this, the child found herself more frightened than ever, and asked her grandfather which one wins. He replied, "The one you feed."

References

Axelrod, R. (2006). *The evolution of cooperation* (Revised ed.). New York: Basic Books.

Barash, D. P. (2003). *The survival game: How game theory explains the biology of cooperation and competition.* New York: Henry Holt.

Barash, D. P. (2012). *Homo mysterious: Evolutionary mysteries.* New York: Oxford University Press.

Barash, D. P., & Webel, C. P. (2009). *Peace and conflict studies* (2nd ed.). Thousand Oaks, CA: Sage Publications.

Bumpus, H. C. (1899). The elimination of the unfit as illustrated by the introduced sparrow. *Biology Lectures in Marine Biology at Woods Hole, Massachusetts, 11,* 209–226.

Clutton-Brock, T. H., Guinness, F. E. & Albon, S. D. (1982). *Red deer: Behavior and ecology of two sexes.* Chicago: University of Chicago Press.

Dawkins, R. (1989). *The Selfish Gene* (Revised ed.). New York: Oxford University Press.

Fry, D. P. (2007). *Beyond war: The human potential for peace.* New York: Oxford University Press.

Hausfater, G. & Hrdy, S. B. (2008). *Infanticide: Comparative and evolutionary perspectives.* New Brunswick, NJ: Aldine Transaction.

Krebs, D. (2011). *The origins of morality: An evolutionary account.* New York: Oxford University Press.

Smith, D. L. (2009). *The most dangerous animal: Human nature and the origins of war.* New York: St. Martin's Press.

Sober, E., & Wilson, D. S. (1999). *Unto others: The evolution and psychology of unselfish behavior.* Cambridge, MA: Harvard University Press.

3

Conflict and Restraint
in Animal Species

Implications for War and Peace

Hanna Kokko

Any casual observer of nature documentaries will easily notice an emphasis on "nature, red in tooth and claw," where one either eats or gets eaten. Biologists tend to accept that much of life behaves in a fairly nasty way toward all other life, while simultaneously marveling at the fantastic adaptations that life's challenges help evolution to produce. For example, bird flight may well have arisen because it allowed birds to flee from predators more efficiently or—when birds switch roles to being predators—to find prey more efficiently; but the consequence is that it also allows the spectacular migration events spanning the entire globe. But is life all about causing damage to other organisms? Asking the same question in a narrower context: how much do aggression and selfish behavior dominate interactions among individuals of the *same* species? These are issues that biologists have discussed at length ever since Darwin provided a logical structure for the evolution of species characteristics in *The Origin of Species* (Darwin, 1859).

Early thinkers in the emerging field of evolutionary biology held very disparate views on this topic. For Thomas Henry Huxley (1888), also known as "Darwin's bulldog," as he saw the value of Darwinian thinking and was not afraid of defending it in public, the phrase "nature, red in tooth and claw" must have felt totally appropriate. In an article titled "The Struggle for Existence," he wrote that in the animal world, beyond the temporary and limited relations of the family, the Hobbesian war of each against all is the normal state of existence. For the former Russian prince and anarchist Petr Kropotkin, however, life was fundamentally cooperative. During his travels in Siberia, he became convinced that life is much more about succeeding in the face of environmental challenges than about outcompeting conspecifics; a herd of ungulates keeping each other warm in a blizzard epitomizes this view (see Dugatkin, 2006).

The arguments of Huxley and Kropotkin were verbal: the quantitative study of evolution was yet to be born. In the following decades evolutionary theory became firmly established, but by now much of the focus of attention of evolutionary biologists was on working out the mathematics of how selection modifies the frequencies of different genotypes. Intriguingly, the study of specific behaviors, aggression among them, became sidelined during this time (review: Kokko & Jennions, 2010). In the 1960s, several authors began finally to ask what rules might govern animal aggression. The arguments provided were initially rather imprecise, based on the logic that too much intraspecific damage would surely be selected against (Huxley, 1966—not the same Huxley as above, but his grandson; Lorenz, 1964, 1965). For example, Konrad Lorenz, the Nobel Prize winning co-founder of ethology, famously discussed the contrast between doves and wolves. Only the latter have dangerous weapons with which they could easily kill conspecifics in the wild, and thus only wolves have evolved "psychological" mechanisms for the good of the species that prevent them from killing pack members that give the appropriate submissive signals (Lorenz, 1964, 1965).

Don't Assume That It's All About Group Performance

No matter how compelling the Lorenzian survival of the species argument may sound, it does not survive closer scrutiny. Today, we know that evolutionary ideas should not be based on the straightforward premise that evolution equips species with traits that are beneficial for the survival of the entire group, population, or species. This is because what is good for the reproductive success of a "lower" entity, such as an individual, may often conflict with what is good for the performance of a higher entity, such as a species. Up to the 1960s, the potential for such conflict was not widely perceived among evolutionary biologists. A massive communication gap appears to have persisted for a surprisingly long time. Work on selection and gene frequencies was largely focused on how organisms evolve to cope with abiotic environmental challenges, and thus it did not occur to mathematically talented researchers to ask what happens if conspecifics interact with each other in potentially damaging ways. Ideas explicitly focused on aggression, on the other hand, were initially developed without much influence of formal evolutionary theory. This allowed researchers such as Lorenz and Huxley to base their publications on the logic that by today's standards appears rather loose: whatever appears beneficial for reproduction or survival in some sense could be favored by selection.

Things came to a head, largely prompted by a book in which Vero Wynne-Edwards, an English zoologist, explicitly argued that adaptations often arise because they benefit groups of individuals, rather than the individuals themselves (Wynne-Edwards, 1962). His contemporaries made use of the same logic, but Wynne-Edwards promoted the idea in such explicit terms that suddenly closer scrutiny appeared appropriate. To use his now famous example: why do many corvids (crows, jackdaws and such) often fly long distances in the evening to roost in the same tree? This question may sound like a trivial detail of animal behavior, but the argument provided by Wynne-Edwards sparked a small revolution in behavioral research—by virtue of being wrong. His hypothesis was that crows do this to be able to estimate if the current population density is about to grow to dangerously high levels, such that further population growth would be unsustainable. According to Wynne-Edwards, avoidance of overbreeding and the resulting depletion of local resources were favored by natural selection.

The counterpoint was provided by George Williams, who in his 1966 book *Adaptation and Natural Selection: A Critique of Some Current Thought* was the first evolutionary biologist who explicitly made the point that selection can very easily favor individual behaviors that are detrimental for groups. His writing made it clear that that the field could no longer afford to ignore explicit mathematical thinking, which means counting copies of genotypes, when making predictions about what should and should not be favored by natural selection in specific circumstances. Whether we are interested in interactions between individuals or the struggle to survive adverse environmental conditions, we must not take an apparent group-level benefit of a certain behavior as evidence that it must have evolved to achieve this function. To use an example from Williams (1966), consider an invisible visitor from Mars who observes panic-stricken humans escaping from a burning theatre. How should our Martian explain this phenomenon?

If the visitor from Mars emphasizes the way the group responded to the stimulus of fire by changing shape from a widely dispersed distribution to dense clusters headed toward the exits, he is likely to be focusing on the wrong level of explanation. A too strong belief in the behavior maximizing the group benefit will make our alien totally miss the point that the sometimes observed behavioral rule, "move toward the doors as fast as possible," is decidedly not the best one that the group could conceivably employ. The rule effectively blocks the exits; thus were the behavior a true adaptation aimed at maximizing group survival, individuals would appear to be in much less of a rush. No wonder that social norms (for instance, those worst-case scenarios cheerfully delivered to us in the form of in-flight safety instructions) try to make us behave more calmly than we are inclined to do, and no wonder we often fail to comply in real life.

As a result of Williams's 1966 book, it became impossible for a biologist to casually assume that any sort of unselfish behavior, limited aggression included, is selected for simply because it appears to benefit the larger social unit in which the individual lives. Importantly, however, this shift was not equivalent to reverting to T.H. Huxley's "nature, red in tooth and claw" worldview. All that happened was the recognition that whether we are arguing for the adaptiveness of a "nasty" or "nice" behavior, we must in each case make the arguments explicit, typically backed up by precise bookkeeping of which individual's genes dominate in future generations when two or more different strategies compete for relative representation in those generations.

This, however, also created a problem, which is best illustrated with aggression as the "nasty" trait. Conceivably, a crow who does not obey the rule "use the roost to gather information about conspecific density, and do not breed if the current population appears too dense," and instead stabs with its sharp beak its sleepy neighbors and takes over all local resources, would be the one whose genes persist: all other types of genes would now be rotting in stabbed crow corpses. We can no longer resort to group-level arguments to explain what keeps overaggressive behavior from spreading. In short, why are so many interactions among animals described as "limited war"? Male kangaroos, for example, famously box using their forelimbs first, and only if neither contestant retreats will the fight eventually escalate to true kickboxing with powerful hind legs, supported by a very sturdy tail.

Limited War? Game Theory Can Explain It

The world did not have to wait for long to find the first satisfactory answer for why limited aggression predominates over escalated fighting among conspecifics. The early half of the twentieth century had seen the birth of *game theory*, a formalism that had its origins in economics. Game theoretic models (particularly in their noncooperative versions) ask what an individual can do to increase one's payoff, when other individuals similarly choose their actions, and individual payoff depends on one's own decision as well as that of others. Importantly, there is no guarantee that the solution maximizes any measure of group performance: trying to run toward the exit as fast as one can might be individually the best option regardless of others' running speed (if others are about to block the entrance, better get out before this happens, so gentlemanly behavior is never rewarded individually). Williams (1966) did not mention game theory, but his example could very well have been interpreted in this light.

Preceded by a paper on sex ratio variation (Hamilton, 1967), a number of papers in the early 1970s imported game theory into the study of animal behavior, with the question of "limited war" now occupying central stage. John Maynard Smith and George Price (Maynard Smith & Price, 1973, Maynard Smith, 1974) provided first a fairly complicated analysis of sequential fights, followed by a simplification by Maynard Smith and Parker (1976) that became the classic Hawk-Dove game (see also Maynard Smith, 1982). Individuals in this dyadic (two-player) model are interested in acquiring a discrete resource item of value V. The value is a measure of how much acquiring this item aids one's reproductive success; V could represent an item of food, a territory, or access to a female. Each individual has two options available: one can play either "hawk," which means being prepared to fight, or "dove," which implies that the individual will only have access to items in which no "hawk" is interested. If another "dove" is interested, the resource is either shared or it is randomly determined which individual gets the item. There are three possible outcomes:

- A dove meets a dove; the expected payoff is $V/2$ for each of them.
- A dove meets a hawk; the dove backs away and has payoff 0, the hawk gains the resource and has payoff V.

- A hawk meets a hawk; a fight ensues, and one of the two individuals wins. Fights are also costly (cost C represents time or energy costs or risks of injury), meaning that the expected payoff is $(V-C)/2$.

Note that it does not matter whether one assumes that the winner hawk gains resource V and the loser pays the full cost C or that both pay a cost of magnitude $C/2$. Assuming that only one randomly chosen hawk can win, the payoff turns out $(V-C)/2$ in either case.

The payoffs of this game are clearly frequency-dependent. In a population consisting of doves, a hawk will have a payoff V that exceeds the payoff of all other (dove) individuals. Assuming that resource acquisition correlates with reproductive success, this result means that hawks propagate their genes more efficiently than doves. Hawks therefore become more common, and they now sometimes encounter other hawks instead of doves. When the proportion of hawks is P, the expected payoff of hawk behavior is $P(V-C)/2 + (1-P)V$. A dove, on the other hand, has payoff $(1-P)V/2$. Both hawks and doves gain more if others are more dove-like; but hawk payoffs decline more rapidly in the presence of other hawks than do payoffs to doves.

This decline eventually stabilizes the proportion of hawks as $P = V/C$, which is less than 1 if $V < C$. Both hawks and doves now have equal payoff $(1-V/C) V/2$, which, importantly, is a fraction $1-V/C$ of the solution that would have maximized the payoff if individuals were somehow selected to maximize group benefit (this implying all individuals are doves; the payoff is then $V/2$ for each individual). There is limited war in the sense that hawks cannot take over the entire population if $V < C$, but simultaneously the costs of war are not limited to zero.

How Spiders and Finches Can Be Hawks and Doves

The hawk–dove game was probably never meant to be more than a caricature of animal behavior: after all, male kangaroos, for example, don't come in two varieties, one that always retreats and the other that always boxes. Intriguingly, at least occasionally it does appear that discrete behavioral types can coexist in a population. In golden orb spiders *Nephila fenestrata* (Figure 3.1), males fall into two categories according to whether they have already mated with a female or not. If they have, they cannot ever mate again, because damage to their genitalia means they are functionally sterile. They can, however, still do something about their fitness: they guard the female they have mated with, fighting against any males who dare to approach her (this makes sense, as rival sperm could otherwise fertilize some of her eggs). At the same time, because mated males' success with any new mates is destined to be low, the cost of fighting, C, also is low for them. Evolutionarily speaking, even if a fight is fatal, the cost of this unfortunate outcome is small if not much could have been achieved by living.

For virgin males, the situation is different. They should not accept the high risks of fighting a mated male who is guarding a female because the virgin males still have mating

FIGURE 3.1 Female golden orb spiders (*Nephila fenestrata*) are worth fighting for. Mated males resemble "hawks" while virgin males act like "doves" in fights over access to a female. (Photo credit: Lutz Fromhage).

capacity left that they can better spend on unmated females or unguarded mated females. By risking injury in a contest, virgin males have much more to lose than mated males. In line with these predictions, Fromhage and Schneider (2005) showed that mated males usually won contests against virgin males, even when the latter were physically superior. This indicates that virgin males use a dove-like approach, and mated males employ a hawk-like strategy in an encounter. Also, Fromhage and Schneider (2005) staged contests between mated males and found that these resulted in high frequencies of injury, again in accordance with the idea of hawk-hawk encounters.

The hawk-like or dove-like behavior of the spiders studied by Fromhage and Schneider (2005) was clearly not genetically fixed, but a flexible (plastic) response to their own mating history. In fact, I am aware of only one example where "hawks" and "doves" are genetically distinct members of the same species. The Gouldian finch *Erythrura gouldiae* is a fantastically colorful species that inhabits northern Australia (Figure 3.2). Both males and females come in three varieties (color morphs): their heads can be red, yellow, or black (Pryke & Griffith, 2007). Of these morphs, yellow is exceedingly rare, and thus the game is mainly played by red and black individuals. The color is determined by an allele on the sex chromosomes, which means that females have one allele for head color—red or black—while males have two, and their heads are black only if they have two copies of the recessive black allele (Pryke & Griffith, 2009a). (In birds, the sex determination system is opposite

FIGURE 3.2 In Gouldian finches (*Erythrura gouldiae*), aggressiveness is influenced by head color. Red-headed individuals behave in a hawk-like fashion, which gives them better access to resources but makes them poorer parents. (Photo credit: Sarah Pryke).

from that of mammals, in which it is the female who has two copies of any gene on the sex chromosomes.)

Detailed observations in the wild as well as in aviaries have revealed that males of the red morph are "hawks," while black males are "doves." These two types of male differ in their breeding strategy: red birds are behaviorally dominant, and thus they are able to outcompete black individuals when nest sites (tree hollows) are scarce. If red males are rare, they thus have a breeding advantage while suffering little cost (Pryke & Griffith, 2009b). However, when red males become common, they appear to suffer increasing costs of meeting other red males. In the case of the Gouldian finch, this cost C does not manifest itself as direct injury; instead offspring production suffers. This appears to result from a trade-off, where spending much effort in aggressive encounters means that brood care suffers (Pryke & Griffith, 2009b).

In principle, either type of male can be a good father: red males provide parental effort comparable to that of black males in environments where competition is low. However, red (but not black) males severely reduce or abandon parental duties in highly competitive environments, particularly when there are many other red males nearby. This covaries with increased testosterone counts and high stress hormone levels, and results in far fewer fledged young per brood when red males live in red-dominated environments (Pryke & Griffith, 2009b). Quite literally, these males "see red" when surrounded by others of their own head color! Since bird studies often find that testosterone inhibits parental care by males (McGlothlin, Jawor, & Ketterson, 2007), it appears that the decline in "hawk" breeding success with an increasing proportion of "hawks" in the population is hormonally mediated. Thus, our understanding in this area has advanced from abstractly formulated V and C values to knowing exactly what mechanisms allow different types to coexist. Aggression is good for nest site acquisition, it is bad for parental performance, and the relative importance of each factor varies with the proportion of "hawks" in the population.

Beyond the First Hawk-Dove Game: A Closer Look at Lethal Fights

Although the above examples are fascinating, it is clearly an oversimplification to assume that all animal contests can be understood as a frequency-dependent game between two types, one more aggressive than the other. Clearly distinct morphs as exist among the Gouldian finch are the exception, not the rule. Sometimes, a behavioral polymorphism is replaced by all individuals appearing hawk-like. For example, lethal fighting is the norm in fig wasps: females routinely fight for the ownership of a fig (where eggs are laid) until only one of them is alive. That evolution permits lethal fighting is not surprising, as $V > C$ predicts that the proportion of "hawks" can increase from any current value P upwards, until $P = 1$ is reached. As stated above, the cost C will be low when one's future life is unlikely to yield reproductive success (if the fight is not won). This can happen when searching for uncontested resources is unlikely to be successful. Such conditions predict the adoption of "desperado" strategies (Grafen, 1987) wherein individuals are willing to risk a lot in a fight, even if the prospects of winning are meager.

A more explicit look at the problem can be obtained by modifying the hawk-dove game such that expected lifetime fitness is $pV + (1 - q)V_0$ (Enquist & Leimar, 1990). Here p is not the proportion of hawks (which we denote as P), but the probability of the focal individual winning a fight. V is the value of the resource over which the contest occurs, and V_0 is the individual's future reproductive success if it does *not* participate in the fight (instead, it could carry on searching, for instance, for uncontested resources). If the individual fights, the value of its future life, V_0, is diminished by a factor q. Fighting thus represents a trade-off: achieving high p probably requires doing something risky (or at the very least wasting time), which increases q and hence diminishes $(1 - q)V_0$.

When is fatal fighting adaptive? Consider the case $p = q = 0.5$. An interpretation of these values is that two "hawks" (individuals who opt to engage in a fight) will carry on until one of them is dead, and the winner has improved its fitness from V_0, the value obtainable without the fight, to $V + V_0$. Given that the winner cannot be predicted in advance, it is on average beneficial for both contestants to fight if the expected value from participating, $(V + V_0)/2$, exceeds the expectation in the absence of the fight, V_0. This simplifies to $V > V_0$. Therefore, one should be prepared to participate in fights where the probability of being killed is 50 percent, if victory more than doubles one's reproductive success (from V_0 to $V_0 + V$ where $V > V_0$).

Of course, one can ask if the winner is expected to be intact enough to make full use of the resource after such a vigorous struggle. Fig wasps seem to manage, but as Lorenz (1964, 1965) already noted, lethal fighting is not really the norm in the animal kingdom. Instead, there are many examples of displays (roaring, strutting) that replace fighting or precede it. Escalation only occurs if neither contestant retreats. These cases differ from the simple hawk-dove game in that there is now the possibility for mutual assessment of strength. Avoidance of conflict can be advantageous for the likely loser as well as for the likely winner. It is not in the interest of an individual to fight in a situation that will lead to a guaranteed loss. Instead, an individual can save time by retreating and searching for resources elsewhere. Similarly it is not in the interest of the stronger opponent to fight if a display of superiority, which avoids any risk of injury, is sufficient to settle the contest.

It is for this reason that individuals often evolve to assess each other's resource-holding power (a technical term that essentially means "strength") before engaging in serious battle. Also, there can be far more stages of escalation in a fight than a straightforward progression from mere looking at each other to maximal use of all weapons available. Optimal behavior in these cases has been modeled with so-called sequential assessment games (Enquist & Leimar, 1983), which predict that contests with great asymmetry in relative fighting ability should end in an early phase, whereas matched individuals may proceed through a series of escalations reaching a final phase of more dangerous fighting. For example, in the cichlid fish *Nannacara anomala*, an analysis of 102 staged fights showed good support for these predictions: contests where the weight asymmetry of fish was minimal led to far longer fights and higher injury scores for the contestants than among pairs with larger weight differences (Enquist, Leimar, Ljungberg, Mallner, & Segerdahl, 1990).

Thus, it appears that animals often avoid fighting when the likely outcome is clear from the start. The group benefit, that is, that animal societies much of the time appear relatively peaceful, is a fortuitous consequence but not the cause of restrained fighting. To go back to the thought experiment of the murderous crow stabbing its sleepy flockmates to death: other crows have powerful beaks too, and it might be quite hard to do this stealthily and repeatedly enough to reduce competition for food for one's own young. Hence, such tendencies are not favored by selection.

The Puzzling Version of Limited War: Uncorrelated Asymmetries

The above section highlighted that conflicts can be settled before they enter an escalated fight stage if there are clear asymmetries between individuals; for example, it may be better for a small fish to swim away as soon as it detects the large territory owner. This is an example of a *correlated asymmetry*, which means that the observable difference (for instance, body length) is a useful predictor of resource holding power and thus the likely outcome of a fight, should one ensue. A more puzzling case is provided by *uncorrelated asymmetries*. Can conflict situations also be settled, to the benefit of both players, if there is an observable asymmetry that does not relate in any way to the fighting abilities of the players?

At first sight, this option appears somewhat bizarre. To use an example by Eshel (2005), suppose that the individual whose thumbs are shorter will always retreat (play "dove") in some populations, whereas in others, the individual with the longer thumbs always retreats. There actually appear to be biologically relevant contests that are settled on the basis of arbitrary asymmetries, although, as we shall see, this may at times be an illusion. By far the most important asymmetry is related to the emergence of *owner-ship*. Individuals, pairs, or entire groups of animals often defend relatively well-delineated areas. If a male bird sings perched on a branch, it is typically sending off two distinct messages: one, that a female is welcome to join him; and two, that any male who thinks about settling here should think twice. There is nothing necessarily physically superior about this bird compared with his neighbor, but if they fight, the one on home ground generally wins. The same bird, in a fight against the same contestant, tends to lose when the home advantage is reversed to favor the neighbor. Ownership, in the form of "I was here first," is often obeyed as a rule that settles conflict (humans included, DeScioli & Wilson, 2011; Stake, 2004).

Ownership can be easy to observe: both the owner and the intruder usually know that the latter is a latecomer. To analyze how this can be useful as a cue that settles conflict and avoids fight costs, consider an extension of the hawk-dove game. In this scenario, in addition to "hawks" that are always aggressive and doves that never are, there could be a type called "Bourgeois" that retreats if it discovers it found the resource as a latecomer and is prepared to fight if it perceives itself to have arrived first. Assuming that fights are sufficiently costly, the Bourgeois strategy can invade a population consisting of pure hawks and doves (Hammerstein, 1981). Something like Bourgeois indeed appears to be going on in now classic experiments on butterflies (a species called the speckled wood, *Pararge aegeria*). This butterfly inhabits brightly sunlit patches in otherwise shady woodlands. Males defend and mate with females who enter the sunlit patches; the relevance of sunlight to the butterfly is clear once one remembers that these are ectothermic (cold-blooded) creatures. Butterfly fights are not very violent affairs; they resemble a war of attrition where rapidly circling flights continue until one individual gives up and flies away. While serious injury is rare, energetic costs, wear and tear, and time costs of such activities may be relevant given the short life of most butterflies.

Who gives up first, and who wins? Nick Davies, who observed fights carefully, observed that the butterfly that had entered the patch first always persisted longer (Davies, 1978). Davies was then able to experimentally trick two butterflies at a time, such that both perceived the other one to be the latecomer. The consequence was similar to the effect of matched-size contests in fish: the contests now lasted much longer, supporting the role of residence asymmetry as a determinant of which individual is expected to respect ownership. The *prior residence effect* has since been found in a large number of animals from polychaete worms to mammals (Kokko, López-Sepulcre, & Morrell, 2006). In its generalized form it predicts that while latecomers might not always retreat without fights, they should, in order to win, have quite a substantial advantage in some *correlated asymmetry* trait, such as body size.

There are, however, practical as well as theoretical problems with the Bourgeois account of territoriality (review: Kokko, in press). In practical terms, it is hard to prove that there really was no correlated asymmetry between the contestants. For example, a butterfly that already has resided in a sunlit patch is warmer, and hence it can be the more agile of the two contestants at the moment the intruder arrives (Stutt & Willmer, 1998). Also, if intrinsically stronger or more motivated individuals win fights, then such individuals accumulate as owners. Under such conditions, intruders might be respecting owners because these are likely to be strong fighters rather than respecting ownership per se. A great deal of empirical effort has been spent to disentangle potential confounding factors. In a recent experiment on the speckled wood butterfly, for example, natural forests have been replaced by large butterfly cages full of artificial Christmas trees, allowing for much greater control over previous experiences and consequent temperature of individuals. It appears now that all individuals appear equally motivated to fight, but the intrinsically aggressive males accumulate as "owners" (Kemp & Wiklund, 2004).

As to the theoretical problem, if the arrival order of the two contestants is really a label as arbitrary as a difference in thumb length, then it is surprisingly hard to see what prevents an *anti-Bourgeois* strategy from spreading. This strategy settles conflicts by using a convention where the latecomer always wins, and the previous owner retreats without fighting. While decidedly paradoxical in its feel (in human societies, nobody agrees to vacate one's dwelling as soon as a random intruder knocks on the door and demands this), the mathematics of anti-Bourgeois is, in simple models at least, equivalent to that of Bourgeois (Kokko et al., 2006; Maynard Smith, 1982). This raises the question of why we do not have, for every species that respects territorial boundaries, another one where all ownership is in continuous flux.

Newer modeling has confronted this problem, showing that the anti-Bourgeois strategy does disappear (that is, being not evolutionarily stable it can be invaded by other strategies) when it is taken into account that a population in anti-Bourgeois flux would have extremely short breeding tenures for individuals. Once this is considered, the prediction is that multiple factors may produce respect for ownership: the prior residence effect on its own can explain ownership respect without producing paradoxical anti-Bourgeois behavior, but respect for ownership is further strengthened if individuals differ in their fighting abilities such that strong individuals accumulate in the owner role (Kokko et al., 2006). The new models also predict that respect is rarely complete, which is in keeping with reality where forceful takeovers occasionally occur despite a clear "home advantage" of the owner (Kokko et al., 2006).

Toward Societies

Much of fighting in nature happens at the individual level: male deer fight to gain ownership of a harem of females in a "winner takes all" fashion, female fig wasps fight similarly over precious figs, and there are also plenty of agonistic encounters between males and females. For example, males of numerous insect species attempt to mount females forcefully, but it is not necessarily in the female's best interest to mate. Mating can take a long time in insects, and being in copula is risky as it compromises mobility—and thus observations and evolutionary reasoning suggest that the female has been selected only to accept a mating when she really needs sperm to fertilize her eggs. Therefore, unreceptive females respond by kicking vigorously. In spiders, females often cannibalize the male instead of allowing him to mate.

In many cases of individuals fighting conspecifics, the exact identity of the opponents does not matter much beyond attending to traits that are useful in predicting the chances of winning. Similarly, in peaceful encounters, such as when flocking behavior brings about safety in numbers (from predation), the identities of conspecifics are largely irrelevant. However, there are also numerous cases where individuals treat each other much better if they are familiar with each other, and agonistic encounters are directed toward unfamiliar conspecifics.

The most obvious possibility is that the conspecifics in question are kin. Parents are obviously selected to behave in a kind manner toward their own genetic descendants, and the reverse is to some extent true as well. Likewise, siblings tolerate each other's presence even though they may compete for the same food delivered to the nest, and in many species cooperation extends to extended family groups. Still, the shield against violence offered by kinship is not foolproof. For example, there is evidence that mothers of a parrot species (*Eclectus roratus*) engage in sex-specific infanticide if there is a late-hatched son in their brood, at least in times when food is scarce and the nest is of poor quality (Heinsohn, Langmore, Cockburn, & Kokko, 2011). (Note that these two risk factors are correlated, since poor nests are attended by fewer males who deliver food to the brood. The female has mated with all these potential fathers). The killing of the son is beneficial for the remaining sister, as she now has sole access to all the food; this beneficial effect is so strong that the mother ends up being more productive if she kills one of her offspring than if she tries to raise both (Heinsohn et al., 2011).

In other species such as herons, the youngsters themselves may be responsible for the death of their sib (Mock, 2004), and siblicide of this sort typically involves pecking the youngest and most defenseless brood member to death. The perhaps most bizarre form of family violence is found in the mound-building ant *Formica exsecta*, where workers—which are always female—raise their brothers to a certain larval stage and then, if food is scarce within the colony, feed these brothers to the more valuable female larvae growing inside the colony (Chapuisat, Sundström, & Keller, 1997). It appears that some "excess" males have no other function in the colony than to serve as a handy protein-rich storage for leaner times!

While rather grotesque forms of conspecific killing can happen within animal soci-eties, kinship can also give rise to great cooperation, including complete self-sacrifice. For example, certain spider females allow their offspring to cannibalize their own body; whether this should be discussed within a chapter devoted to aggression is debatable, as there is no clear conflict between the mother, who would be unlikely to reproduce again even if she was not eaten, and her offspring.

In cases that are more clearly related to aggression, familiarity can sometimes lead to diminished aggression without any influence of kinship. A clear example is the *dear enemy effect*, a form of social recognition where territorial animals become habituated to familiar neighbors. This is distinct from any overall decrease in aggression after territorial boundaries have become established, because the same animals still react aggressively to an unfamiliar territorial song, or one that is heard from a different direction than usual. In some small songbirds, enemies are "dear"—that is, their identity is remembered—even in the following year, after birds have departed their breeding grounds to winter thousands of kilometres away, and returned back to the same location (Godard, 1991).

A clear theme in this chapter is that much of life is not simply "red in tooth and claw" but consists of a much more intricate web of interactions: the key is balancing what can be gained with aggression against the associated costs. A highly intriguing example is the ben-efit of maintaining the "status quo" in territorial animals—exemplified with an animal that indeed fights with massive claws, but usually yellow rather than red (Figure 3.3). Fiddler crabs (*Uca mjoebergi*) living on tidal mudflats totally depend on having access to a burrow that provides shelter from water during the high tide and from predators during the low tide. Digging new burrows in the mud appears to be the less-preferred option compared

FIGURE 3.3 Fiddler crabs (*Uca mjoebergi*) often fight vigorously over access to burrows, which are essential for survival. They have also been shown to assist their neighbors under certain conditions that favor coalition forming. (Photo credit: Tanya Detto).

with fighting for an existing one. Thus, the system allows ample opportunity for watching fight outcomes. Crabs vary in size as they grow from molt to molt, and large crabs often come to help their smaller neighbors when an intruder needs to be chased off (Backwell & Jennions, 2004)—a behavior that extends to cases where different fiddler crab species help each other (Booksmythe, Jennions, & Blackwell, 2010). It appears that having a familiar (and small) neighbor is preferable to new boundary negotiations, as these take time and energy that could be put to better use foraging and breeding.

Although it may be a long step from simple fiddler crab coalitions to the more intricate systems of friendship and mutual dependency that characterize more complex animal societies, the principles are similar. A large chimpanzee troop living in Ngogo, Uganda, for example, has been observed to sometimes attack and kill neighbors, especially when the patrolling situation allows for superiority in numbers. In 2009, this troop finally managed to seize the home range of their rivals, increasing their territory by 22 percent (6.4 square kilometers) and acquiring resources such as fruiting mulberry trees. Interestingly, the Ngogo chimps worked as tightly knit coalitions to kill their opponents (Mitani, Watts, & Amsler, 2010). Given that much of this chapter was about understanding what would happen to a hypothetical selfish crow attempting to kill its conspecifics, it is perhaps paradoxical that the formation of a violent coalition is one of best potential examples of a behavior where individuals perform something costly and the benefit is best understood at the level of the entire group (though not any higher entity such as a species). The selfish behavior in the chimp case would be to not bother participating in a violent attack. It qualifies as selfish as the short-term individual benefit (little risk of injury) combines with the entire group suffering if its territorial area eventually diminishes.

The chimp situation certainly resembles some of the arguments made for the origins of human cooperation, where generosity and solidarity toward one's own has been argued to have emerged in combination with hostility toward outsiders (Bowles, 2008)—though gentler versions of the same argument have also been proposed (e.g., Boyd & Richerson, 2009). The somewhat depressing message from biology is that aggressive interactions, including ones where conspecifics can be killed, are certainly an expected part of life in numerous organisms. The upside is, perhaps, that much of aggressive behavior is also predicted to be very plastic, tending to surface only when the unconscious calculations predict that gentler routes to success are not more profitable. This, of course, is the reason why biology does not at all predict that the "nature versus nurture" debate should be settled in favor of nature only.

References

Backwell, P. R. Y., & Jennions, M. D. (2004). Coalition among male fiddler crabs. *Nature, 430,* 417.

Booksmythe, I., Jennions, M. D., & Backwell, P. R. Y. (2010). Interspecific assistance: Fiddler crabs help heterospecific neighbors in territory defense. *Biology Letters, 6,* 748–750.

Bowles, S. (2008). Conflict: Altruism's midwife. *Nature, 456,* 326–327.

Chapuisat, M., Sundström, L., & Keller, L. (1997). Sex-ratio regulation: the economics of fratricide in ants. *Proceedings of the Royal Society of London B, 264,* 1255–1260.

Davies, N. B. (1978). Territorial defense in the speckled wood butterfly (*Pararge aegeria*): the resident always wins. *Animal Behaviour, 26*, 138–147.

DeScioli, P., & Wilson, B. J. (2011). The territorial foundations of human property. *Evolution and Human Behavior, 32*, 297–304.

Dugatkin, L.A. (2006). *The altruism equation: Seven scientists search for the origin of goodness*. Princeton: Princeton University Press.

Enquist, M., & Leimar, O. (1983). Evolution of fighting behaviour: Decision rules and assessment of relative strength. *Journal of Theoretical Biology, 102*, 387–410.

Enquist, M., & Leimar, O. (1990). The evolution of fatal fighting. *Animal Behaviour, 39*, 1–9.

Enquist, M., Leimar, O., Ljungberg, T., Mallner, Y., & Segerdahl, N. (1990). A test of the sequential assessment game: Fighting in the cichlid fish *Nannacara anomala*. *Animal Behaviour, 40*, 1–14.

Eshel, I. (2005). Asymmetric population games and the legacy of Maynard Smith: From evolution to game theory and back? *Theoretical Population Biology, 68*, 11–17.

Fromhage, L., & Schneider, J. M. (2005). Virgin doves and mated hawks: Contest behaviour in a spider. *Animal Behaviour, 70*, 1099–1104.

Godard, R. (1991). Long-term-memory of individual neighbors in a migratory songbird. *Nature, 350*, 228–229.

Grafen, A. (1987). The logic of divisively asymmetric contests: Respect for ownership and the desperado effect. *Animal Behaviour, 35*, 462–467.

Hamilton, W. D. (1967). Extraordinary sex ratios. *Science, 156*, 477–488.

Hammerstein, P. (1981). The role of asymmetries in animal contests. *Animal Behaviour, 29*, 193–205.

Heinsohn, R., Langmore, N. E., Cockburn, A., & Kokko, H. (2011). Adaptive secondary sex ratio adjustments via sex-specific infanticide in a bird. *Current Biology, 21*, 1744–1747.

Huxley, J. (1966). Introduction: A discussion on ritualization of behaviour in animals and man. *Philosophical Transactions of the Royal Society of London B, 251*, 249–271.

Huxley, T. H. (1888). The struggle for existence: A programme. *Nineteenth Century, 23*, 163–165.

Kemp, D. J., & Wiklund, C. (2004). Residency effects in animal contests. *Proceedings of the Royal Society of London B, 271*, 1707–1711.

Kokko, H. In press. Dyadic contests: Modeling fights between two individuals. In I. C. W. Hardy, & M. Briffa (Eds.), *Animal contests*. Cambridge: Cambridge University Press.

Kokko, H., & Jennions, M. D. (2010). Behavioral ecology: The natural history of evolutionary biology. In M. A. Bell, W. F. Eanes, & D. F. Futuyma (Eds.), *Evolution since Darwin: the first 150 years* (pp. 291–318). Sunderland: Sinauer.

Kokko, H., López-Sepulcre, A., & Morrell, LJ. (2006). From hawks and doves to self-consistent games of territorial behavior. *American Naturalist, 167*, 901–912.

Lorenz, K. (1964). Ritualized fighting. In J. D. Carthy, & F. J. Ebling (Eds.), *The natural history of aggression* (pp. 39–50). London: Academic Press.

Lorenz, K. (1965). *The natural history of aggression* (translated from Das Sogenannte Böse. Vienna: Borotha-Shoeler, 1963).

Maynard Smith, J. (1974). The theory of games and the evolution of animal conflicts. *Journal of Theoretical Biology, 47*, 209–221.

Maynard Smith, J. (1982). *Evolution and the theory of games*. Cambridge: Cambridge University Press.

Maynard Smith, J., & Parker, G. A. (1976). The logic of asymmetric contests. *Animal Behaviour, 24*, 159–175.

Maynard Smith, J., & Price, G. R. (1973). The logic of animal conflict. *Nature, 246*, 15–18.

McGlothlin, J. W., Jawor, J. M., & Ketterson, E. D. (2007). Natural variation in a testosterone-mediated trade-off between mating effort and parental effort. *American Naturalist, 170*, 864–875.

Mitani, J. C., Watts, D. P., & Amsler, S. J. (2010). Lethal intergroup aggression leads to territorial expansion in wild chimpanzees. *Current Biology, 20*, R507–R508.

Mock, D.W. (2004). *More than kin and less than kind: The evolution of family conflict*. Harvard: Harvard University Press.

Pryke, S. R., & Griffith, S. C. (2007). The relative role of male vs. female mate choice in maintaining assortative pairing among discrete colour morphs. *Journal of Evolutionary Biology, 20*, 1512–1521.

Pryke, S. R. & Griffith, S. C. (2009a). Genetic incompatibility drives sex allocation and maternal investment in a polymorphic finch. *Science, 323*, 1605–1607.

Pryke, S. R. & Griffith, S. C. (2009b). Socially mediated trade-offs between aggression and parental effort in competing color morphs. *American Naturalist, 174*, 455–464.

Stake, J.E. (2004). The property "instinct." *Philosophical Transactions of the Royal Society of London B, 359*, 1763–1774.

Stutt, A. D., & Willmer, P. (1998). Territorial defense in speckled wood butterflies: Do the hottest males always win? *Animal Behaviour, 55*, 1341–1347.

Williams, C. G. (1966). *Adaptation and natural selection: A critique of some current thought.* Princeton: Princeton University Press.

Wynne-Edwards, V. C. (1962). *Animal dispersion in relation to social behavior.* London: Oliver & Boyd.

4

An Ethological Perspective
on War and Peace

PETER VERBEEK

When I started out as a researcher and teacher, I was warned not to use the word peace for my research, as it would ruin my chances at a decent career. This was fair warning by good people who had my best interest in mind. They were right, to some extent, as I had a tough time getting my first publication with the word "peace" in the title past gate-keeping editors. It eventually got published, and this first difficult experience, and others that followed it, somewhat paradoxically convinced me that I was on the right track, and that I should continue to try to learn about the nature of peace by observing peace in nature.

I started late in academe, but my interest in the biological basis of peaceful behavior goes back to my early days as a budding naturalist. I spent most of my out-of-school hours either watching the behavior of wild birds and other animals or in front of my aviaries at home observing the behavior of my tropical birds. That is, when I was not taking care of a new litter of puppies. Two early experiences still inspire my work today. The first was the sum of my boyhood observations of nature. Yes, I saw aggression and violent death, some of it rather unsettling, but my main impressions were that nature was wonderfully organized and remarkably peaceful. I thought, then as now, that perhaps we could learn something beneficial from the natural world. My second experience was to become fascinated by the science of ethology.

"War and Peace in Animals and Man"

As a member of a nature-study youth organization I learned about contemporary ethology, the biological study of behavior, and its founders, Konrad Lorenz and Niko Tinbergen. I read *Curious Naturalists* by Tinbergen (1958) and felt like it was written for me. I eventually became a psychobiologist and much of my research training was grounded in the ethological method. This is not to say that the new ethology founded by Lorenz and Tinbergen necessarily led the way toward an understanding of peace in nature. Forty-four years ago Tinbergen wrote that ethology can offer its method and rationale, and also "a little simple common sense, and discipline" to the study of "war and peace in animals and man" (Tinbergen, 1968, p. 1412), but his emphasis was squarely on aggression and war. At the time aggression was still seen as paramount in nature and peace as the mere absence of it. Tinbergen's own ideas about peace centered on how education could help mitigate aggression and thereby promote peace (Tinbergen, 1968).

Tinbergen's focus on aggression and war connect to his experiences during World War II.[1] In 1942 the German authorities replaced various faculty members at Leiden University in the Netherlands with Nazis (Burkhardt, 2005). Tinbergen and 80 percent of his faculty colleagues resigned in protest. He was put in an internment camp that same year. Konrad Lorenz, Tinbergen's trusted partner in the making of ethology and his dear friend, offered to mediate his release but Tinbergen refused special favors from the enemy side. He remained a prisoner until the camp was liberated two years later, but the war continued, and Tinbergen struggled to keep his family from starvation. He also assisted the Dutch resistance (Burkhardt, 2005).

After the war Tinbergen wrote to primatologist Robert Yerkes that "the German terror was unbelievably cruel and a terrible burden," and that, "many of the refined bodily and spiritual atrocities were beyond imagination, and defy description." He told Yerkes that he had "experienced intensities of emotions as I never had before during quiet peace-time," and these had given him "opportunities for many psychological observations of human nature, of my own and of others, often of a not very encouraging nature" (Tinbergen to Yerkes, October 18, 1948, Yerkes Papers, Yale University, cited and discussed in Burkhardt, 2005).

During the war Lorenz had sided with Nazi ideology and this had caused a rift in the fledgling international ethology community. Tinbergen considered his professional relationship with Lorenz to be of great importance for building the new discipline, and about four years after World War II he reconciled with Lorenz. The friendship between the two men endured (Burkhardt, 2005; see pp. 283–308 for a detailed account of the reconciliation process).

Intimately familiar with the horrors of war and the questions they raise about human behavior, Tinbergen was clear on what ethology has to offer to the study of war and peace. He emphasized that it is a systematic and coordinated approach to the study of behavior, *not a set of results* (Tinbergen, 1968; cf. Burkhardt, 2005). The latter was an important concern for him:

> I put so much emphasis on this issue of group territorialism because most writers who have tried to apply ethology to man have done this in the wrong way. They have made the mistake, to which I objected before, of uncritically extrapolating the results of animal studies to man. They try to explain man's behavior by using

facts that are valid only of some of the animals we studied. And, as ethologists keep stressing, no two species behave alike. Therefore, instead of taking the easy way out, we ought to study man in his own right. (Tinbergen, 1968, p. 1414)

The ethological method that Tinbergen referred to is the systematic and complementary investigation of four related aspects of behavior, including the immediate causation of behavior, its development in individuals (together referred to as proximate causation), and the function and evolution of behavior (together: ultimate causation) (Tinbergen, 1963, 1968). Integral to the method is a focus on behavior that occurs in the natural setting of the species. Wherever and whenever possible, naturally occurring variables are experimentally manipulated to further test and isolate proximate causes of behavior, a technique at which Tinbergen excelled.

Tinbergen delivered his call for ethological action on war and peace around the time when *On Aggression* by Lorenz (1966) and *The Naked Ape* by Desmond Morris (1967) were bestsellers. Tinbergen (1968, p. 1411) commented that, "In themselves brilliant, these books could stiffen, at a new level, the attitude of certainty, while what we need is a sense of doubt and wonder, and an urge to investigate, to inquire." This comment still rings true today.

Tinbergen suggested that group territorialism warrants special attention in our search for clues about war, as he believed it to be ancestral in our species. In fact, research on group territorialism in nonhuman primates, in particular chimpanzees (*Pan troglodytes*), is one of the main outcomes of Tinbergen's call for action on "war and peace," and it is to this line of research that I now turn.

Hominoid Warfare?

Chimpanzee sociality is complex and is characterized by close relationships among kin and nonkin, both in the wild (Goodall, 1986; Nishida, 2011), and, when conditions allow for it, in captivity (de Waal, 1982/1998). Chimpanzee communities and captive groups function along something akin to social norms (de Waal, 1991; Rudolf von Rohr, Burkart, & van Schaik, 2011) that are reminiscent of the elementary forms of sociality found in our own species (Verbeek, 2006). Both in the wild and in captivity chimpanzees regularly make peace after fights within the community or group (Arnold, Fraser, & Aureli, 2010), console victims of aggression (Romero, Castellanos, & de Waal, 2011a), appease aggressors to reduce social tension or for political gains (Romero & de Waal, 2011; Romero, Castellanos, & de Waal, 2011b), engage in impartial interventions in complex conflicts that function to restore peace in the community (Rudolf von Rohr, et al., 2012), share and help each other (Pruetz, 2010; Pruetz & Lindshield, 2011; Yamamoto, Humle, & Tanaka, 2009), and warn fellow group members who are ignorant of danger (Crockford, Wittig, Mundry & Zuberbühler, 2012). Chimpanzees collaborate in hunting (Boesch, 1994), manufacture and use tools (Goodall, 1986), and show significant cultural variability among communities in doing so (Whiten et al., 1999).

In captivity, with expert care, chimpanzee males that are strangers to each other can be introduced and live together in newly established social groups without major aggression (Seres, Aureli, & de Waal, 2001). Even after having suffered years of isolation as subjects in invasive biomedical research, chimpanzees can be induced to live with each other in relative peace (Morimura, Idani, & Matsuzawa, 2011; Reimers, Schwarzenberger, & Preuschoft, 2007). By all accounts, chimpanzees are sophisticated social actors for whom the interplay between aggression and peace is a fact of life. In that comprehensive sense chimpanzees closely resemble humans.

Chimpanzee Intergroup Aggression

It is not the complex interplay of aggression and peace in the lives of chimpanzees and humans that draws the most attention in comparative investigations of war and peace. The single aspect of chimpanzee behavior that gets the spotlight in this context is lethal intergroup aggression. Here is an example from Ngogo in Kibale National Park in Uganda, the natural home of a large community of chimpanzees studied for more than 15 years by John Mitani and his colleagues:

> A small party of chimpanzees gathers during the middle of the day. Bartok, the alpha male, grooms quietly with his long-term friend and ally, Hare. The two rest comfortably beside each other, reaffirming their social bond while a third chimpanzee, the beta male Hodge, sits in the distance surveying the group. Just hours earlier, these three joined several other males on a patrol deep into their neighbors' territory, where they encountered, attacked, and killed a rival male. (Mitani, Amsler, & Sobolewski, 2010b, p. 181)

While the opening sentences of this narrative paint a peaceful scene, the closing sentence tells a different story. These Ngogo males are peaceful toward each other, but they are also allies in a coalition of killers. Territorial aggression in wild chimpanzees, some of it lethal, is not restricted to Ngogo and may well be part and parcel of the species (Wilson & Wrangham, 2003). Intergroup aggression has taken different forms and is not restricted to male coalitions. Females have been observed to join males or act by themselves in violent encounters with members of a neighboring community (Boesch et al., 2008). Active support by community members and "strength in numbers" appear to be major factors that affect whether intergroup aggression becomes lethal or whether victims escape relatively unharmed (Boesch et al., 2008).

Playback experiments suggest that males from the Kanyawara community of chimpanzees, Kibale National Park, Uganda, assess their numerical strength before responding aggressively to stranger males. When a recorded pant-hoot call of a single stranger male was played back to parties of various size and sex composition, only parties of three or more males responded with loud calls and by rapidly approaching the speaker (Wilson, Hauser, & Wrangham, 2001). A detailed analysis of 15 years (1992–2006) of data on intergroup encounters confirmed that males from this community were more likely to vocalize in response to hearing calls from stranger males when they had many males in their party (Wilson, Kahlenberg, Wells, & Wrangham, 2012). The same analysis showed that the majority (85 percent) of intergroup encounters involved only acoustic contact. Three out of 120 cases involved physical contact (Wilson, Kahlenberg, Wells, & Wrangham, 2012). In addition to these observed encounters, two intergroup killings were inferred based on circumstantial evidence (Muller, 2002 cited in Wilson et al., 2012; Wrangham, 1999).

Function and mechanism of intergroup aggression. One way to explain lethal intergroup aggression in wild chimpanzees is to assume that it offers benefits such as food and safety that accrue from gaining territory from a neighboring group (Wrangham, 1999). There is evidence that victims of such violence indeed cede parts of their territory to their assailants (Mitani, Watts, & Amsler, 2010a). Continued long-term research will enable the fitness[2] calculus necessary to formally test this functional hypothesis.

A functional explanation addresses only one aspect of causality, and Wrangham (1999) offers a male dominance drive as a proximate psychological mechanism to account for lethal intergroup aggression in chimpanzees. Wrangham suggests that this drive manifests itself as "an appetite for hunting and killing rivals that is akin to predation" (Wrangham, 1999, p. 5) in both intragroup and intergroup contexts. He links it to small raids and ambushes as "the commonest form of combat employed in primitive human warfare" (quoting Keeley, 1996) of which "abundant evidence routinely attests of the blood-lust of the participants" (Wrangham, 1999, p. 5).

Roscoe (2007) argues that it may not be an emotional drive that powers intergroup killing in humans and chimpanzees, but rather an ability to anticipate the benefits that it can bring, and to plan and execute accordingly. He sees this as a form of intelligence that chimpanzees and humans may share. The ability to assess numerical strength during intergroup encounters may be an aspect of such social intelligence.

We now know that numerical strength assessment is not restricted to chimpanzees, as it has recently been observed and experimentally verified in wild white-faced capuchin monkeys as well (*Cebus capucinus*; Meuniera, Molina-Vila, & Perry, 2012). Capuchin monkeys are New World primates and are only distantly related to apes and humans, so this finding tells us something about the convergence of numerical strength assessment in intergroup situations. In white-faced capuchin monkeys both lethal intergroup and lethal intra-group aggression has been observed (Gros-Louis, Perry, & Manson, 2003). Most accounts of lethal aggression in wild nonhuman primates, however, involve isolated cases of intragroup aggression.

Hare, Wobber, and Wrangham (2012) review research from various field sites that show that in bonobos (*Pan paniscus*), a great ape species that is as closely related to humans as chimpanzees, intergroup relations can take various forms, ranging from neighboring communities displaying at each other to physical aggression, and from simple avoidance to peaceful encounters that include play and sex. There is no evidence for lethal aggression in bonobos, but groups of females have been observed attacking and seriously injuring males.

"An appetite for killing" or reluctance to killing? Wrangham (1999) argues that "an appetite for killing" drives intergroup aggression in chimpanzee males and, by extension, in human males. However, as Tinbergen suggested 44 years ago, extrapolating from a particular animal to our own species is problematic. Controversy ensued when evidence of lethal intergroup violence by coalitions of chimpanzee males was used to argue for an innate, lethal-aggressive, predisposition to wage war in human males (Wrangham & Peterson, 1996; cf. McDonald, Navarrete, & Van Vugt, 2012; see Sussman & Marshack, 2010; Wrangham, 2010, for a debate on this issue; and see Prinz, 2012, for a critique of McDonald et al., 2012).

I will now present two examples of lethal aggression between chimpanzee males in captive settings, as I believe that these observations have some bearing on the underlying psychology of lethal aggression. About 25 years ago in Tampa, Florida, I was introduced to Herman, my first chimpanzee friend and teacher of his species' ways. Herman died a violent death at the hand of Bamboo, his male companion at the Lowry Park Zoo (French, 2006). I never met Bamboo, as he arrived at the zoo years after I left Florida, and I am unfamiliar with what may have led up to the fatal fight between the two adult males. The zoo's veterinarian who tried in vain to intervene in the fight later reported that Bamboo was clearly not just upset, but also confused and frightened as he kept returning to the veterinarian with a telling fear grin on his face (French, 2006).

The second example involves a large zoo colony in Arnhem, the Netherlands. Discussed in detail by Frans de Waal (1986; 1982/1998), the case involved the death of Luit, an adult male, after a presumed joint attack by two other adult males, Nikki and Yeroen. De Waal linked the fatal fight to complex power struggles and sexual competition among these males (de Waal, 1986; 1982/1998). The fight took place in the night house where the males usually slept together by their own choice. When the zoo staff found the males in the morning, the fight had ended and "apparently, the males had already reconciled" (de Waal, 1986, p. 243). Moreover, although fatally injured, Luit made great efforts to stay with the other males when the keepers tried to separate them (de Waal, 1986, p. 243).

In these two cases of fatal aggression in captive chimpanzees the assailants displayed conflicting emotions including fear, and, possibly, post-conflict attraction. Their intention to kill cannot be proved. In humans lethal aggression not associated with mental pathology invokes similarly conflicting emotions. Roscoe (2007) cites evidence presented by Browning (1998) of a German reserve police battalion charged with mass-killing Jewish people in the Nazi's "final solution" in Poland. As Roscoe points out, the men in the battalion faced no discernible costs, were in a clear position of power over their victims, and had incentives to participate in these killings (e.g., potential career advancement; removing "a mortal threat," according to Nazi propaganda). Nonetheless, the men experienced great emotional turmoil after conducting their first mass killings ("a sense of shame and horror . . . pervaded the barracks," Browning, 1998, p. 76, cited in Roscoe, 2007).

Psychological wounds of war are nothing new. Ample research shows that the risk for mental health conditions and the need for mental health services among military service members are greater during wars and conflicts, and major depression is highly associated with combat exposure (Milliken, Auchterlonie & Hoge, 2007; Marlowe, 2001; Rosenheck & Fontana, 1999). Extended campaigns in Iraq and Afghanistan have led to high rates of post-traumatic stress symptoms and suicide rates of US Army soldiers that reached a 28-year high (Hoge et al., 2004; Kuehn, 2009; Tanielian, & Jaycox, 2008). Judging from these realistic data, it seems that in times of war, rather than being propelled by an ancestral drive to kill, average human males are reluctant killers for whom the experience of killing may be particularly traumatic (cf. Fry & Szala, chapter 23; Hughbank & Grossman, chapter 25).

The Choice for War

Tinbergen suggested that upsetting of the balance between aggression and fear causes war, and that this is linked to consequences of cultural evolution (Tinbergen, 1968, p. 1415). Irenäus Eibl-Eibesfeldt, a student of Lorenz and pioneer of using ethological methods to study human cultures, reached the following conclusion:

> War, defined as strategically planned, destructive group aggression, is a product of cultural evolution. Therefore, it can be overcome culturally. It makes use of some universal innate human dispositions, such as man's aggressive emotionality and the preparedness for group defense, dominance striving, territoriality, disposition to react to agonal signals from strangers, etc. But all these traits do not lead to warfare. War requires systematic planning, leadership, destructive weapons, and overcoming sympathy through dehumanizing the enemy in advance of the actual conflict. Man easily falls prey to indoctrination to act in supposed group interest (Eibl-Eibesfeldt, 1989, p. 421 cited in Sponsel, 1996).

My interpretation is that we go to war not because we are naturally driven to do so, but because we choose to do so. A choice for war is linked to overcoming fear and empathy, and it is critically important to understand what biological, social-learning, and cultural factors take us there. Comparative findings suggest that both cognitive and emotional factors play a role in how fear and empathy are overcome, some of which are shared with other animals, while others are specific to our own species. An ethological perspective can help delineate these factors through comparative research on other animals. An ethological approach is also of value to sister disciplines working on these issues by clarifying through its method, both conceptually and practically, the distinction between proximate and ultimate explanations of behavior (cf. Scott-Phillips, Dickins, & West, 2011; West, Mouden, & Gardner, 2011). Proximate mechanisms are behavior generators, whereas ultimate functions explain why behaviors are favored by selection (cf. Scott-Phillips, Dickins, & West, 2011; West, Mouden, & Gardner, 2011).

In his 1968 paper calling for action on war and peace Tinbergen proposes two main comparative methods. One is to interpret similarities between species of a different origin as adaptive convergence, and the other is to interpret differences between closely related species as adaptive divergence. As he points out, "by studying the adaptive functions of species characteristics we understand how natural selection can have produced both these divergencies and convergencies" (Tinbergen, p. 1414). Ongoing long-term field research on capuchin monkeys will provide data that can be compared and contrasted with findings from the various chimpanzee field sites. Capuchin monkeys and chimpanzees are distantly related and have a different type of social organization, and similarities as well as differences in intergroup relations among these species can tell us much about the evolution of group territorialism in primates (Crofoot & Wrangham, 2010; Meuniera et. al, 2012). Long-term field research on spider monkeys (*Ateles geoffroyi*; Aureli & Schaffner, 2007) is also of value in this context, considering that this New World monkey shares a fission-fusion lifestyle with chimpanzees. It will be equally important to continue to compare and contrast field data on intergroup relations in chimpanzees and bonobos, as these two species are both closely related to each other and to humans (Furuichi, 2011; Hare et al., 2012). Finally, similarities and differences in intergroup aggression among populations of chimpanzees should be looked at in the context of our increasing knowledge of the genetic variability among populations (cf. Bowden et al., 2012).

Tinbergen (1968) also called for studying our species in its own right. An ethological perspective on war is a natural ally to anthropological field research (e.g., Fry, 2009) and naturalistic work in social psychology (e.g., Bar-Tal, 2004) and peace psychology (e.g., Funkeson, Schröder, Nzabonimpa, & Holmqvist, 2011). An ethological perspective could also be of value to psychologists involved with the new US Army Comprehensive Soldier Fitness Program (Cornum, Matthews, & Seligman, 2011). Data on combat experiences, for example, are important for our developing understanding of how fear and empathy are overcome in lethal combat. Collaborative research of this nature can both help our understanding of war and advance the cause of peace.

Peace in Nature

Defining Peace

Careful and detailed description of behavior is integral to the ethological method and this second major section of the chapter starts with an overview of some common descriptors and an operational definition of peace. After attending the Lorentz Center workshop "Aggression and Peacemaking in an Evolutionary Context" at Leiden University in 2010, I contacted all participants by e-mail and asked them for their personal descriptions of peace. Of the 32 colleagues who replied, 28 (87.5 percent) provided descriptions of peace, which either were coded as *negative peace* (peace = low levels or absence of violence), *positive peace* (peace = active processes aimed at harmonious relations), or both.

There were 12 (42.9 percent) responses that related to positive peace, 7 (25 percent) to negative peace, and 9 (32.1 percent) responses reflected the combined *negative + positive peace* categories. Seventy-five percent of the respondents thus viewed peace as including active behavioral processes. Only three colleagues (10.7 percent) mentioned nature as part of their description of peace and they did so in conjunction with *positive peace*. All other descriptions referred to peace in humans only.

Workshop participant and philosopher David Livingstone Smith pointed out to me that in the English language peace could not be used as a verb. According to Smith the idea of peace seems closely tied to that of passivity or inactivity (personal communication, Feb. 9, 2011). The notion of peace as the mere absence of aggression, "negative peace," further illustrates this passive image.

A rather different view is that of peace as active process. For example, anthropologist Doug Fry proposes,

> When people respect each other that is peace, when people befriend each other
> that also is peace, when people care for each other, naturally, that is peace. Peace is
> not merely the absence of violence and war, but it is the normal state of affairs that
> we are so accustomed to that we take it for granted. Peace entails prosocial values
> that include a concern for others in society. Values such as tolerance for differences,
> acceptance of diversity, support of equality, rights, justice and fairness are peace.
> Peace also entails the nonviolent and prosocial ways that humans can and do
> deal with most conflicts through discussion, mediation, turning the other cheek,
> therapy, ritualization, the courts, and just walking away, all without violence. Peace
> is not an endpoint, but an ongoing process.
>
> (Fry, personal communication, Feb. 15, 2011).

Anthropologist Robert Sussman extends an active view of peace to nature as a whole:

> Peace is the natural condition in which all organisms wish to live and when the
> earth and your particular habitat are in equilibrium. It is the natural state of the
> earth. It would seem that it is what organisms strive for during development, what
> ecosystems attempt to maintain, and what the earth's ecology would like to reach. It
> is the absence of perturbations to systems and the absence of war within society. To
> me and, I think, statistically, it is the norm.
>
> (Sussman, personal communication, Jan. 4, 2011).

Taking cues from my colleagues across disciplines I believe that peace is a natural phenomenon that is modified by culture in both human and nonhuman animals. I argue that in nature peaceful behavior can be a viable strategy that can evolve on its own terms based on its own particular fitness consequences. Peace in this view is not one trait or a particular set of traits and it is not restricted to humans, or the species that we are most comfortable with comparing ourselves to, our fellow primates. Specifically, peaceful behavior is behavior through which individuals, families, groups, communities, or, in the case of humans, nations, experience low levels of aggression and engage in mutually harmonious interactions (Verbeek, 2008).

Increasing evidence suggests that in nature aggression and peace are not antithetical, but rather are linked in recurring relationships. It follows that to understand peace one has to understand aggression and vice versa. In that context aggression can be defined as behavior through which individuals, families, groups, communities or nations pursue active control of resources and the social environment at the expense of others (cf. de Boer in Kruk & Kruk-de Bruin, 2010).

Aggression can be species-typical or species-atypical. The former is context-dependent aggressive behavior that is commonly shown by members of the species, while the latter is aggressive behavior that is infrequently shown by members of the species (cf. Haller & Kruk, 2006; Verbeek, Iwamoto, & Murakami, 2007). Violence, as an example of atypical aggression, is escalated aggressive behavior that is out of inhibitory control (de Boer, Caramaschi, Natarajan, & Koolhaas, 2009). An important question, as we saw earlier, is whether war, as an organized form of lethal aggression, is species-typical or atypical for the human species. Several authors in the present volume also address this question from various angles and perspectives (e.g., Fry & Szala, chapter 23; Sussman, chapter 6).

The distinction between species-typical and species-atypical behavior is important for a proper understanding of both aggression and peace, as early findings suggest that, like aggression, peaceful behavior can be species-typical as well as species atypical (e.g., Sapolsky, 2006). Finally, species-typical behavior, be it aggressive or peaceful, is subject to change over time. In the context of peaceful behavior primatologist Sarah Brosnan contributes the insight, "Peace is a moving target, thus peace includes different frequencies and degrees of conflict for different species, and if a species were to change the frequency of aggression/conflict, the definition of peace for that species would change accordingly" (personal communication, Jan. 4, 2011).

Observing Peace

Much has changed since Tinbergen's 1968 call for action on "war and peace." Theoretically, Hamilton's concept of inclusive fitness (Hamilton, 1964; cf. Scott-Phillips et al., 2011) cleared the way for a truly ethological inquiry of peace in nature and human nature (Verbeek, 2008). Work done on peace from the ethological perspective suggests that peaceful behavior is ubiquitous in nature and can be adaptive and selected for in its own right. We now know, for example, that cooperation occurs at all levels of biological organization from organelles within a single cell to mutualism between different species (cf. Aanen & Hoekstra, 2007).

Examples of peaceful behavior investigated from an ethological perspective include behavior that restores tolerance following conflict and aggression (peacemaking; cf. Silk,

2002a), or reestablishes mutual or reciprocal interests between affiliates (reconciliation; cf., de Waal, 1996). It includes bilateral and integrative forms of conflict management in which both parties win or benefit (cf. Verbeek, Hartup, & Collins, 2000). It also includes social behavior that optimizes relations, through, for example, the pursuit, establishment or deepening of mutual or reciprocal interests, tolerance, helping and sharing (Verbeek, 2008). Reciprocity, altruism, and the social-cultural (Fry, 2006), emotional (e.g., empathy; de Waal, 2008), physiological (e.g. Kogan et al., 2011), and brain mechanisms (Decety & Jackson, 2006; Singer & Lamm, 2009) that underpin these proximate processes of peace in human and nonhuman animals are also being extensively studied.

Whereas four decades ago a biological perspective on peace was barren land, now a thousand flowers bloom, as hardly a week goes by without a new book and multiple publications on some aspect of peaceful behavior, particularly in our own species. A significant subset of these publications is about cooperation in humans, and, building on the age-old notion of a pinnacle spot for humans within nature, presents arguments in favor of a species-specific highly sophisticated form of cooperation in humans that has neither a match nor clearly identifiable shared roots in nature. Much of the work in this area is based on game theory and the testing of theoretical models in computer-animated games (e.g., Bowles & Gintis, 2011; Nowak & Highfield, 2011). Other work in this area focuses on comparisons between the performance of children and laboratory chimpanzees that purport to show that children are superior to chimpanzees in performing experimental helping and sharing tasks (Tomasello, 2009). I take a broader view of interconnectedness of humanity with the rest of nature as shown through observations of peaceful behavior: the ethological way. The next section on the importance of peaceful relationships in a wide range of species further highlights this view.

Relationships and Peace
Kin Relationships

Seeking, making, sustaining, repairing, adjusting, judging, construing, and sanctioning social relationships are crucial for human well-being and survival (paraphrasing Fiske 1992; cf. Verbeek, 2006). But humans are not alone in this. Animals of all kinds of fur and feather depend on mutual relationships for well-being and survival, and across species similar behavioral, neural, hormonal, cellular, and genetic mechanisms have evolved to support social relationships (Cacioppo, Hawkley, Norman, & Berntson, 2011). Across species the adaptive physiological support system for social relations malfunctions in the absence of opportunities to seek and maintain social bonds. Experimental social isolation in animals ranging from fruit flies to pigs produces similar deleterious physiological effects as observed in socially isolated humans (Cacioppo et al., 2011). Kin relationships feature prominently in the lives of many animals, and the notion of inclusive fitness helps to explain the evolution of peaceful behavior within the family realm. Below I present two ethological vignettes that illustrate peaceful aspects of family relations in two mammal species.

Caring for the elderly. Giant otters (*Pteronura brasiliensis*) are cooperative breeders. Offspring reach reproductive maturity by about three years of age and stay with their monogamous parents for up to four years (Davenport, 2010). Family size ranges from about 4 to 10 individuals, and family members work together in sharing food with the youngest members of the family who beg ferociously. With time the breeding pair becomes increasingly skilled at caching fish and navigating the challenges of daily life in the otter habitat. Females are believed to enter menopause similar to human females (Davenport, 2010).

During one longitudinal study of giant otters in Manu National Park, Peru, members of the family were observed to share food with the aging matriarch in response to her, rather discrete, begging (Davenport, 2010). The aging female, who had ceased reproduction, and was experiencing difficulties catching large fish, had never been observed before to beg as she spent much of her life responding to the begging of her children. It is likely that her experience and social information sharing remained important for her family's survival, which can explain the gradual shift in this family from caring for the young to caring for the elderly (Davenport, 2010). These naturalistic observations suggest that peaceful relations among family members of all ages may be important for survival in giant otters.

Females leading the way. In African elephants (*Loxodonta africana*), older matriarchs play an essential role in the survival and well being of families. In this long-lived intelligent species, grandmothers possess the knowledge and ability to make good decisions about where the family should go next to find food or water, and whether or not it is advantageous to join or break away from other families in the ongoing pursuit of resources or safety (Mutinda, Poole, & Moss, 2011). Matriarchs also play important roles in repairing family relations following aggressive conflict. Reconciliation and consolation are often combined in a post-conflict ritual that is initiated by the protesting calls of a victim of aggression. Such events bring together the aggressor and the victim and several family members, including the mother of the victim or other leading females, and the matriarch. The members of the family respond vocally to the victim, and by touching one another and the former opponents peace is effectively restored (Poole, 2011).

Close Relationships Among Nonkin

Close ties in humans and other animals are not limited to kin relationships. For example, similarly as in humans, friendships are an important feature of social life for chimpanzees and other nonhuman primates. Primatologists were initially concerned about anthropomorphizing by using the term "friendship" for the kind of relationships among their subjects that for all intents and purposes function as friendship in the way we would describe it for our own species (Silk, 2002b). Recently, however, the term friendship has become an accepted label to describe bonds between non-related individuals that are characterized by mutual preference, extraordinary proximity, low aggression, high tolerance, and close attachment (Silk, 2002b; cf. Verbeek, 2006; 2008). Long-term ethological studies of the Ngogo chimpanzee community discussed earlier provided evidence for friendships among chimpanzee males that can last from one to ten years (Mitani, 2006; 2009, cited in Seyfarth & Cheney, 2012). Twenty-two out of 28 males studied for an extended period of time formed their longest, closest bond with an unrelated male, and the majority of cooperative behavior was observed between unrelated or distantly related individuals (Mitani, 2009). Friendships among chimpanzees are not restricted to males. A study of 39 females at Ngogo found that females with strong dyadic associations were rarely close kin (Langergraber, Mitani, & Vigilant, 2009; cf. Wittig & Boesch, 2003, cited in Seyfarth and Cheney, 2012).

Cords and Aureli (2000) delineated three fitness-related dimensions of relationship quality: value, compatibility, and security. According to this taxonomy, value refers to its shared usefulness to the partners, while compatibility depends, in part, on individual characteristics of the partners, such as temperament. Security refers to the perceived probability that the relationship will not change for the worse. Multiple studies have now validated this taxonomy and linked it to post-conflict tolerance and relational repair through peacemaking and reconciliation (Arnold et al., 2010; and see below).

In a recent review Seyfarth and Cheney (2012) provide convincing evidence for close friendship-like bonds in a wide range of species. Kin relations explain many close bonds in their review, but, depending on the species, many are also shown to be among unrelated individuals. The authors suggest that "friendships may be generally beneficial for all individuals, and selection may have favored the motivation to form such bonds even when close kin are not available" (Seyfarth & Cheney, p. 161; cf. Cacioppo et al., 2011). Sociality is often assumed to have evolved either to defend resources or to defend against predators. Seyfarth and Cheney's relational hypothesis provides a complementary explanation, and the implications for research on peaceful behavior are clear.

Peacemaking and Reconciliation

Almost 35 years ago Frans de Waal's observations of a large captive group of chimpanzees at the Arnhem Zoo in the Netherlands helped open our eyes to the possibility that peace is as much part of nature as aggression is. In this community individuals involved in a fight would regularly seek each other out afterwards for friendly contact (de Waal & van Roosmalen, 1979). These peaceful reunions between former opponents were labeled "reconciliation" on the assumption that they have a lasting effect on their relationship. A controlled observation method was developed to systematically test their selective occurrence against chance (PC-MC method; de Waal & Yoshihara, 1983; Veenema, Das, & Aureli, 1994).

There are now more than 60 studies providing evidence of post-conflict reconciliation in close to 40 nonhuman primate species, including all major taxonomic groups, from lemurs (including sifaka (*Propithecus verreauxi*) discussed below: Palagi,

Antonacci, & Norscia, 2008) to New and Old World monkeys, to apes and humans (see Arnold et al., 2010; Verbeek, 2008 for reviews). In addition, post-conflict reconciliation has been demonstrated in wolves (*Canis lupus*; Cordoni & Palagi, 2008), domestic dogs (*Canis familiaris*; Cools, Van Hout, & Nelissen, 2008), spotted hyenas (*Crocuta crocuta*; Wahaj, Guse, & Holekamp, 2001); feral horses (*Equus caballus*; Cozzi, Sighierib, Gazzanob, Nicolc, & Baraglib, 2010), domestic goats (*Capra hircus*; Schino, 1998), bottlenose dolphins (*Tursiops truncates*; Holobinko & Waring, 2010; Weaver, 2003), ravens (*Corvus corax*; Fraser & Bugnyar, 2011), monk parakeets (*Myiopsitta monachus*; Morrison, 2009), and cleaner fish and their clients (*Labroides dimidiatus*; Bshary & Würth, 2001).

Several functional hypotheses have been proposed to account for peacemaking and reconciliation. Silk (2002a) suggests that peacemaking signals benign intent after aggression has ended which serves to restore tolerance. Reconciliation, by definition a reconnection, reconnects associates with a shared interest, such as an investment in a mutually beneficial relationship. The Valuable Relationship Hypothesis (de Waal & Aureli, 1997) predicts that conflicts within dyads that have a relationship with important positive fitness benefits for both parties are more likely to be reconciled than conflicts within dyads that have less valuable relationships. Across studies and species this functional hypothesis has abundant support, as kin and friendship relations strongly predict reconciliation (cf. Arnold et al., 2010).

Research on peacemaking and reconciliation in nonhuman primates inspired similar post-conflict research in young children of various cultures, using the same controlled observation methods as developed for the research on nonhuman primates. Verbeek (2008) reviewed post-conflict research on nonhuman primates and children, and compared and contrasted evidence related to the four guiding questions of ethology. Across cultures young children tend to make peace following peer aggression and conflict on average four times of out ten, without any adult intervention. In fact, studies from countries with different social systems, including Japan and the United States, show that teacher intervention in peer conflict decreases the likelihood that the opponents make peace (Verbeek, 2008). As in nonhuman primates, children use both explicit and implicit means of making peace and peer interaction facilitates effective peacemaking. In children and nonhuman primates, peacemaking mitigates anxiety caused by conflict and aggression. Taken together, the comparative evidence suggests that a peacemaking tendency might be a universal feature of early childhood and is molded by culture, as children grow older (Verbeek, 2008).

Tolerance and Peacekeeping

The above sections showed that peaceful behavior is often associated with intraspecific relationships, and areas such as the research on post-conflict behavior that focus on intraspecific relationships are already well-established in the ethology of aggression and peace. Peaceful behavior is not restricted to intraspecific relationships, however, and the study of tolerance and peacekeeping both within and between species is an up-and-coming research area. The following vignettes illustrate the diverse nature of this area.

Sharing Living Space

While territorial toward members of their own species, chimpanzees have been observed to peacefully coexist sympatrically with gorillas (Kuroda, Nishihara, Suzuki, & Oko, 1996; Yamagiwa, Maruhashi, Yumoto, & Mwanza, 1996). Peaceful group encounters within overlapping ranges are not restricted to apes. In Korup National Park, Cameroon, for example, drills (*Mandrillus leucophaeus*) regularly associate with six sympatric monkey species (Astaras, Krause, Mattner, Rehse, & Waltert, 2011), especially with red-capped mangabeys (*Cercocebus torquatus*). Both species exploit the same dietary niche, consuming hard seeds, and, while together, appear to avoid food competition by using different forest strata (Astaras, Krause, Mattner, Rehse, & Waltert, 2011).

Positive aspects of interspecies associations may include improved foraging, increased safety from predators, and social benefits, such as receiving grooming and developmental benefits for the young (Waser, 1987 cited in Verbeek & de Waal, 2002). In Uganda, juveniles of some species commonly play with Colobus monkeys, and the fewer playmates available in the natal group, the more frequently juveniles of sympatric species seek out Colobus peers for play (Waser, 1987 cited in Verbeek & de Waal, 2002).

Dealing with Fission-Fusion

Chimpanzees live in a fission-fusion society and so do spider monkeys (*Ateles geoffroyi*) and some humans. Fusion, the joining of travelling parties and subgroups of members of the same larger community, is often an emotional affair (not unlike coming home for the holidays in humans), and can be a context for aggression. Spider monkeys deal with the threat of aggression at fusion by rapid exchanges of hugs (Aureli & Schaffner, 2007). These hugs in spider monkeys have been compared to our own rapid friendly contact through handshakes, embraces, nose rubbing and kisses, as greetings (Aureli & Schaffner, 2007). Firth (1972) and Kendon & Ferber (1973), both cited in Aureli & Schaffner (2007), interpret such greetings as a "disclaimer of aggression." As in humans, peacekeeping tactics in spider monkeys are not infallible, however, as lethal intra-community aggression has been observed in the species (Campbell, 2006; Valero, Schaffner & Aureli, 2006). In these few instances of lethal aggression, coalitions of adult males attacked and killed sub-adult males. To date, lethal intergroup aggression has not been observed in this species.

Dealing with Strangers

Verreaux's sifaka (*Propithecus verreauxi*) is one of the many lemur species of Madagascar. Sifaka live in multi-male, multi-female groups of which the composition varies from time to time, especially during the mating season (Antonacci, Norscia, & Palagi, 2010). Females are dominant over males and female choice determines mate selection. The males roam during the mating season in pursuit of sexual partners. An ethological study of two sifaka groups near the Mandrare River in Southern Madagascar showed that resident male sifaka use play to make and keep peace with outside males that immigrate into their group (Antonacci, Norscia, & Palagi, 2010). Although aggressive at first toward these new males, resident males soon initiate extensive play bouts with the newcomers and this effectively suppresses further aggression between them. During the transition period when the immigrating males are establishing themselves as new members of the group, resident males groom each other more frequently than usual, thereby solidifying their existing relationships. Sifaka appear to have developed unique behavior patterns to overcome the aversion to strangers that can be found among social animals (Antonacci, Norscia, & Palagi, 2010).

Targeted Interventions

Tolerance and peacekeeping are not restricted to nonhuman primates. Peacekeeping through targeted intervention in aggression, for example, has been observed in fish. "Multies" (*Neolamprologus multifasciatus*) are small shell-dwelling African cichlid fish found in Lake Tanganyika. They live in complex social groups with multiple adult males and females that cooperate in defending their mutual territory against neighboring groups and intruders. At the core the groups are extended families consisting of an established pair and offspring that stayed with their parents beyond sexual maturity (Schradin & Lamprecht, 2000). The membership of these groups is complemented by immigration. Combined field and laboratory studies showed that reproductive females are most likely to immigrate into an established pair or extended family's group territory (Schradin & Lamprecht, 2000). Resident females compete aggressively among themselves and with immigrant females for the shells within the territory that are used for breeding. Resident males intervene in aggressive interactions between females, effectively establishing peace within the group. Controlled experiments confirmed that there were significantly fewer aggressive interactions among reproductive females when the male was present than when he was removed. Peace among females most likely serves the reproductive interests of males (Schradin & Lamprecht, 2000). Similar male peacekeeping behavior has been shown in harem-keeping males of another shell-dwelling Lake Tanganyika cichlid, *Lamprologus ocellatus*, (Walter & Trillmich, 1994). These cases in cichlids illustrate how potentially conflicting reproductive interests between the sexes can serve as a selective basis for peace-keeping behavior.

Inhibiting Cannibalism

A final, striking example of peacekeeping is a strategy in ground beetle larvae that literally saves lives. Naturalistic observations and subsequent experiments show that ground beetle larvae of the species *Chlaenius velutinus* and *Chlaenius spoliatus* practice peace when they meet and touch each other's articulated cerci by refraining from eating each other (Brandmayer, Bonacci, Massolo, & Brandmayer, 2004). Larvae of closely related ground beetle species with non-articulated cerci do not touch cerci when they meet and routinely fight and practice cannibalism. Cannibalism provides high quality food and eliminates competitors, but is costly in terms of inclusive fitness. If there are other food resources available and density is high so encounters are frequent, inhibiting cannibalism through intra-specific recognition can benefit direct fitness (Brandmayer, Bonacci, Massolo, & Brandmayer, 2004). This final example shows that any one type of solution to the fitness problem does not bind nature, and either aggression or peace can be part of the solution.

Future Considerations

Developments in general biology are highly relevant to the future development of a comprehensive ethological approach to "war and peace." Take the case of the "sheep in wolf's clothes," the giant panda (*Ailuropoda melanoleuca*). The recently completed genome of the giant panda shows that genetically the bamboo-eating panda is really a carnivore; in fact, some of the genes necessary for complete digestion of bamboo are missing from its genome (Li, et al., 2010, cited in Lazcano, 2011). Different levels of analysis are necessary, including an analysis of the panda's gut microbiome, and an ethological investigation of what brought about the panda's bamboo feeding behavior (Lazcano, 2011). The point, as biologist Antonio Lazcano (2011, p. 2) puts it, is that "the availability of a completely sequenced genome is not enough to understand the biology of the giant panda or, for that matter, of all animals, including us."

Phenotypic flexibility, defined as the general capacity for change or transformation within genotypes in response to different environmental conditions, can be within single or multiple individuals, and it can be reversible or non-reversible, and seasonably cyclic or consistent (Piersman & van Gils, 2011). The ethologists Piersma and van Gils make a case for behavior as a key aspect of phenotypic flexibility. The key point is that alternative behavioral representations of a single genotype can represent adaptations to new conditions, which subsequently become fine-tuned by natural selection (Piersma & van Gils, 2011). This has implications for our understanding of how the ratio of aggression to peace within as well as across species can vary over time (cf. Brosnan, personal communication, above). A recent comprehensive review of individual differences in cooperative behavior across taxa shows that researchers on peaceful behavior are taking note (Bergmüller, Schürch, & Hamilton, 2010). More generally these two examples reinforce Tinbergen's caution to keep an open mind rather than becoming stifled by a false air of certainty as we pursue biological bases of aggression and peace.

Epilogue

One of the great pioneers of long-term ethological research on wild chimpanzees, Toshida Nishida, wrote, "Chimpanzees are always new to me" (Nishida, 1993, cited in de Waal, 2011). I would like to paraphrase the late Professor Nishida by saying, "Nature is always new to me." While an enduring old-time philosophical school of thought might inspire people to look at nature with a sense of dread, the life work of curious naturalists like Nishida and Tinbergen inspires us to look at nature with a sense of wonder. One of the great wonders of nature is the diverse way by which she goes about the business of propagating life. Integral to nature's life-propagating processes are aggression and peace, which, rather than being antithetical, are linked in recurring relationships that express themselves in flexible phenotypes and evolving genotypes. Up until recently science has focused almost exclusively on the aggressive dimension of natural relationships and has virtually ignored nature's peaceful solutions to the propagation of life. But this is now behind us. A new look at the interplay of aggression and peace in nature will offer us a fresh perspective on the peace in human nature and how to draw on it. Life depends upon it.

Acknowledgements

I thank Douglas Fry and Johan van der Dennen for inviting me to the 2010 Lorentz Center Workshop "Aggression and Peacemaking in an Evolutionary Context" at Leiden University. I am also grateful to Douglas Fry for allowing me to contribute to the present volume, which was inspired by the Leiden workshop. I thank the workshop participants for sharing their thoughts on peace with me. The Harry Frank Guggenheim Foundation supported my work on peacemaking in young children and on species-typical and species-atypical aggression. Miyazaki International College provided me with the opportunity to work on this chapter. Finally, thanks go to Filippo Aureli for his patience and delivery in response to my requests for resources for this chapter, the interpretations of which, warts and all, are entirely mine.

Notes

1. Jan Tinbergen, who, like his brother Niko, was a Nobel Prize Laureate, was similarly motivated to involve his discipline (economics) in a science of peace. He was a founding trustee of Economists for Peace and Security, and the Network of European Peace Scientists (NEPS) continues to organize annual multi-disciplinary conferences on peace science in his name.
2. Fitness here and elsewhere in the chapter refers to inclusive fitness as the sum of direct and indirect fitness. Direct fitness is the number of offspring that reaches reproductive age, while indirect fitness refers to the effect of one individual's actions on everybody's production of offspring, weighted by the relatedness (cf. Scott-Phillips, Dickins & West, 2011).

References

Aanen, D.K., & Hoekstra, R. F. (2007). The evolution of obligate mutualism: if you can't beat 'em, join 'em. *Trends in Ecology and Evolution, 22,* 506–509. doi:10.1016/j.tree.2007.08.007

Antonacci, D., Norscia, I., & Palagi, E. (2010). Stranger to familiar: Wild strepsirhines manage xenophobia by playing. *PLoS ONE, 5(10),* e13218. doi:10.1371/ journal.pone.0013218

Arnold, K., Fraser, O. N., & Aureli, F. (2010). Postconflict reconciliation. In C. J. Campbell, A. Fuentes, K.C. MacKinnon, S. K. Bearder, & R. Stumpf (Eds.), *Primates in perspective 2nd edition*. New York: Oxford University Press.

Astaras, C., Krause, S., Mattner, L., Rehse, C., & Waltert, M. (2011). Associations between the drill (*Mandrillus leucophaeus*) and sympatric monkeys in Korup National Park, Cameroon. *American Journal of Primatology, 73*, 127–134. doi/10.1002/ajp.v73.2

Aureli, F., & Schaffner, C. M. (2007). Aggression and conflict management at fusion in spider monkeys. *Biology Letters, 3*, 147–149. doi:10.1098/rsbl.2007.0041

Bar-Tal, D. (2004). The necessity of observing real life situations: Palestinian Israeli violence as a laboratory for learning about social behavior. *European Journal of Social Psychology, 34(6)*, 677–701. doi:10.1002/ejsp.224

Bergmüller, R., Schürch, R., & Hamilton, I. M. (2010). Evolutionary causes and consequences of consistent individual variation in cooperative behaviour. *Philosophical Transactions of the Royal Society B, 365*, 2751–2764. doi: 10.1098/rstb.2010.0124

Brandmayer, T. Z., Bonacci, T., Massolo, A., & Brandmayer, P. (2004). Peace in ground beetle larvae *Chlaenius spp. Ethology Ecology and Evolution, 16(4)*, 351–361. doi:10.1080/08927014.2004.9522626

Boesch, C. (1994). Cooperative hunting in wild chimpanzees. *Animal Behaviour, 48(3)*, 653–667. doi.org/10.1006/anbe.1994.1285

Boesch, C., Crockford, C., Herbinger, I., Wittig, R., Moebius, Y., & Normand, E. (2008). Intergroup conflicts among chimpanzees in Taï National Park: Lethal violence and the female perspective. *American Journal of Primatology, 70*, 519–532. doi: 10.1002/ajp.20524

Bowden, R., McFie, T. S., Myers, S., Hellenthal, G., Nerrienet, E., Bontrop, R. E., Freeman, C., Donnelly, P., & Mundy, N. I. (2012). Genomic tools for evolution and conservation in the chimpanzee: *Pan troglodytes ellioti* is a genetically distinct population. *PLoS Genetics, 8(3)*, e1002504. doi:10.1371/journal.pgen.1002504

Bowles, D., & Gintis, H. (2011). *A cooperative species: Human reciprocity and its evolution*. Princeton: Princeton University Press.

Browning, C. R. (1998). *Ordinary men: Reserve Police Battalion 101 and the Final Solution in Poland*. New York: Harper Collins.

Bshary, R., & Würth, M. (2001). Cleaner fish *Labroides dimidiatus* manipulate client reef fish by providing tactile stimulation. *Philosophical Transactions of the Royal Society B, 268*, 1495–1501. doi: 10.1098/rspb.2001.1495

Burkhardt, R.W. (2005). *Patterns of behavior: Konrad Lorenz, Niko Tinbergen, and the founding of ethology*. Chicago: University of Chicago Press.

Cacioppo, J. T., Hawkley, L. C., Norman, G. J., & Berntson, G. G. (2011). Social isolation. *Annals of the New York Academy of Sciences, 1231*, 17–22. doi: 10.1111/j.1749-6632.2011.06028.x

Campbell, C. J. (2006). Lethal intragroup aggression by adult male spider monkeys (*Ateles geoffroyi*). *American Journal of Primatology, 68(12)*, 1197–1201. doi: 10.1002/ajp.20305

Cools, A.K.A., Van Hout, A.J.M., & Nelissen, M.H. (2008). Canine reconciliation and third-party-initiated postconflict affiliation: do peacemaking social mechanisms in dogs rival those of higher primates? *Ethology, 114*, 53–63. doi:10.1111/j.1439-0310.2007.01443.x

Cordoni, G., & Palagi, E. (2008). Reconciliation in wolves (*Canis lupus*): new evidence for a comparative perspective. *Ethology, 114*, 298–308. doi:10.1111/j.1439-0310.2008.01474.x

Cords, M., & Aureli, F. (2000). Reconciliation and relationship qualities. In F. Aureli & F. B. M. de Waal (Eds.), *Natural conflict resolution*. Berkeley: University of California Press.

Cornum, R., Matthews, M. D., & Seligman, M. E. P. (2011). Comprehensive soldier fitness. Building resilience in a challenging institutional context. *American Psychologist, 66(1)*, 4–9. doi:10.1037/a0021420

Cozzi, A., Sighierib, C., Gazzanob, A., Nicolc, & C. J., Baraglib, P. (2010). Post-conflict friendly reunion in a permanent group of horses (*Equus caballus*). *Behavioural Processes, 85*, 185–190. doi.org/10.1016/j.beproc.2010.07.007,

Crockford, C., Wittig, R. M., Mundry, R., & Zuberbühler, K. (2012). Wild chimpanzees inform ignorant group members of danger. *Current Biology, 22(2)*, 142–146. doi: 10.1016/j.cub.2011.11.053

Crofoot, M. C. & Wrangham, R. W. (2010). Intergroup aggression in primates and humans: the case for a unified theory. In P. Kappeler & J. Silk (Eds.), *Minding the gap: Tracing the origins of human universals*. New York: Springer.

Davenport LC. (2010). Aid to a declining matriarch in the giant otter (*Pteronura brasiliensis*). *PLoS ONE, 5(6)*, e11385. doi:10.1371/journal.pone.0011385 de Boer, S. F., Caramaschi, D., Natarajan, D., & Koolhaas, J. M. (2009). The vicious cycle towards violence: focus on the negative feedback mechanisms of brain serotonin neurotransmission. *Frontiers in Behavioral Neuroscience, 3(52),*1–6. doi: 10.3389/neuro.08.052.2009

de Waal, F. B. M. (1982/1998). *Chimpanzee politics: Power and sex among the apes.* Baltimore, MD: The Johns Hopkins University Press.

de Waal, F. B. M. (1986). The brutal elimination of a rival among captive male chimpanzees. *Ethology and Sociobiology, 7,* 237–251. doi.org/10.1016/0162-3095(86)90051-8

de Waal, F. B. M. (1991). The chimpanzee's sense of social regularity and its relation to the human sense of justice. *American Behavioral Scientist, 34,* 335–349. doi:10.1177/0002764291034003005

de Waal, F. B. M. (1996). Conflict as negotiation. In W. C. McGrew, L. F. Marchant, & T. Nishida (Eds.), *Great ape societies.* New York: Cambridge University Press.

de Waal, F. B. M. (2008). Putting the altruism back into altruism: The evolution of empathy. *Annual Review of Psychology, 59,* 279–300. doi: 10.1146/annurev.psych.59.103006.093625

de Waal, F. B. M. (2011). Toshisada Nishida (1941–2011): Chimpanzee rapport. *PLoS Biology, 9(10),* e1001185. doi:10.1371/journal.pbio.1001185

de Waal, F. B. M. & Aureli, F. (1997). Conflict resolution and distress alleviation in monkeys and apes. In C. S. Carter, B. Kirkpatrick, & I. Lenderhendler (Eds.), *The integrative neurobiology of affiliation.* New York: Annals of the New York Academy of Sciences.

de Waal, F. B. M. & van Roosmalen, A. (1979). Reconciliation and consolation among chimpanzees. *Behavioral Ecology & Sociobiology, 5,* 55–66. doi: 10.1007/BF00302695

de Waal, F. B. M. & Yoshihara, D. (1983). Reconciliation and redirected affection in rhesus monkeys. *Behaviour, 85,* 224–241.

Decety, J, & Jackson, P. L. (2006). A social-neuroscience perspective on empathy. *Current Directions in Psychological Science, 15(2),* 54–58.doi:10.1111/j.0963-7214.2006.00406.x

Eibl-Eibesfeldt, I. (1989). *Human Ethology.* New York: Aldine de Gruyter.

Firth, R. (1972). Verbal and bodily rituals of greeting and parting. In J. S. La Fontaine (Ed.), *The interpretation of ritual.* London, UK: Routledge.

Fiske, A. P. (1992). Four elementary forms of sociality: Framework for a unified theory of social relations. *Psychological Review, 99,* 689–723.doi: 10.1037/0033-295X.99.4.689

Fraser, O. N, & Bugnyar, T. (2011). Ravens reconcile after aggressive conflicts with valuable partners. *PLoS ONE, 6(3),* e18118. doi:10.1371/ journal.pone.0018118

French, T. (2006). *Elegy for the king and queen.* St. Petersburg Times. Retrieved from http://www.sptimes.com/2006/10/01/news_pf/Tampabay/Elegy_for_the_king_an.shtml

Fry, D. P. (2006) Reciprocity: The foundation stone of morality. In M. Killen & J. Smetana (Eds.): *Handbook of Moral Development.* Mahwah, NJ: Erlbaum.

Fry, D. P. (2009). Anthropological insights for creating non-warring social systems. *Journal of Aggression, Conflict and Peace Research, 1(2),* 4–15. doi: 10.1108/17596599200900008

Funkeson, U., Schröder, E., Nzabonimpa, J., & Holmqvist, R. (2011). Witnesses to genocide: Experiences of witnessing in the Rwandan gacaca courts. *Peace and Conflict, 17,* 367–388. doi: 10.1080/10781919.2011.599736

Furuichi, T. (2011). Female contributions to the peaceful nature of bonobo society. *Evolutionary Anthropology, 20(4),* 131–142. doi: 10.1002/evan.20308

Goodall, J. (1986). *The chimpanzees of Gombe: Patterns of behavior.* Cambridge, MA: Cambridge University Press.

Gros-Louis, J., Perry, S., & Manson, J. H. (2003). Violent coalitionary attacks and intraspecific killing in wild white-faced capuchin monkeys *(Cebus capucinus). Primates, 44(4),* 341–346. doi: 10.1007/s10329-003-0050-z

Haller, J., & Kruk, M. R. (2006). Normal and abnormal aggression: human disorders and novel laboratory models. *Neuroscience and Biobehavioral Reviews, 30,* 292–303. doi:org/10.1016/j.neurobiorev.2005.01.005

Hamilton, W. D. (1964). The genetic evolution of social behavior: I. *Journal of Theoretical Biology, 7,* 1–16. doi:org/10.1016/0022-5193(64)90038-4

Hare, B., Wobber, V., Wrangham, R. W. (2012). The self-domestication hypothesis: Evolution of bonobo psychology is due to selection against aggression. *Animal Behaviour, 83,* 573–585. doi: 10.1016/j.anbehav.2011.12.007

Hoge, C. W., Castro, C. A., Messer, S. C., McGurk, D., Cotting, D. I., & Koffman, R. L. (2004). Combat duty in Iraq and Afghanistan, mental health problems, and barriers to care. *New England Journal of Medicine, 351,* 13–22. doi:10.1056/NEJMoa040603

Holobinko, A., & Waring, G. H. (2010). Conflict and reconciliation behavior trends of the bottlenose dolphin (*Tursiops truncatus*). *Zoo Biology, 29*(5), 567–585. doi: 10.1002/zoo.20293

Keeley, L. H. (1996). *War before civilization*. New York: Oxford University Press.

Kendon, A., & Ferber, A. (1973). A description of some human greetings. In R. P. Michael & J. H. Crook (Eds.), *Comparative ecology and behaviour of primates*. London, UK: Academic Press.

Kogan, A., Saslow, L. R., Impett, E. A., Oveis, C. Keltner, D., & Rodrigues Saturn, S. (2011). Thin-slicing study of the oxytocin receptor (OXTR) gene and the evaluation and expression of the prosocial disposition. *Proceedings of the National Academy of Sciences, 108* (48), 19189–19192. doi:10.1073/pnas.1112658108

Kruk, M. R., & Kruk-de Bruin, M. (2010). *Discussions on context, causes and consequences of conflict*. Leiden: The Lorentz Center, Leiden University.

Kuehn, B. H. (2009). Soldier suicide rates continue to rise: Military, scientists work to stem the tide. *Journal of the American Medical Association, 301*, 1111–1113. doi:10.1001/jama.2009.342

Kuroda, S., Nishihara, T., Suzuki, S., & Oko, R. A. (1996). Sympatric chimpanzees and gorillas in the Ndoki forest, Congo. In W. C. McGrew, L. F. Marchant & T. Nishida (Eds.), *Great ape societies*. New York: Cambridge University Press.

Langergraber, K. E., Mitani, J. C., & Vigilant, L. (2009). Kinship and social bonds in female chimpanzees (*Pan troglodytes*). *American Journal of Primatology, 71*(10), 840–851.doi: 10.1002/ajp.20711

Lazcano A. (2011) Natural history, microbes and sequences: Shouldn't we look back again to organisms? *PLoS ONE, 6(8),* e21334. doi:10.1371/ journal.pone.0021334

Li, R., Fan, W., Tian, G., Zhu, H., He L., et al. (2010). The sequence and de novo assembly of the giant panda genome. *Nature, 463*, 311–317. doi:10.1038/nature08696

McDonald, M. M., Navarrete, C. D., & Van Vugt, M. (2012). Evolution and the psychology of intergroup conflict: the male warrior hypothesis. *Philosophical Transactions of the Royal Society B, 367*, 670–679. doi: 10.1098/rstb.2011.0301

Marlowe, D. H. (2001). *Psychological and psychosocial consequences of combat and deployment, with special emphasis on the Gulf War*. Washington, D.C.: The RAND Corporation, MR-1018/11-OSD, 2001. Retrieved from http://www.rand.org/pubs/monograph_reports/MR1018.11/

Meuniera, H., Molina-Vila, P., Perry, S. (2012). Participation in group defence: Proximate factors affecting male behaviour in wild white-faced capuchins. *Animal Behaviour, 83*, 621–628. doi: 10.1016/j.anbehav.2011.12.001

Milliken, C. S., Auchterlonie, J. L., & C. W. Hoge, C. W. (2007). Longitudinal assessment of mental health problems among Active and Reserve Component soldiers returning from the Iraq War. *Journal of the American Medical Association, 298(18)*, 2141–2148. doi:10.1001/jama.298.18.2141

Mitani, J. C. (2006). Reciprocal exchanges in chimpanzees and other primates. In P. M. Kappeler & C. van Schaik (Eds.), *Cooperation in primates and humans*. Berlin: Springer-Verlag.

Mitani, J. C. (2009). Male chimpanzees form enduring and equitable social bonds. *Animal Behaviour, 77*, 633–640. doi.org/10.1016/j.anbehav.2008.11.021

Mitani, J. C., Watts, D. P., & Amsler, S. J. (2010a). Lethal intergroup aggression leads to territorial expansion in wild chimpanzees. *Current Biology, 20(12)*, R507-R508. doi:10.1016/j.cub.2010.04.021

Mitani, J, C., Amsler, S. J., & Sobolewski, M. (2010b). Chimpanzee minds in nature. In E. V. Lonsdorf, S. R. Ross & T. Matsuzawa (Eds.), *The mind of the chimpanzee. Ecological and experimental perspectives*. Chicago: The University of Chicago Press.

Morimura, N., Idani, G. and Matsuzawa, T. (2011). The first chimpanzee sanctuary in Japan: an attempt to care for the "surplus" of biomedical research. *American Journal of Primatology, 73(3)*, 226–232. doi: 10.1002/ajp.20887

Morris, D. (1967). *The naked ape*. London: Jonathan Cape.

Morrison, L. L. (2009). Sociality and reconciliation in monk parakeets *Myiopsitta monachus* (Master's thesis, University of Nebraska, Lincoln).

Muller, M. N. (2002). Agonistic relations among Kanyawara chimpanzees. In: C. Boesch, G. Hohmann & L. F. Marchant (Eds.), *Behavioural diversity in chimpanzees and bonobos*. Cambridge: Cambridge University Press.

Mutinda, H., Poole, J. H., & Moss, C. J. (2011). Decision making and leadership in using the ecosystem. In C. J. Moss, H. Croze & P. C. Lee (Eds.), *The Amboseli elephants*. Chicago: The University of Chicago Press.

Nishida, T. (1993). Chimpanzees are always new to me. In P. Cavalieri & P. Singer (Eds.), *The great ape project: equality beyond humanity*. London: Fourth Estate.

Nishida, T. (2011). *Chimpanzees of the Lakeshore. Natural history and culture at Mahale*. Cambridge: Cambridge University Press.

Nowak, M. A., & Highfield, R. (2011). *SuperCooperators: Altruism, evolution, and why we need each other to succeed*. New York: Free Press.

Palagi, E., Antonacci, D. & Norscia, I. (2008). Peacemaking on treetops: first evidence of reconciliation from a wild prosimian (*Propithecus verreauxi*). *Animal Behaviour, 76(3)*, 737–747.doi.org/10.1016/j.anbehav.2008.04.016,

Piersma, T., & van Gils, J. A. (2011). *The flexible phenotype*. New York: Oxford University Press.

Poole, J. H. (2011). Behavioral contexts of elephant acoustic communication. In C. J. Moss, H. Croze & P. C. Lee (Eds.), *The Amboseli elephants*. Chicago: The University of Chicago Press.

Prinz, J. (2012). Why are men so violent? [Commentary on the journal article "Evolution and the psychology of intergroup conflict: the male warrior hypothesis"]. *Philosophical Transactions of the Royal Society B, 367*, 670–679. doi: 10.1098/rstb.2011.0301. Retrieved from http://www.psychologytoday.com/print/86893

Pruetz, J. D. (2010). Targeted helping by a wild adolescent male chimpanzee (*Pan troglodytes verus*): evidence for empathy? *Journal of Ethology, 29*, 365–368. doi: 10.1007/s10164–010–0244-y

Pruetz, J. & Lindshield, S. (2011). Plant-food and tool transfer among savanna chimpanzees at Fongoli, Senegal. *Primates*, Online First. doi:10.1007/s10329-011-0287-x

Reimers, M., Schwarzenberger, F., & Preuschoft, S. (2007). Rehabilitation of research chimpanzees: Stress and coping after long-term isolation. *Hormones and Behavior. 51(3)*, 428–435. doi: 10.1016/j.yhbeh.2006.12.011

Romero, T., Castellanos, M. A., & de Waal, F. B. M. (2011a). Consolation as possible expression of sympathetic concern among chimpanzees. *Proceedings of the National Academy of Sciences*, Early Edition. doi/10.1073/pnas.1006991107

Romero, T., Castellanos, M.A., de Waal F. B. M. (2011b). Post-conflict affiliation by chimpanzees with aggressors: Other-oriented versus selfish political strategy. *PLoS ONE, 6(7)*, e22173. doi:10.1371/journal.pone.0022173

Romero, T., & de Waal, F. B. M. (2011). Third-party post-conflict affiliation of aggressors in chimpanzees. *American Journal of Primatology, 73*, 397–404. doi:10.1002/ajp.20912

Roscoe, P. (2007). Intelligence, coalitional killing, and the antecedents of war. *American Anthropologist, 109(3)*, 485–495 doi:10.1525/aa.2007.109.3.485

Rosenheck, R., & Fontana, A. (1999). Changing patterns of care for war-related post-traumatic stress disorder at Department of Veterans Affairs Medical Centers: The use of performance data to guide program development. *Military Medicine, 164(11)*, 795–802.

Rudolf von Rohr, C., Burkart, J. M., & van Schaik, C. P. (2011). Evolutionary precursors of social norms in chimpanzees: a new approach. *Biology and Philosophy, 26*, 1–30. doi: 10.1007/s10539-010-9240-4

Rudolf von Rohr, C., Koski, S. E., Burkart, J. M., Caws, C., Fraser, O. N., Zilterner, A., & van Schaik, C. P. (2012). Impartial third-party interventions in captive chimpanzees: A reflection of community concern. *PloS ONE, 7(3)*, e32494. doi: 10.1371/journal.pone.0032494.

Sapolsky, R. M. (2006). Social cultures among nonhuman primates. *Current Anthropology, 47(4)*, 641–656. doi:10.1086/504162

Seres, M., Aureli, F., & de Waal, F.B.M. (2001). Successful formation of a large chimpanzee group out of two pre-existing subgroups. *Zoo Biology, 20*, 501–15. doi: 10.1002/zoo.10003

Seyfarth, R. M., & Cheney, D. L. (2012). The evolutionary origins of friendship. *Annual Review of Psychology, 63*, 153–177. doi: 10.1146/annurev-psych-120710–100337

Schino, G. (1998). Reconciliation in domestic goats. *Behaviour, 135*, 343–356.

Scott-Phillips, T. C., Dickins, T. E., & West, S. A. (2011). Evolutionary theory and the ultimate proximate distinction in the human behavioral sciences. *Perspectives on Psychological Science, 6(1)*, 38–47. doi:10.1177/1745691610393528

Schradin, C., & Lamprecht, J. (2000). Female-biased immigration and male peacekeeping in groups of the shell-dwelling cichlid fish *Neolamprologus multifasciatus*. *Behavioral Ecology and Sociobiology, 48*, 236–242. doi: 10.1007/s002650000228

Silk, J.B. (2002a). The form and function of reconciliation in primates. *Annual Reviews of Anthropology, 31*, 21–44. doi:10.1146/annurev.anthro.31.032902.101743

Silk, J.B. (2002b). Using the "f" word in primatology. *Behaviour, 139*, 421–446.

Singer, T., & Lamm, C. (2009). The social neuroscience of empathy. *The Year in Cognitive Neuroscience 2009: Annals of the New York Academy of Sciences, 1156*, 81–96.

Sponsel, L. E. (1996). The natural history of peace: A positive view of human nature and its potential. In T. Gregor (Ed.), *The natural history of peace*. Nashville, TN: Vanderbilt University Press, pp. 95–125.

Sussman, R. W., & Marshack, J. L. (2010). Are Humans Inherently Killers? *Global Nonkilling Working Papers, 1*, 7–25.

Tanielian, T., & Jaycox, L. H. (Eds.). (2008). *Invisible wounds of war: Psychological and cognitive injuries, their consequences, and services to assist recovery*. Santa Monica, CA: RAND Corporation. Retrieved from http://www.rand.org/pubs/monographs/2008/RAND_MG720.pdf

Tinbergen, N. (1958). *Curious Naturalists*. London: Country Life.

Tinbergen, N. (1963). On aims and methods of ethology. *Zeitschrift für Tierpsychologie. 20*, 410–433.doi: 10.1111/j.1439–0310.1963.tb01161.x

Tinbergen, N. (1968). On war and peace in animals and man. An ethologist's approach to the biology of aggression. *Science, 160*, 1411–1418. doi:10.1126/science.160.3835.1411

Tomasello, M. with Dweck, C., Silk, J., Skyrms, B., & Spelke, E. (2009). *Why we cooperate*. Boston, MA: MIT Press.

Valero, A., Schaffner, C. M., & Aureli, F. (2006). Intragroup lethal aggression in wild spider monkeys. *American Journal of Primatology, 68(7)*, 732–737. doi:10.1002/ajp.20263

Veenema, H. C., Das, M., & Aureli, F. (1994). Methodological improvements for the study of reconciliation. *Behavioural Processes, 31*, 29–39. Doi:10.1016/0376-6357(94)90035-3

Verbeek, P. (2006). Everyone's monkey: primate moral roots. In M. Killen & J. Smetana (Eds.), *Handbook of moral development*. Mahwah, NJ: Lawrence Erlbaum Associates.

Verbeek, P. (2008). Peace ethology. *Behaviour, 145*, 1497–1524.

Verbeek, P., & de Waal, F.B.M. (2002). The primate relationship with nature: Biophilia as a general pattern. In P.H. Kahn, Jr. & S.R. Kellert (Eds.), *Children and nature. Psychological, sociocultural, and evolutionary investigations*. Cambridge, MA: The MIT Press.

Verbeek, P., Hartup, W. W., & Collins, W. A. (2000). Conflict management in children and adolescents. In F. Aureli & F. B. M. de Waal (Eds.), *Natural conflict resolution*. Berkeley: University of California Press.

Verbeek, P., Iwamoto, T., & Murakami, N. (2007). Differences in aggression among wild type and domesticated fighting fish are context dependent. *Animal Behaviour, 73*, 75–83. doi.org/10.1016/j.anbehav.2006.03.012

Wahaj, S. A., Guse, K.R., & Holekamp, K. E. (2001). Reconciliation in the spotted hyena (*Crocuta crocuta*). *Ethology, 107*, 1057–1074. doi: 10.1046/j.1439–0310.2001.00717.x

Walter, B., & Trillmich, F. (1994). Female aggression and male peacekeeping in a cichlid fish harem: conflict between and within the sexes in *Lamprologus ocellatus. Behavioral Ecology and Sociobiology, 34*, 105–112. doi: 10.1007/BF00164181

Waser, P.M. (1987). Interactions among primate species. In B. B. Smuts, D. L. Cheney, R. M. Seyfarth, R. W. Wrangham, & T. T. Struhsaker (Eds.), *Primate societies*. Chicago: University of Chicago Press.

Weaver, A. (2003). Conflict and reconciliation in captive bottlenose dolphins, *Tursiops truncatus. Marine Mammal Science, 19*, 836–846. doi: 10.1111/j.1748-7692.2003.tb01134.x

West, S. A., El Mouden, C., & Gardner, A. (2011). Sixteen common misconceptions about the evolution of cooperation in humans. *Evolution and Human Behavior, 32*, 231–262. doi: 10.1016/j.evolhumbehav.2010.08.001

Whiten, A., Goodall, J., McGrew, W. C., Nishida, T., Reynolds, V., Sugiyama, Y., Tutin, C.E. G., Wrangham, R. W., & Boesch, C. (1999). Cultures in chimpanzees. *Nature, 399*, 682–685. doi:10.1038/21415

Wilson M. L, Hauser, M. D., Wrangham, R. W. (2001). Does participation in intergroup conflict depend on numerical assessment, range location, or rank for wild chimpanzees? *Animal Behaviour, 61(6)*, 1203–16. doi.org/10.1006/anbe.2000.1706,

Wilson, M. L., Kahlenberg, S. M., Wells, M., & Wrangham, R. W. (2012). Ecological and social factors affect the occurrence and outcomes of intergroup encounters in chimpanzees. *Animal Behaviour, 83*, 277–291. doi: 10.1016/j.anbehav.2011.11.004

Wilson, M. L., & Wrangham, R. W. (2003). Intergroup relations in chimpanzees. *Annual Review of Anthropology, 32*, 363–392. doi:10.1146/annurev.anthro.32.061002.120046

Wittig, R. M., & Boesch, C. (2003). Food competition and linear dominance hierarchy among female chimpanzees of the Tai National Park. *International Journal of Primatology, 24*, 847–867.doi: 10.1023/A:1024632923180

Wrangham, R. (2010). Chimpanzee violence is a serious topic: A response to Sussman and Marshack's critique of demonic males: Apes and the origins of human violence. *Global Nonkilling Working Papers*, *1*, 29–45.

Wrangham, R., & Peterson, D. (1996). *Demonic males: Apes and the origins of human violence*. New York: Houghton Mifflin.

Wrangham, R. W. (1999). The evolution of coalitionary killing. *Yearbook of Physical Anthropology*, *42*, 1–30.

Yamagiwa, J., Maruhashi, T., Yumoto, T., & Mwanza, N. (1996). Dietary and ranging overlap in sympatric gorillas and chimpanzees in Kahuzi-Biega National Park, Zaire. In W.C. McGrew, L.F. Marchant & T. Nishida (Eds.), *Great ape societies*. New York: Cambridge University Press.

Yamamoto, S., Humle T., & Tanaka, M. (2009). Chimpanzees help each other upon request. *PLoS ONE*, *4(*10*)*, e7416. doi:10.1371/journal.pone.0007416

5

Cooperation, Conflict, and Niche Construction in the Genus *Homo*

Agustín Fuentes

Introduction

While it is important to acknowledge the power of a focus on selection and extant Neo-Darwinian theory, we should also emphasize that there is more to evolution than that. Utilizing the traditional concept, a trait-based selection scenario, may be too limiting when thinking about, or modeling, the evolution of complex social systems/organisms. Evolution is ongoing and the contexts, patterns, and mechanisms of evolutionary processes are what should interest us most. This is an argument against the common particularly static take on selection and evolution . . . it is not so much that things have evolved, but that they are evolving.

We are in the midst of significant enhancements in complexity and diversity in evolutionary theory, with the role for behavioral modification of social and ecological spaces, and their inheritance, becoming a key factor. Our grasp of patterns and contexts of selection and the ways in which social, epigenetic and developmental interactors affect outcomes is growing by leaps and bounds. We also are increasingly realizing that social and experiential contexts shape bodies and behavior, affecting trajectories in more substantial manners than previously envisioned. In this chapter I will review current proposals for integrating perspectives from niche construction and multi-inheritance into investigations, models, and explanations for the evolution of human behavior.

Mary Jane West-Eberhard's broad overview (2003) of developmental plasticity and evolution led her to suggest that plasticity is one of the key factors for our understanding of adaptive evolution. She argues, like many other evolutionary biologists, that reducing the processes of development and evolutionary change to genomic levels is not always possible or preferable. These analyses demonstrate that evolved plasticity in development enables the evolution of new or variant, but adaptive, phenotypes without substantial, or even marked, genetic change. This phenotypic plasticity and its relation to ecologies and evolutionary patterns is of core interest in evolutionary theory.

Recent reviews define basic phenotypic plasticity as "the production of multiple phenotypes from a single genotype, depending on environmental conditions" (Miner, Sutlan, Morgan, Padilla, & Relyea, 2005). However, more important than the basic definition is the evidence that a range of organisms express phenotypic plasticity via changes in behavior, physiology, morphology, growth, life history, and demography and that this plasticity can occur in both individually and inter-generational contexts (Jablonka and Lamb, 2005). Research into modeling this plasticity, its potential adaptive value and contexts, and its ecological impact all suggest that phenotypic plasticity is a significant factor for many organisms' evolutionary histories and current behavior/morphology.

Biologists Eva Jablonka and Marion Lamb (2005) call for a renovation in evolutionary theory, a "new" new synthesis in how we model evolution. They argue for recognition of "evolution in four dimensions" rather than a focus on just one. Their main point being that practitioners of traditional Neo-Darwinian approaches focus on one system of inheritance: the genetic system of inheritance. Jablonka and Lamb argue for adding a perspective wherein three other inheritance systems can also have causal roles in evolutionary change. These other systems are the epigenetic, behavioral, and symbolic inheritance systems. Epigenetic inheritance is found in all organisms, behavioral inheritance in most, and symbolic inheritance is found only in humans.

Information is transferred from one generation to the next by many interacting inheritance systems. Variation is also *constructed*, in the sense that which variants are inherited and what final form they assume depend on various filtering and editing processes that occur before and during transmission (Jablonka & Lamb, 2005). This moves past standard Neo-Darwinian approaches. Many organisms transmit information via behavior, thus acquisition of evolutionarily relevant behavioral patterns can occur through socially mediated learning. This transmission of information occurs without having any linkage to genetic systems that natural selection (in a Neo-Darwinian view) can target. Symbolic inheritance comes with language and the ability to engage in information transfer that can be temporally and spatially complex, contain a high density of information, and convey more than material descriptions. This allows for the acquisition and reproduction of a variety of behaviors, perceptions, and beliefs that are potentially beneficial for individual humans and populations and that have no genetic basis or linkage.

Models using this system become more complex than the general reductionist models of Neo-Darwinian behavioral theory (such as kin selection, the favoring of close relatives due to their high degree of shared genotype, for example). However, such models may be better attuned to the actual interactions of systems. Specifically in terms of human evolution, this perspective forces an evolutionary concern with the way in which human bodies and behavioral and symbolic systems construct and interact with social and ecological niches and how, in turn, these systems interact with epigenetic and genetic systems. This perspective blurs any clear prioritization in inheritance systems and forces a move away from approaches that are limited to either social or biological foci.

Building on the work of Richard Lewontin (1983) and earlier perspectives of Ernst Mayr (1963) and Conrad Waddington (1959), and taking from the *extended phenotype* concept of Richard Dawkins (1982), Odling-Smee, Laland, and Feldman (2003) proposed *niche construction* as a significant evolutionary force. Niche construction is the building and destroying of niches by organisms *and* the synergistic interactions between organisms and environments.

Niche construction creates feedback within the evolutionary dynamic, such that organisms engaged in niche construction modify the evolutionary pressures acting on them, on their descendants, and on unrelated populations sharing the same landscape. Niche construction impacts/alters energy flows in ecosystems through ecosystem engineering creating an ecological inheritance and, like natural selection, contributes to changes over time in the dynamic relationship between organisms and environments. Niche construction reflects a synthesis of ecological, biological, and social niches rather than treating them as discreet spheres (e.g., Day, Laland & Odling-Smee, 2003: Fuentes, Wyczalkowski, & MacKinnon, 2010: Kendall, Tehrani & Odling-Smee, 2011).

Odling-Smee et al. (2003) explicitly state that ecological inheritance, via material culture, and niche construction in general can occur via cultural means. They state that humans are the "ultimate niche constructors" and that adding niche construction to attempts to understand human systems makes such attempts more complicated (bypassing more simplistic Neo-Darwinian adaptationist accounts). They see cultural processes as providing a particularly robust vehicle for niche construction. Odling-Smee et al. (2003) propose a specific model for human genetic and cultural evolution that they call a Tri-inheritance vision model.

In the model, human behavior results from information acquiring processes at three levels: population genetic processes, ontogenetic processes and cultural processes. Niche construction in humans emerges from all three of these processes, each of which can impact patterns, contexts, and structure of natural selection. They state "Much of human niche construction is guided by socially learned knowledge and cultural inheritance, but the transmission of this knowledge it itself dependent on preexisting information acquired through genetic evolution, complex ontogenetic processes, or prior social learning" (Odling-Smee et al., 2003, pp. 260–261).

If we see niche construction and multiple lines of inheritance as a core to evolutionary process, then the role of social/symbolic and ecological inheritance and intra- and intergroup interactions and relationships and their impacts on ecosystems come to the forefront in our examinations of evolutionary trajectories and processes, as shown in Table 5.1. This is borne out by a diverse array of recent work (e.g., Bolhuis, Brown, Richardson, & Laland, 2011; Dunbar, Gamble & Gowlett, 2010; Fuentes et. al., 2010; Henrich, 2011; Kendall et al., 2011; Richerson & Boyd, 2005; Wells & Stock, 2007).

TABLE 5.1 **Summaries of Main Points of Emerging Perspectives in Evolutionary Theory**

	Evolution in four dimensions	Developmental systems theory	Niche construction
Focus of selection	Genetic, epigenetic, behavioral, and symbolic systems	Outcome of complex interactions between genic, epigenetic, and behavioral factors	Individual and individual-local ecology interaction (niche)—a focus on Phenogenotypes
Main underlying causes for evolution of human behavior	Combination of genic, epigenetic, behavioral and symbolic inheritance systems	Constant constructing—and being constructed by—demography, social interactions, cultural variations, and manipulation of the environment in intra- and intergroup contexts in addition to the developmental biological and ecological factors throughout the course of life history	Tri-inheritance vision model (TIV) wherein human behavior results from information acquiring processes at three levels: population genetic processes, ontogenetic processes, and cultural processes
Basic premise	<ul><li>there is more to heredity than genes</li><li>some hereditary variations are nonrandom in origin</li><li>some acquired information is inherited</li><li>evolutionary change can result from instruction as well as selection</li></ul>	Evolution is not a matter of organisms or populations being molded by their environments but of organism-environment systems changing over time. This involves: joint determination by multiple causes, context sensitivity and contingency, extended inheritance, development as construction, distributed control, and evolution as construction:	<ul><li>ecosystem engineering</li><li>organisms modify their, and other, organisms' selective environments</li><li>ecological inheritance, including modified selection pressures, for subsequent populations</li><li>is a process, in addition to natural selection, that contributes to changes over time in the dynamic relationship between organisms and environments (niches)</li></ul>

Niche Construction and Human Evolution

The ability of humans to modify their social and physical surroundings is central to any explanation of human behavior. Understanding human evolution requires assessing the interactive and mutually mutable relationship humans have with their social and structural ecologies. We must accept the possibility that selection pressures can be modified as they are occurring and that human response to selective challenges will always fit the expected parameters of the selective force. That is, human toolkits (our bodies and minds) might result in innovation that adds elements into a system that standard evolutionary approaches cannot foresee or do not normally include. For example, behavioral innovation via the use of controlled fire as a response to pressures exerted by climate stress, predation risk, and the extraction of nutrition from complex food sources had impacts on the development of human cognition and adaptive strategies in a diverse array of areas (Gowlett, 2010; Wrangham, 2009).

Humans generally exist in a place where there have been humans previously. The social and ecological landscapes are impacted by the previous generations so that subsequent human generations inherit a known and human-altered landscape and ecology and a substantial amount of information about living in that place (which increases with the advent of even rudimentary language and tool use). Even when moving into new areas, humans carry social and material knowledge of their group with them and pass it on to the generations in the new location. This provides humans with more ways to respond to challenges, and with a more diverse array of means, than other organisms. Given this pattern of shared behavioral plasticity humans may be able to respond at quicker rates than most complex organisms when faced with strong selective challenges; humans can develop multiple responses to the same challenges and potentially share them across individuals and possibly even groups.

Until recently, most hypotheses for the evolution of human behavior relied strictly on natural selection as the only significant evolutionary force in the structuring of human behavior. However, we should also include possible impacts from gene flow and drift in genetic, phenotypic, and behavioral responses. Dual inheritance theory (e.g., Richerson & Boyd, 2005) focuses on the possibility that selection acts on human cultural behavior, and it is highly likely that patterns of flow and drift can impact behavior as well as genotypic factors. Selection need not always be invoked to explain the innovation and spread of behavior. When it is invoked we should also be prepared to include models that accept selection as acting on levels beyond a selfish gene or selfish individual focus (as highlighted by Dunbar, Gamble & Gowlett, 2010; Sober & Wilson, 1998; Odling-Smee et al., 2003; Oyama, Griffiths, & Gray, 2001).

It is most likely that the majority of human responses that result in behavioral change over time are not optimal, even if they do result in adaptation. Successful human responses can reflect a pattern of plasticity and flexibility resulting from a cohort of selection pressures as opposed to specific selection for a particular adaptation in response to a single selective pressure. This suggests that explanations that focus on the link of a particular behavior to a specific adaptive outcome may be poor models for human behavioral evolutionary processes.

In understanding and investigating human evolution, particularly the evolution of the genus *Homo* from the Pleistocene on we need to focus both on continuities and discontinuities in our evolutionary history. Assessing human evolution really becomes a quest to figure out why *Homo* succeeded when all the other hominins went extinct and the hominin's sibling genera (African and Asian great apes) never really made the leap to a broadly successful suite of adaptations (Hare, 2011; Mackinnon & Fuentes, 2011; Malone, Fuentes & White 2012). Mainstream approaches in the inquiry into human evolution frequently look for "big moments," monumental shifts in selection events/ responses that catapult a lineage from one stage to the next. This might not always be the best path to take. Small and/or complex multifaceted changes over time may not leave such dramatic signals and thus a focus on major morphological shifts or the modeling of massive single event behavioral shifts might not be the best way to approach our evolution.

Is it possible that in the mainstream approaches to examining human evolution we have overlooked some core aspects that might be right under our noses; aspects critical to niche construction, behavioral and even symbolic inheritance?

Cooperation and Reciprocity as Core to Human Success

Following Dunbar, Gamble, and Gowlett (2010), Nowak and Highfield (2011), Sussman and Cloninger (2011), and others, I propose that a more comprehensive and inclusive look at intra-, and possibly inter-, group behavior might hold some important answers/concepts to better model human evolution, especially in the areas of aggression and cooperation. More specifically, I argue that we have ignored some important possibilities that emerge from thinking about behavior within and between groups that might provide not only additional information about human evolutionary trends, but also might lead to enhanced explanatory models and insight into modern human behavior.

First, we have to move away from the notion that the basal unit of analysis for human behavior and interaction is the pair, the male-female unit: we do not live in dyads nor have dyads been the main unit of interaction for humans for millions of years (although pair bonds are important for humans). For example, there is emerging consensus that approaches to reconstructing behavior by Pleistocene members of the genus *Homo* are better served by looking at group sizes, social networks, and intergroup interactions and their relationships to changes in the archeological record (tool types, use of fire, etc.) than modeling dyadic interactions between group members (Dunbar, Gamble & Gowlett, 2010, Fuentes 2009).

Expanding outside the "pair focus" might enable us to get a better grasp on why we do what we do, from an evolutionary sense. This implies a shift away from specific trait and sexual selection models as the primary explanatory modes in the evolution of human behavior, such as the explanations proposed by Lovejoy (2009) for pair-bonding and monogamy in early hominins. This does not mean that specific traits and sexual selection are not at play and important, but simply that more comprehensive system processes might also be central to our evolutionary patterns. This is illustrated by Hrdy (2005) and Gettler (2010) when they argue for cooperative breeding and extended male participation in child-care, respectively, in as core factors in human evolution. Hrdy interweaves specific trait-based assumptions about reproductive success and connects their enhancement to a specific scenario of multi-individual allocare. Gettler, in turn, argues for male carrying as a way to reduce reproductive costs on females and increase infant survivorship and suggest that this is part of a network of adaptations that characterize caretaking of high-cost infants in members of the genus *Homo*. Both of these examples use specific behavioral traits in traditional fitness assessments, but they rest the efficacy of the model in the context of multi-individual social networks, forcing a focus on more than dyadic interactions as the basis of their arguments.

Before moving on to present a model for the patterns I suggest, we need to acknowledge a few potential theoretical and ideological stumbling blocks that might affect our abilities to think about human (and primate) evolution. The first is the over-emphasis on the concept of optimality. Do evolutionary processes produce the best outcomes or ones that are just good enough? Largely, the latter. Direct and continuous selection pressure toward optimality can be modeled for any trait in question, but none of these traits occur in a vacuum and it behooves us to remember that optimality modeling is really just a heuristic tool, not a reflection of real systems' operations. If we are always assuming that systems move toward an optimum and that over evolutionary time, traits that persevere are optimal, we might ignore the possibility that there are multiple effective outcomes for a given trait in a given system. We might also make the mistake of describing traits as if they exist by themselves and can be assessed as such, independent of their role and position in a given system. However, if we are not concerned with optimality but rather with system function in the sense of evolutionary sufficiency, we are open to more possibilities for explanation of patterns without denying the possibility that some traits may be approaching optimality in function and/or structure, while others may not be.

The second way to enhance our evolutionary models and insights is to query: what is adaptive? If we are open to the possibility that a myriad of traits (both physical and behavioral) may not be strictly adaptive, but yet still influence the functioning and potential of a given system, we are better positioned to think in terms of multiple systems simultaneously impacting the human evolutionary trajectory. This can go hand in hand with a recognition of plasticity in behavioral patterns as a form of preadaptation which is not optimal, but might be very well suited to an organism that relies on a diverse tool kit for engaging with social and ecological landscapes. Potential for emergent properties and their relation to evolutionary change is important for us to consider. Not all relevant elements in the evolution of systems operate with either directional, disruptive, or stabilizing selection as the only relevant forces on them.

In the investigation of human behavioral evolution, there has traditionally been substantial emphasis placed on direct competition and aggression between dyads and between groups (Fuentes, 2009; Hart & Sussman, 2008). There is mounting evidence from the fossil, archeological, comparative primatological, and modeling literature that this is an incomplete approach at best, and a deleterious approach at worst when investigating human evolution (e.g., Nowak & Highfield, 2011, Sussman & Cloninger, 2011). In this light it is important to point out that conflict/competition are not the *only* drivers in evolutionary systems. We have to consider that there may be a mutual mutability in cooperative and competitive relationships and a degree of plasticity and hybridity in function in addition to our general views of adaptation and strategies. This is not unique to human evolution, since cooperation as a core driver in the evolution of organismal and social systems can be found throughout the animal kingdom (and beyond, e.g., Weiss & Buchanan, 2009). For example, complex social cooperation and reciprocity form the central modes of interaction in many mammalian groups (coyotes, wolves, whales, and meerkats, just to name a few) and are especially important in the daily lives, evolutionary histories, and neurobiologies of the primates (Bekoff 2007, Sussman & Cloninger, 2011, Rilling, 2011, de Waal & Brosnan, 2006).

Finally, we must be wary of the benefits and drawbacks of comparative models, especially with the great apes. Chimpanzee analogies in human evolutions are only partial at best, as the genus *Homo* and the genus *Pan* (consisting of the two species *P. paniscus*, or bonobos, and *P. troglodytes*, or chimpanzees) are extremely different in a wide array of behavioral, ecological, and physiological arenas. Considering the available fossil, physiological, and morphological evidence it is highly likely that each of the African hominoid lineages (chimpanzees/bonobos, gorillas, and humans) are highly derived and that the *recent common ancestor* (RCA) was largely unlike the present forms. This means that behavioral analogies need to be utilized with extreme care. This is very noticeable when it comes to issues of aggression and the *Homo-Pan* comparisons. It should be quite clear at this point that humans and the two *Pan* species may share some similarities, but that behaviorally they are quite divergent in most areas. Simply put, we must stop envisioning chimpanzees and bonobos as a model (behaviorally, morphologically, or ecologically) for the RCA (Ferguson, 2011; Hart & Sussman, 2008). Chimpanzees can provide some good phylogenetic comparisons (as can other primates), but in explaining the radical success of genus *Homo* relative to the other Hominoids we must focus on human derived traits, not only those in common with other primates as has regularly been done with apes (e.g., Dunbar, Gamble & Gowlett, 2010; Hare, 2011; MacKinnon & Fuentes, 2011). We do need to be cautious with the comparative primatological approach as it can misdirect research foci away from important hominin features such as our extreme offspring costs, social plasticity, and niche constructivist tendencies.

Systems Approaches

Human behavior, and the evolution of that behavior, should be examined from a systems perspective; we need to consider what human groups did in the past and what we continue to do. That is, looking at social systems on the whole rather than as a series of dyadic contests or specific concordances (or lack thereof) with optimal predictions may best explain many of the overall behavioral patterns in human and human evolution.

We should be careful, for example, not to use *a priori* modern gender roles and the optimal, or idealized, division of labor as a baseline for the construction of evolutionary "roles" of males and females regarding conflict and cooperation. The expectation of minimal male caretaking of children, the association of males (and not females) with the manufacture and use of tools and other material technical skills including creation of material art, and the expectation of males taking lead roles in group coordination are all assumptions, based on modern gender roles and stereotypes, that are frequently imposed on the human past. The fossil and material record do not provide evidence for the vast majority of the modern gender patterns until very recently (Adovasio, Olga & Jake, 2007). While we can argue for behavioral differences based on size, muscle density, and aspects of reproductive physiology, many of the gender role assignments (from tool-making to sexuality to childcare to group leadership) found in societies today, and assumed to be present in past human groups, are not supported by any fossil or archeological evidence before the last 10 to 20,000 years. There is a pattern wherein the archeological evidence and the comparative primatological approach do not definitively point to one specific way of being successfully human, thus suggesting that what we are looking for may be a conglomerate of behavioral patterns rather than one specific *main* behavior (Ehrlich, 1999; Fuentes, 2009).

So, if there is a broader pattern, or system, apparent in human behavior, what are the characteristics that define this uniquely successful system in *Homo* today? In a nutshell they are: *hyper-cooperation at multiple levels, extensive niche construction, relatively frequent coordinated intergroup violence, symbol use and hyper-complex information transfer, extremely diverse geographic distribution and ecological patterns* (e.g., Dunbar et al., 2010; Fuentes, 2009; Hill, Barton & Hurtado, 2009; Nowak & Highfield, 2011).

Over the last decade or so a number of researchers have reintroduced a focus on cooperative interactions as the focal points for evolutionary questions about human behavior. These foci give us insight into the constituent factors involved in this system. For example, Hrdy (1999, 2005) effectively argues for envisioning humans, and human ancestors, as cooperative breeders. Her basic premise involves the use of multiple caretakers in human groups to ameliorate the costs of large, heavily dependent offspring with very slow developmental trajectories. Hrdy, drawing on ethnographic and evolutionary examples, posits at a system where more individuals than the mother are integral to the successful raising of young. Often these individuals are assumed to be related females (see Hawkes et al., 2003) or maternally related males (i.e., kin selection), however the recent versions of this scenario credit multiple age/sex classes and even non-maternal kin in the group with contributing to the successful rearing, provisioning, and defending of young. Gettler (2010) even provides a strong argument, and evidence, that we should broaden this specifically to include male carrying of young as an important pattern in early members of the genus *Homo*. Here we see that intergenerational cooperation and cooperation between nonkin, or non-close kin, may have emerged as a core process in human evolution that is not best modeled as dyadic interactions or contests.

Fehr and Gintis (2007) and Heinrich et al. (2004) suggest that cooperation is the normative mode of interaction and exchange between human groups. They review a variety of economic experiments conducted across decades and note that the results show consistent deviations from predictions of the *Homo economicus* model (that humans will exhibit "narrowly economically self-interested behavior"). These researchers undertook a cross-cultural experimental study in 15 small-scale societies scattered across the world (in Latin America, Africa, mainland Asia, and Indonesia). Henrich et al. (2004) demonstrate that the central axiom of *Homo economicus* is refuted; they found more variation in behavior across societies than had previously been reported. In fact, selfishness as a primary pattern was not found in any of the societies studied. Rather, patterns of cooperation and social reciprocity were dominant, with much variation in details across society based on integration into world markets, demographic, and other social variables. This does not mean that humans are all egalitarian or selfless, rather it reflects the fact that human societies are based on extensive and extremely complex systems of cooperation and mutual interreliance on one another, such that a consistent selfish behavioral strategy will not be sustainable in human groups. From these results and a survey of the broader literature they argue that both experimental and field data from across the social sciences demonstrate that neither assumptions of narrow economic self-interest, nor evolutionary models based on kinship or reciprocal altruism are sufficient, or effective, explanations to account for the observed patterns of cooperation across human societies (see http://www.hss.caltech.edu/~jensming/roots-of-sociality/).

Looking at the fossil record, Fuentes et al. (2010, see also Fuentes, 2004) and Hart and Sussman (2008) also make the case that cooperative systems were central to the success of earlier hominins and especially the first members of our own genus (e.g., *Homo erectus/ergaster*). These researchers suggest that the selective pressures placed by high predation on early humans had significant effects on their behavior. Specifically, increasingly complex sociality and patterns of intergroup cooperation created a particular niche construction pattern that became a central component of human behavior.

Oka and Fuentes (2011) and Horan, Bulte, and Shogren (2005) extend this concept closer in evolutionary time, arguing that it was the use of long-distance trade routes that enabled humans to out-compete Neanderthals. Comparing and contrasting the effects of feedback from cooperation and its concomitant niche construction on the evolution of two different socio-economic processes, these authors explore the success of Late Pleistocene *Homo sapiens* groups over their contemporaries and the modern day endurance of ethnic traders' networks in east Africa. The main conclusion is that the feedback from intragroup and intergroup cooperation through social networks creates a ratcheting effect on the local ecologies of all groups/organizations responding to similar pressures (predation pressure, socio-political regulation, and/or competition). In such systems the groups that effectively engage in intra- *and* intergroup cooperation have higher potential success than those that do not emphasize cooperation or than those that fail to achieve sufficiently effective group-wide or population-wide cooperative patterns.

This notion of cooperation as a central systemic aspect in human evolution is summarized and supported via mathematical modeling by Nowak in his "supercooperators" theory (see Nowak & Highfield, 2011). Basically, he illustrates via multiple lines of modeling evidence that it is the ability and practice of intense cooperative behavior and patterns of cooperative relationships amongst group members that creates the context for a long-term selective environment (a social and ecological niche) in which the cooperative patterns are a central driver of evolutionary success.

Evolution of the Human System: Cooperation, Conflict, and Niche Construction in the Genus *Homo*

If extensive and substantial cooperation is indeed a core part of the process in human evolution, what might the process by which such a system evolved look like across the last two million years? What would a pattern of niche construction that gives rise to such "super-cooperators" look like?

To assess these questions we need to outline specifically what is proposed to be happening in populations of the genus *Homo* in the Pleistocene (Box 5.1). The fossil and material records suggest that the following patterns emerged in the genus *Homo* between 1.8 million and ~60,000 years ago (see expanded treatments in Fuentes, 2009, 2011): *Increasing brain size (through ~300,000 years ago) extended period of, and effort in, child care, increased cooperative interactions between group members across generations, increased communicative complexity, increased effectiveness at avoiding predation, and allowed for an expansion of the types and patterns of habitats exploited.*

Due to increasing abilities to avoid, combat, or otherwise inhibit the success of predation pressures, members of the genus *Homo* became more costly and predators shifted emphasis to easier prey, reducing the overall selective pressure of predation (Fuentes et al., 2010; Hart & Sussman, 2008). In this context *Homo* experienced increased opportunity for social interactions, range exploration, and testing a variety of novel foraging opportunities. These patterns facilitated, via feedback systems, an emerging higher cognitive

---

BOX 5.1 Core Patterns in the Genus Homo

- Phase I: ~2–.3 MYA
  - Expanding neocortex
  - Intragroup Cooperation and social reciprocity central (Inter- and intrasexual and generational)
  - Increase in material exploitation/manipulation (some specialization/division of labor)
  - Variable intergroup relationships, including cooperation/reciprocity *and* conflict
  - Small-scale trade networks
  - Geographic expansion
- Phase II ~300KYA–40KYA
  - Neurological reconfiguration
  - Increased complexity in social identities and social roles
  - Harsh-ecologies colonization
  - Expanded Trade networks and material exchanges
  - Increased variability in intergroup and inter-regional relationships
- Phase III ~40KYA–recent
  - Increased niche variability and ecological patterns
  - Material inequity and trade expansion/restriction
  - Symbolic-social niche construction
  - Increased male aggression and emergence of complex violence– Large-scale regional polities and emergence of complex peace

functioning via niche construction and its interplay with selection pressures. In this context specific heritable components of human niche construction play core roles. Social traditions such as tool use, manufacture, and trade are inherited and shared among members of groups and local populations. This extends also to the knowledge and use of local areas. As environmental challenges also are increasingly negotiated with information transfer via complex communication patterns, social niches are established in which selection favors gene complexes/physiologies that predispose or facilitate increased cooperation and communication abilities. The use of fire and increased infant survivorship add to the niche constructing capacity via increased capabilities of extra-somatic modification and new demographic structures, which facilitate diversified, and increasingly plastic, patterns of habitat exploitation (e.g., Gowlett, 2010). This series of interconnected processes is tied to an evolving hominin cognition, all of which creates the ongoing feedback in multiple somatic and extrasomatic systems that facilitate multifaceted engagement and success in a diverse array of environments for the genus *Homo*.

Given these patterns and potential processes we can envision a scenario of integrated cooperation as a component of the human niche with central roles for ecological and social inheritance, cross-generational cooperation, the emergence of symbolic identities, and a diverse pattern of intergroup cooperation and conflict across the human species. This pattern begins within the comparative context of primate evolution, becomes more refined in the course of hominin evolution, and emerges in its modern form via the more recent evolution of the genus *Homo* (MacKinnon & Fuentes, 2011).

Primates are characterized by a specific type of "social intelligence" (Dunbar & Shultz, 2007). Many central components of primate cognition emerged in response to the challenging demands of a complex social life, especially the ubiquity of cooperation and competition within the social group (Herrmann, Call, Hernandez-Lloreda, Hare, & Tomasello, 2007; Silk, 2007). There is a ratcheting up of this social complexity in anthropoid primates, which is increased in the Miocene hominoids and exponentially enhanced in hominins (see Malone, Fuentes & White, 2012; MacKinnon & Fuentes, 2011). In this scenario primates are taking the basal complex sociality of mammals and enhancing it by using social networks/contexts as a tool to meet and modify the demands of the environment (the selective landscape). As the local social and biotic environments are being modified selection pressures are altered, thus changing the selective landscapes for the primate populations. Increasing cognitive complexity in the later Miocene hominoids begins to facilitate more intensive use of the social relationships as tools to meet ecological challenges, and thus increased cooperation and reciprocity become central components of behavioral repertoires. This pattern creates a constant feedback between the social and biotic ecologies resulting in niche construction and the continuous modification of selective landscapes. In the hominins, physiological and behavioral adaptations emerge to effectively negotiate the increasingly complex and information-rich social networks where coalitions, multi-party social negotiations, and reciprocity are the primary avenues for social and reproductive success (Dunbar et al., 2010; Nowak & Highfield, 2011). It is at this point in our evolutionary histories that we can begin to see the emergence of unique human characteristics related to conflict and cooperation that eventually involve the use of symbols and language.

As noted above, starting at some point in the early Pleistocene, extended allocare and a shift to more complex manipulation and use of the environmental characterizes the genus *Homo*. This is followed by (and facilitates) a geographic range expansion and increases in tool use/creation and possibly much broader incorporation of extra-somatic materials such as fire. These social and ecological niches facilitate the emergence of increased symbolic and informationally dense communication within and between groups and a significant role for intergroup trade and cooperation (see also Potts, 2004). This period could be seen as the point of emergence of true language. However, it is nearly impossible to test such an assertion using material remains in the fossil record. Finally, the impacts of the previous patterns on ecological, social, and selective processes catalyze the move toward modern human intense reliance on trade, complex inter- and intragroup relationships, and increased scale of conflict and cooperation. It is in our recent evolutionary history that the current versions of human relatively frequent large-scale coordinated lethal aggression (i.e., war) and peace emerge.

War and Peace

The integration of symbolic identities, multipopulation polities, and diverse hierarchical social structures change the ways in which basal patterns of cooperation and competition occur and are perceived by human populations. In the earlier phases of human evolution the types and patterns of relationships between groups were different than those in humans of the last 20,000 years ago or so. In this more recent period of human existence, coordination at larger societal levels begins to be a dominant mode of interaction, whereas previously most interfaces were at small-scale intergroup and interindividual levels. The expansion of human interaction patterns to include larger groups and multiple populations with complex social and economic hierarchies can lead to different patterns and structures of niche construction. This in turn facilitates increased possibilities for differential roles and patterns of exchange within and between social groups impacting the tenor and structure of cooperation and competition.

There is significant contention about the appearance, longevity, context, and patterns of broad-scale political peace and organized warfare/large-scale lethal aggression in humans; this is the first time in human evolutionary history that we see frequent (relative to the previous two million years of human evolution) coordinated intergroup violence. It is important to recognize that these patterns, emerging in this most recent phase of our evolution, are not rooted deep in our evolutionary past but rather are capacities facilitated by the changing demographic, technological, and structural realities of human populations, as a part of the niche we continue to inhabit and alter. While there are countless definitions for "war," Ferguson (2008) provides a basic and useful one: *organized lethal violence by members of one group against members of another group.* By this definition, aside from some populations of chimpanzees, this specific behavior (war) is unique to recent (see Box 5.1—phase 3) populations of the genus *Homo*. Groups of monkeys may fight over food sources, ant colonies fight over space, and many other types of animal groups engage in conflicts, but none of them are planned, organized, and lethal with regularity. This definition also distinguishes war from homicide (single events where an individual is killed by another) (Ferguson, 2008). While warfare is relatively common in recent human history there is very little evidence that wide-scale lethal violence by one group against another characterizes any of the earlier phases of human evolutionary history (Ferguson, 2011; Fry, 2006; Walker, 2001).

In fact, reviewing the available data from the fossil record of humans and other hominins from ~6 million years ago through about 12,000 years ago one finds only a few examples of possible death due to the hand of a conspecific, and many of these can be attributed to cannibalism (either within group or between group) or generalized injuries from interindividual aggression (fights) (Anton, 2003; Ferguson, 2011; Haas & Piscitelli, Chapter 10; Kimble & Delezene, 2009; Tattersal, 1997). Clear evidence of actual deaths from weaponry (i.e., spears and bows and arrows) is only found in modern humans by 8–12,000 years ago. From this point on, most archeological records show some examples of individuals having died at the hands of others (Walker, 2001). The human fossil record supports the hypothesis that while some violence between individuals obviously happened in the past, warfare is a relatively modern human behavior (10–12,000 years old). Thus to seriously investigate war as a major aspect of modern humans we need to consider factors such as ecological and social contexts, group size and population densities, and the differences in conflict versus homicide versus war; we also need to think in terms of human systems and niches, not specific adaptations. Also, it is interesting to note that large-scale coordinated conflicts such as war require that intensive patterns of cooperation are already in place in the society (Ferguson, 2011). War makes use of the human capacity to cooperate but as complex cooperation predates war by many, many millennia, engaging in war cannot be viewed as sparking the origin and evolution of cooperation.

Conclusion

The evolution of human behavioral patterns is complex, but cooperative interactions play a central role. Conflict and competition are ubiquitous in living things, but are not necessarily the main, or only, drivers in the evolution of behavioral systems. In addition to identifying specific adaptation of traits or individual behaviors, our attempts to understand the evolutionary histories of humans must include a systems approach wherein liner models of optimality and traditional presentations of natural selection are not the only processes of relevance. Including the concepts of niche construction and multiple modes of inheritance and the realization that plasticity can be seen as an adaptive pattern in and of itself can enable us to make greater headway in assessing and describing the systems involved in human evolution.

Examining the broad trajectory of human evolution we can see that niche construction, cooperation, and conflict interact, and are intertwined, as a complex system (Kendall et al., 2011). From the fossil and archeological record, and the comparative primatological datasets, we can see that human warfare is an evolutionarily recent phenomenon. It is best seen as emergent from social structures, ecologies, and histories rather than being reflective of specific adaptive patterns of aggression and competition. It is not a basal human aggression that results in warfare or a basic human egalitarianism that results in peace. War and peace emerge from the interactions of patterns of cooperation, shared and disputed ecologies, social, economic, and symbolic histories, and the perceptions of human polities. The social and historical niches we construct and modify interface with the adaptive features of human physiology and behavior, and the ongoing process of evolutionary change, to create systems of integration between cooperation, competition and perception. Understanding these systems will enable us to better model and interpret the human past and present.

References

Adovasio, J. M., Olga, S., & Jake, P. (2007). *The invisible sex: Uncovering the true roles of women in prehistory*. New York: Smithsonian Books.

Anton, S. C. (2003). Natural history of *Homo erectus*. *Yearbook of Physical Anthropology, 46*, 126–170.

Bekoff, M. (2007). *The emotional lives of animals*. Novato, CA: New World Library.

Bolhuis, J. J., Brown, G. R., Richardson, R. C., & Laland, K. N. (2011). Darwin in mind: New opportunities for evolutionary psychology. *PLoS Biology, 9* (7), 1–8.

Dawkins, R. (1982). *The extended phenotype*. New York: Oxford University Press.

Day, R. L., Laland, K. N., & Odling-Smee, J. (2003). Rethinking adaptation: The niche-construction perspective. *Perspectives in Biology and Medicine, 46* (1), 80–95.

de Waal, F. B. M., & Brosnan, S. F. (2006). Simple and complex reciprocity in primates. In P. M. Kappeler & C. P. van Schaik (Eds.), *Cooperation in primates and humans: Mechanisms and Evolutions* (pp. 85–105). New York: Springer.

Dunbar, R., Gamble, C., & Gowlett, J. (2010). *Social brain, distributed mind. Proceedings of the British Academy, 158*. New York: Oxford University Press.

Dunbar, R., & Shultz, S. (2007). Understanding primate brain evolution. *Science, 317*, 1344–1347.

Ehrlich, P. (1999). *Human natures: Genes, cultures and the human prospect*. Washington, DC: Island Press.

Fehr, E., & Gintis, H. (2007). Human motivation and social cooperation: Experimental and analytic foundations. *Annual Review of Sociology, 33*, 43–64.

Ferguson, R. B. (2008). War before history. In P. deSouza (Ed.), *The ancient world at war*. London: Thames and Hudson.

Ferguson, R. B. (2011). Born to live: Challenging killer myths. In R. W. Sussman & C. R. Cloninger (Eds.), *Origins of altruism and cooperation* (pp. 249–270). New York: Springer.

Fry, D. P. (2006). *The human potential for peace*. New York: Oxford University Press.

Fuentes, A. (2004). It's not all sex and violence: Integrated anthropology and the role of cooperation and social complexity in human evolution *American Anthropologist, 106*, 710–718.

Fuentes, A. (2009). *Evolution of human behavior*. New York: Oxford University Press.

Fuentes, A. (2011). *Biological anthropology: Concepts and connections* (second ed.). New York: McGraw-Hill.

Fuentes, A., Wyczalkowski, M., & MacKinnon, K. C. (2010). Niche construction through cooperation: A nonlinear dynamics contribution to modeling facets of the evolutionary history in the genus *Homo*. *Current Anthropology, 51*, 435–444.

Gettler L. T. (2010). Direct male care and hominin evolution: Why male-child interaction is more than a nice social idea. *American Anthropologist, 112*, 7–21.

Gowlett, J. (2010). Firing up the social brain. In R. Dunbar, C. Gamble, & J. Gowlett, (Eds.), *Social brain, distributed mind. Proceedings of the British Academy 158*, 341–366. New York: Oxford University Press.

Hare, B. (2011). From hominoid to hominid mind: What changed and why? *Annual Review of Anthropology, 40*, 293–309.

Hart, D., & Sussman, R. W. (2008). *Man the hunted: Primates, predators, and human evolution*. Boulder, CO: Westview.

Hawkes, K., O'Connell, J. F., & Blurton-Jones, N. G. (2003). Human life histories: Primate trade-offs, grandmothering socioecology, and the fossil record. In P. M. Kappeler & M. E. Pereira (Eds.), *Primate life histories and socioecology* (pp. 204–227). Chicago: University of Chicago Press.

Henrich, J (2011). A cultural species: How culture drove human evolution. *Psychological Science Agenda 25(11)*. http://www.apa.org/science/about/psa/2011/11/human-evolution.aspx

Henrich, J., Boyd, R., Bowles, S., Camerer, C., Fehr, E., Gintis, H., & McElreath, R. (Eds.), (2004). *Foundations of human sociality*. Oxford: Oxford University Press.

Herrmann, E., Call, J., Hernandez-Lloreda, M.V., Hare, B., & Tomasello, M. (2007). Humans have evolved specialized skills of social cognition: The cultural intelligence hypothesis. *Science, 317*, 1360–1366.

Hill, K., Barton, M., & Hurtado, A. M. (2009). The emergence of human uniqueness: Characters underlying behavioral modernity. *Evolutionary Anthropology, 18*, 187–200.

Horan, R. D., Bulte, E., & Shogren, J. F. (2005). How trade saved humanity from biological exclusion: An economic theory of Neanderthal extinction. *Journal of Economic Behavior and Organization, 58*, 1–29.

Hrdy, S. B. (1999). *Mother nature: A history of mothers, infants and natural selection*. New York: Pantheon.

Hrdy, S. B. (2005). Evolutionary context of human development: The cooperative breeding model. In C. S. Carter, L. Ahnert, K. E. Grossmann, S. B. Hrdy, M. E. Lamb, S. W. Porges, & N. Sachser (Eds.), *Attachment and bonding: A new synthesis* (pp. 9–32). Cambridge, MA: MIT Press.

Jablonka, E., & Lamb, M. (2005). *Evolution in four dimensions: Genetic, epigenetic, behavioral, and symbolic variation in the history of life*. Cambridge, MA: MIT Press.

Kendall, J., Tehrani, J. J., & Odling-Smee, J. (2011). Human niche construction in interdisciplinary focus. *Philosophical Transactions of the Royal Society, B, 366*, 785–792.

Kimble, W. H., & Delezene, L. K. (2009). "Lucy" redux: A review of research on *Australopithecus afarensis. Yearbook of Physical Anthropology, 52*, 2–48.

Lewontin, R. (1983). Gene, organism and environment. In D. S. Bendall (Ed.), *Evolution from molecules to men.* Cambridge, UK: Cambridge University Press.

Lovejoy, C. (2009). Reexamining human origins in light of *Ardipithecus ramidus. Science, 326* (5949), 74–74. DOI: 10.1126/science.1175834

MacKinnon, K. C., & Fuentes, A. (2011). Primates, niche construction, and social complexity: The roles of social cooperation and altruism. In R. W. Sussman & C. R. Cloninger (Eds.), *Origins of altruism and cooperation* (pp. 121–143). New York: Springer.

Malone, N. M., Fuentes, A., & White, F. J. (2012). Variation in the social systems of extant hominoids: Comparative insight into the social behaviour of early hominins. *International Journal of Primatology*. Doi:10.10007/s10764-012-9617-0

Mayr, E. (1963). *Animal speciation and evolution*. Cambridge, MA: Harvard University Press.

Miner, B. G., Sultan, S. E, Morgan, S. G., Padilla, D. K., & Relyea, R. A. (2005). Ecological consequences of phenotypic plasticity. *Trends in Ecology and Evolution, 20*(12), 685–692.

Nowak, M. A., & Highfield, R. (2011). *Supercooperators: Altruism, evolution, and why we need each other to succeed.* New York: Free Press.

Odling-Smee, F. J., Laland, K. N., & Feldman, M. W. (2003). *Niche construction: The neglected process in evolution. Monographs in Population Biology, 37*. Princeton: Princeton University Press.

Oka, R., & Fuentes, A. (2010). From reciprocity to trade: How cooperative infrastructures form the basis of human socioeconomic evolution. In R. C. Marshal (Ed.), *Cooperation in social and economic life* (pp. 3–28). Boulder: Altamira Press.

Oyama, S., Griffiths, P. E., & Gray, R. D. (2001). Introduction: What is developmental systems theory? In Oyama, S., Griffiths, P. E. & Gray, R. D. (Eds.), *Cycles of contingency: Developmental systems and evolution* (pp. 1–12). Cambridge, MA: MIT Press.

Potts, R. (2004). Sociality and the concept of culture in human origins. In R. W. Sussman & A. R. Chapman (Eds.), *The origins and nature of sociality* (pp. 249–269). New York: Aldine de Gruyter.

Richerson, P. J., & Boyd, R. (2005). *Not by genes alone: How culture transformed human evolution.* Chicago, IL: University of Chicago Press.

Rilling, J. K. (2011). The neurobiology of cooperation and altruism. In R. W. Sussman & C. R. Cloninger (Eds.), *Origins of altruism and cooperation* (pp. 295–306). New York: Springer.

Silk, J. B. (2007). Social components of fitness in primate groups. *Science 317*(5843), 1347–1351.

Sober, E., & Wilson, D. S. (1998). *Unto others: The evolution and psychology of unselfish behavior.* Cambridge, MA: Harvard University Press.

Sussman, R.W., & Cloninger, R.C. (Eds.), (2011). *Origins of altruism and cooperation.* New York: Springer.

Tattersall, I. (1997). *The fossil trail: How we know what we think we know about human evolution.* New York: Oxford University Press.

Waddington, C. H. (1959). Canalization of development and genetic assimilation of acquired characters. *Nature, 183,* 1654–1655.

Walker, P. L. (2001). A bioarchaeological perspective on the history of violence. *Annual Review of Anthropology, 30,* 573–596.

Weiss, K., & Buchanan, A. (2009). *The mermaid's tale: Four billion years of cooperation in the making of living things.* Cambridge: Harvard University Press.

Wells, J. C. K., & Stock, J. T. (2007). The biology of the colonizing ape. *Yearbook of Physical Anthropology, 134,* 191–222.

West-Eberhard, M. J. (2003). *Developmental plasticity and evolution.* New York: Oxford University Press.

Wrangham, R. (2009). *Catching fire: How cooking made us human.* New York: Basic Books.

PART TWO

Lessons from Prehistory

WAR AND PEACE IN THE PAST

6

Why the Legend of the Killer Ape Never Dies

The Enduring Power of Cultural Beliefs to Distort Our View of Human Nature

ROBERT W. SUSSMAN

Recently it was reported in the *New Scientist* that: "Now a new theory is emerging that challenges the prevailing view that warfare is a product of human culture and thus a relatively recent phenomenon. For the first time, anthropologists, archaeologists, primatologists, psychologists and political scientists are approaching a consensus. Not only is war as ancient as humankind, they say, but it has played an integral role in our evolution" (Holmes, 2008). Furthermore, it has recently been claimed that: "About 30 percent of all men carry what's known as 'the warrior gene'—a tiny bit of DNA that predisposes them to violent behavior" *(National Geographic, 2010)*. First of all, I would question that there is a consensus that "war" is part of our evolutionary (genetic) past and that humans (especially human males) are genetically programmed for war or violence. Secondly, I believe that claims such as these recall an earlier time in US and Western European science, in the early part of the twentieth century, when the Eugenics Movement proposed simplistic and simple-minded genetic explanations of complex human behaviors.

At the height of the Eugenics Movement in the early 1900s, such complex behaviors as the "love of sea" (or thalassophilia) was believed to be a simple Mendelian sex-linked characteristic, especially found in families of naval officers (Davenport & Scudder, 1919). Today, it would seem absurd to claim that such a complex trait as sailing could be determined by simple Mendelian inheritance. Yet, the claim that humans are by nature genetically programmed for war and that human males have a genetic propensity for violence is readily accepted. But what does this mean? Yes, humans can be warlike and violent but they can also be peaceful and non-violent. What does having a propensity for war or being genetically programmed for violence mean? If I am not a violent person, does that mean that I am unfit or not very human? If I have a warrior gene does that mean that I enjoy killing in face to face combat or that I just enjoy pushing a button that drops a bomb? Or does it mean I enjoy sending young men to war so that my business profits? How does this warrior gene or this inherent propensity for warfare and violence manifest itself, precisely? Is it so vague that we can't really know the specific manifestations of this genetic trait? This approach is, of course, what led to the downfall of eugenics—the proposed traits were not really related to genetics but to some vague correlation between the presence of a supposedly hereditary determinant (now called a genotype) and a supposedly relatively invariant adult trait (now called a phenotype) (Allen, 2001), without any concept of how environment influenced this correlation.

Warfaredness (I use the term here in a similar vein to that used by the Eugenics Movement's use of seafaringness or thalassophilia) and killing, or murder, are not genotypes. In fact, there are no specific phenotypes for these complex human behaviors. There is tremendous variation in the expression of these behaviors among different individuals and different *cultures*. If warfare, murder, or homicide is a genetic trait among all humans and not culturally determined, how do we explain the variation in the statistics of these behaviors across different cultures? For example, the homicide rate in Japan is less than one-twelfth that in the United States (0.44 vs. 5.4 killings per 100,000 people per year) (Knauft, 2011). Does this mean that men in the US have a higher rate of genes for killing than do men in Japan, or that more US men have a homicide gene? Are we now going back to a racist, early nineteenth century mentality on these issues? Contrary to *New Scientist*'s assertion that a "consensus" of anthropologists, archaeologists, primatologists, psychologists, and political scientists believe that warfare and violence among humans are hereditary phenomena, I would argue the direct opposite. To me, it is just the fact that the ideas of violence and warfare, the inherent evil of humankind, are so imbedded in our *culture* that it is easy for scientists and the general public to think that these behaviors are a normal, biologically determined, hereditary, and natural part of the human behavioral repertoire (Fry, chapter 1).

In a Levi-Straussian sense, given Western European and United States myths, beliefs and, unfortunately, even practices, "it is easy to think" that humans are by nature violent. Ironically, rather than these traits being genetically determined, the perception that they are "natural or biologically and not culturally determined" is not only *cultural* but is an integral part of a Western European and US *cultural* world view. To me, this misunderstanding is related to the fact that most scientists, and unfortunately, many anthropologists, do not understand the scientific concept of culture and the profound influence that culture has on our way of seeing the world. Since, in our Western European world view, warfare and violence have become accepted as being naturally and biologically determined, it is easy (almost "natural") for us to believe that this is true, even if the data, the scientific evidence, does not support this conclusion. In this chapter, I will demonstrate how the actual evidence does not support the Killer Ape view of humanity. I will consider, first, some of features of this Western view of a violent human nature. Next I will review data from paleontology, primatology, psychology, neurophysiology, sociology, and ethnology that support an alternative view of human nature.

Violence as an Integral Part of Western European World View

Before Darwin, there appears to have been two more prevalent theories of human nature in relationship to violent, aggressive, and cooperative behavior (see Pope, 2005). One of these views saw humans as naturally evil, fallen from grace: the Christian idea of Original Sin. This is represented most vividly in the writings of Thomas Hobbes (1588–1679). He saw humans as violent and aggressive by nature. They were inherently selfish, competitive, and aggressive—"man is a wolf to man." If left to their own devices, humans would kill one another. They are not naturally cooperative but are only made to conform and cooperate by powerful laws. Humans were not seen as being social by nature but only made social by contract. "Individuals will act in their self-interest unless prevented from doing so by a stronger force.... [Government] is established by social contract to bring some degree of security and safety in the face of pervasive human evil and unremitting threats to survival presented by the 'state of nature.' Individuals in the 'state of nature' are beasts" (Pope 2005, pp. 315–316). In this Hobbesian view, truth, goodness, and friendship are values that cannot be realized and an ethics built on cooperation and the common good is hopelessly idealistic.

But this pessimistic and depressing theory was not the only view of the nature of human nature before and during Darwin's time. The other prominent perspective was espoused by Thomas Aquinas following Aristotle, and referred to as Natural Law (Pope, 2005). Natural Law regarded humans as sharing the full repertoire of needs and desires found in other animals, as well as the faculties of nutrition, growth, and reproduction. However, this ancient Western European theory also assumed that human sociality began with sex and childbearing and then extended to the local group. People were seen as thriving in communities and as "political animals." Humans ultimately were seen as social and incomplete without one another. In Natural Law theory: "Sociality is primary; it is essential to human well-being, rooted in biology as well as intelligence, and not a dispensable addition of culture" (Pope, 2005, p. 323).

If one traces these theories into the history of modern biology, we can see that the Hobbesian view has predominated. As stated by Ridley (1996, p. 252): "the Hobbesian diagnosis still lies at the heart of both economics and modern evolutionary biology." He believes that: "Thomas Hobbes was Charles Darwin's direct intellectual ancestor. Hobbes (1651) begat David Hume (1739), who begat Adam Smith (1776), who begat Thomas Robert Malthus (1798), who begat Charles Darwin (1859)" (Ridley, 1996, p. 252). However, Pope sees this as too simplistic a view of Darwin. Darwin had a more nuanced and conflicted view of human nature. Although Darwin was influenced by the Malthusian principle of competition, he also recognized that human beings, like many social animals, basically had a social nature and that this sociality was a product of the evolutionary process and rooted in human nature. He emphasized the benefits conferred on human beings by cooperation and group living. This social nature was an outgrowth of the primitive bonds established from mating, kinship and childrearing. As stated by Darwin (1874, pp. 97, 102):

> Animals of many kinds are social. It has often been assumed that animals were in the first place rendered social, and that they feel as a consequence uncomfortable when separated from each other, and comfortable whilst together, but it is a more probable view that these sensations were first developed, in order that those animals which would profit by living in society, should be induced to live together ... The feeling of pleasure from society is probably an extension of the parental or filial affections ... and this extension may be attributed in part to habit, but chiefly to natural selection.

Thus, although Ridley sees a direct line of thinking to Darwin concerning competition and aggression, it appears Darwin did not particularly lean toward one or the other of these extreme views of human nature. In fact, he was equivocal on these matters. Huxley, on the other hand, in advocating Darwin's theory of Natural Selection, took an unequivocal Hobbesian point of view. In fact, Darwin's most adamant supporter described the processes of evolution in explicitly Hobbesian terms, as the process which permeates the natural world generates an "intense and increasing competition of the struggle for existence" ([1893] 1993, p 36; see also Pope, 2005; Sussman, 1999). In order to prevail against natural individual selfishness and a relentless competitive struggle for existence, human societies must employ laws to suppress the self assertion natural to each individual. Thus, this "nature, red in tooth and claw," "eye for an eye," and "survival of the fittest" view can be traced in Western science to a Hobbesian view of human beings and their "nature" being inherently selfish, competitive and aggressive, if not directly through Darwin, at least through a Huxleyian interpretation of Darwin. Much of modern biology has taken on this Huxleyian view. In fact, currently it appears to be a Hobbesian philosophy that pervades many modern views of human nature and the popular "Man the Hunter" hypotheses (see Kelly, 2000; Hart & Sussman 2009; Pope, 2004; Sussman & Cloninger 2011; and, especially, Fry, 2006, pp. 244–245).

Hobbes, Original Sin, and Theories of Human Evolution

The small-skulled australopithecine discovered in 1924 by Raymond Dart was considered by most of his contemporaries to be a mere ape. While supporters of the Piltdown fossil hominin skull were busy explaining the intellectual endowments of our large-brained ancestors, Dart was convinced his small-brained creature was the first ape-man. At first, Dart theorized that australopithecines were scavengers, eking out an existence in the harsh savanna environment by scavenging small animals (Dart, 1926). It was not until a quarter of a century later, with the discovery in 1953 that Piltdown was a fraud and the unearthing of many more australopithecines, that students of human evolution realized our earliest ancestors indeed were more ape-like than they were like modern humans. This led to a great interest in using primates to understand human evolution and the evolutionary basis of human nature (Sussman, 2000, 2011). With these discoveries began a long list of theories attempting to recreate the behavior, and often the basic morality, of the earliest hominins.

By 1950, Dart developed a new view of hominin behavior based on the fragmented and damaged bones found with the australopithecines, together with dents and holes in these early hominin skulls. From these Dart eventually concluded that this species had used bone, tooth, and antler tools to kill, butcher, and consume their prey, as well as to murder one another. Rather than leaving the trees to search out a meager scavenger's existence in the savannah, Dart espoused that hunting, and a carnivorous lust for blood, drew the man-apes out of the forest and was a main force in human evolution (Dart & Craig, 1959). To Dart, the australopithecines were "Confirmed killers: carnivorous creatures that seized living quarries by violence, battered them to death, tore apart their broken bodies, dismembered them limb from limb, slaking their ravenous thirst with the hot blood of the victims and greedily devouring living writhing flesh" (Dart, 1953, p. 209).

Cartmill (1993) was among the first to point out that Dart's interpretation of early human morality was reminiscent of earlier Greek and Christian views. Dart's (1953) treatise begins with a seventeenth-century quote from the Calvinist writer R. Baxter: "of all the beasts, the man-beast is the worst/to others and himself the cruelest foe." The idea that early hominins were hunters "was linked from the beginning with a bleak, pessimistic view of human beings and their ancestors as instinctively bloodthirsty and savage" (Cartmill, 1997, p. 511).

Dart's evidence for Man the Hunter was not substantive and his particular vision of the human hunter/killer hypothesis did not have much staying power. Upon examination of the evidence, C. K. Brain (1981) noted that the bones associated with the man-apes were exactly like fragments left by leopards and hyenas. It seems that Dart's australopithecines were likely the hunted and not the hunters. Since the 1950s, it seems that the Man the Hunter hypothesis has been revitalized every decade.

In the 1960s, Dart's view was picked up and extensively popularized by the playwright Robert Ardrey (for example, in his bestselling books *The Territorial Imperative* and *African Genesis*). Ardrey (1961) believed it was the human competitive and killer instinct, acted out in warfare, that made humans what they are today:

> We are Cain's children. The union of the enlarging brain and the carnivorous way produced man as a genetic possibility (p. 321).Man is a predator whose natural instinct is to kill with a weapon. It is war and the instinct for territory that has led to the great accomplishments of Western Man. Dreams may have inspired our love of freedom, but only war and weapons have made it ours (p. 324).

The next widely-accepted version of this recurring Man the Hunter theme was presented in the late 1960s by Sherwood Washburn and his colleagues. They claimed that many of the features which define men as hunters again separated the earliest humans from their primate relatives.

> To assert the biological unity of mankind is to affirm the importance of the hunting way of life.... The biology, psychology, and customs that separate us from the apes—all these we owe to the hunters of time past. And, for those who would understand the origin and nature of human behavior there is no choice but to try to understand "Man the Hunter" (Washburn & Lancaster, 1968, p. 303).

Rather than amassing evidence from modern hunters and gatherers to prove their theory, Washburn and Lancaster (1968) used the nineteenth-century concept of cultural "survivals": behaviors that persist as evidence of an earlier time but are no longer useful in society.

Using similar logic for the survival of ancient "learned and pleasurable" behaviors, perhaps it could as easily have been our propensity for dancing rather than our desire to hunt that explains much of human behavior. After all, men and women love to dance; it is a behavior found in all cultures but has even less obvious function today than hunting. Our love of movement and dance might explain, for example, our propensity for face-to-face sex, and even the evolution of bipedalism and the movement of humans out of trees and onto the ground.

Could the first tool have been a stick to beat a dance drum, and the ancient Laetoli footprints evidence of two individuals going out to dance the "Afarensis shuffle?" Although it takes two to tango, a variety of social interactions and systems might have been encouraged by the complex social dances known in human societies around the globe. I am joking, of course, but the evidence for Man the Dancer is just as good (or just as lacking) as it is for Man the Hunter or Man the Killer.

Like Dart, Washburn related human hunting to human morality, both of which had their biological basis in our evolutionary past. The next major scientific statement on the importance of hunting in the formulation of human nature was introduced in the mid-1970s by E. O. Wilson and the other proponents of sociobiology. Wilson (1975) describes a number of behavioral traits (for example, territoriality, aggressive dominance hierarchies, male dominance, male-female bonds) that he claims are found in humans generally and that are genetically-based human universals. These traits are assumed to be biologically fixed characteristics, relatively constant among our primate relatives, and persisting throughout human evolution and in human societies. They are products of our hunting past. For more than a million years, man was a hunter and our "innate social responses have been fashioned largely through this lifestyle" (Wilson, 1975, p. 573).

Following in the Hobbesian tradition, Wilson's (1975, p. 573) observations present the non-consoling thought that "some of the 'noblest' traits of mankind, including

team play, altruism, patriotism, bravery, and so forth, are the genetic product of warfare." These earlier renditions of the Man the Hunter hypothesis have been reviewed
and discussed in detail elsewhere (for example, Cartmill, 1993, 1997; Fry, 2006; Hart &
Sussman, 2005; Hart & Sussman, 2009; Marks, 2002; Sussman, 1999, 2004; Sussman &
Marshack, 2010).

The most recent claim of the importance of hunting and killing and the biological
basis of morality is that of Wrangham and Peterson (1996; see also Ghiglieri, 1999) in their
book, *Demonic Males*. The demonic male theory proposes the following. The split between
humans and common chimpanzees is much more recent than was once believed, only 6–8
million years ago. Furthermore, humans may have split from the chimpanzee-bonobo line
after gorillas, with bonobos separating from chimps only 2.5 million years ago. Because
the common ancestor of all these forms "was barely distinguishable from chimpanzees"
(Wrangham & Peterson, 1996, p. 49), and because the earliest australopithecine was quite
chimpanzee-like, Wrangham (1995 p. 5) speculates that: "The most reasonable view for
the moment is that chimpanzees are an amazingly good model for the ancestor of hominins [and if] we know what our ancestor looked like, naturally we get clues about how it
behaved that is, like modern-day chimpanzees."

Finally, if modern chimpanzees and modern humans share certain behavioral traits,
these traits have "long evolutionary roots" and are fixed, biologically-inherited components of our nature and not culturally determined. Further, the authors of *Demonic
Males* claim that only two animal species—chimpanzees and humans—live in patrilineal, male-bonded communities that exhibit intense territorial aggression, including lethal
raids that seek vulnerable enemies to kill. Since chimpanzees and humans share these
violent urges, the demonic male paradigm emphasizes that chimpanzees and humans also
share an inborn morality.

Thus, according to Wrangham and Peterson (1996), killing and violence are inherited from our ancient relatives. However, Wrangham and Peterson also argue that killing
and violence are traits shared by hominins and chimpanzees that are not byproducts of
hunting. In fact, it is rather this violent nature and natural blood lust that makes both
humans and chimpanzees such good hunters. The bonobo helps them to this conclusion.
They claim that bonobos have lost the desire to kill, as well as the desire to hunt; that
they have suppressed both personal and predatory aggression; that even though bonobos
evolved from a chimpanzee-like ancestor who was both a hunter of monkeys and a hunter
of its own kind, during the evolution of bonobos the males lost the desire to kill each other
and the desire to kill prey; and, finally, that the behavior of bonobos and chimps tells us
that murder and hunting are very similar. Wrangham and Peterson believe that blood lust
ties killing and hunting tightly together, but in this scenario it is the desire to kill that drives
the ability to hunt.

However, chimpanzees have been evolving for as long as humans and gorillas, and
there is no reason to believe that ancestral chimps were highly similar to present-day
chimps. The fossil evidence is extremely sparse for the great apes. It is likely that many

forms of apes have become extinct during millions of years—just as many forms of hominins have become extinct. Furthermore, even if chimpanzees were a good model for the ancestor of humans and a conservative representative of this particular branch of the evolutionary bush, it would not follow that humans would necessarily share specific behavioral traits. As the authors of *Demonic Males* emphasize, chimps, gorillas, and bonobos are all very different from one another in their behavior and in their willingness to kill others of their species. It is exactly because of these differences, in fact, that the authors agree that conservative retention of traits alone cannot explain the drastic behavioral similarities and differences.

On what data is the demonic males theory based? By 2004, there had been only 17 suspected and 12 "observed" cases of adult chimpanzee-chimpanzee killings reported from four of nine chimpanzee long-term research sites. This spanned a total of 215 years of combined observer time at these sites and yields a maximum rate of one chimpanzee killing every 7.5 years (see Ferguson, 2011; Sanz, 2004; Sussman, 2004; Sussman & Marshack, 2010; Wilson & Wrangham, 2003; however, see Wrangham, Wilson & Muller, 2006 and Wrangham, 2010 for a different interpretation). Furthermore, most of the chimpanzee research sites where such data were gathered are highly disturbed by human encroachment and disruption (Sanz, 2004). Critics of Wrangham's interpretation of the causes of these violent events continue to claim that it is *not just past food provisioning* of these chimpanzees that underlies violent episodes, as is claimed by Wrangham (2010). Stress caused by human impact (habitat loss, snare poaching and hunting, epidemics, demographic disruption, impacts of research and tourism, and so on) at these sites is far more invasive and rampant than simply food provisioning (Ferguson, 2011).

I am not claiming that chimpanzees and humans are not violent under certain circumstances, as we all know they are, but that the claims of inherent "demonism" in both chimpanzees and humans are erroneous. Furthermore, research indicates that the neurophysiology of aggression between species (that is, predation) is quite different from spontaneous violence linked to intraspecific aggression by humans (that is, murder) (Archer, 1988; Hart & Sussman, 2005; Worthman & Konner, 1987).

After an examination of ethnographic research on human nomadic foraging societies, Fry (2006, 2011) stresses that virtually all the assumptions of pervasive intergroup hostility in these human groups appear to be flawed to some degree. Counter to the assumptions of ongoing hostile intergroup and interindividual relations and recurring warfare over resources, the typical pattern is for humans to get along rather well, relying on resources within their own areas and respecting the resources of their neighbors. "*In sum, an examination of the actual ethnographic information on simple nomadic foragers suggests that the Pervasive Intergroup Hostility Model rests not on fact but a plethora of faulty assumptions and over-zealous speculation*" (Fry, 2006, p. 183, emphasis in original). Again, this is not to say that humans are never aggressive. In a similar vein, Hinde (2006, p. xii) emphasizes that "We do indeed have propensities to behave assertively and aggressively, but we also have propensities to behave prosocially and cooperatively, with kindness and consideration for others. The very existence of human societies depends on the preponderance of prosocial tendencies over assertive and aggressive ones."

Humans Are by Nature Social and Cooperative: An Alternative Theory

Are views taken from a Man the Hunter perspective supported by any scientific evidence? To assess human behavior, researchers look at our primate roots where sociality may have its origin in the general benefits of mutual cooperation, strong mother-infant bonds, and the evolution of an extended juvenile period in which developing young are dependent on other group members. Naturally-occurring opiates in the brain whose effects are not unlike the restfulness and lessening of unease attained through opium-based narcotics (but without highs, withdrawals, or addiction) may be at the core of innate cooperative social responses (Carter, 1999, Taylor et al., 2000). These could finally explain the evolution not only of cooperation among non-related humans and non-human primates but also of true altruistic behavior. Going one step further, recently Hauser (2006) and Bekoff and Pierce (2009) have provided ample evidence of a moral toolkit in the human brain, a genetic mechanism for acquisition of moral rules.

Researchers have, in fact, identified a set of neuroendocrine mechanisms that might lead to cooperative behavior among related and non-related individuals. In experiments using MRIs, mutual cooperation has been associated with consistent activation in two areas of the brain (specifically, the anteroventral striatum and the orbitofrontal cortex) that have been linked with reward processing. Rilling et al. (2002) and Rilling (2011) have proposed that activation of this neural network positively reinforces cooperative social interactions. Even more compelling, the strength of the neural response increases with the persistence of mutual cooperation over successive trials; it is cumulative and self-reinforcing. Interestingly, a few subjects were able to override the typical proponent emotional response of feeling good when cooperating and instead showed a pleasurable response to not cooperating and to cheating. These atypical subjects scored highest on an independent measure of psychopathic personality (Rilling, 2008). Thus, noncooperation appeared to be a function of psychopathy.

Activation of the brain's reward center may account for why we tend to feel good when we cooperate. Both locations in the brain linked with reward processing are rich in neurons that respond to dopamine, the neurotransmitter known for its role in addictive behaviors. The dopamine system evaluates rewards—both those that flow from the environment and those conjured up within the brain. When the stimulus is positive, dopamine is released. In experiments with rats in which electrodes are placed in the anteroventral striatum, the animals continue to press a bar to stimulate the electrodes, apparently receiving such pleasurable feedback that they will starve to death rather than stop pressing the bar (Angier, 2002). We might say that in some ways we are "wired" to cooperate with each other.

Another physiological mechanism related to friendly affiliation and nurturing is the neuroendocrine circuitry associated with mothering in mammals. Orchestrating the broad suite of these bio-behavioral feedback responses is the hormone *oxytocin*. Oxytocin has been related to every type of animal bonding imaginable—parental, fraternal, sexual, and even the capacity to soothe one's self. It has been suggested that although oxytocin's primary role may have been in forging the mother-infant bond, its ability to influence brain circuitry may have been co-opted to serve other affiliative purposes that allowed the formation of alliances and partnerships, thus facilitating the evolution of cooperative behaviors (Angier, 1999; Carter, 1999; Carter & Cushing, 2004; Taylor et al., 2000; Young, Murphy, Young & Hammock, 2005).

Studies by Charles Snowdon and colleagues on cotton-top tamarin monkeys reveal other hormonal mechanisms critical to cooperation and affiliative behavior (Snowdon, 2011). In these small South American monkeys, males and other helpers, such as older siblings, provide essential infant care. Elevated levels of the hormone prolactin, usually associated with lactation, may be the impetus behind maternal caregiving exhibited by males and siblings. Snowdon has also found correlations of oxytocin and prolactin levels with amounts of friendly social behavior between one adult and another. His experiments indicate that high levels of affiliative hormones may be a result of good quality social interaction suggesting a reward system for positive behavior (Snowden, Ziegler, & Almond, 2006; Snowdon, 2011).

Many cooperative behaviors observed in primates can be explained by individual behaviors that benefit several group members (Sussman & Garber, 2011). Coordinated behaviors such as resource or range defense, cooperative foraging and food harvesting, alliance formation, and predator vigilance and defense can be explained in terms of immediate benefits to both the individual and other group members. Even if the rewards for these behaviors are low level, we should expect cooperation to be common. Thus, many types of social interactions may be best understood in terms of a non-zero-sum game, with multiple winners. Low-risk coalitions in which all participants make immediate gains are widespread in primates (Sussman & Garber, 2011; Watts, 2002) and may explain why non-human primates live in relatively stable, cohesive social groups and solve the problems of everyday life in a generally cooperative fashion. Charles Darwin (1874, p. 102) had this idea long before scientific studies of animal behavior, primatology, or cooperation when he noted that natural selection would opt for "the feeling of pleasure from society."

Even though most nonhuman primates are highly social, investigations into the evolution of primate sociality have tended to focus on aggression and competition instead of cooperation. However, many results from behavioral, hormonal, and brain imaging studies offer a new perspective about primates and their proclivities for cooperation, sociality, and peace. For example, after 16 years research on the behavior and ecology of wild savanna baboons, Silk, Alberts, and Altmann (2003, p. 1231) conclude that social integration even enhances reproductive capabilities in female baboons: "Females who had more social contact with other adult group members and were more fully socially integrated into their groups were more likely than other females to rear infants successfully." De Waal (2006) contends that chimp societies emphasize reconciliation and consolation after conflict; his 40 years of primate behavior observations have documented that concern for others is just natural conduct for our closest primate relatives.

Thus, social animals appear to be wired to cooperate and to reduce stress by seeking each other's company. If cooperation and physical proximity among group-living animals are rewarding in a variety of environmental and social circumstances and if physiological and neurological feedback systems reinforce social tolerance and cooperative behavior, then social living can persist in the absence of any conscious recognition that material gains might also flow from mutual cooperation. Based on the latest research, friendly and cooperative behaviors provide psychological, physiological, and ecological benefits to social primates which are positively reinforced by hormonal and neurological systems.

But, what about violence and war? Why is there an acceptance that humans are innately aggressive and that we characterize our aggressive feelings through violent actions? The general primate physiology does not support this view and leads instead to a belief that cooperation is innate to humans. Why the disconnect? Sometimes putting things in perspective helps. There are more than six billion humans alive today—all are social animals having constant hour-by-hour interactions with other humans. The overwhelming majority of our six billion conspecifics are having days, weeks, even entire lives devoid of violent interpersonal conflicts. This is not to naively underplay crimes, wars, and state-level aggression found in modern times, but it puts them in the domain of the *anomalous.* Why do murder rates vary so greatly from country to country, from culture to culture? Are war, crimes, and violence the genetic, unalterable norm, or are they specific to stresses that occur when too many people want too few resources, or to social inequality, or environmental perturbations, or a plethora of other causes, including atypical psychopathic personalities?

After an exhaustive examination of ethnographic research on modern societies ranging from nomadic foragers to urban industrialized societies, Fry documented the human potential for cooperation and conflict resolution. He stresses that virtually all early studies defining man (only men were defined!) by his capacity for killing appear to be flawed: "War is either lacking or mild in the majority of cultures!" (Fry, 2006, p. 97; see also Fry, 2011). Counter to assumptions of hostility between groups and among individuals and recurring warfare over resources, the typical pattern is for humans to get along rather well, relying on resources within their own areas and respecting resources of their neighbors. After an examination of the actual ethnographic information on nomadic foragers, Fry found the proposition that human groups are pervasively hostile toward one another is simply not based on facts but rather on "a plethora of faulty assumptions and over-zealous speculation." (2006, p. 183). According to Fry (2006, p. 22, emphasis in original), "Conflict is an inevitable feature of social life, but clearly *physical aggression is not the only option for dealing with conflict.*" He summarized his findings by acknowledging the human propensity to behave assertively and aggressively, but adamantly stating that just as inherent is the human propensity to behave *pro*socially and cooperatively, with kindness and consideration for others. Indeed, Fry's work has convinced him that the very existence of human societies is dependent on the preponderance of prosocial tendencies over assertive and aggressive ones.

I am *not* trying to ignore the role of aggression and competition in understanding primate and human social interactions. My perspective, however, is that affiliation, cooperation, and social tolerance associated with long-term mutual benefits form the core of social group living. Our earliest ancestors lived in a world populated by large, fearsome predators. Strong indications from the fossil record and living primate species lead to the conclusion that hominins were regularly hunted and required social organization that promoted inconspicuous behaviors, minimal internal conflicts, and coordinated vigilance (Hart & Sussman, 2009, 2011). What would have been the best strategy to avoid being eaten: conspicuous, violent interpersonal conflicts within the group or high levels of cooperation and reciprocity to facilitate as inconspicuous a presence as possible?

So, What About the Human Biological Propensity for Violence

Thus, it is important to again address, directly, the question of what does it mean for humans to have a biological, genetic propensity for violence, killing, or warfare? How does this concept help us understand human warfare and violence? We are all aware that humans are capable of warfare and violence; it is a part of our behavioral repertoire, part of the human behavioral totipotentiality. Thus, of course it is part of our biology and our inheritance, just as is peaceful behavior and the ability to love (Goldschmidt, 2011). To say that these behaviors are part of our heritage as humans says little to help us understand or explain these phenomena.

Why are some people and some cultures more violent than others? Why do murder rates differ from one country to another? Why is there so much variation among individuals, countries, cultures, and in time and space in the frequency and intensity of these traits? If we all have the same biological propensity for violence and for peace, than we must look for the environment and cultural contexts that underlie the differences in the expression of these traits to gain an understanding of their variable expression. For example, in wealthy countries there is a direct positive relationship between homicide rates, and the incidence of other health and social problems, and inequality in the distribution of wealth (Wilkinson & Pickett, 2009; Munsch & Herrman, 2011). Ultimately, for the most part, it is culture and the environmental context that underlies this variation: biology is the constant (except in exceptional, abnormal circumstances).

> To observe merely that there has been natural selection for capacities to carry on a
> social or cultural activity is of limited significance as long as the variation on which
> selection works occurs in a genetic base that is so general as to serve a great variety

of such activities. Then the range of possible cultural results is not explicable by natural selection. (Bock, 1980, p. 76)

It is time that anthropologists once again understand the profound influence that culture and environment have on human behavior. It also is once again important for anthropologists to teach the importance of the anthropological concept of culture to other scientists and to the public, as we did during the time when the Eugenics Movement and Nazism were conventional wisdom and rampant within the United States and Europe. Ultimately, differences in the expression and frequency of violence among humans will be explained, mainly, by differences in their culture and enculturation, and in their environment, and not in their biology and genetics.

References

Allen, G. E. (2001). Is a new eugenics afoot? *Essays on Science and Society, 294,* 59–61.

Angier, N. (1999). Illuminating how bodies are built for sociality. In R. W. Sussman (Ed.), *The biological basis of human behavior: A critical review* (pp. 350–352). Upper Saddle River, NJ: Prentice Hall.

Angier, N. (2002). Wired by evolution to get along. *The New York Times Large Type Weekly,* 7/29–8/4, p. 24.

Archer, J. (1988). *The behavioural biology of aggression.* Cambridge: Cambridge University Press.

Ardrey, R. (1961). *African Genesis: A personal investigation into the animal origins and nature of man.* New York: Atheneum.

Bekoff, M., & Pierce, J. (2009). *Wild justice: The moral lives of animals.* Chicago: University of Chicago Press.

Bock, K. (1980). *Human nature and history: A response to sociobiology.* New York: Columbia University Press.

Brain, C. (1981). *The hunters or the hunted?* Chicago: University of Chicago Press.

Carter, S. (Ed.). (1999). *Hormones, brain and behavior. Integrative neuroendocrinology of affiliation.* Boston: MIT Press.

Carter, S., & Cushing, B. (2004). Proximate mechanisms regulating sociality and social monogamy in the context of evolution. In R. W. Sussman & A. R. Chapman (Eds.), *Origins and nature of sociality* (pp. 99–121). New York: Aldine de Gruyter.

Cartmill, M. (1993). *A view to a death in the morning: Hunting and nature through history.* Cambridge: Harvard University Press.

Cartmill, M. (1997). Hunting hypothesis of human origins. In F. Spencer (Ed.), *History of physical anthropology: An encyclopedia* (pp. 508–512). New York: Garland.

Dart, R. (1926). Taung and its significance. *Natural History, 115,* 875.

Dart, R. (1953). The predatory transition from ape to man. *International Anthropological and Linguistic Review, 1,* 201–217.

Dart, R., & Craig, D. (1959). *Adventures with the missing link.* New York: Harper.

Darwin, C. (1874). *The descent of man,* Revised Edition. Chicago: The Henneberry Company.

Davenport, C. B. and Scudder, M. T. (1919). *Naval officers: Their heredity and development.* Washington, DC: Carnegie Institution of Washington.

de Waal, F. (2006). *Primates and philosophers: How morality evolved.* Princeton: Princeton University Press.

Ferguson, R. B. (2011). Born to live: Challenging killer myths. In R. W. Sussman & C. R. Cloninger (Eds.), *Origins of altruism and cooperation* (pp. 249–270). New York: Springer.

Fry, D. (2006). *The human potential for peace: An anthropological challenge to assumptions about war and violence.* New York: Oxford University Press.

Fry, D. (2011). Human nature: The nomadic forager model. In R. W. Sussman & C. R. Cloninger (Eds.), *Origins of altruism and cooperation* (pp. 227–247). New York: Springer.

Ghiglieri, M. (1999). *The dark side of man: Tracing the origins of male violence.* Reading, MA: Perseus Books.

Goldschmidt, W. (2011). Notes toward a human nature for the third millennium. In R. W. Sussman & C. R. Cloninger (Eds.), *Origins of altruism and cooperation* (pp. 227–247). New York: Springer.

Hart, D. & Sussman, R. W. (2005). *Man the hunted: Primates, predators, and human evolution*. Boulder: Westview Press.

Hart, D. & Sussman, R. W. (2009). *Man the hunted: Primates, predators, and human evolution*, (Expanded ed.). Boulder: Westview Press.

Hart, D. & Sussman, R. W. (2011). The influence of predation on primate and early human evolution: Impetus for cooperation. In R. W. Sussman & C. R. Cloninger (Eds.), *Origins of altruism and cooperation* (pp. 19–40). New York: Springer.

Hauser, M. (2006). *Moral minds: How nature designed our universal sense of right and wrong*. New York: Harper Collins.

Hinde, R. A. (2006). Foreword. In D. P. Fry, *The human potential for peace: An anthropological challenge to assumptions about war and violence* (pp. xi–xii). New York: Oxford University Press.

Holmes, B. (2008, November 12). How warfare shaped human evolution. *New Scientist, 2682*.

Kelly, R. C. (2000). *Warless societies and the origin of war*. Ann Arbor: University of Michigan Press.

Knauft, B. M. (2011). Violence reduction among the Gebusi of Papua New Guinea—and across humanity. In R. W. Sussman & C. R. Cloninger (Eds.), *Origins of altruism and cooperation* (pp. 203–225). New York: Springer.

Marks, J. (2002). *What it means to be 98% chimpanzee: Apes, people, and their genes*. Berkeley: University of California Press.

Munsch, L. E. & Herrman, H. (2011). Promoting well-being in health care. In R. W. Sussman & C. R. Cloninger (Eds.), *Origins of altruism and cooperation* (pp. 399–416). New York: Springer.

National Geographic (2010, December 14). *Explorer: Born to rage*. Day, P. (Director). T.V. Series, Documentary, National Geographic Channel.

Pope, S. J. (2005). Primate sociality and Natural Law Theory: A case study on the relevance of science for ethics. In R. W. Sussman & A. R. Chapman (Eds.), *Origins and nature of sociality* (pp. 313–331). New York: Aldine de Gruyter.

Ridley, M. (1996). *The origins of virtue*. London: Viking.

Rilling, J. (2008). Neuroscientific approaches and applications within anthropology. *Yearbook Physical Anthropology, 51*, 2–32.

Rilling, J. (2011). The neurobiology of cooperation and altruism. In R. W. Sussman & C. R. Cloninger (Eds.), *Origins of altruism and cooperation* (pp. 295–306). New York: Springer.

Rilling, J., Gutman, D., Zeh, T., Pagnoni, G., Berns, G. & Kilts, D. (2002). A neural basis for social cooperation. *Neuron, 35*, 395–405.

Sanz, C. (2004). *Behavioral ecology of chimpanzees in a Central African forest: Pan troglodytes troglodytes in the Goualougo Triangle, Republic of Congo*. Ph.D. dissertation, Washington University, St. Louis, Missouri.

Silk, J., Alberts, S., & Altmann, J. (2003). Social bonds of female baboons enhance infant survival. *Science, 302*, 1231–1234.

Snowdon, C. (2011). Behavioral and neuroendocrine interactions in affiliation. In R. W. Sussman & C. R. Cloninger (Eds.), *Origins of altruism and cooperation* (pp. 307–331). New York: Springer.

Snowdon, C., Ziegler, T., & Almond, R. (2006). Affiliative hormones in primates: Cause or consequence of positive behavior? Paper presented at the Annual Meeting of the American Association for the Advancement of Science, St. Louis, MO, February.

Sussman, R. W. (1999). The myth of Man the Hunter, Man the Killer, and the evolution of human morality. *Zygon: Journal of Religion and Science, 34*, 453–471.

Sussman, R. W. (2000). Pildown Man: The father of American field primatology. In S. Strum and L. Fedigan (Eds.), *Primate encounters: Models of science, gender, and society* (pp. 85–103). Chicago: University of Chicago Press.

Sussman, R. W. (2004). Are humans inherently violent? In R. Selig, M. London, and P. Kaupp (Eds.), *Anthropology explored: revised and expanded* (pp. 30–45). Washington, DC: Smithsonian Books.

Sussman, R. W., & Cloninger, C. R. (2011). Introduction: Cooperation and altruism. In R. W. Sussman & C. R. Cloninger (Eds.), *Origins of altruism and cooperation* (pp. 1–7). New York: Springer.

Sussman, R. W., & Garber, P. A. (2011). Cooperation, collective action, and competition in primate social interactions. In C. J. Campbell, A. Fuentes, K. C. MacKinnon, S. K. Bearder, & R. S. Stumpf (Eds.), *Primates in perspective*, (2nd ed.) (pp. 587–599). New York: Oxford University Press.

Sussman, R. W. & Marshack, J. (2010). Are humans inherently killers? *Global Nonkilling Working Papers #1* (pp. 7–28). Honolulu: Center for Global Nonkilling.

Taylor, S., Cousino, L., Klein, B., Gruenewals, T., Gurung, R., & Updegraff, J. (2000). Biobehavioral responses to stress in females: Tend-and-befriend, not fight-or-flight. *Psychological Review, 107*, 411–429.

Washburn, S. & Lancaster, C. (1968). The evolution of hunting. In R. Lee & I. DeVore (Eds.), *Man the hunter* (pp. 293–303). Chicago: Aldine.

Watts, D. (2002). Reciprocity and interchange in the social relationships of wild male chimpanzees. *Behaviour, 139*, 343–370.

Wilkinson, R., & Pickett, K. (2009). *The spirit level: Why more equal societies almost always do Better.* London: Allen Lane.

Wilson, E. O. (1975). *Sociobiology: The new synthesis.* Cambridge: Harvard University Press.

Wilson, M. L. & Wrangham, R. W. (2003). Intergroup relations in chimpanzees. *Annual Review of Anthropology, 32*, 363–392.

Worthman, C. M. & Konner, M. J. (1987) Testosterone levels change with subsistence hunting effort in !Kung San men. *Psychoneuroendocrinology, 12*, 449–458.

Wrangham, R. W. (1995) Ape cultures and missing links. *Symbol* (Spring) 2–9, *20*.

Wrangham, R. W. (2010). Chimpanzee violence is a serious topic: A response to Sussman and Marshack's critique of *Demonic males: Apes and the origins of human violence. Global Nonkilling Working Papers #1* (pp. 29–47). Honolulu: Center for Global Nonkilling.

Wrangham, R. W., & Peterson, D. (1996). *Demonic males: Apes and the origins of human violence.* Boston: Houghton Mifflin.

Wrangham, R. W., Wilson, M. L., & Muller, M. N. (2006). Comparative rates of aggression in chimpanzees and humans. *Primates, 47*, 14–26.

Young, L. J., Murphy Young, A. Z. & Hammock, E. A. D. (2005). Anatomy and neurochemistry of the pair bond. *Journal of Comparative Neurology, 493*, 51–57.

7

Pinker's List

Exaggerating Prehistoric War Mortality

R. Brian Ferguson

War, in one form or another, appeared with the first man.
Barack Obama, *Nobel Peace Prize Acceptance Speech*

This chapter is one of a pair (see also Ferguson, chapter 11) that challenge the idea that deadly intergroup violence has been common enough in our species, evolutionary history to act as a selection force shaping human psychological tendencies, toward either external violence or internal cooperation. Broken down, there are three related propositions: (a) war was ubiquitous throughout our species, evolutionary history; (b) war is a natural expression of evolved tendencies toward deadly violence against individuals outside the social group; (c) war casualties were sufficiently high to select for behavioral tendencies conferring reproductive advantage in intergroup competition. For either (b) or (c) to be true, (a) must be true. This chapter and chapter 11 argue that archaeological evidence shows (a) to be false.

Archaeology and Evolutionary Theories

The archaeological record has little to say about questions of intra-species violence over most of human evolution. The evidentiary record prior to the development of states is our best window into early human behavior. If war is our species' natural way, if we are innately inclined to war, it should show up there, in prehistory. For many, many scholars in evolutionary psychology and kindred approaches, it has become accepted as "fact" that war was the rule among prehistoric peoples, and regularly accounted for a very high percentage of all, and especially male, deaths (Fry, chapter 1).

The lineage of theories attributing war to innate predispositions to kill those outside the in-group is deep and broad (Ferguson, 1984a, pp. 8–12; 2001, pp. 106–111; 2011;

Sussman, chapter 6). Fifteen years ago, ethologists, sociobiologists, evolutionary psychologists and others did not have much archaeological data to support their hypothesis of war forever backwards, in which men killed other men to further their own reproductive success. They relied on ethnography, especially of the Yanomami (Chagnon, 1968; 1988), or war-mongering chimpanzees (Goodall 1986) or projections based on the Man the Hunter scenario (Lee & DeVore, 1968; cf. Fry, 2006; Hart & Sussman, 2009). But in 1996, a major book brought archaeology to the fore in this discussion, and seemingly proved the omnipresence of war among non-state peoples.

Keeley's (1996) *War Before Civilization* forcefully asserts that war is and was ubiquitous among non-state peoples. Although most of his material is drawn from ethnography, Keeley's Figure 6.2 (1996, pp. 90–91) graphs percentage of deaths from warfare in nine archaeological cases. Noting that some war deaths would not leave recoverable traces, he concludes that actual prehistoric death tolls "probably ranged from about 7 percent to as much as 40 percent of all deaths." Male percentages, of course, would be greater. This graph is an empirical cornerstone of much subsequent theorizing. (For critiques of Keeley, see Carman & Carman, 2005; Chapman, 1999; Pearson, 2005; Thorpe, 2005).

LeBlanc with Register (2003) followed with a second foundational book, *Constant Battles,* which claims that "*everyone* had warfare in *all* time periods" (2003, p. 8, emphasis in original), and attributes war to the Malthusian tendency of population growth overrunning and degrading natural resources. Both books, as well as many other writings, assert that a neo-Rousseauian tendency—of which I am supposedly the standard bearer—in anthropology and archaeology has artificially "pacified the past." (Keeley, 1996, pp. 17–24, 163–171; LeBlanc, 2007; LeBlanc with Register, 2003, pp. 3–8).[1] In often caustic tones, these and others denounce peace-oriented, politically-correct, advocates-instead-of-scientists, who fail to look for signs of war, or ignore them when found, or define them away as symbolic or ritualistic. In some cases, I believe, the evidentiary "pacification of the past" has been true in *archaeology*—though not in the writings of cultural anthropologists for at least 40 years (see Ferguson 1997; 2006, p. 475). Yet many archaeologists have diligently searched for signs of violence for years, and their work informs this chapter.

Archaeologists accustomed to discussing and debating among themselves seem not to be aware of how central the idea of war forever backwards is in a small industry of scholarship, which claims to plumb the depths of the human mind and behavior. The proposition that war was common and deadly enough to act as a selection mechanism on our species is *axiomatic* in evolutionary psychology. Founders of the field Tooby and Cosmides (2010, p. 191) state the common conception:

War is found throughout prehistory (LeBlanc with Register 2003; LeBlanc 1999; Keeley 1996). Wherever in the archaeological record there is sufficient evidence to make a judgment, there traces of war are to be found. It is found across all forms of social organization—in bands, chiefdoms, and states. It was a regular part of hunter-gatherers life wherever population densities were not vanishingly low, and often even in harsh marginal habitats.

They also invoke chimpanzees and tribal people such as the Yanomami—as do most of the authors noted in this section, in varying combinations. They then use this established "fact" to explain the evolution of a wide range of specialized, innate cognitive modules, including those for hate, anger, coalitional politics, and morality.

Van Vugt (2008, p. 5) premises his argument that human males have an evolved "male warrior complex" with: "Fossil evidence of human warfare dates back at least 200,000 years, and it is estimated that as many as 20–30% of ancestral men died from intergroup violence (Keeley, 1996)." Winegard and Deaner (2010, p. 434) citing Keeley and Bowles (another key writer, see below), claim that "male mortality due to warfare is estimated at between 13 and 30% in traditional societies," and use that to explain "sport fandom." Bracha, Bienvenu, and Eaton (2007, p. 2) state that in "mid-Paleolithic intergroup warfare, victors killed a high percentage of post-pubertal males (estimates range from 15% to 50%) and took reproductive-age females (and some children) captive (LeBlanc with Register, 2003)." Their "Paleolithic-human-warfare hypothesis" is posited to explain "evolved adaptations that lead to blood-injection phobia" among contemporary pre-menopausal women. Boyer and Bergstrom (2011, p. 1037) invoke archaeological findings of high levels of deadly violence to explain the development of threat detection in children; Kanazawa (2009, p. 26–27) to argue that evolved tendencies to capture women in war explains contemporary civil wars; Goetz (2010, p. 16) to construct a theory of status and domestic violence; Snyder, Fessler, Tiokhin, Frederick, Lee, and Navarrete (2011, p. 127) to account for women's fear of crime; Navarrete, et al. (2010, pp. 933–935) to explain gender specific aspects of race bias; and Low (2000, p. 13) as the selective basis for a whole spectrum of innate gender differences. Moreno (2011) argues that mitochondrial haplotypes associated with ritual fighting, murder, and warfare gave the human "culture or tribe" that spread out of Africa a competitive advantage over any others. This list could easily be expanded (also see Jones, De Bruine, Little, Watkins, & Feinberg, 2011, p. 1204; Potts & Haydon, 2008, pp. 152–156; Smirnov, Arrow, Kennett, & Orbell, 2007, p. 929; Wilson, 1999, p. 18), but the point is made—it is taken as established archaeological fact that somewhere around a quarter of all males died in war throughout prehistory, and that such a death rate is more than enough to be a selection mechanism.

This perspective is not confined to evolutionary psychology proper. Several prominent political theorists apply the same data to explain contemporary international relations. Fukuyama (1998, pp. 24–27) combines discussion of chimpanzees and Yanomami with Keeley to make the point that a "feminized" foreign policy could be dangerous in a world of males evolved to be bad. Thayer (2004) is unusual in having read some archaeology beyond the few touchstone pieces, and sometimes seems to say war had a relatively recent inception (2004, pp. 118–119). Yet he falls back on long-term selection by war to explain patterns of contemporary international relations, such as xenophobia and ethnocentrism (2004, pp. 254–261). Gat (2006, p. 12; 2009, p. 574)—whose work has become a foundational source in itself—cites Keeley, LeBlanc, and of course chimpanzees, as having vanquished the neo-Rousseauians. For him, the pervasiveness of war throughout humanity's evolutionary past has produced an integrated motivational complex including practically any reason one could imagine for collective violence (cf. Ferguson 2000). Goldstein (2011, p. 38) prefaces his arguments about stopping war by quoting LeBlanc, "the foremost authority . . . and other experts agree: 'Twenty-Five percent of deaths in warfare [among adult men] may be a conservative estimate. Prehistoric warfare was common and deadly, and no time span of geographical region seems to have been immune.'"

The ubiquity of ancient war is argued to have selected for not only aggressive, violent behavior, but for *cooperation* as well. War is, after all, a supremely cooperative behavior, where one's life or death may depend on the actions of one's fellows. This is not a new idea, but it has been given new salience in a series of publications by Bowles and colleagues (Bowles, 2006; Bowles & Gintis, 2011, pp. 102–196; Choi & Bowles, 2007). Importantly for this chapter, Bowles presents his own compilation of adult mortality due to war (which only partly overlaps with Keeley's) in 15 prehistoric areas (Bowles, 2009, p. 1295). Death rates range from 0 to 46 percent. He and colleagues make a group-selection argument that the average number of deaths in external conflict is capable of explaining the evolution of altruistic, group-beneficial but self-detrimental behaviors—like going to war. Pinker, as usual, has made a big, public splash in the evolutionary pool. In *The Blank Slate* (2002, p. 56), he made his evolutionary position clear, "Hobbes was right, Rousseau was wrong," and approvingly quotes William James: "We, the lineal representatives of the successful enactors of one scene of slaughter after another, must, whatever more pacific virtues we may also possess, still carry about with us, ready at any moment to burst into flame, the smoldering and sinister traits of character by means of which they lived through so many massacres, harming others, but themselves unharmed."

The Better Angels of Our Nature (2011, pp. 1, 48–49), opens with archaeological illustrations of the "shockingly violent" human past. After discussing the supposed evolutionary logic of deadly competition, he returns to archaeology (plus chimpanzees and recent tribals) as the ultimate foundation of his claim that humans naturally tend toward violence—and we still do today—but those primitive impulses have been thwarted and controlled by the forces of modernity. Pinker's list of archaeological evidence, in his Figure 2–2, combines citations from Keeley (1996) and Bowles (2009), producing 21 prehistoric cases, to calculate an average prehistoric death-from-warfare rate as 15 percent (2011, pp. 48–49). The claim that 15 percent of prehistoric populations died in war supports his earlier claim of killer instincts, and provides a springboard for his new book, to show how much nicer we have become than our base nature. This is the most comprehensive list of archaeological data putatively establishing the ubiquity of high-casualty warfare throughout the human past. Given all the publicity for the book, it will surely be widely read, and that is why this chapter is titled Pinker's List.

Archaeologists carefully slogging through the evidence must realize that this is how the findings of their discipline are being portrayed and used to make sweeping claims about human nature and society. Archaeological findings are said to prove that prehistoric people in general were plagued by chronic warfare that regularly claimed about 15 percent of total population, and a quarter or more of the adult men. These numbers have become axiomatic. The point of this chapter, along with chapter 11, is to demonstrate, with abundant evidence, that this "fact"—as widely invoked as it is—is utterly without empirical foundation (see also Dye, chapter 8; Haas & Piscitelli, chapter 10). To use the word favored by opponents of "pacification of the past," the axiom is a *myth*. The clear and present danger is that the past is being artificially "warrified."

This chapter shows that Pinker's List consists of cherry-picked cases with high casualties, clearly unrepresentative of prehistory in general. Chapter 11 shows the results of a more representative approach. By considering the *total* archaeological record of prehistoric populations of Europe and the Near East up to the Bronze Age, evidence clearly demonstrates that war began sporadically out of warless condition, and can be seen, in varying trajectories in different areas, to develop over time as societies become larger, more sedentary, more complex, more bounded, more hierarchical, and in one critically important region, impacted by an expanding state.

The Death List

Pinker's (2011, p. 49) List compiles data from Keeley and Bowles to include 21 cases. One case has no killings, and it will be shown that six more of the 21 cases can be tossed out. The others, valid cases of multiple violent deaths, will be shown to be a very selective compilation of high-killing situations, in no way representative of "typical" war casualties of prehistoric people in general. In the following discussion, cases will be presented in approximate chronological order. The initial number in parentheses is the place of the case in Pinker's List, followed by percentage of deaths, and (K) for the source of Keeley (1996, p. 197) or (B) for Bowles (2009, online supporting material p. 4). (Keeley calculates on the basis of total number of individuals, and Bowles on adults only. That does make a difference, but it is a complication not worth engaging for present purposes).

    (2) 40.7 percent (K) Jebel Sahaba Nubia, Site 117; and (20) 2.3 percent (K) near
        Site 117.

Since it was described in 1968, at the height of Ardrey-ism, Site 117 has stood as the earliest conclusive evidence of war, regularly noted as 12,000–10,000 BC. In the final Paleolithic graveyard, remains of 24 out of 59 men, women and children, have lithic material interpreted as parts of projectiles either embedded in or closely associated with their skeletons. Several are in multiple burials (1968, pp. 990, 993). There is no reason to challenge this as evidence of war, but it is unique in its early occurrence and death rate, and given its importance, some questions do need to be raised.

First is the early date. There is no direct dating of 117 remains. The lithics, however, closely resemble the Qadan industry, estimated at 13,000–5000 BC. If 117 came near the end of this 8,000-year span, it would still be early, but later than other evidence for war from Europe and the Near East. The narrowing of time to 12,000–10,000 BC is based on further similarity of 117 lithics to those of another site, ANE-1. ANE-1 itself is dated by complicated inferences: a lithic sequence and chronology which is "highly tentative," and the relative frequency of associated Late Pleistocene faunal remains, which could coincide with a known Nile aggradation event (Wendorf, 1968, pp. 990–991). The aggradation event, which seems firm around 12,000–10,000 BC (Burleigh & Matthews, 1982, 159–160; Wendorf, Schild, & Haas, 1979, p. 222), is the only basis of putting a year to Site 117. But the linkage is tenuous. This soft dating would not be a big deal, were it not for the fact that on that basis rests 117's claim of being the earliest war anywhere. If the early date is correct, it puts the Jebel Sahaba cemetery within a major ecological crisis, as the Nile cut a gorge that eliminated the previous broad spectrum subsistence base, including marsh resources. After this, the area was entirely abandoned by humans (Ferguson, 2006, pp. 482–483).

Then there are the lithics themselves, 110 associated with skeletons, plus 73 more in the fill (Wendorf, 1968, pp. 959, 982). These are not "arrowheads" but presumably glued or tied to shafts in microlithic fashion. For that purpose, they are remarkably poorly made. Ninety-seven pieces are unretouched chips and flakes (Wendorf, 1968, p. 988). "In a normal assemblage all of these would be classified as debitage or debris, and none would be considered tools" (Wendorf, 1968, p. 991). "Evidently, any pointed thin flake was on occasion employed as a point, and any piece with a thin sharp edge could serve as a barb" (Wendorf, 1968, p. 992). But the lithic material also includes scrapers (Wendorf, 1968, p. 991), and nine cores or core fragments (Wendorf, 1968, pp. 979, 983). Their physical position relative to bones is key for Wendorf, yet some are found inside skulls, with no entry wounds (1968, pp. 971, 973). Classifying all those with associated lithics as war casualties is going too far. Jurmain (2001, p. 20), a judicious specialist in paleo-osteology, concludes the number of violent deaths actually should be counted as 4 out of 41 relatively complete skeletons, or 9.8 percent.

Yet if they were all war deaths, their number raises the question of how that population could have survived. Noting that, Wendorf suggests that this was a special burial area for those who died violently, not for everyone (1968, p. 993). He supports that inference by noting (Pinker case #20) that in a similar cemetery just across the Nile, with 39 skeletons, there was "almost no evidence of violence," with only one likely victim (1968, p. 993). All questions considered, this Nubian record really is overdue for systemic reconsideration—although it seems that the key remains with embedded flakes are now absent from the collection (Judd, 2006, p. 162). Taking it as it has been presented, Site 117 stands as good evidence of very early war, but it is unique in the world for that combination of antiquity and carnage (see Haas & Piscitelli, chapter 10). Pinker's #20 is based on just one individual. In principle, one single violent death in a sample cannot be taken as evidence of war, since one killing could occur in many ways. That brings the list down from 21 to 20 cases.

(21) 0.0 percent (B) Gobero, Niger.

Some 200 individuals were recovered from several lakeside cemeteries from 9700 to 4500 BC. Although there is one triple burial, none show indications of violent death (Sereno et al., 2008, p. 10). This is the only case with no deaths in Pinker's combination of the Keeley and Bowles figures, raising the question of why Bowles included it, when other sequences without signs of violence are not. This brings the number of cases with war to 19.

(4) 22 percent (B) Voloshkoe; and (5) 15.9 percent (K)/ 21 percent (B) Vasilyevka, Ukraine.

Voloshkoe and two cemeteries at Vasilyevka, along the Dnieper rapids, are the earliest European locations showing signs of war. (All European cases are considered in context in chapter 11, and these two, like Jebel Sahaba, are from a period of ecological crisis. Only their unusual character is noted here.) At Voloshkoe, of 19 individuals, 5 have some combination of embedded or associated points and missing appendages (26.3 percent). At Vasilyevka I, 1 (or 2) of 19, and at Vasilyevka III, 5 of 44 have embedded or closely associated points (9.5 percent/11.1 percent for I and III combined (Lillie, 2004, pp. 87–91). (Bowles's percentage is for Vasilyevka III, but based on adults only). These Dnieper sites indicate a very high rate of death by violence, but they are hardly typical. Vasilyevka III is radiocarbon calibrated at 10,000–9,035 BC, and its materials seem somewhat younger than Vasilyevka I and Voloshkoe (Lillie, 2001, pp. 56; 2004, pp. 88–91). That puts the Dnieper rapids warfare right around the transition from Pleistocene to Holocene. Dolukhanov, thoroughly familiar with Eastern European archaeology from Paleo to Neolithic (1997), calls this "the earliest indisputable evidence of warfare" (1999, p. 79). In fact, it is the earliest in all of Europe, (and second earliest in the world). Earlier, contemporary, and later findings discussed in chapter 11 show it to be an outstanding exception to the general record.

(18) 1.7 percent (K) Calumnata, Algeria.

In this case, 2 out of 60 individuals, from 6300–5350 BC, are said to have died from violence, one from a projectile and one from apparently intentional fractures. Keeley, Pinker's source, bases this on a secondary account. The primary source (Dastugue, 1970, pp. 122–126), however, concludes that the irregular cranial fracture probably did *not* come from a weapon, but a collision with something like a jagged rock. (Another individual had a massive fracture suggesting enormous pressure.) As for the flint tip embedded in a vertebrae, given the absence of anything else suggesting war, the author suggests a case of homicide. One death does not indicate war, and the List is down to 18.

(11, 12) 8.0 percent (K) Brittany; and 12 percent (B) Ile Teviec, France.

These two cases in Pinker are actually the same site, which has been presented with different information and dates in Keeley and Bowles. The List is now 17. Teviec, c. 4625 BC, has 23 or 25 individuals (the basis of Keeley's percentage), with 16 adults (the basis of Bowles's). One appears to have died from two projectiles. One has traces of blows on the cranium, and another has a partially healed hole (Dastugue & de Lumley, 1976, p. 617; Newell, Constandse-Westermann, & Meiklejohn, 1979, pp. 132–137; Vencl, 1991, pp. 220, 222). Since there were signs of healing, including this as a death is questionable—but to avoid seeming picky, I leave this case in the List. Teviec takes us into the later European Mesolithic, into major societal changes contemporary with transformations in landscape and food sources associated with mid-Holocene (5000–3000 BC) climate fluctuations in temperature and rainfall (Barber, Chambers, & Maddy, 2004). As discussed in chapter 11, the Mesolithic has acquired a (debated) reputation as being especially violent (cf. Roksandic, 2004), and is said to be the time when war began (Vencl, 1999). Teviec displays signs of "complex hunting and gathering," such as increasing sedentism, reliance on aquatic resources (shellfish), and hierarchical differentiation. (Bender, 1985, p. 23). Ethnographically, complex hunter-gatherers have a well-established reputation of being prone to war, in sharp contrast to nomadic hunter-gatherers (Kelly, 1995, pp. 303, 311–315, Kelly, chapter 9; see also Fry, chapter 1).[2]

(10) 12 percent (B) Bogebakken, Denmark; (9) 13.6 percent (K) Vedbaek, Denmark; and (14) 3.8 percent (K) Skateholm I, Sweden.

Once again, two of Pinker's separate cases, Bogebakken and Vedbaek, are actually one and the same. Now Pinker's tally is cut to 16. Older carbon dates for Vedbaek Bogebakken range from 4300–3800 BC, but calibrated 4800–4400 is more accurate (Schulting, personal communication). In one triple burial of a man, woman, and child, the man has a bone arrowhead between the vertebrae of the neck. Albrethson and Peterson (1976, p. 20) count only that one as due to violence, but given the circumstances, I will settle on a compromise figure of two. Skateholm I, just 80 km. from Vedbaek and perhaps 200 years earlier, has 2 out of 53 individuals with embedded projectile points (Albrethson & Petersen, 1976, pp. 4, 7–8, 14, 20; Newell, Constandse-Westermann, & Meiklejohn, 1979, pp. 47, 50; Price, 1985, pp. 351–352). Both are late Mesolithic, from the Ertebolle tradition, which has produced several other instances of non-lethal violence (Thorpe, 2003, p. 172; 2005, p. 11). But once again, Ertebolle is unusual in that sense. In Thorpe's survey of trauma in Europe and elsewhere, he notes: "reaching southern Scandinavia, the overwhelming impression is of a significantly higher level of conflict visible in the archaeological record than in the areas considered before" (2005, p. 11)—not typical of prehistoric peoples. Even so, in contrast to selecting only sites with signs of violence, if all skeletal remains from the Ertebolle tradition were pooled, then the percentage of violent instances would be much less.

Across the Atlantic: Representative Cases, or Extremes?

The remaining cases from Pinker's combined list take us into the New World (with one exception), and to much more recent times. In several cases, settlement information that was lacking in earlier cases is discussed. The North American record of violence across regions is very complicated, with different kinds of indicators, suggesting different sorts and intensities of violence, present/absent or rising/falling at different times (see Ferguson, 2006, p. 490–495; Lambert, 2002, pp. 211–230). The PaleoIndians of 11000–5000 BC were not free of interpersonal violence. Kennewick Man from 7000–5500 BC (McManamon 1999) and an approximate contemporary from Grimes Burial Shelter (Owsley & Jantz, 2000) both have embedded points. But PaleoIndian remains display a remarkable uniformity of Clovis style tools, "from Maine to Mexico, and from the East Coast to the West," which as Haas (1999, p. 14) emphasizes is uncharacteristic of people who have divided into competitive/violent groups. Evidence of war in the Eastern Woodlands dates to several thousand years before it appears in the American Southwest (Haas, 1999, p. 23). War in the Southwest is one of the best studied of all areas (see Haas, 1990; Haas & Creamer, 1997; LeBlanc, 1999; Rice & LeBlanc, 2001), but it is temporally and geographically complicated, interrupted by long periods of peace. The northern Great Plains has some of the most extreme evidence of mass killings from anywhere in the prehistoric world (see below). Yet in the southern Plains, prior to 500 AD, of 173 skeletal remains, only one shows signs of violent death, a woman with two blows to the head (calculated from Owsley, Marks, & Manhein, 1989, pp. 116–119). The North American record foregrounds the question of representativeness of particular cases.

(16) 5.6 percent (K) Kentucky.

The earliest evidence of war in North America comes from the Eastern Woodlands, where discussion benefits from Milner's (1999, pp. 120–122) exhaustive search for all signs of violence (and see Dye, 2009, pp. 49–85; Dye, chapter 8; Lambert, 2002, pp. 226–227; Milner, 2007, pp. 191–195). In the Early Archaic period, 8500–6000 BC, there are only scattered signs of interpersonal violence, although skeletal remains are limited. In the Middle Archaic, 6000–3000 BC, with greatly expanded skeletal collections, scattered violence continues. The earliest suspicion of war comes from the Windover cemetery in central Florida, about 5400 BC, where 9 of 168 individuals show signs of violence, mostly healed cranial and forearm fractures, but with one embedded point (Dickel, Aker, Baron, & Doran, 1988). A sequence of major climate changes beginning in the mid-Holocene led to extensive landscape modification, which was followed by social transformations in the late Middle and Late Archaic (3000–1000 BC), including larger populations, increased sedentism, a shift to foraging focused on especially favorable locations such as wetlands or rivers surrounded by much less productive regions, incipient cultivation, long distance exchange of elite goods, physical distance between groups, and internal status differentiation (Dye 2009, pp. 51–67; Dye, chapter 8; Winters, 1974, pp. x–xii; Jefferies, Thompson, & Milner, 2005, p. 20; Milner, 2007, pp. 191–192). In other words, the later Middle Archaic has most of the preconditions for war (see chapter 11).

Skeletal indicators of conflict and war increase in this period, though still at far lower levels than found post-500 AD. Pinker's example, Indian Knoll, Kentucky, 4100–2500 BC (Winters, 1974, p. xix), is one of just three cases noted as having multiple deaths, with 48 of 880 burials having embedded points, mutilations, and/or multiple interments (Webb, 1974, pp. 147–155, 173–205).[3] By the subsequent Middle Woodland period (100 BC–400 CE), increased cultivation was accompanied by what seems to be a time of peace. "Skeletons with conflict-related wounds are known from this time horizon, but they are quite uncommon relative to the innumerable burials that have been excavated" (Milner, 1999, p. 122). Violence phased back in during the Late Woodland period (400–1000 CE), leading up to the chronic chiefly warfare and massive fortifications of the Mississippian period, prior to Western contact. Indian Knoll, then, is not representative or typical of prehistoric violence, it is extraordinary in the number and percentage of war deaths, at least until the Mississippian era (see Bridges, 1996; Dye, 2006, 2009).

(9) 22.7 percent–32.4 percent 30 sites from British Columbia, 3500 BC–1774 AD, averages calculated from different sets by (K) and (B).

Both Keeley and Bowles draw on numerous excavations from the Pacific Northwest Coast. In my first publications on war (1983, 1984b), I described a pre-contact pattern of intensive, high casualty warfare, patterned by demographics and resource distribution (such as salmon streams), which affected the whole structure of society, and had roots going back at least three thousand years. I picked this area to study because of the striking intensity of war at the time of Western contact (and after). Archaeological research since then has provided an abundance of evidence from different locales and periods: skeletons with embedded points, multiple traumas, trophy taking, specialized weapons, settlement nucleation, movement to defendable sites, refuges, fortifications, territorial marking and separation, and militaristic iconography (Ames & Maschner, 1999, pp. 195–218; Coupland, 1989; Cybulski, 1992; 1994, pp. 80–83; Lovisek, 2007; Moss & Erlandson, 1992). There is no doubt that specific locations on the Pacific Northwest Coast had casualties at the level claimed to express innate human aggressiveness. But this region cannot be taken as typifying hunter-gatherers throughout prehistory. Instead, the Northwest Coast has become the type-case for "warlike" *complex* hunter-gatherers (Fry, chapter 1).

Another problem is in the *averaging* of cases, which in this rich archaeological record show tremendous variation. The basic picture is outlined by Ames and Maschner (1999, pp. 209–211). There are some suggestions of violence in the sparse archaeological findings prior to 4400 BC, but not enough to draw any conclusions. In the Early Pacific period, 4400–1800 BC, 8 out of 12 adult males show signs of some sort of violence at Namu, not necessarily lethal; but at Blue Jackets Creek series on the Queen Charlotte Islands, there is "virtually no trauma," (Cybulski, 1992, pp. 157–158). Signs of war multiply as populations grow through the Middle Pacific (1800 BC–200/500 AD), though they concentrate in the Northern Coast around Prince Rupert Harbor, where there are iconographic indications of a militaristic ideology. Middle Pacific war signs are much fewer in the south around the Straits of Georgia, where resources are less concentrated and less variable, and their military orientation seems consistent with defense against northern raiders. In the Late Pacific, beginning around 500 CE, with elaborating cultural complexity, major climatic fluctuations, and the inferred arrival of the bow and arrow, there is a profusion of settlement defenses, and war becomes common even in the south. While many details of this complicated picture are debated, it is generally accepted that war developed in some northern locations became more intense over time, and gradually spread to the south. The prehistoric Pacific Northwest Coast was indeed characterized by intensive warfare, but averaging all cases conceals the great spatial and temporal variation. On the question of representativeness, in terms of the high number of victims of violence, and the continuation of war signs (in some areas) for over three thousand years, the Northwest Coast may be fairly characterized as the most warlike region in all North America—except perhaps the region of Central and Southern California, coming up shortly.

(3) 30 percent (B) Sarai Nahar Rai, India.

Geographically interrupting the North American record is a single case from among the voluminous record of South Asian human remains (see Kennedy, 2000). Put at 3140–2854 BC, it is called Mesolithic. The claimed death rate of 30 percent puts this near the top of Pinker's list. This is highly questionable. Three out of the eight well-preserved skeletons are the basis of the claim (Sharma, 1973, pp. 138–139). One is clear-cut, with an embedded microlith. The two others have microliths resting on the pelvic girdle, or alongside the humerus. Not only are microliths found as grave offerings here, but the burials were also packed with dirt from hearths, which contained many microliths from cooking game. Under these circumstances, only the embedded point is good evidence of violence. As noted, one individual is inadmissible as evidence of war. Pinker's List is down to 15.

(15) 6 percent (B) Southern California, 28 sites, 3500 BC–1380 AD; (17) 5 percent (K, B) Central California, 1500 BC–500AD; (13) 8 percent (B) Central California, 1400 BC–235 AD; and (19) 4 percent (B) Central California, 2 sites, 240–1770 AD.

These four cases, including many individual sites, come from western California, spanning about 5,000 years. Pinker's #17 reflects a broad estimate by Moratto (1984, pp. 183–184), summarizing all Central California remains from the Middle Horizon (2000 BC–500 AD), and estimating a prevalence of projectile wounds >5 percent. Pinker's #19, from two Central California sites, is based on reports by Jurmain (1991, 2001). At Ala-329, (500–1700 AD), 10 of 440 individuals, and at CA-SCI-038, (21 BC-1770 AD), 6 of 162 show signs of projectile wounds. The first problem is that Pinker's #13 is based on a study (Andrushko, Schwitalla, & Walker, 2010) of trophy-taking and dismemberment, using a data base of 13,453 individuals from all Central California sites from 3000 BC to 1700 AD. This data set encompasses the times and places covered by Moratto and Jurmain. One could justifiably cite Moratto and Jurmain separately, or Andrushko and colleagues alone, but one cannot count two cases and a summary including those sites as three different studies. Subtracting only one, this brings Pinker's List down to 14.

Both Central and Southern California have long been recognized for exceptional rates of violence among prehistoric peoples. After discussing projectile wounds from other areas, Jurmain (2001, p. 14) comments: "In the New World, the most frequent occurrence of such projectile lesions, however, has been observed at sites in California. Indeed, especially from sites in both central and southern California, the incidence of such lesions is as high as for any region in the world."[4] Andrushko and colleague's (2010, pp. 85, 88, 91) study of mutilation and trophy-taking is powerful evidence for the development of cultural traditions of violence, and probably war. Signs of trophy-taking are found for all times over a five-thousand-year period, (76 individuals, or .56 percent of the sample), but they are entirely absent in Southern California. Within Central California, trophy taking is fifteen times more frequent in the Early/Middle Transition period (500–200 BC) than before or after, which the authors associate with the rise of hierarchical social structure, and migrations of outside groups into the area. Yet other explanations besides war, such as sacrifice or chiefly punishment, should not be ruled out for this kind of data, especially since only 6 of the 76 victims had a projectile point associated with the remains, and considering the nearness of Mesoamerica.[5]

Southern California (Pinker's #15), today known as the Chumash area for its historic population, is also known for violence, but in different forms, and with different timing. The major finding (Lambert, 1997, pp. 82, 89–97) from 30 sites dating from 6000 BC to 1804 AD in the Santa Barbara area and Channel Islands, is a pattern of healed cranial fractures indicating non-lethal fights, compared by the author to the Yanomami. Only 2 percent of the skull fractures are perimortem. As discussed in chapter 11, a consistent record (here 98 percent) of *healed* cranial trauma cannot be taken as a diagnostic of war, since it could equally result from a non-lethal mechanism of conflict resolution (Fry & Szala, Chapter 23). Projectile wounds, in contrast, do suggest lethal intent, and are found in 58 individuals out of 1,744, or 3.3 percent. (Again, Bowles calculates a higher percent by restricting the cases used to adults). Forty-three percent of those have multiple wounds. Projectile wounds come from all periods, but peak dramatically from 580–1380 AD. Given the variability and temporal sweep of these studies, chronological generalizations are difficult. Still, the earliest records show less violence compared to later, and findings are not inconsistent with a major increase in warfare after 500 AD—as already mentioned regarding British Columbian fortifications, and the fading peace of the Eastern Middle Woodlands. Lambert and Walker (1991, pp. 970–971) and Walker & Thornton (2002, p. 515) see localized periods of higher violence as tied to local markers of climatic change and nutritional stress, and to the spread of the bow and arrow (cf. Gamble, 2005). Increasing warfare for a millennium before the European intrusion is common across North America, and major climate change is often temporally linked to those increases. For the current purpose of evaluating Pinker's List, the points are: rates of violence in prehistoric California are far above most comparable North American sites; and within California, they show great variability in practice, and become more common going from earlier to later periods.

(1) 60 percent (K) Crow Creek, South Dakota; (7) 16.3 percent (K) Illinois; and (8) 15 percent (K) Northeast Plains.

At Crow Creek in South Dakota, hundreds were massacred (Willey, 1990, pp. xv, 486). Originally dated to 1325 AD, it is more probably a few decades later (Bamforth, 2006, p. 75). All of the 486 individuals of the agricultural Coalescent Tradition appear to have been killed at the same time. (The 60 percent figure is based on an estimated total village population). This is the highest level of casualties in Pinker's List. It is also "the largest archaeologically recovered massacre in the world" (Willey, 1990, p. xx). The next case is from Norris Farms #36, a cemetery along the middle Illinois River containing 264 burials from about 1300 AD, where 43 individuals appear to have died violently based on projectile points, unhealed major trauma, and/ or animal scavenging marks indicating the bodies were originally left exposed (Milner, Anderson, & Smith, 1991). In Milner's (1999, p. 114) comprehensive survey of war signs in the Eastern Woodlands, he characterizes Norris Farms as the "one notable exception to the general pattern of low casualties." The third case, Northeast Plains, Pinker dates at a mid-point of 1485, but this is another problematic case. The death estimate comes from Keeley, who puts it at 1325–1650 AD, on the sole basis of the following sentence from Wiley (1990, p. xxiv): "Owsley (1988), using a sample of over 700 skeletons from Coalescent Tradition cemeteries, found indications of scalping on as many as 15 percent of the series." "Owsley (1988)" is an abstract of a conference presentation. Repeated efforts to get clarification of the contents of that presentation were unsuccessful. After considering Owsley's publications (1977; 1994a; 1994b), which do not provide any figure or date matching Wiley's description, it seems possible that this figure includes the remains from Crow Creek. Crow Creek, however, is already counted. Since the overlap is not confirmed, this case will remain on the list, but any early Coalescent instances in Owsley's sample would have been subject to the same conditions as applied at Coalescent Crow Creek.

Crow Creek and Norris Farms must be put in context to evaluate their represent-ativeness. In the Eastern forest, the peace of the Middle Woodlands period gave way to returning signs of violence in the Late Woodlands after 500 CE, but greater temporal res-olution is difficult. In the northern Plains, there are very few signs of violence until after 900 AD. In both regions, a major shift to defensively located and fortified villages began around 1050, and continued for centuries (Bamforth, 2006, p. 81; Lambert, 2002, p. 224; Milner, 1999, pp. 122–123). These war signs coincide with the Mississippian period, begin-ning between 800 and 900 AD, and continuing until the invasion of Europeans. From the midwest to southeastern United States, the Mississippian and surrounding traditions were marked (with local variations) by larger populations, big planned settlements, intensive maize cultivation, use of maritime resources, elaborate ceremonialism, mound-building, chiefly hierarchies, and large-scale warfare.

The increase in fortifications coincides with critical climatic instability for larger horticultural populations. Increasingly detailed reconstructions indicate five distinct periods of drought lasting 40 to 60 years between 1030 and 1600 CE (Bamforth, 2006, p. 73). Both Crow Creek (Bamforth, 2006, p. 67) and Norris Farms (Milner et al., 1991, p. 591) skeletons show clear signs of nutritional stress. These late prehis-toric developments come at a time of greatly intensified violence linked to climatic perturbations across much of North America. Yet even in these violent times, Crow Creek and Norris Farms are noted as extreme in their levels of violence (Milner, 1999, pp. 114–117; Lambert, 2002, pp. 225–228). They are not representative, even in this especially violent time.

Conclusion

So let us look back over Pinker's list. Of the original 21, Gobero, Niger is out because it has no war deaths. Three cases, the burial ground across the Nile from Site 117, Sarai Nahar Rai, India, and Calumnata Algeria are all eliminated because they only have one instance of violent death. One site each was dropped because of duplication in Brittany, southern Scandinavia, and California. That leaves two-thirds of the original List, 14 exam-ples, which purportedly represent average war mortality among "prehistoric people." Jebel Sahaba, the two cases from the Dnieper gorge, and Indian Knoll are all highly unusual in their very early dates and number of casualties, when compared to other contemporary locations, including 117's neighbor's cemetery (see Ferguson, chapter 11). Three European sites are from the Mesolithic, which has gained a reputation for violence compared with earlier and later cultures, and two of those are from the Ertebolle tradition, which has an established reputation of being especially violent even within the Mesolithic. Four cases (compiled from many more individual sites) are from the Pacific coast, British Columbia, and Southern-Central California, all of which have higher levels of violence than any other long-term North American sequence, and which still show great variations by time and place. The final three are from Illinois and South Dakota or thereabouts, which, even during the most violent centuries in the entire sequence of prehistoric North America, stand out as the extreme points of warfare killings.

Is this sample representative of war death rates among prehistoric populations? Hardly. It is a selective compilation of highly unusual cases, grossly distorting war's antiquity and lethality. The elaborate castle of evolutionary and other theorizing that rises on this sample is built upon sand. Is there an alternative way of assessing the presence of war in prehistory, and of evaluating whether making war is the expectable expression of evolved tendencies to kill? Yes. Is there archaeological evidence indicating war was absent in entire prehistoric regions and for millennia? Yes. The alternative and representative way to assess prehistoric war mortality is demonstrated in chapter 11, which surveys all Europe and the Near East, considering *whole* archaeological records, not selected violent cases. When that is done, with careful attention to types and vagaries of evidence, an entirely different story unfolds. War does not go forever backwards in time. It had a beginning. We are not hard-wired for war. We learn it.

Acknowledgments

Acknowledgments for both this chapter and chapter 11 are due to Marilyn Roper and Rick Schulting, who read and commented on the manuscripts; to Doug Fry, for his inspiration, editorial advice, and patience; and to the staff at Rutgers University libraries, who made this research possible.

Notes

1. I am the only person identified among "a handful of social anthropologists [who] have recently codified this vague prejudice into a theoretical stance that amounts to a Rousseauian declaration of universal prehistoric peace" (Keeley, 1996, p. 20).
2. Although Kelly (1995) correctively emphasizes the danger of generalizing about nomadic hunter-gatherers, or projecting any contemporary people as representatives of prehistory, they are still the best window we have into ways of life over human evolutionary history.
3. The other two cases are a cluster of seven Late Archaic sites around Kentucky Lake in Tennessee, where 10 out of 439 individuals died violently, or 2.3 percent (Smith, 1997, pp. 250–252); and an unpublished thesis on Creek Tennessee reports three males with points and mutilation in one grave, though no population figures are available (Dye, 2009, p. 62).
4. I could not find enough information to comment on any preconditions for war in times as early as Middle Horizon, although later prehistory (Moratto, 1984, pp. 171–172) is characterized by the Mesolithic/complex hunter-gather-like preconditions of war: seasonal sedentism; broad-spectrum foraging using wetlands and streams, and especially salmon runs like on the Northwest Coast; central locations with "ceremonial lodges or chief's residences;" and occupation by distinct and geographically separated ethnicities (see chapter 11).
5. A more widespread pattern of taking heads as trophies was historically associated with many different California groups, and the similarity of associated ritual across language divides is a good illustration of spreading cultural practices of war (Lambert, 2007).

References

Albrethson, E. A., & Petersen, E. B. (1976). Excavation of a Mesolithic cemetery at Vedbaek, Denmark. *Acta Archaeologica, 47*, 1–28.

Ames, K. M., & Maschner, H. G. D. (1999). *Peoples of the Northwest Coast: Their archaeology and prehistory.* London: Thames and Hudson.

Andrushko, V. A., Schwitalla, A. W., & Walker, P. L. (2010). Trophy-taking and dismemberment as warfare strategies in prehistoric central California. *American Journal of Physical Anthropology, 141*, 83–96.

Bamforth, B. B. (2006). Climate, chronology, and the course of war in the middle Missouri region of the North American Great Plains. In E. N. Arkush, & M. W. Allen (Eds.), *The archaeology of warfare: Prehistories of raiding and conquest* (pp. 66–100). Gainesville, FL: University Press of Florida.

Barber, K. E., Chambers, F. M., Maddy, D. (2004). Late Holocene climatic history of northern Germany and Denmark: Peat macrofossil investigations at Dosenmoor, Schleswig-Holstein, and Svanemose, Jutland. *Boreas, 33*, 132–144.

Bender, B. (1985). Prehistoric developments in the American midcontinent and in Brittany, northwest France. In T. D. Price, & J. A. Brown (Eds.), *Prehistoric hunter-gatherers: The emergence of cultural complexity* (pp. 21–57). Orlando, FL: Academic Press.

Bowles, S. (2006). Group competition, reproductive leveling, and the evolution of human altruism. *Science, 314*, 1569–1572.

Bowles, S. (2009). Did warfare among ancestral hunter-gatherers affect the evolution of human social behavior? *Science, 324*, 1293–1298.

Bowles, S., & H. Gintis (2011). *A cooperative species: Human reciprocity and its evolution.* Princeton: Princeton University Press.

Boyer, P. & B. Bergstrom (2011). Threat-detection in child development: An evolutionary perspective. *Neuroscience and Biobehavioral Reviews, 35*, 1034–1041.

Bracha, H. S., Bienvenu, O. J., & Eaton, W. W. (2006). Testing the Paleolithic-human-warfare hypothesis of blood-injection phobia in the Baltimore EA follow-up study—Towards a more etiologically-based conceptualization of DSM-V. *Journal of Affective Disorders, 97*, 1–4.

Bridges, P. S. (1996). Warfare and mortality at Koger's Island, Alabama. *International Journal of Osteoarchaeology, 6*, 66–75.

Burleigh, R., & K. Matthews (1982). British Museum natural radiocarbon measurements XIII. *Radiocarbon, 24*, 151–170.

Carman, J., & P. Carman (2005). War in prehistoric society: Modern views of ancient violence. In M. P, Pearson, & I. J. N. Thorpe (Eds.), *Warfare, violence and slavery in prehistory: Proceedings of a Prehistoric Society conference at Sheffield University, BAR International Series, 1374*, 217–224. Oxford: Archaeopress.

Chagnon, N. (1968). *Yanomamö: The fierce people.* New York: Holt, Rinehart, Winston.

Chagnon, N. (1988). Life histories, blood revenge, and warfare in a tribal population. *Science, 239*, 985–992.

Chapman, J. (1999). The origins of warfare in the prehistory of Central and Eastern Europe. In J. Carman, & A. Harding (Eds.), *Ancient Warfare* (pp. 101–142). Stroud: Sutton Publishers.

Choi, J-K, & S. Bowles (2007). The coevolution of parochial altruism and war. *Science, 318*, 636–640.

Coupland, G. (1989). Warfare and social complexity on the Northwest Coast. In D. Claire, & B. C. Vivian (Eds.), *Cultures in conflict: Current archaeological perspectives* (pp. 205–214). Calgary: University of Calgary Archaeological Association.

Cybulski, J. S. (1992). *A Greenville burial ground: Human remains and mortuary elements in British Columbia coast prehistory.* Hull, Quebec: Canadian Museum of Civilization.

Cybulski, J. S. (1994). Culture change, demographic history, and health and disease on the Northwest Coast. In C. S. Larsen and G. R. Milner (Eds.), *In the wake of contact: Biological responses to conquest* (pp. 75–85). New York: John Wiley and Sons.

Dastugue, J. (1970). Pathologie des hommes de Columnata. In Chamla, M.C., *Les hommes epipaleolithiques de Columnata (Algerie Occidental). Memoires du Centre de Recherches Anthropologiques Prehistoriques et Ethnographiques, 15*, 118–126.

Dastugue, J., & M-A. de Lumley (1976). Las maladies des hommes prehistoriques du Paleolithique et du Mesolithique. In H. de Lumley (Ed.) *La prehistoire Francaise* (pp. 612–622). Paris: Editions du Centre National de la Recherche Scientifique.

Dickel, D. N., C. G. Aker, B. K. Baron, & G. H. Doran (1988). An orbital floor and ulna fracture from the Early Archaic of Florida. *Journal of Paleopathology, 2,* 165–170.

Dolukhanov, P. M. (1997). Landscape at the Mesolithic-Neolithic transition in the boreal East European plain. In J. Chapman and P. Dolukhanov (Eds.), *Landscapes in flux: Central and Eastern Europe in antiquity,* (pp. 289–306). Oxford: Oxbow Books.

Dolukhanov, P. M. (1999). War and peace in prehistoric Eastern Europe. In J. Carman, & A. Harding (Eds.), *Ancient Warfare* (pp. 73–87). Stroud: Sutton Publishers.

Dye, D. (2006). The transformation of Mississippian warfare: Four case studies from the mid-South. In E. N. Arkush, & M. W. Allen (Eds.), *The archaeology of warfare: Prehistories of raiding and conquest* (pp. 101–147). Gainesville, FL: University Press of Florida.

Dye, D. (2009). *War paths, peace paths: An archaeology of cooperation and conflict in Native Eastern North America.* Lanham, MD: Altamira Press.

Ferguson, R. B. (1983). Warfare and redistributive exchange on the Northwest Coast. In E. Tooker, (Ed.) *The development of political organization in Native North America: 1979 proceedings of the American Ethnological Society* (pp. 137–147). Washington: American Ethnological Society.

Ferguson, R. B. (1984a). Introduction: Studying war. In R. B. Ferguson (Ed.), *Warfare, culture, and environment* (pp. 1–81). Orlando: Academic Press.

Ferguson, R. B. (1984b). A re-examination of the causes of Northwest Coast warfare. In R. B. Ferguson (Ed.), *Warfare, culture, and environment* (pp. 267–328). Orlando: Academic Press.

Ferguson, R. B. (2001). Materialist, cultural and biological theories on why Yanomami make war. *Anthropological Theory, 1,* 99–116.

Ferguson, R. B. (2006). Archaeology, cultural anthropology, and the origins and intensifications of war. In E. N. Arkush, & M. W. Allen (Eds.), *The archaeology of warfare: Prehistories of raiding and conquest* (pp. 469–523). Gainesville, FL: University Press of Florida.

Ferguson, R. B. (2011). Born to live: Challenging killer myths. In R. W. Sussman and C. R. Cloninger (Eds.), *Origins of altruism and cooperation* (pp. 249–270). New York: Springer.

Fry, D. P. (2006). *The human potential for peace: An anthropological challenge to assumptions about war and violence.* New York: Oxford University Press.

Fukuyama, F. (1998). Women and the evolution of world politics. *Foreign Affairs, 77*(5), 24–40.

Gamble, L. H. (2005). Culture and climate: Reconsidering the effect of palaeoclimatic variability among southern California hunter-gatherer societies. *World Archaeology, 37,* 92–108.

Gat, A. (2006). *War in human civilization.* New York: Oxford University Press.

Gat, A. (2009) So why do people fight? Evolutionary theory and the causes of war. *European Journal of International Relations, 15,* 571–599.

Goetz, A. T. (2010). The evolutionary psychology of violence. *Psicothema, 22,* 15–21.

Goldstein, J. S. (2011). *Winning the war on war: The decline of armed conflict worldwide.* New York: Penguin.

Goodall, J. (1986). *The chimpanzees of Gombe: Patterns of behavior.* Cambridge, MA: Belknap Press.

Haas, J. (1990). Warfare and the evolution of tribal polities in the prehistoric Southwest. In J. Haas (Ed.), *The anthropology of war* (pp. 171–189). Cambridge: Cambridge University Press.

Haas, J. (1999). The origins of war and ethnic violence. In J. Carman, & A. Harding (Eds.), *Ancient Warfare* (pp. 11–24). Stroud: Sutton Publishers.

Haas, J., & Creamer, W. (1997). Warfare among the Pueblos: Myth, history, and ethnography. *Ethnohistory, 44,* 235–261.

Jefferies, R. W., V. D. Thompson, & G. R. Milner (2005). Archaic hunter-gatherer landscape use in west-central Kentucky. *Journal of Field Archaeology, 30,* 3–23.

Jones, B. C., DeBruine, L. M., Little, A. C., Watkins, C. D., & Feinberg, D. R. (2011). "Eavesdropping" and perceived male dominance rank in humans. *Animal Behavior, 81,* 1203–1208.

Jurmain, R. (1991). Paleodemography of trauma in a central California population. In D. J. Ortner, & A. C. Aufderhiede (Eds.), *Human paleopathology: Current synthesis and future options* (pp. 241–248). Washington: Smithsonian Institution Press.

Jurmain, R. (2001). Paleoepidemiological patterns of trauma in a prehistoric population from central California. *American Journal of Physical Anthropology, 115,* 13–23.

Kanazawa, S. (2009). Evolutionary psychological foundations of civil wars. *The Journal of Politics, 71,* 25–34.

Keeley, L. H. (1996). *War before civilization: The myth of the peaceful savage.* New York: Oxford University Press.

Kelly, R. L. (1995). *The foraging spectrum: Diversity in hunter-gatherer lifeways*. Washington: Smithsonian Institution Press.

Kennedy, K. A. R. (2000). *God-apes and fossil men: Paleoanthropology in Southeast Asia*. Ann Arbor: University of Michigan Press.

Lambert, P. M. (1997). Pattern of violence in prehistoric hunter-gatherer societies of coastal southern California. In D. L. Martin, & D. W. Frayer (Eds.), *Troubled times: Violence and warfare in the past* (pp. 77–109). New York: Columbia University Press.

Lambert, P. M. (2002). The archaeology of war: A North American perspective. *Journal of Archaeological Research, 10*, 207–241.

Lambert, P. M. (2007). Ethnography and linguistic evidence for the origins of human trophy taking in California. In R. J. Chacon, & D. H. Dye (Eds.), *The taking and displaying of human body parts as trophies by Amerindians* (pp. 65–89). New York: Springer.

Lambert, P. M., & P. L. Walker (1991). Physical anthropological evidence for the evolution of social complexity in coastal Southern California. *Antiquity, 65*, 963–973.

LeBlanc, S. A. (1999). *Prehistoric warfare in the American Southwest*. Salt Lake City: University of Utah Press.

LeBlanc, S. A. (2007). Why warfare? Lessons from the past. *Daedalus*, Winter, 13–21.

LeBlanc, S. A., & Register, K. E. (2003). *Constant battles: The myth of the peaceful, noble savage*. New York: St. Martin's Press.

Lee, R. B., & DeVore, I. (Eds.), (1968). *Man the hunter.* New Brunswick, NJ: Transaction Press.

Lillie, M. C. (2001). Mesolithic cultures of Ukraine: Observations on cultural developments in light of new radiocarbon determinations from the Dnieper Rapids cemeteries. In K. J. Fewster, & M. Zvelebil (Eds.), *Ethnoarchaeology and hunter-gatherers: Pictures at an exhibition, BAR International Series, 955*, 53–63. Oxford: Archaeopress.

Lillie, M. C. (2004). Fighting for your life? Violence at the late-glacial to Holocene transition in Ukraine. In M. Roksandic (Ed.), *Violent interactions in the Mesolithic: Evidence and meaning, BAR International Series, 1237*, 89–93. Oxford: Archaeopress

Lovisek, J. A. (2007). Human trophy taking on the Northwest Coast: An ethnohistorical perspective. In R. J. Chacon, & D. H. Dye (Eds.), *The taking and displaying of human body parts as trophies by Amerindians* (pp. 45–64). New York: Springer.

Low, B. S. (2000). *Why sex matters: A Darwinian look at human behavior*. Princeton: Princeton University Press.

McManamon, F. (1999). The initial scientific examination, description, and analysis of the Kennewick Man human remains. http://www.nps.gov/archeology/kennewick/mcmanamon.htm, accessed 03/07/12

Milner, G. R. (1999). Warfare in prehistoric and early historic eastern North America. *Journal of Archaeological Research, 7*, 105–151.

Milner, G. R. (2007). Warfare, population, and food production in prehistoric eastern North America. In R. J. Chacon, & R. G. Mendoza (Eds.), *North American indigenous warfare and ritual violence*, (pp. 182–201). Tucson: University of Arizona Press.

Milner, G. R, Anderson, E., & Smith, V. G. (1991). Warfare in late prehistoric west-central Illinois. *American Antiquity, 56*, 581–603.

Moratto, M. J. (1984). *California Archaeology*. Orlando: Academic Press.

Moreno, E. (2011). The society of our "out of Africa" ancestors (I): The migrant warriors that colonized the world. *Communicative & Integrative Biology, 4*, 163–170.

Moss, M. L., & Erlandson, J. M. (1992). Forts, refuge rocks, and defensive sites: The antiquity of warfare along the North Pacific Coast of North America. *Arctic Anthropology, 29*, 73–90.

Navarette, C. D., McDonald, M. M., Molina, L. E., & Sidanius, J. (2010).Prejudice at the nexus of race and gender: An outgroup male target hypothesis. *Journal of Personality and Social Psychology, 98*, 933–945.

Newell, R. R., Constandse-Westermann, T. S., & Meiklejohn, C. (1979). The skeletal remains of Mesolithic man in Western Europe: An exhaustive catalogue. *Journal of Human Evolution, 8*, 1–228.

Owsley, D. W. (1977). Ethnographic and osteological evidence for warfare at the Larson Site, South Dakota. *Plains Anthropologist, 22*, 119–131.

Owlsey, D. W. (1988). Osteological evidence for scalping in Coalescent Tradition populations of the Northern Plains. Paper presented at the 46th Annual Plains Conference. (Abstract cited in Willey 1990).

Owsley, D. W. (1994a). Warfare in Coalescent Tradition populations of the Northern Plains. In D.W. Owsley, & R. L. Jantz (Eds.), *Skeletal biology in the Great Plains: Migration, warfare, health, and subsistence* (pp. 333–334). Washington: Smithsonian Institution Press.

Owsley, D. W. (1994b). Osteology of the Fay Tolton Site: Implications for warfare during the Initial Middle Missouri Variant. In D.W. Owsley, & R. L. Jantz (Eds.), *Skeletal biology in the Great Plains: Migration, warfare, health, and subsistence* (pp. 335– 353). Washington: Smithsonian Institution Press.

Owsley, D.W, & Jantz, R. L. (2000). Biography in the bones: Skeletons tell the story of ancient lives and peoples. *Scientific American Discovering Archaeology.* January/February, 56–58.

Owsley, D. W., Marks, M. K., & Manhein, M. H. (1989). Human skeletal samples in the Southern Great Plains. In J. L. Hofman, R. L. Brooks, J. S. Hays, D. W. Owsley, R. L. Jantz, M. K. Marks, & M.H. Manheim (Eds.), *From Clovis to Comanchero: Archaeological overview of the Southern Great Plains* (pp. 111–122). U.S. Army Corps of Engineers, Southwestern Division.

Pearson, M. P. (2005). Warfare, violence and slavery in later prehistory: An introduction. In M. P. Pearson, & I. J. N. Thorpe (Eds.), *Warfare, violence and slavery in prehistory: Proceedings of a Prehistoric Society conference at Sheffield University, BAR International Series, 1374,* 19–33. Oxford: Archaeopress

Pinker, S. 2002. *The blank slate: The modern denial of human nature.* New York: Viking.

Pinker, S. 2011. *The better angels of our nature: Why violence has declined.* New York: Viking.

Potts, M., & T. Hayden (2008). *Sex and war: How biology explains warfare and terrorism and offers a path to a safer world.* Dallas: Benbella Books.

Price, T. D. (1985). Affluent foragers of Mesolithic southern Scandinavia. In T. D. Price, & J. A. Brown (Eds.), *Prehistoric hunter-gatherers: The emergence of cultural complexity,* (pp. 341–363). Orlando, FL: Academic Press.

Rice, G. E., & S. A. LeBlanc (Eds.) (2001). *Deadly landscapes: Case studies in prehistoric southwestern warfare.* Salt Lake City: University of Utah Press.

Roksandic, M. (2004). Introduction: How violent was the Mesolithic, or is there a common pattern of violent interactions specific to sedentary hunter-gatherers? In M. Roksandic (Ed.), *Violent interactions in the Mesolithic: Evidence and meaning, BAR International Series, 1237,* 1–7. Oxford: Archaeopress.

Sereno, P. C., Garcea, E. E. A. A., Jousse, H., Stojanowski, C. M., Saliege, J-F., Maga . . . A. Stivers, J. P. (2008). Lakeside cemeteries in the Sahara: 5000 years of Holocene population and environmental change. *PLoS One,* 3(8), 1–22.

Sharma, G. R. (1973). Mesolithic lake cultures in the Ganga Valley, India. *Proceedings of the Prehistoric Society, 39,* 129–146.

Smirnov, O. H., Arrow, H., Kennett, D. & Orbell, J. (2007). Ancestral war and evolutionary origins of "heroism." *The Journal of Politics, 69,* 927–940.

Smith, M. O. (1997). Osteological indications of warfare in the Archaic period of the Western Tennessee Valley. In D. L. Martin, & D. W. Frayer (Eds.), *Troubled times: Violence and warfare in the past* (pp. 241–265). New York: Columbia University Press.

Snyder, J. K., Fessler, D. M. T., Tiokhin, L., Frederick, D. A., Lee, S. W., & Navarrete, C. D. (2011). Trade-offs in a dangerous world: Women's fear of crime predicts preferences for aggressive and formidable mates. *Evolution and Human Behavior, 32,* 127–137.

Thayer, B. A. (2004). *Darwin and international relations: On the evolutionary origins of war and ethnic conflict.* Lexington, KY: University Press of Kentucky.

Thorpe, I. J. N. (2003). Anthropology, archaeology, and the origin of warfare. *World Archaeology, 35,* 145–165.

Thorpe, I. J. N. (2005). The ancient origins of warfare and violence. In M. P. Pearson, & I. J. N. Thorpe (Eds.), *Warfare, violence and slavery in prehistory: Proceedings of a Prehistoric Society conference at Sheffield University, BAR International Series, 1374,* 1–18. Oxford: Archaeopress.

Tooby, J., & L. Cosmides (2010). Groups in mind: The coalitional roots of war and morality. In H. Hogh-Oleson (Ed.), *Human morality and sociality: Evolutionary and comparative perspectives* (pp. 191–234). New York: Palgrave MacMillen.

Van Vugt, M. (2008). Tribal instincts, male warriors, and the evolutionary psychology of intergroup relations. (Invited paper for Annals of New York Academy of Sciences, Special Issue on "Values and empathy across social barriers"). Retrieved from http://www.professormarkvanvugt.com/files/TribalInstinctsMaleWarriors and The Evolutionary PsychologyofIntergroupRelations-NewYorkAnnalsofAcademyofSciences-2008.pdf (March 30, 2012)

Vencl, S. (1991). Interpretation des blessures causees par les armes au Mesolithique. *L'Anthropologie, 95,* 219–228.

Vencl, S. (1999). Stone age warfare. In J. Carman, & A. Harding (Eds.), *Ancient Warfare* (57–72). Stroud: Sutton Publishers.

Walker, P. L., & Thornton, R. (2002). Health, nutrition, and demographic change in Native California. In R. H. Steckel, & J. C. Rose (Eds.), *The backbone of history: Health and nutrition in the Western Hemisphere*. Cambridge: Cambridge University Press.

Webb, W. (1974). *Indian Knoll*. Lexington: University of Kentucky.

Wendorf, F. (Ed.) (1968). *The prehistory of Nubia*. Dallas: Southern Methodist University Press.

Wendorf, F., Shild, R., & Haas, H. (1979). A new radiocarbon chronology for prehistoric sites in Nubia. *Journal of Field Archaeology, 6*, 219–223.

Willey, P. (1990). *Prehistoric warfare on the Great Plains: Skeletal analysis of the Crow Creek massacre victims*. New York: Garland Publishing.

Wilson, E. O. (1999). *Consilience: The unity of knowledge*. New York: Alfred Knopf.

Winegard, B., & Deaner, R. (2010). The evolutionary significance of Red Sox Nation: Sport fandom as a by-product of coalitional psychology. *Evolutionary Psychology, 8*, 432–446.

Winters, H. D. (1974). Introduction to the new edition, in W. Webb, *Indian Knoll* (pp. v–xxvii). Lexington: University of Kentucky.

8

Trends in Cooperation and Conflict in Native Eastern North America

DAVID H. DYE

While conflict was entwined, if not entrenched, in indigenous eastern North America, so too was the ability to limit the scope of conflict and to engender alliances, coalitions, and cooperation. Patterns of restraint, as well, were in place to constrain overall levels of aggression (Lee, 2007). But these trends changed over time, not only in intensity and scale, but also in their form and structure as social organization coevolved with violence and peace (Table 8.1). Critical junctures in social configurations then correlate with trends in aggression and peacemaking. Documenting these key transitions in the evolution of intergroup conflict and cooperation is crucial for understanding the development of human behavior and its selection for both violent and peaceful relations (Kelly, 2000, p. 159; 2005, p. 15298).

Regional archaeological assessments in areas such as eastern North America provide insightful opportunities for evaluating these transitions and trends, and for avoiding sweeping, continental-scale generalizations of indigenous patterns of aggression and restraint. Complementing the great temporal depth provided by archaeological research, ethnographic reports and ethnohistoric accounts provide important details concerning the political and social organization of eastern North American indigenous people in the post-contact period and their efforts to promote peaceful relationships in the midst of aggression and conflict. Such regional approaches, utilizing both archaeological and ethnographic/ethnohistoric accounts for long-term studies of culture change, provide important opportunities for addressing questions that speak to the human capacity for cooperation and conflict. Based on the work of Fry (2006, 2007, 2011); Kelly (2000, 2005), and others, I present a model of evolving trends in violence and cooperation that incorporates changes in sociopolitical organization. This model accounts for temporal variations in indigenous conflict and cooperation as well as social and political issues.

TABLE 8.1 **Archaeological Periods and Types of Violence and Cooperation**

Years BC/AD	Archaeological Period	Type of Violence	Type of Cooperation	Type of Social Organization
AD 1000–1700	Protohistoric Mississippian	Warfare	Alliances and diplomatic relations	Village agriculturalists
5000 BC–1000 AD	Late Middle Woodland Early Late Middle Archaic	Blood Feuding	Regional alliance and coalition networks	Segmented hunter-gatherer-gardeners
11,000–5000 BC	Early Late Middle Paleoindian Early	Homicide	Alliance, avoidance, cooperation, toleration	Non-segmented, family level foragers

Sponsel (2011) outlines three logical domains that anthropologists face in studying human cooperation and conflict. The first is "killing anthropology," which encompasses studies of violence through archaeological and ethnographic studies. The second, "nonkilling anthropology," challenges "killing anthropology" through the examination of nonkilling societies, and the investigation of nonviolent and peaceful aspects of societies that experience violence. The third domain is "neutral anthropology," which is indirectly relevant to nonkilling with its emphasis on advocacy anthropology and human rights. I suggest a fourth domain should include studies such as the one presented here that investigate the coevolution of cooperation and conflict and social organization.

Three broad cultural trends may be posited for dominant institutions associated with peacemaking and lethal aggression in eastern North America: non-segmented foragers, segmented hunter-gatherer-gardeners, and village agriculturalists. These trends, each to be considered in turn, are not mutually exclusive, but appear to be dominating modes of behavior associated with varying degrees of sociopolitical integration.

Non-Segmental Foragers

Some basic questions are beginning to emerge about aggression and peacemaking among early foragers in eastern North America. What was the nature of intersocietal relations among pioneer hunter-gatherers who crossed through the arctic gateway into the Western Hemisphere? How did conflict and cooperation become transformed as foragers adapted to changing environmental and social conditions? In this section I briefly examine the nature of conflict and cooperation among the earliest inhabitants of North America and attempt to answer some of these questions.

Early foragers who occupied eastern North America during the Paleoindian and Early Archaic periods (11,000 and 5000 BC), were never numerous, leaving only stone tools and the residue from activities associated with butchering game, quarrying flint tools, and camping for short periods of time. Foraging groups, composed of extended families, maintained a high degree of mobility, fluid group membership, and periodic aggregations of multiple families. These gatherings, perhaps lasting for a few weeks, would have been critical for promoting a shared identity and reducing risk and uncertainty by forming and maintaining social and kinship networks that in turn resulted in exchanges of ecological and social information. These social ties would have been reinforced through feasting and ritual (Anderson & Sassaman, 2012). Mechanisms for dampening interfamily conflict and preventing blood feuds would also be critical for maintaining a regional matrix of friendships, kin relations, and trust. The period of early foragers may have been characterized by several modes of conflict and cooperation: homicides, revenge, spontaneous conflicts, and raids. Each trend would be accompanied by associated cooperative institutions that promoted peaceful relations.

Paleoindians in eastern North America would have employed a variety of violent and nonviolent solutions to resolve conflicts and to seek justice based on studies of ethnographically documented hunter-gatherers (Fry, 2006, 2007; Kelly, 2000, 2005). These early foragers lived in an environment that is different from any known today (Meltzer, 2009, pp. 41–43; Speth et al., in press) and may represent a foraging adaptation unlike ones studied by modern researchers. However, they may have exhibited broadly similar responses to violence and conflict resolution as those observed in modern hunter-gatherers.

One solution typically found among family-level foragers is homicides, in which a person with a grievance takes aggressive, unilateral action to punish another individual or to prevail in a dispute (Fry, 2006, p. 23). Aggrieved individuals take justice into their own hands in seeking retribution. Homicides can lead to increased conflict if it is not contained through institutions that ameliorate aggression, such as avoidance, cooperation, friendship, restraint, and trust.

Typically, violence is limited among non-segmented hunter-gatherers because they lack overarching, cohesive kin organizations necessary for coordinating groups larger than the family. Where conflict occurs it is often generated from personal grudges that are reconciled through alliance, avoidance, cooperation, negotiation, toleration, and sometimes homicide. Physical aggression is in fact rare because conflicts are controlled or dampened and peaceful relations are maintained through periodic, large gatherings that further intercommunity networks as the social foundation for ceremonies, cooperation, friendships, gift exchange, and marriage.

Revenge homicide entails organized, planned, and premeditated attacks by family members, rather than the aggrieved individual, against a specific murderer who is explicitly targeted for their prior lethal violence. Kelly (2000, p. 130) argues that feud may well precede "true warfare." And in turn, in the evolution of armed conflict, revenge homicide or "capital punishment" also precedes feud. A homicide is likely to be perceived as an individual loss shared among one's kin rather than as an injury to the social group (Kelly, 2000, p. 47). Justice prevails when only the killer, rather than another family member, is the target of lethal revenge. In such groups social segments are weakly developed or altogether lacking and the sense of justice is achieved when a killer is killed. Balance is thus restored between the families once the homicide is over. The kin groups generally put the matter behind them when punishment has been meted out (Kelly, 2000, p. 111). Relative peace is thus established and maintained because each individual exercises a high degree of personal autonomy to pursue their own personal grievances. In these non-segmented societies authority is minimal and leadership is weakly developed; no one has the authority to adjudicate disputes, hand down enforceable judgments, or call for organized lethal aggression from the social group.

Paleoindian bands, such as Clovis foragers, appear to have been integrated as small, mobile, independent families, loosely connected by extensive kin networks, but with no higher order of social integration than the family, that is, no lineages or clans. Network connections would have been founded upon the circulation of gift exchanges, including red ocher and large, non-utilitarian bifaces knapped from exotic cherts that were often cached. These materials are well-documented in the Paleoindian archaeological record (Speth et al., in press, p. 6). The movement of these valuables over large areas may signify the early establishment of boundaries, the amelioration of occasional conflicts, and the promotion of cooperative relations. Further, the long-distance exchange of symbolic weaponry would have been helpful in establishing exchange partners, creating marriage ties, and furthering conflict resolution across a matrix of kin and social boundaries. Thus, intergroup alliances and coalitions, held together by gift exchanges, may have resulted from open-ended and flexible social relationships during seasonal aggregations of neighboring groups.

Studies of modern hunter-gatherers indicate that lethal conflicts among early, non-segmented foragers upon entering eastern North America may have been restricted to homicides and revenge rather than other forms of aggression such as raids, feuds, or warfare. Upper Paleolithic foragers, in general, had low levels of violence, although conditions favoring sporadic competition may have been present as resource availability fluctuated at any given locale from season to season and year to year.

According to Kelly (2000, p. 135) the initial societies that:

> passed through the Arctic gateway to the New World were thus those that achieved a degree of regional integration through some combination of intermarriage, visiting, gift exchange, joint feasting, and festive intercommunity gathering entailing singing and dancing. Such practices fostered a state of positive peace that provided a basis for sharing and cooperation. In other words, it was not merely the absence of war but the presence of a positive peace that facilitated Upper Paleolithic migration.

Once Paleoindians began to settle in the Eastern Woodlands, they engaged in a generalized foraging strategy within biotic zones characterized by species-rich tundra and temperate forests. In this setting we might anticipate that spontaneous conflicts over access to resources would erupt from time to time. Spontaneous conflicts tend to be found in environments rich in naturally occurring subsistence resources that are dense, diverse, and reliable. The principal trigger is for the parties involved to secure subsistence resources without sharing them. Those participating in such defensive conflicts would be coresidents who routinely hunt or gather together. The weapons employed are implements normally carried for food procurement. Conflict in such cases often takes place at the outer margins of the areas habitually exploited. Spontaneous conflicts over access to resources are a distinctive form of violence, characteristic of a non-segmental type of society that exploits a species-rich environment (Kelly 2000).

When conflicts over access to resources take place among neighboring foraging groups, they typically move apart or settle in unpopulated areas, even if these are less desirable, to avoid or reduce conflict (Fry, 2006, 2007; Johnson, 1982). However, when the establishment of new territories is no longer available, then some degree of tension resulting from population packing may be evident, signaling a progressive intensification of conflict. Unless population numbers are held in check, group size among foragers will increase significantly upon entering lightly or unpopulated, rich resource zones, giving rise to coalitions, defended territories, and elevated competition with neighboring groups.

The incidence and severity of spontaneous conflicts are correlated with the degree to which access to resources is restricted. The frequency of conflict does not covary with population density so much as the frequency and severity of spontaneous conflicts covaries with resource availability (Kelly, 2000). Higher resource restriction or environmental circumscription amplifies the intensity of conflicts (Carneiro, 1988). Thus, the more resources are restricted, the more likely it is that conflict will take place and new mechanisms for alliances and peacemaking will materialize.

Conflicts among foragers may be initiated by neighbors attempting to exploit the resources of another local group, and may expand as relatives and friends on both sides become entangled in bitter disputes. Injuries and fatalities sometimes occur as these intergroup altercations escalate. As populations increased over the centuries after initial settlement due to foraging groups fissioning into new constituent groups, annual hunting and gathering ranges decreased. Over time, the net effect of limited access to resources would result in increased tensions and strained social relations among neighboring bands (Anderson, 1996a, 1996b). Such tensions may have erupted into planned intergroup raids upon encampments, although alliances may have helped ameliorate or dampen hostilities. Such raiding behavior entails preplanned forays into enemy territory for the purpose of killing an unsuspecting individual (Kelly 2000, pp. 138–139). Raiding is thus distinct from spontaneous conflicts over access to resources because the primary purpose of the prototypical raid is payback for prior causalities inflicted upon one's group. Chronic bouts of a raiding style of conflict may give rise to feuding in situations of increased competition over resources.

Segmental Foragers and the Rise of Blood Feuding

The second trend, characteristic of local groups or tribal societies, is kin-based feuding in which aggrieved parties seek personal retaliatory justice from any member of the targeted group through blood revenge over grudges. Feuds may result if revenge follows a homicide and are usually limited to one or two killings at a time. Vengeance is sought after a killing by temporary kin militia. Feuding is an organized means of violence carried out by small, informal, and temporary kin militia groups working under weak chains of command with rudimentary powers of dispersion (Reyna, 1994, pp. 40–43). Generally, one side takes the offensive, but there is no necessary political objective beyond the maintenance of personal or group honor (Boehm, 1987, p. 221). Feuds are often resolved by third-party assisted dispute settlements. Kin group liability for vengeance goes hand-in-hand with the development of descent groups and the conceptualization of marriage as a transaction between social groups (Kelly, 2000, p. 60).

An early example of feuding may be seen in the late Paleoindian Dalton culture (8,500 to 7900 BC) of the Mississippi Valley. Dalton culture is an early expression of tribal organization with all the hallmarks of segmented hunter-gatherers: formal cemeteries, long-distance exchange, symbolic weaponry, and non-egalitarian status relationships (Anderson, 2002). The braided stream regime of the early Holocene Mississippi Valley was one of the richest resource zones in North America. The Mississippi River offered opportunities for population growth, alliances, exchange, and interaction. At about this time the atlatl spread across eastern North America and may have transformed human relations, bringing about differences in alliances, cooperation, hunting patterns, conflict, and territoriality. The late Paleoindian archaeological record "unequivocally speaks of boundaries and alliances" (Sassaman, 2005, p. 83).

Some Dalton locales have produced large and exotic, high-quality lanceolate blades (Koldehoff & Walthall, 2009; Walthall & Koldehoff, 1998). These symbolic oversized blades, measuring up to 38 cm in length, exhibit remarkable workmanship in exotic cherts. The preferred raw material, high-quality Crescent Quarry Burlington chert, located just southwest of St. Louis, was chosen for its superior flint knapping properties. The symbolic blades have been found in more than 30 archaeological sites along a 700 km stretch of the Mississippi Valley (Morse, 1997, p. 17). These unusually large and elaborate bifaces are thought to have been mortuary accompaniments in Dalton cemeteries.

The manufacture and exchange of symbolic weaponry may have helped to create and maintain alliances and to reinforce status differentiation among individual descent groups (Walthall & Koldehoff, 1998, p. 266). The production and exchange of exotic bifaces may have served to integrate kin groups into regional alliance and coalition networks that facilitated information exchange, marriage arrangements, peace maintenance, and resource management. Exchange and manipulation of valuables would have fostered and structured positive social interactions through ritual acts in the context of festive gatherings and gift exchange. Although skeletal evidence is lacking, the large Dalton bifaces may suggest alliances were pursued in the face of an evolving environment of raids and feuds.

The period from about 5000 to 1000 BC (Middle and Late Archaic) witnessed the transition from non-segmental foragers to segmental societies and the transformation of patterns of aggression, alliances, cooperation, conflict, and peacekeeping over a large area of eastern North America. These tribal-like, local groups initially arose in the resource-rich river valleys of the Southeast and Lower Midwest. Key characteristics of tribal groups in the archaeological record include communal rituals, complex monumental earthen construction, symbolic weaponry finely crafted from exotic materials, long-distance exchange, and a feuding style of conflict (Anderson, 2002). These emerging local groups may have been somewhat ephemeral, without a great deal of complexity, longevity, or stability.

Evidence for early complex foragers appears in especially productive resource-rich areas: the Lower Mississippi Valley, Atlantic and Gulf Coasts, and the major river systems of the mid-continent (Arkansas, Missouri, Ohio, and Tennessee Rivers). These factors, coupled with regional population growth, contributed to the emergence of cultural complexity as seen in the growth and elaboration of monumental construction, intercommunity raiding, alliance networks, and long-distance exchange. A fishing, gathering, and hunting economic pattern characterized eastern North American tribal groups, although there is diversity in scale, complexity, and elaboration. What differentiated these populations from earlier foragers is their increased seasonal occupation of base camps, elaboration of communal activities, and heightened differences in wealth or surplus (Anderson & Sassaman, 2012; Caldwell, 1958, p. 21).

By 5000 BC, conflicts appear to have intensified with the development of revenge-based blood feuding in resource-rich areas. Feuding is one outgrowth of increasingly intensified bouts of spontaneous lethal conflict over resources and raiding among segmental groups. One intriguing question is why widespread, complex societies, with the exception of Dalton, first emerged in eastern North America around 5000 BC and not earlier. The answer may lie in widespread aridity and the resulting expansion of pine forests (Delcourt & Delcourt, 2004) that brought about environmental circumscription. Population pressure also may have been a significant variable of cultural elaboration as group circumscription in comparatively resource-rich zones placed pressure on, and generated competition for, resources. As pine forests expanded, populations increased and mobility decreased. Interaction among foragers appears to have intensified, forcing people into more restricted territorial ranges. Critical population density and spacing thresholds were thus reached at a time when climatic uncertainty was increased (Anderson, 2001), fueling collective violence and the necessity for cooperative interaction.

Long-distance prestige goods exchange and monumental construction indicate that a family-level forager organization may have been transcended by segmental forms of tribal social organization, including more complex descent groups such as lineages, clans, moieties, and age grades. Mound centers in eastern Louisiana and southern Florida are examples of complex foragers (Anderson, 2004). Given the labor represented in the construction of mounds and earthworks, these societies appear to be culminations, rather than the beginnings of tribal organization. This initial evidence for widespread tribal social organization is marked by long-distance exchange networks, increased social interaction, subsistence intensification, monumental construction, ceremonial behavior, individual status differences, lapidary crafting, territorial marking by cemeteries, buffer zones, alliances, gift exchange, and intergroup conflict.

Sedentism and the appearance of cemeteries also appear as early as 4000 BC in some resource-rich areas. With the emergence of fixed territories, there may have been competition for resources, resulting in sporadic tribal feuding and territorial marking by mounds and cemeteries. The relatively sudden establishment of cemeteries and burial mounds near resource-rich river valleys seems to mark a dramatic change in the Archaic lifestyle (Charles & Buikstra, 1983). Base camps, and in some instances year-round settlements, flourished because of the diverse and relatively abundant nearby food resources. If a group wished to claim rights of ownership and inheritance to such resources, one logical way to do so would be through maintenance of corporate cemeteries. Prominent Middle Archaic bluff-top cemeteries would be seen then as indicators of hereditary rights by unilineal descent groups to important local resources that were energetically and kinetically defended. Conflict and tensions would have been likely to "erupt into outright violence when people were unwilling or unable to relinquish claims to favorable places; that is, when they could not easily resolve their differences by simply walking away. Conflicts probably broadened and intensified when neighboring groups fell on hard times, making it more difficult for people to move or expand their territories in search of desperately needed food" (Milner, (2004, p. 47).

Worsening intergroup relations coincided with greater exchange in exotic items, suggesting that alliance formation, compensation payments, and diplomatic efforts incorporating gift-giving were becoming necessary and widespread. Distinctive symbolic weaponry continued in importance in the form of hypertrophic or exaggerated biface blades and bannerstones (i.e., atlatl "weights"); both were designed to make emphatic statements about cultural identity, especially in the context of interprovincial alliance and coalitions. Their large size, elaborate shape, skilled craftsmanship, and exotic material transcend the technical requirements or ordinary tolerances for mundane weaponry. Feuding at this time is reflected in buffer zones, mass burials, trophy-taking behavior, and violent deaths based on embedded dart points, skeletal trauma, and scalping. The increase in archaeological evidence for violence suggests that food or other resources may have been contested by local groups, resulting in retaliation for trespass and theft.

The emergence of tribal organization in eastern North America is associated with a rise in violent conflict among hunter-gatherer groups (Bridges, Jacobi, & Powell, 2000; Smith, 1997). Increased exploitation of rich, riverine resources, especially those found in shoal environments, brought about population growth within a circumscribed environment. Economies specializing in intensive harvesting of narrow spectrum subsistence items often exhibit increased conflict resulting from efforts to restrict access to critical resources in favored localities through territorial control. Intergroup conflict may have been based on increased territorial boundary marking and its enforcement (Price and Brown, 1985, p. 12), as well as population growth brought about by innovations in subsistence technology such as storage. The combination of environment and demography may have set the stage for the early appearance of complex forager conflict (Haas, 1999, pp. 22–23), with new forms of conflict resolution.

By 1200 BC local plants, including chenopodium, knotweed, little barley, marshelder, maygrass, sumpweed, sunflower, and local squashes or gourds, were being domesticated by eastern North American populations. Foragers had been collecting these seedy flora as wild plants for millennia, but now gardening was becoming increasingly important. Their nutritional value is extremely high, with some oily seeds like marshelder and sunflower proving to be excellent sources of fat, while starchy seeds such as chenopodium, knotweed, and maygrass were used for their carbohydrates. Harvest yields comparable to those for maize can be obtained from some of these plants (Fritz, 1990). Limited cultivation increased the available food supply and consequently human population levels, tying people to specific tracts of land where their gardens were located. Cultivation resulted in further reducing group mobility (Gremillion, 1996). Evidence for domestication is rare in areas of low population density such as the Atlantic and Gulf Coastal Plains, Florida, the Lower Mississippi Valley, and the Northeast, suggesting that these populations retained a generalized foraging strategy and lower levels of conflict.

Food shortages may have stressed Late Archaic hunter-gatherers between 3000 and 1000 BC, as population increased and well-defined, restricted territories became smaller, bringing about foraging for less-preferred food plants and increased energy expenditure in food collecting and processing. As alternative resource areas became inaccessible, raiding one's neighbors may have become a viable option, relying on gift exchange partnerships and kin networks for transitory alliances and coalitionary support. The demise of bannerstones as an exchange item around 1200 BC signals a change in the components of the interregional alliance protocol, if not the function and nature of the exchange system itself.

Raiding, resulting in violent death and alliance formation, grew in intensity in the Mid-South and Midwest by the Late Archaic period, showing a pattern of feuding characterized by trophy-taking behaviors, human bone modification, mass burials, pincushioning—that is, shooting a person full of arrows—broken and fractured bones, and embedded projectile points. In general, there is a low but sustained level of mortality from violence. Periods of collective violence through organized intergroup raiding by unilineal kin groups apparently took place (Bridges et al., 2000; Jacobi, 2007; Mensforth, 2007), though some examples probably resulted from interpersonal disagreements and social group contests.

Social mechanisms aimed at limiting or controlling violence seems to have resulted from an ecology of blood feuding. Compensation payments in the form of gift exchange would have dampened conflicts, creating a foundation for ritualized gift giving and the social restraint mechanisms that minimized intertribal conflict and violence. Late Archaic mortuary ceremonialism may have provided the context for assuaging intercommunity descent group hostilities and promoting an atmosphere of cooperation and trust among Late Archaic forager-gardeners.

Widespread gift exchange and monumental construction, along with increased emphasis on horticulture and a unilineal descent group political economy, continued in the post-Archaic Woodland period from about 1000 BC to AD 1000. While entrenched feuding would have been difficult to minimize, hostilities and deaths appear to have been dampened through alliances, death compensation payments, exchange relationships, marriage brokering, and ritual practices. The Early Woodland period is an especially important time in the reorganization of cooperation and conflict because it represents a shift in emphasis from a Late Archaic style of feuding or raiding to a Middle Woodland pattern of conflict and cooperation based on complex rituals that underwrote restraint mechanisms.

Between roughly 200 BC and AD 400, many diverse communities interacted with one another in a widespread and extensive exchange system based on shared religious rituals and associated iconography (Anderson & Mainfort, 2002). These Middle Woodland foragers continued to supplement their diet with native cultigens in much the same economic pattern as their Late Archaic and Early Woodland ancestors, and the dispersed community organization did not undergo fundamental changes. Middle Woodland raiding, consistent with tribal intercommunity conflict, is evident in the form of trophy iconography, human skeletal trophies, and combat weapons, both utilitarian and symbolic.

The Middle Woodland period throughout eastern North America is marked by a remarkable cultural florescence of tribal societies that engaged in elaborate mortuary customs, complex exchange networks, and massive earth construction carried out by widespread, interacting, and more or less egalitarian, unilineal descent groups. Some of these kin affiliations appear to have been wealthier and possessed more authority than other descent groups, exercising considerable influence over long-distance exchange, public rituals, and monumental earth construction (Anderson & Mainfort, 2002, p. 10). Mounds and earthworks were focal points for rituals and feasts that integrated dispersed kin-based tribal segments (Knight, 2001). As part of the overall transformation of intersocietal conflict from Late Archaic to Middle Woodland, raiding and attempts at its amelioration may have been increasingly channeled into the ritual requirements of alliance, exchange, and marriage that brought about an atmosphere of friendship, restraint, and trust.

Evidence of Middle Woodland feuding comes from several sources. One important piece of information is the association of human trophies with mound burials. While trophy-taking was a minor element of the Late Archaic mortuary pattern, the use of human trophies as burial accompaniments became a major component of the Middle Woodland mortuary program.

Although few burials indicate evidence of violent death, a large proportion of them are accompanied by modified human remains identified as trophies (Seeman, 2007). Among local groups, bouts of intercommunity conflict are typically interspersed with periods of relative peace. For example, a community might engage in a full spectrum of relationships with neighboring communities. While hostilities may be carried out against enemy communities with whom sporadic exchanges may take place, allied communities may achieve restraint and peaceful relations through regular gift exchange, feasting, ritual performance, and reciprocal kin ties established through strategic marriages.

Conflict and cooperation are continuously present in the building of intercommunity alliances, which embody the sociopolitical dynamics of tribal communities (Redmond, 1998, p. 82). These diplomatic nodes and intercommunity coalitions can be important for mobilizing allied raiding parties in times of conflict, and for seeking aid and refuge in time of danger. Thus, the oscillation between violence and peace in intertribal politics typically swings between one reciprocal form of exchange based on alliances to another based on death compensation.

Near the end of the Middle Woodland period a panregional trend toward larger settlements began taking place. Increased settlement aggregation may have resulted from its high resource potential and from defensive responses to increased competition from other aggregated communities. During the fifth and sixth centuries, nucleated villages began to form in some areas. Dramatic changes took place in eastern North America that transformed a raiding style of intercommunity conflict and its associated ritualized restraint mechanisms and institutions of peacemaking into new opportunities for emerging leadership positions and social hierarchy. As a new political and social order was born, innovative institutions for cooperation and conflict were forged, based on large, sedentary populations and a storable surplus generated from the produce of field agriculture.

Village Agriculture and the Rise of Warfare

The third trend, representative of regional or chiefly societies, is warfare and the complex rituals associated with adoption, gift exchange, and marriages that promote alliances, diplomatic relations, and restraint mechanisms. Unlike blood feuding, warfare is organized violence that affects the balance of power between independent political groups or communities (Reyna, 1994; Wolf, 1987). Warfare has clear political objectives, rather than settling descent group grudges or blood feud scores. Chiefly warfare also differs from family-level homicides and local group feuding in that violence now becomes impersonal lethal aggression between communities, and often results in forced political annexation and onerous tribute payments in the form of material goods and social labor. Peaceful relations among chiefly societies are predicated on the establishment of political alliances among neighboring communities or polities achieved through complex forms of diplomacy and ritual.

During late prehistory large militia groups pursue "national" political policies through organized lethal aggression and alliances. In regional polities the key administrators of justice are public officials who comprise chiefly councils that form a truncated democracy and keep peace through legal procedures. Their purpose is to deliver justice within the polity at a minimal amount of violence (Fry, 2006, pp. 110, 159). However, lethal aggression in the form of torture and death may be meted out to nonkin captured from neighboring polities whose spirits are then adopted upon death. Peace systems, such as the League of the Iroquois, were based on the confederation of interdependent polities who sought cooperation, trust, and peaceful behavior as a strategic necessity, while doling out considerable violence to their enemies through mourning wars which sought captives for condolence rituals (Richter, 1983). Stable peace was achieved among the Iroquois Confederation through three key ingredients: institutionalized restraint, compatible social orders, and cultural commonality (Kupchan, 2010, p. 320).

Warfare and efforts to ameliorate violence were widespread and endemic in the mid-continent from AD 1000 to 1700. The major transformations in domestic life; political, religious, and social organization; and subsistence practices also took place during at this time. Social segmentation increased with the widespread development of unilineal descent, principally matrilocality. The shift to matrilocal postmarital residence patterns is evidenced throughout a large area from the Mississippian Southeast and Lower Midwest to the Upper Midwest Oneota and to the Northeastern Iroquoian-speakers. Matrilocal postmarital residence breaks up fraternal interest groups associated with patrilocal residence and promotes militias of unrelated males who are socialized into priestly and warrior organizations. Matrilocal residence is correlated with violent political conflict because relations with neighboring societies tend to be unstable due to an atmosphere of external aggression (Divale, 1984, p. 205).

Changes in subsistence from hunting and gathering to field agriculture over a large area of eastern North America early in the second millennium provided a storable surplus employed by elites as funding for feasts and rituals that attracted social labor necessary for corporate projects. Settlement patterns shifted from mobile horticulturists to sedentary, palisaded villages or towns in which farmers sequestered themselves. These fortified communities were located in defensive and strategic locales. Consequently, an overall decline and deterioration in health takes place as a result of poor nutrition and crowded living conditions (Steadman, 2011). Archaeological evidence for warfare is abundant in the form of skeletal trauma, fortified towns, widespread combat imagery, and symbolic weaponry, interred as burial accompaniments, displayed as ritual caches, and portrayed in legitimizing iconography. Prestige accruing from war honors becomes a critical cultural currency that warriors were mandated to earn and display in order to be prosperous and successful members of society.

By approximately AD 1050, a major world renewal ritual, the New Fire Ceremony, spreads throughout the Midwest and Southeast, and by around AD 1300 the Calumet Ceremony, an alliance and adoption ritual, emerges in the Upper Midwest. Both ceremonies, and perhaps early forms of the "Plains" Sun Dance, became important formal, ritual restraint institutions for creating and maintaining social and political alliances and coalitions. These new rituals, in part, replaced the Middle Woodland mortuary-based institutions of gift exchange and the adoption that had dampened conflict and promoted cooperation and trust.

With the end of the first millennium, community life, religious institutions, and social organization underwent significant alterations across the midcontinent as regional political hierarchies emerged and settlements became increasingly protected and nucleated. Fortified great towns were vivid reminders to the Mississippian people who lived within their protective confines of the potential violence that loomed on the horizon.

A critical change was taking place in the political landscape at the turn of the first millennium, and that change was evident in the way neighboring polities cooperated with and fought one another.

One primary political benefit of nucleated populations centered on providing chiefly elites with the social labor necessary for aggrandizement strategies, monumental construction projects, and ritual performance. Thus, it is not surprising that regional consolidation and population nucleation were accompanied by large-scale labor projects, elevated status differences, and increases in the production of symbolic weaponry and paraphernalia employed in alliance and war rituals.

Successful military campaigns were often based on a chief's ability to forge effective alliances through war councils. Alliances allowed chiefs to create forces larger than a single polity could effectively field and to concentrate and coordinate political partners as coalition members who could help attack enemy polities and their towns. In the spring of 1543, for example, Hernando de Soto thwarted a coalition of some 20 Lower Mississippi Valley chiefs and their respective polities as they planned a massive, coordinated attack against the Spanish encampment (Hudson, 1997, p. 384).

Warfare and settlement nucleation increased as heroic warrior iconography, long distance exchange, and monumental construction decreased around AD 1400. Substantial increase took place in fortified settlements in the upper Midwest and Northeast as a result of climatic-induced stress on crop yields (Milner, 1999, p. 125). In such cases, territorial conflicts often arose from the need to raid vital stored food surpluses. The overall size of Mississippian towns declined and large centers became nonexistent (Holley, 1999). Many of the great centers such as Moundville had so shrunk from their former political eminence that their hereditary paramountcy lacked any real political power (Knight & Steponaitis, 1998, p. 23).

The Etowah site, located in northwest Georgia, was abandoned, perhaps because of a devastating attack, never to regain its regional importance and preeminence (King, 2003). A number of Mississippian chiefdoms throughout much of the Midsouth and Midwest collapsed in the fourteenth century, leaving the area vacant for some 400 years. This abandonment may have been a consequence of regional devastating multidecadel droughts. The end result was the exacerbation of an already "competitive and often hostile political climate" (Cobb & Butler, 2002, p. 637).

Mississippian elites employed power and ritual strategies that emphasized "more secular measures, including the overt use of force" (Anderson, 1994, p. 137). By AD 1400 emphasis that had been placed upon supernaturally charged prestige goods was replaced by overriding concerns with regional political-military conflict. A competitive landscape generated chiefly struggles as regional elite rivalries escalated. Neighboring polities shifted between transitory alliances and violent warfare to extend or break free from political domination and crippling tribute payments (King, 2006, p. 83).

A pattern of population dispersal in some areas and coalescence in others is reflected in the dramatic and fairly widespread episode of decline and abandonment prior to the arrival of epidemic diseases and European settlers (Smith, 1996, p. 316). Throughout much of the Eastern Woodlands, warfare had developed into a well-orchestrated pattern of offensive and defensive strategies and tactics based on blood revenge, captives, ritual demands, and war honors. Surprise raids, skirmishes, and ambushes were carried out in conjunction with episodic large-scale attacks across broad and extensive buffer zones between neighboring polities. Early European accounts document chiefly forces composed of allies who organized large militias that were equally agile on land and water (DePratter, 1983, pp. 49–55). The fifteenth and early sixteenth centuries witnessed increased tensions and strife. Frequent and perhaps intense warfare is reflected in weapons trauma on skeletal remains (Anderson, 1999, p. 224). Decline of the widespread prestige goods exchange and deteriorating climate almost certainly are linked to the increase in conflict as elite interaction and exchange relations curtailed the ability of chiefs to ameliorate or dampen hostilities with neighboring polities. Complex diplomatic relations facilitated peaceful negotiations by "calm minds" on both sides through peace chiefs and priestly councils (Lee, 2007).

For chiefs to be successful against their enemies they needed a well-coordinated military organization that was based on hierarchical structure and formal institutions. The descent-group-based nature of political organization provided chiefs with a ready-made framework for warrior militias. Hierarchical arrangements provided the organizational capability to create effective chains of command based on graded military ranks. Political efficacy was constructed on formalized and structured balance in the complementary opposition of peace and war based on formal, named dual divisions: the White (peace) and Red (war) organizations (Gearing 1962; Lankford, 2008, pp. 73–97).

Red and white oppositional patterns may be seen in Mississippian utilitarian ritual ware, reflecting the metaphoric imagery of religious beliefs and cosmology coupled with war and peace rituals. To facilitate political action, a widespread protocol based on tightly structured etiquette existed for leaders throughout eastern North America who wished to pursue interpolity diplomatic negotiations (Brown, 2006; Hall, 1997). Rituals associated with establishing peaceful relations and welding binding alliances were complex, elaborate, and symbolic.

European accounts from the sixteenth to eighteenth centuries provide rich ethnohistoric details of stately processions, metaphoric speeches, obligatory feasting, competitive gift exchange, ritual dancing, offerings of tobacco, cleansing through smoking and medicinal drinks, displays of status, mock combat with symbolic weaponry, and adoption of leaders. A primary objective of diplomatic negotiations was an individual's adoption into an unrelated family, a metaphoric act that defined the relationships and obligations between two leaders and their respective communities or polities. A standardized, international set of established rules, employed by strangers to avert violence and to weave alliances, incorporated ritual adoption that was based on earlier Woodland mortuary ceremonialism and spirit adoption (Hall, 1997). The key to proper protocol for "well-mannered" visitations was a complex set of symbolic and ritual behaviors, the ultimate goal of which was to establish and maintain peaceful relations or to form the foundation for political and military alliances. Peacemaking and warfare involved chiefly councils for advice and solutions to persistent and perennial problems that faced ruling elites. With European contact, fundamental changes would be wrought to indigenous institutions through pandemics, slave raids, and European-style warfare.

Conclusion

There is strong evidence for the coevolution of various forms of conflict and degrees of sociocultural integration by indigenous people in eastern North America. Haas notes that "the economic and demographic conditions that are conducive to violence are also conducive to the development of complex, centralized polities" (Haas, 2001, p. 343). The central premise here is that a strong relationship exists between the organizational characteristics of a society and the motives and objectives of aggression and peacemaking. The institutions of diplomacy were fundamentally intertwined with different forms of social organization despite the multiplicity of languages. A principal feature of alliance formation rested on adoption; gift exchange, especially symbolic weaponry; and marriage. Ranging from unsegmented family-level hunters and gatherers to segmented village agriculturalists, kinship bound people in a web of interconnected relationships based on genetic or marriage ties, consanguines or affines, and adoption of the living or the vital forces of the dead.

Conflict and efforts to seek alliances are well-documented archaeologically in eastern North America, beginning with the rise of tribal societies around 5,000 BC. Prior to the beginning of feuding, homicides may have been the primary means of justice seeking. The difference between these early foragers, who sought redress through homicides and revenge, and the later societies with high frequencies of feuding and raiding is the absence of segmentary systems among the former and the presence of segmentary social units within the latter. Unsegmented societies generally lack permanent extended families and the development of lineages or clans. While they sometimes do exhibit homicides, revenge homicides, and group sanctioned executions, organized group violence is rare.

Segmentary social groups, such as tribes and regional polities, exhibit high levels of feuding and death rates per capita, torture, an emerging warrior ethos, and trophy-taking behavior. Feuding often begins in environments rich in resources in which societies "can afford to have enemies for neighbors" (Kelly, 2000, p. 135). Lack of resources encourages cooperation that is mutually beneficial for foragers. As population increases, reliable storage facilities and surplus come into being, bringing about the emergence of segmentary organization and the increased likelihood of feuding. With greater use of base camps in highly productive, resource-rich coastal and riverine environments, evidence for social segmentation and raiding is clearly evident.

The transformation from feuding to warfare among regional polities centered on storable surpluses and the political ambitions of chiefs to consolidate political authority within their polities, as well as to establish external relationships with neighbors through alliances, tribute, or incorporation. Diplomatic negotiation rituals limited violence and promoted peaceful social interactions. Social segmentation became increasingly hierarchical, underwriting both military and diplomatic structures.

Peace is not just an absence of war and violence, but it is "a different way of living with its own distinctive signatures and practices" (Arkush, 2008, p. 564). Peacemaking goes hand in hand with lethal aggression, but the capacity for violence is tempered with the potential for highly elaborated peacemaking institutions. While no society is totally devoid of violence, eastern North American societies were highly skilled at complex rituals and political and social behaviors that ameliorated conflicts, promoted cooperation, and achieved restraint.

Acknowledgments

I would like to express my gratitude to Doug Fry and Johan van der Dennen for their invitation to attend the workshop, "Aggression and Peacemaking in an Evolutionary Context" convened at Leiden University in 2010. Pauline Vincenten's assistance with travel plans to the beautiful and enchanting city of Leiden is most appreciated. My thanks are also extended to Leiden University, the Lorentz Center, and the workshop sponsors for their generous support. I am most grateful to Doug Fry for his invitation to contribute to this volume. Support from Dean Henry Kurtz and Associate Dean Linda A. Bennett, of the College of Arts and Sciences (University of Memphis—Donovan Travel Enrichment Fund), was crucial for travel to The Netherlands. Finally, my appreciation to Brian Ferguson, Doug Fry, Jonathan Haas, Bob Kelly, Charles McNutt, Bob Sussman, and Patty Jo Watson for their comments on this chapter.

References

Anderson, D. G. (1994). *The Savannah River chiefdoms: Political change in the late prehistoric Southeast*. Tuscaloosa: University of Alabama Press.

Anderson, D. G. (1996a). Models of Paleoindian and early Archaic settlement in the lower Southeast. In D. G. Anderson, & K. E. Sassaman (Eds.), *The Paleoindian and early Archaic Southeast* (pp. 29–57). Tuscaloosa: University of Alabama Press.

Anderson, D. G. (1996b). Approaches to modeling regional settlement in the Archaic period Southeast. In K. E. Sassaman, & D. G. Anderson (Eds.), *Archaeology of the Mid-Holocene Southeast* (pp. 157–176). Gainesville, University Press of Florida.

Anderson, D. G. (1999). Examining chiefdoms in the Southeast: An application of multiscalar analysis. In J. E. Neitzel (Ed.), *Great towns and regional polities in the prehistoric American Southwest and Southeast* (pp. 215–241). Albuquerque: University of New Mexico Press.

Anderson, D. G. (2001). Climate and culture change in prehistoric and early historic eastern North America. *Archaeology of Eastern North America, 29*,143–186.

Anderson, D. G. (2002). The evolution of tribal social organization in the Southeastern U.S. In W. A. Parkinson (Ed.), *Archaeology of tribal societies* (pp. 246–277). Archaeological Series 15. Ann Arbor: International Monographs in Prehistory.

Anderson, D. G. (2004). Archaic mounds and the archaeology of Southeastern tribal societies. In J. L. Gibson, & P. J. Carr (Eds.), *Signs of power: The rise of cultural complexity in the Southeast* (pp. 270–299). Tuscaloosa: University of Alabama Press.

Anderson, D. G., & Mainfort, R C., Jr. (2002). An introduction to Woodland archaeology in the Southeast. In D. G. Anderson, & R. C. Mainfort, Jr. (Eds.), *The Woodland Southeast* (pp. 1–19). Tuscaloosa: University of Alabama Press.

Anderson, D. G., & Sassaman, K. E. (2012). *Recent developments in Southeastern archaeology: From colonization to complexity.* Washington, DC: Society for American Archaeology Press.

Arkush, E. (2008).Warfare and violence in the Americas. *American Antiquity, 73,* 560–575.

Boehm, C. (1987). *Blood revenge: The enactment and management of conflict in Montenegro and other tribal societies* (2nd ed.). Philadelphia: University of Pennsylvania Press.

Bridges, P. S., Jacobi, K. P., & Powell, M. L. (2000). Warfare-related trauma in the late prehistory of Alabama. In P. M. Lambert (Ed.), *Bioarchaeological studies of life in the age of agriculture: A view from the Southeast* (pp. 35–62). Tuscaloosa: University of Alabama Press.

Brown, I. W. (2006). The calumet ceremony in the Southeast as observed archaeologically. In G. A. Waselkov, P. H. Wood, & T. Hatley (Eds.), *Powhatan's mantle: Indians in the colonial Southeast* (pp. 371–419). Revised and expanded edition. Lincoln: University of Nebraska Press.

Caldwell, J. R. (1958). *Trend and tradition in the prehistory of the eastern United States.* Springfield: Illinois State Museum.

Carneiro, R. L. (1988). The circumscription theory: Challenge and response. *American Behavioral Scientist, 31,* 497–511.

Charles, D. K., & Buikstra, J. E. (1983) Archaic mortuary sites in the Central Mississippi drainage: Distribution, structure, and behavioral implications. In J. L. Phillips, & J. A. Brown (Eds.), *Archaic hunters and gatherers in the American Midwest* (pp. 117–145). New York: Academic Press.

Cobb, C. R., & Butler, B. M. (2002). The vacant quarter revisited: Late Mississippian abandonment of the Lower Ohio valley. *American Antiquity, 67,* 625–641.

Delcourt, P. A., & Delcourt, H. R. (2004). *Prehistoric Native Americans and ecological change: Human ecosystems in eastern North America since the Pleistocene.* New York: Cambridge University Press.

DePratter, C. B. (1983). Late prehistoric and early historic chiefdoms in the Southeastern United States. Unpublished Ph.D. dissertation, Department of Anthropology. Athens: University of Georgia.

Divale, W. T. (1984). *Matrilocal residence in pre-literate society.* Ann Arbor: UMI Research Press.

Fritz, G. J. (1990). Multiple pathways to farming in precontact eastern North America. *Journal of World Prehistory, 4,* 387–435.

Fry, D. P. (2006). *The human potential for peace: An anthropological challenge to assumptions about war and violence.* Oxford: Oxford University Press.

Fry, D. P. (2007). *Beyond war: The human potential for peace.* Oxford: University of Oxford Press.

Fry, D. P. (2011). Human nature: The nomadic forager model. In R. W. Sussman and C.R. Cloninger (Eds.), *Origins of altruism and cooperation* (pp. 227–248). New York: Springer.

Gearing, F. O. (1962). *Priests and warriors: Social structure for Cherokee politics in the eighteenth century.* Memoir 91. Washington, DC: American Anthropological Association.

Gremillion, K. J. (1996). The paleoethnobotanical record for the Mid-Holocene Southeast. In K. Sassaman, & D. G. Anderson (Eds.), *Archaeology of the Mid-Holocene Southeast* pp. (99–114). Gainesville: University Presses of Florida.

Haas, J. (1999). The origins of war and ethnic violence. In J. Carman, & A. Harding (Eds.), *Ancient warfare: Archaeological perspectives* (pp. 11–24). Stroud: Sutton.

Haas, J. (2001). Warfare and the evolution of culture. In G. M. Feinman, & T. D. Price (Eds.), *Archaeology at the millennium: A sourcebook* (pp. 329–350). New York: Kluwer Academic/Plenum.

Hall, R. L. (1997). *An archaeology of the soul: North American Indian belief and ritual.* Urbana: University of Illinois Press.

Holley, G. R. (1999). Late prehistoric towns in the Southeast. In J. E. Neitzel, (Eds.), *Great towns and regional polities in the prehistoric American Southwest and Southeast* (pp. 23–38). Albuquerque: University of New Mexico Press.

Hudson, C. (1997). *Knights of Spain, warriors of the Sun: Hernando de Soto and the South's ancient chiefdoms.* Tuscaloosa: University of Alabama Press.

Jacobi, K. P. (2007). Disabling the dead: Human trophy taking in the prehistoric Southeast. In R. J. Chacon, & D. H. Dye (Eds.), *The taking and displaying of human body parts as trophies by Amerindians* (pp. 299–338). New York: Springer.

Johnson, G. A. (1982). Organizational structure and scalar stress. In C. Renfrew, M. J. Rowlands, & B. A. Segraves, (Eds.), *Theory and explanation in archaeology: The Southhampton conference* (pp. 389–421). New York: Academic Press.

Kelly, R. C. (2000). *Warless societies and the origin of war.* Ann Arbor: University of Michigan Press.

Kelly, R. C. (2005). The evolution of lethal intergroup violence. *Proceedings of the National Academy of Sciences, 102,* 15294–15298.

King, A. (2003) *Etowah: The political history of a chiefdom capital.* Tuscaloosa: University of Alabama Press.

King, A. (2006). Leadership strategies and the nature of Mississippian chiefdoms in northern Georgia. In B. M. Butler, & P. D. Welch, (Eds.), *Leadership and polity in Mississippian society* (pp. 73–90). Center for Archaeological Investigations, Occasional Paper No. 33. Carbondale: Southern Illinois University.

Knight, V. J., Jr. (2001). Feasting and the emergence of platform mound ceremonialism in western North America. In M. Dietler, & B. Hayden, (Eds.), *Feasts: Archaeological and ethnographic perspectives on food, politics, and power* (pp. 311–333). Washington, D.C.: Smithsonian Institution Press.

Knight, V. J., Jr., & Steponaitis, V. P. (1998). A new history of Moundville. In V. J. Knight, Jr., & V. P. Steponaitis, (Eds.), *Archaeology of the Moundville chiefdom* (pp. 1–25). Washington, D.C.: Smithsonian Institution Press.

Koldehoff, B., & Walthall, J.A. (2009). Dalton and the early Holocene Midcontinent: Setting the stage. In T. E. Emerson, D. L. McElrath, & A. C. Fortier (Eds.), *Archaic societies: Diversity and complexity across the Midcontinent* (pp. 137–151). State University of New York Press, Albany.

Kupchan, C. A. (2010). *How enemies become friends: The sources of stable peace.* Princeton: Princeton University Press.

Lankford, G. E. (2008). *Looking for lost lore: Studies in folklore, ethnology, and iconography.* Tuscaloosa: University of Alabama Press.

Lee, W. E. (2007). Peace chiefs and blood revenge: Patterns of restraint in Native American warfare, 1500–1800. *The Journal of Military History, 71,* 701–141.

Meltzer, D. J. (2009). *First peoples in a New World: Colonizing Ice Age America.* Berkeley: University of California Press.

Mensforth, R. P. (2007). Human trophy taking in eastern North America during the Archaic period: Its relationship to demographic change, warfare, and the evolution of segmented social organizations. In R. J. Chacon, & D. H. Dye, (Eds.), *The taking and displaying of human body parts as trophies by Amerindians* (pp. 222–277). New York: Springer.

Milner, G. R. (1999). Warfare in prehistoric and early historic eastern North America. *Journal of Archaeological Research, 7,* 105–151.

Milner, G. R. (2004). *The moundbuilders: Ancient peoples of eastern North America.* London: Thames & Hudson.

Morse, D. F. (1997). An overview of the Dalton period in northeastern Arkansas and in the southeastern United States. In Dan F. Morse, (Ed.), *Sloan: A Paleoindian Dalton cemetery in Arkansas* (pp. 123–139). Washington, D.C.: Smithsonian Institution Press.

Price, T. D., & Brown, J. A. (Eds.). 1985. *Prehistoric hunter-gatherers: The emergence of cultural complexity.* New York: Academic Press.

Redmond, E. (1998). In war and peace: Alternative paths to centralized leadership. In E. Redmond, (Ed.), *Chiefdoms and chieftaincy in the Americas* (pp. 68–103). Gainesville: University Press of Florida.

Reyna, S. P. (1994) A mode of domination approach to organized violence. In S. P. Reyna, & R. E. Downs, (Eds.), *Studying war: Anthropological perspectives* (pp. 29–65). New York: Gordon and Breach.

Richter, D. K. (1983). War and culture: The Iroquois experience. *William and Mary Quarterly, 40,* 528–559.

Sassaman, K. E. (2005). Structure and practice in the Southeast. In T. R. Pauketat, & D. Di Paolo Loren, (Eds.), *North American archaeology* (pp. 79–107). Cambridge (MA): Blackwell.

Seeman, M. F. (2007). Predatory war and Hopewell trophy-taking. In R. J. Chacon, & D. H. Dye, (Eds.), *The taking and displaying of human body parts as trophies by Amerindians* (pp. 167–189). New York: Springer.

Smith, B. D. (1996). Agricultural chiefdoms of the eastern Woodlands. In B. G Trigger, & W. E. Washburn, (Eds.), *The Cambridge history of the native peoples of the Americas,* Vol. 1, Part 1 (pp., 267–323). New York: Cambridge University Press.

Smith, M. O. (1997). Osteological indications of warfare in the Archaic period of the western Tennessee valley. In D. L. Martin, & D. W. Frayer, (Eds.), *Troubled times: Violence and warfare in the past* (pp. 241–265). New York: Gordon and Breach.

Speth, J. D., Newlander, K., White, A.D., Lemke, A. K., & Anderson, L. E. (in press). Early Paleoindian big-game hunting in North America: Provisioning or politics? *Quaternary International.*

Sponsel, L. E. (2011). The possibilities of a nonkilling anthropology: Challenging the apologists for war and providing a reason and an agenda for peace. Paper presented at the 110th annual meeting of the American Anthropological Association meeting, Montreal.

Steadman, D. (2011). Health hazards models in the middle Cumberland drainage. Paper presented at the Short NSF Team Seminar, School for Advanced Research, "Warfare and the epidemiological transition," Santa Fe.

Walthall, J. A., & Koldehoff, B. (1998). Hunter-gatherer interaction and alliance formation: Dalton and the cult of the long blade. *Plains Anthropologist, 43*, 257–273.

Wolf, E. R. (1987). Cycles of violence: The anthropology of war and peace. In K. Moore (Ed.), *Waymarks: The Notre Dame inaugural lectures in anthropology* (pp. 127–150). Notre Dame: University of Notre Dame Press.

9

From the Peaceful to the Warlike

Ethnographic and Archaeological Insights into Hunter-Gatherer Warfare and Homicide

Robert L. Kelly

In the early twentieth century, hunter-gatherers were considered to have lived Hobbesian lives, a war of all against all. But that view changed dramatically by the 1960s, and especially after the 1966 *Man the Hunter* conference. The Bushmen figured prominently in this makeover, as revealed by the title of Elizabeth Marshall Thomas's 1959 book, *The Harmless People*. And this vision remains popular on the Internet today, where hunter-gatherers are often portrayed as living the lives we all desire, ones of peace, tranquility, and harmony.

But while life in foraging societies is not a Hobbesian hell, neither is it all sweetness and light. Years ago, Carol Ember (1978) and, later, Lawrence Keeley (1996) showed that many foraging societies experience violence that is sometimes lethal. This should surprise no one since lethal violence in small, egalitarian communities can arise from the denial of anger that comes with the politics of nonconfrontation that typify egalitarian societies—one can only keep a lid on animosities for so long. Foraging societies have mechanisms to resolve disputes, and one of these is to vocalize an ethos of non-violence (see Fry, 2006, 2011). Indeed, a few foraging societies known to ethnography experience very little violence (e.g., the Malaysian Batek or the Indian Paliyan; see Endicott & Endicott, 2008; Endicott, chapter 12; Gardner, 2000; Gardner, chapter 15). But for many others, the mechanisms to resolve disputes sometimes fail (Gurven & Kaplan, 2007), and opponents may come to blows. Wrangham, Wilson, and Muller (2006), for example, calculated a median homicide rate of 164/100,000 for foragers; compare this to the 1990s US homicide rate of 5.5/100,000.

But my purpose here is not to ask if foragers are violent or not, but rather what conditions variation in levels of violence. We will look at this from both ethnographic and archaeological perspectives. Although I discuss egalitarian and nonegalitarian foragers below, I do not want the reader to assume that one of these groups represents human nature more than another. Instead, my objective is to show that war and homicide are linked to issues of resource imbalance, and that demonstrations of the frequency of war among foragers or of its antiquity should not lead us to assume that humans have a stronger proclivity for violence than they do for peace.

Ethnographic Data on Homicide and War Among Foragers

Let's first consider the nature of homicide statistics among foragers (Table 9.1). The actual number of murders is low—for example, the San Ildefonso Agta rate of 129/100,000 is based on 11 murders (including at least two by outsiders) over a 43-year period, or about one murder every four years (Early & Headland, 1998). Visit the Agta, or the Ju/'hoansi, or the Hadza most years and you, too, would label them a "harmless people."

By convention, homicide rates are given as the number of murders per 100,000 person-years, but the relevant group size for foragers is far smaller. The "peaceful" Semai, for example, saw only two murders over a 22-year period (Dentan, 1968). But in such a small population Bruce Knauft (1987, p. 458) found these two murders translates into a homicide rate of 30/100,000. But what's the relevant population? Robert Dentan (1988) replied that the base population is larger than Knauft assumed, and that the rate is consequently closer to 1/100,000 (I don't think the data are adequate to calculate an actual rate, though I suspect it is closer to Dentan's estimate). In small groups, it takes only a few deaths to alter the rate significantly. The Hadza rate increases from 6.6 to 40/100,000 if three murders by neighboring Datoga are included (Marlowe, 2010, p. 141; Blurton-Jones, Hawkes & O'Connell, 2002). For the same reason, "extenuating circumstances" can alter the rate. In 5 of the 11 San Ildefonso murders, for example, alcohol was a significant contributing factor (as it is everywhere; see e.g., Marlowe, 2002; Butovskaya, chapter 14; Tonkinson, chapter 13). Would the rate have been lower without the booze? One solution to these issues is to collect data over long spans of time. But since ethnographers cannot be present for decades, this means relying on informants' memories (e.g., Lee, 1979, Table 13.2), which are not always accurate.

Likewise, Lee (1979) argued that to be fair in comparing forager homicide rates to that of the United States we should include people killed in wars; doing so for the Vietnam era Lee found that the US rate was 100/100,000—and would be even higher if we included those who survived what might otherwise have been a lethal attack because of rapid medical care.

The Ache and Hiwi rates stand out in Table 9.1: 500 and 1018/100,000, respectively (the Piegan data reflect one short period of warfare, and are a guess more than an estimate). However, these numbers are not directly comparable to the other figures.

TABLE 9.1 **Homicide Rates Among Hunter-Gatherers with Data
to Calculate Population Pressure**

Group	NAGP[a]	Ratio[b]	Population Density (persons/100km²)	Population Pressure (ln)[c]	Homicide rate[d]	Reference
Hadza	1246	3.8	24	5.284641	6.6	Marlowe, 2010, p. 141
Andamanese	4400	0.5	40	4.007333	20	Keeley, 1996, Table 6.1
Ju/'hoansi[e]	570	3.8	6.6	5.793568	42	Lee, 1979
San Ildefonso Agta	3856	0.4	38	3.703509	129	Early & Headland, 1998, p. 103
Gidjingali	1904	0.4	72.7	2.34908	148	Hiatt, 1965
Tiwi[f]	2273	0.4	37.5	3.188224	160	Keeley, 1996, Table 6.1
Yaghan	484	0.2	4.8	3.004031	169	Cooper,1917, in Wrangham et al., 2005
Yurok	685	0.8	131	1.431078	240	Keeley, 1996, Table 6.1
Casiguran Agta	4512	0.4	87	3.032297	326	Headland, 1989
Murngin	1969	0.4	11.7	4.209402	330	Keeley, 1996, Table 6.1
Modoc	195	0.8	22.9	1.918719	450	Keeley, 1996, Table 6.1
Ache	2480	0.4	14	4.260666	500	Hill et al., 2007
Hiwi	2895	0.3	4.3	5.308153	1018	Hill et al., 2007
Piegan	348	0.2	4.3	2.78415	1000	Keeley 1996, Table 6.1
Batek[g]	3315	0.4	13	4.624973	1	Endicott & Endicott, 2008

[a] From Binford (2001).

[b] Following Keeley's (1988) lead, NAGP is multiplied by a fraction (from Kelly 1983, Table 3, column 5) to reflect the portion of NAGP that is edible by humans and large fauna. The value used for the Hiwi accounts for the fact that large portions of Hiwi territory are not productive (Kim Hill, personal communication, 2011).

[c] Population pressure is (NAGP * ratio)/population density.

[d] Many are warfare deaths alone (especially from Keeley, 1996; Piegan is only warfare deaths); for those, taking intrasocietal deaths into account would increase the rate.

[e] Lee (1979: 398) gives the Ju/'hoansi homicide rate as 29/100,000, based on 22 murders over a 50-year period, 1920–1970. However, he notes that murders ceased about 1955 due to the presence of an outside police force; for a 35-year period this results in a rate of 42/100,000.

[f] For the years1893–1903; this is perhaps too short a time period to establish a "normal" homicide rate.

[g] Endicott and Endicott (2008; see Endicott, chapter 12) do not specifically state that the homicide rate is 0/100,000, but they did seek out instances of violence, recording only a few, and only 1 possible homicide (which for purposes of this table would be counted as infanticide). I gave them a minimal rate of 1/100,000 so that the log could be taken and made comparable to other data in the table.

The Hiwi (precontact) rate includes all violent deaths, including murders by Hiwi, murders by Venezuelans, suicide, and infanticide. Breaking the data down (Hill, Hurtado, & Walker, 2007, Table 4), murders by Hiwi themselves only account for 7 percent of all deaths (8.5 percent if we remove those killed by Venezuelans; 22 percent of all deaths are a result of homicide if we add the Venezuelan murders). Among the Ache, 39 percent of all infant (0–3 years) deaths resulted from infanticide or child homicide (e.g., burial with a deceased parent), and 17 percent of all juvenile deaths (4–14 years). About 9 percent of adult deaths are a result of homicide or club fights (Hill & Hurtado, 1996, Table 5.1). These modified rates of the Hiwi and Ache are closer to that of the Agta, Ju/'hoansi, and Hadza, where violence, not including infanticide, suicide, or external murders, accounts for 3–7 percent of deaths.

Still, there is variability in violent death among foragers, whether we are talking about intragroup murder, warfare, raiding, infanticide, or other child murders. Hill et al. (2007) suggest low homicide rates are a product of colonial intervention and that prehistoric foragers may have witnessed higher rates. An overarching authority to which individuals could petition for redress can restrict violence (Knauft, 1987, p. 476), and such authorities did apparently stem violence among the Ju/'hoansi (Lee, 1979), Ache (Hill & Hurtado, 1996, p. 155), Inuit (Burch, 2007), and Agta (Early & Headland, 1998, p. 115), although we do not know by how much. On the other hand, Blurton-Jones et al. (2002) discount the role of outsiders in maintaining the Hadza's low murder rate.

Foragers tend to have low rates of non-lethal violence (such as fist-fights; Wrangham et al., 2006), but this comes from the cultural denial of aggression in small egalitarian communities rather than the lack of squabbles. Turnbull (1965), for example, recorded a noteworthy dispute every 3–4 days among the Mbuti (see also Ness, Helfrecht, Hagen, Sell & Hewlett, 2010). These disputes were motivated by jealousy (often over women) or some slight, real or perceived. When Jean Briggs (1970) entitled her book on an Inuit family, *Never in Anger* she did not mean that the Inuit are never angry, only that it is inappropriate to show it. The violence that can erupt in foraging communities often has no particular objective other than expressing anger; where that anger becomes lethal, it is "blood drunkenness," a product of rage, not calculated risk, and may even be a form of temporary mental illness (Knauft, 1991, p. 400).

Violence can take many forms, and since these forms can have different proximate causes, it is important to sort them out. Keeley (1996), for example, classifies Australia Aboriginal society as warlike egalitarian foragers, but Fry (2006) demonstrates that most of this fighting was rare, and usually fell under the category of feuding or revenge killings rather than warfare (we will get to a definition of warfare in a moment). Previous cross-cultural studies of war or "intergroup aggression" (e.g., Ember, 1978; Keeley, 1996) do not separate deaths from interpersonal homicide from those resulting from war or raiding. Wrangham et al. (2006), for example, list the Ju/'hoansi's homicides as intergroup aggression when Lee's (1979) account makes it clear that these deaths resulted from individual disputes over women or insults.

In the standard cross-cultural sample (SCCS; Murdock & White, 1969), the reasons given for homicide among nomadic foragers are revenge, disputes over women (including adultery; see e.g., Marlowe, 2010; Lee, 1979), crimes, and execution (see Fry, 2011). These different causes have in common the fact that someone gets hurt (and that it is usually men who do the hurting; Ness et al., 2010), but something is lost by collapsing these different behaviors into a single measure. Unfortunately, it is difficult to separate the different forms of violence with the current data (Table 9.1). Below, we will look at the prevalence of one form of violence, internal warfare among foragers; that will lead us to look at the general homicide statistics in a new light.

Warfare

Put most simply, war is "relatively impersonal lethal aggression between communities" (Fry, 2006, p. 91). "Impersonal" does not mean that warriors are not passionate. In fact, leaders must inspire passion if they want their followers to put their lives on the line and to kill someone who has personally done them no wrong. They accomplish the latter in part by what R. C. Kelly (2000) calls "social substitutability"—the idea that a wrong can be righted by killing anyone in another group containing the offending member or members. War is often fought for revenge, or to retaliate for some slight, but I suspect that for a *group* to be compelled to retaliate, rather than just the offended party, the goal must also be to secure some advantage: to acquire slaves, women, food, territory, or to make a preemptive strike. It is important to separate war from other forms of violence because fighting to secure an advantage and fighting out of passion are two different things (this is the difference between hostile and instrumental aggression; Berkowitz, 1993). There is rarely a direct calculation of risk when a man sets off in a rage to kill his wife's lover or revenge his brother's death, but there is a calculation in warfare, at least by those calling for a raid: is the risk of losing (perhaps one's life) worth the possible benefit of securing an advantage? Such a weighing of costs and benefits means that warfare and perhaps violence in general can be understood from an evolutionary perspective. It becomes complicated, however, because the reason that communities fight is not the reason that the rank-and-file go to war. War requires understanding the relations between the communities involved, but also between the leaders and followers within those communities.

Table 9.2 compiles cross-cultural data on warfare, and its occurrence among egalitarian and nonegalitarian foragers (Fry, 2006, p. 106). Warfare is more common among nonegalitarian hunter-gatherers and less common among egalitarian foragers (R. C. Kelly, 2000; Knauft, 1991). In egalitarian societies, people can level an ambitious and potentially violent man through teasing and ridicule before things get out of hand; or they can "vote with their feet" and move away from troublesome people (Butovskaya, chapter 14; Gardner, chapter 15). Just as there is no overarching mechanism to adjudicate disputes, or punish wrongdoers—and hence stop interpersonal violence—there is also

TABLE 9.2 **Societies listed in the Standard Cross-Cultural Sample by gross social type and presence/absence of warfare (from Fry, 2006, Table 8.3)**

Foraging Social Type	Warfare Absent	Warfare Present
Egalitarian	Ju/'hoansi, Hadza, Aranda, Copper Inuit, Mbuti, Andamanese, Semang, Saulteaux, Vedda, Paiute, Tiwi, Yámana, Slave	Montagnais, Gilyak, Ingalik, Micmac, Botocudo, Kaska, Aweikoma, Yukaghir
Nonegalitarian		Bella Coola, Haida, Gros Ventre*, Yurok, Comanche*, Yokuts, Chiricahua*, Kootenai*, Tehuelche*, Twana, Klamath, Eyak, Eastern Pomo, Aleut

* = equestrian foragers.

no mechanism for building a fighting force. Where others have glossed over foragers as "violent" (Ember, 1978; Keeley, 1996), it is instructive to point out that nomadic, egalitarian foragers do not go to war as much as sedentary, nonegalitarian foragers. Among nonegalitarian foragers, in fact, violence is culturally sanctioned and often raises a man's status (Knauft, 1987). And nonegalitarian foraging societies are universally sedentary peoples. As I have argued elsewhere (Kelly, 1995) sedentary hunter-gatherers arise not from food abundance, but because population density is so high relative to habitable places on the landscape that residential movement is not an option without taking on the violence and risk of displacing another group. War appears when mobility is not an option.

Warfare appears among nonegalitarian societies in part because they are what R.C. Kelly (2000) calls "segmentary societies." These are societies where the concept of "the group" is well-developed, and, consequently, where there is a concept of "group liability" (see also Roscoe [2009] on modular organization). The segments can be organized into a hierarchy: families, villages, and territorial groups. In segmented societies specific families make up a lineage, particular lineages make up a clan, and so on (R. C. Kelly, 2000, p. 45). These kinship units are well-defined, and less susceptible to negotiation. Unsegmented societies are fluid; families and individuals can move among co-residing groups, and the ties that link people together are negotiable (see chapter 27, for example, on the "one country" identification of the Australian Aborigines of the Western Desert). The numbers of people who are mobilized in segmentary organizations reduce the perceived cost of war and could lead to more frequent fighting, but this still begs the question of what leads to war.

The proximate causes of war can be varied, and can be the result of a mere insult, or accusations of witchcraft. Some causes may even seem silly, but at heart they are not. For example, Ames and Maschner (1999, p. 195) recount how the Yakutat Tlingit attacked the Sitka Tlingit because the Sitka had out-sang the Yakutat two years in a row. It seems a silly thing to come to blows over, but in fact the songs are a mere idiom for a far more significant fact. To retaliate after the first year's embarrassment, the Yakutat had learned songs from a neighboring group, but the Sitka had also increased their repertoire with songs from the Aleut. It's not the songs themselves that mattered, but their evidence of friendly connections with others: with their more extensive playlist, the Sitka were proclaiming themselves more powerful than the Yakutat. The Yakutat had to attack and preempt the Sitka's vision of them as weak and vulnerable.

Like any other choice, war has costs and benefits. The most devastating cost of war from the point of view of the participants is obvious: the warriors might die. The benefits are equally obvious: you might win resources—territory, supplies, women, and so on. When does the benefit outweigh the potential cost? It is logical that one set of circumstances would be when the cost of not going to war is starvation. In that case, the *potential* cost of fighting, death, is the same as the *definite* cost of not fighting.

So it is also logical that warfare would be related to a population's demand on food resources (even though the given reason for war might be an insult or accusations of witchcraft). Demand might be measured by population density: as population density increases so too might the likelihood of war. However, in an analysis of the SCCS, including foraging and non-foraging societies, Keeley (1996, Table 8.3) found no evidence for such a relationship. He argued that as societies become larger, the potential for warfare and lethal violence becomes greater (think: mutually-assured destruction). Under such conditions, societies find ways to short-circuit aggression, through feasting or other "appeasement" rituals, and hence warfare declines at high population densities.

However, population density is not an adequate measure of pressure on the food base (see Keeley, 1996). High population density may simply reflect that there is a lot of food on the landscape which can be converted into more people. Instead, the critical variable is *population pressure*. Population pressure is roughly a measure of how much food is available per person. Following Keeley's (1988) approach, we obtain a rough measure of population pressure by dividing the net above-ground productivity (NAGP) of the group's environment by the population density. In this case, I followed Keeley's (1988) lead by first multiplying the NAGP by a fraction (from Kelly, 1983, Table 9.3, column 5) to reflect the portion of NAGP that is edible by humans and large fauna. We then take the log of the first value divided by the second; the *higher* the value, the *greater* the food availability per person and the *lower* the population pressure. Does population pressure correlate with warfare?

Table 9.3 shows a sample of 19 Standard Cross-Cultural Sample (SCCS) societies for which there are appropriate data. The warfare measure is variable 768 in the SCCS: "conflict between communities of the same society." Conflict was measured along a 4 point scale: 1=once a year, 2=once every five years, 3=once every generation, 4=rare or never. There is *no* significant relationship between the incidence of internal warfare and population density (r_s = −0.28, n = 19, t = −1.20; p = .35).

However, there is a correlation between this measure of warfare and population pressure (r_s = 0.62, t = 3.3, n = 19, p = .006; Figure 9.1A; see also R. C. Kelly, 2000). As population pressure increases, communities fight more. It may seem odd that the Comanche appear more "peaceful" (conflict once every generation) than some other foragers in Figure 9.1A given their reputation as fierce, even vicious warriors, However, they do rank high in the SCCS for *external* warfare (variable 774, once a year). The population pressure measure used here does not account for the pressure placed on the Comanche by advancing Euroamerican society. If it could, it would almost certainly push this case further to the left on the graph.

The Klamath are the most warlike of societies in this sample—and they also score as violent in terms of external warfare (same as the Comanche). The Klamath raided each other and their neighbors for slaves that were sold for horses and guns. Whether this thirst for horses and guns was a product of Euroamerican encroachment or increasing pressure on the food base is not clear. It is clear, however, that their high level of conflict is not unexpected given their level of population pressure. Other societies living under high population pressure may have "solved" the problem of warfare with other social mechanisms, such as the Yokuts mourning ceremony (Wallace, 1978).

TABLE 9.3 Societies from the Standard Cross-Cultural Sample with Data to Calculate
Population Pressure, and Coded for Variable 768, Conflict Between Communities of the
Same Society (see Table 9.1 for variable definitions)

Group	NAGP	Ratio	Population Density (persons/100km²)	Population Pressure (ln)	v768
Ju/'hoansi	570	3.8	6.60	8.28	4
Mbuti	2242	0.4	17.00	6.45	4
Semang	3315	0.4	17.57	6.81	4
Andamanese	4400	0.4	86.00	5.50	2
Tiwi	2273	0.3	37.50	5.39	2
Gilyak	417	0.2	19.31	3.07	2
Ingalik	416	0.7	2.71	5.78	3
Copper Eskimo	42	0.7	0.43	4.22	2
Saulteaux	411	0.2	1.20	5.84	3
Slave	172	0.2	1.00	4.64	2
Eyak	573	0.2	5.86	4.36	3
Bellacoola	769	0.2	13.00	4.08	2
Yurok	685	0.5	131.00	3.16	2
Yokuts (Lake)	115	0.5	38.10	2.90	3
Klamath	286	0.8	25.00	3.82	1
Gros Ventre	391	0.35	3.37	5.31	4
Comanche	696	4.3	2.33	9.46	3
Chiricahua	485	0.7	1.16	7.98	4
Yámana	484	0.2	4.68	4.13	3

To summarize so far, it is not useful to ask whether hunter-gatherers (inclusive of egalitarian and nonegalitarian types) are peaceful or warlike; we find evidence for both among them. The better question is: when do foragers resort to war? From this small sample, the answer appears to be: when population pressure forces people to weigh the potential benefits of warfare higher than its potential cost.

This simple analysis agrees with Ember and Ember's (1992) broader cross-cultural one. Here they found that war was associated with societies that were impacted by periodic natural disasters, and, to a lesser extent, with societies that were characterized by a mistrust of nature and of other peoples. However, they did not argue that war happened as a result of natural disasters—which would make sense in light of this chapter's conclusion, but as a hedge against them. Given how the data were collected (see Ember & Ember, 1992, p. 256) I suspect it likely that people who feel threatened by natural disasters are impacted by such disasters frequently enough that it would be hard to separate war generated by fear of disaster from war generated by actual disaster without analyzing each instance of violence. In fact, the Embers' variable that measures the "threat of disaster" predicts war as well as a variable that measures the actual occurrence of disasters.

Homicide

We can take the same approach to general homicide rates since we can expect the tensions that erupt in interpersonal violence to be linked to overall societal stress, which could in

(A)

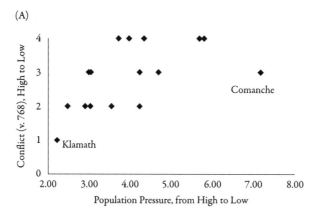

(B)

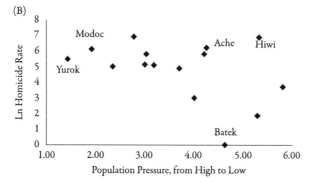

FIGURE 9.1 A. The relationship between population pressure and warfare (SCCS variable 768, conflict between communities of the same society: 1—yearly, 2—once every 5 years, 3—once every generation, 4—rare or never). B. The relationship between population pressure and homicide rates in a sample of foraging societies.

turn be linked to population pressure. Recall, though, that some of these estimates include those who died from warfare (so this is not an entirely separate test from above).

Figure 9.1B shows the relationship between homicide rates (from Table 9.1) and population pressure. This relationship is not significant (p = .12, n = 15, r = .41). However, the outstanding case is that of the Hiwi, whose rate would be lower if, as noted above, we could remove the effects of outsiders and infanticide; the same is true for the Ache estimate. If we remove the greater outlier, the Hiwi, the relationship is significant (p = .03, n = 14, r = .58): homicide rates increase with population pressure (from our discussion above, it is likely that both the Hiwi and Ache data should be lower to make them comparable to most of the others). On the other end of the population pressure spectrum, the Yurok and Modoc might be expected to have higher rates of homicide—on the order of 10,000/100,000 based on a projection from Figure 9.1B, but as noted above, these might be societies where social mechanisms ameliorate disputes formerly settled by violence. Under such high rates virtually everyone in the population would be affected by a death and that could lead people to pressure leaders to negotiate a solution that did not involve further bloodshed. Figure 9.1B suggests that homicide frequencies level out at a rate of 1000/100,000, meaning that may be the upper end of homicide/warfare death rates. Such high rates of death in warfare are rare events (Pinker, 2011; see also chapter 1); neither the Piegan nor the Hiwi could probably sustain a homicide/warfare death rate of 1000/100,000 for several generations without going extinct.

In sum, hunter-gatherers will always have some minimal level of violence that results from the rage that builds up among people in small groups who cannot avoid stepping on each other's toes. Homicide above this level and more serious violence such as warfare increase with increasing population pressure. At some level of pressure, people will weigh the benefits of violence higher than the potential cost. It is perhaps under such circumstances that groups form which are segmental, that permit social substitutability, and hence are primed for war.

The SCCS was put together with avoidance of "Galton's problem" in mind by including ethnographic cases that were not culturally or historically linked so that the sample does not overrepresent one particular geographic region or culture (it does not achieve this perfectly). But the sample did not consider whether the ethnographic data are comparable. For example, the SCCS contains both the Ju/'hoansi and the Gros Ventre. Data on the Ju/'hoansi were collected by ethnographers who witnessed a "living" foraging society (though the homicide data are from informants' memories); data on the Gros Ventre comes largely from Kroeber's (1908) ethnography, in which he is upfront about not witnessing anything that he writes about—it is all based on informant memory. Given potential issues with the ethnographic sample, perhaps archaeological data might be a better source of information (see Ferguson, chapter 11; Fry, chapter 1; Haas & Piscitelli, chapter 10).

The Archaeological Record

In the past few decades, primatologists have documented "coalitionary" killings between groups of chimpanzees, who along with bonobos are humanity's closest biological relatives (see reviews in Wilson, chapter 18; Wrangham & Peterson, 1996; Wrangham, 1999; R. C. Kelly, 2005). Wrangham argues that if reproductive fitness is correlated with food supply, and if the food supply is a function of territory size, then chimpanzees could be expected to increase their territorial size by decimating or driving out a neighboring chimpanzee group whenever advantage seems to be on their side, namely, when a party of chimps comes upon a lone foreign chimp. Wrangham suggests that this means that such coalitionary killing was probably present among our earliest human ancestors. But R. C. Kelly (2005; see also Fry, chapter 1) debates whether such coalitionary killing would be common among simpler foraging societies that lacked segmentary social organization (which was most likely true for early *Homo* and the australopithecines, if, indeed, they had anything that would be recognizable to an anthropologist as social organization). R. C. Kelly does not debate that increasing a group's foraging area increases reproductive fitness. In fact, he argues that foragers who lack segmentary social organizations use coalition-building forces to permit access to another group's territory and to make full use of their own territory's border regions; the ethnographic record is replete with evidence of such mechanisms, including trade, feasts, name relationships, and so on (R. L. Kelly, 1995, pp. 185–189; Tonkinson, chapter 13). Putting theoretical arguments aside, then, what is the direct evidence for warfare in prehistory?

Direct evidence for warfare among humans comes primarily from two sources. First are the physical traces left behind on human skeletal remains, evidence of perimortem injuries that likely caused death, including cranial fractures and indentations, nasal and facial fractures, and projectile points embedded in bone; or defensive "parrying" wounds such as cutmarked phalanges and fractured radii and ulnae. Second is evidence of defensive structures—structures in defensible locations such as butte tops, or ones with walls, moats, bastions, and so on. Two additional sources are weapons and iconography, but these are less useful for foragers who generally lack specialized instruments of war (but not always) and who did not invest much time in the production of art, including that which glorified war and conquest (see Lambert, 2007).

Unfortunately, the exigencies of preservation are such that the further we go back in time, the less skeletal material there is for us to examine. Prior to 50,000 years ago most skeletal remains are in secondary contexts, and it is difficult to separate the effects of post-depositional processes from those of violence. The skeletal record picks up with Neandertal remains, but skeletal data are rare prior to about 25,000 years ago, and are restricted mostly to Europe, northern Africa, and southwest Asia (see Haas & Piscitelli, chapter 10). A considerable percentage of these bear evidence of bone fracture, but these are interpreted to be largely the result of a rough, outdoor lifestyle and of the close hunting of large game, rather than interpersonal violence or warfare (but see Walker, 2001; review in McCall & Shields, 2008).

For those time periods where we have an adequate sample, the evidence for violence increases—perhaps as early as 35,000 years ago (Keeley, 1996, p. 37). Otterbein (2004) claims that warfare was widespread along the Nile in the Upper Paleolithic, but I am not convinced by the evidence he musters; nor am I convinced that warfare or ambushes were as widespread as he argues from the meager archaeological data for the Upper Paleolithic. Virtually all the skeletal evidence can be accounted for by interpersonal violence within groups, such as disputes over women. However, one case does point to warfare, that of the 12,000–14,000-year-old cemetery at Jebel Sahaba in northern Sudan (Wendorf, 1968; Ferguson, chapter 7; Haas & Piscitelli, chapter 10). Here, 41 percent of 59 individuals, including men, women, and children, apparently died of violence. Some individuals had multiple points in the torsos or embedded in bone. Many had healed parry fractures pointing to earlier violent events, and the children were killed execution-style with points embedded in the head or cervical vertebrae.

But documenting early evidence of violence or warfare only tells us the sad fact that humans have beaten on one another for a long time. What we need is a diachronic analysis of warfare, evidence for its frequency across time, in circumstances where we can determine if it is endemic, or if it is associated with population pressure.

In many places in the world, the literature on warfare focuses on those periods for which it is common; these tend to be agricultural and/or pastoral societies. The best place to examine evidence of prehistoric warfare among hunter-gatherers is North America, where a good portion of the continent was inhabited by hunter-gatherers up until contact, and where the prehistoric archaeology is fairly well-known. Fortunately, these data have been synthesized by Patricia Lambert (2002; see also, 1997, 2007).

For the Arctic, the Northwest Coast, and California—places whose prehistory is entirely that of hunter-gatherers—Lambert shows that evidence of warfare is generally restricted to the late Holocene, and especially the 1000 years or so prior to European contact (warfare continues after contact in many places as well, between indigenous groups and Europeans, and among indigenous groups). In the Arctic, evidence of violence appears about 3500 BP; but the first defended locations appear much later, about 1700 BP, and do not become common until 900 BP. The best evidence of a massacre—annihilation warfare—is found at the 700 BP Saunaktut site.

On the Northwest Coast, evidence for violence appears as early as 9400 years ago, in the Kennewick burial, a man who carried a stone point embedded in his hip for some number of his last years. More evidence appears during times when we have a larger burial population. During the Early Pacific Period, 6400 to 3800 BP, 21 percent of burials showed evidence of violence (Ames & Maschner, 1999, p. 209), though these are concentrated at one location. During the Middle Pacific Period (3800–1500 BP), this figure increases to 48 percent along the north coast (south coast burials show a lower incidence of violence). Definite defensive sites appear about 2200 BP, and become common during the Late Pacific period (1500 BP to contact), with most dating to 1100 to 800 BP. Villages become larger after 1700 BP, suggesting an increase in population generally and an increase in aggregation, and weapons that we suppose were used exclusively for war (e.g., slate daggers and stone clubs) make their appearance (Maschner, 1997). Unfortunately, a change in custom to above-ground burials after 1500 BP leaves us without our best source of information for the frequency of violence, but the existence of weaponry, armor, and defended locations suggests it became common, if not endemic, in the last 1000 years. The incidence of violence increased after contact with European colonial powers (Ferguson, 1983) but seems to have been an increase in an already existing practice.

In California, evidence of warfare does not appear until about 1500 BP, when cranial vault fractures increase in frequency. On the Channel Islands, defended locations are occupied, and projectile injuries are found in about 10 percent of burials, from 1500 to 700 BP. By 950–700 BP, the Channel Islands are abandoned, possibly due to drought. Lambert (2007) shows a dramatic increase in the frequency of projectile injuries in the Late Middle Period (~1500 to 600 BP) in southern California, along with evidence of subsistence stress (e.g., cribra orbitalia). Evidence for violence then declines during the Late Period (600 BP to contact). Lambert attributes the violence to a growing population size, but also to multiple droughts during the Medieval Climatic Warming. Violence declined somewhat during the Late Period as climate improved, and as various social mechanisms (e.g., hierarchy and trade) appeared that may have been a response to the previous high incidence of violence (see Jurmain et al., 2009 for a contrasting case from the San Francisco Bay area).

Finally, data from the northwestern Plains (primarily Wyoming, but including portions of southern Montana, western South Dakota and Nebraska, and northeastern Colorado), also point to an increase in violence associated with high population density relative to carrying capacity. Figure 9.2 shows the summed probability values of calibrated, taphonomically-corrected and standardized radiocarbon dates from a large sample of archaeological sites in the Bighorn Basin in northwestern Wyoming (Kelly, Surovell, Shuman, & Smith, n.d.), and those from a set of 39 human burials from across the northwestern Plains. The radiocarbon dates on these sites shows several peaks in population—about 10,700, 9200, 4500, and 1250 BP. Although these data are derived from the Bighorn Basin alone, other data suggest that they are roughly accurate for most if not all of the northwestern Plains, especially the late prehistoric peak in population. The peak at 9200 is present only in caves and rock shelters, and probably represents a geographic rearrangement of population rather than a regional increase. We assume that the other peaks represent regional increases in the human population. (The final population decline began about 1050 BP and continued through at least 850 BP. The apparent continuation of the decline to 500 BP may be partly the result of a bias against dating the uppermost occupations in stratified sites and using European trade goods to date the final 200 years in the sequence.)

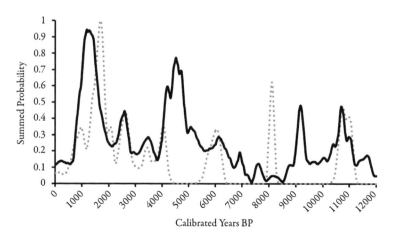

FIGURE 9.2 Graph showing the calibrated, taphonomically-corrected, standardized, and 200-yr smoothed, summed probability values of radiocarbon dates in the Bighorn Basin, northwest Wyoming (solid line), showing population peaks at 10,700, 9200, 4500, and 1250 BP, and (dashed line) similarly calculated frequency of radiocarbon dates for 39 dated human burials in the northwestern plains (burial data from Scheiber, 2008).

Although 706 burials are recorded for the northwestern plains (Scheiber, 2008), only 39 have been radiocarbon-dated, and 199 cannot be ascribed to a time period based on associated artifacts. The dated sample is obviously smaller than we would prefer, and undoubtedly introduces some bias. For example, the peak in burials at about 8200 (Figure 9.2) probably reflects a bias toward the dating of burials that for some reason (e.g., stratigraphy) suggest considerable age. The lack of burials in the middle Archaic, in association with the 4500 BP population peak, is intriguing. This gap is not simply a matter of dating bias on the part of archaeologists because very few burials (3) of those that are not radiocarbon-dated can be ascribed to the middle Archaic on the basis of grave goods (Scheiber, 2008, Table 2.2). Instead, the gap may reflect a change in burial practices (e.g., platform or tree burials) that did not result in the preservation of human remains.

For our purposes, though, what matters is that evidence for interpersonal violence appears to be associated with the late prehistoric peak in population—about 1250 BP (Scheiber, 2008; Gill, 2010). This evidence includes severe unhealed skeletal injuries and, in one-third of sites containing burials, projectile points embedded in bone or recovered in what would have been the torso. Cranial and facial traumas are biased toward males at this time (Gill, 2010). Although the largest sample of burials (257) comes from the protohistoric period, there is far less evidence of violence in this sample than in the late prehistoric sample (93 burials).

The incidence of violence as evidenced by the human skeletal record, therefore, peaks in the late prehistoric period. It is at this time that other cultural groups apparently moved into the Northwestern Plains. What are called "Avonlea" groups may have migrated southward from Saskatchewan, and pottery-producing peoples from the Plains may have moved into southeastern Wyoming. Although it is debated, Numic-speaking peoples (notably, the Shoshone) may have migrated in from the Great Basin to the southwest. Such emigrants may have been partly responsible for the late prehistoric population peak. It is also in the late prehistoric period that defensible locations such as butte tops are commonly occupied (Kornfeld et al., 2010, p. 130), some of which continue to be used into the protohistoric period (Schroeder, 2010).

The late prehistoric population peak is intriguing because the radiocarbon record with its peaks at 10,700, 4500, and 1000 BP can be well-predicted by the climate variables of temperature and moisture (Kelly et al., n.d.). The decline that begins about 1000 BP is associated with the onset of a more arid climate—one typical of the Medieval warming of the western United States—that significantly reduced carrying capacity just as the human population reached its greatest peak.

These archaeological studies generally find that warfare peaks with a peak in population and, for southern California and the northwestern plains, an increase in environmental stress. A similar process seems to be at work in eastern North America during the Archaic (Dye, 2009, Chapter 4; and see Dye, chapter 8 of this volume). We suggested above that warfare exists where the benefit of such violence outweighs the potential cost;

the ethnographic data suggest that these conditions hold when population pushes the limits of an environment's carrying capacity. The archaeological data generally support this hypothesis.

Conclusion

Aggression appears in many species, suggesting that it has a long evolutionary history (Barash, chapter 2; Fry & Szala, chapter 23; Kokko, chapter 3). More specifically, it is sufficiently common among primates that it is almost certainly a proclivity that goes back at least as far as a shared ancestor between humans and the other apes (Walker, 2001; Wrangham & Peterson, 1996). It is part of our behavioral repertoire, and at times serves us well. But perhaps just as common as aggressive behaviors are mechanisms such as threat and submission displays that limit the chance of injuries or death (Fry & Szala, chapter 23; Kokko, chapter 3). Therefore, demonstration of the antiquity of violence does not tell us the causes of warfare and is not evidence that a proclivity for violence is any stronger in humanity than is one for peacefulness and cooperation (Barash, chapter 2; Verbeek, chapter 4).

Violence is largely a behavioral choice, especially when associated with warfare. Many men have gone to war, killed their fellow humans, and then returned home to live lives of utter peace and kindness. If such behavior is a "choice," then I doubt that warfare and homicide, even if prevalent in the past, created the conditions for the evolution of altruistic behaviors (contra Bowles, 2009; see also Fry, chapter 1). Even with a genetic proclivity for violence, we can eradicate it if we remove the conditions that make war seem unavoidable. High levels of competition set the stage for warfare. But it is not only "trouble" that leads to war, but also the realistic *threat* of trouble and consequently the perceived need to take preemptive action. For foragers, competition is generated by a growing human population without a concomitant increase in the food supply or, worse, environmental conditions that reduce the food supply. Other circumstances, such as trade imbalances that create large discrepancies in the perceived material conditions of life, could also create the crucial sense of threat, a sense that one is always on the brink of disaster.

What is the larger lesson then? The key, I believe, to understanding warfare is that it is based on the vision that cooperation is a losing option and that trying to displace or dominate rather than work with a neighbor is the only viable course of action (see Fry, chapter 27). Steven Pinker's (2011) recent compilation suggests that violence is declining (in all sorts of ways) and that one factor operating against war is trade and other exchanges. Under some conditions, working with rather than against another group makes the most sense—from both a personal and evolutionary point of view. This is where anthropology needs to do what it does best: under what conditions does the benefit of cooperation outweigh the benefit of competition, and, assuming that we would like to rid the world of war, how do we encourage those conditions for cooperation?

References

Ames, K., & Maschner, H. D. G. (1999). *Peoples of the Northwest Coast: Their archaeology and prehistory*. London: Thames & Hudson.

Berkowitz, L. (1993). *Aggression: Its causes, consequences, and control*. New York: McGraw-Hill.

Binford, L. (2001). *Constructing frames of reference*. Berkeley: University of California Press.

Blurton Jones, N., Hawkes, K., & O'Connell, J. (2002). Antiquity of postreproductive life: Are there modern impacts on hunter-gatherer postreproductive life spans? *American Journal of Human Biology, 14*,184–205.

Bowles, S. (2009). Did warfare among ancestral hunter-gatherers affect the evolution of human social behaviors? *Science, 324*: 1293–1298.

Briggs, J. (1970). *Never in anger: Portrait of an Eskimo family*. Cambridge: Harvard University Press.

Burch, E. S., Jr. (2007). Traditional native warfare in western Alaska. In R. Chacon & R. Mendoza (Eds.), *North American indigenous warfare and ritual violence* (pp. 11–29). Tucson: University of Arizona Press.

Dentan, R. (1968). *The Semai: A nonviolent people of Malaya*. New York: Holt, Rinehart & Winston.

Dentan, R. (1988). Reply to Knauft. *Current Anthropology, 29*, 625–729.

Dye, D. H. (2009). *War paths, peace paths: An archaeology of cooperation and conflict in the native eastern North America*. Lanham, MD: Altamira.

Early, J. D., & Headland, T. N. (1998). *Population dynamics of a Philippine rain forest people*. Gainesville: University of Florida Press.

Ember, C. (1978). Myths about hunter-gatherers. *Ethnology, 17*, 439–448.

Ember, C., & Ember, M. (1992). Resource unpredictability, mistrust, and war: A cross-cultural study. *Journal of Conflict Resolution, 36*, 242–262

Endicott, K., & Endicott, K. L. (2008). *The Headman was a woman: The gender egalitarian Batek of Malaysia*. Long Grove, IL: Waveland Press.

Ferguson, R.B. (1983). Warfare and redistributive exchange on the Northwest Coast. In E. Tooker (Ed.), *The development of political organization in native North America* (pp. 133–147). Washington, DC: American Ethnological Society.

Fry, D. P. (2006). *The human potential for peace*. Oxford: Oxford University Press.

Fry, D. P. (2011). Human nature: The nomadic forager model. In R. W. Sussman & C. R. Cloninger (Eds.), *Origins of altruism and cooperation* (pp. 227–247). New York: Springer.

Gardner, P. (2000). Respect and nonviolence among recently sedentary Paliyan foragers. *Journal of the Royal Anthropological Institute, 6*, 215–236.

Gill, G. W. (2010). Advances in northwestern plains and Rocky Mountain bioarchaeology and skeletal biology. In M. Kornfeld, G. C. Frison, & M. L. Larson (Eds.), *Prehistoric hunter-gatherers of the high plains and Rockies* (pp. 531–552). (Third ed.). Walnut Creek, CA: Left Coast Press.

Gurven, M., & Kaplan, H. (2007). Longevity among hunter-gatherers: a cross-cultural review. *Population and Development Review, 33*, 321–365.

Headland, T. N. (1989). Population decline in a Philippine negrito hunter-gatherer society. *American Journal of Human Biology, 1*, 59–72.

Hiatt, L. (1965). *Kinship and conflict: A study of an aboriginal community in Northern Arnhem Land*. Canberra: Australian National University Press.

Hill, K., & Hurtado, M. (1996). *Ache life history: The ecology and demography of a foraging people*. New York: Aldine de Gruyter.

Hill K., Hurtado, A. M., & Walker, R. S. (2007). High adult mortality among Hiwi hunter-gatherers: implications for human evolution. *Journal of Human Evolution, 52*, 443–454.

Jurmain, R., Bartelink, E. J., Leventhal, A., Bellifemine, V., Nechayev, I., Atwood, M. & DiGiuseppe, D. (2009). Paleoepidemiological patterns of interpersonal aggression in a prehistoric central California Population from CA-ALA-329. *American Journal of Physical Anthropology, 139*, 462–473.

Keeley, L. (1988). Hunter-gatherer economic complexity and "population pressure": A cross-cultural analysis. *Journal of Anthropological Archaeology, 7*, 373–411.

Keeley, L. (1996). *War before civilization*. Oxford: Oxford University Press.

Kelly, R. C. (2000). *Warless societies and the origin of war*. Ann Arbor, MI: University of Michigan Press.

Kelly, R. C. (2005). The evolution of lethal intergroup violence. *Proceedings of the National Academy of Sciences, 102*(43), 15294–15298.

Kelly, R. L. (1983). Hunter-gatherer mobility strategies. *Journal of Anthropological Research*, 39, 277–306.

Kelly, R. L. (1995). *The foraging spectrum: Diversity in hunter-gatherer lifeways*. Washington, DC: Smithsonian Institution Press.

Kelly, R. L., Surovell, T., Shuman, B., & Smith, G. (n.d.). A continuous climatic impact on Holocene human population in the Rocky Mountains. Submitted to *Proceedings of the National Academy of Sciences*.

Kornfeld, M., Frison, G. C., & Larson, M. L. (2010). *Prehistoric hunter-gatherers of the high plains and Rockies*. (Third ed.). Walnut Creek, CA: Left Coast Press.

Knauft, B. (1987). Reconsidering violence in simple human societies: Homicide among the Gebusi of New Guinea. *Current Anthropology*, 28, 457–500.

Knauft, B. (1991). Violence and sociality in human evolution. *Current Anthropology*, 32, 391–428.

Kroeber, A. (1908). Ethnology of the Gros Ventre. *Anthropological papers of the American Museum of Natural History*, 1, 141–281.

Lambert, P. (1997). Patterns of violence in prehistoric hunter-gatherer societies of coastal southern California. In D. L. Martin & D. W. Frayer (Eds.), *Troubled times: Violence and warfare in the past* (pp. 77–109). Amsterdam: Gordon and Breach Publishers.

Lambert, P. (2002). The archaeology of war: A North American perspective. *Journal of Archaeological Research*, 10, 207–241.

Lambert, P. (2007). The osteological evidence for indigenous warfare in North America. In R. J. Chacon & R. Mendoza (Eds.), *North American indigenous warfare and ritualized violence* (pp. 202–221). Tucson: University of Arizona Press.

Lee, R. B. (1979). *The !Kung San: Men, women and work in a foraging society*. Cambridge: Cambridge University Press.

Marlowe, F. (2002). Why the Hadza are still hunter-gatherers. In S. Kent (Ed.), *Ethnicity, hunter-gatherers, and the "other": Association or assimilation in Africa* (pp. 247–275). Washington DC: Smithsonian Institution Press.

Marlowe, F. (2010). *The Hadza: Hunter-gatherers of Tanzania*. Berkeley: University of California Press.

Maschner, H. D. G. (1997). The evolution of northwest coast warfare. In D. L. Martin & D. W. Frayer (Eds.), *Troubled times: Violence and warfare in the past* (pp. 267–302). Amsterdam: Gordon and Breach Publishers.

McCall, G., & Shields, N. (2008). Examining the evidence from small-scale societies and early prehistory and implications for modern theories of aggression and violence. *Aggression and Violent Behavior*, 13, 1–9.

Murdock, G. P., & White, D. R. (1969). Standard Cross-Cultural Sample. *Ethnology*, 9, 329–369.

Ness, N., Helfrecht, C., Hagen, E., Sell, A., & Hewlett, B. (2010). Interpersonal aggression among Aka hunter-gatherers of the Central African Republic: Assessing the effects of sex, strength, and anger. *Human Nature*, 21, 330–354.

Otterbein, K. F. (2004). *How war began*. College Station: Texas A&M Press.

Pinker, S. (2011). *The better angels of our nature: Why violence has declined*. New York: Viking.

Roscoe, P. (2009). Social signaling and the organization of small-scale society: The case of contact-era New Guinea. *Journal of Archaeological Method and Theory*, 16, 69–116.

Scheiber, L. (2008). Life and death of the Northwestern plains: Mortuary practices and cultural transformations. In G. W. Gill & R .L. Weathermon (Eds.), *Skeletal biology and bioarchaeology of the Northwestern Plains* (pp. 22–41). Salt Lake City: University of Utah Press.

Schroeder, B. (2010). *Plan of attack, the Alcova Redoubt: A protohistoric fortification in central Wyoming*. Unpublished MA thesis, Department of Anthropology, University of Wyoming.

Thomas, E. M. (1959). *The harmless people*. New York: Knopf.

Turnbull, C. (1965). *Wayward servants: The two worlds of the African pygmies*. Garden City, N.Y.: Natural History Press.

Walker, P. L. (2001). A bioarchaeological perspective on the history of violence. *Annual Review of Anthropology*, 30, 573–596.

Wallace, W. (1978). Southern Valley Yokuts. In R. Heizer (Ed.), *Handbook of North American Indians, Vol. 11: California* (pp. 448–461). Washington, DC: Smithsonian Institution Press.

Wendorf, F. (1968). Site 117: A Nubian final paleolithic graveyard near Jebel Sahaba, Sudan. In F. Wendorf (Ed.), *The Prehistory of Nubia*, Vol. 2 (pp. 954–995). Dallas: Southern Methodist University Press.

Wrangham, R. (1999). The evolution of coalitionary killing. *Yearbook of Physical Anthropology*, 42, 1–30.

Wrangham, R., & Peterson, D. (1996). *Demonic males: Apes and the evolution of human violence*. Boston: Houghton Mifflin.

Wrangham, R. W., Wilson, M. L. & Muller, M. N. (2006). Comparative rates of violence in chimpanzees and humans. *Primates*, 47, 14–26.

10

The Prehistory of Warfare

Misled by Ethnography

Jonathan Haas and Matthew Piscitelli

Warfare is not an endemic condition of human existence but an episodic feature of human history (and prehistory) observed at certain times and places but not others.
Kelly, 2000, p. 75

Recent years have witnessed a resurgence of archaeological and anthropological studies of warfare. One of the critical issues is a fundamental question about the origins and ubiquity of war in human history. There are basically two schools of thought on this issue. One holds that warfare has origins that go into the deep history of humanity. In this interpretation warfare, as an integral part of human culture, goes back at least to the time of the first thoroughly modern humans and even before then to the primate ancestors of the hominid lineage. The second position on the origins of warfare sees war as much less common in the cultural and biological evolution of humans. Here, warfare is a latecomer on the cultural horizon, only arising in very specific material circumstances and being quite rare in human history until the development of agriculture in the past 10,000 years.

The question of how, why, and when warfare first started in human populations and even in primate populations is not a trivial one. Indeed, it has immediate relevance to understanding warfare in the contemporary world and to policy makers who wage that war. If the first school of thought is correct and warfare is and always has been a prevalent part of human existence and may have biological roots in our primate ancestors, then it becomes less incumbent on us to look for the "root causes of war" (Berenson, 1996). In an analysis Berenson did for the Pentagon of the root causes of war, he used the archaeological and anthropological literature on warfare to argue that warfare is inherent to the human species. If the Pentagon and other policy makers consider warfare to be innate, then there is no fundamental reason to look for the immediate cause of war on the ground. (This is certainly an oversimplification, but it does promote the notion that much of human behavior is based on biology and thus inherent and not in need of further explanation or understanding.) On the other hand, if warfare is *not* an inherent component to humanity, but rather, an irregular cultural phenomenon that comes and goes as material circumstances change, then it becomes much more important to understand the reasons *why* people come to fight at some points in human history and don't fight at others. The question of the intensity, chronology, and frequency of warfare in humanity is ultimately an empirical one that can be answered only by research and not by theorizing, speculation, or assertion. To address the issue empirically, we must ultimately turn to the archaeological record of the human past, as it is only in prehistory that we find the actual record of the origins of war.

For more than 15 years now, the archaeology of warfare has been co-opted by over-reliance on both ethnography and primate ethology. Scholars have tried to supplement an absence of archaeological evidence of warfare with implied parallels between ancient hunters and gatherers and contemporary hunters and gatherers as well as primates, primarily chimpanzees. Archaeologists have long used ethnography to fill in perceived gaps in the archaeological record, sometimes successfully and sometimes not. In 1978, Martin Wobst addressed the problems of relying too heavily on ethnography:

> If archaeologists consume ethnographically derived theory without prior testing, there is a great danger that they merely reproduce the form and structure of ethnographically perceived reality in the archaeological record. This form and structure may spuriously confirm the ethnographically derived theoretical expectations, in a never ending vicious circle (Wobst, 1978, p. 303).

He goes on to point out that hunters and gatherers recorded in the "ethnographic present," that is, the nineteenth and twentieth centuries "were intimately tied into continent-wide cultural matrices, be it through the world market or through other direct and indirect contacts with more complex societies" (Wobst, 1978, p. 303). The main point of Wobst's article is that historic and contemporary ethnographies of hunters and gatherers are not appropriate models for the vast majority of human history when hunters and gatherers lived without the influence of colonial powers or other more complex polities.

Wobst's warning came at a time of intellectual upheaval in archaeology, when archaeologists were searching for ways to bring more "life" to the archaeological record. They were using ethnoarchaeology, ethnographic analogy, and experimental archaeology to make inferences about the nature of prehistoric peoples. Indeed, such bridging arguments have proved very valuable in interpreting some kinds of phenomenon in the archaeological record. Binford's study of Nunamiut hunters, for example, gave archaeologists insights into the distribution of artifacts in temporary campsites (Binford, 1978). Unfortunately, there was also rampant misuse of the ethnographic record as well. Archaeologists finding inevitable gaps in the archaeological record turned to the ethnographic record to fill in the holes. One of the best instances of this would be the effort to define the social organization of past hunters and gatherers. Archaeologists jumped onto the evolutionary models of Steward (1956), Service (1962), and Fried (1967), which provided very convenient models for pigeonholing prehistoric societies. Hunters and gatherers nicely fit into the Patrilineal/Patrilocal Band category of Steward and Service or the Egalitarian category of Fried. With these ethnographically derived models in hand, archaeologists felt confident in inferring whole suites of characteristics for their prehistoric societies. At the most basic level, for example, prehistoric hunters and gatherers, inferentially, were patrilocal, patrilineal, and egalitarian. Wobst was then one of the first to call such blanket inferences into question. Others followed as archaeologists found that the ethnographic models didn't "fit" the archaeological data and that there was far greater diversity in the archaeological record than was seen in the ethnographic present of the late nineteenth and twentieth centuries. The ethnographic models also failed to either consider or successfully filter out the influence of centuries of colonialism and contact with state-level societies on historically known hunters and gatherers.

Since the 1970s, most archaeologists working on hunters and gatherers have moved beyond ethnographic analogies for making inferential statements about the nature of hunting and gathering societies. There is one glaring exception to this understanding of a major disconnect between past and present hunters and gatherers, and this is in the realm of warfare. Since Keeley (1996) published *War Before Civilization: The Myth of the Peaceful Savage*, archaeologists, anthropologists, and other social scientists studying the origins of warfare have found the archaeological record somehow lacking in their efforts to understand the beginnings of warfare in the ancient past. To fill in the perceived gaps, they have persistently turned to the historic record of hunters and gatherers, and in doing so have fallen into the trap of ethnographic tyranny.

The Tyranny of the Ethnographic Record of Warfare

The impact of this misuse of modern ethnographic and ethological studies has been significant in recent considerations of the origins of warfare in the archaeological past. In *War Before Civilization*, Keeley (1996) was updating the long-neglected field of the archaeology of warfare. He develops an excellent methodology for looking at warfare in the archaeological record and uses diverse data sets to present multiple case studies of prehistoric warfare in different parts of the world. He is also able to show unequivocally that there was significant warfare at different times and places in the archaeological record of prehistory. This was highly significant at the time, as there had been a 30–40 year hiatus in the anthropological literature looking at possible patterns of warfare in prehistory. His attack on the "myth of the peaceful savage" was a considered one, given an implicit sense in the discipline that warfare was a malady of the modern world. It is intellectually interesting that in the first half of the twentieth century prehistoric warfare was accepted as a given, but in the second half the study of conflict in the ancient past slowed to a trickle. Keeley starts out with good intentions: "If uncivilized societies were very peaceful before literate observers could record them, archaeology should be able to provide the documentation" (Keeley, 1996, p. 23). But in the very next sentence he succumbs to the allure of the rich ethnographic literature: "The evaluation of these ideas (and, of course, any ideas contrary to them) requires careful surveillance of both ethnographic and archaeological data, with special attention to questions of how recent tribal and ancient prehistoric warfare was actually conducted and what the direct results of such conflicts were" (Keeley, 1996, p. 24).

He then goes on to cite three different cross-cultural ethnographic studies of "tribal and state" societies, all of which describe the ubiquity of warfare. Keeley subsequently reinforces his conclusion that "several cross-cultural ethnological and historical surveys indicate that more than 90 percent of all known societies have been at war at least once a generation" (Keeley, 2001, p. 334). Interestingly, for the few societies that lack warfare, Keeley brings in the effects of outside states and imposed conflict: "Most of these peaceful societies were recently defeated refugees living in isolation, lived under a 'king's peace' enforced by a modern state, or both" (Keeley, 1996, p. 28).

The surrounding context of the non-peaceful societies, however, is never questioned. Yet all the societies in these cross-cultural surveys have been heavily impacted in similar ways and such impacts must be accounted for in such analyses.

More recently, Otterbein (2004; see also, 1970 and 2009) undertook another extensive review of archaeological and ethnographic literature in *How War Began*. Otterbein specifically mentions the prevalence of two kinds or periods of warfare-related "military organizations" in the history of humankind:

> . . . one of which can be found two million years ago, at the dawn of humankind, and the other five thousand years ago. It is the thesis of this book that early warfare arose first among hunting peoples, who sometimes had lethal encounters with other hunting peoples, and later among peaceful agricultural peoples, whose societies first achieved statehood and then proceeded to embark on military conquests (Otterbein, 2004, p. 3).

Both of these theories are scientifically testable. For the first, one must go back in time and look in the archaeological record for evidence of that "military organization" and "lethal encounters" two million years ago. The second is a bit more complex in that you would want to find archaeological evidence of those "peaceful agricultural peoples" antecedent to states and then evidence for military organizations embarking on conquest. Of particular interest in the present context is the effort by Otterbein to argue for the presence of warfare at the "dawn of humankind."

Rather than going back and looking first at the archaeological record from two million years ago, he instead looks at the ethnography of hunters and gatherers in the ethnographic present. Like Keeley, Otterbein looks at comparative literature and concludes that warfare is closely correlated with big game hunting. Using this simple correlation, he goes back into the past and notes that there was heavy reliance on big game hunting through much of that two-million-year period and therefore there was an abundance of warfare. Only with this up-front confirmation of his initial hypothesis does he then turn to look for empirical evidence in the archaeological record. First, he looks at rock art, and cites two somewhat ambiguous cases in French caves from the Upper Paleolithic—a period of 30,000+ years—of unarmed individuals punctured by shafts. His other evidence of warfare comes from depictions of armed conflict in rock art from Spain, which does appear to represent armed conflict, and from more ambiguous scenes of violence from Australia (see Fry, 2006), comes from significantly later times, after the Upper Paleolithic in the last 10,000 years, a time closing in on Otterbein's second period and kind of warfare. This latter period of warfare corresponds to the post-agricultural revolution, about which all scholars tend to be in general agreement that there is empirical evidence of a global increase in conflict, except, perhaps, in Australia, where agriculture was not adopted.

Next, in his global survey of the archaeological evidence of early warfare during the two-million-year period, Otterbein (2004, p. 73) cites but a single article (Bachechi, Fabbri, & Mallegni, 1997) to come up with only six instances worldwide where individuals were found with imbedded projectile points (Otterbein states there are seven cases, but Bachechi et al. [1997] only list six instances of embedded tools in human bone and two in non-human bone). From this scant archaeological evidence, he goes on to conclude: "The presence of points in bones, I believe, confirms that the rock art does indeed represent actual killings, whether they be executions, ambushes, or battles" (2004, p. 73). Based then on two depictions in rock art, and six cases of projectile points in human bones, Otterbein concludes "What has been found suggests widespread killing in the Upper Paleolithic" (2004, p. 75). He goes on to make a huge presumptive leap from killing to warfare: "The majority of hunting and gathering bands have warfare; those with the greatest reliance on hunting engage in warfare more frequently than those that are primarily gatherers. This pattern probably also holds true for the Upper Paleolithic" (Otterbein, 2004, p. 77).

More recently, Otterbein (2011, p. 439; see also Carbonell et al., 2010) has made the argument that evidence for cannibalism at one site in Spain from 800,000 years ago constitutes "the earliest known evidence for warfare." Ultimately, Otterbein's argument that warfare has characterized humankind for the past two million years is based on extremely scant archaeological evidence and almost complete reliance on contemporary hunting bands.

One of the biggest concerns with such ethnographically-based cross-cultural comparisons can be seen in the way it is used by other scholars trying to interpret the archaeological record. As but one example of the misuse of existing cross-cultural comparisons, Tuggle and Reid (2001) discuss conflict and defense at the fourteenth century A.D. site of Grasshopper Pueblo in the American Southwest. Specifically, they cite Keeley and other cross-cultural summaries to declare armed conflict as "virtually a human universal." They then go on to actually *assume* the presence of conflict: "...we take a simple approach to the problem: we assume that conflict of some sort was a component of the prehistoric social system and thus we develop a model based on the evidence that is consistent with this assumption" (Tuggle & Reid, 2001, p. 85). There would seem to be an inherent danger of such an argument in that if we can *assume* the presence and ubiquity of warfare, we never have to actually *explain* why warfare and conflict start or stop (cf. Haas and Creamer 1993).

In making these assessments, Keeley, Otterbein, and others rely on the same cross-cultural studies that have been carried out using mostly the comparative database of the Human Relations Area Files (HRAF) (see Otterbein, 1989; Ember & Ember, 1992; Ember, 1978; Ross, 1983, 1985; see also Naroll, 1966). These comparative works using hunting and gathering groups, as well as other kinds of more sedentary agricultural groups, have been cited frequently by archaeologists studying warfare. Indeed, they all provide valuable information about the nature and frequency of warfare in historically known societies. One of the positive qualities of HRAF is that the data format makes it possible to review a particular attribute, such as warfare, across many cultures and world areas. What this format does not facilitate is placing these individual and independent cases in context. Thus, while such studies do a reasonable job of surveying a broad spectrum of ethnographic literature, they make no effort to place any of the different societies into a broad, global, historical context.

We would not say that there is no value in studying warfare amongst historic and modern hunters and gatherers. In general, contemporary and historic ethnographic information can offer great insights into why people—in simple or complex societies—engage in warfare and make peace. Recent comparative ethnographic studies of warfare in historic societies, such as those by Kelly (2000) or Fry (2007), contribute greatly to our understanding of why people come to fight in the contemporary world. They have also demonstrated that the supposed ubiquity of warfare in hunting and gathering societies is itself a "myth"—to turn Keeley's words around. These studies, however, do not go beyond the data to make sweeping inferences about the past based on the present. The problem with using ethnographic and ethnohistoric comparisons to make inferences about the past, no matter how many cultures are included and how prevalent warfare may or may not be, is that no historically known societies reasonably reflect conditions that prevailed over the vast majority of human existence on earth.

Keeley, Otterbein, and followers (see LeBlanc, 1999; Chacon & Mendoza, 2007; Bowles, 2009; Smith, 2009; Guilaine & Zammit, 2005; Nielsen & Walker, 2009), in turning to the historic ethnographic record to support their claims of the ubiquity of warfare in the prehistoric past, fail to consider how hunters and gatherers of the "ethnographic present" may be profoundly different from hunters and gatherers of the more distant archaeological past. How many of these societies were surrounded and circumscribed by existing states; pushed by the rippling effects of other refugees; armed by traders; provoked, directly or indirectly, by missionaries; cut off from traditional lands? The short answer to this question is that *all of them*, by the very fact of having been described and published by anthropologists, have been irrevocably impacted by historic and modern colonial nation states (see Dickson, 1990).

Many tribal type societies (meaning here any society without the formal bureaucratic organization of a state) have been affected by state societies for at least 5000 years. The early incursions of ancient Egypt into northern Africa, for example, impacted much of North Africa. They were followed by the waves of Islamic conquests in the seventh and eighth centuries AD. These expanding states had significant direct impact on tribal people throughout northern Africa and unknown, indirect rippling effects in other parts of the continent. There were also expansive states and Empires well before European contact in the Americas. The Wari, Chimu, and Inca of South America, as well as the Maya, Toltecs, and Aztecs of Mesoamerica, for example, all had economic, political, and religious tentacles extending far out into distant tribal societies in both North and South America. While some effort has been made to look at the possible influence of Mesoamerican and Andean polities in adjoining areas, such studies have only minimally addressed the impact of these states on local patterns of warfare.

One illustrative example of this kind of precontact state influence is the pattern of cannibalism manifested in the American Southwest, during the eleventh and twelfth centuries AD. Both Keeley (1996, p. 105) and LeBlanc (1999, pp. 169–176) conclude it is an important period of tribal violence in their discussions on the archaeological evidence of cannibalism. But neither considers the extent to which it may have been influenced or provoked by the contemporaneous Toltec empire of Mesoamerica (cf. Turner & Turner, 1999, (pp. 464–469). Yet Turner and Turner (1999, 464–469), who have studied cannibalism extensively in the Southwest, specifically consider possible influences of Mesoamerican state polities on cannibalism. In their analysis, they find that a majority of the cannibalism is associated with the florescence of the renowned culture of Chaco Canyon. They then point to the strong connections between Chaco and Mesoamerica and conclude that this connection had a major impact on the cannibalism in Chaco.

Beyond such influence of early states, the colonial expansion of European polities in recent centuries encompassed the entire inhabitable planet. Literally no cultures, no matter how isolated, have been immune to the touch and influence of colonialism. Indeed, anthropology itself is the social science of colonialism, arising as an intellectual discipline to address the diverse peoples and cultures encountered throughout the non-Western world. The process of colonialism around the world had profound impacts on every tribal society encountered. Some of the impact came directly from the effects of conquering armies, epidemic diseases, voracious traders, and evangelical missionaries. More indirect influence, much harder to assess, came from the removal of vast tracts of land previously available in the expansion and contraction of Native peoples, circumscription of Native peoples by colonial powers or adjuncts, introduction and spread of foreign domesticated plants and animals, spread of foreign trade goods and weapons, and simply through contact with colonized peoples.

The Actual Archaeological Record

Looking across the vast landscape of the past 200,000 years (or even the last 2,000,000 years for that matter) for most of that time, humans existed in extremely low densities across the continents. The emergence of modern *Homo sapiens sapiens* in Africa some 200,000 plus years ago is not marked anywhere in the archaeological record by an explosion of population. There have indeed only been a handful of human remains and archaeological sites that date more than 20,000 years old in Africa, an area of 30,000,000 sq km. While negative evidence is not by itself proof of an absence of warfare, it nevertheless bears directly on the relative density of humans on the continent during this very long period. There is nothing at all to indicate any kind of population pressure or possible scarcity of resources. There is also a complete lack of evidence of concrete social units above the level of a family or immediate family group for this same period. Who then, exactly, would have been fighting whom and for what possible reason? This question intensifies when the early humans crossed over into Europe, perhaps 60,000 years ago. Once onto the new continent, an area of over 10,000,000 sq km, they encountered small populations of Neanderthals in some parts of Europe and the Middle East. Outside Africa, there was not another living person anywhere on the planet! All of Asia, with another 44,000,000 sq km, was empty. When people finally got to the Western Hemisphere, with 42,000,000 sq km, it too was devoid of people.

Estimating populations and population densities, even in the recent archaeological record, is a notoriously difficult proposition. It depends a great deal on getting a "complete" picture of how many people are living in any given area at any given period of time. Since most archaeological dating techniques rarely allow for specificity beyond 50 years—2.5 generations—most estimates are broad generalizations. Numerous scholars have attempted to estimate population growth of hominids over the past million years or so, but their estimates vary widely. Deevey (1960) estimates that for the period from about 200,000 years ago to 12,000 years ago, the human population density was only .04 people per sq km. Birdsell (1972) gives a similar estimate. Hassan (1981, pp. 196–200), based on modern ethnographic analogs (with all the incumbent problems as discussed above), calculates population estimates from *optimum carrying capacity* of the different environmental biomes as different parts of the world opened to humans. From this he estimates the world could have supported a population of about 6 million people 200,000 years ago and 8 million people 10,000 years ago. These figures yield a population density of .100 for the beginning of this period and .115 for the end. Hassan's estimates are all based on historic/modern hunters and gatherers and represent maximum figures if every environmental niche was filled to capacity the moment it became available as the ice age passed. (See also Binford, 2001 for a similar analysis and similar population estimates.)

More recently an estimate of population in Europe during the upper Pleistocene has been developed based on more than a century of archaeological excavation and survey .(Bocquet-Appel, Demars, Noiret, & Dobrowsky, 2005). Here again, Bocquet-Appel and colleagues use ethnographic analogy, but in this case it is used more productively.

They look at the relationship between site size and resident population of modern hunt-ing and gathering communities. They then use these figures on historic site size and den-sity as a proxy of population for prehistoric densities based on the size of archaeological sites. Bocquet-Appel and colleagues estimate that in the Aurignacian (40,000–31,000 Cal BC) the population of Europe was approximately 4400 individuals and by the Late Glacial (17,000–11,000 Cal BC) that population had grown to approximately 29,000. This latter figure works out to a population density of .003 people per square kilometer. There have been more upper Pleistocene sites found in Europe than any other part of the world. It seems likely that other world areas would have had lower population densities until rela-tively recently. Conversely, it is highly unlikely that other world areas would have had pop-ulation densities higher than those found in Europe, again until relatively recently. Using the .003 figure as an average, there would have been upwards of 132,000 people in all of Asia, 126,000 people in the Americas, and 90,000 people in Africa. Adding in smaller populations for Australia and the rest of the world, the total number of humans on the planet would have been something less than 500,000.

Whether one relies on the optimum carrying capacity figures of Hassan (1981) or the archaeologically derived figures of Bocquet-Appel, et al. (2005) the population of the world prior to the onset of the Neolithic was extremely low. Under either scenario, Figure 10.1 represents an accurate chart of the world's population from the emergence of modern *Homo sapiens sapiens* to the present day. This chart illustrates two things clearly: First, for 190,000 years of human existence on the planet, low population densities obviated all the proposed biological or cultural reasons for warfare and intraspecific conflict; second, all of the ethnographic accounts of hunters and gatherers as well as all ethological accounts of primates fall into the final tiny fraction of the demographic chart when the global human population is exponentially greater than the low population densities of the more distant past. Since 8000 BC (10,000 years ago) on all continents, the population of the world has grown exponentially.

In trying to look at warfare in the past, one major question is how to recognize it in the archaeological record. This topic has been addressed extensively by a number of archae-ologists (Vencl, 1984; Wilcox & Haas, 1994; Keeley, 1996; LeBlanc, 1999). Generally, warfare is recognized archaeologically by some combination of multiple lines of evidence, including defensive site locations and architectural features, "parry fractures" (fractures to the ulna), blows to the frontal bone, zones of "no-man's-land," art depicting warriors and battles, and systematic burning of sites. The further back you go in time, the more dif-ficult it may be to fully reconstruct combined suites of such characteristics, but warfare, when present, is not invisible in the archaeological record. When the actual archaeological record over the past 200,000 years is examined for empirical evidence of warfare and con-flict, the data say a lot about the appearance and frequency of warfare in the past.

In looking for archaeological indicators of warfare, a fairly clearly line can be drawn at approximately 8000 BC (10,000 years ago). After 8000 BC there is evidence of signifi-cant, though localized, warfare in several parts of the world (see Keeley, 1996; Otterbein,

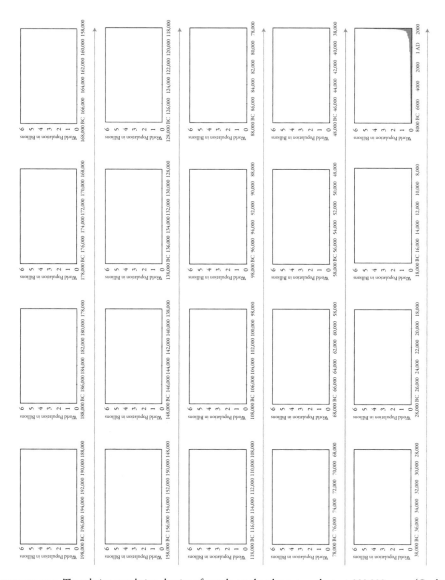

FIGURE 10.1 The relative population density of people on the planet over the past 200,000 years. (Credit: Jonathan Haas).

2004; Bachechi et al., 1997; Bowles & Gintis, 2011; Roper, 1969; Kelly, 2000; Haas, 2001; Thorpe, 2005, 2008; Raaflaub & Rosenstein, 2001; Carman & Harding, 2004; Martin & Frayer, 1998). From 8,000 BC onward, at different times and places around the world, there begins a steady—if episodic—trickle of such indicators of warfare and conflict. In no world area is there an unbroken lineage of warfare with the markers of conflict rising and falling as demographic and economic circumstances change. An important milestone in looking at the origins of warfare in humans is 8000 BC, as it stands at the very end of the Mesolithic and beginning of the Neolithic periods. It also marks major changes in the trajectory of human history, as humankind was reaching the upper demographic limits of sustainable hunting and gathering around the world. People were in the throes of the transition from a hunting-and-gathering, nomadic lifestyle to an agricultural and settled lifestyle. There is little disagreement over the rising prevalence of warfare and conflict after 8000 BC. For present purposes, however, it is the period *before 8000 BC* that is of greatest interest. Looking back at the very long stretch of time between 200,000 and 10,000 years ago, the archaeological evidence for warfare melts away.

Generally for this early time period, two types of evidence are used to identify conflict, and more indirectly, warfare in the past: rock art and violence in human skeletal remains. The rock art evidence is particularly telling. Those who argue for the ubiquity of warfare throughout human history all tend to cite the same sources. Three caves in France, Cosquer, Cougnac, and Pech Merle, have rock art that is frequently cited as evidence of violence. A total of four figures are singled out as indicators of humans punctured by spears. None of these figures, however, is clearly human and indeed two of them have tails (Figures 10.2 and 10.3) (see Clottes & Courtin, 1996, pp. 156–158). One of these (Figure 10.3), at Pech Merle, is described by Giedion (1962, pp. 460–462) thusly:

> It is not headless but has a birdlike head; in other respects it is drawn partly as an animal and partly as a human being. Again the body is traversed by long lines. These are so far from being straight that Lemozi [1929] took their curvature to represent a bow and arrows carried by an archer. They certainly do not represent arrows, spears, or any weapons in the ordinary sense. They are irregularly curved and are symbols: magic missiles, magic lines of force, magic emblems of fertility. A curving line to the rear might hint at an animal tail.

Yet another figure, called "The Killed Man" (Figure 10.4) from Cosquer cave, shares more characteristics with a chamois (or "goat-antelope" as shown in Figure 10.5 for

FIGURE 10.2 Figure from Cougnac cave, France. Note the tail. (Credit: Jill Seagard, The Field Museum; redrawn from Clottes and Courtin 1996).

FIGURE 10.3 Figure from Pech Merle cave, France. Note the tail. (Credit: Jill Seagard, The Field Museum; redrawn from Clottes and Courtin 1996).

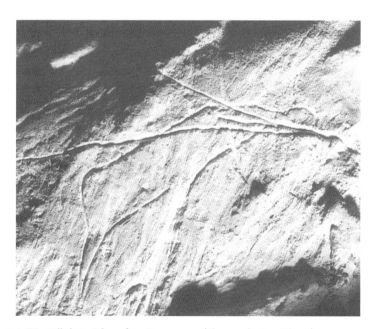

FIGURE 10.4 "The Killed Man" figure from Cosquer cave. (Photo credit: Jean Clottes).

comparative purposes) than with a human figure. Not mentioned in the discussions of warfare/conflict is the fact that two of the four figures repeatedly cited are directly associated with prey animals. Figure 10.2 is integrated within the upper body of an elephant, while Figure 10.6 (from Cougnac) lies within the body of an elk.

FIGURE 10.5 This figure from Cosquer cave, France, is a chamois, or goat antelope. Compare its features with "The Killed Man" shown in Figure 10.4. (Photo credit: Jean Clottes).

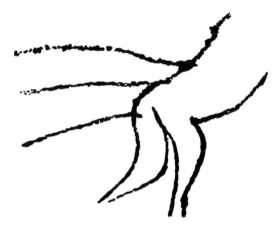

FIGURE 10.6 Figure from Cougnac cave. (Credit: Jill Seagard, The Field Museum; redrawn from Clottes and Courtin 1996).

This ambiguous and extremely limited evidence of violence against or between humans lies in stark contrast to the *thousands* of highly explicit images in many caves of a wide range of animals that were found and hunted by the prehistoric residents (Giedion, 1962; Clottes & Courtin, 1996). They also contrast with a florescence of clear images of warfare, conflict, fighting, and warriors found in cave art *after 8000 BC* (see Nash, 2005). At the same time, even if for the sake of argument the very few examples (Figures 10.2,

10.3, 10.4, and 10.6) are accepted as evidence of violence in cave art, they stand more as a testament to the rarity of conflict rather than to its ubiquity.

Turning from the ambiguous evidence of rock art to more direct evidence of violence in skeletal remains, there is again a but a tiny number of cases of violence in skeletal remains that are mentioned over and over by multiple authors. These would include individual skeletons with imbedded projectile points at two Italian sites of Grotta de San Teodoro (Bachechi et al., 1997) and Grotta dei Fanciulli (Dastugue & de Lumley, 1976), and two Ukrainian sites, Voloshskoe (Danilenko, 1955), and Valil'evka (Telegin, 1961). Dolní Věstonice in the Czech Republic (Trinkaus & Jelinek, 1997) has multiple individuals (3) in a single burial, which is interpreted by some as a sign of conflict, though there is no sign of violence to the skeletal remains. No attempt was made to distinguish warfare versus disease as equally plausible reasons for three individuals dying at one time.

The single case that goes beyond one or two skeletons with imbedded stone tools/points is the universally cited Jebel Sahaba in Sudan, occupied approximately 12,000–14,000 years ago (Wendorf, 1968). Among the 58 human skeletons recovered from this site, there were multiple examples of "parry" fractures, stone implements embedded in bone, and points found within body cavities (Wendorf, 1968; Anderson, 1968). Jebel Sahaba is of interest to the present discussion in particular as it is clearly not anything like a typical, nomadic hunting and gathering site characteristic of the Upper Paleolithic in other parts of the world (see also Ferguson, chapter 7). The presence of an actual graveyard with 58 excavated burials indicates intensive and long-term use. In discussing possible causes of the conflict at the site, Wendorf makes a case that sounds very much like the causes of warfare in later, more sedentary societies. He states:

> . . . population pressures may have become too great with the deterioration of the Late Pleistocene climate and the effects which this had on the herds of large savanna-type animals which were the primary source of food at this time. With this situation, the few localities which were particularly favorable for fishing would have been repeatedly fought over as other sources of food became increasingly scarce (Wendorf, 1968, p. 993).

This description of the causes of warfare at Jebel Sahaba outlines a specific set of circumstances that arose at a particular point in time and brings in increased population pressure with resources scarcity, the two elements that consistently combine to provoke warfare with greater frequency in the later Neolithic and thereafter.

With Jebel Sahaba as a notable exception, the evidence for conflict between humans in the archaeological record appears to be scant. However, it is reasonable to ask whether the sparsity of evidence is merely a factor of the sparsity of human remains from the period before 8000 BC. It turns out there is no comprehensive catalog of all the remains of *Homo sapiens sapiens* that have been excavated around the world. For this chapter, we conducted an extensive—though no claim is made for comprehensive—survey of skeletal remains listed in existing catalogues or original site reports. This search of multiple sources of data revealed that, globally, at least 2,930 skeletal remains of *Homo sapiens sapiens* have been recovered at over 400 archaeological sites dating prior to 8000 BC/10,000 BP in the following citations (Alexeeva, Bader, Buzhilova, Kozlovskaya, & Mednikova, 2000; Alciati, Delfino, & Vacca, 2005; Anokovich, et al., 2007; Arensburg & Bar-Yosef, 1973; Bachechi et al., 1997; Balout, 1954; Barker et al., 2007; Barton, et al, 2008; Bar-Yosef & Gopher, 1997; Belfer-Cohen, Schepartz, & Arensburg, 1991; Binford, 1968; Boule, Vallois, & Verneau, 1934; Bresson, 2000; Camps, 1974; Chamberlain & Williams, 2001; Chamla, 1970, 1978; Churchill, Franciscus, McKean-Peraza, Daniel, & Warren, 2009; Conard & Bolus, 2003; Danilenko, 1955; Duarte, Pettitt, Souto, Trinkhaus, van der Plicht, & Zilhão, 1999; Einwöger, Friesinger, Handel, Neugebauer-Maresch, Simon, & Teschler-Nicola, 2006; Eshed, Gopher, Galili, & Hershkovitz, 2004; Formicola, Pettitt, Maggi, & Hedges, 2005; Gambier & Houët, 1993; Gambier, Valladas, Tisnerat-Laborde, Arnold, & Bresson, 2000; Garralda, 1991; Grifoni, Borgognini, Formicola, & Paoli, 1995; Grine et al., 2007; Grun, Beaumont, & Stringer, 1990; Hachi, 1996; Henry-Gambier, 2001; Henry-Gambier & Sacchi, 2008; Herschkovitz, Frayer, Nadel, Wish-Baratz, & Arensburg, 1995; Holt & Formicola, 2008; Hovers, 2009; Hublin, 1993; Jacobi & Higham, 2008; Kauffman, 1988; Kennedy, Roertgen, Chiment, & Disotell, 1987; Kennedy & Zahorsky, 1997; Lumley, 1976; Mallegni, Bertoldi, & Manolis, 2000; Mallegni & Fabbri, 1995; Mariotti, Bonfiglioli, Facchini, Condemi, & Belcastro, 2009; Matsumura & Pookajorn, 2002; McDermott, Stringer, Grün, Williams, Din, & Hawkesworth, 1996; Meier, R. J., Sahnouni, Medig, & Derradji, 2003; Meiklejohn, Pardoe, & Lubell, 1979; Meiklejohn, Bosset, & Valentin, 2010; Minellono, Pardini, & Fornaciari, 1980; Morel, 1993; Moser, 2003; Oakley & Campbell, 1967; Oakley, Campbell, & Molleson, 1971, 1975; Orschiedt, 2000; Pardoe, 1995; Perrot, 1966; Pettitt, Richards, Maggi, & Formicola, 2003; Pettitt & Trinkaus, 2000; Pond, 1928; Ramirez Rozzi, d'Errico, Vanhaeren, Grootes, Kerautret, & Dujardin, 2009; Rougier et al., 2007; Sereno et al., 2008; Shackelford, 2007; Shang, Haowen, Shuangquan, Fuyou, & Trinkaus, 2007; Schulting, Trinkaus, Higham, Hedges, Richards, & Cardy, 2005; Soficaru, Petrea, Dobos, & Trinkaus, 2007; Stock, Pfeiffer, Chazan, & Janetski, 2005; Susuki & Hanihara, 1982; Svoboda, 2008; Svoboda, 1997; Telegin, 1961; Trinkaus & Svoboda, 2006; Ullrich, 1992; Vercellotti, Alciati, Richards, & Formicola, 2008; Wendorf, 1968; Wendorf & Schild, 1986; Wu, 1982). While many of the earliest known remains consist of isolated finds with little skeletal material, later archaeological contexts exhibit a greater number of individuals. Like the rock art data, the small number of skeletal finds mentioned above, showing ambiguous signs of conflict (Jebel Sahaba excepted), come from a comparatively small number of sites. (It should also be noted that again with the exception of Jebel Sahaba, none of the often-cited examples in art or skeletal remains would be accepted as evidence of warfare—as opposed to violence or even accidents—in later time periods.) Rather than demonstrating the commonness of ancient warfare amongst humans, consideration of the entire archaeological data set shows the opposite. Unfortunately, the full body of cave paintings and rock art along with the full body of skeletal remains from hundreds of archaeological sites have not been considered in studies attempting to argue for the prevalence of war throughout human history. Comparing the total number of known individuals before 8000 BC to the small sample of remains showing signs of violence demonstrates the infrequency of warfare or conflict in the ancient past. The archaeological record is *not silent* on the presence of warfare in early human history. Indeed, this record shows that warfare was the rare exception prior to the Neolithic pressures of population densities and insufficient resources for growing populations.

Rather than fighting with each other under extremely low population densities and no viable competitors for an abundance of food and game, humans would have relied on neighbors for cooperative ventures, such as hunting large game, or for the potential pool of mates. It is interesting and relevant to note in this regard that throughout Europe and large tracts of Asia all the way to Siberia, the time period from about 40,000 years ago to 25,000 years ago was all characterized by the same material cultural tradition—the Aurignacian. If you cross over into the Americas, you find a similar pattern of a continent-wide material culture during the period from 13,500 to 13,000 years ago, when all peoples across the entire continent of North America were producing remarkably similar and distinct "Clovis" projectile points. In South America all peoples were producing similar "Fishtail" points. Everyone, across continental spaces and over long stretches of time, was making the same kinds of tools. There is a glaring lack of any kind of analog in the ethnographic record for this kind of continental distribution of remarkably similar material culture. All of the issues of group boundaries, "traditional enemies," different ethnicities, and territoriality are simply incompatible with a model of open continent-wide social networks.

The contrast between the realities of the archaeological record and the notion of the universality of warfare in humans is seen in the recent book by Thayer, *Darwin and International Relations: On the Evolutionary Origins of War and Ethnic Conflict*. Thayer makes broad proclamations about the early origins of conflict:

> "From the Pliocene until very recent history many resources were scarce for all humans. Indeed, people in many parts of the world today face shortages of what may be considered basic resources, such as land and clean water. Resources may be rare or hard to come by, or they may be plentiful enough but access to them is controlled, perhaps by a hostile tribe. The origins of warfare are grounded in one's egoism—the human desire to gain or defend the resources needed to feed and protect a family, other relatives, and then one's group" (Thayer, 2004, p. 108).

Here is the ultimate confusion of the present with the past. Thayer is correct in pointing out that land and water are scarce today in the twenty-first century, with a global population of almost seven billion people, but provides no basis at all for inferring similar

scarcity for the far distant past, when population densities of hominids were a tiny fraction of that number. There is also no evidence at all in the archaeological record of "hostile
tribes" controlling water or land. Thayer ultimately wants to attribute warfare to biological
foundations of humans, their immediate hominid ancestors, and ultimately to their primate roots as witnessed in the warfare of *Pan troglodytes*, the chimpanzee.

It is worthwhile noting that the ethological data on chimpanzees and other primates
are not dissimilar to the ethnographic record in offering minimal insights into the extent
and nature of *prehistoric* warfare in *Homo sapiens sapiens*. Primate populations around the
world have been contaminated by millennia of predation, circumscription, and contraction of resource zones caused by humans. This topic, however, is beyond the bounds of the
present chapter.

Conclusions

So why is it so important to critically examine the relevance of hunter-gatherer ethnographies to studies of the history of warfare in humankind? The biggest problem with using
historical ethnographies to make inferences about patterns of *past* human behavior is that
they burden us with pictures only painted in the light of the modern, dense, colonial world
of nation states. To carry the analogy one step further, it is as if we tried to give a picture of
life on earth based only on what could be seen on one rainy day, an hour after sunset. Our
view of the world would be gloomy and dim and would never tell us of a sunny morning or
a snowy night. Another problem with the major studies based on ethnographies is that lots
of other scholars take them as gospel. Declaring that warfare is rampant amongst almost
all hunters and gatherers (as well as those cunning and aggressive chimpanzees) fits well
with a common public perception of the deep historical and biological roots of warfare
(e.g., Smith, 2009; Bowles & Gintis, 2011; Thayer, 2004; Otterbein, 2004; Dennen, 1995;
Pinker, 2011). The fact that there is extremely limited empirical evidence of any warfare
among past hunters and gatherers is pushed to the wayside as an intellectual inconven-
ience. Unfortunately, the presumed universality of warfare in human history and ancestry
may be satisfying to popular sentiment; however, such universality lacks empirical support.
Drawing such false conclusions ultimately does not help us to understand *why humans
go to war, why wars start and stop, and what is the role of warfare* in either the biological
or cultural evolution of humanity. As scholars of warfare, it is incumbent upon us to not
make faulty assumptions about the ubiquity of warfare in humanity based on misleading
comparisons between the ancient past and the modern hunters and gatherers and our primate relatives.

To return again to the analysis of Wobst, the study of warfare in the human past is
being constrained by the tyranny of the ethnographic record. By confining ourselves only
to the record of the modern world and historical depth of written history we are disal-
lowing 98 percent of human history, diversity, and creativity, as well as our incredible
uniqueness as primates. Assuming that warfare has been a constant since the beginning

of human history, based on the present, relieves us of responsibility for investigating the causes of war and the potential for peace (Fry, 2007). Yet these are exactly the issues that we need to address in the present world of pervasive warfare. Furthermore, archaeologists are the ones who are going to have to address the epochal period of human history before the advent of agriculture and development of complex polities. In spite of protestations to the contrary by non-archaeologists and even some archaeologists, there is in fact a substantial body of data from around the globe that is relevant to questions about the origins and role of warfare in the long history of modern humans on the planet. Ultimately, we would argue that the root causes of warfare are to be found in demographic and economic pressures on specific populations at specific points in their respective history. Equally, waves of peace can be explained by looking at the material conditions of life in those same historical trajectories.

References

Alexeeva T. I., Bader, N., Buzhilova, A. Kozlovskaya, M, & Mednikova, M. (2000). *Homo sunghirensis: Upper Paleolithic man: Ecological and evolutionary aspects of investigation.* Moscow: Scientific World.

Alciati, G., Pesce Delfino, V. & Vacca, E. (2005). Catalogue of Italian fossil human remains from the Palaeolithic to the Mesolithic. *Journal of Anthropological Sciences* (Supplement 84, p. 184).

Anderson, J. E. (1968). Late Paleolithic skeletal remains from Nubia. In F. Wendorf (Ed.), *The Prehistory of Nubia*, (pp. 996–1040). Dallas: Southern Methodist University Press.

Anokovich, M. V., Sinitsyn, A., Hoffecker, J., Holliday, V., Popov, V., Lisitsyn, S., . . . & Praslov, N. D. (2007). Early upper Paleolithic in Eastern Europe and implications for the dispersal of modern humans. *Science, 315,* 223–226.

Arensburg, B. & O. Bar-Yosef (1973). Human remains from Ein Gev I: Jordan Valley, Israel. *Paléorient 1,* 201–206.

Bachechi, L., Fabbri, P., & Mallegni, F. (1997). An arrow-caused lesion in a late Upper Paleolithic human pelvis. *Current Anthropology, 38*(1), 135–140.

Balout, K. (1954). Les Hommes Préhistoriques du Maghreb et du Sahara: Inventaire Descriptif et Critique. *Libyca, 2,* 214–424.

Barker, G., Barton, H., Bird, M. Daly, P., Datan, I., Dykes, A., . . . & Turney, C. (2007).The "human revolution" in lowland tropical Southeast Asia: the Antiquity And Behavior of Anatomically Modern Humans at Niah Cave (Sarawak, Borneo). *Journal of Human Evolution, 52*(3), 243–261.

Barton, R.N.E., Bouzouggar, A., Humphrey, L.T., Berridge, P., Collcutt, S.N., Gale, R., Parfitt, S., Parker, A.G., Rhodes, E.J., Schwenninger, J.L. (2008). Human burial evidence from Hattab II Cave (Oued Laou-Tétuoan, Morocco) and the question of continuity in Late Pleistocene-Holocene mortuary practices in Northwest Africa. *Cambridge Archaeological Journal, 18,* 195–214.

Bar-Yosef, O., & Gopher, A. (Eds.). (1997). *An early Neolithic village in the Jordan Valley, Part 1: The archaeology of Netiv Hagdud.* Cambridge, MA: Peabody Museum of Archaeology & Ethnology.

Belfer-Cohen, A., Schepartz, L., & Arensburg, B. (1991). New biological data for the Natufian populations in Israel. In O. Bar-Yosef & F. R. Valla (Eds.), *The Natufian culture in the Levant* (pp. 411–424). Ann Arbor: International Monographs in Prehistory.

Berenson, P. J. (1996). *The root causes of war.* Report submitted to the U.S. Department of Defense.

Binford, L. R. (1978). *Nunamiut ethnoarchaeology.* New York: Academic Press.

Binford, L. R. (2001). *Constructing frames of reference: An analytical method for archaeological theory building using ethnographic and environmental data sets.* Berkeley: University of California Press.

Binford, S. R. (1968). A structural comparison of disposal of the dead in the Mousterian and the Upper Paleolithic. *Southwestern Journal of Anthropology, 24*(2), 139–154.

Birdsell, J. B. (1972). *Human evolution: An introduction to the new physical anthropology.* Chicago: Rand McNally.

Bocquet-Appel, J.-P., Demars, P.-Y., Noiret, L., & Dobrowsky, D. (2005). Estimates of Upper Palaeolithic meta-population size in Europe from archaeological data. *Journal of Archaeological Science, 32,* 1656–1668.

Boule, M., Vallois, H., & Verneau, R. (1934). Le Grottes Paleolithiques des Beni-Segoual Algerie. *Archives de l'Institut de Paleontologie Humaine, 13,* 83–239.

Bowles, S. (2009). Did warfare among ancestral hunter-gatherers affect the evolution of human social behaviors? *Science 324,* 1293–1298.

Bowles, S., & Gintis, H. (2011). *A cooperative species: Human reciprocity and its evolution.* Princeton: Princeton University Press.

Bresson, F. (2000). Le Squelette du Roc-de-Cave (Saint-Cirq-Madelon, Lot). *Paleo, 12,* 29–60.

Camps, Gabriel (1974). *Les Civilisations Préhistoriques de L'Afrique du Nord et du Sahara.* Paris, France: Doin.

Carbonell, E., Ccáceres, I., Lozano, M., Saladié, P., Rosell, J., Lorenzo, C, . . . & María Bermúdez de Castro, J. (2010). Cultural cannibalism as a paleoeconomic system in the European lower Pleistocene: The case of level TD6 of Gran Dolina (Sierra de Atapuerca, Burgos, Spain). *Current Anthropology, 51*(4), 539–549.

Carman, J., & Harding, A. (Eds.). (2004). *Ancient warfare: Archaeological perspectives.* Gloucestershire, UK: Sutton Publishing.

Chacon, R. J., & Mendoza, R. (Eds.). (2007). *North American indigenous warfare and ritual violence.* Tucson: The University of Arizona Press.

Chamberlain, A.T., & Williams, J. (2001). A gazetteer of English caves, fissures and rock shelters containing human remains. Capra [online], created June 1, 2001, viewed September 15. 2011. http://capra.group.shef. ac.uk/1/caves.html

Chamla, M.C. (1970). Les hommes Épipaléolithiques de Columnaa. *Mémoires du Centre de Recherches Anthropologiques Préhistoriques et Ethnographicques Algérie, 15,* 5–115.

Chamla, M.C. (1978). Le Peuplement de l'Afrique du Nord de l'Epipaleolithique a l'Epoque Actuelle. *L'Anthropologie, 82,* 385–430.

Churchill, S. E., Franciscus, R., McKean-Peraza, H., Daniel, J., & Warren, B. (2009). Shanidar 3 Neandertal rib puncture wound and Paleolithic weaponry. *Journal of Human Evolution, 57*(2), 163–178.

Clottes, J., & Courtin, J. (1996). *The cave beneath the sea: Paleolithic images at Cosquer.* Paris, France: Harry N. Abrams.

Conard, N. J., & Bolus, M. (2003). Radiocarbon dating the appearance of modern humans and timing of cultural innovations in Europe: New results and new challenges. *Journal of Human Evolution, 44*(3), 331–371.

Danilenko, V. N. (1955). Voloshskji Epipaleoliticheskij Mogil'nik. *Sovetskaja Etnografija, 8,* 56–61.

Dastugue, J., & de Lumley, M. (1976). Les maladies des hommes préhistoriques de Paléolithique et du Mésolithique. In J. Guilaine, (Ed.), *La prehistoire Française* (Vol. I, pp. 621–622). Paris, France: Editions du Centre National de la Recherche Scientifique.

Deevey, E. S. (1960).The human population. *Scientific American 203,* 195–204.

Dennen, J. M. G. van der (1995). *The origin of war: The evolution of male-coalitional reproductive strategy.* Groningen, The Netherlands: Origin Press.

Dickson, D. (1990). *The dawn of belief: Religion in the Upper Paleolithic of southwestern Europe.* Tucson: University of Arizona Press.

Duarte, C., Maurício, J., Pettitt, P., Souto, P., Trinkhaus, E., van der Plicht, H., & Zilhão, J. (1999). The early Upper Paleolithic human skeleton from the Abrigo do Lagar Velho (Portugal) and modern human emergence in Iberia. *PNAS, 96*(13), 7604-7609.

Einwöger, T., Friesinger, H., Handel, M., Neugebauer-Maresch, C., Simon, U., & Teschler-Nicola, M. (2006). Upper paleolithic infant burials. *Nature, 444,* 285.

Ember, Carol R. (1978). Myths about hunter-gatherers. *Ethnology, 17*(4), 439–448.

Ember, C. R., & Ember, M. (1992). Resource unpredictability, mistrust, and war. *The Journal of Conflict Resolution, 36*(2), 242–262.

Eshed, V., Gopher, A., Galili, E., & Hershkovitz, I. (2004). Musculoskeletal stress markers in Natufian hunter-gatherers and Neolithic farmers in the Levant: The upper limb. *American Journal of Physical Anthropology, 123*(4), 303–315.

Formicola, V., Pettitt, P., Maggi, R., & Hedges, R. (2005).Tempo and mode of formation of the late Eipgravettian necropolis of Arene Candide Cave (Italy: Direct radiocarbon evidence. *Journal of Archaeological Science, 32,* 1598–1602.

Fried, M. H. (1967). *The evolution of political society: An essay in political anthropology*. New York: Random House.

Fry, D. P. (2006). *The human potential for peace: An anthropological challenge to assumptions about war and violence*. New York: Oxford University Press.

Fry, D. P. (2007). *Beyond war*. New York: Oxford University Press.

Gambier, D., & Houët, F. (1993). France: Upper palaeolithic hominid remains an up-date. *Anthropologie et Préhistoire* (Supplement 6).

Gambier, D., Valladas, H., Tisnérat-Laborde, N., Arnold, M., & Bresson, F. (2000). Datation de Vestiges Humains Présumés du Paléolithique Supérieur par la Méthode du Carbone 14 en Spectrométrie de Masse par Accélerateur. *Paleo, 12*, 201–212.

Garralda, M. D. (1991). Spain: Hominid remains an up-date. *Anthropologie et Préhistoire*, (Supplement 4).

Giedion, S. (1962). *The eternal present: The beginnings of art*. New York: Random House.

Grifoni Cremonesi, R., Borgognini Tarli, S.M., Formicola, V., & Paoli, G. (1995). La seplture epigravettiana scoperta nel 1993 Nella Grotta Continenza di Trasacco (L'Aquila). *Rivista Di Antropologia, 73*, 223–225.

Grine, F. E., Bailey, R.M., Harvati, K., Nathan, R., Morris, A., Henderson, G., Ribot, I., & Pike, A. (2007). Late Pleistocene human skull from Hofmeyr, South Africa, and modern origins. *Science, 315*, 226–229.

Grun, R., Beaumont, P., & Stringer, C. (1990). ESR dating evidence for early modern humans at Border Cave in South Africa. *Nature, 344*, 537+.

Guilaine, J., & Zammit, J. (2005). *The origins of war: Violence in prehistory*. Oxford: Blackwell Publishing.

Haas, J. (2001). Warfare and the evolution of culture. In G. M. Feinman & T. D. Price (Eds.), *Archaeology at the millennium: A sourcebook* (pp. 329–350). New York: Kluwer Academic/Plenum Publishers.

Haas, J., & Creamer, W. (1993). Stress and warfare among the Kayenta Anasazi of the Thirteenth Century AD *Fieldiana 21*. Chicago: Field Museum of Natural History.

Hachi, S. (1996). L'Ibéromaurusien, Découverte des Fouilles d'Afalou (Bèdjaîa, Algérie). *L'Anthropologie, 100*, 55–77.

Hassan, F. A. (1981). *Demographic archaeology*. New York: Academic Press.

Henry-Gambier, D. (2001). *La sépulture des enfants de Grimaldi (Baoussé-Rouseè, Italia)*. Paris, France: Reunión des Musées Nationaux.

Henry-Gambier, D., & Sacchi, D. (2008). La Crouzade V-VI (Aude, France): Un des plus anciens fossiles d'anatomie moderne en Europe occidentale. *Bulletins et Mémoires de la Société d'Anthropologie de Paris* [online], *20*(1–2), created 24 April 24, 2009, viewed September 15, 2011. Retrieved from http://bmsap.revues.org/6054

Herschkovitz, I., Frayer, D., Nadel, D., Wish-Baratz, S., & Arensburg, B. (1995). Ohalo II H2: A 19,000-year-old skeleton from a water-logged site at the sea at Galilee, Israel. *American Journal of Physical Anthropology, 96*(3), 215–234.

Holt, B. M., & Formicola, V. (2008). Hunters of the ice age: The biology of upper Paleolithic people. *Yearbook of Physical Anthropology, 51*, 70–99.

Hovers, E. (2009). *The lithic assemblages of Qafzeh Cave*. New York: Oxford University Press.

Hublin, J.-J. (1993). Recent human evolution in Northwestern Africa. In M. J. Aitken, C. B. Stringer, & P. Mellars (Eds.), The origins of modern humans and the impact of chronometric dating (pp. 118–131). Princeton: Princeton University Press.

Ingham, K. (1975). *The Kingdom of Toro in Uganda*. London: Methuen.

Jacobi, R. M., & Higham, T. (2008).The "red lady" ages gracefully: New ultrafiltration AMS determinations from Paviland. *Journal of Human Evolution, 55*(5), 898–907.

Kauffman, D. (1988). New radiocarbon dates for the Geometric-Kebaran. *Paléorient 14*, 107–109.

Keeley, L. (1996). *War before civilization: The myth of the peaceful savage*. New York: Oxford University Press.

Keeley, L. (2001). Giving war a chance. In G. Rice & S. LeBlanc (Eds.), *Deadly landscapes: Case studies in prehistoric Southwestern Warfare*, (pp. 331–342). Salt Lake City: University of Utah Press.

Kelly, R. C. (2000). *Warless societies and the origin of war*. Ann Arbor: University of Michigan Press.

Kennedy, K., Roertgen, S., Chiment, J., & Disotell T. (1987). Upper Pleistocene fossil hominids from Sri Lanka. *American Journal of Physical Anthropology 72*(4), 441–461.

Kennedy, K., & Zahorsky, J. (1997). Trends in prehistoric technology and biological adaptations: New evidence from Pleistocene deposits at Fa Hien Cave, Sri Lanka. In *Proceedings of the 13th Conference of the European Association of South Asian Archaeology*, Vol. 2. (pp. 839–853).

LeBlanc, S. (1999). *Prehistoric warfare in the American Southwest*. Salt Lake City: University of Utah Press.

Lémozi, A. (1929). *La Grotte-Temple du Peche-Merle. Un nouveau sanctuaire prééhistorique*. Paris, France: Picard.

Lumley, H. de (1976). *La Préhistoire française: Civilisations paléolithiques et mésolithiques de la France*, Centre National de la Recherche Scientifique. Paris, France: Editions du C.N.R.S.

Mallegni, F., Bertoldi, F., & Manolis, S. (2000). Paleobiology of two Gravettian skeletons from Veneri Cave (Parabita, Puglia, Italy). *Homo, 51*, 235–257.

Mallegni, F., & Fabbri, P. F. (1995). The human skeletal remains from the Upper Palaeolithic burials found in Romito Cave (Papasidero, Cosenza, Italy). *Bulletin et Memoires de la Societe d'Anthropologie de Paris, 7*, 99–137.

Mariotti, V., Bonfiglioli, B., Facchini, F., Condemi, S., & Belcastro, M. G. (2009). Funerary practices of the Iberomaurusian population of Taforalt (Tafoughalt; Morocco, 11–12,000 BP): New hypotheses based on a grave by grave skeletal inventory and evidence of deliberate human modification of the remains. *Journal of Human Evolution, 56*(4), 340–354.

Martin, D. L. & Frayer, D. (Eds.). (1998). *Troubled times: Violence and warfare in the past*. Amsterdam, Netherlands: Gordon & Breach.

Matsumura, H., & Pookajorn, S. (2002). A morphometric analysis of the Late Pleistocene human skeletons from the Moh Kwiew Cave in Thailand (abstract). *Anthropological Science, 111*(1), 141.

McDermott, F., Stringer, C. B., Grün, R., Williams, C., Din, V., & Hawkesworth, C. (1996). New Late Pleistocene uranium-thorium and ESR dates for the Singa hominid (Sudan). *Journal of Human Evolution, 31*(6), 507–516.

Meier, R. J., Sahnouni, M., Medig, M., & Derradji A. (2003). Human skull from the Taza locality, Jijel, Algeria. *Anthropologischer Anzeiger, 61*, 129–140.

Meiklejohn, C., Pardoe, C., & Lubell, D. (1979). The adult skeleton from the Capsian site of Aïn Misteheyia, Algeria. *Journal of Human Evolution, 8*(4), 411–426.

Meiklejohn, C., Bosset, G., & Valentin F. (2010). Radiocarbon dating of Mesolithic human remains in France. *Mesolithic Miscellany, 21*(1), 10–56.

Minellono, F., Pardini, E., & Fornaciari, G. (1980). Le Seplture Epigravettiane di Vado all'Arancio (Grosseto). *Rivista di Scienze Preistoriche, 35*, 3–44.

Morel, P. (1993). Une Chasse à l'ours Brun il y a 12000 Ans: Nouvelle Découverte à la Grotte du Bicho (La Chaux-de-Fonds). *Archäologie der Schweiz 16*(3), 110–116.

Moser, J. (2003). *La Grotte d'Ifri n'Ammar, Tome 1, L'Ibéromaurusien*, Vol. 8. Aichwald, Germany: Allgemeine und Vergleichende Archäologie.

Naroll, R. (1966). Does military deterrence deter? *Trans-Action, 3*(2), 14–20.

Nash, G. H. (2005). Assessing rank and warfare strategy in prehistoric hunter-gatherer society: A study of representational warrior figures in rock-art from the Spanish Levant. In P. Pearson & I. Thorpe (Eds.), *Warfare, violence and slavery in prehistory* (pp. 75–86). BAR International Series 1374. Oxford: Archaeopress,

Nielsen, A., & Walker, W. (2009). *Warfare in cultural context: Practice, agency, and the archaeology of violence*. Tucson: University of Arizona Press.

Oakley, K., & Campbell, B. (Eds.) (1967). *Catalogue of fossil hominids. Part I: Africa*. London: Trustees of the British Museum (Natural History).

Oakley, K., Campbell, B., & Molleson, T. (Eds.) (1971). *Catalogue of fossil hominids. Part II: Europe*. London: Trustees of the British Museum (Natural History).

Oakley, K., Campbell, B., & Molleson, T. (Eds.) (1975). *Catalogue of fossil hominids. Part III: Americas, Asia, Australia*. London: Trustees of the British Museum (Natural History).

Orschiedt, J. (2000) Germany: Hominid remains an up-date. *Anthropologie et Préhistoire* (Supplement 10).

Otterbein, K. F. (1970). *The evolution of war: A cross-cultural study* (Second ed.). New Haven, CT: Human Relations Area Files Press.

Otterbein, K. F. (1989). Socialization for war. Appendix E in the evolution of war: A cross-cultural study, (Third ed.). New Haven, CT: Human Relations Area Files Press.

Otterbein, K. F. (2004). *How war began*. College Station: Texas A&M University Press.

Otterbein, K. F. (2009). *The anthropology of war*. Long Grove, IL: Waveland Press.

Otterbein, K. F. (2011). The earliest evidence for warfare?: A comment on Carbonell et al. *Current Anthropology, 52*(3), 439.

Pardoe, C. (1995). Riverine, biological and cultural evolution in Southeastern Australia. *Antiquity, 69*(265), 696–713.

Perrot, J. (1966). Le gisement natoufien de Mallaha(Eynan), Israel. *Anthropologie, 70*, 437–483.

Pettitt, P. B., Richards, M., Maggi, R., & Formicola, V. (2003). The Gravettian Burial known as the Prince (Il Principe): New evidence for his age and diet. *Antiquity, 77*(295), 15–19.

Pettitt, P.B. & Trinkaus. E. (2000). Direct radiocarbon dating of the Brno 2 Gravettian human remains. *Anthropologie, 38*, 149–150.

Pinker, S. (2011). *The better angels of our nature: Why violence has declined.* New York: Viking Press.

Pond, A. W. (1928). A contribution to the study of prehistoric man in Algeria, North Africa. Beloit, WI: The Logan Museum.

Raaflaub, K. A. & Rosenstein, N. (2001). War and society in the ancient and medieval worlds: Asia, the Mediterranean, Europe, and Mesoamerica. Cambridge: Center for Hellenic Studies.

Ramirez Rozzi, F., d'Errico, F., Vanhaeren, M., Grootes, P., Kerautret, B., & Dujardin, (2009). Cutmarked human remains bearing Neandertal features and modern human remains associated with the Aurignacian at Les Rois. *Journal of Anthropological Sciences, 87*, 153–185.

Roper, M. (1969). A survey of the evidence for intrahuman killing in the Pleistocene. *Current Anthropology, 10*(4), 427–460.

Ross, M. (1983). Political decision making and conflict: Additional cross-cultural codes and scales. *Ethnology, 22*(2), 169–192.

Ross, M. (1985). Internal and external violence: Cross-cultural evidence and a new analysis. *Journal of Conflict Resolution, 29*(4), 547–579.

Rougier, H., Milota, S., Rodrigo, R., Gherase, M., Sarcină, L., Moldovan, . . . & Trinkhaus, E. (2007). Peştera cu Oase 2 and the cranial morphology of early modern Europeans. *PNAS, 104*(4), 1165–1170.

Sereno, P., Elena A. A. Garcea, Hélène Jousse, Christopher M. Stojanowski, Jean- Francois, . . . & Jeffrey P. Stivers (2008). Lakeside Cemeteries in the Sahara, 5000 years of Holocene population and environmental change. *PLoS ONE 8*(3), e2995.

Service, E. (1962). *Primitive social organization: An evolutionary perspective.* New York: Random House.

Steward, J. (1956). *Theory of culture change.* Urbana: University of Illinois Press.

Shackelford, L. (2007). Regional variation in the postcranial robusticity of Late Upper Paleolithic humans. *American Journal of Physical Anthropology 133*(1), 655–668.

Shang, H., Haowen, T., Shuangquan, Z., Fuyou, C., & Trinkaus, E. (2007). An early modern human from Tianyuan Cave. *PNAS, 104*(16), 6573–6578.

Schulting, R., Trinkaus, E., Higham, T., Hedges, R., Richards, M., & Cardy B. (2005). A Mid-Upper Palaeolithic human humerus from Eel Point, South Wales, UK. *Journal of Human Evolution*, 48(5), 493–505.

Smith, D. L. (2009). *The most dangerous animal: Human nature and the origins of war.* New York: St. Martin's Press.

Soficaru, A., Petrea, C., Dobos, A., & Trinkaus, E. (2007). The human cranium from Peştera Cioclovina Ucastă, Romania: Context, age, taphonomy, morphology, and paleopathology. *Current Anthropology, 48*(4), 611–619.

Stock, J. T., Pfeiffer, S., Chazan, M., & Janetski, J. (2005). F-81 skeleton from Wadi Mataha, Jordan, and its bearing on human variability in the Epipaleolithic of the Levant. *American Journal of Physical Anthropology 128*(2), 453–465.

Susuki, H., & Hanihara. K. (Eds.) (1982). *The Minatogawa man: The Upper Pleistocene man from the Island of Okinawa.* University Museum Bulletin 19. Tokyo: University of Tokyo.

Svoboda, J. (2008). The Upper Paleolithic burial area at Predmostí: Ritual and taphonomy. *Journal of Human Evolution, 54*(1):15–33.

Svoboda, J. (Ed.). (1997). *Pavlov I-Northwest. The Upper Paleolithic Burial and its Settlement Context.* The Dolní Věstonice Studies 4. Brno, Czech Republic: Academy of Sciences of the Czech Republic.

Telegin, D. J. (1961). Vasilivs'kij Tretij Nekropol'n Nadporizhzhi. *Arxeolojia, 13*, 3–19.

Thayer, Bradley A. (2004). *Darwin and international relations: On the evolutionary origins of war and ethnic conflict.* Lexington: The University Press of Kentucky.

Thorpe, I. (2005). The ancient origins of warfare and violence. In P. Pearson & I. Thorpe (Eds.), *Warfare, violence and slavery in prehistory* (pp. 1–18). BAR International Series 1374. Oxford: Archaeopress,

Thorpe, I. (2008). Anthropology, archaeology, and the origin of warfare. *World Archaeology, 35*(1), 145–165.

Trinkaus, E. & Jelinek. J. (1997). Human remains from the Moravian Gravettian: The Dolni Vestonice 3 postcrania. *Journal of Human Evolution, 33*(1), 33–82.

Trinkaus, E., & Svoboda, J. (2006). *Early modern human evolution in Central Europe: The people of Dolní Věstonice & Pavlov*. New York: Oxford University Press.

Tuggle, H., & J. Reid (2001). Conflict and defense in the Grasshopper region of East- Central Arizona. In G. Rice & S. LeBlanc (Eds.), *Deadly landscapes: Case studies in prehistoric southwestern warfare*, (pp. 85–108). Salt Lake City: University of Utah Press.

Turner, C., & Turner, J. (1999). *Man corn: Cannibalism and violence in the prehistoric American Southwest*. Salt Lake City: University of Utah Press.

Ullrich, H. (1992). Armenia, Azerbaijan, George, Russia, Ukraine & Uzbekistan. Hominid remains an up-date. *Anthropologie et Préhistoire* (Supplement 5, p. 91).

Vencl, S. (1984). War and warfare in archaeology. *Journal of Anthropological Archaeology 3*, 116–132.

Vercellotti, G., Alciati, G., Richards, M., & Formicola, V. (2008). The Late Upper Paleolithic skeleton Villabruna 1 (Italy): A source of data on biology and behavior of a 14,000 year-old hunter. *Journal of Anthropological Sciences, 86*, 143–163.

Wendorf, F. (1968). Site 117: A Nubian final paleolithic graveyard near Jebel Sahaba, Sudan. In F. Wendorf (Ed.), *The prehistory of Nubia* (pp. 954–995). Dallas: Southern Methodist University Press.

Wendorf, F., & Schild, R. (1986). *The Wadi Kubbaniya skeleton: A late Paleolithic burial from southern Egypt*. Dallas: Southern Methodist University Press.

Wilcox, D., & Haas, J. (1994). The scream of the butterfly: Competition and conflict in the prehistoric southwest. In G. Gumerman (Ed.), *Themes in Southwestern Prehistory*, (pp. 211–238). Santa Fe: School of American Research Press.

Wobst, M. (1978). The archaeo-ethnology of hunter-gatherers or the tyranny of the ethnographic record in archaeology. *American Antiquity 43*(2), 303–309.

Wu, R. (1982). Paleoanthropology in China, 1949–1979. *Current Anthropology 23*(5), 473–477.

11

The Prehistory of War and Peace in Europe and the Near East

R. Brian Ferguson

This second of two companion chapters intends to demonstrate that prehistoric war was not ubiquitous, that it is in fact rare in very early archaeological records, and becomes common only over time. It makes that claim based on a proper method, of compiling and comparing the *total* record regarding war and peace, from across regions of Europe and the Near East.

This chapter challenges the repeated refrain of "absence of evidence is not evidence of absence." War does leave behind recoverable evidence. True, in some cases, war could be present but for some reason not leave traces. However, comparison of many, many cases, from all different regions, shows some clear patterns. In the earliest remains, other than occasional cannibalism, there is no evidence of war, and barely any of interpersonal violence. In Europe's Mesolithic, war is scattered and episodic, and in the comparable Epipaleolithic of the Near East, it is absent. Neolithic records vary, but all except one begin with at least a half a millennium of peace, then war appears in some places, and over time war becomes the norm. War does not extend forever backwards. It has identifiable beginnings.

Even in later periods, when war clearly is present, casualties rarely (though sometimes) reach levels that have been recorded among recent tribal peoples.[1] When considered against the total record, the idea that 15 percent of prehistoric populations died in war (see Ferguson, chapter 7) is not just false, it is absurd. Moving beyond that easily falsified point, and the *assumption* that war at some level was always present, opens up interesting questions about early war, how it relates to broader anthropological theory, and to the really broad question of whether it is human nature to make war.

The plan is simple: starting with Europe, then moving on to the Near East, in all cases, all available evidence of war and/or interpersonal violence will be considered, contextualized, and evaluated as to the presence or absence of war. Discussion of Europe begins with the Paleolithic, then the Mesolithic, and for Neolithic times, becomes regionally specific, moving around the continental regions in a big circle: Greece, Italy, France, Iberia, England, Northern Europe, and Eastern Europe. With each region, I will begin with evidence from the earliest Neolithic, and move forward through the end of the Neolithic to the Chalcolithic and, sometimes, Early Bronze Age. The Near Eastern section, after a brief encounter with Neanderthals, starts with the Epipaleolithic Natufians. Three regions emerge as significant in the Near East—the Southern Levant, the Anatolian highlands, and an area I will call the northern Tigris. Each will be considered and compared following standard periodization: the Pre-Pottery Neolithic A, Pre-Pottery Neolithic B, Pottery Neolithic, Chalcolithic, and Early Bronze Age. In both Europe and the Near East, the literature reviews begin without signs of war, and end in periods when war is unambiguously established and often a dominant factor in social life.

Theory

My position is that human beings have no evolved predisposition to inflict deadly violence on people outside their own social group (Sussman, chapter 6; Fry & Szala, chapter 23). Human behavior is plastic, open equally to both altruistic cooperation and deadly conflict. I also subscribe to Marx's 8th thesis on Feuerbach, "all social life is essentially practical." As a broad generalization, war starts when those who start it believe that course is in their own, practical self-interest. Practicality is culturally and historically specific. Evaluations and decisions—*agency*—occurs and is structured by existing social relations and cultural psychology, within the context of concrete historical circumstances. The theoretical challenge is to elucidate in a cross-culturally consistent way the interrelationship between this enormous conjuncture of material, social, and symbolic variables (Ferguson, 1984; 1988; 1990; 1992; 1995; 2003a; 2006a; 2009). One particularly relevant point is that as war is woven through the fabric of social life, it becomes not only a cultural possibility, but even a cultural necessity (1999). But war is by no means inevitable. "Even at relatively advanced levels of sociocultural evolution, there is no reason, theoretically, to deny the possibility of peaceful societies. Indeed, there may be alternative peaceable and militaristic *trajectories* of evolution" (Ferguson, 1994, p. 103).

This general understanding of war, developed through ethnology, is applied to the archaeological record in earlier publications (Ferguson, 1997; 2001a; 2003b; 2006b; 2008). From study of the earliest evidence of violence from around the world, I (Ferguson, 2008, pp. 24–26) settle on several *preconditions,* which in varying combinations make the observed onset of warfare more likely: geographic concentration of critical resources, sedentism, high population density, food storage and/or livestock, social divisions creating separate collective identities,[2] social and political hierarchy or ranking, monopolizable long-distance trade in valuable prestige goods, and major ecological reversals affecting food production. Obviously, all these variables may be causally interrelated, and affect possibilities for war not singly but in systemic interaction.

Although there are some exceptions, developments in some or all of these areas regularly precede any evidence that can be construed as warfare. Yet there are other cases where some or all of these preconditions exist for extended periods, apparently without war. The preconditions may be necessary, but not sufficient to explain the onset of war in archaeological sequences. There is something lacking in these preconditions as an explanation of war.

Part of that is omitting the factors that lead to peace. One of the main developments in the anthropology of war in the past two decades is appreciation that peace is an active state, with its own preconditions, independent of those that lead to war (Dye, 2009; Fry, 2006; Gregor, 1996; Sponsel & Gregor, 1994; Ury, 2002). Fry (2007, pp. 207–229) boils down this wide-ranging, complex literature into a few general categories: social ties that cross-cut and connect different social groups, mutual interdependence and cooperative effort, attitudes and beliefs that valorize peace and stigmatize violence, authoritative institutions that can prevent resort to attack, and established processes to resolve conflicts for the common good. These may not be obvious within the accumulated knowledge of archaeology, but they are not impossible to investigate (see Dye, chapter 8). They will only be found if they are looked for. In this chapter, I argue that some evidence suggests that one region, the Near East's Southern Levant, does have "peace signs," that fit with an extraordinarily long existence without any persuasive evidence of war.

Evidence

Numerous excellent reviews of archaeological evidence and ambiguities concerning war are available (Chapman, 1999; Jackes, 2004; Jurmain, 1999; Knusel, 2005; Milner, 2005; Schulting, 2006; Smith, Brickley, & Leach, 2007; Walker, 2001). Here I will discuss mainly the issues relevant for assessing the presence of war in this chapter.

Evidence comes in four categories. One, artistic representation of combat or killing is the least common in earlier records discussed here, appearing only in later Neolithics or the Copper Age. Another, technology, is more useful, but often ambiguous. Chapman (1999, pp. 107–112) distinguishes tool-weapons, clearly used for work but also usable for killing people; weapon-tools, probably used for fighting but possibly for work; and weapons proper, such as swords. The presence of a great many tool-weapons is only a weak positive for war, but their absence is a strong negative. Maces are weapons-tools, and they merit special consideration.

Mace-heads are often the earliest weapon-tool in archaeological recovery. Yet mace-heads are often so small or lightly constructed that they appear to be symbolic. Symbolic of what? Of military prowess, or of legitimate *authority*—as used today by royalty, legislatures, and courts. Maces can be weapons of war, yet my university has a mace. Yes, there is an implication of power backed by force, but that can apply to mandatory decisions. Authority to settle conflicts is, as Hobbes illuminated, the very antithesis of war. In the Near East, there is a profusion of maces, but deaths possibly attributable to a mace-blow are exceedingly rare. Without other evidence, a mace-head, particularly lightly made, cannot be taken as diagnostic of war. What is needed is for scholars to indicate the robustness of a mace head, how big and heavy is it, and particularly, would the shaft be large enough to withstand a blow. If the pattern in the artifact assembly is that they are all ceremonial and there are no combat mace-heads, the obvious inference is that they are symbols of authority. In this chapter, the presence of maces is often noted, but only a few times can their utility be ascertained.

Settlement data is a broader source of insight. It can range from conclusive to suggestive, though this kind of evidence is variable, usually non-existent, in earlier remains. Fortifications can be clear-cut, though village enclosures of simple walls, hummocks, or ditches are often ambiguous. The interpretive issue, militarily speaking, is that a ditch or mound around a village could be more advantageous for attackers than residents. If attackers got there first, which is likely with the element of surprise, either would provide cover for raining projectiles into the settlement. But erect a palisade on top of an encircling mound, especially with dogs to bark if anyone tries to scale it—then that is protection. Add multiple encirclements, elaborated gates, or bafflements, and the presence or potential of war is obvious. Yet even nondefensive enclosures may have military significance. A major contrast between Neolithic Europe and some areas of the Near East is that the former saw a widespread pattern of enclosures defining and separating local communities, which did not develop in the latter. That may have been a critical difference in their diverging trajectories of war and peace.

Skeletal remains can be conclusive indicators of interpersonal violence. Recovery is always an issue, especially when dealing with fragments. Embedded projectile points or their cuts are clear signs of deadly violence. As often noted, only about one in three or four projectiles will impact bone (Milner, 2005, pp. 150–151). That does not mean a general rule of multiplying the noted dead by three. Many war victims are hit by multiple projectiles, increasing the likelihood of being evident. Many are killed by blows to the head, which are hard to miss with a skull. Points in soft tissue may be extracted, but many still appear closely associated in graves. Whether these are grave offerings or are from wounds is a judgment call, but many do get counted. In the famous Jebel Sahaba remains (Ferguson, chapter 7), for instance, the great majority of inferred killings are from associated, not embedded, points.

Blunt force trauma is often difficult to interpret, especially if healed. Parry fractures of the forearm can be accidental (see Jurmain, 1999, pp. 215–223), as can be compression fractures of the skull.[3] Even where a clear pattern of cranial injury is apparent, healed fractures may come from ritualized club fights, as among the Surma (Abbink, 1999) or Mursi (Turton 1979, pp. 197–201), domestic violence, as in the American southwest (Martin, 1997; also Novak, 2006), or sacrifice, as in ancient Peru (Verano, 2001). "The fact that— apart from mass grave contexts—a large proportion of cranial injuries are healed could suggest a more controlled form of violence in which the death of the participants was not seen as appropriate" (Schulting, 2006, pp. 228). To make the point more bluntly, there is no practice of tribal warfare I know of that would result in a high frequency of healed but few, or no, perimortem cranial fractures. If warriors get close enough to land such a blow, they kill.

A pattern of healed cranial fractures does indicate violence. It does not indicate war; indeed it may represent a way of dealing with conflict without killing.

A single case of traumatic death, from a projectile or a blow, by itself cannot be taken as evidence of war. Either could result from interpersonal violence, social execution, or even an accident. That is why the few but often-listed (Ferguson, 2006b, pp. 480–481; Roper, 1969, pp. 447–448; Thorpe, 2005, pp. 8–9) cases of single Paleolithic individuals with embedded points are destined to remain ambiguous. There is also a real danger of false positives of war. If within-group homicides were occurring in the ancient past as they do among the Gebusi and some other ethnographically known peoples (Knauft, 1987), that would be very difficult to distinguish from those caused by external enemies.

Dismemberment consistent with trophy-taking (see Chacon & Dye, 2007) can be good evidence of war, yet separation of the head or other body parts is often part of mortuary customs, quite common in the Near East. People killed in war may not appear in cemeteries, lying where they fell, which might be inferred by a notable absence of warrior-age men among remains. Then again, dead warriors may receive special attention in interment, as suspected at Jebel Sahaba (although I know of no other case of a "warriors' cemetery"). Multiple burials may be used to infer war deaths, but only when signs of violence are known for the site. Otherwise, disease or some other catastrophe is just as likely, at least in the Neolithic (Schulting, 2006, pp. 231–232). The origin of domestication also appears to be the origin of several infectious diseases, although processes now appear more complex than the old idea of transmission from herd animals (Pearce–Duvet, 2006; Wolfe, Dunavan, & Diamond, 2007).

Cannibalism has its own problems. After a long history of seeing signs of cannibalism in every fractured prehistoric bone, criteria for diagnosis have become much more precise (Knusel & Outram, 2006). The enduring problem, however, is inferring whether the dead were enemies killed in war, or members of the group consumed in mortuary rites (see Conklin, 2001, pp. xiii–xxxi). Knusel and Outram's (2006, p. 266) review concludes: "One of the enduring problems with records of cannibalism is that the mortuary type of cannibalism, endo-cannibalism, is confused with exo-cannibalism;" and suggests a key variable for identifying the latter is signs of violent death (p. 263). Without that, evidence of cannibalism just raises a big question, and especially so when found in hominins prior to modern *Homo sapiens*.

Evidence that can indicate war will vary by location and time. Sometimes only skeletons are available, sometimes few skeletons are found and settlement or other remains have to suffice. It is often the case that war may be deduced only by a pattern of inconclusive but suggestive clues, though a pattern of such clues can raise inferences from "war possible" to "likely." As Pearson (2005, p. 24) puts it:

> There is no standard "cook book" formula of middle range theory to provide a
> cut-and-dried clinical diagnosis of warfare, violence or slavery from archaeological
> remains: each case has to be built up as a closely argued and richly textured
> contextual regional study which draws on multiple strands of evidence which, when

analyzed in isolation, are often inconclusive and ambiguous. In many cases the evidence must be argued on a balance of probabilities.

The common refrain of "absence of evidence is not evidence of absence" is certainly true for any one or a few excavations. But if the absence of evidence is reported by scholars who have looked for it in many sites, without any persuasive indicators of war, than pleading scholarly "pacification of the past" amounts to "warrification of the past." That is especially so in an area sequence that goes from no evidence to clear evidence of war, without an abrupt increase in material recovery; or by comparison within one period where war-signs are overt in some situations, but entirely lacking in others.

The remainder of this chapter demonstrates an alternative to that used in Pinker's List (Ferguson, chapter 7), of selectively presenting cases with exceptionally high rates of violence as representative (Fry, chapter 1). The whole records of both Europe and the Near East will be surveyed, not only for evidence of war, but also to take seriously the absence of evidence. When this even-handed approach is employed, the development of war out of a warless background is shown again and again. Referring back to the two questions animating chapter 7 (Ferguson): does the presence of prehistoric warfare indicate a human tendency to kill outsiders? Does prehistoric war indicate a selective mechanism capable of shaping the evolution of human nature? The answer to both is a resounding no.

Europe

The earliest suggestions of war in Europe are quite old indeed. Remains of 11 young individual's from Gran Dolina, dated to around 780,000 BP, show good indications of a pattern of cannibalism (Fernandez-Jalvo, Y., Diez, J. C., Caceres, I, & Rossell, J., 1999). Carbonell, Caceras, Lozano, Saladie, Rosell, Lorenzo . . . & Bermudez de Castro (2010) speculate that because the bones were disposed like those of game animals, this indicates a pattern of one group hunting others, both for nutrition and to reduce competition. Otterbein (2011), whose theory of war says that it was normal among ancient game hunters, jumps in to "conclude that the earliest evidence of warfare has been found." But *Homo antecessor* is a different species, with a cranial capacity around 1000 cc, teeth like African *Homo erectus*, and of questionable placement in human ancestry, though they may be ancestral to Neanderthals (White & Folkens, 1999, p. 499). There is no indication of how these individuals died, and as noted, humans sometimes eat their own. This does not demonstrate war. There are also the enigmatic (though not cannibalized) findings from Sima de los Huesos, Spain (probably >300,000 BP), where all eight craniums have erosion depressions. There are no traumatic fractures in post-cranial remains from 33 individuals, and the depressions seem to be due to scalp inflammations, which might be due to blows, or maybe to infections (Perez, P.-J., Martinez, A., & Arsuaga, J. L., 1997, p. 417).

Middle and Upper Paleolithic

Whether Neanderthals at Krapina ate each other has been debated for years without res-olution (Berger & Trinkaus, 1995; Estabrook & Frayer, 2012; Knusel & Outram, 2006, pp. 266–267; Trinkaus, 1985; Villa, 1992, pp. 96; White, 2001), though another case of Neanderthal cannibalism seems more secure (Defleur, White, Valensi, Slimak, & Cregut-Bonnoure, 1999). The same problem persists—cannibalism does not demonstrate war. One indication of some sort of violence among Neanderthals is the young adult from St. Cesaire who has a healed skull fracture, probably from a sharp object (Zollikofer, C. P. E., Ponce de Leon, M. S., Vandermeersch, B., & Leveque, F., 2002). Although some Neanderthal skeletons do show high levels of trauma, these do not fit the profile of war wounds. Berger and Trinkaus (1985) find them resembling those of modern rodeo riders, suggesting Neanderthals had more problems with mammals with four legs rather than those with two.

Turning to modern humans, Upper Paleolithic cave art is frequently cited as evi-dence of violence or war. But as discussed in Ferguson (2006, pp. 181–182), the bent or wavy lines that pass over, around, into, and through the human figures are starkly differ-ent from the straight, V-tipped lines portrayed as hitting large animals in another cave. What those non-spear-like lines depict is an open question (Haas & Piscitelli, chapter 10). In Gough's Cave, Somerset, England, from the very end of the Pleistocene 11,000–9500 BC, the remains of five individuals show signs of processing for consumption, suggest-ing cannibalism. The same problem persists here as always: cannibalism does not mean war, although in this case, one of the individuals may show signs of trauma (Andrews & Fernandez-Jalvo, 2003; Heath, 2009, pp. 16–18).

From the testimony of the bones, the European late Upper Paleolithic has two or three individuals with embedded points. At Grimaldi, Italy (Dastugue and de Lumley, 1976, p. 617), a child had a point embedded in the vertebra, probably lethal. At San Teodoro (Bachechi, Fabbri, & Mallegni, 1997), a (probable) female had a lithic point embedded in the hip, but with healing. A century ago at Montfort Saint-Lizier in France, a surface find produced a human vertebra with an embedded point (Guilaine & Zammit, 2005, p. 50), but this may be Mesolithic (Thorpe, 2003a p. 152).

In the Czech Republic, one area has been cited by Keeley (1996, p. 37) and LeBlanc with Register (2003, p. 124) as substantiating the claim of Paleolithic warfare, Predmosti and Dolni Vestonice (25,000–23,000 BC). LeBlanc with Register claim these sites have "almost every line of evidence for warfare" including large longhouses, a wall or fence of mammoth bones, mass burials of "fighting age men," head wounds, and location on a high point that was defendable against spear throwers. These claims are evaluated elsewhere (Ferguson, 2006, pp. 505–507). Not one is accurate. Instead, there were small huts, a long-term cemetery but no mass interment, no wall, cranial trauma only of a minor sort, and location partway up a slope with higher ground right behind it (and see Gamble, 1999, pp. 386–414; Svoboda, Lozek, & Vlcek, 1996). There is one triple burial with some unusual aspects (Alt, Pichler, Vach, Klima, Vlcek, & Sedlmeier, 1997; Formicola, 2001), but nothing suggesting deadly violence. The only other possible contender for Paleolithic warfare (it is on the cusp of the Mesolithic) are the Dnieper rapids sites discussed in Pinker's List (Ferguson, chapter 7). I will revisit it below as Mesolithic.

Holt and Formicola's (2008, pp. 87–91) table of Upper Paleolithic skeletal remains tallies 103 from Europe, including Grimaldi and San Teodoro (but apparently not Montfort). Calculating on that basis, the only reported death from violence is the Grimaldi child, amounting to just under 1 percent. Brennan (1991) directly examined all available Middle and Upper Paleolithic remains (including Neanderthals) from southwestern France, a total of 209 though most very fragmentary, and found a total of five fractures of any sort, concluding "the absence of a single parry fracture or wound to the left side of the head in my sample seems to belie some of the previously held notions in the literature of bestial behavior and violence for this time period." Holt and Formicola's (2008, p. 80) review of Middle to Upper Paleolithic cases across Europe found numerous traumas, but "with the exception of the fracture affecting the ulna of CV 15 that could represent a parry fracture, there is no evidence of deliberate injury." In an overview of the eastern European Paleolithic, Dolukhanov (1999, p. 77) concludes that "in no case could one find any evidence of inter-group conflict." Surveying the total record Dastugue and de Lumley (1976, p. 612) conclude "the first *Homo sapiens* do not seem to have led the warrior's life so often attributed to them, for their pathology is not marked by a traumatology other than that caused by the accidents of everyday life."

The European Paleolithic is our best record of lifeways before the massive transformations of the Holocene. The commentators just quoted are not pacifiers of the past. They are scholars who have searched for signs of violence, and did not find it. Looked at every way the evidence allows, the entire Paleolithic record produces just one individual, a child, killed by other humans. "Absence of evidence is not evidence of absence," the proponents of war forever backwards claim. And given the relatively limited amount of evidence, it would be foolish to assert that there was *no* war in the Paleolithic. Yet the evidence from the European Paleolithic that could show signs of deadly violence, does not. Compare this to signs of trauma in cases selected for Pinker's List, or those to come in this chapter. There is no support here for war as an expression of innate human tendencies, or a selective force driving human psychological evolution, and certainly not for the claim of 15 percent war mortality.

Mesolithic

The start of the Mesolithic is associated with the transition from the Pleistocene to Holocene, conventionally dated to 8000 BC, but calibrated to 9,500 (Anderson, Maasch, Sandweiss, & Mayewski, 2007, pp. 3–4). This foraging epic ends at different times as agriculture develops or spreads across Europe. The European Mesolithic, generally, is a time of increasing complexity. The concept of complexity among hunter-gatherers is hotly debated, in its definition, in its variables, and in its causal connections, including climatic effects (Cohen, 1985; Hayden, 1995, pp.15–86; Kelly, 1995, pp. 303–331; Price and

Brown, 1985; Sassaman, 2004). But in most formulations, some basic parameters appear: higher populations, more sedentism, foraging concentrated on spatially limited and highly productive sites, food storage, definition of more distinctive social groups, and sociopolitical hierarchy. These all apply, with local variations, to the European Mesolithic. They are also preconditions for the development of warfare, as with ethnographically known *complex* hunter-gatherers, which are widely known for making war (Kelly, 1995, pp. 303, 311–315).

Vencl (1999, pp. 59, 70; also Dolukhanov, 1999, p. 77; Thorpe, 2003a, p. 155; Vencl, 1983:121) sees the Mesolithic as "the formative period of warfare," though others caution against overgeneralizing the evidence of violence (Chapman, 1999, pp. 105–106; Roksandic, 2004a, 2004b; Thorpe, 2005, pp. 10–11). As noted above, preconditions are only necessary, not sufficient, conditions for war. The entire package of traits may be oriented to nonviolent coping with subsistence variability. In Europe, some Mesolithic societies made war, or may have, but others did not. The following survey, in rough chronological order, demonstrates that variation and the perils of averaging, while contradicting the idea that warfare was a general characteristic of prehistoric peoples.

Lethal wounds in 11 of 82 individuals from three cemeteries on the Dnieper rapids were noted in chapter 7 as the earliest evidence of war in Europe. From around 10,000 BC, these have been called both Epipaleolithic (Lillie, 2001, p. 55) and Mesolithic (Dolukhanov, 1999, p. 79). Whichever, it was a time of "deep ecological and sociocultural crisis" (1999, p. 78) for peoples in steppe environments, with decreasing resource productivity, a shift to plant gathering, disintegration of larger communities, migrations, and signs of hierarchy and tribal differentiation. War may have been waged to get access to favorable locations (Stanko, 1997, pp. 259–260). That seems likely along the rapids. Right at the end of the last Ice Age, "as soon as the glaciers melted, at least three skull-and-face types . . . occupied different cemeteries and were buried in different poses" (Anthony, 2007, p. 157). On the middle Danube, the Iron Gates Gorge of Serbia-Romania is a comprehensively excavated record of the Mesolithic to Early Neolithic settlements (Radovanovic, 1996). Four-hundred-eighteen individuals, including 263 adults, were recovered from six cemeteries on the right bank of the river, 8200–5500 BC. Of the adults, six (2.3 percent) showed signs of violent injury, with two probable deaths, one from a cranial blow, and one from a projectile. There was no temporal clustering, but they all preceded the development of farming in the area (Roksandic, Djuric, Rakocevic, & Seguin, 2006, pp. 340–345). Roksandic (2006, p. 177) concludes that these are unrelated incidents that "could have as easily happened within the community as with members of other groups." In contrast, downstream from the Gorge, at Schela Cladovei (7303–7545 cal BC), of 57 individuals, 5 have fatal injuries, from skull fractures and projectiles, and 14 others have non-lethal trauma. Seven of the total are from Schela Cladovei III, and appear to be from the same time. Roksandic et al. (2006, pp. 345–347) infer that this represents a "localized and temporarily restricted" episode of warfare (2004, p. 72). Projectiles per individual are 0.0 percent at Lepenski Vir (n = 103) and .8 percent at Vlasac (n = 118) in the Gorge, and

10.7 percent at Schela Cladovei III (n = 28) (Roksandic et al., 2006, p. 117). (Roksandic et al. use these findings to argue against the idea that the Mesolithic was characterized by endemic warfare).

In Greece, Franchthi Cave has 3 of 6 adults (7600–7200 BC) with traumatic injuries (Angel 1969:380). The single lethality is later than the others, from a time when subsistence had undergone a marked shift to marine resources. More intriguingly, that time also sees a proliferation of obsidian from Melos, demonstrating sea-born trade (Jacobsen 1969:376; 1973:82–85). In the Near East, monopolization of trade in obsidian is associated with the development of war.

There is possible cannibalism of three infants and five adults at Perrats in France in the seventh millennium, with the usual question—how did they die (Boulestin, 1999)? The most famous instance of Mesolithic violence is Ofnet, Bavaria, where two "nests" of skulls and skull fragments of 33/34 individuals were found close to each other, dating to around 5700 BC (Frayer, 1997, p. 187). The demographic profile is unusual, with young people and females predominating. Fourteen have definite, and two more possible, perimortem fractures, most on the back of the head, possibly from polished stone axes known from the later Mesolithic. Frayer (1997, pp. 208–209) believes all in each pit were interred simultaneously, inferring a "massacre." But Orschiedt (2005, pp. 68, 72) challenges that inference with evidence of sequential interments. This makes a difference—is it one big massacre, or a smaller one with later burials added? Going with the high number of 34 killings amounts to more deaths than from all other European Mesolithic sites *combined* (see below). Although clear evidence of multiple killings makes Ofnet strong evidence for war, what really happened there remains a mystery.

Three cases from Pinker's List are next. The late Mesolithic Ertebolle period of northern Germany, Denmark, and southwest Sweden is conventionally dated to 4500–3200 BC, calibrated at 5400–3900 (Richards, Price, & Koch, 2003, p. 288). (By 5000 BC, war was already well established among *Linearbandkeramik* LBK agriculturalists not far away—discussed below). Ertebolle culture was characterized by most of the complex hunter-gatherer package: local population growth, more permanent settlement, exploitation of fish in estuarine environments, trade in exotic goods, general social complexity—though apparently not much hierarchy (Nash, 2003, p. 160; Price, 1985, pp. 350–355, 360). As noted in chapter 7, Ertebolle culture has the reputation of being especially violent. But besides the violent deaths at Bogebakken (2 or 3 of 22) and Skateholm (2 of 53), other reported signs of violence (Bennike, 1985, pp. 98–115; Thorpe, 2003b, p. 172) involve healed skull fractures. Bennike (1985, p. 101) found these to be very common, but notes that most were found in the middle of the frontal bone. "If a large part of these injuries should have been the result of fighting, one would surely have expected to find a greater number on the left side, but strangely enough that is not the case here." Subsequent unwounded finds lowered the average of trauma, but it "still remains high within the context of prehistoric Europe" (Schulting, 2006, p. 227). So how warlike was the Ertebolle, really? Outside Scandinavia, the Teviec region in

Brittany presents evidence suggesting war, with 1 or 2 individuals out of 23–25. Teviec too looks complex, with increasing sedentism, a focus of restricted aquatic resource, and social hierarchy (Bender, 1985, p. 23)

Iberia presents powerful negative evidence. From shell middens along the Muge and Sado Rivers in Portugal, 5500–3500 BC, examination of 308 individuals produced a total of 14 traumatic injuries. Post-cranial breaks seem accidental, but six healed depressions on the cranial frontal bone are likely due to blows (Cunha, Umbelino, & Cordasco 2004). Conflict, violence, yes, but no traumatic deaths are indicated.

A major cemetery at late Mesolithic (4000 BC) Oleneostrovski mogilnik in northern Russia reveals a very large, complex forager center, in a particularly rich boreal zone, immersed in long-distance trade of lithic materials (O'Shea, 1984, 29, 35). Trauma is not described, or denied, among its 170 individuals, though O'Shea spends several pages discussing the burials and possible social relations between groups. Dolukhanov (1999, 80) characterizes the area as "comparatively harmonious." Besides those cases, an "exhaustive catalogue" of Mesolithic remains (Newell, Constandse-Westermann, & Meiklejohn, 1979, pp. 39, 97) remains found two other probably lethal injuries: a pre-Ertebolle man from Gotland Sweden, c. 6000 BC, with a point embedded in the pelvis, and an unhealed skull fracture in a man of Cheddar, England, c. 7130 BC (Heath, 2009, p. 19–20). Vencl's (1991, p. 220) review adds one more, a woman from Popova, Russia, during the Boreal phase (7000–6000 BC), with a point in her shoulder. Of course, single deaths do not demonstrate the presence of war.

Considering the standard claim discussed in Pinker's List, of 15 percent average prehistoric war casualties, what does this amount to? Radovanic (1996, pp. 295–297) tabulates 1,107 individual remains from "formal disposal areas" for all of Europe. (This is not a complete list of all human remains.) His table includes all of the European cases in Pinker's List (number of deaths = 16), the Danubian cases (n = 7, including two singletons), and Ofnet (n = 14/34). Totaling those deaths plus Franchthi in Greece and the three single individuals just noted allows the following calculations against the total figure of 1,073 Mesolithic individuals: 3.7 percent with the low estimate for Ofnet (n = 41), 5.5. percent with the high estimate for Ofnet (n = 61), and 2.4 percent for all skeletal remains excluding Ofnet (n = 27). These figures include six single lethalities, which may not represent war. This death rate is much greater than for the Paleolithic, but the "violent" Mesolithic is reputed to be the time when war began—not as a general trend, evidently, but in some times and places.

The Neolithic

A highly simplified European framework dates the Early Neolithic to 5500–4200 BC, the Middle Neolithic to 4200–2800 BC, and the Late Neolithic to 2800–2200 BC (Christensen, 2004, p. 129), but dates vary considerably, with agriculture in the Aegean beginning at least a thousand years earlier than in Northwestern Europe (Gkiasta, Russel, Shennan, & Steele, 2003, p. 57–58; Parkinson & Duffy, 2007, p. 99). At equally varying dates starting in the later fifth millennium, most of Europe passes from the Neolithic to the Chalcolithic, or Copper Age, and from that to the Bronze Age. By those Ages, war had become a cultural obsession across Europe.

Before the Mesolithic got that reputation, the Neolithic was seen as the time of the origin of war. There is certainly a lot more evidence for it (Christensen, 2004; Guilaine & Zammit, 2005; Pearson, 2005). The Neolithic record is vastly more abundant than that of the Mesolithic, but with major gaps, regional and temporal variations, and causal complications. Many more skeletons are available, but numbers vary considerably along with changes in mortuary customs. Technology gives strong clues for war. A profusion of tool-weapons in the earlier Neolithics are joined over time by weapon-tools—daggers, axes, and maces. But the greatest source of information about the presence of war comes from settlements.

Villages are commonly enclosed by ditches and mounds, but whether these are for-tifications or ritual centers without defensive design has been debated heatedly (Carman and Carman, 2005, p. 219; Christensen, 2004, p. 142–152; Golitko & Keeley, 2007, p. 336–338; Keeley, 1996, p.18; Thorpe, 2005, p. 1–2; Whittle, 1985). Some are clearly geared for defense, others are not, and many are ambiguous. Building enclosures or mounds involve a great deal of coordinated, collective labor. When they appear across a landscape, its local groupings have become something more than ad hoc collections of families, prob-ably lineages or clans. Ritual activity is to be expected. Parkinson and Duffy's (2007) conclusions, after surveying Europe and beyond, seem reasonable: European enclosures represent more segmental social organization. Heightened group identity can be the social basis of either cooperation or violent competition, "different faces of intergroup interac-tion, one peaceful, the other violent" (p. 127). I would add that they are evidence for war only when they incorporate clear defensive preparations.

What follows is a tour around Europe, assessing the total war record rather than listing the most violent cases. A few extraordinarily violent events are reported, most from the final Early Neolithic LBK culture of northern Europe. Those killings are often cited as evidence of the high casualties of prehistoric war. Put in context, they stand out as far from normal. The overall record will reveal—with gaps as encountered in the literature—very limited violence or killings in the earliest Neolithic, with more signs of institutional-ized warfare developing through the Middle and Late Neolithic (with some exceptions), and being obvious in the elaborating weaponry of the Copper, Bronze, and Iron Ages. Coverage stops there, when war was firmly ensconced.

Southern Europe

In Greece, some Neolithic sites date to as early as the late tenth millennium, but more appear in the later ninth, probably representing diffusion/migration from Anatolia (Gkiasta et al., 2003, p. 57; Ozdogan, 2011). Although there are suggestions of defen-sive ditches in some Early Neolithic (6600–5700 BC) sites in Thessaly, trenches are more common in the Middle (5700–5350), and walls are more common in the Late and Final

Neolithic (5350–3200). Sesklos on Thessaly has an enclosure of debated purpose, but it was destroyed at the end of the Middle Neolithic. The sparse skeletal evidence of violent death, shifts in tools towards weapons, and settlement clustering with vacant spaces between, all became more common and pronounced through the Middle and into the Late and Final Neolithic (Andreaou, Fotiadis, & Kotsakis, 1996, pp. 541–543, 547; Kokkinidou & Nikolaidou, 1999, pp. 92–97; Runnels, Payne, Rifkind, White, Wolf, & LeBlanc, 2009, pp. 172–189). Yet one skeletal collection from Late/Final Neolithic Alepotrypa Cave has 9 of 69 individuals with small, healed cranial depressions, but still no indications of violent death (Papathanasiou, 2005:225). In the Early Bronze Age (3250–2250), walls are larger and more obviously defensive, with bastions (Andreou et al., 1996, p. 547). By the late Bronze Age and into the Early Iron Age, warrior burials are major cultural statements, though carrying different meanings (Whitley, 2002).

One line of the spreading Neolithic package through Europe went from Greece across the northern Mediterranean rim (Rowley-Conway, 2011). In Italy, limited evidence of cultivation begins in the period 6500–6200 BC, but by 5700 it was thriving. Around then, in the Tavolieri plain (and in some but not all other eastern Mediterranean sites) ditches surround the earliest farming villages. This is a good illustration of ambiguous enclosures, with defensive purpose very questionable. In some sites, houses within a village have additional open-C ditches around them too (Robb, 2007 pp. 91–95, 261–265; Skeates, 2000, p. 162). At almost every excavation, there are indications that houses were burned upon abandonment, but the careful tending of fires required indicates deliberate acts by those moving on, rather than an attack (Robb, 2007 p.89).

I am not aware of any data that indicates temporal trends in conflict over the entire Neolithic, and the advent of collective violence remains fundamentally ambiguous. "Evidence is sparse. There is no iconography or elaboration of material culture related to weaponry until the Late Neolithic" (Robb, 2007, p. 258). Analysis of the limited and fragmentary skeletal remains from Neolithic and later Italy indicates a substantial percentage of cranial and post-cranial trauma, though cause is unknown. Robb (1997, p. 134) notes cranial trauma is greater in the Neolithic taken as a whole than in the Bronze and Iron Ages, reputed to be very warlike—"actual violence, as far as cranial trauma reflects it, and the perceived threat of violence, as reflected in defensive architecture, appear to have declined precisely as the cultural celebration of violence increased" (p. 136).[4] By the Copper Age, metal daggers and other weapons are prominent (Robb, 2007, p. 300). "Otzi," the famous "ice man" of the Tyrolean Alps, is dated to 3360–3100 BC, around the Neolithic/Copper Age transition (Rom, Golser, Kutshera, Priller, Steier, & Wild, 1999). He was killed by an arrow in the back (Nerlich, Peschel, & Egarter-Vigl, 2009).

In France, the local Neolithic develops in the seventh millennium (Gkiasta et al., 2003, p. 58), and is often pegged to around 6000 BC. In southern France, the cave of Fontbregoua contained remains of 8 to 14 individuals. Careful analysis indicates cannibalism, from what is stratigraphically indicated to be of one moment (Villa et al., 1986; Villa, 1992, pp. 99–100). While cannibalism does not necessarily indicate war, it surely can be a result of it. War seems more likely in this case because new dating has moved this from around 3930 BC, to around 5000 (Le Bras-Goude et al., 2010, p. 174), which makes it roughly contemporary with massacres at Tallheim and Schletz-Asparn in Germany and Austria (see below). Yet human remains are not mixed with animal remains (mixing being an accepted indicator of cannibalism), and there is no evidence of violent death (Knusel & Outram, 2006, 263). Besides that extraordinary event, in a survey of all Neolithic human remains from France, some 2000–3000 individuals, 48 had projectile wounds, including healed ones. Taking the median for individuals, that amounts to 1.9 percent, with some unknown fraction of those were healed. The vast majority is post-3500, but since there are far fewer remains from before that date, it is impossible to divine a trend in that data.

In the Middle Neolithic, from the late fifth millennium, among the few skeletons available there seems to be a high frequency of trauma, and enclosures develop protective outerworks at gates (Christensen, 2004, pp. 137, 150). When skeletal remains increase, the most violence at any one site in France is from the third millennium Baumes-Chaudes cave, where of 300–400 individuals, 17 had arrow injuries, and a *copper* dagger was stuck in a thorax (Guilaine & Zammit, 2005, 125–143). Another late burial has six skeletons, two with embedded points, but all killed with cranial blows (Birocheau, Convertini, Cros, Duday, & Large 1999). Over the third millennium, locations associated with the sometimes similar Funnel Beaker and widely-flung Corded Ware Culture (also known as the Battle-Axe Culture), provide all sorts of war signs—wounds, weapons, fortifications, art—as war and warriors are glorified (Guilaine & Zammit, 2005, pp. 158 ff.). Champ Durand, 3300–3000 BC, has a massive system of defense in depth trenches, walls, and palisades (Christensen, 2004, p. 152).

In Iberia, the Neolithic package of cultivation, domesticated animals, and ceramics arrived, probably with colonizers from the sea, sometime around 5500 BC. Aspects were rapidly adopted by local foragers, and quickly spread outwards (McClure, Molina Balaguer, & Bernabeu Auban, 2008, pp. 326–327). Only in the Late Neolithic (c. 3400 BC), going into the early Chalcolithic (c. 2950 BC)—a time of population expansion, massive social transformation, and growing hierarchy—are there good indications of war. First, settlements move to defendable, but nonfortified locations. Arrowheads are mass-produced, and along with daggers are prominent as grave goods. In some areas, hillforts appear in the early third millennium—as they do at this time elsewhere in the Western Mediterranean (Oosterbeek, 1997)—including the spectacular construction of Los Millares (Aranda Jimenez, & Sanchez Romero 2005). But those developments are post-Neolithic.

Projectile wounds are rare. From Portugal, there are only two individuals, one of them from the LN/Chalcolithic transition, 3500–2500 BC. In Basque Spain, at San Juan Ante Portam Latinum, (Final Neolithic 3300–3000 BC), of 338 individuals, there are arrow wounds in 12 persons, with 7 or 8 surviving (Fernandez Crespo, 2007). Twenty km away at Longar, 4 of 112 individuals have embedded points, but at 2400 BC, that is well into the Chalcolithic (Armendariz et al., 1994). Silva and Marques (2010, pp.187–189) note three additional Spanish sites with single arrow wounds, but conclude that overall, such trauma is less common in Iberia than in France.

In the gorges of Castallon on Spain's western Levant are famous rock paintings depicting both warfare and executions. These extensive portrayals cannot be directly dated, but a variety of considerations have practically ruled out any time prior to the earliest Neolithic (Christensen, 2004, p. 135; Fairen, 2004, pp. 4–7; Guilaine & Zammit, 2005, p. 121; Nash, 2005, pp.:75, 79).

More precise dating is not possible, and they could come from any time up to Copper Age, a span of some 3,000 years. Several features in *some* of the portrayals suggest Final Neolithic or early Chalcolithic social organization: large parties of warriors, signs of rank (headdresses), and expressions of authority (as in executions) (Nash, 2005). A dominant arrow form resembles those of the Chalcolithic (McClure et al., 2008). The prevalence of hunting scenes, which once was the basis of Mesolithic or even Paleolithic dates, is actually quite consistent with Chalcolithic/Bronze Age iconography elsewhere, which associates both warfare and hunting with male valor (Guilaine & Zammit, 2005, pp. 167–173). But as far as I know, there are no suggestions of hill forts in this art, and the fighting portrayed is open battle. For that reason, I would guess they are no later than the early Chalcolithic.

Northern Europe (Loosely Defined)

The Neolithic developed rather late in the British Isles, but war followed more quickly on its advent than elsewhere. Agriculture spread rapidly around 4000 BC (with significant local variations) (Thomas, 2007). Although it has been looked for, there is no evidence of war between farmers and foragers. There are tool-weapons of axes and arrows, but of course those can be used for work, and temporal distribution or any change from early to late Neolithic is not clear. The earliest farmers did not live free of violence, however. There are a few embedded projectile points, and others found loose in burials suggest wounding. Blunt instrument trauma is common. Systemic reexamination of cranial remains 4000–3200 cal BC, often putting together fragments, produced about 350 individuals, 31 of whom had identifiable trauma. The researchers estimated that in about 2 percent of the total sample, the fractures may have caused death, and 4–5 percent were healed (Heath, 2009, 34–42). That is a high proportion of deadly strikes compared to other patterns of cranial trauma discussed elsewhere in this chapter, and so more suggestive of war.

Although many early sites were enclosed, there is a consensus that they were not designed for defense (Schulting & Wysocki, 2005, pp. 108–109, 132). Around the middle fourth millennium, however, major hill fort defenses appear at different locations across southern England (Heath, 2009, pp.43–55; Schulting & Wysocki, 2005, p. 108). Two massive structures, Crickley Hill and Hambledon Hill, show clear signs of attack and destruction, the latter about 3400 cal BC (Mercer, 1999, p. 156), and among four bodies buried together at Fengate, one had an embedded point (Pryor, 1976). In an unusual development, after 3200 BC, almost all the major hillforts are abandoned, and signs of warfare virtually disappear from the later Neolithic, returning only in the Middle Bronze Age after 1500 BC (Mercer, 2007, pp. 123–124, 148; c.f. Heath, 2009, pp. 65 ff.). Given that other preconditions of war are present throughout that hiatus, this period merits further investigation as possibly a time when forces of peace overcame those of war.

We now come to the most investigated Neolithic culture, and the most debated-on war, for all of Europe, the *Linearbandkeramik*, or LBK. Developed around 5700 BC in Hungary, this represent a distinct wave of Neolithization that rapidly spread across northern Europe—through some combination of migration and exchange, and absorption or displacement of local Mesolithic peoples (Rowley-Conway, 2011). Ultimately, by about 5000 BC, a remarkably uniform LBK tradition occupied most areas from Ukraine to the Paris basin (Gkiasta et al., 2003; Price, Wahl, & Bentley, 2006, pp. 260–261). Earlier LBK settlements in the east have few enclosures or skeletal indications of violence, and stayed that way later on. But in the western extensions, later LBK settlements are more often enclosed, and some are clearly fortified with stockpiles of arrowheads (Keeley, 1997, pp. 307–312; Golitko & Keeley, 2007, pp. 332, 338).

The most dramatic evidence of war in all of Neolithic Europe comes from three western LBK sites, Talheim, Schletz-Asparn, and (perhaps) Herxheim (Golitko & Keeley, 2007, pp. 333–335; Guilaine & Zammit, 2005, pp. 86–95). In each, large numbers of skeletons are found with obvious signs of violence. There is general agreement that Talheim and Schletz-Asparn were slaughters, and marks of the killing instruments show they were done by other LBK people. Herxheim is more complicated, at first interpreted as the biggest massacre of all; then reconsidered as a central burial place for a large surrounding population that did not die violently but whose bones were processed for burial; but also with interpretations of sacrifice and/or cannibalism (Boulestin, Jeunesse, Haack, Arbogast, & Dermaire, 2009; Orschiedt, Hauber, Haidle, Alt, & Buitrago-Tellez, 2003; Orschiedt & Haidle, 2007). The three sites are very close in time, just around 5000 BC (Wild et al., 2004, p. 384), roughly contemporary with the Fontbregoua cannibalism in southern France. This dramatic coincidence suggests some common factor, and climate change disruption of subsistence has been proposed (Gronenborn, 2007; Teschler-Nicola et al., 1999), though the connection is tenuous. On the other hand, late LBK settlements had grown to high density in favorable zones, so perhaps were sensitive to disruption; and within those areas, local communities had developed levels of alignment, clans and beyond (Bogaard, Krause, & Strien, 2011), well-suited for war.

Other Middle/Late LBK sites contain skeletal remains that might, or might not, reflect multiple killings. Interpretation is key, and some scholars are pushing back against current trends to argue that "violence and warfare are not interwoven with the late and terminal phases of LBK" (Gronenborn, 2007, p. 19). But there is a lot of evidence to argue against in the later, western LBK. Skeletal trauma (including non-lethal) for all LBK sites reaches 20 percent. For the western extensions alone, including the massacres, it hits an astonishing 32 percent. Taking out Talheim, Schletz-Asparn, and Herxheim, brings the overall total down to 6.2 percent. For the eastern areas alone, it is only 2 percent (Golitko & Keeley, 2007, p. 335)—which is not that much, since this includes all kinds of trauma. On the point of nonlethal trauma, 4 out of 71 individuals (54 adults) from Neolithic northeast Hungary, 5860–4380 BC, including pre- and post-LBK, have skeletal trauma indicating violence, some with multiple fractures, but none of these traumas appears to be the cause of death (Ubelaker, Pap, & Graver, 2006, pp. 250–251). However, as bad as the western LBK ended up, the cultural tradition began peacefully.

The massacres coincided with the end of the Early Neolithic, as Northern Europe broke up into distinctive local traditions. Generalization is difficult, but different areas follow the expected long-term shift toward war. In Poland's Lengyel Culture, 4700–4000 BC, one site is on a defendable location, ditched and palisaded, with burned houses, skeletal violence, and battle-axes. It is the only such site on the Polish plain (Lorkiewicz, 2011, p. 429). However, that pattern of defendable fortified sites is more common in late Lengyel sites, perhaps linked to major climatic change and/or developing social hierarchy. Elaboration of defenses progresses into the Copper Age (Pavuk, 1991). Lengyel sites in Austria and Slovakia show signs of violence and possibly massacres (Vencl, 1999, pp. 64, 69). Estergalyhorvati in Hungary had 25–30 haphazardly dumped bodies, at least two of which had perimortem injuries (Makkay, 2000; Schulting, 2006, p. 231). In the Netherlands, northwest of the old LBK area, a cemetery at Schipluiden from 3600–3400 BC has seven individuals. One double grave includes a person with a deadly skull fracture, and other remains show additional signs of violence (Smits & Van der Flucht, 2009). In Denmark, within the fourth millennium Funnel Beaker Neolithic, sites from 3500–3100 BC have many clearly fortified sites and battle-axes (Andersen, 1993, pp. 101–103).

In the Late Neolithic verging into the Chalcolithic, the Corded Ware/Battle-Ax Culture (2800–2200 BC) spread from Holland to Russia. Although fortifications cease to be built, battle-axes are found in the graves of roughly one in ten men. Actual levels of killing in Corded Ware times are still foggy, but one German site, c. 2800 cal BC, has 13 bodies in multiple graves, with multiple signs of deadly trauma (Meyer, Brandt, Haak, Ganslmeier, Meller, & Alt, 2009). Somewhat later in the even more widespread Bell Beaker culture, axes are surpassed by daggers and spears. In Scandinavia, the Bell Beaker from 2350 BC up to the Early Bronze Age around 1700, the diagnostic of different sub-periods is changing styles of stone dagger and spear heads (Vandkilde, 2006). Christensen (2004, p. 154) interprets these seemingly contradictory trends in fortifications and weapons as signaling a shift to open battle, involving a military elite.

Eastern Europe

Closing the circle and moving from the northwestern to Eastern Europe, we return to the areas previously discussed for Mesolithic violence, around the Dnieper rapids. Skeletons from the final Mesolithic and early Neolithic have no signs of violence (Lillie, 2004, p. 92). Around the Iron Gates Gorge between Serbia and Romania, there is no trauma during the time early farmers coexisted with foragers (Roksandic et al., 2006, p. 347). Referring to the Iron Gates, but commenting more broadly about Eastern Europe, Chapman (1999, pp. 140–141) emphasizes that some very early farming sites are surrounded by ditches of unknown purpose but that different indicators of war trend upward through the Neolithic into the Chalcolithic, when as usual, there appears an apparent cultural emphasis on marshal values (Chapman, 1999, pp.140–141).

Between the Danube and Dnieper, east of the LBK and later Lengyel areas, a non-LBK Neolithic tradition, the Cucuteni-Tripolye culture, developed from 5500 BC or sometime later. Earliest finds are associated with mountain passes that may have channeled trade. They expanded and replaced or absorbed the Bug-Dneister culture, into parts of Ukraine, Moldava, and Romania. No indications of war are reported. But the Middle Cucuteni-Tripolye, 4440–3810 BC, saw a shift to internal social hierarchy or even stratification, larger settlements, extensive fortifications, weapons, and skeletal trauma, with the most militaristic areas facing cultural boundaries with non-Cucuteni-Tripolye groups. By late Cucuteni-Tripolye, 3780–3320 BC, there were stone ramparts and population replacements. Cucuteni-Tripolye gave way to the Corded Ware/Battle-Ax culture that spread—although with surprisingly few signs of actual war—across northern Europe, and passed into the Copper Age, with its well-defined military elite (Anthony, 2007, pp. 162–174; Dolukhanov, 1999, pp. 81–87, cf. Gimbutas 1991).

Below the Cucuteni-Tripolye, in northeast Bulgaria, the Neolithic began in the earlier sixth millennium, and the Chalcolithic by around 4900 BC, considerably ahead of other areas previously discussed (Ivanova, 2007). There is no evidence for warfare in the later sixth millennium, and no fortifications. That changed abruptly in the early fifth millennium Chalcolithic, which is characterized by remarkable social complexity and clear hierarchy and wealth differences. Scattered settlements nucleated into dense networks in defendable locations, possibly as deliberate acts of colonization, stayed in place for centuries, and erected major fortifications. Yet initially, there are few signs of actual war, in killings or destruction. Those came later. After 4500 BC, new weapons appear or proliferate—heavy arrowheads, javelins, maces, axes of stones and metal. For 4350/4300 BC, numbers of skeletons with deadly wounds may be found in or around burned structures of subsequently abandoned tells (Anthony, 2007, pp 225–227). Even though 4300 is an earlier end-point than most other time lines considered, in Bulgaria it was almost into the Bronze Age, and time to stop this tour.

Vencl (1999, p. 71) sums up the European record: by the Late Neolithic and Copper Age, "a complete and definitive set of archaeological war attributes developed, fully corresponding to the evidence from later periods when war and warfare are attested by written sources." Then comes the Bronze Age, with its military aristocracy. In contrast to the ad hoc, locally variable fighting of the earlier Neolithic, war by then was a self-sustaining cultural system, adapting and evolving across all of Europe (Harding, 1999; Kristiansen, 1999; Kristiansen & Larrson, 2005; Osgood & Monks, with Toms, 2000). To get to written history, Europe still has to pass through the chaotic, violent end of the Bronze Age—with climate change strongly implicated in its "collapse"—and then the Iron Age, with its disciplined infantries and new manifestations of warriorhood (Drews, 1993; Randsborg, 1995, 1999; Whitley, 2002). There are real questions about the lethality of the later wars of the metal ages—how much of the population fought, did they fight often, and how many were killed? Did a military elite maintain their dominance but also find ways to limit actual wars? While war was clearly a major presence across European cultures, it is not at all clear that a great many people died in combat. But war in the metal ages is beyond the scope of this chapter, except to note that it is, at once, the end product of millennia of war development, and a foundation of classical views of "the warlike barbarian," and the idea that humans have "always" made war.

Considering prehistoric war in Europe, many authors confirm Keeley's characterization of a prior "pacification of the past," as scholars overlooked evidence of violence and war. But the tide is well-turned.[51] More than a decade of studies has documented the existence of war (or stressed the military possibilities of ambiguous evidence, or imagined it almost everywhere based on dubious analogy with twentieth century ethnography). Conclusions are always subject to interpretation and debate, and complicated by many lacunae in data. But in my assessment, there are some clear regularities, which I will state here as generalizations.

The European Paleolithic has few signs of violent injury, including one killed child, but excepting the ambiguous cases of cannibalism, no evidence of war. The Mesolithic provides several instances of multiple deaths strongly suggesting war, but these are scattered across the continent and millennia. The earliest centuries of farming exhibit, in some places, some signs of individual violence, but no evidence that persuasively establishes the existence of war, although war in the initial Neolithic is a possibility in England. In all other regions, after 500–1000 years or more without it, clear evidence of war appears in skeletons and settlements, in some places but not others. As time goes on, more war signs are fixed in all potential lines of evidence—skeletons, settlements, weapons, and sometimes art. But there is no simple line of increase: the violence around 5000 BC in the western LBK was far worse than what followed, and other areas had ups and downs in active war. Even unmistakable evidence of the cultural presence of war does not indicate how much actual killing took place. Whatever the actual death toll, by the final Neolithic/Chalcolithic transition, a culture of war was in place across all of Europe, becoming more prominent in the Bronze and Iron Ages.

Because of space limitations, discussions of war evidence has made only limited references to what I argue as preconditions for war, which vary greatly by area, and are often debatable both in interpretation and dating. Yet I will hazard another set of generalizations for the European Neolithic, acknowledging that there are numerous exceptions and arguable points. By the time war signs appear, so do several sociodemographic changes, with settlements becoming bigger, denser, and more permanent. Livestock herds get larger, and harvests more likely to be stored and managed than consumed by individual households. Local social segmentation—often marked by enclosures—and/or migrations increase definition of and distinction between local groups and even larger networks. Networks of long-distance trade in exotic valuables appear (though I did not find a single study suggesting trade control could be a source of warfare, as I will argue for the Near East). Local groups begin the Neolithic with virtually no discernible hierarchy, and end it with clear inequality, and an apparent military elite. The latter is reflected by the end of some Neolithics, in a culture of war, with veneration of weapons and warriors, as characterized the subsequent Copper and Bronze Ages. Finally, environmental perturbations are associated with several points of transition and conflict, though cases are too variable, and sometimes temporally fuzzy, to make much of a conclusion. The preconditions for war grow in tandem with the development of war.

Considering the significance of the war-forever-backwards image both for evolutionary theories of human nature and popular understanding of war in our own culture—it may be time for European archaeologists to move beyond refuting the pacified past, to address the question of whether European prehistory shows that war actually had a beginning, and to follow the trail as it spread and intensified. Of course, some will always assert, "absence of evidence is not evidence of absence." But considering how many scholars have been diligently searching for signs of violence, and considering how multistranded and convincing is the later evidence of war, usually without any dramatic increases in recovery (with exceptions, such as pre/post 3500 skeletons in France), is such a stance justified? Or is it a presumptive "warrification" of the past?

It would be preposterous to imagine that Europe is representative of other places. European sequences are manifestly *in*applicable to prehistoric North America (Ferguson, chapter 7), and assuredly will be elsewhere. The theory of unilineal evolution died a long time ago. All world areas will have their own characteristics. The following section turns to another region that has been equally investigated by archaeology, the Near East. The record is very different from Europe's, and it provides even better proof of the absence or limitation of war in earlier prehistory.

The Near East

Discussion of the Near East focuses on the Levantine corridor, a rich belt running through Israel, Jordan, Lebanon, and Syria; or bordered by Sinai on the south, the Mediterranean on the west, the Taurus-Zagros Mountains on the north, and the Syro-Arabian desert to the east (Goring-Morris, Hovers, & Belfer-Cohen, 2009, p. 185). The mountains and plateaus of Turkish Anatolia are also covered here. Through these discussions focusing on war, three different areas emerge as significant: Anatolia, the northeastern Levant, which I will refer to as the northern Tigris area, and the Southern Levant. The three areas will be shown to have very distinctive war histories. Most important, the discussions that follow build a case that the Southern Levant developed an enduring "peace system," ways of dealing with conflict without resorting to war, which only ended with Egyptian imperial expansion.

Paleolithic

The Near Eastern Middle Paleolithic is especially noteworthy for the long coexistence of Neanderthals and modern *Homo sapiens*. Humans were present from about 120,000 BP and disappeared around the onset of glacial conditions c. 80,000, at an apparent "dead end." They reappeared in the Levant about 50,000. Neanderthals were present from 120/112,000 BP, and disappear around 47,000 BP (Churchill, Franciscus, & McKean-Peraza, 2009, pp. 163–169; Shea & Sisk, 2010, p. 116). Shea (2003, pp. 369–372) argues that in competition over the constricted resources, the reappeared *Homo sapiens* had an advantage in using projectiles instead of the thrusting spears of Neanderthals. But was that competition expressed just in an advantage in hunting, or did it involve interspecific violence?

The *Homo* individual Skhul IX, 130–100,000 BP, was claimed to have spear wounds, but these are more likely marks from pickaxes during excavation (Churchill et al., 2009, pp. 175–176). However, at Shanidar in northern Iraq, 51000–47000 BP or older, a partially healed injury in the rib of an old (41–42-year-old) Neanderthal male, is clearly from a weapon. This is "the oldest case of human interpersonal violence" (Trinkhaus & Zimmerman, 1982, pp. 62, 72). Experimental comparisons suggest it is from a throwing spear, not a thrusting spear (though it is possibly from a knife, and there is no evidence that modern humans were actually in northern Iraq at this time) (Churchill, Franciscus, & McKean-Peraza, 2009, pp. 63–165, 174–176). While far from conclusive, this provides some support for the old idea of interspecies violence.

Natufians

After that, there is no information relevant to this study until arriving at the late Epipaleolithic, 13,100–9600 cal BC, and the people we call Natufian. Mostly settled, complex hunter-gatherers exploiting an abundant range of resources, some Natufian settlements were small and temporary, but others reached 1000 m² with about 150 residents. Over time, settlements expanded into different areas, shaped by population growth, local ecology, and climatic perturbations. Trade in exotic stone such as obsidian developed, with some indication of regional cultural differentiation, but with no persuasive evidence of social ranking as found among some other complex hunter-gatherers (Bar-Yosef, 1998, pp. 162–167; Henry, 1985, pp. 374–378; Goring-Morris, Hovers, & Belfer-Cohen, 2009, pp. 198–207).

Skeletal remains have been recovered of more than 400 Natufians. One female of 35–40 years from Nahal Oren apparently died from a blow to the head (Ferembach, 1959, p. 67). Three small samples also indicate the presence of violence, sometimes deadly. One of seven individuals, an unsexed adult, from around 10000 BC, had two healed and one unhealed cranial fractures, possibly the cause of death (Webb & Edwards, 2002). A reexamination of 17 individuals, from around 9100 BC, found an embedded lunate point with no signs of healing in a vertebra of a mature adult male. Two others among the five adult males had healed cranial trauma (Bocquentin & Bar Yosef, 2004). In another study, 5 of 30 adult male skulls (16.7 percent) and 3 of 15 adult females (20 percent) had healed trauma, though only 1 of 487 upper limbs had a fracture (Eshed, Gopher, Pinhasi, & Hershkovitz, 2010, pp. 125, 127). Conflict, violence? Yes. But Bar-Yosef, who has called for a deliberate effort to de-pacify the past (2010a), considering all that is known about Natufians, concludes that there is no evidence supporting the interpretation of war, just personal violence (2010b, p. 72). LeBlanc (2010, p. 41) posits three possible indicators of warfare among people such as the Natufian: settlements on defendable sites, deadly skeletal trauma, and specialized or stockpiled weapons, yet even this champion of de-pacification does not cite any instances. In contrast to the European Mesolithic, there is no evidence of war among Natufians.

Pre-Pottery Neolithic A

Bar-Yosef (2011) argues that climate change drove subsistence and settlement changes among the Natufians, and eventually a shift toward domestication (and later changes). Unlike all other farmers discussed in this chapter, the people of the Levant did not acquire domesticants from elsewhere. They did it themselves. Although the "Neolithic package" as it spread through Europe is usually marked by the presence of pottery, in the Near East ceramics appeared thousands of years after the domestication of plants and animals. The first phase, the Pre-Pottery Neolithic A (PPNA), can be roughly dated as 9600–8500 BC. There are different centers, the Northern Levant, Southern Levant (where Natufian continuity is very clear), Upper Tigris, and Middle Euphrates. Each has shared and distinctive characteristics, including experimentation in a variety of domesticants, while at the same time continuing with extensive hunting and gathering.

Compared to the Natufian, PPNA population is denser, and with larger settlements of commonly 150–300 people. Evenly spaced villages cluster in favorable lowland environments near rivers, and are abandoned after a few centuries. A hierarchy of settlement sizes is apparent, down to small seasonal sites, with storage and cultic constructions in the larger ones. They are not in defendable locations, and without any indication of surrounding ditches or walls. Except by distance between major centers, there are no major cultural breaks. All areas are marked by convergence in technologies, and are linked in trade of exotic materials such as salt, bitumen, sea shells, and above all, obsidian, coming from multiple sources (Bar-Yosef, 2011, pp. 181–182; Belfer-Cohen & Goring-Morris, 2011, p. 213; Goring-Morris et al., 2009, pp. 208–211; Goring-Morris & Belfer-Cohen, 2011, pp. 200–201). Nothing in the construction or distribution of settlements suggests the presence of war.

A few of the largest sites appear to be nodes in trade networks, and probably cultic centers (Belfer-Cohen & Goring Morris, 2011, p. 213). Evidence for communal production and distribution, and for collective ceremonialism, is a persistent characteristic of the early Near East. My argument is that they are part of a peace system, resolving potential conflict and avoiding war. At the very start of the PPNA around 9650 BC, Wadi Faynan 16 in Jordan has a large public structure with a complex internal structure (Mithen, Finlayson, Smith, Jenkins, Najjar, and Maricevic, 2011). The purpose is not obvious, but a ritual center seems likely. A more clear-cut (and amazing) ritual center is Gobekli Tepe in southeastern Turkey, centrally located on high ground visible for miles around, from 9130–8650 BC (Mithen, Finlayson, Smith, Jenkins, Najjar, & Maricevic, 2011, p. 360). It seems to have been free-standing, without accompanying settlement. No settlement remains have been found, and its monumental construction suggests a massive work commitment from populations throughout the surrounding area, leading to the inference that it was a means of creating a shared identity and culture at the very transition to the Neolithic (Schmidt, 2010, 253–254).

Jericho in Jordan is the best known settlement of the PPNA, reaching 500 inhabitants. After some centuries, the people of Jericho constructed a wall and a central tower, which was often taken as the earliest evidence of warfare, unique for its milieu (Roper, 1975, pp. 304–306). Bar-Yosef (1986) reanalyzed those constructions, and found them unsuited for defense, and more likely for protection against flooding and mudflows, an interpretation that has been widely accepted. Over 500 burials at Jericho have been recovered from all periods (including PPNB), with some multiple burials. One burial that has 30 individuals lacks any sign of violence, which suggests that they died in an epidemic (Rollefson, 2010, p. 62). LeBlanc (2010, p. 45) mentions "a few . . . healed skull fractures" from Jericho and one other site, without elaboration.

Another huge, long-inhabited and very well-investigated PPNA site is Abu Hureyra in Syria. On a terrace above a flood plain, there are no signs of walls or towers. With up to 3,000 inhabitants in clearly planned structures, there must have been some form of authority. Yet there is no sign of social hierarchy—which suggests an alternative to standard evolutionary models that connect authority to chiefs. Authority may be vested in village councils of elders or lineage representatives, who live as others do. Recognized authority can be a precondition of peace. At Abu Hureyra, remains of approximately 162 individuals include multiple burials but they have no signs of violence. Disease seems likely. Points are found in a few burials, but their positioning suggests they are grave offerings, along with other objects (Molleson, 1994, p. 70; Moore, Hillman, & Legge, 2000, pp. 3–4, 279, 294, 494–495, 505). One young man, however, has an embedded point that was clearly lethal. "This is the only evidence that we have found for death by violence" (Moore et al., 2000, p. 288).

From the Southern Levant, several small sites spanning PPNA and PPNB yield 34 skulls for osteological analysis. One has a healed cranial fracture (Eshed, Gopher, Pinhasi, & Hershkovitz 2010, pp.123, 127, 129). That is the paltry sum of evidence for war in the Levantine PPNA. The PPNA lasted for only 1,100 years, but that much time was more than enough in Europe for clear signs of war to emerge among Neolithic people.

This absence of evidence gains significance in contrast to the earliest Neolithic in the northern Tigris area, northern Iraq. The Late Round House Horizon seems to develop out of the local Epipaleolithic Zarzian. Considerable differences exist on dates. Goring-Morris et al. (2009, pp. 210, 212) go for calibrated 9750–8750, making it contemporary with the PPNA of the Levant. Village sites are located on the ecotone between floodplains and the Taurus. Two sites are important for evidence of war, the smaller and earlier Qermez Dere, and the nearby and later but overlapping Nemrik 9.

Qermez Dere is on high ground, with panoramic views of all approaches, and is protected on three sides by a steep drop. There are a few mace-heads, which may or may not be weapons of war. More significantly, it has a "spectacular development of projectile points" without any evident changes in hunting. Many points have broken tips, and may have "impacted with the settlement" (Watkins, 1992, pp. 68–69; Watkins, Baird, & Betts, 1989, p. 19). Nemrik 9 is bounded by steep wadis. It has mace heads, but also has skeletons with associated points (and no other grave goods) (Kozlowski, 1989, pp. 25–28). One male skull contained two points, a second skeleton had a point in the pelvic area, and a third had a broken point next to a broken arm. These points are of a type that is unusual locally, suggesting that attackers had come from some distance (Rollefson, 2010, p. 63). This convergence of different kinds of evidence supports the inference of war, the earliest in the Near East. Why war first appeared here is anyone's guess. Later firsts in the evolution of war from this same area are associated with the long-distance trade in Anatolian obsidian, as later routes went right through this area. But obsidian was rare at Qermez Dere (Watkins et al., 1989, p. 22) and not mentioned at Nemrik 9 (Kozlowski, 1989, pp. 27–28).

Pre-Pottery Neolithic B

The second phase of the Pre-Pottery Neolithic, PPNB, lasted longer, 8500–6400 cal BC. This was the early Holocene climatic optimum, especially favorable to cultivation—"a time of plenty as conditions improved from one year to the next" (Goring-Morris & Belfer-Cohen, 2011, p. 202). Cultivation shifted from earlier local experimentation to heavy reliance on cereals. Domesticated animal herds increased, use of wild resources declined, and the population exploded. Villages grew in size and stayed put for many centuries—still regularly spaced and with smaller settlements grading out from larger— and populations colonized formerly marginal areas. With northern and southern variations, some long-settled locations were abandoned, possibly due to changing water tables (Bar-Yosef, 2011, p. 182; Goring-Morris et al., 2009, pp. 212–214). Within this panorama, a new phenomenon of "mega-sites" approaching urban proportions developed and spread, transforming the social landscape, expanding "on an almost 'unlimited' scale in terms of food resources, due to the presence of various ungulates . . . and the availability of arable lands" (Gebel, 2004, p. 4).

Across a mosaic of locally specific adaptations, a deeply entwined interaction sphere of exchange and cultural convergence developed that extended past the old PPNA areas to include Anatolia and Cyprus (Asouti, 2006; Goring-Morris & Belfer-Cohen, 2011, p. 202). Still, no fortifications or territorial separations are noted, at least until (possibly) the end, even though the presence of war is sometimes assumed (e.g., Gebel, 2004, p. 9). In contrast, major ritual centers—consistent with the generally pronounced cultic

orientation of PPNB remains—developed *between* major population centers, especially in the Northern Levant and southern Anatolia, which imply social cooperation
across large areas. Gobekli Tepe, which began in the late PPNA, continued on, but other
centers such as Nevali Cori and Cayonu became more common in the PPNB, often
between settlements, often on high ground visible for miles around (Belfar-Cohen &
Goring-Morris, 2011, pp. 213–214; Bodet, 2011; Erdogu, 2009, pp. 130–131, Kuijt &
Goring-Morris, 2002, p. 419).

Roper's (1975, pp. 311–312) pioneering survey of signs of war in the Near East
finds nothing for a millennium after the questionable early wall of Jericho, the original
mega-site, but some possibilities from the late seventh millennium. Extensively quoting
Kenyon's report, the first ten PPNB occupation levels have no hint of a wall, but Phase
XII and XIII trenches found massive stone slabs sloping up on top of fill, which Kenyon
interpreted as defensive. Not likely. The structure was built in the midst of domestic units.
The land behind it was filled in to its top, with house structures then built right up to the
edge. Everything looks like a terrace, not a defensive wall. Besides that, for this key case,
the extensive skeletal collection from PPNB Jericho does not display signs of violence, and
multiple burials could be from epidemics.

Beidha (Southern Levant) level IV c. 6900–6600 BC is another candidate for
war. Beidha was burned, with some culturally new elements found after, yet there are
also continuities. With no clear signs of fortifications or of any violence in skeletal
remains, war remains nothing more than a possibility (Roper, 1975, pp. 312–313). Ras
Shamra (Northern Levant) c. 6436 BC, possibly an early seaport, has a surrounding
glacis of stone slabs over dirt, but that could be to prevent inundations (Roper, 1975,
pp. 313–314). In Turkey Mellaart (1975, pp. 90 ff) has interpreted Catalhuyuk joined
structures with roof entrances as defensive—a point that seems destined to intermina-
ble debate—and a similar interpretation has been offered for aceramic Haclilar c. 7040
BC. Roper (1975, p. 316) notes the doubts, and considering all four sites, concludes
that "there is no conclusive evidence . . . that warfare was feared or practiced, though it
is likely." These four sites are frequently noted as evidence of Near Eastern warfare. It is
not much of a record.

Post-Roper's-survey, Ghwair I, a smaller site from southern Jordan (Southern Levant,
as are other PPNB sites to follow), 6800–6300 BC, has one infant with elaborate grave
goods, and an elderly female with a point embedded inside her jaw (Simmons & Najjar,
2006, p. 90). At late PPNB Basta in Jordan, of 29 skulls, five had healed minor cranial
fractures (Schultz, Berner, & Schimdt-Schultz, 2004, p. 260). Another boy was killed by
a blow to the head (Rollefson, 2010, p. 63). The violence at both those sites would be
consistent with pronounced internal hierarchy. Late PPNB Ba'ja, a small site in mega-site
times, is on a terrace in nearly vertical sandstone formations, approachable only through
a steep and narrow passage. It certainly could be called defendable, and in that quality is
noted as unique within its time. But from photographs, Ba'ja's terrace seems to be the only
habitable ground in the vicinity, at least with access to water. No traces of contemporary

settlements have been found anywhere around them (Bienert & Gebel, 2004, pp. 119, 121, 135; Gebel, & Bienert 1997, pp. 223, 229).

Ba'ja, Basta, and Beidha are not far apart, and this confluence of inconclusive clues makes it a promising area to look for concrete evidence of war. Yet as it stands, there is really nothing in any of those sites that even probably support the conclusion that war was present. The mega-sites should be able to raise a few hundred fighting men, and the effects of fighting at that scale most likely would be seen. On the contrary, in the north Jordan valley from the PPNB through the Pottery Neolithic, the countryside was spotted with small settlements in flat ground near water without any defensive characteristics (Roper, 1975, p. 31). In sum, there is no persuasive evidence of war in the PPNB from the Southern Levant to Anatolia. Kuijt and Goring-Morris (2002, p. 421) sum up the record for the entire Levant Pre-Pottery Neolithic, both A and B. They note the "near-total absence of evidence for interpersonal or intercommunity aggression in the PPN." Starting with the Natufian in 13100 BC, the close of the PPN around 6400 BC makes 6700 years in the Southern Levant without any good evidence of war.

Pottery Neolithic

The end of the PPNB, often called "collapse," included abandonment of many long-settled sites, and was close to and quite possibly related to the major climatic reversal and aridity in the eastern Mediterranean, known as the "8200 cal yr BP event" (Clare, 2010, pp. 15–17; Rollefson, Simmons, & Kafafi, 1992, p. 468; Weninger et al., 2006). The Pottery Neolithic, 6400–4500 cal BC (Goring-Morris et al. 2009:190), post-8.2 K cal BC, is marked most obviously by the development and immediate spread of pottery. It also saw a shift to smaller settlements, the digging of wells, more reliance on pastoralism, and sharp differentiation of local cultures. With climate-forced competition, invested labor in wells and livestock, and cultural differentiation, one might expect the emergence of warfare.

But war is not apparent in the record of the Southern Levant PN. Roper (1975, p. 317) notes settlements are small, on low, watered land. There is no sign of fortifications in the sixth millennium after the questionable wall at PNNB Jericho. Archaeological excavation in the Southern Levant has been intense in recent decades, as more real estate is developed (Rowan & Golden, 2009, p. 2). But 35 years after Roper, the evidence has not changed.

'Ain Ghazal was a central Jordan mega-site and major ritual center that was not abandoned with the PPNB "collapse." Occupied from 7250–5000 BC, no walls are indicated until Pottery Neolithic times (5500–5000 BC), when "stone enclosure walls abound . . . but just what these features enclosed is difficult to determine" (Rollefson et al., 1992, p. 450). As these walls are found throughout the settlement, it is hard to see anything that suggests a defensive purpose (Rollefson, 1997). Differential burial of 112 skeletons suggest two classes of people, perhaps "a two-tiered 'patron-client' population" (Rollefson et al., 1992, p. 463). One of the "trash burials" has a thin flint blade, snapped at both sides, going through the skull (Rollefson, 2010, p. 63). It could be a killing, except "it is not entirely clear if this was intentional or rather the result of post-depositional processes (Kuijt & Goring-Morris, 2002, p. 422). What 'Ain Ghazal may be indicating is some form of hierarchy in a ritual-oriented central place, and increasing control as an alternative to warfare even in tough times for subsistence.

Although Clare (2010, pp. 18–19, 20, 23) takes a generally hawkish position in interpreting evidence for war, and points out a few possible indicators which are "to say the least, ambiguous," he recognizes a total absence of any "obvious fortification structures," a general reduction (with local variations) of tool-weapons of knives and arrowheads without any increase in sling ammunition, and concludes "harmonious times for the southern Levant might even be suggested, at least during the PN, and this is indeed the picture that is beginning to emerge." Clare suggests that climatically driven hard times may have led to new forms of cooperation.

The issue of maces is fully joined in the Pottery Neolithic Southern Levant (Rosenberg, 2010, pp. 210–211, 214). Many maceheads are found, but they are small (most under 5 cm in diameter) and with very thin shaft holes (most 10–15 mm, some down to 6 mm). These maces could not "withstand a serious blow." He concludes, "most early maceheads were never used in combat." Rosenberg speculates on possible ritual uses. A reasonable interpretation is that they were symbols of authority. This does not necessarily imply social ranking or "chiefs." It could be the authority of a community, represented by elders and wise people, perhaps with cultic backing (Kuijt & Goring-Morris, 2002, pp. 420–423). As noted previously, recognized authority is a way of regulating conflict, and could be central to avoiding war. Maces may be part of a system of peace. Adding the PPN to what came before in the Southern Levant, that makes 8600 years without signs of war.

Yet across the *northern* Near East, evidence for war is substantial in the Pottery Neolithic. Around the northern Tigris, close to Qermez Dere at the border between mountains and plains, is seventh millennium Tell Maghzaliyah. Several centuries after it was first occupied, a major defensive wall was raised, possibly with one or more towers (Bader, 1993, pp. 64–66). This is the earliest known fortification in Mesopotamia (Munchaev, 1993, p. 250), and may be the earliest in the Near East. Maghzaliyah appears to be of different cultural tradition then Qermez Dere, with some Anatolian affinities, and its people had a thousand times more obsidian (Watkins et al., 1989, p. 22). This is the *debouchment* where Anatolian trade comes down to the plains. Maghzaliyah could be a node in what would become (if it was not already) an enduring system of long-distance trade routes in Anatolian obsidian (Healey, 2007, pp. 262–263), certainly the most important exotic good in the Neolithic (Yellin et al., 1996, p. 366). Cross-culturally, different aspects of trade control are often critical issues in practices of war (see Ferguson, 1999, pp. 414–415). A linkage is suggested in this case, since erection of the wall coincided with a dramatic shift from obsidian to flint, suggesting that somebody was cutting into the flow of trade from Anatolia (Bader, 1993, p. 66).

Turning to Anatolia itself, the origin of Neolithic ways is still poorly understood. In central Anatolia, clear indicators of a Neolithic way of life appear near the end of the Pre-Pottery Neolithic, between 7400–7100 cal BC. Settlements remain small and sporadic until about 6500, around the start of the PN, with level 6 at Catalhuyuk—which as noted early is perennially debated as an exemplar of war. A significant development for this chapter's interest in peace is that communal ritual centers disappear from Anatolia over the PN, with religious practices moving into domestic contexts (Ergogu, 2009, 129). If major ritual centers had unified scattered people, their decline could make war more likely. Yet the painted representations at Catalhuyuk do not suggest war. There are life scenes of hunting, of domesticated plants and animals, and of vultures picking flesh from headless bodies—but no portrayals of war (Erdogu, 2009, pp.133–135). The vulture scenes could stand as a warning against it. They may have had reason to worry. War was on the way.

A case has been made (Ozdogan, 2011) and challenged (Asouti, 2009; Thissen, 2010) that climatic deterioration associated with the 8200 cal K BP event drove late Neolithic subsistence shifts within Anatolia, and the spread of domestication from there to the Balkans. Consistent with that line of thinking, Clare et al. (2008, pp. 71–77) discuss four Late Neolithic/Early Chalcolithic sites in the densely settled Lake District (Pisidia) of the south-western Anatolian plateau: Hacilar, Kurucay Hoyuk, Hoyucek Hoyuk, and Bademagaci Hoyuk. Between them are multiple indicators of war: major conflagrations, some with unburied bodies, some with a subsequent hiatus or replacement by another group, fortifications with walls and towers, and large numbers sling missiles. During (2011, pp. 72–73) questions the defensive interpretation of structures at Hacilar and Kurucay (and elsewhere) and argues that the postulated signs of war postdate 6000 BC, centuries too late to be linked to the 82 cal K event. These are valid points. The most compelling evidence from war at Hacilar (II) is dated to 5600 BC (Roper, 1975, p. 321).[6]

Signs of war in other Anatolian sites also date to the early sixth millennium. Domuztepe of the Halaf culture has a pit (5700–5600 BC) with 40 possible victims of violence (Erdal, 2012, p. 2). Guvercinkaya, 5210–4810 BC, was built on top of a steep rock outcropping. During (2011, p. 75) emphasizes that a nearby contemporary settlement was not fortified, but that would be consistent with fortifications on trade nodes. Down from the highlands on the coast, between Anatolia and Cyprus, the port settlement of Ras Shamra was destroyed by fire around 5234 BC. An apparent defensive wall went up somewhat later, possibly associated with arrival of Halafians, a people originating in Northern Mesopotamia (Akkermans 2000), who seem to have brought war along with them (Roper, 1975, p. 318). The Halafian culture is not well-understood, but they had an unusual immersion in obsidian commerce. "They apparently engaged in directionally controlled, nonreciprocal, extensive trade which seems to have been more structured and more intensive (e.g., imported obsidian comprising three-fourths or more of the chipped stone industry) than we might expect in a tribal society" (Watson & LeBlanc, 1990, pp. 137).

While climatic deterioration may be related to this widespread pattern of war, a much stronger causal connection appears to involve key nodes of the trans-Anatolian obsidian trade. Obsidian from Anatolia was found all over the Near East. Pisidia was not a center of obsidian production, which came from Central Anatolia (Clare, Rohling, Weninger, & Hilpert, 2008, p. 82). Sources of critical goods usually do not control trade, those at passage bottlenecks do. Ozdogan (2011, p. 55) notes final Neolithic "turmoil" in Anatolia, and that for the first time, there appears to be monopolization of trade patterns. Monopolization is the key link between war and trade.

On the Turkish coast, Mersin XX was destroyed and then reoccupied by Halafians. A similar sequence occurred at Chagar Bazar in northern Syria, and level 8 of Sakce Gozu. Below the mountains but close by, Ras Shamra Vb, also on the coast, and basal Tell Halaf (c. 5837 BC) appear to be "fortified Halafian settlements." "It is significant that all the sites that exhibit destruction or have fortifications are located on the east-west overland trade route (or subsidiary connections to this route)" (from Nineveh in northern Iraq through the Northern Levant, to Mersin, and up through the Taurus). "One may hypothesize that the Halafians wanted and took control of a portion of this great trade route" (Roper, 1975. pp. 323–325). Sixth millennium Halaf may be the first cultural group to expand via war.

The Chalcolithic and Early Bronze Age

The Anatolian trade network and accompanying warfare continued during the Chalcolithic (4500–3300 BC), with (probable) fortifications at Cadir Hoyuk and Kurucay level 6 (During 2011, p. 75). The Early Bronze Age Anatolia trade network included a wide array of materials and products. It expanded to reach from the northern edge of Mesopotamia to the Aegean and Greece (including Troy), and was characterized by centralized urban centers with massive fortifications (Sahoglu, 2005, pp. 339–341). "Signs of systematic violence become ever more pervasive in Anatolia during the Bronze Age (ca. 3000–1200 BC), starting especially in the EBA (ca. 3000–2000)" (Erdal, 2012, p. 2).

Considering this record against all the other records examined here leads to a major conclusion: by the early sixth millennium, along the trade corridors of Anatolia, the Western world's first widespread, enduring social system of war had begun. The inclusion of Troy serves to extend that point: this is the start of a system of war that flows down in a river of blood to our present.

On the Turkish coast around 4300 BC, Mersin was a true fort or citadel, with firing ports, offsets covering turns in walls, a protected gateway and tower, and possible barracks for specialized soldiers (cf. During, 2011, pp.74–75). After about a century, Mersin was destroyed, and the site occupied by Ubadian people (Roper, 1975, pp. 328–329). At the eastern end of the Northern Levant, even more dramatic developments ensued in the Late Chalcolithic.

In northeast Syria, close to the earlier Tell Maghzaliyah and Qermez Dere, Tell Brak and Hamoukar were emerging as urban centers by 4200 BC. Each was a major entrepôt for northern obsidian (Khalidi, Graute, & Boucetta, 2009; Oates, 1982, p. 62). Tell Brak was most probably situated to control trade, given its strategic location on a key river crossing between the Anatolian passes and the north, the Syrian route to the

Levant, and southward toward Mesopotamia. Hamoukar was on another choke point in the passage to Mesopotamia. At Brak were found not only masses of obsidian, but great caches of other prestige goods, fabulous items such as an obsidian and white marble chalice, seal impressions revealing two levels of control, "industrial" buildings, and a "feasting hall" that may have served travelers. Findings at Brak particularly (but the less excavated Hamoukar looks similar), have upended conventional notions of southern Mesopotamia as the heartland of cities, preceding known southern developments by several centuries. Monumental in every way, Brak at its peak around 3400 BC covered 55 hectares, including sprawling low-density "suburbs" around its center. The emerging question is: were they states (Oates, McMahan, Karsgaard, al-Quntar, & Ur, 2007; Gibson, Al-Azm, Reichel, Quntar, Franke, Khalidi, & Hartnell, 2002; Ur, Karsgaard, & Oates 2001)?

Surrounding Tell Brak were massive fortifications, with towers, gates, and guardhouses (Oates et al. 2007, p. 588–589). Four mass graves have been found from 3800 to 3600. The two best known suggest a simultaneous interment of hundreds, with demographic patterns and casual disposal suggesting purposeful killing rather than an epidemic. Based on several factors—such as the absence of peri-mortem skeletal trauma and the formidability of defenses—researchers speculate that this represents internal violence rather than attacks from the outside (McMahon, Soltysiak, & Weber, 2011). That is not far-fetched, given Gilgamesh's oppression of his own people to build his massive walls (Gardner & Maier, 1985, pp. 57, 67),[7] and the possibility that local food production was stressed by cooling and increased aridity (McMahon et al., 2011, p. 217). Hamoukar, however, was attacked by outsiders. Recent excavations indicate that around 3500 BC, a massive bombardment by thousands of sling bullets weakened its 10-foot-high wall, which then collapsed in a conflagration. Subsequent levels were dominated by Uruk pottery, suggesting the south had conquered the northern trade portal to Mesopotamia (Bower, 2008; University of Chicago, 2005).

The northern Near East exhibits a long and clear trajectory to the sort of war known from the beginning of written history. But the last stop on this survey is extremely different. The record from Southern Levant in the Chalcolithic (4500–3500 BC) is best known from central Jordan. The period saw major population growth, development of transhumance and partial separation of pastoralist groups, and local cultural differentiation. Yet there were strong intra-regional similarities in ceramics, iconography, and mortuary custom. Craft specialization and mass-production grew, local and long-distance trade continued. Settlements had two tiers, and many were built according to set plans. Prestige goods and elaborate tombs suggest inequality, though its character, and whether there were "chiefs," is debated (Golden, 2010, pp. 9, 181, 190; Kerner, 1997, pp. 467–469; Levy, 1993, pp. 227–232; Rowan & Golden, 2009, pp. 69). This combination leads some to expect warfare (Golden, 2010, pp. 201). Yet the evidence of war is just not there, while evidence for a continuation of managed relations between local groups is.

The Jordan Valley was filled with unfortified settlements on the valley floor, near water. Cemeteries are often (not always) unassociated with settlements, suggesting people from different locales shared them. "Public sanctuaries," open air structures for ritual performances, were common, and some were also apart from any settlement, such as Tuleilat Ghassul, with its plastered walls "depict[ing] ceremonial processions, mythical figures and strange animals" (Levy, 1993, pp. 235–236). Tulleilat Ghassul and Tell 'Abu Hamid had major structures which could be "temples and/or administrative buildings," and "huge storage pits and large vessels." One interpretation is unification and joint administration of regional clusters (Ibrahim, 2010, pp. 82–83).

"[E]vidence for widespread site destruction, perimeter walls or other defensive features is currently lacking" (Rowan & Golden, 2009, p. 71). There is one "warrior burial," so-called because of the presence of a complex bow, but there is no reason to think it was used for anything but hunting (Golden, 2010, p. 66). Its presence does raise one important comparative point. In contrast to the European record, the Late Neolithic/Chalcolithic/Early Bronze Age "cult" of weapons and warriors is absent from the Near East (at least as far as this study goes, leaving out imperial Egypt). There are plenty of mace heads in the Chalcolithic (Rosenberg, 2010), but copper maces, once again, seem more associated with authority or ceremony than war (Tadmor, 2002, p. 241).

The sole evidence of deadly violence in the Southern Levant Chalcolithic comes from Shiqmim in the Negev, a site occupied from 4500–3200 cal BC. One adolescent has three unhealed cranial fractures, clearly the cause of death, which might have been caused by a mace (though the big hole seems rather large for that). The researchers conclude that this implies war. "Thus, the integration of simple autonomous village communities into larger more complex chiefdom organizations . . . was accompanied by warfare and violence" (Dawson, Levy, & Smith, 2003, p. 118). This is a good illustration of the current "warrification" of the past. One killing of a youth does not suggest war.

Why would war be endemic in the north, and absent in the south? Two factors may be involved in this striking contrast. One is the region's marginality to the massive currents of northern trade. In the later Neolithic, mid-fifth millennium (e.g., 5561–5317 cal BC), Hagoshrim in northern Israel was a major entrepôt for Anatolian materials, with more than 8000 items of obsidian recovered, continuing a pattern that went back to the Natufian (Rosenberg, 2010, pp. 283, 290). A thousand years later, Chalcolithic Gilat (4500–3500 cal BC), in the Negev had only rare pieces of obsidian, and those became more scarce over time. The Southern Levant had become a backwater to the great northern networks. During the Chalcolithic, worked Levantine copper began going to Egypt (Ibrahim, 2010, p. 83), and by the Early Bronze Age, Egypt would be the focus of its trade networks—with tragic consequences.

The second reason may be the persistence of a ritually reinforced system of maintaining peace between local communities. Besides Tell 'Abu Hamid and Tuleilat Ghassul and other open-air sites between settlements, Gilat, located at the border of the agricultural coastal plain and pastoralist hills, was a major ritual center (Levy, 1993, p. 236; 2006), and a center of a local exchange in cultic objects (Yellin, Levy, & Rowan, 1996, pp. 361, 366–367). As it was at the end of the line from Anatolia, there would be no reason to fight over trade control and no diffusion of war from violent neighbors; while locally, ceremony and exchange integrated communities.

This absence of war signs continues into the start of the Bronze Age, where major, urban settlements arose in the midst of smaller and mobile groups. During the later Early Bronze Age Ia (3500–3300 BC, though dates vary[8]), Megiddo and Bet Shean—both in the center of Jordanian population and astride the main trade routes—developed into massive sites. Megiddo appears to have originated as a free-standing, extramural ritual center, but in the process of developing its huge structures, a sprawling settlement arose around it (Halpern, 2000, 536). At 50 hectares, Megiddo was nearly as large as its contemporaries Tell Brak and Hamoukar—but what a difference! Megiddo was a cultic center with a major, pillared temple, located at a transition between hilly pastoral areas and alluvial sites, where collective rituals "cement[ed] social relationships and promote[ed] solidarity between groups who did not come into contact on a day-to-day basis." Bet Shean, in the center of agriculture, had major grain-storage facilities and served as a "redistribution facility" (Greenberg, 2003, pp. 18–19). Finkelstein and Ussishkin (2000, p. 584) interpret central Jordan as "a fully developed territorio-political entity, centered at Megiddo." Seen in light of Southern Levant history, Megiddo and other centers may represent a culmination of an ancient system of resolving potential conflicts through peaceful means. That was about to end.

War in a Tribal Zone

Late in the EBIb (3300–3050 BC), Megiddo and other major sites (Tell Shalem, possibly Jericho and Tell-Erani) were fortified, as were many smaller settlements. Many settlements constructed walls in late EBIb. Subsequently, in EBII, Megiddo, Bet Shean, and other places were abandoned. Walled settlements became the rule in central Jordan, even around small sites, and some locales show signs of destruction. The defenses that archaeologists have sought in vain for thousands of previous years are suddenly evident all over the place. After local population had swelled in the EBIb, it crashed in EBII, falling by a third or more. Some indications suggest that groupings of local settlement were taking on new territorial definition (Eisenberg, 1996; Finkelstein & Ussishkin, 2000, p. 584; Greenberg, 2003, p. 20; Ibrahim, 2000; Paz, 2002, pp. 238–240, 245–251; de Miroschedji et al., 2001, p. 84).

It is often assumed that signs of war are absent in earlier remains because the type of evidence which could show war only comes in later times. My point has been that frequently, signs of war appear without any increase in physical recovery. The Southern Levant is the best possible illustration of that point. Fortifications go from none-detected to ubiquitous in only about a century, with no increase in archaeological discovery. Unmistakably, war had arrived, in a dramatic and abrupt transition. What happened? Comparative history combined with the local chronology of events suggests one very likely answer: newly imperial Egypt turned central Jordan into a Tribal Zone.

A Tribal Zone is an area of non-state peoples affected by the proximity of a state. These are best known from the expansion of Europe, but tribal zones surround ancient states as well (Ferguson, 1993; Ferguson & Whitehead, 1999). Cross-culturally and pan-historically, a new state presence transforms war that is ongoing, frequently intensifies it, and sometimes generates war where none existed. The latter pertains here. War is affected via many interaction processes—demographic, economic, political, and ideological. The exogenous factors do not supplant local dynamics, but set them on new trajectories in a multidimensional dialectic of social change. Thus, a study such as by Philip (2003, pp. 112–113), which situates the construction of walls in relation to changes in agriculture, and the emergence of social and symbolic identification with local communities, is complemented with a tribal zone approach, which asks: why now (and see Levy 1993)? Tribal zones across cultures and times exhibit remarkable similarities in process, and those regularities inform inferences in the following discussion.

In what would become known as Canaan, pre-dynastic Egypt had a long history of seemingly balanced, mutually beneficial trade, greatly facilitated by the use of donkeys by the late Chalcolithic (de Miroschedji, 2002, 40–44). The central Jordan valley was a land of "fantastic wealth" (Paz, 2002, p. 225), producing olive oil, wine, and metals, which its craftsmen were extremely skilled in working (Levy, 1993, pp. 242–243). Relations went through a "complex process" during the time of Egyptian consolidation, from sporadic contacts before 3500, to "entrepreneurs with royal affiliations" from 3500 to 3200, "to an extensive network of royal outposts [3200–3000] (complemented by the appearance of Southern Levantine traders and craftsmen at Maadi)" (Joffee 2000: 118). Maadi, near contemporary Cairo, rose to major scale based on its connections to the Southern Levant. Over time, the biggest traders in Egypt became emerging royal lines (Trigger, Kemp, O'Connor, & Lloyd, 1983, pp. 26, 59).

In Jordan, Egyptian goods proliferated in EBIa (de Miroschedji et al. 2001:98). Around 3500 BC, southwest of the central population area and along the land route from Egypt, an Egyptian village, Tell Ikhbeineh was established around 3500. Around 3300, the start of the EBIb, Tell es-Sakan was founded as what appears to be an administrative center. In the EBIb, Egyptian colonization was "so dense that it is as if the oriental frontier of Egypt had moved east to incorporate not only the northern Sinai, but also the south-west of Canaan." By late EBIb, a hierarchy of settlements with administrative centers is apparent. Mixing, probably with intermarriage, was happening. By late EBIb some dozen sites, mostly north of es-Sakan and toward the center of population, had much imported Egyptian material along with local products —in contrast to more central Jordanian sites with few Egyptian goods, and those usually of the elite sort (de Miroschedji, 2002, pp. 42–44; and see Braun, 2002). The earlier signs point to a balanced, voluntary relationship, though, over time, tipping toward more Egyptian extractive control. One sign of increasing unilateralism is that the major Canaanite production center in Maadi came to an end by the start of EBIb (Tadmore, 2002, p. 247).

Egypt itself was going through momentous transformation. The consolidation of Egypt and rise of dynastic power is a long process, starting around 3500 BC. There are many ambiguities, unknowns, and debates on who, how, and when. Given the ambiguities and local variations and complexities, no one can assign fractions to the role of cultural spread, mercantile consolidation, and military conquest or hegemony. It does seem to be generally accepted, however, that conquest warfare was important in the final stages of unification. The culmination of state building is associated with Egypt's Naqada III, just as colonization expanded in the EBIb of Jordan. The whole Nile was more or less unified by the time of Narmer in 3050 BC, although it may have been earlier, under his predecessor the Scorpion King. The time of the Pharaohs had begun (Joffee, 2000; Trigger et al. 1983, pp. 44–60; Watrin, 2002). Their ruling world view emphasized the duality of Egypt versus all outsiders, including Asiatics of Canaan, that order must be imposed, that interference with trade was to be severely punished, and that war against enemies would be total (Gnirs, 1999 pp. 72–75). By the start of the First Dynasty, Egyptian forces were conquering areas of Nubia, and in later Early Dynastic times, external punitive expeditions could reach genocidal proportions (Trigger et al., 1983, pp. 61–63).

Narmer's name appears in Levantine sites at the end of EBIb (Braun 2009:29). Clearly, relations with the locals had taken on a very new character. Around 3200, Ikhbeineh was abandoned. About that same time, epochal events occurred. A defensive wall went up around the Egyptian center at Tell es-Sakan, possibly with an outer bastion. Roughly a century later, a more substantial wall replaced it, this time with a glacis, making a total height of 5–6 meters, with a bastion and postern. Between 3000 and 2900, fortified es-Sakan was abandoned (de Miroschedji & Travaux, 2000, 31; de Miroschedji et al., 2001, pp. 80, 84, 90, 98–101). That and later events are beyond the scope of this chapter.

What was happening among the locals? At late EBIb Megiddo, Level XVIII has been radiocarbon dated to cal 3320–3097 BC (Finkelstein & Ussishkin, 2000, pp. 577, 579), or so close to the Egyptian fortification that sequencing the two is impossible. XVIII Megiddo raised a huge defensive wall, originally 4–5 meters thick, then increased to eight meters, with a minimum height (what is preserved) of over 4 meters. Urgency is apparent. The wall surrounded the central temple. It cut through the existing house structures that led down the slopes, destroying many of them. Excavators commented on how poorly built it was. On a slope so steep, it quickly needed reinforcement. It was made in vertical sections with seams in between. Its neat stone facade covered a weak fill of dirt and rubble (Finkelstein & Ussishkin, 2000, pp. 579–583; Loud, 1939, pp.66, 70). What would one expect for the first fort they ever built?

Even more remarkable are two of the artifacts found in the cultic center: a very functional bronze spear head, and a ceremonial *sword* of pure copper, embellished with silver (Loud, 1948, plates 173, 283). These are the first clear weapons ever found in the Southern Levant, but they may not be unique. The "Kfar Monash Hoard" of bronze tools includes axes, daggers, and spearheads, though whether this comes from EBIb or later is disputed (Tadmor, 2002). What is not disputable, is that just as Egypt was making its transition to Pharoahs and empire, at Megiddo, weapons of war were incorporated into the most important cultic center in the land indicating a major shift in their cognized world.

Of course, no one can know the politics and history leading to this radical shift in Jordanian orientation. But developments in Egypt, and some standard lessons of Tribal Zones, suggest an answer. As Egypt developed toward greater centralization, incorporation, and militarism, the centuries-old trading relationship with Canaan gave way to tribute (see Watrin, 2002). Such has happened in countless imperial situations. No more Mister Nice Guy. Colonizers declare they are now in charge, and the locals better pay up, or suffer killings, destructions of villages, and not improbably in this case, sending captives back to Egypt as slaves. The extractive products of olive oil, wine, and metals, the tributary focus of Egyptian expansion, could only be realized upon the mundane necessities of imperial operations: local manpower and food. Those are precisely what local settlement walls protected (Philip, 2003 p. 114). If it went as other tribal zones have gone, when Egyptian troops began exemplary punishments, local people were forced into war in defense. It is also expectable that Egyptians operated with local allies joined to them through a history of marriage and exchange, thus spreading war through the fabric of local social relations. Centers of local unity and resistance would be special targets (Levy, 1993, p. 243).

In the next phase, Early Bronze Age II, Megiddo and Bet Shean were completely abandoned, though no signs of destruction have been found thus far (Greenberg, 2003, p. 20). Population of the Jordan Valley plummeted, and every village in the central area was fortified; many villages were razed, many abandoned. The former settlement distribution suggesting areal unification around main ritual centers was replaced by spatial clustering and separation of local settlements (Finkelstein & Ussishkin, 2000, p. 584; Greenberg, 2003, pp. 21–24; Halpern, 2000, p. 537; Paz, 2002, pp. 248–251). "The Tribal Zone" is called that because colonial expansion typically leads to tribalization, the generation of new tribal entities. The Southern Levant is well known in history for its tribes. Perhaps this is where they began.

Yes, this is speculation, but it is closely tied to data and dates, and consistent with a body of theory derived from many colonial situations. It is able to explain the unprecedented turn to militarism in the Southern Levant, which is strangely un-noted in recent debates about prehistoric war in the Near East. The imposed hegemony of Egypt was "the end of independent social evolution in the country" (Levy, 1993 p. 243). "[T]he flourishing pattern of hundreds of unfortified settlements was never seen again" (Paz, 2002, p. :255). The Southern Levantine mechanisms, which I hypothesize avoided war for millennia, were destroyed in the cauldron of a Tribal Zone. Megiddo is the namesake of the prophesied war that ends the world. In the sense of a world free of war, Armageddon already happened, at the end of Early Bronze Age Ib.

Near East Conclusion

A recent issue of *Neo-Lithics*, stimulated by the writings of Keeley, LeBlanc, Otterbein and others, represents a collective effort to "de-pacify" the past by seeking out any possible evidence of war in the Near Eastern Neolithic. Although some authors remain skeptical, the enthusiasm of others raises the specter of "warrifying" prehistory. So Bar-Yosef (2010a, pp. 7–8) suggests that abandonment of long-established settlements in itself might reflect war; and Roscoe (2010, p.66) argues that the fact of settlement nucleation indicates the need to defend against attacks. Both, of course, have other explanations. On the other hand, Otterbein (2010, p. 56) finds that the evidence produced does nothing to contradict his theory that war was absent during the era when plants and animals were domesticated. LeBlanc, after reviewing possible signs of war from the entire Near East (almost all of which has been covered in this chapter), concludes: "Evidence does exist, it is just not particularly strong." Keeley (1996, p. 38), in contrast, previously concluded there was little evidence of war in the Near East until "the later Neolithic and in the Bronze Age." Many of the authors ringingly call for more systematic searching for any possible signs of war.

By all means, search. Look everywhere. But understand that findings, or lack thereof, are two-sided. LeBlanc (2010, p. 46) claims "We will never be able to show that there was absolutely no warfare even if there was none" (2010, p. 46). Yet dedicated searching that fails to produce evidence *does* support the theory that war was not present. Indeed, the hypothesis "war was not present" is eminently testable and easily falsified, like the "all swans are white" hypothesis. It is the opposite position, that "war was present even when we cannot provide evidence," which is unfalsifiable, and so unscientific. If archaeologists would go beyond the mantra "absence of evidence is not evidence of absence," and focus instead on regional and temporal variations in the evidence that *does* exist, some very interesting issues could be joined.

Seen in terms of war, the Near East has at least three significant regions. One is the northern Tigris. Four superlatives come from less than 90 miles apart. The first strong evidence for war in the Near East is from Qermez Dere and Nemrik 9 in the tenth into ninth millennium, contemporary with the PPNA. The earliest fortification in Mesopotamia, and possibly the Near East, is found at Tell Maghzaliyah from the seventh millennium. From 3800 3500 BC come the first mass burials, at Tell Brak, and the first conquest of a major urban center, at Hamoukar. The last two, and probably Maghzaliyah, were related to the trade routes that came down from Anatolia. That is not evident at Qermez Dere and Nemrik 9, but the tight geographic association is suggestive.

Anatolia is another region of war. Neolithic signs appear in the late eighth millennium, but a major transition dates to around 6500 BC. Regardless of the verdict on Catalhuyuk and war, by around the start of the sixth millennium in the Pottery Neolithic, clear signs of war appear in multiple sites, several suggesting military expansion by Halafians. These continue through subsequent periods, and spread out to encompass trading centers across the Northern Levant from the Mediterranean to Iraq, and northward to the Aegean and

Greece. The relatively short span (centuries not millennia) between the start of agriculture and war in Anatolia is similar to time-frames in Europe. This widespread, enduring pattern is the beginning of an unbroken lineage of war that comes down to the modern world. Yet even in the northern Tigris and Anatolia, to the stopping point of this research at least, there is no apparent development of a cult of war, weapons, and warriors, as appeared in Europe's final Neolithic and continued through the Chalcolithic and Bronze Age. That is a major contrast.

It is the Southern Levant that presents the most intriguing findings. From the time of the Natufians, beginning around 13100 BC, up to the Early Bronze Age IIb around 3200 BC, there are only a handful of violent deaths indicated by skeletal remains: two Natufians (an unsexed adult and an older woman) with unhealed cranial fractures and one adult male with an embedded point; a lethal wound—maybe—at 'Ain Ghazal; an elderly woman with a point in her jaw at Ghwair; a boy killed by a blow to the head at Basta; and an adolescent male killed by multiple blows at Shiqmim. I may have missed some reports; other killings no doubt could be found by careful reexamination of museum skeletons, more will be unearthed in the future, and overall, skeletal remains are not all that common in the Near East. Nevertheless, seven instances from nearly 10,000 years, with only one or two adult males, is a remarkable record—against the presence of war.

As for fortifications or deliberate destructions in the Southern Levant, Roper (1975), culling earlier reports, found only Beidha and Jericho that rose to the level of "suspicious," and nothing persuasive has been added to that since 1975, even considering Ba'ja and Basta. Compare that to the recent proliferation of findings of war from the northern Tigris, Anatolia and its environs, and tribal zone Jordan. Although population distributions and urban concentrations change greatly by period, at all times it seems that villages were distributed according to available resources, not in defendable locations, and were uniformly without fortifications. The only notable weapon-tools are maces, which generally seem too frail for combat, and which may symbolize authority and so the *prevention* of war. Even tool-weapons such as arrowheads are not especially prominent, particularly in later periods. One can repeat "absence of evidence is not evidence of absence," but why are all lines of evidence for war consistently absent in the Southern Levant, when they are so abundant in other areas of the Near East and in Europe?

Evidence of war may yet turn up in the Southern Levant. No system is perfect. With all the times of population growth, climatic reverses, and anthropogenic resource degradation, there certainly was potential were great reasons for collective conflict. But even if a case or two does appear, that would not change the general finding of peace, and the striking contrast between the Southern Levant and other areas. As it stands today, the archaeological record supports a remarkable point, one worth not just recognizing, but heralding. For 10,000 years in the Southern Levant, *there is not one single instance where it can be said with confidence, "war was there."* Am I wrong? Name the place.

Conclusion: Toward an Archaeology of Peace

The case has been forcefully made that archaeologists "pacified the past" by not looking for signs of war, or neglecting them when found. Sometimes that has been true. But also true is that in many places and periods, evidence simply does not appear, even when diligently sought—in striking contrast to plenty of other places where war signs are very clear. The weight of this negative evidence may be hard to bear for those who believe war flows out of human nature, or is an inescapable shadow of social existence. But as those who invoke biological predispositions for killing commonly intone, a scientific approach to human existence means facing up to facts, however unpleasant.

In many early times and places, an absence of war is theoretically consistent with the absence of preconditions for war. Yet early war is far less common than its preconditions. They are necessary but not sufficient to explain its presence. That is true for the ethnographic universe as well. A central question in the anthropology of war has been, why does war happen, when most people, most of the time, are at peace? One answer is that war is not chosen lightly. War is costly, risky in the extreme, and usually decided upon only after conflicted local politics. Archaeology brings in another kind of inhibition, not applicable to most ethnographically known cases. Non-state peoples of the past 500 years have lived in a world long turned to war. They are not exemplars of our very distant past, not our "contemporary ancestors" (Ferguson, 2006, pp. 477–480, 497–499, and see endnote 1). Going to war would be immeasurably more difficult in a prehistoric situation of social conflict which did not already have a history of collective attacks. If a people had never *heard of* going out and slaughtering neighbors, it would be a daunting task to convince them that it was a good idea. There would be no prisoners' dilemmas. There would be no culture of war, no valorization of warriors.

But more than that, before war became "normal," there may have been developed cultural systems to prevent conflict from turning into collective violence. Cross-cultural research tells us that there are factors and forces which promote peace, which are quite distinct from those that encourage war. The comparative record from Europe and the Near East suggests that these could be investigated, if archaeologists recognized the possibility, and chose to investigate them. There could be an *archaeology of peace* (Dye, chapter 8).

It might start with the formulation: if archaeological recovery is sufficient so there is a good chance of finding signs of war if war was present; if this absence of evidence extends over time and place to a number of sites; if the preconditions of war are markedly and in combination present; and if there are other comparable regions in which signs of war are repeatedly found; then it may be hypothesized that elements of the local culture combined in a system to maintain peace and prevent war. This might apply to much of pre-war Europe and the Near East (and to post-3200 BC England), but the best example comes from the Southern Levant.

Referring back to Fry's (2006) broad categories of peace-promoting factors, many of them are apparent, or potentially recoverable, in the Southern Levant. Signs of cross-cutting ties and interdependence are legion. Despite periods of cultural differentiation, common patterns from tool manufacture to mortuary customs are found spanning much of the Near East from the Epipaleolithic onward, and remain the rule in the Southern Levant. Intermarriage and movement between areas are not demonstrated given current evidence, but are possibly approachable through DNA or tooth enamel studies. Trade connected all areas, without indications of monopolistic control.

In the later Southern Levant, local trade networks continued even as longer-distance trade shifted from Anatolia to Egypt, with cultic objects prominent. Communal storage and redistribution is associated with later central sites, which also seem intended to span the potential divide between farmers and herders. Perhaps the most striking contrast between European and Levantine Neolithics is that village enclosures—communal projects demarcating discrete local identities—are not found in the latter. Even though early unfortified European enclosures were not suitable for defense in war, they may have been critical in fixing local identification and separation—us, as opposed to them—in developing European cultures.

In many areas of the Near East, some form of social authority is clear in many pre-planned settlement constructions, and is strongly suggested by the widespread occurrence of maces unsuitable for actually hitting anybody. Yet the type of ostentatious chiefly lifestyle that in other parts of the world is often associated with war is rarely evident until the Chalcolithic, if then; and burials of warriors with weapons, common in Europe, are notably absent. Values promoting peace are not recoverable artifacts. But extramural public ritual spaces, built collectively and lacking anything of a martial flavor, suggest a value on harmony; and possibly served as locations where conflicts were authoritatively addressed. Collective burial sites also may have symbolically unified multiple communities.

My suggestion is that as archaeologists search for signs of war, they also consider the possibility that humans are capable of systematically dealing with conflict in peaceful ways. People of the Southern Levant domesticated nature. It is a pessimistic view indeed to presume they were not also capable of domesticating conflict. Pessimistic, but perhaps understandable. Across all of Europe and the Near East, war has been known from 3000 BC, or millennia earlier, present during all of written history. No wonder we think of it as "natural." But the prevalent notion that war is "just human nature" is empirically unsupportable. The same types of evidence that document the antiquity of war refute the idea of war forever backwards. War sprang out of a warless world. Humankind has suffered infinite misery because systems of war conquered our social existence. Better understanding of what makes war, and what makes peace, is an important step toward bringing peace back.

Dedication

This chapter is dedicated to my brilliant friend, Neil Lancelot Whitehead.

Notes

1. If the earliest archaeological records contain little evidence of warfare, the question becomes: how did war become so common in later sequences, and in ethnographically observed peoples? First, because over time around the world, the preconditions of war (below) became more widespread in more places. Then, from the earlier areas of warfare, war spread outwards, due to interaction with war-making groups—making peaceful trajectories less viable—and/or spreading of the preconditions. A third long-term change is the impact of ancient states on non-state peoples in their peripheries, along their trade routes, or subject to their predation. The final factor is the intensively disruptive impact of European colonialism. For all these reasons, the common practice of inferring a high level of prehistoric warfare by invoking practices of tribal peoples in recent centuries is, to put it mildly, invalid. That is a central point of Ferguson (2006; see also Haas & Piscitelli, chapter 10).
2. Kelly's (2000) theoretical elaboration on group definition and the development of war is important: substitutability of intended victims, group liability for offenses, and responsibility for revenge are what distinguished war from other sorts of violence. But these conditions are not archaeologically recoverable.
3. One study of Iberian remains (Jimenez-Brobeil, du Souich, & Al Oumaoui, 2009, pp. 467–469) from seven periods, ranging from Neolithic to the first half of the twentieth century, found 71 instance of cranial trauma in 677 individuals, every one of them healed. Interestingly, the early twentieth century had by far the highest rate of injury. Walker (1997, p. 158) presents a composite representation of skull fractures in modern Americans that in an archaeological context could casually be interpreted as evidence of war.
4. That is consistent with the profound ambiguity of actual combat deaths in the metal ages, even though by then war was clearly a cultural preoccupation.
5. A new volume (Schulting & Fibiger 2012) of European archaeological studies of war appeared after this chapter was completed.
6. In the Taurus Mountains of northwest Iran, sixth millennium Hajii Firuz Tepe is said by LeBlanc (2010, p. 45) to have "an extremely high incidence of violent deaths." Given the time and location, that would not be a surprise. But I could not find such a claim in his source. Voigt (1983, pp. 78–94, 342) just reports the sort of disarticulation sometimes found in ossuary reburials, while a discussion of pathology notes two forearm fractures, and a few other accidental breaks.
7. "Gilgamesh does not allow the son to go with his father; day and night he oppresses the weak … Gilgamesh does not allow the young girl to go with her mother, the girl to the warrior, the bride to the groom" (Gardner & Maier, 1985, p. 67). This sounds much like the compulsory incorporation of young men and women into fighting and production regiments as the Zulu passed from chiefdom to state (Guy, 1981, pp. 40–46).
8. Period and subperiod divisions vary by report by 50 to 250 years. This makes reconstruction at *historical* levels of resolution impossible. For most general dates concerning parallel developments in the Southern Levant and Egypt, I rely on de Miroschedji (2002, p. 40) and de Miroschedji et al. (2001, p. 80).

References

Abbink, J.G. (1999). Violence, ritual, and reproduction: Culture and context in Surma dueling. *Ethnology, 38,* 227–242.

Akkermans, P. M. (2000). Old and new perspectives on the origins of the Halaf culture. In *La Djezire et l'Euphrate syriens de la protohistoire a la fin du IIe millenaire av.J.-C. (Subartu VII),* 43–54.

Alt, K. W., Pichler, S., Vach, W., Klima, B., Vlcek, E., & Sedlmeier, J. (1997). Twenty-five thousand-year-old triple burial from Dolni Vestonice: An Ice-Age family? *American Journal of Physical Anthropology, 102,* 123–131.

Andersen, N. H. (1993). Causewayed camps of the Funnel Beaker Culture. In S. Hvaas, & B. Storgaard (Eds.), *Digging into the past: 25 years of archaeology in Denmark* (pp. 100–151). Copenhagen: The Royal Society of Northern Antiquaries.

Anderson, D. G., Maasch, K. A., Sandweiss, D. H., & Mayewski, P. A. (2007). Climate and culture change: Holocene transitions. In D. G. Anderson, K. A. Maasch, & D. H. Sandweiss (Eds.), *Climate change and cultural dynamics: A global perspective on mid-Holocene transitions* (pp. 1–23). Amsterdam: Elsevier.

Andreaou, S., Fotiadis, F., & Kotsakis, K. (1996). Review of Aegean prehistory V: The Neolithic and Bronze Age of northern Greece. *Journal of Archaeology, 100,* 537–597.

Andrews, P., & Fernandez-Jalvo, Y. (2003). Cannibalism in Britain: Taphonomy of the Creswellian (Pleistoene) faunal and human remains from Gough's Cave (Somerset, England). *Bulletin of the Natural History Museum, London, 26*, 59–81.

Angel, J. (1969). Human skeletal material from Franchthi Cave, (Appendix II in T. Jacobsen, Excavations at Porto Cheli and Vicinity, Preliminary Report, II: The Franchthi Cave, 1967–1968). *Hesperia, 38*, 343–381.

Anthony, D. W. (2007). *The horse, the wheel, and language: How Bronze-Age riders from the Eurasian steppes shaped the modern world.*. Princeton: Princeton University Press.

Aranda Jimenez, G., & Sanchez Romero, M. 2005). The origins of warfare: Later prehistory in southeastern Iberia. In M. P. Pearson, & I. J. N. Thorpe (Eds.). *Warfare, violence and slavery in prehistory: Proceedings of a Prehistoric Society conference at Sheffield University, BAR International Series, 1374*, 181–194. Oxford: Archaeopress.

Armendariz, J., Irigarai, S., & Etxeberria, F. (1994). New evidence of prehistoric arrow wounds in the Iberian peninsula. *International Journal of Osteoarchaeology, 4*, 215–222.

Asouti, E. (2006). Beyond the Pre-Pottery Neolithic B interaction sphere. *Journal of World Prehistory, 20*, 87–126.

Asouti, E. (2009). The relationship between early Holocene climate change and Neolithic settlement in central Anatolia, Turkey. Current issues and prospects for future research. *Documenta Praehistorica, 36*, 1–5.

Bachechi, L., Fabbri, P-F., & Mallegni, F. (1997). An arrow-caused lesion in a late Upper Palaeolithic human pelvis. *Current Anthropology, 38*, 135–140.

Bader, N. O. (1993). Summary of the earliest agriculturalists of northern Mesopotamia. In N. Yoffee, & J. J. Clark (Eds.), *Early stages in the evolution of Mesopotamian civilization: Soviet excavations in northern Iraq* (pp. 64–88). Tucson: University of Arizona Press.

Bar-Yosef, O. (1986). The walls of Jericho: An alternative interpretation. *Current Anthropology, 27*, 157–162.

Bar-Yosef, O. (1998). The Natufian culture in the Levant, threshold to the origins of agriculture. *Evolutionary Anthropology, 6*, 159–167.

Bar-Yosef, O. (2010a). Warfare in Levantine Early Neolithic: A hypothesis to be considered. *Neo-Lithics, 1/10*, 6–10

Bar-Yosef, O. (2011). Climatic fluctuations in the Levant: The outer envelope. *Current Anthropology, 52 supplement 4*, 175–193.

Bender, B. (1985). Prehistoric developments in the American midcontinent and in Brittany, northwest France. In T. D. Price, & J. A. Brown (Eds.), *Prehistoric hunter-gatherers: The emergence of cultural complexity* (pp. 21–57). Orlando: Academic Press.

Belfar-Cohen, A., & Goring–Morris, A. N. (2011). Becoming farmers: The inside story. *Current Anthropology, 52 supplement 4*, 209–220.

Bennike, P. (1985). *Paleopathology of Danish skeletons*. Copenhagen: Akademisk Forlag.

Berger, T. D., & Trinkaus, E. (1995). Patterns of trauma among the Neanderthals. *Journal of Archaeological Science, 22*, 841–852.

Bienert, H-D., & Gebel, H. G. K. (2004). Summary on Ba'Ja 1997, and insights from the later seasons. In H-D. Bienert, H. G. K. Gebel, & R. Neef (Eds.), *Central settlements in Neolithic Jordan, Studies in Early Near Eastern Production, Subsistence, and Environment, 5*, 119–144. Berlin: Ex Oriente.

Birocheau, P., Convertini, F., Cros, J-P., Duday, H., & Large, J-M. (1999). Fosse et sepultures du Neolithique recent aux Chatelliers du Vieil-Auzay (Vendee); Aspects structuraux et anthropologiques. *Bulletin de la Societe Prehistorique Francaise, 96*, 375–390.

Bocquentin, F., & Bar-Yosef, O. (2004). Early Natufian remains: evidence for physical conflict from Mt. Carmel, Israel. *Journal of Human Evolution, 47*, 19–23.

Bodet, C. (2011). The megaliths of Gobekli Tepe as a mirror of kinship structures and a promoter of social rules. *Peneo, 3(1)*, 1–15.

Bogaard, A., Krause, R., & Strien, H-C. (2011). Towards a social geography of cultivation and plant use in an early farming community: Vaihingen an der Enz, south-west Germany. *Antiquity, 85*, 395–416

Boulestin, B. (1999). *Approache taphonomique des restes humains: Le cas de Mesolithiques de la grotte des Perrats et le probleme du cannibalism en prehistoire recent Eureopeenne, BAR International Series, 776*. Oxford: Archaeopress.

Boulestin, B., Zeeb-Lanz, A., Jeunesse, C., Haack, F., Arbogast, R-M., & Denaire, A. (2009). Mass cannibalism in the Linear Pottery Culture at Herxheim (Palatinate, Germany). *Antiquity, 83*, 968–982.

Bower, B. (2008). Dawn of the city: Excavations prompt a revolution in thinking about the earliest cities. *Science News, 173 (6)*, 90–92.

Braun, E. (2002). Egypt's first sojourn in Canaan. In E. C. M. van den Brink, & T. E. Levy (Eds.), *Egypt and the Levant: Interrelations from the 4th through the early 3rd millennium BC* (pp. 173–189). London: Leicester University Press.

Braun, E. (2009). South Levantine Early Bronze Age chronological correlations with Egypt in light of the Narmer serekhs from Tel Erani and Arad: New interpretations. *British Museum Studies in Ancient Egypt and Sudan, 13*, 25–48.

Brennan, M. U. (1991). Health and disease in the Middle and Upper Paleolithic of southwestern France: A bioarcheological study. Doctoral dissertation, New York University. Ann Arbor: University Microfilm.

Carbonell, E., Caceras, I., Lozano, M., Saladie, P., Rosell, J., Lorenzo, C. . . . & Bermudez de Castro, J.M. (2010). Cultural cannibalism as a paleoeconomic system in the European Lower Pleistocene: The case of level TD6 of Gran Dolina, (Sierra de Atapuerca, Burgos, Spain). *Current Anthropology, 51*, 539–549.

Carman, J., & Carman, P. (2005). War in prehistoric society: Modern views of ancient violence. In M. P. Pearson, & I. J. N. Thorpe (Eds.), *Warfare, violence and slavery in prehistory: Proceedings of a Prehistoric Society conference at Sheffield University, BAR International Series, 1374*, 217–224. Oxford: Archaeopress.

Chacon, R. J., & Dye, D. (Eds.). (2007). *The taking and displaying of human body parts as trophies by Americans.* New York: Springer.

Chapman, J. (1999). The origins of warfare in the prehistory of Central and Eastern Europe. In J. Carman, & A. Harding (Eds.), *Ancient Warfare* (pp. 101–142). Stroud: Sutton Publishers.

Christensen, J. (2004). Warfare in the European Neolithic. *Acta archaeologica, 75*, 129–136.

Churchill, S. E., Franciscus, R. G., & McKean-Peraza, H. A. (2009). Shanidar 3 Neandertal rib puncture wound and paleolithic weaponry. *Journal of Human Evolution, 57*, 163–178.

Clare, L. (2010). Pastoral clashes: Conflict risk and mitigation at the Pottery Neolithic transition in the southern Levant. *Neo-Lithics, 1/10*, 13–31.

Clare, L., Rohling, E. J., Weninger, B., & Hilpert, J. (2008). Warfare in late Neolithic/early Chalcolithic Pisidia, southwestern Turkey. Climate induced social unrest in the late 7th millennium cal BC. *Documenta Praehistorica, 35*, 65–92.

Cohen, M. N. (1985). Prehistoric hunter-gatherers: The meaning of social complexity. In T. D. Price, & J. A. Brown (Eds.), *Prehistoric hunter-gatherers: The emergence of cultural complexity* (pp. 99–119). Orlando: Academic Press.

Conklin, B. A. (2001). *Consuming grief: Compassionate cannibalism in an Amazonian society.* Austin: University of Texas Press.

Cunha, E., Umbelino, C., & Cardoso, F. (2004). About violent interactions in the Mesolithic: The absence of evidence from the Portuguese shell middens. In M. Roksandic (Ed.), *Violent interactions in the Mesolithic: Evidence and meaning, BAR International Series, 1237*, 41–46. Oxford: Archaeopress.

Dastugue, J., & de Lumley, M-A. (1976). Les maladies des hommes prehistoriques du Paleolithique et du Mesolithique. In H. de Lumley (Ed.), *La prehistoire francaise: Tome I, les civilizations Paleolithiques et Mesolithiques de la France*, 612–622. Paris: Edition du Centre National de la Recherche Scientifique.

Dawson, L., Levy, T. E., & Smith, P. (2003). Evidence of interpersonal violence at the Chalcolithic village of Shiqmim (Israel). *International Journal of Osteoarchaeology, 13*, 115–119.

Defleur, A., White, T., Valensi, P., Slimak, L., & Cregut-Bonnoure, E. (1999). Neanderthal cannibalism at Moula-Guercy, Ardeche, France. *Science, 286*, 128–131.

de Miroschedji, P. (2002). The social-political dynamics of Egyptian-Canaanite interaction in the Early Bronze Age. In E. C. M. van den Brink, & T. E. Levy (Eds.), *Egypt and the Levant: Interrelations from the 4th through the early 3rd millennium BC* (pp. 40–57). London: Leicester University Press.

de Miroschedji, P., & Travaux, P. (2000). Travaux archaeologiques a Tell Sakan (Bande de Gaza) en 1999. *Orient Express, (2)*, 30–32.

de Miroschedji, P., Sadeq, M., Faltings, D., Boulez, V., Naggiar-Moliner, L, Sykes, N., & Tenberg, M. (2001). Les fouilles de Tell es-Sakan (Gaza): nouvelles donnees sur les contacts egypto-cananeens aux I've-IIIe millenaires. *Paleorient, 27*, 75–104.

Dolukhanov, P. M., 1999. War and peace in prehistoric Eastrn Europe. In J. Carman, & A. Harding (Eds.), *Ancient Warfare* (pp. 73–87). Stroud: Sutton Publishers.

Drews, R. (1993). *The end of the Bronze Age: Changes in warfare and the catastrophe ca. 1200 BC.* Princeton: Princeton University Press.

During, B.S. (2011). Fortifications and fabrications: Reassessing the emergence of fortifications in prehistoric Asia Minor. B. S. During, A. Wosskink, & P. M. M. G. Akkermans, (Eds.), *Correlates of complexity: Essays in archaeology and Assyriology dedicated to Diederik J.W. Meijer in honor of his 65th birthday.* Leiden: Nederlands Instituut voor het Nabije Oosten.

Dye, D. H. (2009). *War paths, peace paths: An archaeology of cooperation and conflict in Native Eastern North America.* Lanham, MD: Altamira.

Estabrook, V. H., & Frayer, D. W. (2012). Trauma in the Krapina Neandertals: Violence in the Middle Paleolithic. In C. Knusel, & M. Smith (Eds.), *A history of conflict: osteology and "traumatized bodies" from earliest prehistory to the present.* Oxford: Routledge, forthcoming

Eisenberg, E. (1996). Tel Shalem–soundings in a fortified site of the Early Bronze Age IB. *Atiqot 30,* 1–24.

Erdal, O. D. (2012). A possible massacre at Early Bronze Age Titris Hoyuk, Anatolia. *International Journal of Osteoarchaeology 22,* 1–21.

Erdogu, B. (2009). Ritual symbolism in the early Chalcolithic period of Central Anatolia. *Journal for Interdisciplinary Research on Religion and Science, 5,* 129–151.

Eshed, V., Gopher, A., Pinhasi, R., & Hershkovitz, I. (2010). Paleopathology and the origin of agriculture in the Levant. *American Journal of Physical Anthropology, 143,* 121–133.

Fairen, S. (2004). Rock art and the transition to farming: The Neolithic landscape of the central Mediterranean coast of Spain. *Oxford Journal of Archaeology, 23,* 1–19.

Ferguson, R. B. (1984). Introduction: Studying war. In R. B. Ferguson (Ed.), *Warfare, culture, and environment* (pp. 1–81). Orlando: Academic Press.

Ferguson, R. B. (1988). War and the sexes in Amazonia. In R. Randolph, D. Schneider, & M. Diaz (Eds.), *Dialectics and gender: Anthropological approaches* (pp. 136–154). Boulder, CO: Westview.

Ferguson, R. B. (1990). Explaining war. In J. Haas (Ed.), *The anthropology of war* (pp. 22–50). New York: Cambridge University Press.

Ferguson, R. B. (1992). A savage encounter: Western contact and the Yanomami warfare complex. In R. B. Ferguson, & N. L. Whitehead, *War in the tribal zone: Expanding states and indigenous warfare* (pp. 199–227). Santa Fe: School of American Research Press.

Ferguson, R. B. (1993). When worlds collide: The Columbian encounter in global perspective. *Human Peace, 10*(1), 8–10.

Ferguson, R. B., (1994). The general consequences of war: An Amazonian perspective. In S. P. Reyna, & R. E. Downs, *Studying war: Anthropological perspectives* (pp. 85–111). Langhorne, PA: Gordon and Breach.

Ferguson, R. B. (1995). *Yanomami warfare: A political history.* Santa Fe: SAR Press.

Ferguson, R. B. (1997). Violence and war in prehistory. In D. L. Martin, & D. W. Frayer (Eds.), *Troubled times: Violence and warfare in the past* (pp. 321–355). Langhorne, PA: Gordon & Breach.

Ferguson, R. B. (1999). A paradigm for the study of war and society. In K. Raaflaub, & N. Rosenstein (Eds.), *War and society in the ancient and medieval worlds: Asia, the Mediterranean, Europe, and Mesoamerica* (pp. 409–458). Cambridge, MA: Center for Hellenic Studies and Harvard University Press.

Ferguson, R. B. (2003a). Introduction: Violent conflict and control of the state. In R. B. Ferguson (Ed.), *The state, identity, and violence: Political disintegration in the post-Cold War era,* (pp. 1–58). New York: Routledge.

Ferguson, R. B. (2003b). The birth of war. *Natural History* (July/August), 28–35.

Ferguson, R. B. (2006a). Tribal, "ethnic," and global wars. In M. Fitzduff, & C. Stout (Eds.), *The psychology of resolving global conflicts: From war to peace; Vol. 1: Nature vs. nurture,* 41–69. Westport, CT: Praeger Security International.

Ferguson, R. B. (2006b). Archaeology, cultural anthropology, and the origins and intensification of war. In E. N. Arkush, & M. W. Allen (Eds.), *The archaeology of warfare: Prehistories of raiding and conquest* (pp. 469–523). Gainesville: University of Florida Press.

Ferguson, R. B. (2008). War before history. In de Souza, P. (Ed.), *The ancient world at war: A global history* (pp. 15–27). London: Thames & Hudson.

Ferguson, R. B. (2009). Ten points on war. In A. Waterston (Ed.), *The anthropology of war: Views from the frontline* (pp. 32–49). New York: Berghahn.

Ferguson, R. B., & Whitehead, N. L. (1999). The Violent edge of empire. In R. B. Ferguson, & N. L. Whitehead (Eds.), *War in the tribal zone: Expanding states and indigenous warfare* (1–30). Santa Fe: School of American Research Press.

Fernandez Crespo, T. (2007). Final Neolithic multiple burials in the upper Ebro Valley: The case of San Juan Ante Portam Latinam (Basque Country, Spain). EEA Summer School eBook 1:55–63. Retrieved from http://eaa.elte.hu/FERNANDEZ.pdf, accessed March 24, 2010

Fernandez-Jalvo, Y., Diez, J. C., Caceres, I., & Rossell, J. (1999). Human cannibalism in the Early Pleistocene of Europe (Gran Dolina, Sierra de Atapuerca, Burgos, Spain). *Journal of Human Evolution, 37,* 591–622.

Finklestein, I., & D. Ussishkin (2000). Archaeological and historical conclusions. In I. Finkelstein, D. Ussishkin, & B. Halpern (Eds.), *Megiddo III: The 1992–1996 seasons* (pp. 576–605). Jerusalem: Emery and Claire Yass Publications in Archaeology.

Ferembach, D. (1959). Note sur un crane brachycephale et deux mandibules du mesolithique d'Israel. *Israel Exploration Journal, 9,* 65–73.

Formicola, V., Pontrandolfi, A., & Svoboda, J. (2001). The Upper Paleolithic triple burial of Dolni Vestonice: Pathology and funerary behavior. *American Journal of Physical Anthropology, 115,* 372–379.

Frayer, D. W. (1997). Ofnet: Evidence for a Mesolithic massacre. In D. L. Martin & D. W. Frayer (Eds.), *Troubled times: Violence and warfare in the past* (pp. 181–216). Amsterdam: Gordon & Breach.

Fry, D. P. (2006). *The human potential for peace: An anthropological challenge to assumptions about war and violence.* New York: Oxford University Press.

Fry, D. P. (2007). *Beyond war: The human potential for peace.* New York: Oxford University Press.

Gamble, C. (1999). *The paleolithic societies of Europe.* Cambridge: Cambridge University Press.

Gardiner, J., & Maier, J. (1985). *Gilgamesh.* New York: Vintage.

Gebel, H. G. K. (2004). Central to what? The centrality issue of the LPPNB mega-site phenomenon in Jordan. In H. D. Bienert, Gebel, H. G. K., & Neef, R. *Studies in early Near Eastern production, subsistence, and environment* (pp. 1–19). Berlin: Ex Orient.

Gebel, H. G. K., & Beinert, H-D. (1997). Ba'ja hidden in the Petra Mountains. Preliminary report on the 1997 excavations. In H. G. K. Gebel, Kafafi, Z., & Rollefson (Eds.), *The prehistory of Jordan, II. Perspectives from 1997* (pp. 221–262). Berlin: Ex Oriente.

Gibson, M., Al-Azm, A., Reichel, C., Quntar, S., Franke, J. A., Khalidi, L. . . . & Hartnell, T. (2002). Hamoukar: A summary of three seasons of excavation. *Akkadica, 123,* 11–34.

Gimbutas, Marija. (1991). *The civilization of the goddess.* San Francisco: Harper Collins.

Gkiasta, M., Russell, T., Shennan, S., & Steele, J. (2003). The Neolithic transition in Europe: The radiocarbon record revisited. *Antiquity, 77,* 45–67.

Golden, J. (2010). *Dawn of the Metal Age: Technology and society during the Levantine Chalcolithic.* London: Equinox.

Gnirs, A. M. (1999). Ancient Egypt. In K. Raaflaub, & N. Rosenstein (Eds.), *War and society in the ancient and medieval worlds: Asia, the Mediterranean, Europe, and Mesoamerica* (pp. 71–104). Cambridge, MA: Center for Hellenic Studies and Harvard University Press.

Golitko, M., & Keeley, L. H. (2007). Beating ploughshares back into swords: Warfare in the *Linearbandkeramik. Antiquity, 81,* 332–342.

Goring-Morris, A. N., & A. Belfer-Cohen (2011). Neolithization process in the Levant: The outer envelope. *Current Anthropology, 52* supplement 4, 195–208.

Goring-Morris, N., Hovers, E., & Belfer-Cohen, A. (2009). The dynamics of Pleistocene and early Holocene settlement patterns and human adaptations in the Levant: An overview. In J. J. Shea, & D. E. Lieberman (Eds.), *Transitions in prehistory: Essays in honor of Ofer Bar-Yosef* (pp. 185–223). Oakville, CT: Oxbow Books.

Gregor, T. (Ed.). (1996). *A natural history of Peace.* Nashville: Vanderbilt University Press.

Greenberg, R. (2003). Early Bronze Age Megiddo and Bet Shean: Discontinuous settlement in sociopolitical context. *Journal of Mediterranean Archaeology, 16,* 17–32.

Gronenborn, D. (2007). Climate change and socio-political crises: Some cases from Neolithic central Europe. In T. Pollard, and I. Banks (Ed.), *War and sacrifice: Studies in the archaeology of conflict* (pp. 13–32). Leiden: Brill.

Guilaine, J., & Zammit, J. (2005). *Origins of war: Violence in prehistory.* Oxford: Blackwell.

Guy, J. J. (1981). Production and exchange in the Zulu kingdom. In J. P. Peires (Ed.), *Before and after Shaka: Papers in Nguni history* (pp. 33–48). Grahamstown, South Africa; Institute of Social and Economic Research, Rhodes University.

Halpern, B. (2000). Centre and sentry: Megiddo's role in transit, administration and trade. In I. Finkelstein, Ussishkin, D. & Halpern, B. (Eds.), (2000) *Megiddo III: The 1992–1996 seasons* (pp. 535–575). Jerusalem: Emery and Claire Yass Publications in Archaeology.

Harding, A. (1999). Warfare: A defining characteristic of Bronze Age Europe? In J. Carman, & A. Harding (Eds.), *Ancient Warfare* (pp. 157–173). Stroud: Sutton Publishers.

Hayden, B. (1995). Pathways to power: Principles for creating socioeconomic inequalities. In T. D. Price, & G. M. Feinman (Eds.), *Foundations of social inequality* (pp. 15–86). New York: Plenum Press.

Healey, E. (2007). Why is there so much obsidian at Tell Magzhaliyah? *Systems techniques et communautes de Neolithique preceramique au Proch-Orient, actes du 5e Collogue international Frejus*, 255–265. Antibes: Editions APDCA.

Heath, J. (2009), *Warfare in prehistoric Britain*. Gloucestershire: Amberly.

Henry, D. O. (1985). Preagricultural sedentism: The Natufian example. In T. D. Price, & J. A. Brown (Eds.), *Prehistoric hunter-gatherers: The emergence of cultural complexity* (pp. 365–383). Orlando: Academic Press.

Holt, B. M., & Formicola, V. (2008). Hunters of the Ice Age: The biology of Upper Paleolithic people. *Yearbook of Physical Anthropology*, *51*, 70–99.

Ibrahim, M. M. (2010). The Jordan Valley during the Early Bronze Age. In E. Kaptijn, & L. Petit (Eds.), *A timeless vale: Archaeological and related essays on the Jordan Valley in honor of Gerrit van der Kooij on the occasion of his sixty-fifth birthday*. Leiden: Leiden University Press.

Ivanova, M. (2007). Tells, invasion theories and warfare in fifth millennium BC north-eastern Bulgaria. In T. Pollard, & I. Banks (Eds.), *War and sacrifice: Studies in the archaeology of conflict* (pp. 33–48). Leiden: Brill.

Jackes, M.K. (2004). Osteological evidence for Mesolithic and Neolithic violence: Problems of interpretation. In M. Roksandic (Ed.), *Violent interactions in the Mesolithic: Evidence and meaning, BAR International Series*, *1237*, 23–39. Oxford: Archaeopress.

Jacobsen, T. (1969). Excavations at Porto Cheli and Vicinity, Preliminary Report, II: The Franchthi Cave, 1967–1968. *Hesperia*, *38*, 343–381.

Jacobsen, T. (1973). Excavations in the Franchthi Cave, 1969–1971, Part I. *Hesperia*, *42*, 45–88.

Jimenez-Brobeil, S.A., du Souich, P., & al Omaoui, I. (2009). Possible relationship of cranial traumatic injuries with violence in the south-east Iberian peninsula from the Neolithic to the Bronze Age. *American Journal of Physical Anthropology*, *140*, 465–475.

Joffe, A. H. (2000). Egypt and Syro-Mesopotamia in the 4th millennium: Implications of the new chronology. *Current Anthropology*, *41*, 113–123.

Jurmain, R. (1999). *Stories from the skeleton: Behavioral reconstruction in human osteology*. Amsterdam: Gordon and Breach Publishers.

Keeley, L. H. (1996). *War before civilization: The myth of the peaceful savage*. New York: Oxford.

Keeley, L. H. (1997). Frontier warfare in the early Neolithic. In D. L. Martin, & D. W. Frayer (Eds.), *Troubled times: Violence and warfare in the past* (pp. 303–320). Langhorne, PA: Gordon & Breach.

Kelly, R. C. (2000). Warless societies and the origin of war. Ann Arbor: University of Michigan Press.

Kerner, S. (1997). Status, perspectives and future goals in Jordanian Chalcolithic research. In H. G. K. Gebel, Kafafi, Z., & Rollefson, G. O. (Eds.), *The Prehistory of Jordan, II: Perspectives from 1997*. Berlin: Ex Oriente.

Khalidi, L., Graute, B., & Boucetta, S. (2009). Provenance of obsidian excavated from late Chalcolithic levels at the sites of Tell Hamoukar and Tell Brak, Syria. *Archaeometry*, *6*, 879–893.

Knauft, B. M. (1987). Reconsidering violence in simple human societies: Homicide among the Gebusi of New Guinea. *Current Anthropology*, *28*, 457–500.

Knusel, C. J. (2005). The physical evidence of warfare—Subtle stigmata? In M. P. Pearson, & I. J. N. Thorpe (Eds.), *Warfare, violence and slavery in prehistory: Proceedings of a Prehistoric Society conference at Sheffield University, BAR International Series*, *1374*, 49–65. Oxford: Archaeopress.

Knusel, C. J., & Outram, A. K. (2006). Fragmentation of the body: Comestibles, compost, or customary rite? In R. Gowland, & C. Knusel (Eds.), *Social archaeology of funerary remains* (pp. 253–276). Oxford: Oxbow Books.

Kokkinidou, D., & Nikolaidou, M. (1999). Neolithic enclosures in Greek Macedonia: Violent and non-violent aspects of territorial demarcation. In J. Carman, & A. Harding (Eds.), *Ancient Warfare* (pp. 89–99). Stroud: Sutton Publishers.

Kozlowski, S. K.. (1989). Nemrik 9, a PPN Neolithic site in northern Iraq. *Paleorient*, *15*, 25–31.

Kristiansen, K. (1999). The emergence of warrior aristocracies in later European prehistory and their long-term history. In J. Carman, & A. Harding (Eds.), *Ancient Warfare* (pp. 175–189). Stroud: Sutton Publishers.

Kristiansen, K., & Larsson, T. B. (2005). *The rise of Bronze Age society: Travels, transmissions and transformations*. New York: Cambridge University Press.

Kuijt, I., & Goring-Morris, N. (2002). Foraging, farming, and social complexity in Pre-Pottery Neolithic of the Southern Levant: A review and synthesis. *Journal of World Prehistory*, *16*, 361–440.

Le Bras-Goude, G., Binder, D., Zemour, A., & Richards, M. P. (2010). New radiocarbon dates and isotope analysis of Neolithic human and animal bone from the Fontbregoua Cave (Salernes, Var, France). *Journal of Anthropological Sciences*, *88*, 167–178.

LeBlanc, S. A. (2010). Early Neolithic warfare in the Near East and its broader implications. *Neo-Lithics, 1/10,* 40–49.

LeBlanc, S. A., with Register, K. E. (2003). *Constant battles: The myth of the peaceful, noble savage.* New York: St. Martin's Press.

Levy, T. E. (1993). Cult, metallurgy and rank societies—Chalcolithic period (ca. 4500–3500). In Levy, T. E. (Ed.), *The archaeology of society in the Holy Land* (pp. 227–243). New York: Facts on File.

Lillie, M.C. (2001). Mesolithic cultures of Ukraine: Observations on cultural developments in light of new radiocarbon determinations from the Dnieper Rapids cemetaries. In K.J. Fewster, & M. Zvelebil (Eds.) *Ethnoarchaeology and hunter-gatherers: Pictures at an exhibition, BAR International Series, 955,* 53–63.

Lillie, M.C. (2004). Fighting for your life? Violence at the late-Glacial to Holocene transition in Ukraine. In M. Roksandic (Ed.), *Violent interactions in the Mesolithic, BAR International Series 1237,* 86–93. Oxford: Archeopress.

Lorkiewicz, W. (2011). Unusual burial from an early Neolithic site of the Lengyel culture in central Poland: Punishment, violence, or mortuary behavior? *International Journal of Osteoarchaeology, 21,* 428–434.

Loud G. (1939). *Megiddo II: Seasons of 1935–39. The University of Chicago Oriental Institute Publications, Volume LXII..* Chicago: University of Chicago Press.

Loud, G. (1948). *Megiddo II: Seasons of 1935–39, Plates. The University of Chicago Oriental Institute Publications, Volume LXII.* Chicago: University of Chicago Press.

Makkay, J. (2000). *An early war: The late Neolithic mass grave from Esztergalyhorvati.* Budapest: published by the author.

Martin, D. L. (1997). Patterns of violence in prehistoric hunter-gatherer societies of coastal southern California. In D. L. Martin, & Frayer, D. W. (Eds.), *Troubled times: Violence and warfare in the past* (pp. 77–109). Langhorne, PA: Gordon and Breach Publishers.

McClure, S. B., Molina Balaguer, L., & Bernabeu Auban, J. (2008). Neolithic rock art in context: Landscape history and the transition to agriculture in Mediterranean Spain. *Journal of Anthropological Archaeology, 27,* 326–337.

McMahon, A., Soltysiak, A., & Weber, J. (2011). Late Chalcolithic mass graves at Tell Brak, Syria, and violent conflict during the growth of early city-states. *Journal of Field Archaeology, 36,* 201–220.

Mellaart, J. (1975) *The Neolithic in the Near East.* New York: Scribners.

Mercer, R. J. (1999). The origins of warfare in the British Isles. In J. Carman & A. Harding (Eds.), *Ancient Warfare* (pp. 143–156). Stroud: Sutton Publishers.

Mercer, R. J. (2007). By other means? The development of warfare in the British Isles 3000–500 BC. In T. Pollard, & I. Banks, *War and sacrifice: Studies in the archaeology of conflict* (pp. 119–151). Leiden: Brill.

Meyer, C., Brandt, G., Haak, W., Ganslmeier, R., Meller, H., & Alt, K.W. (2009). The Eulau eulogy: Bioarchaeological interpretation of lethal violence in Corded Ware multiple burials from Saxony-Anhalt, Germany. *Journal of Anthropological Archaeology, 28,* 412–423.

Milner, G. R. (2005). Nineteenth-century arrow wounds and perceptions of prehistoric warfare. *American Antiquity, 70,* 144–156.

Mithen, S. J., Finlayson, B., Smith, S., Jenkins, E., Najjar, M., & Maricevic, D. (2011). An 11600 year-old communal structure from the Neolithic of southern Jordan. *Antiquity, 85,* 350–364.

Molleson, T. (1994). The eloquent bones of Abu Hureyra. *Scientific American,* August, 70–75. Moore, A. M. T., Hillman, G. C., & Legge, (Eds.). (2000). *Village on the Euphrates.* Oxford: Oxford University Press.

Moore, A. M. T., Hillman, G. C., & Legge, A. J. (2000). *Village on the Euphrates.* Oxford: Oxford University Press.

Munchaev, R. M. (1993). Some problems in the archaeology of Mesopotamia in light of recent research. In N. Yoffee, & J. J. Clark (Eds.), *Early stages in the evolution of Mesopotamian civilization: Soviet excavations in northern Iraq* (pp. 249–256). Tucson: University of Arizona Press.

Nash, G. (2003). Settlement, population dynamics and territoriality during the late south Scandinavian Mesolithic. In L. Bevan, & J. Moore (Eds.), *Peopling the Mesolithic in a northern environment, BAR International Series, 1157,* 159–170.

Nash, G. (2005). Assessing rank and warfare-strategy in prehistoric hunter-gatherer society: A study of representational warrior figures in rock-art from the Spanish Levant, southeastern Spain. In M. P. Pearson, & I. J. N. Thorpe (Eds.), *Warfare, violence and slavery in prehistory: Proceedings of a Prehistoric Society conference at Sheffield University, BAR International Series, 1374,* 75–87. Oxford: Archaeopress.

Nerlich, A. G., Peschel, O., & Egarter-Vigl, E. (2009) New evidence for Otzi's final trauma. *Intensive Care Medicine, 35,* 1138–1139.

Newell, R. R., Constandse-Westermann, T. S., & Meiklejohn, C. (1979). The skeletal remains of Mesolithic man in Western Europe: An exhaustive catalogue. *Journal of Human Evolution, 8,* 1–228.

Novak, S. A. (2006). Beneath the facade: A skeletal model of domestic violence. In R. Gowland, & C. Knusel (Eds.), *Social archaeology of funerary remains* (pp. 238–252). Oxford: Oxbow Books.

Oates, D. (1982). Tell Brak. In J. Curtis (Ed.), *Fifty years of Mesopotamian discovery: The work of the British School of Archaeology in Iraq, 1932–1982* (pp. 62–71). London: The British School of Archaeology in Iraq.

Oates, J., McMahan, A., Karsgaard, P., al-Quntar, S., & Ur, J. (2007). Early Mesopotamian urbanism: A view from the north. *Antiquity, 81,* 585–600.

Oosterbeek, L. (1997). War in the Chalcolithic? The meaning of the west Mediterranean hillforts. In J. Carman (Ed.), *Material harm: Archaeological studies of war and violence* (pp. 116–132). Glasgow: Cruithne Press.

Orschiedt, J. (2005). The head burials from Ofnet cave: An example of warlike conflict in the Mesolithic. In M. P. Pearson, & I. J. N. Thorpe (Eds.), *Warfare, violence and slavery in prehistory: Proceedings of a Prehistoric Society conference at Sheffield University, BAR International Series, 1374,* 67–73). Oxford: Archaeopress.

Orschiedt, J., & M. N. Haidle (2007). The LBK enclosure at Herxheim: Theatre of war or ritual center? References from osteoarchaeological investigations. In T. Pollard, & I. Banks (Eds.), *Warfare and sacrifice: Studies in the archaeology of conflict* (pp. 153–167). Leiden: Brill.

Orschiedt, J., Hauber, A., Haidle, M. N., Alt, K. W., & Buitrago-Tellez, C. H. (2003). Survival of a multiple skull trauma: The case of an early Neolithic individual from the LBK enclosure at Herxheim (Southwest Germany). *International Journal of Osteoarchaeology, 13,* 375–383.

Osgood, R., Monks, S. with Toms, J. (2000). *Bronze Age warfare.* Gloucestershire: Sutton Publishing.

O'Shea, J. (1984). Oleneostrovski mogilnik: Reconstructing the social and economic organization of prehistoric foragers in northern Russia. *Journal of Anthropological Archaeology, 3,* 1–40.

Otterbein, K. F. (2010). Early warfare in the Near East. *Neo-Lithics, 1/10,* 56–58.

Otterbein, K. F. (2011). The earliest evidence for warfare? A comment on Carbonell et al. *Current Anthropology, 52,* 439.

Ozdogan, M. (2011). Archaeological evidence on the westward expansion of farming communities from eastern Anatolia to the Aegean and the Balkans. *Current Anthropology, 52* supplement 4, 415–430.

Papathanasiou, A. (2005). Health status of the Neolithic population of Alepotrypa Cave, Greece. *American Journal of Physical Anthropology, 126,* 377–390.

Parkinson, W., & Duff, P. R. (2007). Fortifications and enclosures in European prehistory: A cross-cultural perspective. *Journal of Archaeological Research, 15,* 97–141.

Pavuk, J. (1991). Lengyel-culture fortified settlements in Slovakia. *Antiquity, 65,* 348–357.

Paz, Y. (2002). Fortified settlements of the EB IB and the emergence of the first urban system. *Tell Aviv, 29,* 238–261.

Pearce-Duvet, J. M. C. (2006). The origin of human pathogens: Evaluating the role of agriculture and domestic animals in the evolution of human disease. *Biological Reviews, 81,* 369–382.

Pearson, M. P. (2005). Warfare, violence and slavery in later prehistory: An introduction. In M. P. Pearson, & I. J. N. Thorpe (Eds.), *Warfare, violence and slavery in prehistory: Proceedings of a Prehistoric Society conference at Sheffield University, BAR International Series, 1374,* 19–33. Oxford: Archaeopress.

Perez, P-J. Gracia, A., Martinez, I., & Arsuaga, J. L. (1997). Paleopathological evidence of the cranial remains from the Sima de los Hueso Middle Pleistocene site (Sierra de Atapuerca, Spain). Description and preliminary inferences. *Journal of Human Evolution, 33,* 409–421.

Philip, G. (2003). The Early Bronze Age of the Southern Levant: A landscape approach. *Journal of Mediterranean Archaeology, 16,* 103–132.

Price, T. D. (1985). Affluent foragers of Mesolithic southern Scandinavia. In T. D. Price, & J. A. Brown (Eds.), *Prehistoric hunter-gatherers: The emergence of cultural complexity* (pp. 341–363). Orlando: Academic Press.

Price, T. D., & Brown, J. A. (1985). Aspects of hunter-gatherer complexity. T. D. Price, & J. A. Brown (Eds.), *Prehistoric hunter-gatherers: The emergence of cultural complexity* (pp. 3–20). Orlando: Academic Press.

Price, T. D., Wahl, J., & Bentley, R. A. (2006). Isotopic evidence for mobility and group organization among Neolithic farmers at Talheim, Germany, 5000 BC. *European Journal of Archaeology, 9,* 259–284.

Pryor, F. (1976). A Neolithic multiple burial from Fengate, Peterborough. *Antiquity, 50,* 232–233.

Radovanovic, I. (1996). *The Iron Gates Mesolithic.* Ann Arbor: International Monographs in Prehistory.

Randsborg, K. (1995). *Hjortspring: Warfare and sacrifice in early Europe. Aarhus: Aarhus University Press.*

Randsborg, K. (1999). Into the Iron Age: A discourse on war and society. In J. Carman, & A. Harding (Eds.), *Ancient Warfare* (pp. 191–202). Stroud: Sutton Publishers.

Richards, M. P., Price, T. D., & Koch, E. K. (2003). Mesolithic and Neolithic subsistence in Denmark: New stable isotope data. *Current Anthropology, 44,* 288–295.

Robb, J. (1997). Violence and gender in early Italy. In D. L. Martin, & D. W. Frayer, (Eds.) *Troubled times: Violence and warfare in the past* (pp. 111–144). Langhorne, PA: Gordon and Breach.

Robb, J. (2007). *The early Mediterranean village: Agency, material culture, and social change in Neolithic Italy.* New York: Cambridge University Press.

Roksandic, M. (2004a). Introduction: How violent was the Mesolithic, or is there a common pattern specific to sedentary hunter-gatherers? In M. Roksandic (Ed.), *Violent interactions in the Mesolithic: Evidence and meaning, BAR International Series, 1237,* 1–7. Oxford: Archaeopress.

Roksandic, M. (2004b). Contextualizing the evidence of violent death in the Mesolithic: Burials associated with victims of violence in the Iron Gates Gorge. In M. Roksandic (Ed.), *Violent interactions in the Mesolithic: Evidence and meaning, BAR International Series, 1237,* 53–74. Oxford: Archaeopress.

Roksandic, M. (2006). Violence in the Mesolithic. *Documenta Praehistorica, 33,* 165–182.

Roksandic, M., Djuric, M., Rakocevic, Z., & Seguin, K. (2006). Interpersonal violence at Lepenski Vir Mesolithic/ Neolithic complex of the Iron Gates Gorge (Serbia-Romania). *American Journal of Physical Anthropology, 129,* 339–348.

Rollefson, G. (1997). Changes in architecture and social organization at 'Ain Ghazal. In *The prehistory of Jordan, II: Perspectives from 1997, Studies in Early Near Eastern Production, Subsistence, and Environment, 4,* 287–307. Berlin: Ex Oriente.

Rollefson, G. (2010). Violence in Eden: Comments on Bar-Yosef's Neolithic warfare hypothesis. *Neo-Lithics, 1/10,* 62–65.

Rollefson, G., Simmons, A. H., & Kafafi, Z. (1992). Neolithic cultures at 'Ain Ghazal, Jordan. *Journal of Field Archaeology, 19,* 443–470.

Rom, W, Golser, R., Kutschera, W., Priller, A., Steier, P., & Wild, E.M. (1999). AMS 14C dating of equipment from the Iceman and of spruce logs from the prehistoric salt mines of Hallstatt. *Radiocarbon, 41,* 183–197.

Roscoe, P. (2010). War, community, and environment in the Levantine Neolithic. *Neo -Lithics 1/10,* 66–67.

Roper, M. K. (1969). A survey of the evidence for intrahuman killing in the Pleistocene. *Current Anthropology, 10,* 427–459.

Roper, M. K. (1975). Evidence of warfare in the Near East from 10,000-4,300 BC. In Nettleship, M. A., Dalegivens, R., & Nettleship, A. (Eds.), *War, its causes and correlates* (pp. 299–340). The Hague: Mouton Publishers.

Rosenberg, D. (2010) Early maceheads in the Southern Levant: A "Challcolithic" hallmark in Neolithic context. *Journal of Field Archaeology, 35,* 204–216.

Rowan, Y. M., & J. Golden (2009). The Chalcolithic period of the southern Levant: A synthetic review. *Journal of World History, 22,* 1–92.

Rowley-Conway, P. (2011). Westward ho! The spread of agriculturalism from central Europe to the Atlantic. *Current Anthropology, 52 supplement 4,* 431–451.

Runnels, C. N., Payne, C., Rifkind, N. V., White, C., Wolff, P., & LeBlanc, S. A. (2009). Warfare in Neolithic Thessaly: A Case Study. *Hesperia, 78,* 167–194.

Sahoglu, V. (2005). The Anatolian trade network and the Izmir region during the Early Bronze Age. *Oxford Journal of Archaeology, 24,* 339–361.

Sassaman, K. E. (2004). Complex hunter-gatherers in evolution and history: A North American perspective. *Journal of Archaeological Research, 12,* 227–280.

Schmidt, K. (2010). Gobekli Tepe—The stone age sanctuaries. New results of ongoing excavations with a special focus on sculptures and high reliefs. *Documenta Praehistorica, 37,* 239–256.

Schulting, R. (2006). Skeletal evidence and contexts of violence in the European Mesolithic and Neolithic. In R. Gowland and C. Knusel, *Social archaeology of funerary remains* (pp. 224–237). Oxford: Oxbow Books.

Schulting, R., & Fibiger, L. (Eds.). (2012). *Sticks, stones, and broken bones: Neolithic violence in European perspectives.* Oxford: Oxford University Press.

Schulting, R., & Wysocki, M. (2005). "In this chambered tumulus were found cleft skulls...": An assessment of the evidence for cranial trauma in the British Neolithic. *Proceedings of the Prehistoric Society, 71,* 107–138.

Schultz, M., Berner, M., & Schmidt-Schultz, T. H. (2004). Preliminary results on morbidity and mortality in the late PPNB population from Basta, Jordan. In H. D. Bienert, H. G. K. Gebel, & R. Neef (Eds.), *Central settlements in Neolithic Jordan: Proceedings of a symposium held in Wadi Musa, Jordan, 21st-25th of July 1997* (pp. 259–269). Berline: Ex Oriente.

Shea, J. J. (2003). The Middle Paleolithic of the east Mediterranean Levant. *Journal of World History, 17,* 313–394.

Shea, J. J., & Sisk, M. L. (2010). Complex projectile technology and Homo sapiens dispersal into Western Eurasia. *Paleoanthropology,* 2010, 100–122.

Simmons, A. H., & Najjar, M. (2006). Ghwair I: A small, complex Neolithic community in Southern Levant. *Journal of Field Archaeology, 31,* 77–95.

Silva, A. M., & Marques, R. (2010). An arrowhead injury in a Neolithic human axis from the natural cave of Lapa do Bugio (Seimbra, Portugal). *Anthropological Science, 118,* 185–189.

Skeates, R. (2000). The social dynamics of enclosure in the Neolithic of the Tavoliere, south-east Italy. *Journal of Mediterranean Archaeology, 13,* 155–188.

Smith, M. J., Brickley, M. B., & Leach, S. L. (2007). Experimental evidence for lithic projectile injuries: Improving identification of an under-recognized phenomenon. *Journal of Archaeological Science, 34,* 540–553.

Smits, L., &. van der Plicht, H. (2009). Mesolithic and Neolithic human remains in the Netherlands: Physical anthropological and stable isotope investigations. *Journal of Archaeology in the Low Countries, 1,* 55–85.

Sponsel, L. E., & Gregor, T. (Eds.) (1994). *The anthropology of peace and non-violence.* Boulder, CO: Lynne Rienner Publishers.

Stanko, V. (1997). Landscape dynamics and Mesolithic settlement in the north Pontic steppe. In J. Chapman, & P. Dolukhanov (Eds.), *Landscapes in flux: Central and Eastern Europe in Antiquity* (pp. 253–262). Oxford: Oxbow Books.

Svoboda, J., Lozek, V ., & Vlcek, E. (1996). *Hunters between east and west: The Paleolithic of Moravia.* New York: Plenum.

Tadmor, M. (2002). The Kfar Monash hoard again: A view from Egypt and Nubia. In E. C. M. van den Brink, & T. E. Levy (Eds.), Egypt and the Levant: Interrelations from the 4th through the early 3rd millennium BC (pp. 239–251). London: Leicester University Press.

Teschler-Nicola, M., Gerold, F., Bujatti-Narbeshuber, M., Porhaska, T., Latkoczy, C., Stingeder, G., & Watkins, M. (1999). Evidence of genocide in 7000 BP--Neolithic paradigm and geo-climatic reality. *Collegium Anthropologicum, 23,* 437–450.

Thissen, L. (2010). The Neolithic-Chalcolithic sequence in the SW Anatolian lakes region. *Documenta Praehistorica, 37,* 269–284.

Thomas, J. (2007). Mesolithic-Neolithic transitions in Britain: From essence to inhabitation. *Proceedings of the British Academy, 144,* 423–439.

Thorpe, I. J. N. (2003a). Anthropology, archaeology, and the origin of warfare. *World Archaeology, 35,* 145–165.

Thorpe, I. J. N. (2003b). Death and violence—The later Mesolithic of Southern Scandinavia. In L. Bevan, & J. Moore (Eds.), *Peopling the Mesolithic in a northern environment, BAR International Series, 1157,* 171–180.

Thorpe, I. J. N. (2005). The ancient origins of warfare and violence. In M. P. Pearson, & I. J. N. Thorpe (Eds.), *Warfare, violence and slavery in prehistory: Proceedings of a Prehistoric Society conference at Sheffield University, BAR International Series, 1374,* 1–18. Oxford: Archaeopress.

Trigger, B. G, Kemp, B. J., O'Connor, D., & Lloyd, A. B. (1983). *Ancient Egypt: A social history.* New York: Cambridge University Press.

Trinkaus, E. (1985). Cannibalism and burial at Krapina. *Journal of Human Evolution, 14,* 203–216.

Trinkaus, E., & Zimmerman, M. R. (1982). Trauma among the Shanidar Neandertals. *American Journal of Physical Anthropology, 57,* 61–72.

Turton, D. (1979). War, peace and Mursi identity. In F. Katsuyoshi, & D. Turton (Eds.), *Warfare among East African herders, Senri Ethnological Studies no. 3,* 179–210. Osaka: National Museum of Ethnology.

Ubelaker, D. H., Pap, I., & Graver, S. (2006). Morbidity and mortality in the Neolithic of northeastern Hungary. *Anthropologie, 44,* 241–257.

University of Chicago. (2005). University of Chicago-Syrian team finds first evidence of warfare in ancient Mesopotamia. Retrieved from http://www-news.uchicago.edu/releases/05/051216.hamoukar.shtml (Accessed July 7, 2011).

Ur, J. A., Karsgaard, P., & Oates, J. (2001). Early urban development in the Near East. *Science, 317,* 1188.

Ury, W. L., (Ed.). 2002. *Must we fight? From the battlefield to the schoolyard—A new perspective on violent conflict and its prevention*. Cambridge, MA: Program on Negotiation, Harvard Law School.

Vandkilde H. (2006). A review of the early Late Neolithic period in Denmark: Practice, identity and connectivity. Retrieved from www. jungstein.uni-kiel.de/pdf/2005-vankilde.low.de.pdf (accessed April 12, 2012)

Vencl, S. (1983). War and warfare in archaeology. *Journal of Anthropological Archaeology*, 3, 116–132.

Vencl, S. (1991). Interpretation des blessures causees par les armes au Mesolithique. *L'Anthropologie*, 95, 219–228.

Vencl, S. (1999). Stone age warfare. In J. Carman, & A. Harding (Eds.), *Ancient Warfare* (pp. 57–72). Stroud: Sutton Publishers.

Verano, J. W. (2001). The physical evidence of human sacrifice in ancient Peru. In E. P. Benson, & A. G. Cook (Eds.), *Ritual sacrifice in ancient Peru* (pp. 165–184). Austin: University of Texas Press.

Villa, P. (1992). Cannibalism in prehistoric Europe. *Evolutionary Anthropology*, 1, 93–104.

Villa, P., Courtin, J., Helmer, D., Shipman, P., Bouville, C., Mahieu, E., Belluomini, G., & Branca, M. (1986). Un cas de cannibalisme au Neolithique. *Gallia Prehistoire*, 29, 143–171.

Voigt, M. M. (1983). *Hajji Firuz Tepe, Iran: The Neolithic settlement*. Philadelphia: The University Museum.

Walker, P. L. (1997). Wife beating, boxing, and broken noses: Skeletal evidence for the cultural patterning of interpersonal violence. In In D. L. Martin & D. W. Frayer (Eds.), *Troubled times: Violence and warfare in the past* (pp. 145–175). Amsterdam: Gordon & Breach.

Walker, P. L. (2001). A bioarchaeological perspective on the history of violence. *Annual Review of Anthropology*, 30, 573–596.

Watkins, T. (1992). Pushing back the frontiers of Mesopotamian prehistory. *Biblical Archaeologist*, 55, December, 176–181.

Watkins, T., Baird, D., & Betts., A. (1989). Qermez Dere and the early aceramic Neolithic of N. Iraq. *Paleorient*, 15, 19–24.

Watrin, L. (2002). Tributes and the rise of a predatory power: Unraveling the intrigue of EB I Palestinian jars found by E. Amelineau at Abydos. In E. C. M. van den Brink, & T. E. Levy (Eds.), *Egypt and the Levant: Interrelations from the 4th through the early 3rd millennium BC* (pp. 450–463). London: Leicester University Press.

Watson, P. J., & LeBlanc, S. A. (1990). Girikihaciyan: A Halafian site in southeastern Turkey. Los Angeles: University of California, Institute of Archaeology, Monograph 33.

Webb, S. G., & Edwards, P. C. (2002). The Natufian human skeletal remains from Wadi Hammeh 27 (Jordan). *Paleorient*, 28, 103–124.

Weninger, B., Alram-Stern, E., Bauer, E., Clare, L., Danzeglocke, U., Joirs, O. . . . . van Andel, T. (2006). Climate forcing due to the 8200 cal yr BP event observed at Early Neolithic sites in the eastern Mediterranean. *Quarternary Research*, 66, 401–420.

White, T.C. (1992). *Prehistoric cannibalism at Mancos 5MTUMR-2346*. Princeton: Princeton University Press.

White, T. D., & Folkens, P. A. (1999). *Human osteology*, second edition. New York: Academic Press

Whitely, J. (2002). Objects with attitude: Biographical facts and fallacies in the study of Late Bronze Age and Early Iron Age Warrior graves. *Cambridge Archaeological Journal*, 12, 217–232.

Whittle, A. (1985). *Neolithic Europe: A survey*. Cambridge: Cambridge University Press.

Wild, E. M., Stadler, P., Hausser, A., Kutschera, W., Steier, P., Teschler-Nicola, M., Wahl, J., & Windl, H. J. (2004). Neolithic massacres: Local skirmishes or general warfare in Europe? *Radiocarbon*, 46, 377–385.

Wolfe, N. D., Dunavan, C. P., & Diamond, J. (2007). Origin of major human infectious diseases. *Nature*, 447, 279–283.

Yellin, J., Levy, T. E., & Rowan, Y. M. (1996). New evidence on prehistoric trade routes: The obsidian evidence from Gilat, Israel. *Journal of Field Archaeology*, 23, 361–368.

Zollikofer, C. P. E., Ponce de Leon, M. S., Vandermeersch, B., & Leveque, F. (2002). Evidence for interpersonal violence in the St. Cesaire Neanderthal. *Proceedings of the National Academy of Science*, 99, 6444–6448.

PART THREE

Nomadic Foragers

INSIGHTS ABOUT HUMAN NATURE

12

Peaceful Foragers

The Significance of the Batek and Moriori for the Question of Innate Human Violence

KIRK ENDICOTT

Introduction

The question of whether humans—or at least human males—are innately inclined toward violence will never be resolved by studying the behavior of chimpanzees. Humans and chimpanzees have evolved independently for six to eight million years (Sussman & Hart, 2010, p. 63; Marlowe, 2010, p. 1), and there is no reason to believe that their behavioral tendencies have not diverged as much as their physical characteristics during that vast period of time (Barnard, 2011, pp. 18–28). This was dramatically confirmed by the attempt of American researchers to raise a chimpanzee, Nim, as if he were human, which revealed insurmountable differences between the innate behavioral patterns of chimps and humans (Hess, 2008). The place to look for human behavioral propensities is obviously in the human species itself (Fry, 2006, p. 165). If the behaviors that we gloss as "violence" and "aggression" are inherited tendencies rather than learned by individuals, then they must have been favored by natural selection, and, except for the last 10,000 years or so, that selection took place mostly in the context of small, nomadic groups living by hunting and gathering.

One of the most valuable methods for reconstructing the social setting in which human evolution took place is the "ethnographic analogy," which involves generating hypotheses about the cultures and behaviors of prehistoric peoples by comparisons with still-existing peoples living in similar environments and using similar technologies (Marlowe, 2010; Fry, 2011; Barnard, 2011; but see Wylie, 1985 on the limitations of the ethnographic analogy in archaeology). Not all historically documented hunting and gathering societies provide good models for early human and protohuman societies, however. For example, the well-known mounted buffalo hunting peoples of the North American

Great Plains followed a way of life that came into existence only a few hundred years ago, after the Native Americans gained access to horses from Spanish colonists in the American Southwest. Also, "complex" hunting and gathering societies, such as those of the Pacific Northwest, which had sedentary villages and social hierarchy, could probably have existed in only a few highly productive environments in prehistoric times (Marlowe, 2010, pp. 256–262; Fry, 2011). The best models for ancient human and protohuman societies, then, would be hunting and gathering peoples living in Africa and in similar environments in other parts of the world (Marlowe, 2010). Most of those societies live (or lived) in small, egalitarian, nomadic groups.

The majority of small-scale nomadic hunting and gathering societies that have been documented by anthropologists engage in little or no fighting between groups (Fry, 2011). What little violence takes place among adults results from personal conflicts that do not escalate into feuds or wars between groups. These societies generally try to suppress violence within and between neighboring groups because cooperation (for example, sharing food), more than competition, promotes the survival of groups and individuals (Howell & Willis, 1989, pp. 19–22; Carrithers, 1989; Marlowe, 2010, pp. 225–254). The general peacefulness of nomadic hunter-gatherers may be due merely to the absence of the conditions that, in other types of societies, lead to collective violence. For example, Kelly argues that nonviolent forager societies are those that are "unsegmented," that is, without rigidly bounded corporate groups above the level of the family and local community that could become the units of group conflict (2000, pp. 44–45, 73). Similarly, Otterbein contends that peoples who engage in violent conflict between bands are those in which bands contain "fraternal interest groups," "localized groups of related males who can resort to aggressive measures when the interests of their members are threatened" (Otterbien, 2004, pp. 5; also 46, 80, and *passim*). A few nomadic foraging societies, such as the Paliyan of India (Gardner, 2000, 2004, 2010), deliberately and consciously suppress violence of any kind, thus creating and maintaining an ethos of peacefulness.

In this paper I examine two hunting and gathering societies, the Batek of Malaysia and the Moriori of the Chatham Islands, which actively suppress all violence inside and between groups. I attempt to determine the specific conditions that cause their deliberate pursuit of peace and the means by which they achieve it. I end by addressing the question of whether Batek and Moriori practices and beliefs shed any light on social relations in early human and protohuman societies.

The Batek

The People

The Batek are one of the twenty or so cultural-linguistic groups making up the Orang Asli (Malay for "Original People") of Peninsular Malaysia. They are classified as members of the Semang or Negrito category of Orang Asli, and they speak a language in the Northern

Aslian stock of the Mon-Khmer language family. Numbering about 700–800 persons, they live in the lowland tropical rainforest in a contiguous area at the intersection of the states of Kelantan, Pahang, and Terengganu. This chapter focuses on those Batek who were living in the upper Lebir River watershed, Kelantan, in the 1970s, when they had only occasional contact with outsiders, mainly Malay traders of forest products.

The economy of the Lebir Batek in the 1970s was based on hunting and gathering; collecting and trading forest products, such as rattan and fragrant wood; and occasional stints of swidden horticulture at the behest of the Department of Orang Asli Affairs (JHEOA). The staple carbohydrates in their diet included wild yams, seasonal fruits, rice and flour obtained by trade, and wild vegetables such as mushrooms and palm hearts. Their main sources of meat were monkeys, gibbons, and birds, which they killed by means of bamboo blowpipes and poisoned darts, and fish obtained by nets and hook and line (Endicott, 1984).

The Lebir people lived in temporary camps, with each conjugal family housed in lean-to shelters covered with palm leaf thatch. The 90 or so people living on the upper Lebir usually formed between two and four camps, and there was constant movement of individuals and families between camps. Camps often contained parts of extended families, but there were no rigid kinship criteria for membership. Residence in a camp was based purely on the wishes of individuals and families. Camps usually lasted from one to two weeks, until the food and other resources in the immediate vicinity became depleted, after which the occupants moved to another location or split up and joined other existing camps. Although camps were voluntary associations, residents were expected to share any excess food obtained and to cooperate and help other camp members if needed (Endicott, 2011).

No Batek person had political power over anyone else. Although they had nominal headmen (Malay *penghulu*), who were appointed by the Department of Orang Asli Affairs, the headmen had no authority within Batek society. Natural leaders, usually respected older people of either sex, had some influence, but they could not impose their wishes on others. Most decisions about what work to do, where to move, and so on were made by individuals or married couples, often after consultation with other camp residents. Batek highly valued their personal autonomy (Endicott, 2011).

Batek religion was based on a belief in a number of specialized superhuman beings that inhabited the forest, firmament, and underworld. They were thought to be responsible for many natural phenomena, both beneficial and detrimental to the Batek. The most important superhuman being was Gobar, the thunder god, who was involved in sending honey bees and the blossoms of wild fruit trees to earth, but who also caused thunderstorms to punish people who broke certain prohibitions (called *lawac*), ranging from laughing at butterflies to violence. A female underground deity, Ya' ("Grandmother"), assisted Gobar by causing floods to well up beneath the offender's camp. The creator god, Tohan, also punished disrespectful acts (*tolah*) by causing offenders to incur diseases or accidents. Batek communicated with the superhuman beings through dreams and self-induced trances in night-long singing sessions in which they asked for such things as abundant supplies of wild fruits or help in curing diseases (Endicott 1979).

Batek Attitudes Toward Violence

Batek considered all violence, aggression, and coercion of any kind, both toward group members and toward outsiders, absolutely unacceptable (Endicott & Endicott, 2008, p. 50; Endicott, 2011, p. 74). Like the Semai and most other Orang Asli, they saw themselves as peaceful, and they regarded violence and threats of violence as something only outsiders (*gob*) or unsocialized children would do. Even Batek hunting—shooting small, arboreal game with poisoned darts—is not very violent compared to other methods of killing game, and they do not consider it a form of violence (see Howell, 1989, p. 51 for the similar Chewong attitude toward hunting). One Batek man told me that the ancestors had forbidden Batek to engage in war. Even hitting someone was seen as a serious breach of Batek moral obligations—the Batek term *sakel* means both to hit and to kill—and also a threat to cosmic order. Batek considered violent acts to be both *lawac*, punished by the thunder god and the underworld deity, and *tolah*, punished by the creator god Tohan. Although the disease sent by Tohan would afflict only the offender, the violent thunderstorms and upwelling floods sent by Gobar and Ya' could destroy entire camps and kill all their inhabitants. Batek regarded violent behavior as a sign of madness. I was told that if a person were violent during life, the superhuman beings would refuse to take the offender's shadow soul to the afterworld after death. The shadow soul was doomed to roam the forest as a malevolent ghost.

Suppression of Violence

Batek taught their children to be nonviolent from an early age (K. L. Endicott, 1986, pp. 11–12; Endicott & Endicott, 2008, pp. 122–123). Babies and young children sometimes hit each other, fought over things, and threatened to hurt each other. People regarded this as normal but something that they would grow out of. Usually, when children behaved aggressively, parents and other adults would calmly separate them, try to divert their attention, or laugh at them, making light of whatever seemed so important to the child. Very occasionally we saw a frustrated parent hit or roughly treat a child who was behaving aggressively, to "show them how it felt," but physical punishment was not a standard component of Batek childrearing. By age four or so, Batek children had learned that fighting was not something Batek do. Significantly, they never saw aggression among adults, which could have served as a model for their own behavior. In 2008, writer and human rights advocate Edith Mirante visited some Batek living on a side-stream of the Tembeling River in Pahang. At one point she noticed some little girls acting out Thai boxing moves they had seen on a DVD. Her English-speaking Batek guide, Kumbang, "then gave a speech to the teenaged boys [and, presumably, the girls] about how violence was not the Batek way and even if they saw foreigners fighting in movies, it was not right for them to do that in real life" (Mirante, 2012).

Disputes between Batek adults were infrequent, but occasionally arose over such matters as adultery, broken promises, insults, envy, and hoarding food instead of sharing. People used several nonviolent ways of resolving or managing such conflicts. One method was for the disputants to air their grievances publically in camp, a process reminiscent of Ju/'hoansi "talks" or "shouts" (Marshall, 1976, pp. 290, 293). This enabled the disputants to vent their anger or frustration and to put their case before the court of public opinion. Although Batek leaders did not have the authority to impose settlements on the antagonists, they and other camp members might offer possible solutions. If the consensus of opinion clearly favored one party, the offender might accept that opinion and try to make amends. Because violent acts of individuals were thought to endanger whole groups, camp members brought strong social pressure to bear on the antagonists to settle their dispute peacefully.

If public discussion did not resolve the dispute, one or more of the antagonists might move to another camp, which is the usual safety valve for nomadic foraging peoples. Apparently some people who did not like each other avoided camping together in the first place. One case of adultery illustrates the informal processes by which conflicts were resolved peacefully. A young woman was discovered to have had sex with a man other than her husband. When the word got out, she and her paramour moved to her father's camp, while her husband stayed in their original camp. After about a week, she returned to the shelter she shared with her husband. She was very quiet and unobtrusive at first, until the anger of her husband and his relatives died away. We heard later that the wife's lover had apologized to the woman's husband, but he continued to live in another camp.

In the management of disputes, reestablishing peace was the paramount goal. Except for religious prohibitions, the Batek did not have abstract ideas of justice that had to be enforced by means of punishments, nor did they think of offenses as requiring revenge or retribution (see Bonta, 1996, pp. 404, 409, 415). People were expected to keep their anger under control and to avoid disrupting the harmony of the group. To the hypothetical question of how people would deal with a persistently violent person, I was told that they would abandon that person, fleeing if necessary. The threat of ostracism is a powerful sanction, since in such a society one's long-term survival depends on cooperation with others (Bonta, 1996).

Batek methods of suppressing violence were highly effective. We heard of only a few instances of adults committing acts of violence. While we were there but living in a different camp, we heard that a mother had hit her toddler with a stick and knocked him unconscious. Apparently she was taking out her anger against her husband on the child. Other camp members took care of the injured child and bawled out the mother. We were told that she had done something similar before, actually killing two of her young children. People attributed her actions to bouts of insanity. We were also told of an incident a few years earlier in which two young men fought over one man's wife. An older man tried to break up the fight, warning them of the cosmic consequences, but most of the camp residents fled to high ground, fearing that the earth deity would punish them by sending an upwelling flood to engulf the camp. In 1990, I heard that a Batek man living in Terengganu had beaten his wife. She had left him and moved to a camp on the upper Aring River, where she was living happily as a single mother.

Effects of the Suppression of Violence

The Batek prohibition on violence ensured that social life in camps was generally harmonious. No one had to fear being hurt by anyone else. This prohibition enhanced the personal autonomy of all Batek—one of their basic values—because it meant that no one could coerce another to do anything against their wishes. Even children had great freedom and independence. The prohibition on violence also contributed to the equality of the sexes by preventing men from using force against weaker women.

Reasons for Batek Nonviolence

Probably the original reason the Batek prohibited fighting with outsiders was the fear that they would be killed or enslaved. Like other Orang Asli, they were victims of slave raiding by Malays during the nineteenth and early twentieth centuries (Endicott, 1983; Dentan, 2008). Groups of well-armed slave raiders would usually attack Orang Asli camps or settlements while the inhabitants were sleeping. They would kill all the adults and carry off the children to be sold or raised as household servants. Although historical records of the Batek are rare, there is some evidence that some nineteenth-century Batek tried to defend themselves from slave raiders by force, while others entered into relationships with Malay villagers, who offered them some protection in exchange for forest products and help in harvesting crops. When the Russian explorer and ethnographer N. von Mikluho-Maclay traveled through the Batek area in 1875, he found that the local Malays distinguished between "wild" Batek (*Orang Sakai-liar*), who lived deep in the forest and avoided all contact with Malays, and "tame" Batek (*Orang Sakai-jina*), who were nomadic but maintained some contacts with Malay villagers. He writes, "If the *Orang Sakai-jina* are somewhat dependent upon the Malays, the *Orang liar* remain decidedly hostile to them, and never lose an opportunity of taking revenge on these people" for, among other things, trying to "capture their children in order to keep or sell them as slaves" (Mikluho-Maclay 1878, p. 213; Endicott, 1997, pp. 40–42). It is conceivable that some so-called wild Batek attempted to protect themselves by ambushing slave raiders and other intruders using blowpipes and poisoned darts or bows and poisoned arrows (which they no longer make and use). In 1990, a Batek man told me a story, which may or may not be true, of how a Batek man once shot and killed a "wicked" Malay man with a poisoned arrow.

Nevertheless, by the end of the nineteenth century, the most common means of defense against outside aggressors seems to have been hiding in the interior of the forest, where most Malays were reluctant to go, and remaining ready to move at a moment's notice. Batek say that during the slave-raiding period, they confined their trade to a few trusted villagers with whom they had only intermittent contacts. Even after slave raiding ceased in the early twentieth century, the Batek preserved the memory of it in stories they told to their children. They continued to flee from outsiders during World War II, when Japanese soldiers occupied the area immediately to the west of the Batek, and during the Communist insurrection (called the Emergency) that followed from 1948 to 1960 (Endicott, 1997).

Fear of outsiders probably also intensified the tendency for Batek to turn to each other for support, support that would be compromised by internal conflict (see Dentan, 2010, p. 153). As late as the 1970s, the Batek taught their children to fear and distrust outsiders and never to act aggressively toward them. Outsiders, along with tigers and the thunder god, were used as bogeymen to frighten children into obedience. However, Batek fear of outsiders did not seem to be as strong as it apparently was among the Semai, who had been caught in the crossfire between Communist guerrillas and government forces during the Emergency (Dentan, 1968; Robarchek, 1994). In the 1970s Batek living on the Lebir and Aring Rivers in Kelantan had fairly cordial relations with Malays, especially the forest product traders.

The main reason Batek prohibit violence with other Batek seems to be that they recognize the importance of maintaining good relations with the people upon whom they depend for survival. They know that fighting would weaken the social bonds within their camps and among their people as a whole. For the same reason, competition of any kind was virtually absent from Batek life. Like the Semai (Robarchek, 1994), their sense of security depended on the support of their own group. Although Batek tried to be self-reliant, their survival over the long term, through good times and bad, depended upon the cooperation of others, living in groups, sharing food and possessions, and helping each other when needed (see Sussman & Hart, 2010, p. 72).

Batek have also benefited from maintaining peaceful relations with other Orang Asli peoples in the past. For example, during the disruption of the Japanese invasion in the 1940s, some Batek fled up the Nenggiri River and stayed with Temiar villagers. More recently there has been intermarriage between Batek of the Lebir and Tembeling Rivers and the Semaq Beri people, who live to the south and east. Hunter-gatherers like Batek and swiddeners like Semai and Temiar occupy complementary ecological niches or ways of exploiting the rainforest environment (Benjamin, 1985, 1987). Mutually beneficial trade of forest products (e.g., rattan, bamboo, resin) for agricultural products has probably gone on for a long time (Dunn, 1975).

Another reason for the lack of violence among the Batek was that some of the causes of conflict in other tribal groups were absent. For example, there was no competition for scarce resources. The wild foods that they consumed and the forest products (e.g., rattan) that they traded for foods such as rice were widely scattered and readily available to all. There were no crucial, scarce resources that could have been monopolized by force and claims of exclusive ownership. There were also no enduring and sharply bounded corporate groups that could compete for resources and no sense of group culpability for individual conflicts, which could lead to feuding or even war. There were no ambitious leaders seeking to aggrandize themselves by extending their authority over others. And finally, there were no beliefs in witchcraft or sorcery that would have to be suppressed or punished by violence.

The Moriori

The People

The Moriori were the original inhabitants of the Chatham Islands, a small cluster of islands located 533 miles east of the South Island of New Zealand. The Moriori were an offshoot of the ancestral Maori who probably migrated to the Chatham Islands from the east coast of New Zealand's South Island (Sutton, 1980, p. 87, 1982, p. 83). The Moriori language can be considered a dialect of Maori or a separate but closely related language (Sutton, 1980, pp. 70–74; Clark, 1994), and the earliest artifacts found on Chatham and Pitt Islands show strong affinities with the Archaic material culture of New Zealand. The early immigrants to the South Island lived mainly by mobile hunting and gathering because most parts of the South Island were too cool to grow the tropical crops brought by their ancestors. Their prey included seals and moas, huge flightless birds that were soon hunted to extinction (Bellwood, 1978, pp. 135–143). There is some disagreement among scholars about the dates of the Moriori migration to the Chathams, but it probably took place between 1400 and 1600 AD, during the early period of exploration and settlement in the South Island (Irwin & Walrond, 2009, p. 4; McFadgen, 1994, pp. 35–37; Belich, 1996, p. 65; Sutton, 1980, pp. 78, 87). Probably only a few voyaging canoes reached the Chathams. The settlers were later prevented from returning to New Zealand by the absence on the Chathams of trees suitable for the construction of voyaging canoes (Welch & Davis, 1870–1871, p. xcix, ciii; Skinner, 1919; Sutton, 1980, 1982, p. 83). By the time of European contact in 1791, the only watercraft in use in the Chathams were raft-like constructions of sticks, flower stems, and reeds encasing flotation organs from kelp (Welch & Davis, 1870–1871, p. xcix; Shand, 1894, pp. 85–86; Skinner, 1919; Sutton, 1980, p. 82). Thus, the Classic Moriori culture developed in isolation after 1400 to 1600 AD (Sutton, 1980).

The climate of the Chathams was also too cold for the cultivation of tropical crops (Shand, 1894, p. 80, 1896, p. 14; Skinner, 1923, pp. 15, 53), so the Moriori reverted to a fully foraging economy based on harvesting seals, pelagic birds (e.g., albatrosses), fish, shellfish, terrestrial birds, wild vegetables (e.g., fern roots), and occasionally beached whales (Welch & Davis, 1870–1871, p. xcviii; Shand, 1894, pp. 80–82; Sutton, 1980, p. 80–83, 1982, pp. 78–83; King, 2000, pp. 23–24). Seals were the most important year-round resource in the prehistoric period. However, the seal population declined precipitously between 1809 and 1839 due to European and American sealers killing them off (Shand, 1894, p. 83; Skinner, 1923, pp. 30–31). Apparently food was plentiful before the arrival of Europeans (Welch & Davis, 1870–1871, p. cii), however, as there is no evidence of severe food shortages. The population density was only 5.4 persons per square mile overall

(Sutton, 1982, p. 94), which, in that relatively food-rich environment, seems to have been below the long-term carrying capacity.

The Moriori procured their food on a daily basis, "and their time was well filled up, on the whole, in fishing in all its branches, snaring and killing birds, digging fern-root, cutting firewood, etc." (Shand, 1894, p. 87). Some hunting methods, such as expeditions to albatross colonies on off–shore islets, were cooperative (King, 2000, p. 26). Most foods were eaten immediately, as only a few foodstuffs—including whale blubber, baby albatrosses, and karaka berries (*Corynocarpus laevigata*)—were suitable for storage (Shand, 1894, pp. 80–81). Generally speaking, each family was responsible for gathering its own food (Skinner & Baucke, 1928, pp. 371, 377). However, some foods, such as karaka berries, were shared throughout the residential group (Skinner & Baucke, 1928, pp. 377), and large windfalls, such as beached whales, were shared far beyond the immediate local group (Shand, 1894, p. 89; Skinner, 1923, p. 50; Skinner & Baucke, 1928, pp. 361, 365, 376).

The Moriori population was probably about 2000 at the time of European contact in 1791 (Sutton, 1980, p.68). Only the two largest islands, Chatham and Pitt, were permanently inhabited. The population was divided into seven "tribal areas," which were mostly located around the coast near seal rookeries (Skinner & Baucke, 1928, 377–378; Sutton, 1980, p. 85, 1982, pp. 83–4). The tribes were named cognatic (bilateral) descent groups of people descended from a common ancestor. Cognatic descent groups provide individual members with some choice of whether to reside with kin on the mother's or father's side. Exogamy rules required that people marry outside their extended family or tribe, so some people had relatives in more than one tribe (Skinner, 1923, p. 50–51; Skinner & Baucke, 1928, pp. 369, 377). Within the tribes, people usually lived in extended family groups of 30 to 50 persons (Sutton, 1982, p. 84). Before European contact residence was semi-sedentary: small groups had villages near seal rookeries and also seasonal camps, many evidenced by large middens of shells and bones (Shand, 1894, p. 79; Sutton, 1982, pp. 80, 87). According to Skinner, "[T]he Moriori social group was . . . largely migratory, building rough houses for winter occupation but deserting them during the greater part of the year, moving from beach to lagoon, from lagoon to uplands, and from uplands to coast again, as the food supply fluctuated season by season" (1923, p. 15). Their most substantial houses were A-frame roofs without walls, thatched with leaves and rushes (Skinner, 1923, 74–77). Tribes had exclusive rights to the food and resources in their area (Shand, 1894, pp. 88–89; Skinner, 1923, p. 50), but within the tribal area ownership of resources was communal, except for a few family-owned resources (Skinner, 1923, p. 53). Residence groups were largely self-sufficient in food and raw materials (Sutton, 1980, p. 85, 1982, p. 82).

Like the Maori, the Moriori maintained a social distinction between chiefs and commoners into the historical period, but among Moriori there was no class of slaves (Shand, 1894, p. 88; Skinner, 1923, p. 51). "In each tribe there was a chief who was the eldest born of the principal family" (Shand, 1894, 87). However, unlike the Maori, Moriori society became more egalitarian over time, as evidenced by the changing nature of grave goods and other status markers (Sutton, 1980, p. 83–84, 1982, p. 83; King, 2000, pp. 25–26). Also, political leadership weakened as time went on. Apparently, people with chiefly status were respected, but not obeyed. According to Baucke, subclans were "subject to the founders' authority; they owed him allegiance and respect, yet were independent of control" (Skinner & Baucke, 1928, p. 377). Welch and Davis went so far as to say that "[t]he Moriori do not appear to have any hereditary chiefs or leaders . . ., it appears that their usual method was to elect such as was considered most useful. Thus anyone who was distinguished for stature or prowess, or as a successful bird-catcher or fisher, was usually chosen as leader, but did not possess more than ordinary power, being simply looked upon as a leader or judge" (1870–1871, p. c). Within residential groups, "[c]ommunity decisions were made collectively, and elders were senior members of the group whose powers were persuasive rather than arbitrary and hereditary. Leaders worked on subsistence tasks alongside their followers; they were not tattooed; nor did they typically wear distinctive clothing and ornaments" (King, 2000, p. 25).

Moriori religion was based on belief in good and bad spirits and the Polynesian gods of departments of nature (Welch & Davis, 1870–1871, pp. xcix–c; Shand, 1894, pp. 89–92; Skinner, 1923, pp. 55–64). "They believed that all food was given them by a good spirit named Atua, which is the Maori word for God" (Welch & Davis, 1870–1871, p. xcix). Spirits of the newly dead were thought to be responsible for sending whales ashore (Welch & Davis, 1870–1871, pp. xcix–c; Shand, 1894, pp. 88–89). The Moriori performed numerous rituals before and after hunting and gathering various foods, all of which seem to have been dedicated to their spiritual guardians, such as Pou, the god of fish, and Tangaroa, the god of the sea (Skinner, 1923, p. 61; Skinner & Baucke, 1928, pp. 359, 362, 378). If the rites were not performed properly, the deities might withhold the food or even destroy the offenders by means of wind and storms (Skinner & Baucke, 1928, p. 378; Sutton, 1980, p. 84). "[T]here is evidence that supernatural sanctions rather than political power were important in handling wrongdoing and regulating resource exploitation" (Sutton, 1982, p. 84, see also 1980, p. 84).

Moriori Attitudes Toward Violence

At the time of first European contact (1791), Moriori retained some traces of a violent past (Skinner, 1923, pp. 22–30). The Moriori who met the first British sailors to land on Chatham Island seemed bewildered, and they gestured as if to ask whether they had come from the sun. After the sailors made some unsuccessful attempts to trade trinkets for Moriori clothing and equipment, the atmosphere turned hostile. The Moriori rushed at the sailors' cutter, "brandishing their spears and clubs with much vociferation" (King, 2000, p. 42). The sailors were forced to fire their muskets, loaded with small shot, at the attackers in an attempt to fend them off, and, to their regret, one Moriori man was killed (Welch & Davis, 1870–1871, p. civ; King, 2000, p. 42–46). These events were very similar to Captain Cook's first encounters with Maori groups in his exploration of New Zealand in 1769 (Salmond, 1991). Even after the Moriori had established friendly relations with European visitors in the early nineteenth century, they preserved stories of earlier fighting among themselves (Shand, 1894, p. 92; Skinner, 1923, p. 100–101), and they also still remembered numerous war chants (Shand, 1894, p. 92; King, 2000, p. 26).

However, by the time of European contact, "[a]ccording to tradition (and the archaeological record does not contradict it), Moriori had . . . abolished lethal combat between and within kin groups, a feature of their culture that was unusual in Polynesia" (King, 2000, p. 26; see also Welch & Davis, 1870–1871, p. c; Shand, 1894, p. 78, 1896, pp. 29–30; Williams, 1898, 345; Sutton, 1980, pp. 84–85, 1982, p. 84; but cf. Skinner, 1923, p. 42). Supposedly, during the early days of their occupation of the Chatham Islands, some tribes engaged in warfare with each other (Skinner & Baucke, 1928, pp. 376–377). Alarmed at the scale of bloodshed, some of the elders tried to put limits on the fighting, for instance, by prohibiting pursuit of the beaten, but they were unable to stop the fighting altogether. Then, during one fierce battle,

> a chief, Nunuku, related to both contestants, but joining neither side, stood upon the shore to view the fight, and seeing the slaughter and impending Wheteina defeat, his heart welled with pity for the senseless carnage, and like another Telemachus leapt between the ranks and yelled: "Stop! End it! Each side retire!"

> Stricken with stupefaction at this apparition, without striking a further blow, they so retired. "Follow me!" Palsied with a fear of the unknown, they followed. When they reached the shore he cried: "You Rauru, sit there; you, Wheteina, here!" They sat accordingly. "Onlookers, gather all arms and stack them there!" Obediently the arms were stacked. "Build a fire and cast the arms on top!" The fire was built, the spears and claymores of wood were burnt, yet no word was spoken in protest. "Rauru! Wheteina! arise and meet!" They arose and met. "Touch nose to nose!" Nose to nose was touched. "Listen all! From now and forever, never again let there be war as this day has been! From today on forget the taste of human flesh! Are you fish that eat their young?"

> So it was there agreed that because men get angry and during such anger feel the will to strike, that so they may, but only with a rod the thickness of a thumb, and one stretch of the arms in length, and thrash away, but that on an abrasion of the hide, or first sign of blood, all should consider honor satisfied. "And," said the teller, "all obeyed! Why? Because of the Nunuku curse: 'May your bowels rot the day you disobey!'" (Skinner & Baucke, 1928, p. 377; see also Shand, 1894, p. 78; King, 2000, p. 26)

Whether or not this story is historically true, the Moriori seem to have taken it seriously. "Tradition and historical evidence suggests that Nunuku's injunction was largely honored" (King, 2000, p. 26). Anger and hostility continued to arise, but were expressed in nonviolent ways. For example, people sometimes carried out curses and antagonistic rituals against other groups, "in which they went through and recited incantations for the success of their party, just as if in actual warfare" (Shand, 1894, p. 78). This is reminiscent of a Maori practice in which a group would launch a revenge expedition against an enemy, but only go through the rituals, without actually attacking (Vayda, 1960, p. 44).

While violence was declining in the Chatham Islands, Maori violence apparently increased in New Zealand after the ancestors of the Moriori left. During the early settlement period in New Zealand, "[f]ighting seems to have been uncommon and episodic, and the early settlements do not appear to have been fortified" (Salmond, 1991, p. 38; see also Vayda, 1960, p. 12). But, by the time the first Europeans reached New Zealand, in 1642, the Maori attitude toward strangers was anything but friendly. When Dutch explorer Abel Tasman's two ships sailed into a bay on the north coast of the South Island, they were greeted by a flotilla of Maori canoes filled with armed warriors shouting war chants. The next morning two canoes came out and lurked near the ships, their occupants repeating their challenging chants and gestures. Suddenly one canoe rammed the explorers' small cockboat, knocking the quartermaster overboard, and the Maori warriors killed three sailors and mortally wounded another. The Dutch quickly weighed anchor and sailed away. They named the site of their encounter "Murderers Bay" (Salmond, 1991, pp. 75–84). By the time Captain Cook arrived in 1769, warfare between subtribes (*hapu*) was endemic. Most settlements had fortifications (*pa*) to which they could retreat when attacked (Salmond, 1991). The intensification of violent conflict that took place in New Zealand bypassed the Moriori who by then were living in isolation in the Chatham Islands.

Suppression of Violence

We have no direct information about how Moriori raised their children to be nonviolent. Apparently Moriori parents were indulgent and loving and let their children have a lot of freedom (Skinner & Baucke, 1928, p. 371). However, as children learned the skills of adults, they also learned the beliefs and rituals connected with those activities. Presumably they were also taught the prohibition on violence.

The Moriori used several methods to resolve conflicts while limiting violence. As mentioned above, disputants were allowed to fight but only with sticks the thickness of a thumb and an arm span in length; they had to stop fighting as soon as any blood was spilled. This ensured the survival of the disputants (Shand, 1894, pp. 78, 84; King, 2000, p. 26), and it also prevented an interpersonal dispute from escalating into a group conflict—a feud or war. They punished theft by ridicule, giving the thief a derogatory name, rather than by corporal punishment (Skinner & Baucke, 1928, p. 375–376). Incest was punished by banishment, but the offender could move to another tribe (Skinner & Baucke, 1928, p. 376). The cognatic descent system would have ensured that most people would have relatives in different locations whose groups they could join. They punished murder by ostracism (Skinner & Baucke, 1928, p. 376; King, 2000, p. 26). An informant told Baucke why they refused to use capital punishment on a murderer, saying: "'Why slay this for that which cannot be returned—to life?'" (Skinner & Baucke, 1928, p. 366). In the only recorded case of murder, the groups of the victim and the offender agreed that they and all other groups should drive the murderer away from all birding and fishing places and all human company. This caused him to commit suicide by jumping into a blowhole. "This instance may be taken for a standard pattern how the Moriori punished murder. By this indirect method of forcing the culprit to kill himself, Nunuku's edict was obeyed, and justice was satisfied" (Skinner & Baucke, 1928, p. 376). Apparently their methods of suppressing violence were effective, as "there is no record of their ever again breaking the law of Nunuku" after their clash with Lieutenant Broughton's party in 1791 (King, 2000, p. 50).

Reasons for Moriori Nonviolence

At the time of the Maori invasion (see below), some Moriori said that the prohibition on killing was intended "to prevent a small population of related people destroying themselves in a chain of blood feuds" (King, 2000, p. 61). Probably they also realized that feuding undermined valuable cooperation within and between groups, e.g., sharing large windfalls of food. Apparently the decision to abolish violence was made on the basis of experience and rational discussion of its advantages and disadvantages.

Also, some of the usual causes of armed conflict in small-scale societies were absent in the Chathams and in the Moriori culture. For example, food was plentiful, widely dispersed, and freely available. There was no competition over scarce, localized resources that could conceivably have been subject to exclusive ownership claims and defended by force. Also the lack of sharply defined interest groups and strong leaders probably reduced any tendency there might have been to go to war with other groups.

The Fate of the Moriori

When Maori from Taranaki in the North Island of New Zealand heard of the existence of the Chatham Islands and the Moriori from European sealers and Maori seamen in 1835, 900 Maori commandeered a British ship and went there armed with guns, clubs, and axes (Shand, 1892a,1892b, 1892c, 1893; Skinner, 1923, pp. 34–35; King, 2000, pp. 53–66). The invaders claimed all the land and the Moriori people as slaves. When the Maori first arrived, about 1000 Moriori met and decided that they would not fight the Maori but would offer peace, friendship, and sharing of the land and resources instead (King, 2000, pp. 60–66). Some younger men argued that the edict of Nunuku did not apply in these circumstances, but older leaders considered nonviolence to be a moral imperative, necessary for the *mana* (spiritual power and integrity) of the people. Before the offer of peaceful coexistence could be made, however, the Maori attacked, killing and eating about 300 Moriori and enslaving the remainder. The Moriori population plunged rapidly after that, due to disease, Maori brutality, overwork, and despair (Welsh & Davis, 1870–1871, p. cvii; Skinner, 1923, p. 8; Sutton, 1980, p. 87; King, 2000, pp. 63–67). The last full–blooded Moriori person died in 1934 (King, 2000, p. 187).

Similarities Between the Batek and Moriori Cases

The similarities between these two examples of peaceful hunting and gathering societies reveal some of the conditions that can give rise to nonviolent practices and ethics and provide insight into how such systems can be maintained.

Environments

Although the particular resources in the Malaysian rainforest and the Chatham Islands were very different, in both environments critical resources were scattered evenly in space. In the Batek case, there were no local concentrations of critical resources susceptible to claims of exclusive ownership and control by any one group. In the Moriori case, the seal rookeries that the people depended upon were localized, but there were enough of them scattered around the islands to provide for the various tribes and local groups. Both environments provided adequate resources to support the existing populations, so there was no internal competition over scarce resources, which could have led to violent conflict (Otterbein, 1985; Dentan, 2010, p. 152).

Both the Batek and Moriori lived in isolation from other potentially dangerous peoples, protected from outsider attack by natural barriers, a situation in which, according to Otterbein, groups do not need military organizations (2004, p. 82). The Batek deliberately hid in an environment that was hard for outsiders to penetrate. The Moriori, by an accident of history, were isolated on islands distant from all other peoples.

Economies

Both the Batek and Moriori were immediate-return foragers who did not accumulate large surpluses of stored food or other resources. Both peoples lived in small groups that were economically self-sufficient. Individuals in both societies depended upon their residential groups for survival and were thus motivated to maintain harmonious relations with other group members. Batek depended upon the food-sharing network in case their individual foraging efforts fell short, and the general cooperation of camp members helped in numerous ways, including protecting them from dangerous animals, such as tigers and elephants. Moriori also shared food, though not as fully as the Batek, and they benefited from cooperation in various economic endeavors, such as expeditions to catch immature albatrosses. Neither economy produced the surpluses necessary to support nonproductive classes, such as rulers or warriors, which are often implicated in intergroup violence.

Social Systems

Batek and Moriori corporate groups were only weakly developed. Batek did not have descent groups, and camp-groups continually changed in composition. Rights to resources resided in the ethnic group as whole, not particular groups or individuals. Moriori lived in extended family groups, and they were members of cognatic descent groups, termed "tribes" in the literature. These groups were not rigidly bounded, however, because individuals had some choice of which group to live with and which tribe to identify with. Tribes *did* claim joint ownership of resources in bounded areas, but they also shared access to some resources, such as beached whales, with other groups. Thus, the Batek fit Kelly's category of "unsegmented societies," which he associated with nonviolence (Kelly, 2000, pp. 44–67), but the Moriori, arguably, did not. However, both lacked "fraternal interest groups," which Otterbein regards as the main agents of violence and killing within and between foraging bands (Otterbein, 2004). Both played down the idea of group responsibility for individual acts of violence, which is the basis of feuds and wars (Knauft, 1994, p. 51).

Both Batek and Moriori societies were egalitarian. The Batek emphasized individual autonomy in their social relations and respect for everyone, including children. The Moriori retained traces of the typical Polynesian ranking by degrees of hereditary *mana*, but these distinctions weakened over time until they were almost inconsequential. Political leadership was weak among both peoples. Batek "headmen" and natural leaders had no authority; their leadership consisted only of influence. Similarly, Moriori had hereditary "chiefs" and chosen task leaders, but they did not have power over others. Neither society offered the possibility of an ambitious leader fomenting violence for his (or her) own aggrandizement, which seems to have been common among the Classic Maori.

Attitudes Toward Violence

Both the Batek and the Moriori considered interpersonal violence to be a threat to their survival. They saw violence not only as a disruption of the internal harmony and cooperation on which they depended for survival (Howell & Willis, 1989, pp. 19–22; Carrithers, 1989), but also as a violation of the cosmic moral order. Their extreme fear of violence was probably due to their ancestors having experienced horrendous violence in the past, the Moriori from their own former feuding and warfare and the Batek from having been victims of violent slave raiders. They perpetuated this fear and communicated it to their children through their oral traditions.

Methods of Restraining Violence

Both peoples embedded their restraints against violence within their religious worldview (Knauft, 1994, p. 45; Howell & Willis, 1989, p. 25). The Batek believed that their ancestors forbade them to wage war, and the Moriori culture hero Nunuku forbade intergroup fighting and cannibalism. Both also believed that superhuman beings would punish violent acts, thus easing the need for human sanctions. Batek deities were thought to cause violent people to die from illness or devastating storms. Moriori believed that Nunuku's curse would kill offenders by rotting their bowels. The only humanly imposed punishment for violence was separation of murderers from society (ostracism) (see Bonta, 1996, p. 409).

Both peoples devised ways of settling disputes that limited violence. The Batek used camp-wide discussions and separation to defuse potentially violent conflicts. The Moriori used limited stick fighting to settle angry disputes between individuals, making sure that the dispute did not linger on or spread to other people.

Relevance for Human Behavioral Evolution

Both the Batek and Moriori cultures differed from those of our ancient ancestors in various ways, but, in spite of those differences, I think their cases can shed light on the social environment in which prehistoric humans and protohumans evolved. This study suggests that small-scale hunting and gathering groups living in environments with evenly scattered resources, local sufficiency of resources, and natural protective barriers against potentially violent groups would probably have favored suppression of violence within the group and with neighboring groups. Internal violence would only have weakened group cohesion and cooperation, which promote individual and group survival in foraging societies.

There is also evidence from recent hunter-gatherers that foraging societies living in areas where resources fluctuate unpredictably from year to year (e.g., Kalahari Desert, Western Desert of Australia) tend to develop friendly ties with adjacent groups, thus ensuring reciprocal access to others' resources in time of need (see, e.g., Peterson, 1975; Cashdan, 1983; Endicott & Endicott, 1986; Tonkinson, 1991, pp. 53–54). Only groups living off concentrated scarce resources that could be defended in times of shortages would be motivated to attack adjacent groups and to aggressively defend their own resources.

In theory, archaeologists and paleontologists should be able to work out whether specific groups were more likely to have been peaceful or violent by examining the characteristics of their environments—for example, whether critical resources were scattered or concentrated—and physical traces of their behavior, such as settlement patterns. This in turn could help to determine whether human ancestors evolved in predominantly violent or peaceful circumstances, which bears on questions about the nature of human aggression.

In my opinion, selection for violent behavior among our protohuman and human ancestors would not have been strong and similar everywhere. It might have been favored in some circumstances, but not in others, such as those in which the Batek and Moriori lived. This corresponds to the outcome we see in the human species today: some individuals are inclined to be violent, but the majority are not (Carrithers, 1989; Fry, 2006, 2007; Sussman & Hart, 2010). If selection for violent individuals had been strong during human evolution, we would be a "hyperaggressive" species (Seville Statement on Violence, in Silverberg & Gray, 1992, p. 296), like wolves, whereas, in reality most humans are peaceful most of the time. Whether violence is common or not in a given group depends on environmental circumstances and social and cultural arrangements, not the genetic makeup of the population.

Acknowledgements

I presented earlier versions of this chapter at the workshop on "Aggression and Peacemaking in an Evolutionary Context" at the Lorentz Center, Leiden University, Leiden, The Netherlands on October 20, 2010 and at the American Anthropological Association annual meeting in Montreal, Quebec in a session entitled "Challenging the Legacy of Innate Depravity: The New Tidemark of the Nonkilling Paradigm" on November 16, 2011. I thank the participants in those meetings and especially Douglas Fry for valuable suggestions. I am also grateful to my research assistant, Jennifer Koester, for her thorough review of the literature on the Moriori and other peaceful foraging groups, and to Judy Huntsman, Douglas Sutton, and Benjamin Davies for their helpful comments on the draft paper. I thank all my Batek friends for their generous hospitality and assistance during my fieldwork between 1971 and 2004. I also thank the Economic Planning Unit (EPU) of the Prime Minister's Office and the Department of Orang Asli Affairs (JHEOA) for granting me permission to conduct research with the Batek. I gratefully acknowledge financial support for my fieldwork from the U.S. National Institute of Mental Health, the University of Malaya, the Australian National University, the Fulbright-Hays Commission, the American Social Science Research Council, and the Claire Garber Goodman Fund of Dartmouth College.

References

Barnard, A. (2011). *Social anthropology and human origins*. Cambridge: Cambridge University Press.

Belich, J. (1996). *Making peoples: A history of the New Zealanders from Polynesian settlement to the end of the nineteenth century*. Auckland, New Zealand: Allen Lane, Penguin Press.

Bellwood. P. (1978). *The Polynesians: Prehistory of an island people* (Revised ed.). London, England: Thames and Hudson, Ltd.

Benjamin, G. (1985). In the long term: Three themes in Malayan cultural ecology. In K. L. Hutterer, A. T. Rambo, & G. Lovelace (Eds.), *Cultural values and human ecology in Southeast Asia* (pp. 219–278). Ann Arbor: Center for South and Southeast Asian Studies, University of Michigan.

Benjamin, G. (1987). Ethnohistorical perspectives on Kelantan's prehistory. In Nik Hassan Shuhaimi bin Nik Abd Rahman (Ed.), *Kelantan zaman awal: Kajian arkeologi dan sejarah di Malaysia* (pp. 108–153). Kota Bharu, Malaysia: Perbadanan Muzium Negeri Kelantan.

Bonta, B. D. (1996). Conflict Resolution among peaceful societies: The culture of peacefulness. *Journal of Peace Research*, 33(4), 403–420.

Carrithers, M. (1989). Sociality, not aggression, is the key human trait. In S. Howell & R. Willis (Eds.), *Societies at peace: Anthropological perspectives* (pp. 187–209). New York: Routledge.

Cashdan, E. (1983). Territoriality among human foragers: Ecological models and an application to four Bushman groups. *Current Anthropology*, 24(1), 47–66.

Clark, R. (1994). Moriori and Maori: The linguistic evidence. In D. G. Sutton (Ed.), *The origins of the first New Zealanders* (pp. 123–135). Auckland: Auckland University Press.

Dentan, R. K. (1968). *The Semai: A nonviolent people of Malaya*. New York: Holt, Rinehart & Winston.

Dentan, R. K. (2008). *Overwhelming terror: Love, fear, peace, and violence among Semai of Malaysia*. Lanham, MD: Rowman & Littlefield.

Dentan, R. K. (2010). Nonkilling social arrangements. In J. Evans Pim (Ed.), *Nonkilling societies* (pp. 131–182). Honolulu: Center for Global Nonkilling.

Dunn, F. L. (1975). *Rain-forest collectors and traders: A study of resource utilization in modern and ancient Malaya*. Kuala Lumpur, Malaysia: Malaysian Branch of the Royal Asiatic Society.

Endicott, K. L. (1986). Batek socialization and kinship. In *Precirculated papers*. London, UK: Fourth International Conference on Hunting and Gathering Societies, London School of Economics and Political Science.

Endicott, K. M. (1979). *Batek Negrito religion: The world-view and rituals of a hunting and gathering people of Peninsular Malaysia*. Oxford: Clarendon Press.

Endicott, K. M. (1983). The effects of slave raiding on the Aborigines of the Malay Peninsula. In A. Reid & J. Brewster (Eds.), *Slavery, bondage and dependency in Southeast Asia* (pp. 216–245). St. Lucia, Australia: University of Queensland Press.

Endicott, K. M. (1984). The economy of the Batek of Malaysia: Annual and historical perspectives. *Research in Economic Anthropology, 6,* 29–52.

Endicott, K. M. (1997). Batek history, inter-ethnic relations, and subgroup dynamics. In R. Winzeler (Ed.), *Indigenous peoples and the state: Politics, land, and ethnicity in the Malayan Peninsula and Borneo* (pp. 30–50). New Haven, CT: Yale University Southeast Asia Studies.

Endicott, K. M. (2011). Cooperative autonomy: Social solidarity among the Batek of Malaysia. In T. Gibson & K. Sillander (Eds.), *Anarchic solidarity: Autonomy, equality, and fellowship in Southeast Asia* (pp. 62–87). New Haven, CT: Yale University Southeast Asia Studies.

Endicott, K. M. & Endicott, K. L. (1986). The question of hunter-gatherer territoriality: The case of the Batek of Malaysia. In M. Biesele, R. Gordon, & R. Lee (Eds.), *The past and future of !Kung ethnography: Critical reflections and symbolic perspectives: Essays in honour of Lorna Marshall* (pp. 137–162). Hamburg, Germany: Helmut Buske Verlag.

Endicott, K. M. & Endicott, K. L. (2008). *The headman was a woman: The gender egalitarian Batek of Malaysia.* Long Grove, IL: Waveland Press.

Fry, D. P. (2006). *The human potential for peace: An anthropological challenge to assumptions about war and violence.* New York: Oxford University Press.

Fry, D. P. (2007). *Beyond war: The human potential for peace.* New York: Oxford University Press.

Fry, D. P. (2011). Human nature: The nomadic forager model. In R. W. Sussman and C. R. Cloninger (Eds.), *Origins of cooperation and altruism* (pp. 227–247). New York: Springer.

Gardner, P. (2000). Respect and nonviolence among recently sedentary Paliyan foragers. *Journal of the Royal Anthropological Institute, 6* (2), 215–236.

Gardner, P. (2004). Respect for all: The Paliyans of South India. In G. Kemp and D. P. Fry (Eds.), *Keeping the peace: Conflict resolution and peaceful societies around the world* (pp. 53–71). New York: Routledge.

Gardner, P. (2010). How can a society eliminate killing? In J. Evans Pim (Ed.), *Nonkilling societies* (pp. 185–194). Honolulu: Center for Global Nonkilling.

Hess, E. (2008). *Nim Chimpsky: The chimp who would be human.* New York: Bantam Books.

Howell, S. (1989). "To be angry is not to be human, but to be fearful is": Chewong concepts of human nature. In S. Howell & R. Willis (Eds.), *Societies at peace: Anthropological perspectives* (pp. 45–59). New York: Routledge.

Howell, S. & Willis, R. (1989). Introduction. In S. Howell & R. Willis (Eds.), *Societies at peace: Anthropological perspectives* (pp. 1–28). New York: Routledge.

Irwin, G. & Walrond, C. (2009). When was New Zealand first settled?—The date debate. In *Te ara—The encyclopedia of New Zealand.* Retrieved from http://www.TeAra.govt.nz/en/when-was-new-zealand-first-settled/1

Kelly, R. C. (2000). *Warless societies and the origin of war.* Ann Arbor: University of Michigan Press.

King, M. (2000). *Moriori: A people rediscovered* (Revised ed.). Auckland, New Zealand: Penguin Books.

Knauft, B. M. (1994). Culture and cooperation in human evolution. In L. E. Sponsel & T. Gregor (Eds.), *The anthropology of peace and nonviolence* (pp. 37–67). Boulder: Lynne Rienner.

Marlowe, F. W. (2010). *The Hadza: Hunter-gatherers of Tanzania.* Berkeley: University of California Press.

Marshall, L. (1976). *The !Kung of Nyae Nyae.* Cambridge: Harvard University Press.

McFadgen, B. G. (1994). Archaeology and Holocene sand dune stratigraphy on Chatham Island. *Journal of the Royal Society of New Zealand, 24*(1), 17–44.

Mikluho-Maclay, N. von. (1878). Ethnological excursions in the Malay Peninsula—November 1874 to October 1874. (Preliminary communication). *Journal of the Straits Branch of the Royal Asiatic Society, 2,* 205–221.

Mirante, E. (2012). *The wind in the bamboo: A journey in search of Asia's "Negrito" indigenous people.* Bangkok: Orchid Press.

Otterbein, K. F. (1985). *Evolution of war: A cross-cultural study* (Second ed.). New Haven, CT: Yale University Press.

Otterbein, K. F. (2004). *How war began.* College Station: Texas A&M University Press.

Peterson, N. (1975). Hunter-gatherer territoriality: The perspective from Australia. *American Anthropologist, 77,* 53–68.

Robarchek, C. A. (1994). Ghosts and witches: The psychocultural dynamics of Semai peacefulness. In L. E. Sponsel & T. Gregor (Eds.), *The anthropology of peace and nonviolence* (pp. 183–196). Boulder: Lynne Rienner Publishers.

Salmond, A. (1991). *Two worlds: First meetings between Maori and Europeans 1642–1772.* Honolulu: University of Hawaii Press.

Shand, A. (1892a). The occupation of the Chatham Islands by the Maoris in 1835. Part I—The migration of Ngatiawa to Port Nicholson. *Journal of the Polynesian Society, 1*(2), 83–94.

Shand, A. (1892b). The occupation of the Chatham Islands by the Maoris in 1835. Part II—The migration of Ngatiawa to Chatham Island. *Journal of the Polynesian Society, 1*(3), 154–163.

Shand, A. (1892c). The occupation of the Chatham Islands by the Maoris in 1835. Part III—The Jean Bart incident. *Journal of the Polynesian Society, 1*(4), 202–211.

Shand, A. (1893). The occupation of the Chatham Islands by the Maoris in 1835. Part IV—Intertribal dissensions. *Journal of the Polynesian Society, 2*(2), 74–86.

Shand, A. (1894). The Moriori people of the Chatham Islands: Their traditions and history. Chapter I. Introduction. *Journal of the Polynesian Society, 3*(2), 76–92.

Shand, A. (1896). The Moriori people of the Chatham Islands: Their traditions and history. Chapter VIII. Ko hokorongo-tiringa. The migration of the Moriois to the Chatham Islands. *Journal of the Polynesian Society, 5*(1), 13–32.

Silverberg, J. & Gray, J. P. (Eds.). (1992). *Aggression and peacefulness in humans and other primates*. New York: Oxford University Press.

Skinner, H. D. (1919). Moriori sea-going craft. *Man, 19*, 65–68.

Skinner, H. D. (1923). The Morioris of Chatham Islands. *Memoirs of the Bernice P. Bishop Museum, IX*(I), 1–140.

Skinner, H. D. & Baucke, W. (1928). The Morioris. *Memoirs of the Bernice P. Bishop Museum, IX*(5), 342–384.

Sussman, R. W. & Hart, D. (2010). Gentle savage or bloodthirsty brute? In J. Evans Pim (Ed.), *Nonkilling societies* (pp. 55–80). Honolulu: Center for Global Nonkilling.

Sutton, D. G. (1980). A culture history of the Chatham Islands. *Journal of the Polynesian Society, 89*(1), 67–93.

Sutton, D. G. (1982). Towards the recognition of convergent cultural adaptation in the subantarctic zone. *Current Anthropology, 23*(1), 77–97.

Tonkinson, R. (1991). *The Mardu Aborigines: Living the dream in Australia's desert* (Second ed.). Fort Worth: Holt, Rinehart & Winston.

Vayda, A. P. (1960). *Maori Warfare*. Wellington, New Zealand: The Polynesian Society.

Welch, E. A. & Davis, J. B. (1870–1871). An account of the Chatham Islands: Their discovery, inhabitants, conquest by the Maories, and the fate of the aborigines. *Journal of the Anthropological Society of London, 8*, xcvii–cviii.

Williams, J. W. (1898). Notes on the Chatham Islands. *Journal of the Anthropological Institute of Great Britain and Ireland, 27*, 343–345.

Wylie, A. (1985). The reaction against analogy. *Advances in Archaeological Method and Theory, 8*, 63–111.

13

Social Control and Conflict Management Among Australian Aboriginal Desert People Before and After the Advent of Alcohol

ROBERT TONKINSON

"Traditional" Social Control and Conflict Management

Introduction

The ancestors of the Aborigines probably entered Australia more than 50,000 years ago and soon occupied the entire continent, where, as far as we can deduce from the available archaeological and mitochondrial DNA evidence, they remained undisturbed by outside influences until just a few centuries ago. Today, the two Indigenous minorities, Aborigines and Torres Strait Islanders, number about 575,000 people out of a total population of 22.7 million. Most Aboriginal people now live in major cities and regional centers, like the rest of the population. The lowest population densities are in the arid interior, where the Western Desert region alone covers about one sixth of the continent, by far its largest single Aboriginal cultural bloc (Figure 13.1). This region is the last Australian frontier: a few of the older Mardu still alive today were already adults when they encountered their first "whitefellas," as recently as the 1970s.

Prior to European incursion, the rhythm of aggregation and dispersal framing nomadic hunter-gatherer lives in this vast arid region heavily favored the dispersal mode of adaptation: exactly what one would expect given its sparse and extremely irregular rainfall. Other key characteristics were high mobility levels and very low population densities, which, together with the unpredictable rainfall pattern, rendered the defense of territory unthinkable (Gould, 1969; Tonkinson, 1988a). No group could be reliably self-sufficient

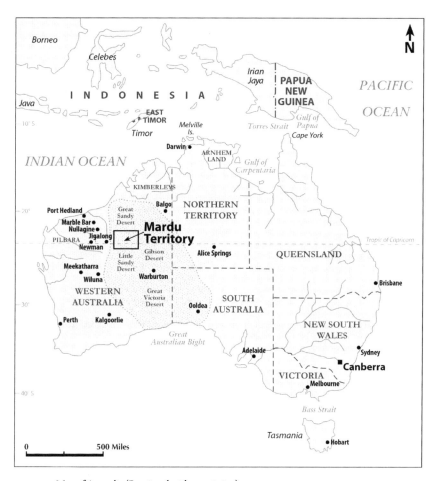

FIGURE 13.1 Map of Australia (Reprinted with permission).

within its homeland area. Understandably, people spent almost all of their time in small, labile bands of about fifteen to thirty, which varied in size and composition over time. For all the mobility, though, the strong recognition of wider homogeneities—the fact that people knew and felt themselves to be part of a much wider "society"—engendered a deep-rooted social identity extending way beyond the level of the small local group.

Despite a dominant ethos of "traditional" life as egalitarian and peaceful, neither condition was absolute. In the Western Desert language there are words for "fighting" but none for either "feud" or "warfare" (or suicide, for that matter). Egalitarianism was on occasion, and infrequently, overridden by hierarchy, most notably in two different social situations: during domestic disputes when men strongly assert their superior rights, to the disadvantage of women; and in the organization and activation of a complex, multifaceted and pervasive religious life. In this culturally preeminent arena, both male and female ritual hierarchies structure much of what happens but, predictably, senior men are in firm control of both the agenda and the secrets and mechanisms of power. Peaceful equilibrium, though underwritten by a battery of individual predispositions and inhibitions and collective values and behaviors, was likewise punctuated at times by short bursts of conflict and confrontation. These upsets resulted from individual volatility, which could rapidly generate and escalate tensions to a high and potentially violent pitch. Disequilibrium of this kind triggered rapid reactions on the part of the non-combatants present, whose varied responses would be guided primarily by considerations of kinship, and predominantly in a manner favoring a rapid, and lasting, cessation of hostilities.

Throughout Australia, Aboriginal societies were integrated primarily by shared religion, worldview, classificatory kinship, marriage, and exchange (see Berndt & Berndt, 1988). People lived their entire lives within a universe of kin; "strangers" existed, but no interaction with them was conceivable until the appropriate kin relationship had been arrived at. The kinship system was, in effect, the fundamental blueprint for structuring interpersonal behavior. Every kin term designates a status, which inescapably entails particular obligations and responsibilities. Potentially tense relationships tend to feature avoidance or restraint, while at the opposite end of the spectrum are obligatory joking and physical horseplay. Classificatory kinship converts "stranger" to "kin," giving people a ready-made egocentric framework of reference. This grid not only positions all others in relation to oneself but also provides a guide to behavioral patterns appropriate to each dyadic relationship. These conventions in turn make for peaceable interaction as the norm and impart a sense of belonging.

Knowing how kinship works is essential for understanding the dynamics of how and why people behave as they do during disputes. Depending upon specific kinship links to the combatants, there are those who may chastise, restrain, substitute for and defend, incite and inflame, appeal to reason and calm, and so on. Kinship norms are occasionally ignored in the heat of the moment, so one's ability to predict likely behavior would also depend on an intimate knowledge of people's personalities and past reactions to aggravation and stress.

A major characteristic of Desert ritual activity is the division of the society into moieties, formed by the intermarrying pairs of sections in a four-section system (see Tonkinson, 1987, 1991). Certain stages of the male initiation process entail ritualized conflict among particular kin of opposite moieties. For example, shortly after the sudden seizing of a supposedly unaware youth prior to the long chain of events leading to his circumcision, several of the "mourners" moiety, related as classificatory "fathers" attack members of the other ritual category, the "activists," throwing boomerangs (all purposely aimed to miss) and haranguing them loudly for undue haste in "grabbing" this initiate without sufficient prior consultation with the relevant kin. As a rule, no one is physically harmed; this aggressive behavior exemplifies mock conflict, which also occurs in some other ceremonial contexts.

The second major plank of conformity was a profoundly spiritual religion and worldview centered on the core cultural symbol commonly called "the Dreaming," which both underpins and permeates the entire cultural fabric (Stanner, 1958; Maddock, 1982). Adults "follow the Dreaming" by reproducing forms believed to have been instituted by the great ancestral creative beings, which are credited with leaving behind the first humans while simultaneously endowing them with their homelands, dialect, cultural and organizational forms, and moral codes (Tonkinson, 2011). These precepts, today commonly referred to by Desert Aborigines as "the Law," had to be obeyed; if not, it was believed, the flow of power from the spiritual realm in response to ritual could be interrupted, with consequences believed to be fatal for both social and natural environments. Typically, Law-breakers were expected to take full responsibility for their transgressions, and their offenses carried a range of penalties, up to and including being put to death—though this was apparently rare. For example, when eloping lovers were eventually caught, both could expect grievous bodily harm or even death at the hands of the woman's husband and his kin. The theft of sacred objects, allegedly rare, was a male capital offense, as was, for women, any trespass on men's secret-sacred territory and/or witnessing of men's secret-sacred activities or paraphernalia.

The Individual, Ethos and Emotion

The ideal Desert adult is *kurntawinti* "having, knowing shame/embarrassment," the essence of humanness, and is sensitive to others, agreeable, unassuming, self-effacing, generous, always ready to fulfil ritual and kinship obligations, an active provider as parent, child of aged parents, and in-law, demonstrating compassion for others and respect for their integrity. One's status is divorced from material possessions, personality, and creativity. A vigorous elder who successfully manages several wives, and/or whose religious knowledge is great, may be admired, but achieved statuses such as these matter little in everyday life. Desert people are typically gregarious, love animated discussion and repartee, and are highly alert to what transpires in their environmental, social, and spiritual surroundings. They share with many other hunter-gatherers a readiness to joke about themselves and others alike.

Potentially disruptive emotions and behaviors of course existed: active dislike, jealousy, greed, envy, promiscuity, and malicious gossip. There is also a condition known as *yurntiri*, "aggressive sulking," which attracts attention to the aggrieved person, so that others are moved to elicit said grievances. This response thus saves the disgruntled person from broaching the matter first, since in Desert society public speaking is for most people a painful and embarrassing ordeal. Appropriate verbal style in such situations is a quiet, self-effacing, and rather apologetic delivery. People are always heard out in public meetings, and every effort is made to obtain consensus when decisions are being made. In reality, however, "consensus" often means merely that those who have been arguing against the majority cease raising their objections publicly, so in actuality the matter may not be finally resolved at this point.

Managing Interpersonal Conflict

Most Desert adults are agreeable people, quick to laugh and joke, but when shamed or angered by something they tend to be quickly aroused and verbally aggressive, sometimes in ways suggesting that physical violence is inevitable. Attempts at self-infliction of injuries may occur as a demonstration of anguish over the sickness or death of a relative; also, certain kin will routinely vent their anger on others who have allegedly failed in their duty of care to kin. Intense hostility resulting from seemingly minor upsets can quickly escalate to rowdy confrontations. Yet such outbursts are not characteristic of everyday life; people are quick to calm down again, and give no indication that they harbor grudges.

The unstated aim of the many conventions surrounding disputes between males is for them to be aired verbally rather than physically: protagonists broadcast their grievances and accusations publicly, at high volume and with maximum menace, and satisfaction is gained from the drama of confrontation itself. The largely predictable series of events evidences a pronounced ritualization of such conflicts. At times, however, control slips and fights may escalate; for example, an unleashed boomerang can go astray, resulting in an injury to an innocent bystander, which might take matters in new directions. Once combatants are face to face, both males and females of the appropriate kinship categories will intervene to separate them and prevent them from launching weapons. Women often play a key role in men's fights by doggedly clinging to the combatants, pinning down their arms and dislodging spears from spear-throwers. However, there will be other kin present whose relationship to an antagonist requires active encouragement of physical punishment in certain disputes, especially when his or her opponent's guilt is obvious to all.

Generally, though, Desert Aboriginal ethos heavily favors the rapid suppression of conflict (Tonkinson, 2004). If a rift has been serious (for example, a spear fight between two brothers), the pair may be required to engage in a ritualized exchange of secret-sacred objects, which renders further conflict unthinkable. If one man is judged by the group to be clearly in the wrong, he faces the onerous task of carving the object, which has been cut and shaped by the offended party. When a dispute arises from an obvious or admitted offense, the wronged person obtains satisfaction from the exposure of the offense to public notice and the punishment and group censure of the offender. Few transgressions can remain private because everyone, from an early age, can read the ground like a map, and gossip is commonplace (and greatly enjoyed). A Law-breaker may flee and join relatives in a distant group after severe wrongdoing, but eventually he or she will have to face accusers and accept punishment. Although a prudent withdrawal may result in the ultimate clash being less intense than it would otherwise have been in the heat of the moment, most Law-abiding people stay and confront the problem. This path of action is doubtless prompted by fear of sorcery or "revenge expeditions." People are alert to both these hazards, and should some omen arouse suspicions, a *maparn* (diviner-curer), if available, may be summoned to repel the threat magically.

Equilibrium in Desert society is best served by the rapid, relatively bloodless defusing of tensions and the restoration of good feelings toward others with whom one has had differences, but serious breaches invite severe retribution. Adult male offenders who are judged to be guilty by their own local group typically step forward into a public space to await their punishment, carrying only a narrow wooden shield. Sometimes, the expiatory encounter will involve a group of people whose kin relationships to the offender designate them as punishing agents. They will stand in a group at a distance and throw spears at the upper body of the offender, who parries them with his shield until he is eventually wounded. A more common procedure, though, is that the offender offers himself submissively, head bowed and thigh held motionless, ready to receive the initial clubbing and jabs from stabbing spears carefully guided into the leg to avoid arteries. Some of his "brothers" and "grandfathers" will surround him, ready to protect him from overzealous punishers. The multiple spear-wound scars that every old Desert man and woman proudly carried as a testament to youthful rebellion also indicate the popularity of this form of punishment—favored because the jabbing spear can be guided accurately to its target, whereas thrown missiles are far more unpredictable. Within domestic groups, particularly, a quick-tempered outburst may lead to blows being struck, and sometimes women are severely beaten by their husbands. Verbal exchanges may prompt physical abuse when a woman swears at her spouse and thus embarrasses him in front of co-wives, children, and other nearby families, who are certain to be paying close attention. The husband has the right to engage in such behavior, so others tend not to intervene, regardless of whether or not they judge the wife to be in the wrong. Close kin intercede to restrain a man only if he appears to be seriously injuring his wife, but women can and do arm themselves and fight back, though they should not initiate physical attacks on their husbands.

In Desert society, older men, especially, may have more than one wife, though more than three would be rare. Traditionally, older wives would welcome the economic contribution and assistance of younger co-wives, whose junior status meant subservience to their elders. Although fights among co-wives were said to be uncommon, jealousy at times inflames passions, and women may attack co-wives, or more commonly, rivals for the affections of their lovers. When Desert women fight each other, for whatever reason, the conflicts may be bloody and intense; they wield clubs or digging sticks, inflicting wounds to the scalp and upper body, or use their hands and teeth as weapons. Women's fights within or between families are usually regarded by the local community as less serious than men's, and if short-lived may be viewed as light entertainment by men (other than their husbands, usually). Sometimes, though, their ferocity may cause other women to become involved, and, should the altercation continue, men may physically intervene if their shouted epithets and threats are ignored. Women very quickly put such altercations, even quite bloody ones, behind them; I have seen women the following morning, still bearing blood-stained hair and clothes from their fight, sitting together chatting by the fire as if nothing amiss had happened.

Female conflicts appear to involve fewer conventions than those between males, but commonly a woman who is clearly at fault must bow her head and accept the first blow uncontested. She thus admits guilt and offers "satisfaction" to her opponent, regardless of who fares better in the ensuing club fight. The only men's weapons women are permitted to use are clubs. A young woman who commits the serious offense of having sexual intercourse deemed incestuous under the rules of classificatory kinship usually bears a much heavier burden of blame than does her male partner. Initially standing alone and unaided by senior female kin, she faces the savage attacks of women related to her lover as "mothers" and "sisters." Ignoring kinship conventions is tantamount to animality, and those who persist in such relationships threaten the very integrity of the social fabric, thus inviting grievous injury or death. While casual affairs are frequent and widely tolerated, passionate attachments that may threaten the marriage bond will be dealt with decisively.

Intergroup Conflict

Given the homogeneity of Western Desert societies and the constraining power of kinship relatedness, intergroup conflict was uncommon. The attribution of most unexpected deaths to sorcery, plus the belief that close relatives cannot resort to this practice, means that distant groups were generally blamed. Self-help on the part of an offended person or family would have been the norm against alleged offenders, if identified. Expiatory measures were available, including the preemptive punishment of an own-group member adjudged guilty of an offense against a member of some other group; or, if the offender is a man, he may be induced to face the wronged group. Disputes could stem either from an actual event, as for example, when a member of one elopes with the wife of a member of the other, or could derive from an alleged offense, such as a sorcery attack, an attempted or actual ambush by a "revenge expedition" (a small group of men sent by an aggrieved party from a different group to punish someone who has allegedly wronged that person), or some alleged failure to reciprocate adequately or Lawfully. Short of physical combat—or following it, if cool heads have not prevailed—other measures exist to help effect enduring settlements. Again, the most binding and permanent sanction is the cutting, exchange, and carving of secret-sacred objects by members of the two disputing groups. If the elders cannot resolve the matter to the satisfaction of both groups, the only solution would be to delay adjudication until the next "big meeting."

The "Big Meeting"

This Desert institution, which is vital to the integration of Desert societies at large, is held two or three times a year at different sites throughout the region. A number of groups from contiguous areas assemble at a prearranged venue in order to conduct the business of the society at large: the exchange of gifts, information, rituals, and sacred objects; the initiation of male novices; the performance of other rituals; the planning of future meetings; betrothals, and so on. Every big meeting begins with a ceremonial welcome staged by the host group, then a ritual response by the visitors, then the formal introduction of any "strangers" from further afield. What takes place next is an institution vital to the success of the big meetings: the airing and adjudication of outstanding disputes, with each group of litigants in turn putting its case to the large assembly, which is the closest physical approximation to "society" that the Western Desert people achieve. Everyone present who has a case to answer must come forward and face their accusers, answer the charges, then take whatever punishment is meted out, with the assembly acting as judge and jury. Proceedings usually end with all attending groups united, seated in a single circle, grieving and wailing for recently deceased persons, over whom accusations of murder may have been aired at the meeting. No serious ritual business—and there is always much to follow—can be conducted until the air is cleared and "stomachs" (believed to be the seat of the emotions in most of Aboriginal Australia), are "calm." The vital arena of ritual activity is also protected from violence: it is forbidden to argue or fight anywhere within earshot of such activity, and conflict of any kind is unthinkable in men's secret-sacred areas and during ritual performances. Discord would not only upset the mood of the occasion but could also result in the failure of the ritual to achieve its objectives by angering those omnipresent spiritual powers whose cooperation is being invoked.

The Post-Contact Era and the Impacts of Alcohol

The foregoing description of social control and conflict management in Western Desert "traditional" culture has suggested a number of mutually reinforcing dispositions, norms, values, and behaviors that work to minimize both interpersonal and intergroup conflict. Given the exceptionally marginal ecological setting, protracted feuding and boundary maintaining behaviors would be suicidal. The situational and shifting nature of leadership, in combination with the dominance of classificatory kinship in structuring interpersonal relations, ensures that cooperation is the dominant mode of social being. The intrusion of Europeans and alcohol in the early twentieth century heralded a massive period of reaction and adjustment.

Alcohol's Impacts on Indigenous Minorities in Australia, New Zealand, and Canada

For the world's indigenous peoples, and especially among former hunter-gatherer peoples, alcohol's impact has been devastating. Considerations of space preclude a global overview in this chapter, so I confine my discussion to an important study comparing the use of alcohol in three British Commonwealth countries; in all three it is the most common drug used by their Indigenous peoples. In this highly informative work, anthropologists Sherry Saggers and Dennis Gray (1998) emphasize the need to situate alcohol consumption patterns within a broader sociohistorical frame of colonialism and its enduring deleterious impacts, especially the emergence and intractability of structural inequalities. The authors allow Indigenous voices to give substance to the major social, cultural, health, and economic consequences of misusing alcohol. Its abuse is, of course, not confined to these minorities, but constitutes a major social problem for all three nations and incurs massive costs. However, the relative impacts of these factors become vividly clear when statistics for the non-Indigenous majorities are compared with those of Indigenous minorities.

Saggers and Gray (1998, p. 191) note that, although several theories have been advanced as to why some peoples seem more prone to alcohol misuse than others, in their view the key to understanding lies in historical forces and resultant structural conditions, such as displacement, marginalization, political impotence, and lack of access to economic resources—the origins of which lie in British colonial history and the widespread dispossession of indigenous peoples. The authors note that, "Violence, inadequate parenting, threats to culture and tradition, sickness and premature death are all part of the drinking cultures embedded within many indigenous communities" (1998, p.190). These pathologies feed into the prejudices of the majority populations, to the detriment of those many Indigenous people who are teetotallers living peaceable lives.

In Australia, proportionally fewer Indigenous than non-Indigenous people drink or use drugs, but those who do are more likely to do so at dangerous levels. Saggers and Gray (1998, p.192) estimate that 25 to 50 percent of illness and death among Indigenous people in all three countries is alcohol-related. Statistics show that a far greater proportion of Indigenous than non-Indigenous deaths are alcohol-related (Saggers & Gray, 1998, p.124). For example, in the period 2005 to 2009, data from the five Australian states that collect statistics on alcohol-related deaths reveal that the rate for Indigenous people averaged 7.5 times that for non-Indigenous people (Commonwealth of Australia, 2011, 10.29).

On a whole range of indicators, including health status, level of education, house ownership, income, unemployment, violence, crime rates, and suicide, Indigenous people in all three countries fare much more poorly than the majority population. Discrepancies in life expectancy between non-Indigenous and Indigenous Australians, at 18–20 years (when Saggers and Gray were writing) are much higher than in New Zealand, where the gap was 7 years for Maori men and 8.5 years for Maori women (and for both was declining steadily), and in Canada, where the gap is 10 years. However, Saggers and Gray note that the *general* pattern of Indigenous health is similar in all three countries (1998, p.123). In Indigenous Australia, more women than men abstain from alcohol, but most who do so are middle-aged or older. Saggers and Gray (1998, p. 193) cite research showing that children are experimenting with alcohol and other drugs at an increasingly early age, with those in the 10–13 years age bracket exposed to the greatest risk. Despite huge expenditure on prevention and health education, and a host of strategies and interventions aimed at reducing the deleterious impacts of alcohol in all three nations, no major or decisive breakthroughs have yet been achieved (see Saggers and Gray, 1998, Ch. 8 on what is being done and Ch. 9 on program evaluations).

In what follows I return to the Western Desert case and the accelerated rate of change that has been experienced by the Mardu people, particularly in the last few decades. Major economic developments, predominantly in the mining sector, have turned the northern part of Western Australia into a giant quarry, supplying massive quantities of minerals, most particularly iron ore, to a vigorous and voracious world market, currently dominated by China. Huge royalty monies are beginning to flow to Aboriginal land councils and community organizations throughout the region. The problem of how to redistribute this bonanza equitably, down to the level of the individual, is perhaps the biggest challenge faced by the mining industry, state and federal authorities, and the Indigenous beneficiaries.

After the Desert Exodus

Much has changed since Aboriginal groups began to leave their Desert homelands in the early decades of the twentieth century and eventually settled on cattle stations and mission settlements along the fringes of the desert (Tonkinson, 2007a). Today, increasing numbers of their descendants are living in public housing in towns, but many others now live in their own homeland communities, on land deemed theirs by the national Native Title process. Since the 1970s, Desert communities have been structured along Western-oriented administrative lines, controlled by elected Aboriginal councils that have become increasingly preoccupied by bureaucratic dealings with the outside world and assisted by non-Aboriginal staff in positions such as community advisor, project officer, mechanic, bookkeeper, and so on, and with mostly non-Aboriginal resident government employees, such as nurses, schoolteachers, and, in some cases, police. These communities feature Western-style housing, well-equipped schools, clinics, electricity, television, telephones, computers, supermarkets, art centers, and so on. In the last two decades, most families have acquired four-wheel drive vehicles, which have greatly increased their mobility and range of travel (see Tonkinson, 2007b).

A casual visitor to any of these communities may have difficulty detecting that important cultural continuities remain, other than hearing people speak in their own language. Kinship still structures most social interaction among Mardu, and despite what may look like a great deal of Westernization (in clothing, foods, vehicles, the amount of English used, and so forth), "the Dreaming" and "the Law" remain important, as does the strong pull of being with one's close kin and in one's own country. Most adults would still regard their religious life, with its strong focus on male initiation, as of greater cultural significance than what they term "whitefella business," even as the latter increasingly demands and engages their attention.

Changes in health status have everywhere been major and predominantly negative, despite considerable expenditure on medical services in remote areas. Becoming sedentary greatly reduced exercise levels and, despite the continuance of hunting and gathering practices, albeit with vehicles and rifles today, people's diets have changed radically. Their low-sugar, low-fat desert regime was replaced by "rations," regular distributions of white flour, powdered milk, canned meat, sugar, tea, jam, and tobacco. In recent decades, easy access to Western junk foods has markedly accelerated the number of overweight and obese people. Also, by the early 1970s alcohol was becoming more readily available to Desert people, who had begun to acquire motor vehicles, so the stage was set for a rapid deterioration in health levels. Alcohol has had the same devastating effect on community life as elsewhere in Aboriginal Australia, where it remains the most serious problem confronting Indigenous Australians, both male and female (see Tonkinson, 1990, pp. 125–47 on Mardu women and change). Drinking has been unquestionably bound up with historical circumstances that were conducive to feelings of alienation and hopelessness in the face of racism. Alcohol has featured prominently in Australia since day one of

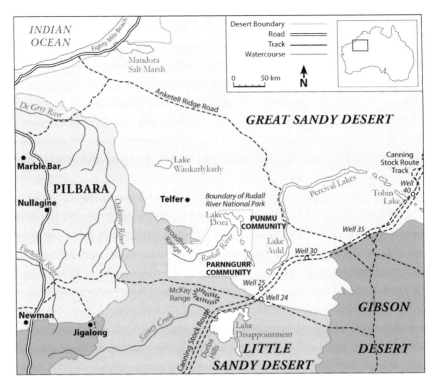

FIGURE 13.2 Map of the Mardu region (Reprinted with permission).

British settlement, and today Australia is one of the highest per capita alcohol-consuming nations in the world.

Jigalong

My fieldwork since 1963 has been with the Mardu people, Desert immigrants who began to settle at Jigalong (see Figures 13.1 and 13.2), now regarded by many Mardu as a kind of ancestral home even though it lies just west of the desert itself. Begun as a camel-breeding and maintenance depot on the Rabbit Proof Fence (a futile attempt to keep rabbits out of farming areas), it became a Christian mission in 1946 after the closure of the depot (Tonkinson, 1974, 2011). School-aged children were put into dormitories and able-bodied men were encouraged to find work as laborers on pastoral properties in the surrounding area. By the time the missionaries departed, in 1969, Jigalong's population had grown to about 350, and numbers continued to swell following job losses on pastoral properties after 1968, when equal wages laws were extended to Aboriginal workers (see Bunbury, 2002). Income from various welfare payments thus became (and still remains) the backbone of the local economy, which switched to a cash base in the early 1970s (Tonkinson, 1978). Having an assured income altered Mardu spending patterns and enabled more of them to purchase vehicles, thus increasing their mobility, but also their access to alcohol, which had always been totally banned in mission times.

Excessive alcohol use among many Aboriginal Australians is certainly linked to their colonized status as an alienated and socioeconomically deprived minority, subject to continuing prejudice and social exclusion from the broader Australian society. Disproportionately high incarceration rates of Aboriginal Australians are predominantly either directly or indirectly linked to alcohol. Western Desert people are socialized to experience powerful feelings of shame/embarrassment if their behavior violates social norms or if they witness other people failing to exercise self-control. Drunks are not held fully responsible for their actions because they are deemed entirely different beings from their sober selves. Unfortunately, this perception of them prompts their fellows to physically distance themselves from such extremely shameful behavior. In Western Desert culture, to lack shame (*kurntaparni* or *parnuparnu*) is to be like an animal, emphatically not human. Violent assault and sexual offenses committed by the inebriated are proof to their fellow Mardu that drunks are not themselves. The loss by drunks of their self-control was so deeply embarrassing that people would flee rather than confront disruptive inebriates, sometimes with in fatal consequences (Tonkinson, 2007a).

The varied mechanisms of social control I have just discussed for the "traditional" situation have, to differing degrees, been weakened in the post-contact era. A powerful legacy of paternalism before the 1970s undoubtedly contributed to the community's felt inadequacy to deal with a number of emerging problems, most notably alcohol. Today, kinship remains very significant for Mardu interaction and feelings of security, but the system's rules cannot be so effectively enforced, and there are now perhaps greater potential sources of conflict. Some brief examples follow:

a.   Notions of individual autonomy mean that young people want to choose their own partners and marry age-mates and, in the case of males, begin to cohabit at a much younger age than before, but also increasingly in contravention of the kinship rules governing "correct" marriage partners, which formerly would have resulted in aggressive intervention by parents and other elders;

b.   Male initiation continues, but in an increasingly attenuated form that reduces the control elders can exert over youngsters;

c.   Mobility has increased because of greater access to motor vehicles and also because of opportunities to live in towns, often away from the authority of kin;

d.   The form of Western housing that now prevails means greater privacy but also overcrowding, with attendant stresses, and a greater risk of fights not being adequately controlled by relevant kin;

e.   Alcohol availability exacerbates most of these dangers; its disinhibiting effects allow jealousy and anger to be acted out more readily, while onlookers are loath to intervene. Angry inebriates often jump into cars and drive away, or do wheelies, or worse, when drunk. Drinking and driving on remote roads, especially at night, has led to many fatal accidents;

f. Sorcery suspicions are escalated as many young people die in accidents, and from ill-
    nesses such as heart, liver, and renal failure. Such deaths require explanation, and alco-
    hol may fuel accusations and revenge fights;

g. Tedium and boredom are rife, and indulgence in drinking is a major form of recreation
    and bonding among younger people, leading to some of the situations just outlined.

At Jigalong, uncontrolled alcohol-related fighting and drunk-driving led to a large
increase in injury and death. Although the community Council never allowed the sale
of alcohol there, rules forbidding its presence in the settlement were never consistently
enforced. In recent times, a police post was established, although there are only about 300
residents; this is an indication of a failure to manage the violent and disruptive behavior
of inebriated people. Liquor is banned from all the Mardu settlements in the desert; and
as a result, it has to be bought at outlets 150 kilometres and more away, so drinking is a
periodic activity in all three Desert Mardu communities today. All Mardu communities
have experimented with many different strategies in recent decades to deal with this most
serious of their problems. Unfortunately, they have yet to develop a successful one—and
the same could be said of the overwhelming majority of Aboriginal communities in remote
Australia where alcohol remains a scourge.

Christianity

The rapid and widespread acceptance of Christianity in Oceania stands in notable contrast to its failure, until relatively recently at least, to gain a solid foothold in Aboriginal
Australia. To a great extent, Christian proselytizing fell on barren ground, seemingly
unable to dislodge an indigenous religious system so pervasive and integrated that it was
synonymous with, and inseparable from, the fabric of life itself. At Jigalong, although
Mardu adults won their battle to protect their core religious values, rituals, and the Law,
some understandings about Christianity were retained among the dormitory children, who of all the Mardu were the most strongly exposed to fundamentalist Christian
teachings. In the 1980s, the Mardu and many other remote Aboriginal communities
across Australia's north and center were caught up in a nationwide evangelical movement. However, those who began professing Christian beliefs did not therefore abandon the Law, since the less judgmental denominations could accommodate the notion
of "two laws" by proposing that Jesus "put" everything on earth, including Aboriginal
religion. Significantly, most churches active in the Western Desert are totally opposed
to alcohol, so for those battling with addiction the support of the church community
offered a way to help them "get off the grog," and some have successfully given up alcohol. Missionaries (often Pacific Islanders) are again resident in Jigalong, and the number
of professed Christians, particularly women, has increased. The churches that are active
in the wider region offer one way to help Mardu cope with unemployment, boredom,
indirection, and an increasing truncation of the traditional religious life (cf. Tonkinson,
1988b, 2007b, 2007c).

Involvement with Australian Law

Another significant change to Mardu society that has a bearing on conflict and peace-making is their relationship to the Australian legal system. Aboriginal people generally are arrested, convicted, and imprisoned at rates that far exceed their proportion of the populations. Among the crimes for which they are punished, violent offenses, usually involving spouses, partners, and other kin, are common. There are often clashes between Aboriginal Law and the nation's legal system. A recent example that is still unresolved occurred in a community on the eastern side of the desert, but the issues it raises are similar across the Western Desert region. While in the town of Alice Springs (Northern Territory), a young man was killed in a fight with two other young men from his home community. The police charged the offenders, but one was released on bail and a feud developed between his family and that of the victim. There was so much discord and fighting that the offender and his family left the community and crossed the border into another state. The victim's family claimed that all they wanted was for a "payback" ceremony, in which he and/or members of his family would be punished (beaten with clubs, and possibly speared in the leg). There has been protracted argument as to whether such punishment, seen by many community members as a way of restoring harmony, should be countenanced by the authorities. The offender and his family have now returned, but the feud continues.

Conclusion

Today, most Mardu reside either in three Desert communities (Jigalong, Parnngurr, Punmu) or in towns, and there is constant movement between town and desert homelands. Throughout the Western Desert region, mobility rates continue to be extremely high, with an expanded range of movement facilitated by four-wheel drive vehicles. Most Mardu now living in towns remain in, but not of, them, culturally segregated not only by their visibility and distinctly Aboriginal behavior but also by entrenched racist attitudes among many of their non-Aboriginal neighbors. A major hindrance to more effective Mardu adaptation is the failure of a viable civil society to emerge. People often seem acutely aware of straddling "two laws," attempting to preserve their traditions and identity while at the same time being embedded in a powerfully assimilative Australian nation. Although traditional methods for managing conflict and maintaining a peaceful society have not disappeared, they are severely challenged, and the disinhibition that accompanies drinking gives rise to high levels of involvement with police.

In her groundbreaking work at the Numbulwar community in northern Australia, Burbank (2006, 2011) employs schema theory to link patterns of family relationship to the reluctance of Aboriginal people to participate in Western arrangements. Burbank argues that emotional incompatibility between the cultural self and Western structuring of others leads Aboriginal people to feel that there is no logic to justify their participation in these alien institutions. Certainly, in the comparable Mardu case, a powerful nexus constituted predominantly by kinship, country, and the Law frames a worldview that readily partakes of elements of Western *material* culture but remains surprisingly impervious to much else. Despite two decades of exposure to television and videos, for example, Mardu of all ages evince remarkably little interest in what is "out there" in the wider world. Deep differences in value systems persist, as does the absence of motivation or desire to become more like "whitefellas," whom Mardu view as irredeemably different (Tonkinson & Tonkinson, 2010). Of course, these same virtues that firmly ground Mardu people and have great survival value may be viewed negatively as impediments by powerful non-Indigenous critics and others bent on accelerated assimilation as the best solution to the "Aboriginal problem."

References

Berndt, R. M., & Berndt, C. H. (1988). *The world of the first Australians*, revised ed. Canberra: Aboriginal Studies Press.

Burbank, V. K. (2006). From bedtime to on time: Why many Aboriginal people don't especially like participating in Western institutions. *Anthropological Forum, 16*, 3–20.

Burbank, V. K. (2011). *An ethnography of stress: The social determinants of health in Aboriginal Australia.* New York: Palgrave Macmillan.

Bunbury, B. (2002). *It's not the money—it's the land.* Fremantle: Fremantle Arts Centre Press.

Commonwealth of Australia (2011). *Overcoming Indigenous disadvantage: Key indicators 2011.* Canberra: Productivity Commission.

Gould, R. A. (1969). *Yiwara: Foragers of the Australian desert.* New York: Scribner.

Maddock, K. (1982). *The Australian Aborigines: A portrait of their society*, 2e. Melbourne: Penguin.

Saggers, S., & Gray, D. (1998). *Dealing with alcohol: Indigenous usage in Australia, New Zealand and Canada.* Cambridge: Cambridge University Press.

Stanner, W. E. H. (1958). The Dreaming. In W. A. Lessa and E. Z. Vogt (Eds.), *Reader in comparative religion* (pp. 513–525). New York: Harper and Row.

Tonkinson, M., & Tonkinson, R. (2010). The cultural dynamics of adaptation in remote Aboriginal communities: policy, values and the state's unmet expectations. *Anthropologica, 52*, 67–75.

Tonkinson R. (1974). *The Jigalong Mob: Aboriginal victors of the desert crusade.* Menlo Park: Cummings.

Tonkinson, R. (1978). Aboriginal community autonomy: myth and reality. In M. C. Howard (Ed.), *"Whitefella business": Aborigines in Australian politics* (pp. 93–103). Philadelphia: Institute for the Study of Human Issues.

Tonkinson, R. (1987). Mardujarra kinship. In D. Mulvaney & J. White (Eds.), *Australians to 1788* (pp. 196–219). Vol.1, Australians: a Historical Library. Sydney: Fairfax, Syme & Weldon.

Tonkinson, R. (1988a). Egalitarianism and inequality in a Western Desert culture. *Anthropological Forum, 5*, 545–558.

Tonkinson, R. (1988b). One community, two laws: aspects of conflict and convergence in a Western Australian Aboriginal settlement. In B. Morse and G. Woodman (Eds.), *Indigenous Law and the State* (pp. 395–411). Dordrecht: Foris.

Tonkinson, R. (1990). The changing status of Aboriginal women: "free agents" at Jigalong. In R. Tonkinson & M. C. Howard (Eds.), *Going it alone? Prospects for Aboriginal autonomy: Essays in honour of Ronald and Catherine Berndt* (pp. 125–147). Canberra: Aboriginal Studies Press.

Tonkinson, R. (1991). *The Mardu Aborigines: Living the dream in Australia's desert*, (2nd ed.). Fort Worth: Holt, Rinehart & Winston. (Originally published 1978; since 2002, published by Thomson Wadsworth/ Cengage Learning).

Tonkinson, R. (2004). Resolving conflict within the Law: The Mardu Aborigines of Australia. In G. Kemp & D. P. Fry (Eds.), *Keeping the peace: Conflict resolution and peaceful societies around the world* (pp. 89–104). London: Routledge.

Tonkinson, R. (2007a). Aboriginal "difference" and "autonomy" then and now: Four decades of change in a Western Desert society. *Anthropological Forum, 17*, 41–60.

Tonkinson, R. (2007b). The Mardu Aborigines: On the road to somewhere. In G. Spindler & J. E. Stockard (Eds.), *Globalization and change in fifteen cultures: Born in one world, living in another* (pp. 225–255). Belmont, CA: Thomson Wadsworth.

Tonkinson, R. (2007c). *Homo Anthropologicus* in Aboriginal Australia: "Secular missionaries," Christians and morality in the field. In J. Barker (Ed.), *The anthropology of morality in Melanesia and beyond* (pp. 171–189). Aldershot: Ashgate.

Tonkinson, R. (2011). Landscape, transformations and immutability in an Aboriginal Australian culture. In P. Meusburger, M. Heffernan & E. Wunder (Eds.), *Cultural memories* (pp. 329–345). Dordrecht: Springer.

14

Aggression and Conflict Resolution Among the Nomadic Hadza of Tanzania as Compared with Their Pastoralist Neighbors

MARINA L. BUTOVSKAYA

Introduction

Evolutionary psychologists as well as behavioral ecologists and human ethologists view various forms of human aggression as evolutionarily advantageous traits and as important predictors of success both in traditional and modern industrial societies (Archer, 2004; Archer & Thanzami, 2007; Buss & Duntley, 2006). The emphasis is made on relationships between aggression and intrasexual competition for mates (predominantly among males) and on securing valuable resources (Archer & Thanzami, 2007; Buss & Duntley, 2006). Aggression may be used as an instrument of status acquisition and as a tactic for enhancing reproductive success. This is especially relevant for men (Chagnon, 1979). Given a high probability of both positive and negative selective pressures in the course of evolution, it is not surprising that a meta-analysis of 24 genetic studies of aggression revealed that heritability accounts for about 50 percent of the variance in aggression (Miles & Carey, 1997; Rhee & Waldman, 2002), and that the genetic component of aggressive behavior is higher in males (Craig & Halton, 2009).

Aggressive behavior in humans is highly sexually dimorphic. In virtually all cultures, males exhibit more physical same-sex violence than women (Archer 2004; Björkqvist, 1994; Butovskaya, Timentschik, & Burkova, 2007; Butovskaya, Burkova, & Mabulla, 2010; Daly & Wilson, 1988), which is likely due to greater male impulsiveness and greater female fear of physical danger (Daly & Wilson, 2001; Knight, Guthrie, Page, & Fabes, 2002).

Verbal and indirect or relational aggression (gossiping and spreading rumors directed toward damaging another's self-esteem and reputation, ostracism, breaking confidences, talking loudly enough for others to hear negative information about a target) is more frequent in women's conflicts (Owens, Shute, & Slee, 2000). This is true both of modern Western cultures (Björkqvist, 1994; Hines & Fry, 1994; Werner & Crick, 1999) and of small-scale societies (Shostak, 1981; Geary, 1998; Peters, 1998). For example, gossiping strategies were more frequently used as an instrument of competition with other women in the Ju/'hoansi (Shostak, 1981). Shostak (1981, p. 170) reported that polygynous marriages among the Ju/'hoansi normally result in tensions, and senior wives frequently resort to gossiping, making the life of a new co-wife and her husband intolerable until he breaks the new marriage. Similar functions of women's gossip were reported for the Yanomamö and Zinacanteco Indians, for instance (Geary, 1998, pp. 48–250; Peters, 1998, pp. 116–117).

The evolutionary model predicts more direct and severe competition over sexual partners in men (Daly & Wilson, 1988; Fry, 2007). As the ethnographic evidence suggests, conflicts over access to females occurs even in simple and egalitarian hunter-gatherer societies, and most cases of homicide, rare as they are, relate to reproduction and jealousy (Knauft, 1991; Boehm, 1999; Holmberg, 1969; Fry, 2007; Butovskaya: personal observation among the Hadza). Also, researchers recently working with the Hadza concluded that the homicide rate in this culture is much higher than it was previously believed; in fact, it is higher than in the United States (Marlowe, 2010). It is not clear whether a similar homicide level was typical of Hadza society in the past or whether it has resulted from recent social transformations following contact with neighboring societies, interethnic marriages, socialization in a multiethnic environment of boarding schools, and so forth.

Of course, apart from aggression, humans, like other gregarious animals, possess other means of coping with conflicts (de Waal, 2000; Aureli, Cords, & van Schaik, 2002; Butovskaya, Verbeek, Ljungberg, & Lundardini, 2000; Verbeek, Hartup, & Collins, 2000). Post-conflict reunion depends on factors such as individual recognition and personal social relationships (Cords & Aureli, 2000; Aureli et al., 2002; Butovskaya, 2001). It is not easy to study post-conflict interactions among adult humans in natural settings, but post-conflict reunions in children were studied by ethological methods in several countries including Russia (Russians and Kalmyks), Sweden, the United States, Italy, and Japan (Butovskaya & Kozintsev, 1999; Ljungberg, Westlund, & Lindqvist, 1999; Ljungberg, Horowitz, Jansson, Westlund, and Clarke, 2005; Butovskaya et al., 2000; Butovskaya, 2001; Verbeek & de Waal, 2001; Fujisawa, Kutsukake, & Hasegawa, 2005, 2006). In recent decades, peacemaking has been shown to be one of the main stress-reduction mechanisms in post-conflict interactions in both non-human primates and humans (Aureli & Smucny, 2000; Butovskaya et al., 2000; Butovskaya, 2008). Specifically, the tension-reduction hypothesis of post-conflict affiliation was recently applied to children using both the direct ethological observation method (Fujisawa et al., 2005) and hormonal methods based on saliva cortisol and dehydroepiandrosterone sulfate

(DGEA-S) measurements in boys (Butovskaya, 2008; Butovskaya, Boyko, Selverova, & Ermakovo, 2005).

It was concluded that reconciliation in children is mainly motivated by two factors. The emotional factor relates to the fear of damaging valuable social bonds: children are more attached to friends, and conflicts with them are more stressful than those with other group members (Butovskaya & Kozintsev, 1999; Butovskaya, 2001, 2008). The second factor is rational and is based on cultural norms, specifically on the idea that group membership is valuable; therefore any threat to group integration causes anxiety and uncertainty (Butovskaya, 2008).

This study addresses cultural norms related to aggression and conflict management in the Hadza, who are nomadic hunter-gatherers, and recent transformations resulting from ethno-tourism and contacts with neighboring groups such as interethnic marriages and socialization in the multiethnic environment of boarding schools. Aggression and conflict management among the Hadza will be compared to that observed in a neighboring society, the Datoga, who are semi-nomadic pastoralists.

The Hadza: Cultural Background

The Hadza, also known as Hadzapi, Tindiga, Kindiga, Kangeju, and Wahi, are one of the few groups preserving a traditional way of life in East Africa (Woodburn, 1979, 1982). They practice an immediate-return economy (Woodburn, 1982, 1998; Marlowe, 2010) similar to that practiced by the San of Namibia before the 1970s (Blurton Jones, Smith, O'Connell, Hawkes, & Kamuzora, 1992; Marlowe, 2002; Woodburn, 1988). The Hadza live near Lake Eyasi in northwestern Tanzania, and their language (Hadzane, Hadzapi) is distantly related to the San language (Woodburn, 1977). At present, the total number of Hadza is about 1000. Some 350–400 Eastern Hadza still practice traditional foraging (Butovskaya & Mabulla, 2008).

The Hadza were subjected to selective pressures similar to those experienced by Paleolithic humans (Blurton Jones, Hawkes, & O'Connell, 2002; Marlowe, 2010). Particularly, the high level of pathogenic stressors, and the limited access to medical help were the main causes of high mortality: 46 percent of individuals in this population died before the age of 15 (Blurton Jones et al., 2002).

The Hadza society is markedly egalitarian, relatively peaceful, and has only nominal leadership (Woodburn, 1982, 1988; Marlowe, 2002, 2010). On the other hand, in terms of Gardner's classification (Gardner, 1972, 1991, 1999), the Hadza culture is individualistic. Individuals are relatively unrestricted in their behavior; one can express dissatisfaction, verbal aggression, and anger openly; and one may easily leave after conflict. Mate choice among the Hadza may be a selective factor aimed against aggressive and impulsive individuals. Both sexes consider peaceful character an important criterion in marital partner choice (Marlowe 2004; personal observations), and our respondents often mentioned their ex-partners' quick temper as the main reason of divorce.

Why Do Hadza Fight?

Although virtually all anthropologists who have studied the Hadza described them as peaceful, this does not imply that Hadza never fight. One of the main reasons that Hadza fight appears to be jealousy. Either spouse may resort to physical aggression on finding their partner with a lover somewhere in the bush. Later, unless a divorce ensues, both spouses sometimes recall such episodes humorously. One man demonstrated a scar on his elbow, commenting that he had obtained it for adultery, and his wife said on another day that she had injured both him and his mistress with a stone. The mistress never showed up in the camp again. Another man told me that he had once been engaged in a duel, the cause of which was jealousy: his rival, who had recently arrived at the camp, had tried to court his girlfriend. Rivals fought by hitting with bows, injuring each other (my informant demonstrated a long scar on his head) until other men stopped them. Eventually my respondent married this girl, and his former rival became his friend.

Some women and men reported that they had divorced because their former spouses had beaten them. Other reasons for violence among spouses include disregard of household duties and child neglect. One man told me he had once kicked his wife at night because she had not reacted to their baby's crying; when he asked her to feed the child, she flatly refused. Among other causes of violence between band members and between local residents and visitors are disputes over food and personal belongings. Both juvenile and adult males said they had fought with unfamiliar Hadza over a hunting kill or honey. If fighting occurred in the bush and was not stopped by others, the men eventually made peace and shared the meat or the honey. One man told me that a few months ago a fellow from the same camp had stolen one kilo of honey from him. He realized this because the thief's children were eating honey, and he knew that the man had not obtained any honey in recent days. They started fighting with bows, the thief was injured, and other men intervened to stop the aggression. Afterwards, the elders assembled, discussed the case, and demanded that the thief compensate the owner with five kilos of honey. The elders also sentenced the thief to a fine of 20,000 Tanzanian shillings (equivalent to $13). Some men reported that they had fought with men who had stolen their bows or arrows. In such cases, other camp members usually separated the fighters, and thieves were forced to return what they had stolen. Fights between women were typically over a piece of stolen jewelry or a digging stick. Again, others usually stopped the fight, and the belongings were returned to the owner.

Our data suggest that in a number of cases fighting was triggered by alcohol intoxication. Either the Hadza have become more aggressive than they used to be, or their peacefulness was overestimated. In any case, according to Marlowe (2010, p. 141), the homicide rate among the Hadza (mainly motivated by jealousy) is equivalent to approximately 6.6 per 100,000 per year (or two killings in a 30-year period in the entire population).

And still the Hadza are a relatively peaceful and tolerant people. They do resort to aggression at the inter-individual level, but blood revenge is not practiced. Likewise, no

FIGURE 14.1 Hadza men broke up the quarrel between two boys and explained to the one who had stolen an arrow from his friend that he should never steal arrows again. (Photo Credit: Marina Butovskaya.)

instances of intergroup warfare or raiding have been reported. The main reasons for tolerance between the groups are rooted in Hadza social organization, specifically in bilateral descent, the same as in most nomadic foraging societies (Fry, 2011; Knauft, 1991; Marlowe, 2005); multilocal residence whereby relatives are spread widely across different bands (Marlowe, 2005); and lack of patrilineal kin groups of any type (Fry, 2011).

Means of social integration specific to Hadza culture include the *epeme* dance (Woodburn, 1964). This ceremony not only unites people but "heals those who have violated *epeme* rules and brings good luck in future hunting" (Marlowe, 2010, p. 60). Food sharing with a former opponent is also typical. Older people usually intervene in the conflicts of children and adolescents, convincing them to reconcile (Figure 14.1). Many of our respondents were able to remember such episodes in the past and commented that later former opponents became their close friends.

Children and Adolescents: Aggression and Conflict Resolution

Given the generally accepted view of the Hadza as an egalitarian and peaceful people, we examined the differences between Hadza children and adolescents and their peers from neighboring societies. The study was conducted at the Endamagha boarding school in Mangola, Northern Tanzania in 2005–2006 (Butovskaya et al., 2010). This primary school was founded in 1971, originally intended for Hadza children settled in Endamagha, but currently two-thirds of the pupils are not Hadza (Marlowe, 2010, p. 32). Today about

20 percent of Hadza under 60 years of age and 40 percent of Hadza under 30 years of age have had some schooling (mainly in Endamagha or Mongo wa Mono), although in most cases they studied for no more than two years (Marlowe, 2010, p. 36).

In our sample, children from two traditional East African cultures are represented: the peaceful, egalitarian, and predominantly monogamous Hadza hunter-gatherers; and the Datoga, who are belligerent and polygynous semi-nomadic pastoralists (Woodburn, 1964, 1982; Blurton Jones et al., 1992; Borgerhoff Mulder, 1992; Marlowe, 2002; Butovskaya, 2011). All subjects were asked to fill out the Swahili version of the Self-Estimated Conflict Behavior inventory originally developed by Björkqvist and Österman (1998). Also, each child was asked to report how many times he or she had engaged in certain behaviors over the previous week (see Butovskaya et al., 2010, for more details).

Distinct gender differences in patterns of aggression were found in Hadza children. Hadza boys reported a higher frequency of physical (t = 2.923, p = 0.004) and indirect aggression (t = 1.997, p = 0.047), compared to girls (Butovskaya et al., 2010). In the Datoga children, no significant gender differences were found for any behavior. Although, all the children we studied were living together in the same dormitory and interacting on a daily basis, significant cultural differences were found with regard to aggression and conflict resolution (Butovskaya et al., 2010). Hadza boys rated themselves higher on verbal (t = 3.395, p = 0.001), indirect aggression (t = 2.109, p = 0.036) and constructive conflict resolution (t = 3.082, p = 0.002) than did their Datoga peers. These findings are in line with our direct observations in Hadza camps: quarrelling and spreading rumors about rivals are common and tolerated by group members, while direct physical aggression is considered unacceptable. Among the Datoga, by contrast, both verbal and especially indirect aggression are considered provocative, and are usually followed by a physical attack. In fact, according to cultural norms, the recipient of such behavior must retaliate physically to save face.

In girls, behavioral differences are apparent as well. Compared to their Datoga peers, Hadza girls rated themselves higher on verbal aggression (t = −2.901, p = 0.004), physical aggression (t = −3,836, p = 0,000), and indirect aggression (t = −4.163, p = 0.000) (Figure 14.2). One teenage Datoga girl told me that she recently fought with her peer because the latter offended her by saying aloud that she was weak and timid. These differences are likely attributable to lifestyle: Hadza women rarely resort to physical aggression but may be verbally aggressive as well as spread rumors freely. Also, Datoga women can hardly leave their homes after conflict, whereas Hadza women are free to live in another camp for some time in such cases.

When data on both the cultures are analyzed together regarding participation in constructive conflict resolution (reported for the previous week) and third-party intervention (mean scores), the frequencies of these behaviors were found to be higher in boys than in girls (constructive conflict resolution: t = 2.255, p = 0.025; third-party intervention: t = 2.064, p = 0.04). It has been suggested that girls are usually more sociable than boys based on data mainly from industrial countries (Butovskaya & Demianovitsch,

FIGURE 14.2 A Datoga girl (seated) intervened in a fight between her younger relatives and beat the aggressor with a small stick. (Photo Credit: Marina Butovskaya.)

2002; LaFreniere et al., 2002; Butovskaya et al., 2007). The present findings question this assumption (Butovskaya et al., 2010). Gender differences in aggression and peacemaking are apparent in Hadza children and adolescents. Importantly, although children at the boarding school reproduce certain cultural stereotypes of conflict resolution, they appear well adjusted to the multiethnic environment.

Hadza Children and Adolescents: Boarding School Versus Bush Camp

To investigate possible differences in the behavior of Hadza children between those living at the boarding school and those living in the bush, we administered the same questionnaire in both locations. The data were collected between 2007 and 2009. In the bush camps, all children were orally asked the questions, as illiteracy precluded the use of a written questionnaire. The sample includes 178 schoolchildren (80 boys and 98 girls) and 59 children from the bush (34 boys and 25 girls).

Hadza boys in school or bush were not significantly different, except for the occurrence of third-party interventions, which happened more frequently in the school environment (Table 14.1). This difference may be due to the fact that at school the

TABLE 14.1 **Differences in Aggression and Post-Conflict Interactions in Male Hadza Children and Adolescents from Boarding School and from the Bush Camps**

Mean Scores[1] /Mean Number of Times in the Last Week[2]		N	Mean	Standard Deviation	t
Verbal aggression[1]	School	78	2.04	0.90	−0.60
	Bush	34	2.21	1.51	
Indirect aggression[1]	School	77	1.94	1.12	0.59
	Bush	33	1.79	1.24	
Physical aggression[1]	School	78	2.06	1.05	−0.51
	Bush	34	2.21	1.47	
Constructive conflict resolution[1]	School	78	3.01	1.34	1.88
	Bush	34	2.44	1.58	
Third-party intervention[1]	School	78	2.74	1.21	2.10*
	Bush	34	2.18	1.36	
Withdrawal[1]	School	78	2.69	1.37	1.02
	Bush	34	2.38	1.518	
Victimization[1]	School	78	1.97	1.24	−0.21
	Bush	33	2.03	1.29	
Physical aggression[2]	School	80	1.64	2.11	−0.74
	Bush	34	1.91	1.68	
Indirect aggression[2]	School	80	1.76	2.08	−1.87
	Bush	34	2.74	2.72	
Conflict solved in constructive way[2]	School	80	3.13	2.76	0.87
	Bush	34	2.62	2.90	
Protecting someone of your peers[2]	School	80	3.56	2.35	0.95
	Bush	34	3.12	2.28	
How many times others protect you from physical aggression[2]	School	80	3.54	2.39	1.17
	Bush	34	2.94	2.55	

Table note 1. Keyed to the first list of variables, the ratings were:1 = never; 2 = seldom; 3 = sometimes; 4 = quite often;
5 = very often.
Table note 2. Keyed to the second list of variables, the values are means for the number of times in the last week.
t = t-test for independent samples;
Equal variances not assumed;
*– P <0.05 (two-tailed).

density of children is much higher, and as a rule aggressive interactions took place in close proximity to peers, while in the bush fights were usually at a distance from potential third-party interveners.

The behavior of Hadza schoolgirls was different from that of their bush peers, pertaining to some behaviors. The schoolgirls were more verbally aggressive than the bush girls but, importantly, they also reconciled with former opponents more frequently (Table 14.2). Hadza schoolgirls intervened in the conflicts of other children and stopped fights more frequently than did Hadza girls in the bush. Also, they were much more often likely to protect others and be protected by others when attacked than were the bush girls (Table 14.2).

In total, it may be concluded that girls appeared to be much more sensitive to changes in social environment and changed their behavior in school settings more significantly than boys did. Because most subadults usually return to bush camps

TABLE 14.2 **Differences in Aggression and Post-Conflict Interactions in Female Hadza Children and Adolescents from Boarding School and from the Bush Camps**

Mean Scores[1] /Mean Number of Times in the Last Week[2]		N	Mean	Standard Deviation	t
Verbal aggression[1]	School	98	2.12	1.03	4.08***
	Bush	25	1.40	0.71	
Indirect aggression[1]	School	98	1.82	1.02	0.67
	Bush	26	1.65	1.13	
Physical aggression[1]	School	98	1.88	0.96	0.47
	Bush	25	1.76	1.13	
Constructive conflict resolution[1]	School	98	2.90	1.53	3.98***
	Bush	26	1.88	1.04	
Third-party intervention[1]	School	98	3.06	4.66	1.35
	Bush	25	2.32	1.41	
Withdrawal[1]	School	97	2.66	1.31	1.85
	Bush	25	2.12	1.31	
Victimization[1]	School	98	2.09	1.22	1.23
	Bush	25	1.76	1.20	
Physical aggression[2]	School	98	1.47	1.55	−0.44
	Bush	25	1.60	1.26	
Indirect aggression[2]	School	98	1.35	1.53	−1.13
	Bush	25	1.72	1.46	
Conflict solved in constructive way[2]	School	98	2.92	2.15	3.18***
	Bush	25	1.80	1.38	
Protecting someone of your peers[2]	School	98	3.43	3.05	2.83**
	Bush	24	2.17	1.58	
How many times others protect you from physical aggression[2]	School	98	3.37	2.64	3.26**
	Bush	25	2.00	1.63	

Table note 1. Keyed to the first list of variables, the ratings were: 1 = never; 2 = seldom; 3 = sometimes; 4 = quite often;
5 = very often.
Table note 2. Keyed to the second list of variables, the values are means for the number of times in the last week.
t = t-test for independent samples;
Equal variances not assumed;
*– P <0.05 (two-tailed);
** – P<0.01(two-tailed);
*** – P<0.005 (two-tailed).

after graduating from primary or in some cases secondary school, behavioral patterns acquired at school may gradually become standard in camps. Indeed, the social behavior of the Hadza youth, at least of the girls, may be undergoing transformation. Instead of separating after conflicts, former female partners had become competent in peacemaking and both sexes may be acquiring the ability to stop the fights of others. The newly acquired strategies appear to be very useful because Hadza frequently interact with members of other cultures and are gradually shifting from the nomadic to the sedentary lifestyle.

As more and more children are being educated at the boarding school and at least the behavior of girls seems to be different in the school environment than in the bush, perhaps social relationships in Hadza camps will change gradually as more and more school-educated children return to the bush camps. At least among females, there could be a shift in the future toward the use of verbal aggression, conflict resolution, and third-party interventions in accordance with what is reflected within the boarding school context.

Adults: Aggression in the Traditional Settings

Data on 129 adult Hadza males (mean age: 34±13) and 104 females (mean age: 35±16) were collected between 2007 and 2009. All subjects were interviewed with regard to ethnicity and various behaviors, particularly those related to conflict. The respondents were asked if they had fought with other Hadza and their responses coded on the following three-option scale: never, only in childhood or adolescence, or continues to fight at present. Additionally, self-ratings on aggression were obtained using the Buss and Perry (1992) Aggression Questionnaire (AQ), which has four subscales for assessing physical aggression, verbal aggression, anger, and hostility.

The Hadza display significant sex differences in aggressive behavior. While 50.4 percent of males had either fought in the past or currently continue the practice, the corresponding percentage for the females was 29.1 percent. Of the fighters, 16.5 percent of the men and 10.0 percent of the women reported having fought with same-sex individuals during the same or previous year. Similar figures were obtained for self-ratings on the four subscales of the Buss and Perry AQ (Table 14.3). Males and females differed significantly in their self-ratings of physical and verbal aggression, but not for anger or hostility (Table 14.3). Males scored higher for both physical and verbal aggression than did the females. We did not evaluate indirect aggression in this study, but the results of interviews suggest that the Hadza do not find this type of aggression abusive and mostly ignore it. Also, they are tolerant to ridicule. At least four adult men recalled that when they had reacted aggressively in response to being ridiculed by peers, their

TABLE 14.3 **Male and Female Self-Ratings on the Buss-Perry Aggression Questionnaire for the Hadza Sample**

Subscale	Sex	N	Mean	Standard Deviation	t
Physical aggression	Males	129	26.17	5.58	2.20*
	Females	104	24.61	5.24	
Verbal aggression	Males	129	16.75	3.91	2.08*
	Females	104	15.58	4.59	
Anger	Males	128	19.12	4.82	−0.82
	Females	104	19.68	5.51	
Hostility	Males	129	24.09	5.61	0.75
	Females	103	23.47	6.73	

Equal variances not assumed
* $P < 0.05$ (two-tailed)

TABLE 14.4 **Male and Female Self-Ratings on the Buss-Perry Aggression Questionnaire for the Datoga Sample**

Subscale	Sex	N	Mean	Standard Deviation	T
Physical aggression	Males	101	28.4059	5.14816	−0.15
	Females	123	28.5122	5.29052	
Verbal aggression	Males	102	17.7059	4.15918	−0.14
	Females	123	17.7805	3.79719	
Anger	Males	101	22.3861	4.64106	−0.59
	Females	123	22.7398	4.14459	
Hostility	Males	101	32.6337	6.34149	−1.82
	Females	122	34.0410	4.97497	

Equal variances not assumed
* P <0.05 (two-tailed)

TABLE 14.5 **Correlation Coefficients for the Buss-Perry AQ Subscales and Age for Hadza Males**

		Physical aggression	Verbal aggression	Anger	Hostility	Age
Physical aggression	Pearson Correlation	1	.421(**)	.553(**)	.568(**)	−.057
Verbal aggression	Pearson Correlation			.330(**)	.441(**)	.028
Anger	Pearson Correlation				.598(**)	−.202(*)
Hostility	Pearson Correlation					−.109

Due to missing data, correlation coefficients are calculated based on at least 128 cases out of the total male sample size of 152.
** Correlation is significant at the 0.01 level (2-tailed).
* Correlation is significant at the 0.05 level (2-tailed).

parents immediately discouraged their aggressive responses by saying that "everyone is free to criticize others."

Table 14.4 presents the results of the four Buss-Perry AQ subscales for the Datoga sample. No significant differences between Datoga men and women were found related to physical aggression, verbal aggression, anger, or hostility. A non-significant trend can be noted regarding hostility, with Datoga women exhibiting a higher mean score than the men.

Male Hadza displayed lower self-ratings on all four scales of the AQ than did the Datoga males: physical aggression ($t = −3.174$, $p = 0.002$); verbal aggression ($t = −1.974$; $p = 0.049$); anger ($t = −5.307$, $p = 0.000$); hostility ($t = −6.196$, $p = 0.000$). Similarly, female Hadza were significantly less aggressive than Datoga females: physical aggression ($t = −5.555$, $p = 0.000$); verbal aggression ($t = −3.788$; $p = 0.000$); anger ($t = −4.685$, $p = 0.000$); hostility ($t = −8.948$, $p = 0.000$). Importantly, Hadza females rated themselves significantly lower on physical and verbal aggression than did males, whereas no sex differences on these scales were found in the Datoga. Consequently,

TABLE 14.6 **Correlation Coefficients for the Buss-Perry AQ Subscales
and Age for Hadza Females**

		Physical aggression	Verbal aggression	Anger	Hostility	Age
Physical aggression	Pearson Correlation	1	.460(**)	.562(**)	.610(**)	−.075
Verbal aggression	Pearson Correlation			.548(**)	.666(**)	−.046
Anger	Pearson Correlation				.640(**)	−.072
Hostility	Pearson Correlation					−.171

Due to missing data, correlation coefficients are calculated based on at least 103 cases out of the total male sample size of 123.
** Correlation is significant at the 0.01 level (2-tailed).
* Correlation is significant at the 0.05 level (2-tailed).

gender asymmetry in the aggression expressed toward same-sex peers is greater among the monogamous Hadza than among the polygynous Datoga. At the same time, adult Hadza females may counteraggress, or even initiate physical aggression toward males (mainly their spouse s), whereas adult Datoga females never direct physical aggression toward the opposite sex (Butovskaya, 2012). On the whole, however, our data support the conclusion that the Hadza foragers are significantly less aggressive than are the Datoga pastoralists.

Hadza self-ratings on all four AQ scales correlate significantly with each other for both males and females. In males, a significant negative correlation was found between anger and age (younger males lose their temper more readily) (Table 14.5). In females, a non-significant trend (p = .085) hints at the possibility that hostility might decrease with age (Table 14.6).

Modern Hadza: Aggression and Alcohol

In 2011, we interviewed 152 adult Hadza (83 men and 69 women) from eleven camps at Gorofani, Mangola (53 men and 43 women) and from four camps at Gidamilanda (30 men and 26 women). The two areas had differential access to alcohol. The Mangola Hadza were only 10 to 12 km away from sources of alcohol, whereas the nearest ready source of alcoholic beverages for the Gidamilanda Hadza was approximately 30 km away. It turned out that virtually all money obtained from tourists was spent on cheap alcohol. In the past, Hadza did not consume any alcohol and no cultural norms regulating its consumption existed. Having taken to drinking, they are unable to stop and go on until all the money is spent or until they pass out (Marlowe, 2010; personal observations). In the last few years, drinking caused the death of some males. In Mangola, at least four people were killed in conflicts when drunk, in the village and in the camps. Unfortunately, egalitarianism and the food-sharing tradition play a negative role in the spread of alcoholism among the Hadza, particularly among juveniles. Adults not only share alcohol equally among themselves, but also give it to 12–13-year-old boys. Some Hadza confessed to me that they liked alcohol more than anything else (Frank Marlowe, personal communication dated June 30, 2011, has heard similar statements from the Hadza). Such people can hardly be discouraged from drinking. Hadza living 10–12 km away from Gorofani, Mangola, are regularly seen in local pubs and never miss local markets, where alcohol is available.

Data on alcohol consumption, violence, and certain daily activities of Hadza males and females living in Mangola and Gidamilanda are presented in Table 14.7. The percentage of females regularly consuming alcohol in Mangola is about 24 times the percentage of female drinkers in Gidamilanda, and for men, the corresponding difference between Mangola and Gidamilanda is almost five times (Table 14.7).

While it can hardly be assumed that interpersonal aggression was absent among the Hadza in the past, it seems likely that rates of physical aggression have dramatically increased in recent years. Present-day Hadza in Mangola frequently fight when drunk. Others usually try to stop the fighting. On the next day, aggressors seldom if ever apologize. When I asked such men if they were ashamed, they replied, "We all understand that a drunk is unaware of what he/she is doing, so one ought to excuse him/her, and on the next day one should behave as if nothing had happened." One young man from Gidamilanda, who had been visiting his relatives in Mangola and drinking there heavily, ran amok upon returning to his camp at night. He was abusing innocent people, some of whom were already resting in their huts. He set two huts on fire (luckily, no one was injured) and attacked several camp members. Eventually most people fled the camp, thus demonstrating a typical example of the type of conflict avoidance that is much reported among nomadic forager societies (Ichikawa, 1999; Gardner, 1972, 1991, 1999; Turnbull, 1965; Fry, 2007, pp. 173, 184, 185). The next day the camp head called a local "mganga" (healer) of Sukuma origin to cure the man's madness. When we visited this camp a few days later, the man behaved gently and peacefully again, but several other camp members who had fled did not return.

Drinking appears to have produced a dramatic impact on Hadza mentality. Under the influence of alcohol many Hadza have turned into bullies, hostile to outsiders and camp members alike. A drunk can be recognized already at a distance. Normally the Hadza are

TABLE 14.7 **Alcohol and Aggression: Hadza from Mangola (Surroundings of Gorofani) and Gidamilanda Compared**

Place	Sex	Alcohol consumption	Fights (overall percent with injuries)	Fight between spouses (overall percent with injuries)	Hunting nowadays	Big game hunting in the past
Mangola	Men	79.30%	51.0% (17.0% of cases)	36.20% (3.6% of cases)	81.13%	58.5%
(Gorofani)	Women	95.4%	11.3% (3.7% of cases)	3.5% (5.3% of cases)		
Gidamilanda	Men	17%	13.3% (3.3% of cases)	5.0% (0.0% of cases)	93.3%	66.7%
	Women	4.0%	11.54% (0.0% of cases)	9.1% (0.0% of cases)		

gentle; they are not noisy when they talk, joke, and laugh. When drunk, they quarrel, shout, and kick. Interviews conducted in 2011 showed that Hadza injure each other mainly when they are drunk. When fighting, they use their hands, stones, knives, bows and arrows, and burning branches. While taking anthropometric measurements we found that many adult Hadza had burns on the chest, shoulders, hips, and elsewhere. Most of these burns had been inflicted during alcohol-related violence. One-half (51 percent) of adult men from Mangola reported that they had fought at least once during the past year. The rate is about four times higher than for Gidamilanda males. Over the past year, some 17 percent of the Hadza men at Mangola were injured during fighting, compared to 3.3 percent of the men in Gidamilanda. The percentage of Hadza women who reported injuries sustained during fighting was lower in both locations. At Mangola, 3.7 percent of the females reported that they had been injured during fights with other females (in all cases at least one fighter was drunk). Among the Gidamilanda females, no one was injured during fighting (Table 14.7).

Along with the increase of general violence at Mangola, the rate of physical aggression between spouses also has increased (Table 14.7). In most cases, conflicts were exacerbated by inebriation. One or both spouses were heavily drunk and unable to control themselves. One man told me that about three years ago he had gotten drunk and started abusing his wife. As she did not react, he bit off a piece of her ear. The sight of blood sobered him, and he rushed to the bush to collect medical herbs to stop the bleeding. Since that time, as he commented, he has not quarreled with her anymore. I tend to believe him because I have more than once witnessed him being tender to his wife.

As the interviews with married Hadza at Mangola (47 men and 40 women) indicate, 37.5 percent of wives and 36.2 percent of husbands were the objects of violence in disputes with their spouses (with hands, teeth, sticks, bows and arrows, and stones being used in the attacks). Family violence is normally symmetric, and in every third family both spouses were injured (Table 14.7). By contrast, at Gidamilanda (with a sample of 20 husbands and 22 wives), the number of males who reported having fought with their wives was seven times less than at Mangola, and the respective number for females was four times less. No one was injured in those conflicts (Table 14.7).

Family violence patterns among the Hadza differ from those among the Datogas. Datoga males often beat their wives and, as my interviews indicate, the practice is still viewed as a legitimate sanction approved by both sexes. While fights between the Hadza spouses are mostly symmetrical, meaning that wives are able to reciprocate or even are the first to attack, family violence among the Datoga is always asymmetrical, with wives being the only targets of attack (Butovskaya, 2012). Here, too, alcohol is one of the key factors behind male violence. But unlike the situation with the Hadza, the woman's personal ratings regarding physical aggression are reliable predictors of her partner's violence. The number of co-wives is another significant predictor of the frequency and severity of wife battering among the Datoga (Butovskaya, 2012).

Cultural mechanisms of control over violence against women are well-developed in the Datoga because male violence against wives has been a threat to social stability in this culture. Our informants explain that a man who has physically abused his wife must pay a fine (for example, a cow, sheep, goat, or some honey) both to the woman and to her relatives. Our data suggest that the severity of wife battering was the only significant predictor of the amount of the fine to be paid to the in-laws. As in many cultures, a Datoga woman's relatives can protect her rights. The gender asymmetry in power control in Datoga households, then, is limited by cultural norms, providing a certain amount of personal freedom for women.

The impact of ethno-tourism on the social behavior of Datoga pastoralists of Mangola appears to be different than that experienced by the Hadza. Datoga men and women spend the additional money on food, clothes, medicines, and households items rather than on alcohol. Datoga women also have become more independent and can earn their own money by selling souvenirs to ethno-tourists.

Discussion and Conclusions

The data on the Hadza and the Datoga confirm the idea that aggression is a flexible adaptation, not an obligate behavior (Fry, 2007, p. 185). Traditional Hadza may be classified as an egalitarian, tolerant, and autonomous people. They tend to cope with conflicts by avoidance and tolerance, as members of most nomadic forager societies do (e.g., Ju/'hoansi, Efe, Aka, Mbuti, Paliyan, Netsilik, Montagnais-Naskapi) (Ichikawa, 1999; Gardner, 1972, 1991, 1999; Turnbull, 1965; Fry, 2007, pp. 184, 185). In conflict situations, the Hadza, like other nomadic foragers, prefer to retire (Fry, 2007, p. 173), and most men and women have never killed anybody. Blood revenge is not practiced. Under these circumstances, the lack of special conflict resolution techniques and the aggressor's impunity do not endanger social security. As in the past, criticism and ridicule serve as forms of social control (Boehm, 1999, p. 75) and are still efficient unless alcohol is involved. Today alcohol abuse is a serious problem facing the Hadza, as drunks often become violent. Most Hadza enjoy drinking and display little ability to control their alcohol intake, even though most of them know about the ensuing dangers such as injuries and homicide, which have recently risen following the rise of alcohol consumption. Some Hadza comment that if they had been abused by drunken partners or friends they would ignore such incidents the next day because they know that inebriated persons lack of self-control. Although the Hadza, like the Paliyan, do relate violence to alcohol consumption (Gardner, 1972), unlike the Paliyan, the Hadza do not curtail their drinking for that reason.

The Datoga semi-nomadic pastoralists living in the same region are more aggressive than the Hadza. Their attitude toward aggression and the ways they cope with it are different, too. Ridicule and joking are viewed as overt aggression among the Datoga. Individual violence among the Datoga has been restricted by the system of fines and ultimately by ostracizing the habitual aggressors. Violence among Datoga spouses is highly asymmetrical and is virtually always directed against women (Butovskaya, 2012). But husbands are far from being unrestricted in their aggression: efficient mechanisms of control over a husband's violence exist in the form of compensation to be paid to the victim herself as well as to her relatives (Butovskaya, 2012).

Data on Hadza schoolchildren revealed a number of transformations in their aggression and conflict resolution strategies following contacts with their non-Hadza peers. It was more obvious for girls. These newly acquired strategies among the schoolgirls may be gradually spreading within bands once the girls return to the bush, and they may provide an additional possibility of conflict resolution options in addition to avoidance. Hadza school boys demonstrated a higher level of third-party intervention compared to those in the bush, and a higher level of constructive conflict resolution compared to their Datoga peers, although an increase in the frequency of this pattern at school compared to that in the bush did not reach a level of significance. Finally, if alcohol consumption by the Hadza is not limited in the near future, violence may continue to rise. In that case, new conflict management strategies learned through socialization in the multiethnic school environment may become very useful.

Acknowledgments

My thanks go to D. Fry for inviting me to participate in this book and for all his valuable comments and suggestions on an earlier version of this chapter. This study was supported by grants: RFHR, № 08-01-00015e, RFBR № 12-01-00032a, Federal innovation program, № 16.740.11.0172 and the grant from Basic Sciences to Medicine. The field study was approved by the COSTECH of Tanzania. I am especially grateful to my students V. Burkova, D. Dronova, and M. Drambjan for assistance with data collection, as well as to R. Butovsky and D. Karelin for their help in the field, to Prof. A. Mabulla for his cooperation and valuable help over the years, to my field assistant Momoya Merus, and especially to my Hadza friends for their tolerance and cooperation.

References

Archer, J. (2004). Sex differences in aggression in real-world settings: A meta-analysis review. *Review of General Psychology, 8*(4), 291–322.

Archer, J., & Thanzami, V. L. (2007). The relation between physical aggression, size and strength, among a sample of young Indian men. *Personality and Individual Differences 43*(3), 627–633.

Aureli, F., Cords, M., & van Schaik, C. (2002). Conflict resolution following aggression in gregarious animals: A predictive framework. *Animal Behaviour, 63*, 1–19.

Aureli, F., & Smucny, D. (2000). The role of emotion in conflict and conflict resolution. In F. Aureli & F. B. M. de Waal (Eds.), *Natural conflict resolution* (pp. 199–224). Berkeley: University of California Press.

Björkqvist, K. (1994). Sex differences in physical, verbal and indirect aggression: A review of recent research. *Sex Roles 30*(3/4), 177–88.

Björkqvist, K., & Österman, K. (1998). *Scales for research on interpersonal aggression.* Vasa, Finland: Åbo Akademi University.

Blurton Jones, N. G., Hawkes, K., & O'Connell, J. (2002). Antiquity of postreproductive life: Are there modern impacts on hunter-gatherer reproductive life span? *American Journal of Human Biology, 14*, 184–205.

Blurton Jones, N. G., Smith, L. C., O'Connell, J. F., Hawkes, K., & Kamuzora, C. L. (1992). Demography of the Hadza: An increasing and high density population of savanna foragers. *American Journal of Physical Anthropology, 89*(2), 159–181.

Boehm, C. (1999). *Hierarchy in the forest.* Cambridge, MA: Harvard University Press.

Borgerhoff Mulder, M. (1992). Demography of pastoralists: Preliminary data on the Datoga of Tanzania. *Human Ecology, 20*, 383–405.

Buss, D. M., & Duntley, J. D. (2006). The evolution of aggression. In M. Schaller, D. T. Kenrick, & J. A. Simpson (Eds.), *Evolution and social psychology* (pp. 263–86). New York: Psychology Press.

Butovskaya, M. L. (2001). Reconciliation after conflicts: Ethological analysis of post-conflict interactions in Kalmyk children. In J. M. Ramirez, & D. R. Richardson (Eds.), *Cross-cultural approaches to aggression and reconciliation* (pp. 167–190). Huntington, NY: Nova Science.

Butovskaya, M. L. (2008). Reconciliation, dominance and cortisol levels in children and adolescents (7–15-year-old boys). *Behaviour, 145*, 1557–1576.

Butovskaya, M. L. (2011). Reproductive Success and Economic Status among the Datoga—Semi-Sedentary Pastoralists of Northern Tanzania. *Ethnographic Review, 4*, 85–99.

Butovskaya, M. L. (2012). Wife-battering and traditional methods of its control in contemporary Datoga Pastoralists of Tanzania. *Journal of Aggression, Conflict, and Peace Research, 4*, 28–44.

Butovskaya, M. L., Boyko, E. J., Selverova, N. B. & Ermakova, I. V. (2005). The hormonal basis of reconciliation in humans. *Journal of Physiological Anthropology, Applied Human Sciences, 24*, 333–337.

Butovskaya, M. L., Burkova, V. N., & Mabulla, A. (2010). Sex differences in 2D:4D ratio, aggression and conflict resolution in African children and adolescents: A cross-cultural study. *Journal of Aggression, Conflict and Peace Research, 2*(1), 17–31.

Butovskaya, M. L., & Demianovich, A. N. (2002). Social competence and behavior evaluation (SCBE-30) and socialization values (SVQ): Russian children ages 3 to 6 years. *Early Education and Development, 13*(2), 153–170.

Butovskaya, M. L., & Kozintsev, A. G. (1999). Aggression, friendship, and reconciliation in Russian primary schoolchildren. *Aggressive Behavior, 25*, 125–139.

Butovskaya, M. L., & Mabulla, A. (2008). Processes of social transformation among the Hadza of Northern Tanzania (Materials of complex anthropological study). In A. P. Bujilova (Ed.), *Interdisciplinary investigations in archaeology* (pp. 121–140). Moscow: Paralleli Press.

Butovskaya, M. L., Timentschik, V., & Burkova, V. (2007). Aggression, conflict resolution, popularity, and attitude to school in Russian adolescents. *Aggressive Behavior 33*(2), 170–183.

Butovskaya, M. L., Verbeek, P., Ljungberg, T. & Lunardini, A. (2000). Multicultural view of peacemaking among young children. In F. Aureli & F. B. M. de Waal (Eds.), *Natural conflict resolution* (pp. 423–450). Berkeley: University of California Press.

Chagnon, N. A. (1979). Is reproductive success equal in egalitarian societies? In N. A. Chagnon & W. Irons (Eds.), *Evolutionary biology and human social behavior: An anthropological perspective* (pp. 374–401). North Scituate, MA: Duxbury.

Cords, M., & Aureli, F. (2000). Reconciliation and relationship qualities. In F. Aureli & F. B. M. de Waal (Eds.), *Natural conflict resolution* (pp. 177–198). Berkeley: University of California Press.

Craig, I. W., & Halton, K. E. (2009). Genetics of human aggressive behaviour. *Human Genetics, 126*(1), 101–113.

Daly, M., & Wilson, M. (1988). *Homicide.* New York: Aldine de Gruyter.

Daly, M., & Wilson, M. (2001). Risk-taking, intrasexual competition, and homicide. In J. A. French, A. C. Kamil, & D. W. Leger (Eds.), *Evolutionary psychology and motivation* (pp. 1–36). Lincoln: University of Nebraska Press.

de Waal, F. B. M. (2000). Primates—a natural heritage of conflict resolution. *Science, 289*, 586–590.

Fujisawa, K., Kutsukake, N. & Hasegawa, T. (2005). Reconciliation pattern after aggression among Japanese preschool children. *Aggressive Behavior, 31*, 138–152.

Fujisawa, K., Kutsukake, N. & Hasegawa, T. (2006). Peacemaking and consolation in Japanese preschoolers witnessing peer aggression. *Journal of Comparative Psychology, 120*, 48–57.

Fry, D. P. (2007). *Beyond war: The human potential for peace.* Oxford: Oxford University Press.

Fry, D. P. (2011). Human nature: The nomadic forager model. In R. W. Sussman, & C. R. Cloninger (Eds.), *Origins of altruism and cooperation* (pp. 227–247). New York: Springer.

Geary, D. C. (1998). *Male, female: The evolution of human sex differences.* Washington, DC: American Psychological Association.

Hines, N. J., & Fry, D. P. (1994). Indirect modes of aggression among women of Buenos Aires, Argentina. *Sex Roles, 30,* 213–236.

Holmberg, A. (1969). *Nomads of the long bow: The Siriono of Eastern Bolivia.* New York: American Museum of Natural History.

Ichikawa, M. (1999). The Mbuti of Northern Congo. In R. B. Lee & R. Daly (Eds.), *The Cambridge encyclopedia of hunters and gatherers* (pp. 210–214). Cambridge: Cambridge University Press.

Gardner, P. M. (1972). The Paliyans. In M. C. Bicchieri (Ed.), *Hunters and gatherers today: A socioeconomic study of eleven such cultures in twentieth century* (pp. 404–450). New York: Holt, Rinehart & Winston.

Gardner, P. M. (1991). Forager's pursuit of individual autonomy. *Current Anthropology, 32*(5), 543–572.

Gardner, P. M. (1999). The Paliyan. In R. B. Lee & R. Daly (Eds.). *The Cambridge encyclopedia of hunters and gatherers* (pp. 261–264). Cambridge: Cambridge University Press.

Knight, G. P., Guthrie, I. K., Page, M. C., & Fabes, R. A. (2002). Emotional arousal and gender differences in aggression: A meta-analysis. *Aggressive Behavior, 28*(5), 366–393.

Knauft, B. (1991). Violence and sociality in human evolution. *Current Anthropology 32*(4), 391–428.

LaFreniere, P., Masataka, N., Chen, Q., Dessen, M., Atwanger, K., Butovskaya, M. L., Schreiner, S., Montirosso, R., & Frigerio, A. (2002). Cross-cultural analysis of social competence and behavior problems in preschoolers. *Early Education and Development, 13*(20), 201–220.

Ljungberg, T., Horowitz, L., Jansson, L., Westlund, K., & Clarke, C. (2005). Communicative actors, conflict progression, and use of reconciliatory strategies in pre-school boys—a series of random events or a sequential process? *Aggressive Behavior, 31,* 303–323.

Ljungberg, T., Westlund, K., & Lindqvist Forsberg, A. J. (1999). Conflict resolution in 5-year- old boys: Does post-conflict friendly, prosocial behaviour have a reconciliatory role? *Animal Behaviour 58,* 1007–1016.

Marlowe, F. (2002). Why Hadza are still hunters-gatherers. In S. Kent (Ed.), *Ethnicity, hunter gatherers and the other: Association or assimilation in Africa* (pp. 247–275). Washington: Smithsonian Institution Press.

Marlowe, F. (2004). Mate preferences among Hadza hunter-gatherers, *Human Nature 15(4),* 365–376.

Marlowe, F. (2005). Hunter-gatherers and human evolution. *Evolutionary Anthropology 14,* 54–67.

Marlowe, F. (2010). *The Hadza: Hunter-gatherers of Tanzania.* Berkeley: University of California Press.

Miles, D. R., & Carey, G. (1997). Genetic and environmental architecture of human aggression. *Journal of Personality and Social Psychology, 72*(1), 207–217.

Owens, L. R., Shute, R., & Slee, P. (2000). "Guess what I just heard!": Indirect aggression among teenage girls in Australia. *Aggressive Behavior, 26,* 67–83.

Peters, J. F. (1998). *Life among the Yanomami.* Peterborough, ON: Broadview Press.

Rhee, S. H., Waldman, I. D. (2002). Genetic and environmental influences on antisocial behavior: A meta-analysis of twin and adoption studies. *Psychology of Bulling, 128,* 490–529.

Shostak, M. (1981). *Nisa: The life and words of a !Kung woman.* New York: Vintage Books.

Turnbull, C. M. (1965). The Mbuti Pygmies of the Congo. In J. Gibbs (Ed.), *Peoples of Africa* (pp. 279–318). New York: Holt, Rinehart & Winston.

Verbeek, P., de Waal, F. B. M. (2001). Peacemaking among preschool children. *Journal of Peace Psychology, 7,* 5–28.

Verbeek, P., Hartup, W. W., & Collins, W. A. (2000). Conflict resolution in children and adolescents. In F. Aureli & F. B. M. de Waal (Eds.), *Natural conflict resolution* (pp. 34–54). Berkeley: University of California Press.

Werner, N. E., & Crick, N. R. (1999). Relational aggression and social psychological adjustment in a college sample. *Journal of Abnormal Psychology, 108,* 615–623.

Woodburn, J. (1964). *The social organization of the Hadza of north Tanganyika.* (Unpublished doctoral dissertation, Cambridge University).

Woodburn, J. (1977). The East African click languages: A phonetic comparison. In A. Tucher (Ed.), *Zur sprachgeschichte und ethnohistorie in Afrika* (pp. 300–323). Berlin: Reimer Verlag.

Woodburn, J. (1979). Minimal politics: The political organization of the Hadza of North Tanzania. In W. A. Shack, & P. S. Cohen (Eds.), *Politics in leadership* (pp. 244–266). Oxford: Clarendon Press.

Woodburn, J. (1982). Egalitarian societies. *Man, 17,* 431–451.

Woodburn, J. (1988). African hunter-gatherer social organization: Is it best understood as a product of encapsulation? In T. Ingold, T. D. Riches, & J. Woodburn (Eds.), *Hunters and gatherers v.1: History, evolution and social change* (pp. 43–64). Oxford: St. Martin's Press.

Woodburn, J. (1998). Sharing is not a form of exchange: An analysis of property sharing in immediate-return hunter-gatherer societies. In C. M. Hanned (Ed.), *Property relations: Renewing the anthropological tradition* (pp. 48–63). Cambridge: Cambridge University Press.

15

South Indian Foragers' Conflict Management in Comparative Perspective

PETER M. GARDNER

Eighteen different foraging peoples were among the so-called "hill tribes" that once inhabited the scattered, forested ranges in India's four southernmost states. Although a few are near neighbors to one another, the overall picture is one of dispersal across a region that is both extensive and diverse. It extends about 900 km from north to south and it varies from virtual rainforest in certain coastal ranges facing the Arabian Sea on the west to open stands of dry, thorny growth in the lower hills facing the great eastern plain. Some foragers even dwell now on the plain. Despite substantial differences of flora and fauna among their habitats, divergence of their Dravidian languages and dialects, and local variation in the contact they have had with other tribal peoples and the ancient culture of the plains, there are notable similarities in how they have managed to deal with conflict traditionally. This may come as a surprise to those who have read about some of these long-separated cultures and who have come to think of them in terms of features that made each account distinctive.

Cultures of 6 of the 18 cultures have been described sufficiently well to be included in this comparison. Starting with the less-acculturated southernmost foragers and moving north, the respectful, plural forms of terms they use for themselves are Malapandaram, Paliyar, Kadar, Kattunayaka/Jenu Kurumba/Jenu Kuruba (treated by those who study them as one and the same peoples), Yanadi, and Chenchu.

All have experienced great culture change during the past century. Yet government-sponsored surveys published between 1909 and the 1940s and professional ethnographic research from 1940 onward provide us with a clear picture of both the previous social values held by these forest peoples and the repertory of techniques they once employed when faced with interpersonal difficulties. Readers familiar with accounts of

Paliyar conflict management (Gardner, 1966, 1985, 2000a, 2000b, 2004, 2010; Norström, 1999, 2001, 2003) may be interested to learn that, scattered as they have long been, the foragers covered in this chapter exhibit a region-wide style—and it is a style that is the precise opposite of the authoritarian one that dominates the surrounding, largely Hindu society.

Most of the specifics to be taken up here under the headings "Social Values" and "Techniques for Managing Conflict" are, of course, not unique to South India's foragers, or even to foragers in general. At the end of the chapter, for the sake of perspective, comparative notes will be provided on foragers elsewhere and pertinent theoretical works.

Social Values

Although we have had diverse cultural and social anthropological training—in different eras and in a variety of scholarly traditions—we ethnographers speak with one voice as to the significance of a cluster of related values that help shape how South India's foragers deal with interpersonal conflict. There are three key values, each having to do with a different facet of individualism, these being pursuit of independence, self-reliance, and equality.

Independence

The idea that people ought to be independent or autonomous in their decision-making has been shown to be universal to our sample of South Indian foragers. In the approximate chronological order of the initial field studies, this value was reported for Chenchu (Fürer-Haimendorf, 1943), Kadar (Ehrenfels, 1952), Yanadi (Raghaviah, 1962; Rao, 2002), Paliyar (Gardner, 1966; Norström, 1999, 2001), Kattunayaka/Jenu Kuruba (Bird-David, 1987; Misra, 1969), and Malapandaram (Morris, 1982). As the matter was put in an early ethnography, "The Chenchu is a child of nature and through every vein of his body runs the instinct to follow his own inclinations. Even his hours of leisure emanate that same spirit of independence, individualism and spontaneity which characterizes his more serious activities" (Fürer-Haimendorf, 1943, p. 237). And Ehrenfels (1952, p. 127) argues that the seeming "laxity" of Kadar, rather than being indicative of recent disintegration, is a sign of "persistence" of "the typical aboriginal love for freedom."

In four instances, it was specified that even young children should be treated thus, these cultures being Chenchu (Fürer-Haimendorf, 1943), Yanadi (Rao, 2002), Paliyar (Gardner, 1966; Norström, 2001), and Malapandaram (Morris, 1982). Two quotations should convey the idea adequately. Morris described achievement of independence by Malapandaram children thus, "By the age of five or six, a Hill Pandaram child acts almost as if he were an independent person. . . . Children are treated as autonomous individuals, and are not taught, or expected to obey their elders" (1982, pp. 146–147). As for school-age Yanadi children, they "attend school when they feel like and cannot be coerced by their parents" (Rao, 2002, p. 95).

Self-Reliance

Placing a premium on individuals being self-reliant or self-sufficient in their routines is reported to be important to Chenchu (Fürer-Haimendorf, 1943), Paliyar (Gardner, 1966; Norström, 1999), Malapandaram (Morris, 1982), and Kattunayaka/Jenu Kurumba (Bird-David, 1983; Demmer, 1997). And, it is hard not to conclude that this value also underlies the Kadar "love for freedom" and the readiness of individuals of both sexes to move at will (Ehrenfels, 1952, p. 127). Again, let me offer two examples, the first about adult Kattunayaka: "When asked why he did not borrow from his brother some wood which he could return the very next day Maran answered that if he did so people would laugh at him, saying he was not a 'person' if he could not collect his own firewood" (Bird-David, 1983, p. 78). As for Paliyar, after protracted observational study of a number of families, I described the very early age at which self-reliance is first witnessed among them thus: "The child's attempts at . . . self-reliance are reinforced by adult expectations and lack of supervision. A 2 or 3 year old child may play . . . with [machete-like] bill hooks without supervision from adult relatives who are present, and a 5 year old may climb unwatched to the top of a tree [or start] a fire . . . for cooking" (Gardner, 1966, p. 392).

A contributing factor to a child's development of self-reliance may be its social learning. It is well-documented that Chenchu, Paliyar, Malapandaram, and Kattunayaka children get almost no verbal lessons from parents, because learning even critical subsistence tasks is left largely up to them. In culture after culture, they master procedures both by what are initially playful imitations of the actions of parents and older children and by trial and error (Bird-David, 1983; Fürer-Haimendorf, 1943; Gardner, 1972, 2000b; Morris, 1982; Naveh, 2007; Norström, 2003). Achieving understanding is altogether another matter. It depends on children drawing inferences privately, inferences that will not routinely be challenged or corroborated by others. The resulting meanings and understandings will be more personal and idiosyncratic than most anthropological models acknowledge. Naveh (2007, pp. 90–91) has gone into the matter of interpersonally variable knowledge and learning in some depth, ". . . there is no essentialistic way to set up, say, a pig trap; however Chenan's way . . . can be observed and known *while* being with him when he is setting up such a trap. Karian's way . . . may be quite different. . . ." And, "adult men refrained from actively instructing Suresh2 [Naveh's label] and his friend Balan in their attempts to construct traps" (2007, p. 93).

Equality

Equality is reported to be important to Chenchu (Fürer-Haimendorf, 1943), Kadar (Ehrenfels, 1952), Paliyar (Gardner, 1966, 1972), Malapandaram (Morris, 1982), and Kattunayaka/Jenu Kurumba (Bird-David, 1988, 1996, 1999; Demmer, 1996, 2004). And there is at least "an element of equality" within Yanadi households (Rao, 2002, p. 126). This is one subject about which Paliyar occasionally voice an explicit standard. To use their wording, one must avoid *tarakkoravaa*, which means literally, "to lower or diminish [another person] in level," in other words, to put them down or be disrespectful (Gardner, 2000b, p. 85). It is a general admonition that covers both gender and age equality. Ehrenfels, besides referring to, "the economic and customary equality of the sexes," made a similar point to the Paliyar one, that Kadar are "sensitive to overbearing, assuming or condescending behaviour" (1952, pp. 133, 140). As for specifics on the other cultures, Fürer-Haimendorf said that, "the equality of status of husband and wife is strongly emphasized" (1943, p. 107), and Demmer reported that, "they have a marked egalitarian understanding of themselves" (1996, p. 191). Young children are explicitly said to have rights equal to others in some of the cultures. Morris has made this observation on Malapandaram, "Over the age of about eight all members of a . . . community treat each other more or less as equals" (1982, p. 151). And I have written this of Paliyar, "Everyone merits equal respect by virtue of being a person. While infants and young children have not yet begun making decisions or handling power, let it at least be understood that even nonrelatives will step in if needed to guarantee their right to respect and protection" (Gardner, 2000b, pp. 85–87).

Techniques for Managing Conflict

The impact of these values on conflict management is that they define in firm and absolute terms what kinds of response to conflict are socially acceptable and unacceptable. Most importantly, they specify that no one has legitimate power over any other person, not even elders over youths, parents over their own children, or one spouse over the other. They leave room only for an acephalous or anarchic social system in the original Greek sense, namely, a group without a chief or head.

How is it, then, that we ethnographers *all* encountered talk of headmen when we began our fieldwork with these South Indian foragers? Looking at the overall set of beliefs and the actual social practices, most of us eventually concluded that such talk had to be explained as a culture contact phenomenon. Jenu Kuruba told Misra that they had a headman, yet there was a lack of agreement as to both who occupied the position and what such a person did. Misra concluded that they "might have taken the term from the neighbouring people but have not been able to fit it in their own system" (1969, p. 206). Others of us had similar experiences and drew the same conclusion. Over a century ago, the Maharaja of Cochin appointed a Kadar headman to administer the tribe. While Kadar themselves seek to appear "civilized" in the eyes of plains dwellers they encounter, not so much as a semblance of this leadership could be seen in 1947, when Ehrenfels began his research (1952). Administrators and police are said to have attempted to appoint Malapandaram and Yanadi as headmen in order to "control" their communities (Morris, 1982; Raghaviah, 1962), yet actual control was not achieved. Finally, traders such as Forestry officials or forest produce contractors and their agents have informally named cooperative Paliyar, Kattunayaka, Chenchu, and Malapandaram as headmen to facilitate extraction of forest goods (Bird-David, 1999; Fürer-Haimendorf, 1943; Gardner, 1972, 2000a; Morris, 1982). The fact remains, nonetheless, that while the latter appointees had been picked because they had the amiability and skills needed to coax a few of their fellows to join a work party, it was only in the Chenchu case that doing such coordinating had afforded these foremen slight financial advantages, prestige, or a degree of power within their own communities. Although Fürer-Haimendorf used the word "authority" more than once to describe their power, when it came to his case studies of inheritance and dispute resolution, he made it amply clear that no one had the right to such a position and all that the so-called "head-men" could achieve was modest influence at best (1943; see also Ehrenfels, 1952). In the eyes of their fellows, they lacked authority in the sense of *legitimate* power. Near the other end of the rather short power continuum, the one to three Paliyar who served thus as fore-men in any particular group were often moved to clown or put on a special show of humil-ity in order to cope with the position's mere appearance of inequality. Despite decades of outsiders tinkering with all these foragers' social systems, not a single person could claim a mandate to give orders within his or her band or community at the time when we did our studies. Behaving in such a manner could simply not be reconciled with fundamental social values.

Culture-by-culture, the review of techniques used in managing conflict reveals a degree of variation in the lists. Close examination of the data suggests that this is due mainly to certain techniques being absent or unreported, rather than being the product of divergent alternatives. What the cultures definitely do share is what the ethnographers generally highlight as the most basic technique: self-restraint.

Self-Restraint

There are several ways of exhibiting self-restraint, practiced alone or in combination. Three of them are especially important: separation, silence, and tolerance. First, people will walk away from those who threaten or offend them. They will leave for minutes, months, or as long as it takes either for the threat to subside or for their own anger to dissipate. Over minor matters, just turning away may suffice. As illustrated in Figure 15.1, in the face of murder or threatened violence by outsiders, separation can last several years.

Although data suggest that Chenchu and Yanadi when feeling disrespected may be a bit more prone than the other South Indian foragers to confront or to attack their antagonist in anger (Fürer-Haimendorf, 1943; Raghaviah, 1962), offended individuals in those two cultures, as well as in the other cultures we are reviewing, tend routinely to pull back from disrespect. The mode of documentation varies. Rather than generalizing about Chenchu practices, Fürer-Haimendorf (1943) offers a number of their life stories that illus-trate married couples and others separating quickly over jealousy or disagreements. Misra (1970) and Bird-David (1995), by contrast, generalize about withdrawal from conflict by Jenu Kuruba/Kattunayaka without going into specifics. In the cases of Kadar and Yanadi, we have both case descriptions and overviews. First, Ananthakrishna Iyer (1909, p. 21) told us of Kadar that "when any harsh words are used, they simply move away from one place to another. One forest to them is as good as another." Then Ehrenfels (1952) provided us with a number of Kadar life stories that illustrate couples and others separating quickly

FIGURE 15.1 Paliyans may sleep in a different place each night when fleeing violent outsiders. I met up with this
elusive sub-band only by traveling with a friend of theirs.

over jealousy or disagreements. Between the two of them, Raghaviah and Rao dealt with
the Yanadi approach similarly. Raghaviah said, "If you are angry with the Yanadi, he simply turns his face away and keeps himself out of your sight for a while until your temper
cools down and you yourself invite him for a talk" (1962, p. 224). And he provided us
with Yanadi life histories that illustrated this (1962). Rao saw the overall picture much as
Raghaviah had (1983). Fürer-Haimendorf and Morris report that Malapandaram separate
over conflict (Fürer-Haimendorf, 1960; Morris, 1982), but Morris goes on to say correctly
that they are mobile for other reasons, such as subsistence, as well (1982). Finally, Paliyar
are said to separate in response to conflict (Gardner, 1969, 1985; Norström, 2003) and
systematic study of all of my documented cases of Paliyar managing disrespect revealed
that 52 % of the time moving away was the immediate or eventual response of the offended
party (Gardner, 2004). And this would be a yet higher percentage if we took into account
instances in which the response was merely turning away—a functional equivalent of actual
departure. Furthermore, grandmothers or other available adults have been seen carrying or
leading off Paliyar children who are too young to be able to walk away from misbehaving
parents on their own (Gardner, 2000a). Such rescue has been witnessed too when bystanders realized that a woman had become so agitated by her husband that she had lost sight
of the needs of the baby that she carried; women rushed to her side anxiously and, always
with the mother's cooperation, gently took over care of the little one (Gardner, 2004). It
is a consistent picture.

    Second, there is silence. People in three of the cultures tend to refrain from discuss-
ing a past or present threat, injury, or personal offense. Even less likely are suggestions,

criticism, and ridicule—the sorts of domineering talk that they hear incessantly from outsiders. Indeed, repeated discussion of the demeanors of others is what has made one elderly Paliyar peripheral to his community; he seemed never to learn that his loud pointed commentaries were deemed by all others to be offensive and alienating. Paliyar who sense that they have been treated with disrespect generally hold back from any verbal rejoinder, any gesture such as a shaken fist, or any appeal to nearby relatives or neighbors at the time of the incident (Gardner, 2000b). In my experience, the only clue that there had been trouble was often the sight of Paliyar walking away from others without a word. As witnesses who are not directly involved tend also to hold back from discussing inappropriate behavior, how does an anthropologist learn the facts? I discovered quickly that children who have yet to develop mature restraint often take delight in talking about a drama they have just seen; overhearing their chatter often informed me just well enough to make it possible for me to approach one of the more forthcoming adults and discretely elicit a bit more detail (2004). Bird-David describes a general lack of gossip amongst the Kattunayaka (1994). And Demmer, who is concerned with angry talk, reports that Jenu Kurumba view openly articulated anger as a threat and "neither side wants those emotions and nobody admits having such bad emotions. Instead, everybody is rather concerned with denying those feelings" (2001, p. 487). This, naturally, dampens conversation. He gives the impression that rhetoric and argument take place mainly in their rituals. It must be admitted nonetheless that, on occasion, extreme distress can push injured parties in these cultures over a threshold, their restraint giving way to a long, agonized or angry outburst, perhaps with tears. If this does eventuate, it will generally go unanswered.

Third, the foragers throughout the region are *said* in our ethnographies to put up with irregular behavior such as incest, murder, and theft by their fellows. Is this believable? Could they really dismiss such problems by saying, "it is not my business"? In order to put our ethnographic reports in perspective, we have to realize three things: that the foragers expect to see individual behavioral differences, that kinship violations should not be appraised from an outsider's viewpoint, and that some irregular behavior is primarily a concern of the deities.

It has been said of Chenchu, whether in economic activities or recreation, each is "an individualist who likes to follow the trend of his own inclinations" (Fürer-Haimendorf, 1943, p. 266); Yanadi create innovative art as an aspect of their "extreme individualism" (Raghaviah, 1962, p. 404); and Paliyar are said to "foster individuality," use novel, playfully figurative speech in many contexts (Gardner, 2000b, p. 177), and express delight when their fellows cultivate individual postures and steps in circle dances while keeping time to the common beat.

In every culture under discussion the foragers have had long-term contact with Dravidian speaking outsiders, whose so-called Dravidian kinship system entails preferential cross-cousin marriage. Those outsiders not only classify sexual relations or marriage with parallel cousins (or parallel sibling's child) as virtually incestuous, they find it beyond belief that their forest neighbors would view such unions differently. Thus, they tend to be quick to condemn seemingly deviant tribal marriages they become aware of (Gardner, 1988). Outsiders are vocal about other prescriptions too, that husbands be senior to wives, that polyandry is irregular, and so on. Anthropologists would be wise to keep this acculturation pressure from the plainsmen in mind as we try to interpret remarks about foragers' supposed "irregularities." Although the foragers half-heartedly and inexpertly affect the standard South Indian kinship in contact situations, to protect themselves from humiliating criticism, this does not mean that any but the most acculturated take the priorities of plains dwellers seriously. So, reports that Chenchu, Jenu Kuruba, Paliyar, and Malapandaram "condone" or "tolerate" unions their neighbors regard as improper (Fürer-Haimendorf, 1943; Misra, 1970; Gardner, 2000a; Morris, 1982) are of no help whatsoever in establishing what the foragers themselves consider to be acceptable behavior.

Given the deities' concern with human behavioral propriety, it would be important to ascertain what it means to say that humans are tolerant. We might begin with a list of what the forest deities punish. The precise list varies slightly, but in all the cultures being examined people say that their deities punish by illness or death offenses on the order of incest, theft, murder, taboo violation, or neglect in making offerings (Bird-David, 1996; Ehrenfels, 1952; Fürer-Haimendorf, 1943; Gardner, 1995; Morris, 1981; Rao, 1983, 2002). We must, of course, recognize differing cultural definitions of incest. It is co-habiting in "permanent liaisons and not merely . . . casual sexual encounters" between primary relatives that is deemed irregular by Malapandaram (Morris, 1981, p. 209). And Paliyar not only have a 12% incidence of marriage with stepsons or stepdaughters, but such unions are above criticism and some individuals state a preference for them because of their durability (Gardner, 1972, 2009). This institution is found amongst Malapandaram, too, and what appear to be individual instances of such marriages have been recorded amongst Kadar and Jenu Kuruba, as well (Ehrenfels, 1952; Misra, 1970; Morris, 1982). Whatever the cultural definitions of incest are, with deities said to be monitoring what people define as lapses, surely human intervention is simply not called for. Saying "it is not my business" might be a brief way of saying "this is a matter for the deities, not me, to handle." We should not lose sight of that. Apart from irrelevant violations of rules that underlie the kinship system of their neighbors, we find the following. In our ethnographic accounts, occasional jealous accusations and verbal or mild physical abuse (e.g., a slap) of husband or wife in response to actual or suspected extramarital sex were reported among all but the Malapandaram (Bird-David, 1987; Ehrenfels, 1952; Fürer-Haimendorf, 1943; Gardner, 2000a; Misra, 1969; Raghaviah, 1962; Rao, 2002); the distress is usually said to have been brief, not lasting. What foragers themselves call incest can occur. I knew personally a Paliyar case of mother-son sex leading to pregnancy (Gardner, 2000b), and there were alleged cases of father-daughter and brother-sister incest among Malapandaram (Fürer-Haimendorf, 1960; Morris, 1982). As for divine punishment, the young Paliyan man who initiated the incest just mentioned suffered for weeks from disabling boils on his legs, these being widely interpreted as a response of one of the deities. Returning to the question as to whether people really are tolerating or condoning irregular behavior, let us reexamine the earlier quotation, "it is not my business." It was an elderly Paliyar who first told me this, calmly and with a smile, after his young wife had brought home a yet younger lover, creating a polyandrous household. As he did not grit his teeth and say, "the gods will get them," he surely exhibited greater forbearance than we would expect from most husbands on this planet.

Two aids to self-restraint were seen amongst Paliyar. First, people feeling really agitated rubbed blossoms of a ubiquitous leguminous flower on their foreheads, for what they described as its tranquilizing effect. Second, they refrained from drinking alcohol that could be obtained quite readily from co-workers in plantations. They believed realistically that it would undermine their efforts to maintain self-control.

Conciliation

It is only in the southernmost cultures that there is positive evidence of conflict being eased by conciliators. Such specialists may go unnoted elsewhere, because their position is informal and voluntary, and it is only infrequently that one sees them participating in easing a difficult situation. Because it is skillful use of wit or diplomacy that allows them to step forward in this role and effectively replace tense faces with smiles, Paliyar sometimes describe them as "people with good heads." This makes the outsiders' term "headman" an apt label (Gardner, 1972, 2000b) and it is irrelevant to Paliyar that the very same term may be used for foremen. After all, it is surely skilled people with good heads who are able to coordinate work parties in a good-natured, non-authoritarian way. Either way, those who occupy either position lack authority of any sort within their own community, no matter what those who hire the foremen believe. Norström (2003) also makes brief reference to conciliators easing relations amongst Paliyar, and Morris (1982) does the same for Malapandaram, whose disputes are "often" handled thus.

Calling the Deities

The deities live in another realm, but there is no question that they are imminent, that they are deeply concerned with the behavior of those they often refer to as their "grandchildren," and that the deceased usually end up in the same realm where they dwell. The foragers have frequent direct contact with deities by means of (a) what tend to be night-time shamanistic sessions to deal with illness and misfortune (Bird-David, 1996; Demmer, 2007; Gardner, 1991a; Morris, 1982; Rao, 1983); (b) offerings to them after hunts, when honey collecting, or at first fruit ceremonies (Ehrenfels, 1952; Demmer, 1997; Fürer-Haimendorf, 1943, 1960; Gardner, 2000b); and (c) propitiation of them at somewhat Hinduized daylong communal festivals at which every family may have to be represented (Bird-David, 1996; Ehrenfels, 1952; Gardner, 1991a). Whether it is ancestral spirits, nature deities, or locally important Hindu deities who are called by their shamans, in culture after culture people ask for diagnoses of illness, explanations of illness and death, and protection or relief from other problems, such as predators, lack of rain, or social difficulties. During interchanges they have with these deities, people usually have to deal with the deities' anger over neglect of the usual offerings, breaches of social norms, or violations of taboos. Sometimes there is a complex problem, such as improper behavior that has led to a magical attack and consequent illness. Deities have the power to ascertain causes and rectify such problems, but this almost always necessitates humans promising to be more careful in their social lives and more attentive to providing the deity with its customary offerings. In all of the cultures except that of the Chenchu, there is direct, oral communication. Chenchu achieve some of the same ends by first using divination to learn which deity has caused an illness, and then by promising offerings if the patient recovers (Fürer-Haimendorf, 1943). Some of us documented specific instances in which domestic quarrels, lack of appropriate sharing within the group, contact with outsiders leading to adoption of their practices, and simple disregarding of customary practices have been identified by the deities as causes for concern (Bird-David, 1996; Gardner, 1991a; Morris, 1982; Rao, 1983). These make it apparent that achieving direct contact with the deities can justifiably be listed as one of the techniques for managing social problems. It may be of interest to comparative scholars that shamans among the Yanadi and Jenu Kurumba are not just possessed by the deities, as in the other cultures being reviewed, but the shamans' spirits make journeys to the land of the deities in the same way that spirits of circumpolar and Onge shamans do (Pandya, 1993).

Community Gathering

A rarely used and possibly new way of responding to conflict is an assembly of community members, or *kuttam*. If it is indeed a new institution, it may be an egalitarian version of the Indian panchayat, or council of elders. To my knowledge, assemblies of this sort have only been documented amongst Yanadi and Paliyar (Gardner, 2004; Rao, 2002), unless we consider the clan meeting of the Chenchu as a functional equivalent (Fürer-Haimendorf, 1943). Unlike the Indian panchayats, these assemblies have no authority to make decisions, but, after watching one of them review a dispute in 2001, I agree with Fürer-Haimendorf that they may serve as a means by which the principal parties can weigh public opinion and make personal decisions on whether or not to back down. That would, of course, be fully in keeping with the tribal values.

Weighing the Success of Their Efforts

One measure of success of south Indian foragers in their quest for a respectful society is the absence of homicide. Fürer-Haimendorf wrote that, "no case of [Chenchu] murder or manslaughter has occurred on this side of the Kistna [River] within the memory of the present generation" (1943, p. 169). Kadar knew only of cases of murder or violent revenge in the towns of the outside world, but none, even in distant bands, within their own society (Ehrenfels, 1952). Those who have had intimate long-term relations with Paliyar, such as a teacher, an aging forestry officer, an experienced forest produce contractor, and I, are in agreement that murder is absent among them (Gardner, 2004). And Morris says of Malapandaram, "murder seems to be unknown in their society" (1981, p. 209). Given the general respect for others that is central to their sets of values, and given their techniques for managing conflict, it seems that foragers in the south Indian forests achieve an extraordinarily peaceful anarchy, one in which people are able to head off any escalation of conflict.

Except for Chenchu, who acquired muzzle-loaders in the 1870s and, for a few years, exacted tribute from pilgrims they escorted to forest temples (Thurston & Rangachari, 1909), these foragers uniformly retreat from others rather than confronting them. War is totally beyond the pale for them. And, in recent times, all but the Yanadi and Chenchu lack bows and arrows.

Yet, a big question remains. Is there surreptitious revenge? I interviewed a few Paliyar men about their dreams and most reported instructive fantasies. One prominent type entailed the dreamer flying over the heads of certain men (notably over individuals I myself had come to see as unusually capable). Another type involved the dreamer enjoying a revenge affair with the wife of a man who had previously had a liaison with the dreamer's wife (Gardner, 2000b). They commonly laughed with telling discomfort after recounting these.

If there are latent stresses, and surely we would expect them, is there more than fantasy revenge going on? The south Indian foragers live in precisely the kind of society that Whiting (1950) and Swanson (1960) had in mind when they tested cross-cultural samples to see whether people in societies that lacked authorities and superordinate social punishment tended to deal with conflict by resort to sorcery. Both found significant positive associations.

It is common to hear the foragers' neighbors talking of sorcery in the hills, with Kurumba, especially, being feared as practitioners (Dubois, 1906; Rivers, 1906). Almost certainly as a result of the sensitivity of this subject, most ethnographies lack much detail. Ehrenfels merely mentions the beliefs of outsiders regarding Kadar sorcery and seems not to have any Kadar sources (1952), Raghaviah says sorcery is "widely believed in" by Yanadi (1962, p. 379), and it is only Fürer-Haimendorf, Demmer, and I who have provided any real specifics. Fürer-Haimendorf heard of several recent deaths that were interpreted to be the result of sorcery (1943). I found it easy to elicit details of two techniques Paliyar know, then heard allegations of two contemporary sorcery attacks plus a case of a person beseeching a deity to strike a community with an epidemic (2000b). And Demmer wrote that *all* Jenu Kurumba deaths are viewed as probable results of sorcery, people even attributing a snakebite death to that cause (1999). Directly relevant to the subject of this paper, Demmer's impressive, word-by-word transcript of an entire shamanistic session makes it clear that social and moral conflicts underlie these Jenu Kurumba magical attacks. As he puts it, "the social dimension is of paramount importance" (2007, p. 32). The sequence of social conflict leading in turn to sorcery, a snakebite, a death, then a diagnostic séance that revealed the original conflict, has brought us right back to the idea that calling the deities is a mechanism for managing conflict. It is important to point out that, unlike what happened in premodern Europe and Africa, sorcerers in tribal South India do not themselves face retribution. We see no angry finger pointing. A conversation with the deities and a promise to do better close the matter.

There is enough sharing of values and conflict management techniques in our accounts of South Indian foragers that we can talk *at most* of variation of a theme. Surprisingly, we ethnographers, with training from the 1930s to the 2000s, in Vienna, Philadelphia, London, Lucknow, Cambridge, Stockholm, Heidelberg, and Haifa, and having different topical interests, have been able to achieve near consensus about the basic social life of scattered South Indian foragers we have studied. That speaks to the veracity of our accounts. Although those we studied cope with challenges without benefit of authorities, strict socialization, or a well-defined set of rules, they manage as individuals to achieve a workable and unusually peaceful life amongst themselves. There are few cultures on this planet in which children can expect comparable respect and protection. As loose as their various social systems may be, to say merely "they manage" must be viewed as a gross understatement.

Comparative Notes

Worldwide ethnographic and theoretical research is useful in giving us an overall perspective on the conflict management of South Indian foragers.

Ethnographic Parallels

Le Clercq (1910, pp. 242–243) wrote that Mi'kmaq in Eastern Quebec, "hold it as a maxim that each one is free: that one can do whatsoever he wishes: and that it is not sensible to put constraint upon men" and "they let every one do as he pleases, ... the fathers and the mothers do not dare to contradict their children, but permit their misbehaviour. ..." We get similar accounts from across the North American Subarctic. A 1913 study of northern Athapaskans closed thus, "Individualism seems to be the keynote to the interpretation of this culture. The individual is ... coerced by no authority" (Mason, 1946, p. 43). Social life in the region was also labeled "atomistic" (Hallowell, 1946; Honigmann, 1946, 1949). Dehcho Dene, Dene K'e, and Dene Tha (once known collectively by the pejorative exonym, "Slave"), especially, have sets of values and conflict management techniques that correspond closely to those found in South India. There is general agreement that they value individual autonomy, self-reliance, or responsibility for one's own life (Gardner, 1976; Goulet, 1998; Helm, 1961; Honigmann, 1946;); Helm described equality between spouses and work mates (1961); and I found that they pursue and reward individuality (Gardner, 2006). Instead of relying on authorities, they employ self-restraint when difficulties arise. They walk away from those who behave unacceptably (Gardner, 2006; Helm, 1961; Honigmann, 1946;). They are as taciturn as Paliyar, for they pass neighbors and relatives without saying anything, enter one another's houses silently, and even refrain from interrupting a former speaker's deliberate silence (Christian & Gardner, 1977; Gardner, 1976, 2006; Helm, 1961; Honigmann, 1946). Finally, they tolerate irregular behavior and they fear the actions of those adept at handling "power"—their version of sorcery (Helm, 1961; Honigmann, 1946).

The shellfish gathering Yamana of southern Tierra del Fuego live in a social world shaped by personal independence, small self-reliant families, and general equality. They, too, are a near-silent people who avoid gossip, offer one another conciliation when there is friction, and expect their deity to punish misbehavior. During their initiation rites, elders teach young men the value of behaving peacefully. When a killing does occur, they allow regulated revenge by a kinsman, but that closes the matter (Gusinde, 1961 [1937 orig.]).

There are numerous other partial parallels around the world. Bleek said of !Kung in Angola, "Chiefs are non-existent, but deference is paid to the patriarch of any small group, though his authority is very limited" (1928, p. 109). Later ethnographers of the Kalahari San generally concur with this and eventually provide much more detail (Lee, 1982). They exhibit tolerance, for example (Lee, 1979; Marshall, 1960; Schapera, 1930). Birket-Smith (1929, p. 260) found that Caribou Inuit, "know no government. Here . . . is a society which is entirely built up on that voluntary agreement of which Kropotkin dreamt . . . everyone enjoys full individual freedom." Some Inuit also practice highly regulated revenge. In addition, there are several cultures for which there is good documentation of children learning largely by observation and self-reliance, such as Ngatatjara, Gwich'in, Dehcho Dene, Dene Tha, and Aka; they closely echo what we saw in South India (Christian & Gardner, 1977; Gardner, 1976, 2002; Gould, 1968, 1969; Goulet, 1998; Helm, 1961; Hewlett, 1991; Hewlett & Cavalli-Sforza, 1986; Nelson, 1973). There is no question that many of the traits we have been examining are functionally related to one another. Building a culture around valuing the individual puts distinct limits on how social problems can be dealt with and this, in turn, limits the overall shape of the system. Nonetheless, contrasting practices such as walking away from problems and taking carefully limited revenge certainly illustrate that there are workable options. Although Goulet might disagree (1998), most subarctic ethnographers would find another striking contrast, between the positive social atmosphere of a South Indian camp and the more guarded or suspicious tone of interaction in a subarctic settlement.

Theoretical Contributions

For 75 years anthropologists have been theorizing about the nature and variation of Holocene foragers. We have produced: (a) global generalizations about them, (b) diverse simple typologies, most based on just one or two hypothesized causal factors, and (c) complex, relatively open approaches to the nature and causes of their variation. Each of these has some relevance to questions raised by the South Indian materials.

In a rigorous cross-cultural comparative study using a large sample, Barry, Child, and Bacon (1959) showed that both sexes in hunting and fishing cultures (having low accumulation of food resources), when compared with children in cultures with animal husbandry, are under much higher socialization pressure for self-reliance. In an informal overview, Service (1966) characterized all the well-studied non-sedentary foragers as being nomadic, having simple material culture, small communities, vague group boundaries, domestic families as the only consistent face-to-face groups, and a lack of specialized economic, political, or religious institutions. Lee and DeVore (1968) agreed with Service's first three points and added that foragers are egalitarian, flexible in response to variable resources, unconcerned about food resources, and able to use individual mobility in place of authorities to resolve conflict. Leacock and Lee (1982, pp. 7–8) repeated several of these same points and added strong anti-authoritarianism; "cooperation in conjunction with great respect for individuality;" permissive child-rearing practices; retreat from conflict; and use of humor, talk, and ritualization in dealing with antagonisms. Finally, Foley (1988) contended that, by contrast with Pleistocene big game hunters, recent foragers responded to newly warmed environments and loss of megafauna by increased use of plant foods, equal involvement of both sexes in the food quest, development of small and flexible bands, and egalitarianism. Despite overlap among these findings and the degree to which they reflect South Indian foragers' independence, self-reliance, equality, respect for individuality, and use of mobility in response to conflict, we must not draw premature conclusions, because foragers are actually far more diverse than suggested by any of these statements.

Three of the several simple typologies addressed the contact circumstances we find in South India. (1) Hickerson (1960) held that invasive settlers cause social fragmentation and individualism among Subarctic foragers and, using a world sample, Service (1962) claimed that it also causes depopulation, relocation, and social disorganization in place of orderly patrilocal residence. At face value these look relevant, but are we not finding coherent systems rather than chaos and social collapse? (2) Involvement in a market economy is said to lead to emphasis on the nuclear family, individual decision-making, and nomadism (Bose, 1956; Fox, 1969; Kroeber, 1928; Leacock, 1954; Steward, 1936, 1955). This is plausible. (3) There is a set of varied interdisciplinary theories, holding that enclaved, subordinated peoples respond to intercultural pressure by withdrawal, aloofness, individualism, egalitarianism, and non-violence (Gardner, 1966; Gillin, 1942; James, 1961; Miller & Dollard, 1941; Scott, 2009). These remain untested.

In the 1990s new questions were being asked in review articles and conference papers. Recent wisdom is that foragers, as well as the factors that help shape them, are highly diverse (Burch, 1994; Feit, 1994; Kelly, 1995). My own examination of 12 theories about supposed individualism, egalitarianism, and flexibility of foragers supported this (Gardner, 1991b). It also revealed two things. First, most of the theories' main arguments complement rather than contradict one another. They are not really rival theories. Because our theorists made a collective case for many economic, social, conflict-handling, and intellectual variables being causally interrelated in a web-like fashion, many aspects of such cultural systems might be joint products of several factors working together. Second, using what Murdock (1981) deemed to be the "best described" foraging culture from each of the world's 37 cultural provinces having foragers, according to his coding of traits, 9 were both individualistic and egalitarian, 9 were only egalitarian, 2 were only individualistic, and the remaining 17 were neither (Gardner, 1991b). Use of rigorous sampling promises us more constrained, more valid generalizations than did the simple typologies that focus overly on cultures with which the authors are most familiar.

Closing Thoughts

Although South Indian foragers resemble certain foragers elsewhere, especially those in the North American Subarctic, they stand out nevertheless for the extreme effectiveness with which they manage conflict. They also share much with one another, raising the possibility that they represent scattered instances of one and the same culture. I would say that this is unlikely for two reasons. First, most of them have long been some distance apart. Some Malapandaram do intermarry with southern Paliyar (Morris, 1982), and Yanadi have a tradition of having once been Chenchu. Even so, these particular pairs exhibit antipathy toward one another, as do southern and northern Paliyar. In most instances most have been isolated from one another for centuries, if not millennia, by farming peoples on the intervening plains. Additionally, they have their own identities, they speak different languages or dialects, and they also have some notable cultural differences. For instance, in five of the cultures for which we have good data on principles for distributing the meat of large game animals, these differ strikingly.

It is possible to speak more decisively about degrees of similarity than about reasons for them. Questions as to why they have similar ways of keeping the peace may be just as difficult to answer at this time as questions about why many Algonkian and Athapaskan speakers in North America's Subarctic have such similarities across thousands of kilometers, or why northern Athapaskans and Navajo have comparable resemblances, despite more than a millennium of separation.

References

Ananthakrishna Iyer, L. K. (1909). *The Cochin tribes and castes* (I). Madras: Higginbotham.

Barry, H., Child, I. L., & Bacon, M. K. (1959). Relation of child training to subsistence economy. *American Anthropologist, 61*, 51–63.

Bird-David, N. (1983). Wage gathering: Socio-economic changes and the case of the food-gatherer Naikens of South India. In P. Robb (Ed.), *Rural South Asia: Linkages, change and development* (pp. 57–88). London: Curzon Press.

Bird-David, N. (1987). Single persons and social cohesion in a hunter-gatherer society. In P. Hockings (Ed.), *Dimensions of social life: Essays in honor of David Mandelbaum* (pp. 151–165). Berlin and New York: Mouton de Gruyter.

Bird-David, N. (1988). Hunter-gatherers and other people: A re-examination. In T. Ingold, D. Riches, & J. Woodburn (Eds.), *Hunters and gatherers 1: History, evolution and social change* (pp. 17–30). Oxford: Berg.

Bird-David, N. (1994). Sociality and immediacy: Or, past and present conversations on bands. *Man (N.S.), 29*, 583–603.

Bird-David, N. (1995). Hunter-gatherers' kinship organization: Implicit roles and rules. In E. N. Goody (Ed.), *Social intelligence and interaction: Expressions and implications of the social bias in human intelligence* (pp. 68–84). Cambridge: Cambridge University Press.

Bird-David, N. (1996). Puja or sharing with the gods?: On ritualized possession among Nayaka of South India. *The Eastern Anthropologist, 49* (3–4), 259–276.

Bird-David, N. (1999). Animism revisited: Personhood, environment, and relational epistemology. *Current Anthropology, 40*, supplement 67–91.

Birket-Smith, K. (1929). *The Caribou Eskimos: Material and social life and their cultural position* (Thule Expedition, Report 5). Copenhagen: Gyldendalske Boghandel.

Bleek, D. F. (1928). Bushmen of Central Angola. *Bantu Studies, 3,* 105–125.

Bose, N. K. (1956). Some observations on nomadic castes of India. *Man in India, 36* (1), 1–6.

Burch, E. S. Jr. (1994). The future of hunter-gatherer research. In E. S. Burch, Jr. & L. J. Ellanna (Eds.), *Key issues in hunter-gatherer research* (pp. 441–455). Oxford: Berg.

Christian, J. M. & Gardner, P. M. (1977). *The individual in Northern Dene thought and communication: A study in sharing and diversity* (Canadian Ethnology Series, paper 35). Ottawa: National Museums of Canada.

Demmer, U. (1996). *Verwandschaft und sozialität bei den Jenu Kurumba: Vom arbeiten, vom teilen und von (un) gleichheit in einer Südindischen sammler-und jägergesellschaft.* Stuttgart: Franz Steiner Verlag.

Demmer, U. (1997). Voices in the forest: The field of gathering among the Jenu Kurumba. In P. Hockings (Ed.), *Blue mountains revisited: Cultural studies on the Nilgiri Hills* (pp. 164–191). Delhi: Oxford University Press.

Demmer, U. (1999). How to make the spirit of the dead happy. In E. Schömbucher & C. P. Zoller (Eds.), *Ways of dying: Death and its meaning in South Asia* (pp. 68–87). Delhi: Manohar.

Demmer, U. (2001). Always an argument: Persuasive tools in the death rituals of the Jenu Kurumba. *Anthropos, 96,* 475–490.

Demmer, U. (2004). Visual knowledge: A test case from South India. *Visual Anthropology, 17* (2), 107–116.

Demmer, U. (2007). The power of rhetoric: Dialogue and dynamic persuasion in healing rituals of a South Indian community. In U. Demmer & M. Gaenszle (Eds.), *The power of discourse in ritual performance* (pp. 26–53). London: LIT.

Dubois, J. A. (1906). *Hindu manners, customs and ceremonies* (3rd ed.). Oxford: The Clarendon Press.

Ehrenfels, U. R. (1952). *Kadar of Cochin.* Madras: University of Madras.

Foley, R. (1988). Hominids, humans and hunter-gatherers: An evolutionary perspective. In T. Ingold, D. Riches, & J. Woodburn (Eds.), *Hunters and gatherers 1: History, evolution and social change* (pp. 207–221). Oxford: Berg.

Fox, R. G. (1969). "Professional primitives": Hunters and gatherers of nuclear South Asia. *Man in India, 49* (2), 139–160.

Fürer-Haimendorf, C. von (1943). *The Chenchus: Jungle folk of the Deccan.* London: Macmillan.

Fürer-Haimendorf, C. von (1960). Notes on the Malapantaram of Travancore. *Bulletin of the International Committee on Urgent Anthropological and Ethnological Research, 3,* 45–51.

Gardner, P. M. (1966). Symmetric respect and memorate knowledge: The structure and ecology of individualistic culture. *Southwestern Journal of Anthropology, 22* (4), 389–415.

Gardner, P. M. (1969). Paliyan social structure. In D. Damas (Ed.), *Contributions to Anthropology: Band societies* (National Museums of Canada, Bulletin 228) (pp. 153–67). Ottawa: National Museums of Canada.

Gardner, P. M. (1972). The Paliyans. In M. G. Bicchieri (Ed.), *Hunters and gatherers today: A socioeconomic study of eleven such cultures in the twentieth century* (pp. 404–447). New York: Holt, Rinehart & Winston.

Gardner, P. M. (1976). Birds, words, and a requiem for the omniscient informant. *American Ethnologist, 3,* (3), 446–468.

Gardner, P. M. (1985). Bicultural oscillation as a long-term adaptation to cultural frontiers: Cases and questions. *Human Ecology 13,* 411–432.

Gardner, P. M. (1988). Pressures for Tamil propriety in Paliyan social organization. In T. Ingold, D. Riches, & J. Woodburn (Eds.), *Hunters and gatherers 1: History, evolution and social change* (pp. 91–106). Oxford: Berg.

Gardner, P. M. (1991a). Pragmatic meanings of possession in Paliyan shamanism. *Anthropos, 86,* 367–384.

Gardner, P. M. (1991b). Foragers' pursuit of individual autonomy. *Current Anthropology, 32* (5), 543–572.

Gardner, P. M. (1995). Illness and response among South Indian foragers. *Medical Anthropology, 16,* 119–139.

Gardner, P. M. (2000a). Respect and nonviolence among recently sedentary Paliyan foragers. *Journal of the Royal Anthropological Institute 6,* (2), 217–236.

Gardner, P. M. (2000b). *Bicultural versatility as a frontier adaptation among Paliyan foragers of South India.* Lewiston, N. Y.: Edwin Mellen Press.

Gardner, P. M. (2004). Respect for all: The Paliyans of South India. In G. Kemp & D. P. Fry (Eds.), *Keeping the peace: Conflict resolution and peaceful societies around the world* (pp. 53–71). New York: Routledge.

Gardner, P. M. (2006). *Journeys to the edge: In the footsteps of an anthropologist.* Columbia: University of Missouri Press.

Gardner, P. M. (2009). Quasi-incestuous Paliyan marriage in comparative perspective. *The Open Anthropology Journal, 2,* 48–57.

Gardner, P. M. (2010). How can a society eliminate killing? In J. Evans Pim (Ed.), *Nonkilling societies* (pp. 185–194). Honolulu: Center for Global Nonkilling.

Gillen, J. (1942). Acquired drives in culture contact. *American Anthropologist, 44* (4), 545–554.

Gould, R. A. (1968). Chipping stones in the outback. *Natural History, 77* (2), 42–49.

Gould, R. A. (1969). *Yiwara: Foragers of the Australian desert.* New York: Charles Scribner's Sons.

Goulet, J-G. A. (1998). *Ways of knowing: Experience, knowledge, and power among the Dene Tha.* Lincoln: University of Nebraska Press.

Gusinde, M. (1961). *The Yamana: The life and thought of the water nomads of Cape Horn* (transl. of 1937 German ed. by F. Schütze). New Haven: Human Relations Area Files.

Hallowell, A. I. (1946). Some psychological characteristics of the northeastern Indians. In F. Johnson (Ed.), *Man in Northeastern North America* (Papers of the R. S. Peabody Foundation for Archaeology, No. 3) (pp. 195–225). Andover: Phillips Academy.

Helm, J. (1961). *The Lynx Point people: The dynamics of a Northern Athapaskan band* (National Museum of Canada, Bulletin 176). Ottawa: Dept. of Northern Affairs and Natural Resources.

Hewlett, B. S. (1991). *Intimate fathers: The nature and context of Aka Pygmy paternal infant care.* Ann Arbor: University of Michigan Press.

Hewlett, B. S., & Cavalli-Sforza, L. L. (1986). Cultural transmission among Aka Pygmies. *American Anthropologist, 88,* 922–934.

Hickerson, H. (1960). The feast of the dead among the seventeenth-century Algonkians of the upper Great Lakes. *American Anthropologist, 62,* 81–107.

Honigmann, J. J. (1946). *Ethnography and acculturation of the Fort Nelson Slave* (Yale University Publications in Anthropology, No. 33). New Haven: Yale University Press.

Honigmann, J. J. (1949). *Culture and ethos of Kaska society* (Yale University Publications in Anthropology, No. 40). New Haven: Yale University Press.

James, B. J. (1961). Social-psychological dimensions of Ojibwa acculturation. *American Anthropologist, 63,* 721–746.

Kelly, R. L. (1995). *The foraging spectrum: Diversity in hunter-gatherer lifeways.* Washington: Smithsonian Institution Press.

Kroeber, A. L. (1928). *Peoples of the Philippines* (revised ed.). New York: American Museum of Natural History.

Leacock, E. (1954). *The Montagnais "hunting territory" and the fur trade* (American Anthropological Association Memoir 78).

Leacock, E. & Lee, R. (1982). Introduction. In E. Leacock & R. Lee (Eds.), *Politics and history in band societies* (pp. 1–20). Cambridge: Cambridge University Press.

Le Clercq, C. (1910). *New relation of Gaspesia: With the customs and religion of the Gaspesian Indians* (transl. of 1691 French ed. by W. F. Ganong). Toronto: The Champlain Society.

Lee, R. (1979). *The !Kung San: Men, women, and work in a foraging society.* Cambridge: Cambridge University Press.

Lee, R. (1982). Politics, sexual and non-sexual, in an egalitarian society. In E. Leacock & R. Lee (Eds.), *Politics and history in band societies* (pp. 37–59). Cambridge: Cambridge University Press.

Lee, R. B. & DeVore, I. (1968). Problems in the study of hunters and gatherers. In R. B. Lee & I. DeVore (Eds.), *Man the hunter* (pp. 3–12). Chicago: Aldine.

Marshall, L. (1960). !Kung Bushman bands. *Africa, 30* (4), 325–355.

Mason, J. A. (1946). *Notes on the Indians of the Great Slave Lake area* (Yale University Publications in Anthropology, No. 34). New Haven: Yale University Press.

Miller, N. E. & Dollard, J. (1941). *Social learning and imitation.* New Haven: Yale University.

Misra, P. K. (1969). *The Jenu Kuruba* (Bulletin 18, 3). Calcutta: Anthropological Survey of India.

Misra, P. K. (1970). Economic development among Jenu Kurubas. *Man in India, 50* (1), 78–86.

Morris, B. (1981). Hill gods and ecstatic cults: Notes on the religion of a hunting and gathering people. *Man in India, 61* (3), 203–236.

Morris, B. (1982). *Forest traders: A socio-economic study of the Hill Pandaram.* London: Athlone Press.

Murdock, G. P. (1981). *Atlas of world cultures.* Pittsburgh: University of Pittsburgh Press.

Naveh, D. (2007). *Continuity and change in Nayaka epistemology and subsistence economy: A hunter-gatherer case from South India* (unpublished doctoral dissertation, Haifa University, Haifa).

Nelson, R. K. (1973). *Hunters of the northern forest: Designs for survival among the Alaskan Kutchin.* Chicago: University of Chicago Press.

Norström, C. (1999). Increasing competition, expanding strategies—Wage work and resource utilization among the Paliyans of South India. In T. Granfelt (Ed.), *Managing the globalized environment: Local strategies to secure livelihoods* (pp. 66–87). London: IT Publications.

Norström, C. (2001). Autonomy by default versus popular participation: The Paliyans of South India and the proposed Palni Hills sanctuary. In I. Keen & T. Yamada (Eds.), *Identity and gender in hunting and gathering societies* (pp. 27–51). Osaka: National Museum of Ethnology.

Norström, C. (2003). *"They call for us": Strategies for securing autonomy among the Paliyans, hunter-gatherers of the Palni Hills, South India* (Stockholm Studies in Social Anthropology, 53). Stockholm: Stockholm University.

Pandya, V. (1993). *Above the forest: A study of the Andamanese ethnoanemology, cosmology, and the power of ritual.* Delhi: Oxford University Press.

Raghaviah, V. (1962). *The Yanadis.* New Delhi: Bharatiya Adimjati Sevak Sangh.

Rao, N. S. (1983). Rangam of the Yanadi of Sriharikota. *The Eastern Anthropologist, 36* (3), 223–235.

Rao, N. S. (2002). *Ethnography of a nomadic tribe: A study of Yanadi.* New Delhi: Concept Publishing Company.

Rivers, W. H. R. (1906). *The Todas.* London: Macmillan.

Schapera, I. (1930). *The Khoisan peoples of South Africa: Bushmen and Hottentots.* London: George Routledge.

Scott, J. C. (2009). *The art of not being governed: An anarchist history of Upland Southeast Asia.* New Haven: Yale University Press.

Service, E. R. (1962). *Primitive social organization: An evolutionary perspective.* New York: Random House.

Service, E. R. (1966). *The hunters.* Englewood Cliffs: Prentice-Hall.

Steward, J. H. (1936). The economic and social basis of primitive bands. In R. H. Lowie (Ed.), *Essays in anthropology presented to A. L. Kroeber* (pp. 331–350). Berkeley: University of California Press.

Steward, J. H. (1955). *Theory of culture change.* Urbana: University of Illinois Press.

Swanson, G. (1960). *The birth of the gods; The origin of primitive beliefs.* Ann Arbor: University of Michigan Press.

Thurston, E. & Rangachari, K. (1909). *Castes and tribes of Southern India* (2), Madras: Government Press.

Whiting, B. B. (1950). *Paiute sorcery.* New York: Viking Fund Publications in Anthropology.

16

The Biocultural Evolution of Conflict Resolution Between Groups

Christopher Boehm

Introduction

Moralistic "social control" serves primarily as a means by which human groups try to protect themselves from social deviants (Black, 2011). At the same time, coming down hard on deviants serves as a general damper on the social conflicts that always arise within human groups (Boehm, 1982), while such conflicts also are reduced by direct attempts at mediation (Fry, 2000). Both conflict and active conflict management are universal within human groups, including hunter-gatherer bands.

Here, in an evolutionary framework, I will link conflict and conflict management within groups to the same pair of behaviors when they take place between groups. This analysis will require dealing with a large evolutionary picture, which at the level of phylogenetics involves behavioral preadaptations and at the level of culture and psychology involves people making generalizations that allow predictable, highly routinized peacemaking *within* groups to serve as a generalizable model for the less predictable conflict management that takes place *between* groups.

As evolutionary background I begin by focusing on human hunter-gatherers and on chimpanzees and bonobos, the two African great apes with whom we share the greatest amount of DNA, to see what these three species are capable of in matters related to intergroup conflict and its management, and social control. After isolating some relevant social-sanctioning behaviors that were likely in our shared ancestor, a larger question to be asked will be: how could becoming moral have changed us, in our species' potential for both external conflict and external peacemaking?

Rules for Behavioral Reconstruction

A basic assumption is that evolutionary processes are sufficiently "conservative" (see Wrangham, 1987) that highly probable ancestral reconstructions are possible with respect to certain major patterns of social behavior. Thus, "behavioral phylogenetics" (Brosnan, 2006) enables us to look at living clades like African great apes (e.g., Wrangham & Peterson, 1996) to see if certain behaviors are shared within the living clade and therefore are very likely—given the parsimony with which evolutionary processes work—to relate to a shared ancestor. On this basis, I shall briefly discuss several primitive behavior patterns as likely preadaptations, not only for today's moralized social control and conflict resolution, but also for the shameful consciences that humans have uniquely evolved (see Boehm, 2012a).

Our specific interest will be in reconstructing, as of 5 to 7 MYA, some political propensities of Ancestral *Pan* (defined in Boehm, 2004)—the ape from which today's bonobos, chimpanzees, and humans are descended (see Ruvolo, Disotell, Allard, Brown, & Honeycutt, 1991). The parsimony principle is statistical, and the larger the clade the more secure the reconstructive analysis. Because here we are dealing with a rather small clade, I will take the additional, conservative measure of using only least common denominators in the behavioral reconstructions that follow.

Ancestral Antecedents for Conflict and Peacemaking

Ancestral *Pan* was essentially given to hierarchy. Chimpanzees and even bonobos are distinctly hierarchical, and while nomadic human foragers behave antihierarchically and do so to great effect, they have to work hard to maintain their egalitarian orders in the face of would-be alpha bullies, while later human societies like primitive kingdoms in fact can become very hierarchical, indeed (Boehm, 1999). Thus, Ancestral *Pan* surely was quite hierarchical (see Knauft, 1991), with an alpha-male system, and this strong *potential* for hierarchy development has continued all the way down the line for humans (Boehm, 1999) even though it is so variably expressed.

In conservatively reconstructing Ancestral *Pan's* degree of xenophobia and intergroup aggression, bonobos will be the limiting factor. In human hunter-gatherers and chimpanzees the males are known to collaborate in attacking members of neighboring communities, and they sometimes eliminate such groups (e.g., Burch, 2005; Goodall, 1986). However, male bonobos do not approach being so ferocious. Indeed, often enough two bonobo groups may meet and intermingle with sexual contact—even though often the males of the groups may carefully stay apart (see Furuichi, 2011; Kano, 1992; de Waal & Lanting, 1997). However, when foraging parties from less friendly bonobo communities meet, there are definite signs of xenophobic territoriality: both parties will vocalize hostilely, as larger parties chase away less sizable ones, or much smaller parties may simply go silent and retreat. In this context Kano (1992) reports seeing a member of his study group wounded after a noisy confrontation between two sizable parties.

By the conservative reconstruction rules I am using here, we must say that Ancestral *Pan* was only as prone to intergroup conflict as is seen at the bonobo level, which would preclude patrols and the surprise-attack, lethal raiding type of "warfare" practiced by chimpanzees and some human foragers. However, within their groups humans and chimpanzees, and also bonobos, readily fight, and many of the scars bonobos bear likely come from serious fighting (de Waal & Lanting, 1997). It is this readiness to do combat that enables the bonobo females to form effective alliances and, in feeding contexts, to successfully challenge the supremacy of the larger males—who do not form such alliances (Furiuchi, 2011; deWaal & Lanting 1997).

Was there ancestral peacemaking? Within the group, wild and captive chimpanzee alpha males routinely become active and sometimes quite forceful as third-party peacemakers (Boehm, 1994; de Waal, 1996), while similar behaviors are reported but much more rarely for wild bonobos (Kano, 1992). In being egalitarian, hunter-gatherers suppress any strong development of the alpha-male role, so such power-based interventions are rare—but humans do have third-party mediators who serve as verbally persuasive peacemakers (Fry, 2000). In addition, in all three species dyadic reconciliations take place without third-party assistance (e.g., Fry, 2000; de Waal, 1996), so ancestral tendencies to make peace within the group were prominent and they were expressed both triadically and dyadically.

Did such conflict-management tendencies extend to conflicts between different territorial communities? There is no sign of this in the two apes, but some human foragers, when they fight or raid, call truces as certain Inuit do (e.g., Burch, 2005), or they can ceremonially resolve intercommunity feuds as in the Andamans (Sarkar, 1990; Lebar, 1972; Radcliffe-Brown, 1933). Thus active *intergroup* peacemaking would appear to be a derived behavior, developed only by humans, and later we will examine some of the ethnographic details for mobile hunter-gatherers.

Overall, this behavioral-phylogenetic approach will permit the coming evolutionary arguments to be based on homology, and hence will allow us to identify some important preadaptations (Mayr, 1983). In a nutshell, the conservative historical starting point is a markedly hierarchical, moderately territorial Ancestral *Pan* that was capable of wounding and likely killing other members of the same group, and actively tried to damp or reconcile such conflicts, while all it experienced in tense intergroup skirmishes were possible male-male woundings,[1] and it had no mechanism for peacemaking at the intergroup level.

Antecedents for Gaining Power Through Social Control

We now turn to a primitive (ancestral) type of "social control" by groups, which involved the use or threat of force by subordinate coalitions to sometimes counter the actions of those who individually outranked them. We begin this reconstruction by assessing human foragers. As egalitarians, economically independent, nomadic human hunter-gatherer band members practice moralistic social control that involves ostracism, shaming, banishment, or capital punishment (Boehm, 2000), and a major focus of all this sanctioning is to cut down would-be "alpha males" —individuals who would usurp the egalitarian orders that are so predictably enforced in such societies (Boehm, 1999, 2012b).

Foraging bands do this routinely and often, and the chief target for capital punishment is a male who tries to intimidate or boss his peers (Boehm, 1993; Erdal & Whiten, 1994). Similarly, bonobos form female coalitions, which in feeding contexts routinely level the power between themselves and the physically stronger males; in one instance, a sizable female coalition gang-attacked a resented male so strongly that he was badly wounded and was never seen again (Parker, 2007). Wild chimpanzees occasionally form still larger coalitions (male or male-and-female) that attack disliked former or incumbent alpha males, and either the male disappears (e.g., Goodall, 1992; Nishida, 1996) or he is killed (Ladd, 2011), while in captivity the females routinely form powerful coalitions that prevent an alpha male from brutalizing females as is his wont (de Waal, 1996). Only with humans, however, does a reversal of the direction of dominance become so definitive, among adult males, that subordinate coalitions actually gain ascendancy. This is done moralistically, with the help of capital punishment (Boehm, 1993).

In all three species such conflictive "sharing of power" takes place predictably, and on this basis Ancestral *Pan* would have had at least a nonmoral version of antihierarchical group "social control." This involved strategic use of coalitional power to curb strongly disliked dominance behaviors, and it is very likely that at least occasionally such sanctioning would have become lethal. Because warfare involves the lethal use of coalitional power, this can be seen as a likely preadaptation for warfare as human groups practice it (see Boehm & Flack 2010), particularly since Ancestral *Pan* had at least some moderate territorial tendencies.

Antecedents for Moral Behavior

In humans both intergroup conflict and intergroup peacemaking have important moral components, but Ancestral *Pan* was not moral (Boehm, 1999). In becoming "moralized," ancestral tendencies to xenophobia have been transformed into ethnocentrism, which combines a visceral, fearful dislike of culturally-different outgroupers with colorful cultural elaboration and predictable moral disdain (LeVine & Campbell 1972). This moral dimension is important—especially as it developed in conjunction with symbolic language; indeed, ethnic strangers sometimes become so culturally demonized that they are viewed as being no better than animals—while predictably they are at least seen as being culturally different and therefore morally inferior. One effect of ethnocentrism is that enemies can be killed with very little compunction because moral rules about killing "people" do not fully apply (see also Sober & Wilson 1998).

In and of itself, human morality has some important ancestral precursors or building blocks, including the empathy, self-recognition, and perspective taking (Flack & de Waal 2000) which could have helped along the evolution of a moralistic conscience (see also Boehm, 2008, 2012b). Our conscience is not primitive but derived, for by no means do chimpanzees or bonobos internalize group "rules," or exhibit a sense of shame that is coupled with blushing (Boehm, 2012b). Basically, the social order in their groups is based merely in hierarchical relations of dominance and submission (Goodall, 1982; see also Boehm & Flack, 2010)—and hence just upon power that engenders fear reactions.

How different does a conscience make us? Bonobos and chimpanzees do at least impose predictable "rules" on others—both as individuals and sometimes as groups— which means that as individuals they respond fearfully to the "rules" of others. The same is true of humans. And if we define the evolutionary conscience (see Alexander, 1987) mainly in terms of psychological functions that involve sophisticated social strategizing and self-inhibition, this fear component also continues in punishment-aversive humans today. What makes us so different is a unique, blushing sense of shame (see Boehm, 2012b) that couples with our *internalization* of rules (Gintis, 2003)—in the sense that one *identifies* emotionally and positively with the same rules that one must cope with and submit to. There is no very apparent precursor in Ancestral *Pan* for either of these developments, and as will be seen they brought some important ramifications for the issue of human war and peace, for both activities have moral as well as political dimensions.

Hunting as a Preadaptation for Conspecific Killing

We cannot say that Ancestral *Pan* hunted collectively or in a well-coordinated way as groups, for basically bonobos seem to hunt solo. But when dangerous power-scavenging and later pursuit hunting became part of the human repertoire (see Stiner, 2002) we may assume that there was some combination of teamwork and likely some personal self-endangerment in the acquisition of sizable mammals (see Kelly, 1995). This cooperation, along with the exposure to danger and the explicit objective of killing, would seem to articulate quite easily into "raiding" or "warfare" patterns, while an accompanying "merit system" might have stimulated and prestigiously rewarded both types of behavior.

Weapons, and Understanding of Death

When Levine and Campbell published *Ethnocentrism* in 1972, this landmark cross-cultural study showed that as a species humans have a strong, morally-mediated sense of in-versus-out group; we have already discussed the consequences for intergroup conflict. The underlying *xenophobia* (see Holloway, 1974), and with it the negative social discount that is applied to out-groupers, goes back 5 to 7 MYA. This reaction to members of other groups makes them much easier to kill when conflicts arise.

Another major difference is weapons (see also Wrangham & Glowacki, 2012), which humans use in combat and chimpanzees and bonobos do not. For at least 400,000 years thrusting or projectile weapons designed to kill animal prey at a safe distance (e.g., Thieme, 1997) have enabled human foragers to kill other humans without grappling dangerously at close quarters, and as hunters they always have such weapons at the ready—whether they practice intergroup killing or not—and they are skilled in their use. Such weapons are used routinely to riskily kill sizable and sometimes quite dangerous mammals, which obviously could include a fellow human being who is armed.

Another difference is that humans understand the act of killing in its finality. It is true that chimpanzees (Goodall, 1986) or even probably bonobos (Parker, 2007) may wound an individual to death, but they appear not to "understand" death in terms of administering an efficient *coup de grace*—an instinctual behavior that they, unlike full social carnivores like lions, have not evolved (Verbeek, chapter 4). Humans, by contrast, do understand in some practical way the finality involved, and we have strong moral rules against killing within the group. An understanding of death not only makes unrestrained lethal attacks against other groups more efficient; this same understanding also makes the potentially dire consequences of intergroup violence fully comprehensible to group members, as a matter of ultimate loss.

Thus, even as hunter-gatherers worry about conflicts within the group turning homicidal, they also understand the risks in making lethal attacks on neighbors (Fry & Szala, chapter 23). As will be seen, in spite of predictable and well-reckoned costs over half of the foraging societies surveyed do engage in armed, lethal intergroup conflict. At the same time, however, a similar number of these societies engage in peacemaking activities that reduce combat's economic and energetic costs—and also reduce casualties due to wounding or death.

Balance of Power

When two sizable chimpanzee patrols at Gombe sight one another in no man's land they vocalize aggressively or else one slinks away, depending on the numbers involved. Two groups of approximately equal size will simply reach a standoff and, after displaying, mutually retreat (Wrangham, 1999; see also Boehm, 1991; Goodall, 1986), but a sizable patrol spotting a lone enemy attacks. When hostile bonobo foraging parties meet at a frontier, they vocalize antagonistically and if one party is smaller it withdraws first (Kano, 1992), while much smaller parties may just withdraw silently (Furuichi, 2011). So far, at the intergroup level no observed or probable lethal attacks have been reported.

Wilson and Wrangham (2003) suggest that such apes are capable of accurately assessing the relative strengths of their own and competing groups, and field experiments have born this out for chimpanzees. Indeed, chimpanzees will not attack their neighbors unless they have overwhelming numerical superiority (Wilson, chapter 18).

In contrast, the potential for full battlefield warfare, putting all the males of both groups at risk, seems to be present only in humans. A dramatic example would be the nomadic Inuit-speaking Iñupiaq foragers of Northwest Alaska: with them, while a successful surprise attack can wipe out an entire band, an alert enemy will quickly line up to engage in battle, and in fighting both sides may suffer serious casualties if their primitive body armor fails to stop enemy arrows (Burch, 2005). These may well be the hunter-gatherers whose pattern of fighting comes the closest to fulfilling a modern definition of intensive warfare (see Otterbein, 1974), for their attacks are actually genocidal—both in intention and sometimes in effect—and all the males of two groups may fight at the same time.

Thus there is something in the makeup of humans that allows us, under conditions of strong competition and hostility, to go beyond careful, relatively safe asymmetrical raiding, and rush into an even battle knowing that casualties on both sides are likely. It is possible that using projectile weapons gives the illusion of keeping violence more at a distance, but there is also warrior prestige: good warriors, like good hunters, regularly receive an elevated social status, and are well thought of morally because of their arduous and risky occupation. In addition, and perhaps equally important, culturally-elaborated motives of revenge spur not only warfare and raiding, but also protracted feuds that involve chains of related killings (Boehm, 2011; e.g., Lee, 1979). Individually chimpanzees and bonobos are prone to retaliate for prior aggression, but they don't collectively elaborate these tendencies culturally, for instance by counting their dead or planning revenge attacks.

Ancestral Social Control as a Major Preadaptation

Human foragers form latent or overt political coalitions when they behave as moral communities to sanction deviants; an obvious instance would be a well-documented !Kung attack on a serial killer who everyone agreed had to go. This began with the delegated would-be executioner's using a poisoned projectile weapon, but the dying bully wounded a bystanding woman and killed her husband before, finally, the entire band converged to administer the *coup de grace* (Lee, 1979). In another case, a Mbuti Pygmy man cheated flagrantly during a net hunt and, while his family-faction stood to one side and did not try to support him, other band members took turns in shaming him and threatening him with banishment (Turnbull, 1961). In other cases, as with the initial attack by the !Kung executioner, one man is delegated by the group to slaughter a habitual bully or a dangerous psychotic, as with the Inuit of Central Canada (see Balikci, 1970; van den Steenhoven, 1957, 1959, 1962). Thus, social sanctioning can be either truly collectivized or it can simply represent the will of a moral majority with delegated individuals taking the necessary measures.

This means that within their bands, prehistoric hunter-gatherers who were culturally-modern like ourselves already had a cognitive model with respect to acting as a coalition in order to attack and kill a member of the same species, in this case a member of the same group whose dangerous deviance (or, more rarely, psychosis) made him almost an "outsider," structurally speaking (e.g., Black, 2011). We have seen that similar dynamics pertain to Ancestral *Pan*, and in humans such dynamics make it an easy transition to collectively kill a true outsider from another group, especially if his alien ethnicity or language automatically makes him a candidate for strong ethnocentric hostility.

Motives of Revenge

In band-level societies the smallest and most basic social unit is the family, and in just a few environments people cannot aggregate regularly in the multifamily bands (Gould, 1982) that are preferred. Here, however, we will be dealing with multifamily bands of the nomadic type (see Hill, et al. 2011). When I refer to intergroup conflict, I refer to any attack between members of two different multifamily bands that normally camp separately and tend to share meat separately.

Among humans, agricultural tribesmen are known for their vendettas, but hunter-gatherers, too, can engage in chains of revenge killings (see Boehm, 2011). When a male forager kills another male, he can expect close male kin of his victim to retaliate, and usually he moves away, using avoidance as a shield (Knauft, 1991). Revenge killings can take place within the same band, between two neighboring bands in the same cooperating social network or language group, or between neighbors who are ethnically different or economically separate.

When thinking about factors that make for warfare up to and including pitched battles, an important consideration is this penchant for retaliation—which in tribal humans in particular can be very long-lasting (e.g., Boehm, 1986; Chagnon, 1983; see also Otterbein & Otterbein, 1965). Retaliatory targeting often is reckoned rather precisely, in terms of one death deserving another, but among tribesmen like the Yanomamo it can become generalized to entire groups (e.g., Chagnon, 1983). In hunter-gatherers often a single retaliation settles the score (e.g., Lee, 1979), and among them often the target is just the actual killer—but not always by any means (see Kelly, 2000).

Revenge would appear to be not only a factor in intergroup fights developing, but a major motivation in the *continuation* of intergroup hostilities in small-scale societies once they have started. While the great majority of extant mobile foragers certainly don't have Iñupiaq-style warfare at the level of pitched battles, once an intergroup killing does take place, the probability of continuing hostilities can be high because a predictable human reaction to another's killing one's loved one seems to be a combination of grieving loss and retaliatory vindictiveness (Boehm, 2011; Fry, chapter 1; Fry & Szala, chapter 23). After first vengeance is achieved, if an honor-based counterreaction is part of the cultural pattern this can easily produce a long and costly chain of revenge attacks, and such chains may require deliberate intervention to stop them.

One way to roughly differentiate hunter-gatherer "feuding" from "raiding" or "warfare" would be simply to count conflicts with carefully kept scores based on one-at-a-time killings as feuds, while larger attacks with more generalized revenge themes can run along a continuum from raiding to warfare—with warfare being seen as conflicts between whole local groups with at least one of the groups fully mobilized to attack.[2]

In considering the difference between finite, targeted feuding and raiding or warfare, Kelly (2000) raises the important issue of "social-substitutability" in conflict situations. Usually when one forager kills another, the latter's kin will try to return the favor by killing the killer and often that, by cultural definition, is the end of it. However, in some cases the killer's close male kin may become equally liable, and sometimes even all the males in his community may become liable. In such cases, once a return killing has been accomplished, there can be a solid cultural basis for further, *generic* killing (of males, usually) between entire groups. This can shade into lethal raids or into primitive types of warfare, up to and including what the indisputably warlike Iñupiaq practice (see Wrangham and Glowacki, 2012).

On this basis it can be said that there is a continuum that runs from a single killing in retaliation for a previous killing, which by custom concludes the conflict, to extended chains of back-and-forth individual killings, to the transformation of such patterns through social substitutability (see Boehm, 2011; Kelly, 2000) so that entire kin groups or even entire bands or networks of ethnically-similar bands can become all but perpetually involved in low-level conflict unless some means of pacification exists. This means that in spite of the anthropological penchant for clear typologies, we are basically dealing with continua here, along several dimensions.

It bears emphasis that even though intergroup conflict labeled as revenge killing, raiding, or warfare is not universally reported among hunter-gatherers (see Ember, 1978), many preconditions congenial to the development of "warfare" or "raiding" are present in foragers who do not practice either. These include forming aggressive and potentially lethal coalitions in dealing with serious deviants *within* their bands, and in the fact that kin-retaliation against individuals after a homicide seems to be such an extremely strong tendency (Knauft, 1991). This is the case among "Late-Pleistocene Appropriate" (LPA) foragers everywhere (Boehm, 2011)—be the killing within a band or between bands. By the same token, peacemaking within the group provides a widespread and possibly universal "cognitive model" for trying to make peace *between groups*—should this aspect of social problem-solving come into play. Presently, I shall support this hypothesis with ethnographic data from a systematic survey of these LPA foragers.

Realities of Band-Level Conflict, Then and Now

Bowles (2006, 2009) has made a remarkable analysis of Late-Pleistocene hunter-gatherer warfare consequences, and it would appear that throughout the changeable and protracted Pleistocene Epoch there could have been frequent junctures at which resource scarcity alone would have spurred serious intergroup competition. Probably there were also benevolent phases when previously decimated populations could expand without need for "territorial conflict," but once population pressure arrived, and especially when the resources in question were clustered enough to be readily defensible (e.g., Dyson-Hudson & Smith, 1978), armed conflict could have been profitable to the winners as individuals or as groups—be the competition between bands or between regional "nexuses" of bands (Heinz, 1972).[3]

In considering whether ethnographically-studied foragers can provide reasonable proxies for this relatively recent past, I believe that certain contemporary foragers can in fact serve as Late Pleistocene models, as long as the reconstruction applies just to prehistoric humans who were culturally modern—i.e., going back to about 45,000 BP (Klein, 1999) or somewhat earlier. However, such reconstructions must not be made in terms of absolutes or universals, but rather in terms of strong central tendencies (Boehm, 2002). Elsewhere (Boehm, 2008, 2012b), I have suggested that if one considers only economically and politically independent foragers who are both nomadic and egalitarian, one can look for strong, *core* central tendencies in their socioeconomic behavior (e.g., Steward, 1955), and confidently transpose those core patterns—again, as strong central tendencies rather than as universals—into the culturally-modern human past.

This involves removing from the ethnographically-studied world corpus of over 300 exclusively-foraging hunter-gatherers (see Binford, 2001) any decidedly inappropriate types, such as foragers who also practice horticulture or trade food with horticulturalists, foragers long engaged with the fur trade, mounted hunters, and sedentary foragers who store food and eventually lose their egalitarian ethos and develop hereditary leaders. (These last two types are exceptionally bellicose.) LPA foragers, then, are pure foragers who are economically independent, politically egalitarian, and spatially mobile, and whose subsistence fits with what we know of *Homo sapiens* between 45,000 BP and 15,000 BP.[4]

The Potential for Group Conflict

Studies that address hunter-gatherer conflict, by Otterbein and Otterbein (1965), Otterbein (1970), Ember (1978), Keeley (1996), Kelly (2000, 2005), Bowles (2006, 2009), Boehm (2011), and Pinker (2011), use widely differing definitions of "warfare," while basically the samples of foraging societies used in these studies have not been keyed to the conservative restrictions used here—even though in most cases about half of the foragers sampled would qualify as "LPA." Out of well over 100 identifiable LPA foragers, the database I have been building for the past 10 years has involved coding in detail the sociopolitical patterns for 49 of these societies. I have mentioned already that just over half of them report casualties resulting from between-group encounters,[5] but there are two reasons to believe that this figure is likely to be seriously incomplete. First, contact with punitive external authorities can quickly suppress actual homicide rates, and second, as mentioned above, people quickly become so reticent about previous patterns of homicide that ethnographic reports often will be seriously incomplete— unless ethnographers have been present at contact, as often in the Arctic (e.g., van den Steenhoven, 1959) or in Australia, or unless an exceptional ethnographic investigation takes place (Lee, 1979).

Based on this detailed coding project (the 49 LPA societies are listed in Appendix A), information about interband conflict is as follows.

Table 16.1 reflects accounts of some type of forager intergroup conflict, with such conflict being reported on all continents populated by hunter-gatherers and in over half of the 49 societies surveyed. In the interest of simplification I have merged all types of intergroup conflict, which range from single revenge killings to limited raids to whole-group intensive warfare. Although societies not reporting such conflict may be inherently "peaceable," other likely possibilities include their being extremely isolated, one party's using spatial avoidance to avoid political strife with a feared neighbor, or two parties avoiding each other.

Table 16.2 shows reports of avoidance, but note that there is considerable overlap between the societies listed in Tables 16.1 and 16.2: in societies with intergroup fighting males often also use avoidance strategies, although in three cases (Gilyak, Iglulik, and Tiwi) avoidance does seems to be the sole strategy reported. I must qualify this finding by pointing out that ethnographies are not always complete in their political coverage. It must be kept in mind, as well, that avoidance is not always possible.

The winning vs. losing patterns covered in Table 16.3 contrast with the more usual conflict patterns that continue or are resolved without the advantage going to one party. Some

TABLE 16.1 **Interband Conflict in 49 LPA Societies**

Africa:	Dorobo, G/wi, Hadza, !Ko, !Kung, Naron
Arctic:	Copper, Coronation Gulf, Ingalik, MacKenzie Delta, Netsilik, Northwest Alaska, Nunamiut, Nunivak, Pacific, Polar, Quebec, Utku
Asia:	Jarawa, Manus
Australia:	Dieri, Euahlayi, Murngin, Pintupi, Tasmanians, Walbiri,
N, America:	Yumans
S. America:	Ona, Yahgan
Total = 29 (59%)	

TABLE 16.2 **Use of Avoidance to End Conflict**

Africa:	Dorobo, G/wi, Hadza, !Kung
Arctic:	Copper, Coronation Gulf, Gilyak, Iglulik, Northwest Alaska, Nunamiut, Quebec
Asia:	*None*
Australia:	Murngin, Pintupi, Tasmanians, Tiwi, Walbiri
N. America:	*None*
S. America:	Yahgan
Total = 17 (35%)	

TABLE 16.3 **Winning or Losing a Conflict***

Africa:	Dorobo, !Kung
Arctic:	Northwest Alaska, Nunamiut
Asia:	*None*
Australia:	Tasmanian, Walbiri
N. America:	Yumans
S. America:	Yahgan
Total = 8 (15%)	

*The majority of these wins and losses involve natural
resources.

of these one-sided outcomes are reported as being about contested resources, but for this to
be possible, again, the resources in question must be clumped enough and dense enough to
be defensible (Dyson-Hudson & Smith 1978). This is not always the case. However, such
territorial displacement is reported, if rather rarely, on five out of six continents.

Because these data are from today's LPA foragers, it is appropriate to consider the
rather different climatic conditions that prevailed in the Late Pleistocene (see Burroughs,
2005). During that climatically unpredictable epoch our culturally-modern forbears probably would have been fighting more often as competing groups, especially at junctures
when populations had had time to expand during good times and then rather quickly had
to compete sharply for resources when drastically changing climates created abrupt down-
turns in resources. Such junctures could have been fairly frequent, and, because at times
they coincided with dangerous population bottlenecks (Burroughs 2005), sporadically
resource competition could have become seriously intensive.

While Bowles (2009) has made the case that such conflict might have been sufficient to drive group selection to reach significant levels, firm archaeological evidence of
"warfare" (in the form of massacres) only goes back about 15,000 years (see Keeley, 1996;
Ferguson, chapters 7 & 11; Haas & Piscitelli, chapter 10). Given a major data hiatus in this
respect, the large-sample ethnological reconstruction methodology I am employing here
could be important, in that a substantial worldwide sampling permits a reasonably reliable
Pleistocene behavioral assessment. I believe that this method can be used conservatively in
reconstructing sociopolitical patterns for at least the past 45,000 years, and given the probably understated figures in the first three tables it seems likely that well over half of all Late
Pleistocene hunter-gatherers were to some degree fighting at the group level.

I emphasize that a maximally conservative Late-Pleistocene reconstruction can reach
back reliably only to humans who were culturally modern, and that it must be limited to
central tendencies. Thus, for at least from 45,000 BP to 15,000 BP, or a bit later, it seems
likely that in all human societies a combination of chronic male competition over females
and recurrent intensive resource competition were stimulating some level of lethal conflict between bands, and that strong tendencies to lethal retaliation sometimes would have
tended to keep such patterns in place over time, including in times of plenty, unless some
effective method of pacification was available.

Rates of Intergroup Homicide

Three general criteria should be fulfilled if figures are to be reasonably representative of what foragers were doing 45,000 BP. First, they must include homicide between LPA groups but exclude those within a band. Second the conflicts must be with other LPA foragers, not with types of people who came on the scene later. And third, they must fit the LPA category in the interest of making the assessment conservative.

With its focus on the peacemaking aspect of intergroup conflict, the present investigation uses only about half of the total coded information I have on intergroup conflict per se. This is because of the steep time demands of manually extracting coded information from the database. Appendix B shows the portion of the coding protocol for my project for which data have been assembled, specifically, information used here was extracted from item 7, "Conflict Resolution between Groups," which includes "Warfare Outcomes" but provides little idea of casualty rates or exact types of conflicts. While these categories were chosen because of a focus on conflict management, in the future I hope to extract coded data for item 6, "Conflict between Groups," which will permit making distinctions between feuding, raiding, and warfare types of activities and perhaps will permit a tentative assessment of casualty rates in terms of rough central tendencies.

While the limited coded data that are assessed here and are reflected in Tables 16.1–16.6 do not yield rates of killing between groups, they do enable me to construct a general preliminary profile of hunter-gatherers' intergroup hostility patterns as of up to at least 45,000 years ago. The biases used in sampling (see Appendix A) should not affect the overall picture, which shows that 59 percent of the LPA forager sample has enough lethal intergroup conflict for this to be reported in an ethnography. To extrapolate to the pre-Holocene past, it would appear that many but by no means all hunter-gatherers were likely to be fighting at the intergroup level in some way. However, a fair part of this fighting could have involved just single acts of revenge.

It seems likely that changeable Late-Pleistocene differences of subsistence pattern and subsistence opportunity could have affected these patterns, sometimes for the better and sometimes for the worse. I have mentioned that climate swings were likely to have caused populations to grow and then contract, as a direct function of resource availability, and the more crowded phases could have exacerbated the patterns of intergroup conflict arrived at here for foragers operating in the Holocene. At the same time, when resource competition became sharp and lethal hostilities resulted, the revenge factor that I have emphasized could have helped to keep such conflicts going even when resources became adequate again. However, in this respect, it is of interest that in Table 16.3, which treated winning or losing conflicts mainly in terms of loss or gain of resources, only a small portion of the conflicts engaged in by almost two-thirds of my sample of 49 societies were designated as involving winners or losers.

A conflict with an unresolved outcome can continue all but indefinitely, and it is my hypothesis that once a conflict gets started—be it because of male competition over females or because of competition for resources or whatever—the revenge factor can hold that conflict in place strongly unless there is some effective mode of avoidance or pacification. The consideration of peacemaking between groups that follows is based on all of the coded data I have that is relevant, and it will become clear that LPA foragers who fight usually try to negotiate as they go along, and sometimes manage to conclude a real peace.

The Potential for Peacemaking

In setting forth these facts and theories about Late Pleistocene intergroup conflict, I have said little about the "peace" side of the equation so far, but several things are worth noting. One is that the well-developed type of truces that are found so widely in warlike pastoral-nomadic tribal societies (e.g., Evans-Pritchard, 1940), or in shifting-cultivation tribal societies (Chagnon, 1983), or in transhumant pastoralist societies that farm (Boehm, 1986), or in sedentary agricultural societies (e.g., Sahlins, 1967) are found also among certain nomadic LPA foragers like the aforementioned Iñupiaq of Northwest Alaska. Another is that hunter-gatherers sometimes go beyond trucemaking to sue for permanent peace; these patterns will become apparent in Tables 16.5 and 16.6.

Table 16.4 shows general frequencies for varied attempts to negotiate intergroup conflicts. The total is 29 societies, as with Table 16.1, but with some differences in the societies reporting this. Thus, just as with disputes *within* bands, many interband conflicts can be negotiated in some way. With respect to these negotiations, overall the geographic distributions are so extensive that such behavior would not appear to be a regional invention but rather a strong tendency that is based on a combination of innate human proclivities, similarities in foragers' political situations, and the remarkable efficiency of human problem-solving inventiveness.

With respect to temporary truces, Inuit speakers in Northwest Alaska annually call off all of their genocidal hostilities on a regional basis for a few weeks, in the summer, in order to hold trade fairs at which food and commodities from different regions are exchanged. This takes place reliably in spite of the fact that intensive and genocidal warfare is taking place across the region during the rest of the year. As another example, two hostile Yahgan groups in Terra del Fuego suspend their fighting temporarily when a whale beaches in one of their territories, in order to ensure future reciprocation in kind (Cooper,

TABLE 16.4 **Negotiations Take Place in 49 LPA Societies**

Africa:	Dorobo, Hadza, !Ko, Kung, Naron
Arctic:	Copper, Coronation Gulf, Gilyak, Labrador, MacKenzie Delta, Pacific, Polar, Netsilik, Northwest Alaska, Utku, West Greenland
Asia:	Andaman, Arioto, Jarawa, Manus, Nicobar
Australia:	Dieri, Euahlayi, Murngin, Pintupi, Tasmanians, Walbiri
N. America	*None*
S. America:	Ona, Yahgan
Total = 29 (59%)	

TABLE 16.5 **Truces Temporarily Suspend Hostilities in 49 LPA Forager Societies**

Africa:	Dorobo
Arctic:	Northwest Alaska, Polar, Utku
Asia:	Andaman, Jarawa, Nicobar
Australia:	Dieri, Euahlayi, Murngin, Tasmanians, Walbiri
N. America	*None*
S. America:	Yahgan
Total = 13 (27%)	

TABLE 16.6 **Formal Peace Meetings**

Africa:	!Ko
Arctic:	Copper, Gilyak, Northwest Alaska, West Greenland
Asia:	Andaman, Manus
Australia:	Murngin, Tasmanians
N. America:	*None*
S. America:	*None*
Total = 8 (16%)	

1946; Gusinde, 1961). The logic of the situation dictates a truce, since one group cannot eat an entire whale before it spoils; because the two sides reciprocate over time, this is a win-win situation, and in both cases the truces are based on major economic incentives. In Table 16.5 such truces, while not very frequent, are reported on five out of six continents,[6] so such behavior cannot be attributed just to regional political exigencies or to localized cultural traditions.

In current usage, "peace" seems to mean either that a conflict is effectively ended or at least reliably suspended, or it can mean that intergroup conflict doesn't exist in the first place. When peace is actively created between fighting groups (see Table 16.6), it is likely that the same ideologies that so strongly support conflict resolution within the group are being applied in a similarly problem-solving fashion, but obviously in a between-group context. Formal peace meetings are found on all of the continents for which five or more cultures were able to be sampled, and it is important to draw the distinction between a truce, which merely interrupts an ongoing conflict pattern, and trying to put a real end to the conflict.

In assessing Table 16.6, it is clear both that hunter-gatherers sometimes do try to create peace and succeed in doing so when a conflict has been ongoing, but also that such negotiations appear to result somewhat more often in a temporary suspension of hostilities (see Table 16.4), as opposed to a definitive resolution of the conflict.

Peacemaking's Deep Background

My suggestion has been that in a phylogenetic sense human conflict resolution within groups—a primitive ancestral behavior—is more basic than conflict resolution between groups (a derived behavior). If we go back to our conservative assessment of Ancestral *Pan*, the finding there was that while between groups no frequent, active, and *lethal* conflict could be stipulated, deliberate mechanisms to suspend or resolve whatever intergroup hostilities did exist were not present, either—even though *within the group* peacemaking behavior did exist. The fact that neighboring bonobo groups sometimes "intermingle" (Furuichi, 2011) is intriguing, and suggests a rough parallel with the trucemaking patterns in Northwest Alaska and Tierra del Fuego. However, its political dynamics remain to be understood.[7] Furthermore, since chimpanzees lack any mingling pattern with respect to males, such mingling cannot be proposed as ancestral—even though chimpanzee females (like bonobo females) do emigrate at adolescence.

With human foragers, negotiations of some type (including truces and peacemaking) are found in more than half of the LPA societies surveyed (59 percent). However, Table 16.6 tells us that formal and effective peacemaking is reported only for a few of these 29 societies. I must emphasize that geographically, the fact that only two-thirds of the world's culture areas (Africa, the Arctic, Asia, and Australia) are represented probably is not terribly significant, because at present only three LPA cultures have been sampled from North and South America (see Appendix A) because of the rigorous selection criteria specified in Appendix A.

Ethnographic Examples of Between-Group Peacemaking

To complement the statistical analysis, some exemplification will be useful. Peacemaking after two different forager groups fight can be routinized through rituals. Off the coast of India, the Andaman Islanders fought a great deal (Kelly, 2000), and when they decided to make peace women did the arranging (Lebar, 1972) and a dance was held, with weapons being ceremonially exchanged by both sides (Radcliffe-Brown, 1933). It is worth mentioning that the burden (and glory) of active intergroup aggression falls mainly on males.

This same ethnographer describes some of the social functions involved: the peace-making dance gives expression to collective anger, which then dies down and wrongs are forgotten and forgiven, and the purpose of this rite is to abolish a condition of enmity and replace it with friendship. I must point out immediately that the purposes and also the emotional dynamics are all but identical to those that pertain—in general—to resolving a dispute between individuals *within* a band (see Fry, 2000), and also to composing blood feuds (Boehm, 2011).

At the tip of Tierra del Fuego the Yaghan fight with neighbors, but also share certain marine resources such as the beached whales mentioned above. Hostilities are suspended for such sharing, and also, apparently, in times of extreme food stress (Cooper, 1946; Gusinde, 1961). On the other hand, among the same people making peace in the face of a chain of revenge killings (with social substitutability) can involve unending payment of material goods (Gusinde, 1961) if the payer wishes to avoid lethal retaliation, so feud-resolution appears to be inconclusive. Likewise, among tribal pastoralists or agriculturalists who feud, resolving vendettas can range from temporary measures of payment that merely delay the retaliation (e.g., Peters, 1967), to blood-money settlements that are seen as definitive (Boehm, 1986; Hasluck, 1954) and are fairly successful in resolving the conflict.

Perhaps the most developed instance of hunter-gatherer trucemaking in the ethnographic literature is that of the aforementioned NW Alaskan Iñupiaq, nomads who use large hide boats or sleds to bring substantial quantities of commodities to a large coastal market or "trade fair" every summer, with sometimes over 1000 persons attending. Because some Iñupiaq bands have maritime adaptations and others go hunting inland, there is great economic advantage in such trade (Burch, 2005), and even with quite a large number of bands involved, remarkably a sizable foraging population that includes many friendly and many highly unfriendly bands renders itself permeable, as a whole, to safe travel. Because so many of these bands engage in the genocidal intercommunity attacks described earlier, the success of a general truce may seem improbable, but in fact this takes place every summer with three weeks' safe passage to and from the fair, and with mortal enemies mingling at market. As the general truce finishes, lethal hostilities are resumed.

This trucemaking serves as a testimonial to the possibilities of expedient hunter-gatherer peacemaking when motivation is sufficient. On the far side of the Arctic, in West Greenland, there are also regional trade fairs, along with "courts" that settle disputes through drum songs (Birket-Smith, 1924). But there a general truce is not needed to guarantee the safety of the parties involved, since intensive intergroup conflicts like those of the Iñupiaq are lacking. Thus, globally the varieties of intergroup peacemaking, while not often described in detail ethnographically, are diverse.

As an African example, !Ko Bushmen's bands are organized into nexuses or clusters of friendly bands, while relations between bands in different nexuses are tense. There, interpersonal strife at the between-nexus level is taken as a problem to be solved actively, and the respective headmen try to talk things out and restore amicable relations. This suggests, again, that principles and methods of peacemaking within bands can be applied not only within a friendly nexus, but also between the larger regional nexuses in spite of ethnocentric hostilities.

In the Australian desert, the Murngin experience long-term vendettas between groups, with high casualties. When ready, they engage in peacemaking ceremonies that involve the killers offering themselves as targets for spearing, which up to a point they try to avoid by dodging. A successful dodger will eventually have to allow a spear to hit him, however, to resolve the political tension and the feud, and in some cases a killer may actually be killed during the ceremony (Chaseling, 1957; Warner, 1937). This ritual is called a *makarata*. The Murngin *gaingar* is a ritualized "war game" that involves fairly large scale ritualized fighting (see also Fry, 2009) with the intention to express conflict without too many casualties; this serves as a means of drastically ameliorating the damage ensuing from all-out "warfare," and such deliberately limited conflict is also found among tribesmen and non-LPA foragers; for instance, counting coup by Plains mounted horsemen (e.g., Wallace & Hoebel, 1952) and also low-casualty "great fights" practiced by highland New Guinea horticulturalists (Heider, 2006; Roscoe, Chapter 24). Such ritualized conflicts can be seen as a compromise between all-out fighting and conflict-free peacemaking (Fry & Szala, Chapter 23). The Murngin also may send food and tobacco as ritualized compensation, and if the entire group is willing to partake, the feud is actually resolved.

When killings seem likely among the Murngin, avoidance out on the Australian desert may also solve a potentially disruptive and costly problem. Because feuds can be protracted and intergroup attacks can even become genocidal with respect to males (Warner, 1937), avoidance is an efficient strategy if peacemaking cannot be accomplished.

Integrating the Analysis

Looking to the social and political dynamics found in LPA foraging bands, I emphasize that these can be projected at least 45,000 years into the past, in terms of strong central tendencies. Certain aspects of the typical local ethos or worldview are prominent. One is that male political equality is all but sacred (Boehm, 1999). Another is that personal altruism is heavily endorsed (Boehm, 2008), along with social harmony (Sober & Wilson, 1998). Another is that group cooperation makes for useful safety nets (Alexander, 1987). The result is a strong aversion to within-group conflict, which translates into active attempts to distract or separate the protagonists or to actively mediate and compact a dispute (see Fry, 2000). And one basic reason to resolve conflicts among armed hunters is that death is understood and the life of any group member is valued morally. As we have seen, killing outgroup members can be far less controversial.

From an evolutionary perspective, conflict between groups can be *bilaterally* quite costly in energy and lives, even though in strategizing each side will seek to minimize its own casualties. But major one-sided gains can also be made from such conflict, as opposed to conflict *within* bands, which is always costly to the entire group involved. Thus, while intragroup conflict is always actively headed off or resolved if possible, simply because band communities recognize the costs of internal strife, intergroup conflict is different. For one thing, as Table 16.3 demonstrated, it can in fact be highly profitable in evolutionary terms of competition for individual (and group) reproductive success (Boehm, 1992, 1999), in terms of both differential casualty rates and territorial/resource gains. For another, the intended damage accrues to outsiders who are less than fully human because of the ethnocentric discount, so such losses are not necessarily contradictory in terms of the moral values placed on human life. Furthermore, functionally, conflict with outsiders tends to strengthen social solidarity and cooperation within the band (Boehm & Flack 2010).

Group members basically want the groups they live in to be internally at peace. This is based on an appreciation of social harmony and the deliberate enhancement of cooperation: the active "tweaking" of indigenous social systems in this direction is done through preemptive moralizing in favor of altruistic cooperation (see Campbell, 1975; see also Boehm, 2008), and also through active conflict management (Fry, 2000). While this is universally true of peace *within* bands, it *can* apply also to more extended political relations. This would be particularly the case in situations of microecological unpredictability where interband networks result in vital safety nets and hence interdependency. The *hxaro* system of the !Kung Bushmen (Wiessner, 2002) provides a well-studied example, and similarly regional trading-cum-security-networks are found, for instance, in Aboriginal Australia (see Lourandos, 1997) and in Northwest Alaska (Burch, 2005). A proposition worth testing may be that where people in neighboring groups have a great deal to gain from cooperation, peacemaking efforts may be more prominent and intergroup conflict more subdued.

One might surmise that there should be an either-or choice between setting up friendly, cooperative relations with neighbors, as opposed to fighting with them, but in fact the ultra-warlike Iñupiaq can do both within the same ethnic-linguistic region. A given band will never be at war with all of its neighbors, so that in times of localized hardship, families can seek refuge with associated families in those bands that in fact are friendly, while avoiding those with which genocidal hostilities prevail (see Burch 2005).

In terms of strong central tendencies, LPA foraging societies often can pacify and resolve lesser disputes that occur within their bands at close quarters, which threaten both the quality of social life and efficient group cooperation. They do so moralistically (Boehm, 2000). However, because of revenge motives *lethal* fights within the group are dealt with differently: the relatives of the victim are left to exact vengeance, while killers usually use long-distance avoidance to avert further conflict.

When lethal conflicts erupt *between* groups, they are accompanied by similar motives of revenge, which tend to perpetuate the conflicts even though they may have started due to a single instance of, say, two males competing for a female. When competition for scarce natural resources enters the picture, this, along with ongoing needs for vengeance, can keep an ongoing conflict pattern strongly in place. However, even in environments given to scarcity, as with the Bushmen, understandings can be reached about use of natural resources that avert fighting; thus, basically the defense of resource boundaries can be social (see Cashdan, 1983), rather than military.

Violent intergroup conflicts are cited in more than half the LPA sample, as is the case for intergroup conflict-management negotiations (which may or may not succeed in creating peace). Thus, there is a pronounced tendency among the 49 LPA cultures for both of these types of behavior to be present, and realistically the fact of often incomplete ethnographic coverage could make these tendencies still more pronounced. This strong central tendency to both fight (see also Bowles, 2009) and negotiate can be projected confidently back to prehistoric culturally-modern humans, and probably beyond to include the entire Late Pleistocene. It was local conditions of scarcity or accidents of homicide—in conjunction with continuing revenge motives—that could have made for not infrequent and protracted intergroup conflicts, which, if they became too costly, were sometimes susceptible to pacification.

This phylogenetic treatment suggests strongly that both aggression and peacemaking *within* groups were ancestral, and that as primitive traits both have been part of the human potential ever since. Because humans are so good at generalizing and at imaginatively solving social problems, at some point in evolutionary time peacemaking began to be practiced also at the between-group level. Thus, it is suggested that the same human capacity for social analysis of economic costs and benefits and the same preference for peaceful relations that are obtained so predictably within groups, can also be directed at conflicts between groups. The more recent seeds of such behavior, and also of modern waging of war and peacemaking, as well, are to be found in the political patterns represented in the six tables, by the same type of forager that most recently evolved our genes for us.

The finding here is that intergroup conflict and external peacemaking would both seem to have been prominent in human political life, back to at least 45,000 BP and probably earlier. But because such conflicts were among nomads, a portion of the conflict would have been obviated by avoidance, without need for active intergroup conflict management in the form of truces and peace pacts. As some foragers, like those in the Pacific Northwest, became sedentary, and as others became sedentary agriculturalists, territorial competition—exacerbated by motives of revenge—often became both widespread and chronic, even though systems of trucemaking and peacemaking also continued as a means of management and sometimes resolution.

Conclusion

LPA hunter-gatherers are highly moralistic in their judgment of other people; they gossip accordingly, and they can become vehement when groups come down hard on deviants. Curiously, however, when a major conflict threatens the integrity of a cooperating band these moral feelings are largely set aside because the primary objective becomes to manage the conflict, not to decide who is the moral offender. Thus, in intergroup conflicts, there is already an established intragroup method of conflict management, which often can be generalized to an external conflict in case avoidance doesn't resolve the problem.

Questions of "war," "peace," and "human nature" are obviously complicated in terms of ethnographic analysis. But generalizations are possible even when the behaviors in question lack universality. Here I have adduced one set of generalizations from primitive ancestral behaviors, which takes us back 5 to 7 million years, while another set, based on the LPA forager survey, takes us back to 45,000 BP when our modern gene pool was basically in place. One finding is that the roots of intergroup conflict were already in place 5 to 7 million years ago. Another is that important parallels exist between the ways that modern humans have pacified conflicts within their groups and how they have done this when groups fight with one another.

Appendix A
Roster of 49 LPA Societies

Africa: 6 societies

Bushmen—!Ko
Bushmen—!Kung
Bushmen—G/wi
Bushmen—Naron
Dorobo
Hadza

Arctic: 24 societies

Gilyak
Inuit—Alaskan (North)
Inuit—Alaskan (NW)
Inuit—Alaskan (SW)
Inuit—Asiatic
Inuit—Baffinland
Inuit—Bering Strait
Inuit—Caribou
Inuit—Copper
Inuit—Coronation Gulf
Inuit—Greenland
Inuit—Greenland (East)
Inuit—Greenland (West)
Inuit—Iglulik
Inuit—Ingalik
Inuit—Labrador
Inuit—Mackenzie Delta
Inuit—Netsilik
Inuit—Nunamiut
Inuit—Nunivak
Inuit—Pacific
Inuit—Polar
Inuit—Quebec
Inuit—Utku

Asia: 6 societies

Andaman Islanders—Arioto
Andaman Islanders—Jarawa
Andaman Islanders—Nicobar
Andaman Islanders—Onges
Andaman Islanders—General
Manus

Australia: 10 societies

Australian Aborigines—Dieri
Australian Aborigines—Euahlayi
Australian Aborigines—Gidjingali
Australian Aborigines—Murngin
Australian Aborigines—NW Aus
Australian Aborigines—Pintupi
Australian Aborigines—Tasmanians
Australian Aborigines—Tiwi
Australian Aborigines—Walbiri
Australian Aborigines—Yiwara

North America: 1 society

Plateau Yumans

South America: 2 societies

Ona
Yahgan

Note: From a total of over 100 LPA societies the 49 listed above have been selected on the basis of: 1) geographic representation; 2) completeness of ethnographic description; and 3) a bias in favor of societies that were studied at contact or soon after contact.

Appendix B
Coding Topics

7. Conflict Resolution between Groups
7.0 Bilateral Negotiations
7.00 Negotiations on the battlefield
7.01 Negotiations off the battlefield
7.1 Third party negotiations with mediator
7.2 Truces
7.3 Formal peace meetings

7.4 Payment of compensation

7.5 Prisoner exchange

7.6 Warfare outcomes

7.60 Conflict continues with no resolution attempted

7.61 Conflict just trails off

7.62 One group avoids the other

7.63 Conflict turns into alliance against mutual enemy

7.64 One side wins in some way

7.65 One side loses significant territory

7.66 Casualties: dead; wounded; enslaved

7.67 Truce suspends the conflict temporarily

Notes

1. See Wrangham and Peterson (1996) for ancestral modeling that gives more weight to chimpanzee behavior. Given sufficient research time, the bonobo's potential for lethal-attack behavior might have to be rated as somewhat higher. This was the case with chimpanzees.
2. There are many and varying definitions of feuding, raiding, and warfare, but in this case basically I am using those found in Boehm (1986).
3. This Bushman-specific term can be generalized to mean a cluster of bands within which cordial relations exist in comparison with adjacent clusters with which relations are distant or hostile.
4. LPA foragers did not have domesticated animals, with the exception of dogs, used by most Inuit, which were domesticated in the Late Pleistocene.
5. In reading the tabulations it must be kept in mind that random sampling was not used; thus, there is only one culture representing North America while 24 Arctic cultures have been included in the sample of 49 societies.
6. There is only one LPA society coded for North America; see Appendix A. Curiously, ethnographic reports for the Andamans and the Nicobar include mentions of truces but not of intergroup conflict. This supports my suggestion that were the ethnography more complete, figures in all of the tables would be more inclusive.
7. One possibility would be that the less xenophobic groups may have fissioned recently.

References

Alexander, R. D. (1987). *The biology of moral systems.* New York: Aldine de Gruyter.

Balikci, A. (1970). *The Netsilik Eskimo.* Prospect Heights: Waveland Press.

Binford, L. R. (2001). *Constructing frames of reference: An analytical method for archaeological theory building using hunter-gatherer and environmental data sets.* Berkeley: University of California Press.

Birket-Smith, K. (1924). Ethnography of the Egedesminde District with aspects of the general culture of West Greenland. *Meddelelser om Greenland, 66,* 3–476.

Black, D. (2011). *Moral time.* Oxford: Oxford University Press.

Boehm, C. (1982). The evolutionary development of morality as an effect of dominance behavior and conflict interference. *Journal of Social and Biological Sciences, 5,* 413–422.

Boehm, C. (1986). *Blood revenge: The enactment and management of conflict in Montenegro and other tribal societies.* Philadelphia: University of Pennsylvania Press.

Boehm, C. (1991). Response to Knauft, Violence and sociality in human evolution. *Current Anthropology, 32,* 411–412.

Boehm, C. (1992). Segmentary "warfare" and the management of conflict: Comparison of East African chimpanzees and patrilineal-patrilocal humans. In A. Harcourt & F. B. M. de Waal (Eds.), *Us against them: Coalitions and alliances in humans and other animals* (pp. 137–173). Oxford: Oxford University Press.

Boehm, C. (1993). Egalitarian behavior and reverse dominance hierarchy. *Current Anthropology, 34*, 227–254.

Boehm, C. (1994). Pacifying interventions at Arnhem Zoo and Gombe. In R. W. Wrangham, W. C. McGrew, F. B. M. de Waal & P. G. Heltne (Eds.), *Chimpanzee cultures* (pp. 211–226). Cambridge: Harvard University Press.

Boehm, C. (1999). *Hierarchy in the forest: The evolution of egalitarian behavior.* Cambridge: Harvard University Press.

Boehm, C. (2000). Conflict and the evolution of social control. *Journal of Consciousness Studies, 7,* 79–183.

Boehm, C. (2002). Variance reduction and the evolution of social control. Paper presented at Santa Fe Institute, 5th annual workshop on the co-evolution of behaviors and institutions, November 2002, Santa Fe. (Posted at Santa Fe institute web site).

Boehm, C. (2004). What makes humans economically distinctive? A three-species evolutionary comparison and historical analysis. *Journal of Bioeconomics, 6,* 109–135.

Boehm, C. (2008). Purposive social selection and the evolution of human altruism. *Cross-Cultural Research, 42,* 319–352.

Boehm, C. (2011). Retaliatory violence in human prehistory. *British Journal of Criminology, 51,* 518–534.

Boehm, C. (2012a). Ancestral hierarchy and conflict. *Science, 336,* 844–847.

Boehm, C. (2012b). *Moral origins: The evolution of altruism, virtue, and shame.* New York: Basic Books.

Boehm, C., & Flack, J. (2010). The emergence of simple and complex power structures through social niche construction. In A. Guinote (Ed.), *The social psychology of power* (pp. 46–86). New York: Guilford Press.

Bowles, S. (2006). Group competition, reproductive leveling, and the evolution of human altruism. *Science, 314,* 1569–1572.

Bowles, S. (2009). Did warfare among ancestral hunter-gatherers affect the evolution of human social behaviors? *Science, 324,* 1293–1298.

Brosnan, S. F. (2006). Nonhuman species' reactions to inequity and their implications for fairness. *Social Justice Research, 19,* 153–185.

Burch, E. S., Jr. (2005). *Alliance and conflict: The world system of the Iñupiaq Eskimos.* Lincoln: University of Nebraska Press.

Burroughs, W. J. (2005). *Climate change in prehistory: The end of the reign of chaos.* Cambridge: Cambridge University Press.

Campbell, D. T. (1975). On the conflicts between biological and social evolution and between psychology and moral tradition. *American Psychologist 30*:1103–1126.

Cashdan, E. (1983). Territoriality among human foragers: Ecological models and an application to four bushman groups. *Current Anthropology, 24,* 47–66.

Chagnon, N. (1983). *Yanomamo: The fierce people.* New York: Holt, Rinehart and Winston.

Chaseling, W. S. (1957). *Yulengor: Nomads of Arnhem Land.* London: The Epworth Press

Cooper, J. M. (1946). The Yahgan. *Bureau of American Ethnology, Bulletin 143,* vol. 1, pp. 81–106. Washington: Smithsonian Institution.

de Waal, F. B. M. (1996). *Good natured: The origins of right and wrong in humans and other animals.* Cambridge: Harvard University Press.

de Waal, F. B. M., & Lanting, F. (1997). *Bonobo: The forgotten ape.* Berkeley: University of California Press.

Dyson-Hudson, R. & Smith, E. A. (1978). Human territoriality: An ecological reassessment. *American Anthropologist, 80,* 21–41.

Ember, C. R. (1978). Myths about hunter-gatherers. *Ethnology, 17,* 439–448.

Erdal, D., & Whiten, A. (1994). On human egalitarianism: An evolutionary product of Machiavellian status escalation? *Current Anthropology, 35,* 175–184.

Evans-Pritchard, E. E. (1940). *The Nuer: A description of the modes of livelihood and political institutions of a nilotic people.* New York: Oxford University Press.

Flack, J. C., & de Waal, F. B. M. (2000). "Any animal whatever": Darwinian building blocks of morality in monkeys and apes. *Journal of Consciousness Studies, 7,* 1–29.

Fry, D. P. (2000). Conflict management in cross-cultural perspective. In F. Aureli & F. B. M. de Waal (Eds.), *Natural conflict resolution* (pp. 334–351). Berkeley: University of California Press.

Fry, D. P. (2009). *Beyond war: The human potential for peace.* Oxford: Oxford University Press.

Furuichi, T. (2011). Female contributions to the peaceful nature of bonobo society. *Evolutionary Anthropology, 20,* 131–142.

Gintis, H. (2003). The hitchhiker's guide to altruism: Gene-culture coevolution and the internalization of norms. *Journal of Theoretical Biology, 220,* 407–418.

Goodall, J. (1982). Order without law. In M. Gruter & P. Bohannan (Eds.), *Law, biology and culture: The evolution of law* (pp. 50–62). Santa Barbara: Ross-Erikson.

Goodall, J. (1986). *The chimpanzees of Gombe: Patterns of behavior.* Cambridge: Belknap Press.

Goodall, J. (1992). Unusual violence in the overthrow of an alpha male chimpanzee at Gombe. In T. Nishida, W. C. McGrew, P. Marler, M. Pickford & F. B. M. de Waal (Eds.), *Topics in primatology, volume 1: Human origins* (pp. 131–142). Tokyo: University of Tokyo Press.

Gould, R. A. (1982). To have and have not: The ecology of sharing among hunter-gatherers. In N. M. Williams & E. S. Hunn (Eds.), *Resource managers: North American and Australian hunter-gatherers* (pp. 69–91). Boulder: Westview Press Inc.

Gusinde, M. (1961). *The Yamana: The life and thought of the water nomads of Cape Horn.* New Haven: Human Relations Area Files.

Hasluck, M. (1954). *The unwritten law in Albania.* Cambridge: Cambridge University Press.

Heider, K. G. (2006). *The Dugum Dani: A Papuan culture in the highlands of West New Guinea.* New York: Aldine.

Heinz, H. J. (1972). Territoriality among the bushmen in general and the !Ko in particular. *Anthropos, 67,* 405–416.

Hill, K. R., Walker, R., Božičević, M., Eder, J., Headland, T., Hewlett, B., Hurtado, A. M., Marlowe, F., Wiessner, P. & Wood, B. (2011). Coresidence patterns in hunter-gatherer societies show unique human social structure. *Science, 331,* 1286–1289.

Holloway, R. L. (1974). *Primate aggression, territoriality, and xenophobia.* New York: Academic Press.

Kano, T. (1992). *The last ape: Pygmy chimpanzee behavior and ecology.* Stanford: Stanford University Press.

Keeley, L. H. (1996). *War before civilization.* New York: Oxford University Press.

Kelly, R. C. (2000). *Warless societies and the evolution of war.* Ann Arbor: University of Michigan Press.

Kelly, R. C. (2005). The evolution of lethal intergroup violence. *Proceedings of the National Academy of Sciences, 102,* 15294–15298.

Kelly, R. L. (1995). *The foraging spectrum: Diversity in hunter-gatherer lifeways.* Washington: Smithsonian Institution Press.

Klein, R. G. (1999). *The human career: Human biological and cultural origins.* Chicago: University of Chicago Press.

Knauft, B. M. (1991). Violence and sociality in human evolution. *Current Anthropology, 32,* 391–428.

Ladd, S. & Maloney, K. Chimp murder in Mahale. Retrieve from http://www.nomad-tanzania.com/blogs/greystoke-mahale/murder-in-mahale

Lebar, F. M., ed. (1972). *Ethnic groups of insular Southeast Asia,* vol 1: Indonesia, Andaman islands, and Madagascar. Part II: Andaman-Nicobar. Human Relations Area Files Press.

Lee, R. B. (1979). *The !Kung san: Men, women, and work in a foraging society.* Cambridge: Cambridge University Press.

LeVine, R. A., & Campbell, D. T. (1972). *Ethnocentrism: Theories of conflict, ethnic attitudes, and group behavior.* New York: Wiley.

Lourandos, H. (1997). *Continent of hunter-gatherers: New perspectives in Australian prehistory.* Cambridge: Cambridge University Press.

Mayr, E. (1983). How to carry out the adaptationist program? *American Naturalist, 121,* 324–334.

Nishida, T. (1996). The death of Ntologi, the unparalleled leader of M group. *Pan Africa News, 3,* 4.

Otterbein, K. F. (1974). The anthropology of war. In J. J. Honigmann (Ed.), *Handbook of social and cultural anthropology* (pp. 923–958). Chicago: Rand McNally.

Otterbein, K. F. (1970). *The evolution of war: A cross-cultural study.* New Haven: HRAF Press.

Otterbein, K. F., & Otterbein, C. S. (1965). An eye for an eye, a tooth for a tooth: A cross-cultural study of feuding. *American Anthropologist, 67,* 1470–1482.

Parker, I. (2007). Swingers: Bonobos are celebrated as peace-loving, matriarchal, and sexually liberated. Are they? *New Yorker, July 30, 82,* 48–61.

Peters, E. L. (1967). Some structural aspects of the feud among the camel-herding Bedouin of Cyrenaica. *Africa, 37,* 261–282.

Radcliffe-Brown, A. R. (1933). *The Andaman islanders.* Cambridge: Cambridge University Press.

Ruvolo, M., Disotell, T. R., Allard, M. W., Brown, W. M., & Honeycutt, R. L. (1991). Resolution of the African hominoid trichotomy by use of a mitochondrial gene sequence. *Proceedings of the National Academy of Science*, *88*, 1570–1574.

Sahlins, M. D. (1967). The segmentary lineage: An organization of predatory expansion. In R. Cohen & J. Middleton (Eds.), *Comparative political systems: Studies in the politics of pre-industrial societies* (pp. 89–119). Garden City: Natural History Press.

Sarkar, J. (1990). *The Jarawa*. Calcutta: Seagull Books.

Sober, E. & Wilson, D. S. (1998). *Unto others: The evolution and psychology of unselfish behavior*. Cambridge: Harvard University Press.

Steward, J. H. (1955). *Theory of culture change*. Urbana: University of Illinois Press.

Stiner, M. C. (2002). Carnivory, coevolution, and the geographic spread of the genus *homo*. *Journal of Archaeological Research*, *10*, 1–63.

van den Steenhoven, G. (1957). *Research report on Caribou Eskimo law*. The Hague: G. van den Steenhoven.

van den Steenhoven, G. (1959). *Legal concepts among the Netsilik Eskimos of Pelly Bay, Northwest territories*. Canada department of northern affairs, N.C.R.C. Report 59–3.

van den Steenhoven, G. (1962). *Leadership and law among the Eskimos of the Keewatin district, Northwest territories*. Rijswijk: Excelsior.

Thieme, H. (1997). Lower Paleolithic hunting spears from Germany. *Nature, 385*, 807.

Turnbull, C. M. (1961). *The forest people*. Garden City: Natural History Press.

Wallace, E., & Hoebel, E. A. (1952). *The Comanches: Lords of the South Plains*. Norman, OK: University of Oklahoma Press.

Warner, W. L. (1937). *A Black Civilization: A social study of an Australian Tribe*. New York: Harper and Brothers.

Wiessner, P. (2002). Hunting, healing and *hxaro* exchange: A long-term perspective on !Kung (ju/'hoansi) large-game hunting. *Evolution and Human Behavior, 23*, 407–436.

Wilson, M. L. & Wrangham, R. W. (2003). Intergroup relations in chimpanzees. *Annual Review of Anthropology, 32*, 363–392.

Wrangham, R. W. (1987) African apes: The significance of African apes for reconstructing social evolution. In W. G. Kinzey (Ed.), *The evolution of human behavior: Primate models* (pp. 282–296). Albany: SUNY Press.

Wrangham, R. W. (1999). The evolution of coalitionary killing: The imbalance-of-power hypothesis. *Yearbook of Physical Anthropology, 42*, 1–30.

Wrangham, R. W. & Glowacki, L. (2012). Intergroup aggression in chimpanzees and war in nomadic hunter-gatherers: Evaluating the chimpanzee model. *Human Nature, 23*, 5–29.

Wrangham, R. W. & Peterson, D. (1996) *Demonic males: Apes and the origins of human violence*. New York: Houghton Mifflin.

17

The 99 Percent—Development and Socialization Within an Evolutionary Context

Growing Up to Become "A Good and Useful Human Being"

Darcia Narvaez

In comparison to our pre-agriculture foraging cousins we are far from virtuous and might even be considered to have lost our minds, if not our humanity (Sahlins, 2008).[1] In fact, we are quite immoral, wicked, and stupid if we use anthropological reports of those who live like our presumed nomadic foraging, gatherer-hunter[2] ancestors as a baseline. How did this come to be? How do modern Westerners differ socially and morally from those who live like our distant ancestors and what might account for the differences? In this chapter, I compare the ancestral social environment, as known from extant small-band gatherer-hunter cultures from around the world, with the contemporary Western social environment (focused mostly on the United States, which continues to export its views and lifestyle to the rest of the world).

Apprehending an appropriate baseline for judging social functioning is critical for understanding how cultural practices influence human nature and personality. Unfortunately, many popularized evolutionary theorists today ignore or keep shifting the baseline used for comparison. Most commonly, they assume that today's human behavior is normal and normative and then try to explain it as adaptive. There is a lack of awareness of how different the social environment was for our ancestors and how this forms a different human nature. Because the small-band gatherer-hunter context encompassed 99 percent of human genus existence, I take it as the baseline range for human society and human development with their corresponding influences on human nature.[3]

The ancestral lifestyle and its implications are often ignored or confused by what I call Hobbesian evolutionary psychology (H-EP; a subset of evolutionary psychology).

This view is Hobbesian (Hobbes, 1651/ 2010) because it often concludes that humans are naturally selfish and aggressive and need extensive social controls to behave well (e.g., Pinker, 2011). H-EP typically transposes the behaviors and personalities of modern Westerners and Western social environments onto the past and explains how today's behaviors were adaptations made in the ancestral environment ("environment of evolutionary adaptedness," Bowlby, 1951; Hartman, 1939). This H-EP reasoning is totally backwards. The contemporary Western social environment creates individuals and personalities quite different from the ancestral social environment, influencing human development, capacities, and culture.

Common Characteristics of Small Band Gatherer-Hunter Life

Small-band gatherer-hunter societies, found all over the world, developed strikingly similar cultures. Here I discuss several generalized characteristics of these societies, relying heavily on Ingold (1999) and others who summarize or report their own anthropological data on gatherer-hunter societies (e.g., Marshall, 1979; Shostak, 1981; Thomas, 1989). Small-band gatherer-hunters (SBGH) refers to immediate-return societies (vs. delayed-return societies who invested in cultivation, domestication, or resource accumulation) who were foragers with few possessions.[4] Table 17.1 provides a summary of comparisons discussed.

Companionship Culture

One of the most notable features of SBGH life is a *companionship* lifestyle (Gibson, 1985). It represents a boundaryless context that involves nonexclusive intimacy and face-to-face connection that is constituted by a sharing of food, movement, residence, company, and memory (Bird-David, 1994; Ingold, 1999). Companionship is voluntary and terminable, preserving individual autonomy. As an immediate-return society, egalitarianism is assumed and predominant. The formal structures of *kinship* culture "places people from birth in determinate relations with fixed, lifelong commitments" (Ingold, 1999, p. 404), whereas in SBGH there is an absence of formal, adjudicated commitments. In contrast to delayed-return societies with their hierarchies and fixed relations, some argue that SBGH live socially but without a society at all, an arrangement representing the minimal necessary and sufficient characteristics of a society (Ingold, 1999; Wilson, 1988). SBGH individual freedom is unknown to us today, but may be sought as people move from rural communities to the anonymity of the city.

Despite the evidence to the contrary, H-EP assumes the predominance in the ancestral environment of the type of patriarchal, male-dominated family structure that we assume to be normal today in the West (nuclear family, mom and dad in charge), which is only a recent historical development (Coontz, 1992). H-EP uses a baseline derived from

TABLE 17.1 **Comparison of Two Types of Living**

	Small-band gatherer-hunters	United States Today
Social embeddedness	High	Low
Social support	High	Low
Socially purposeful living	Normative	Non-normative
Community social enjoyment	Every day	Rare (spectator sports, religious services)
Boundaries	Fluid, companionship culture	Rigid kinship culture, social classes
Physical contact with others	Considerable (sleeping, resting, sitting, dancing)	Minimal
Relations with other groups	Cooperative	Competitive attitude although cooperative action
Individual freedom	Extensive (freedom to leave, to play, freedom of activity; no coercion)	Primarily free to make consumption choices (freedom to move if adult)
Relationships	Egalitarian (no one bosses anyone)	Hierarchical (adults over children, boss over worker, teacher over student)
Contact with other ages	Multi-age group living day and night	Rare outside of family home
Role models	Virtuous	Frequently vicious within popular and news media
Cultural mores	Generosity and cooperation are fostered and expected	Selfishness and stubbornness are expected and fostered by popular culture
Immorality	Cheating, abuse, aggression were not tolerated	Cheating, abuse, aggression expected
Natural world	Embeddedness in and partnership with nature	Detachment from, control and fear of nature

Sources for information include those cited in the text and *The Cambridge Encyclopedia of Hunters and Gatherers* (Lee & Daly, 1999).

these more recent social structures, projecting onto the past a scenario like today's of sexual restriction and competition, assuming sexual competitiveness for virginity, and emphasizing the timing of first sexual behavior. H-EP assumes mate competition and male desire to control female reproduction to ensure genetic dominance. In contrast, among SBGH, sexual relations are widespread with experimentation at all ages (e.g., Everett, 2009). As with our bonobo cousins, individuals do not wait for the right fertile mate. Sexual relations are more about pleasure than control. Moreover, there is no evidence to show that SBGH males are concerned about whose child was theirs, but evidence to the contrary—communal living means collective breeding and alloparenting (Hrdy, 2009). Women control reproduction themselves—they are responsible for killing a newborn who is defective or unable to be cared for by the community.

From the hypotheses that are tested in H-EP, it is clear that they are missing an understanding of the SBGH baseline. Otherwise, for example, why else would they hypothesize a male preference for virginity, a concern of settled societies, not SBGH? In fact, the patriarchy and male dominance H-EP assumes to be normal is about 6000 years old (called the "Great Reversal" by Campbell, 1959–1968) and is non-universal since it does not exist among SBGH.

Personhood and Individualism

SBGH members value individualism but it is of a different nature than the individualism of the modern Western world. Ingold (1999, p. 407) points out the differences: the

Westerner is considered to be rational, self-contained, and autonomous, "locked within the privacy of a body," "standing against" and competing for the "rewards of success" with "an aggregate of other such individuals" in the society; Westerners have anonymous, "brittle, contingent, and transient" relationships that lack "direct, intersubjective involvement" (Ingold, 1999, p. 407).

In contrast, SBGH do not experience a dichotomy between public and private, self and society: "Every individual comes into being as a center of agency and awareness within an unbounded social environment which provides sustenance, care, company, and support. All people and things known, used or made are drawn into the person's subjective identity" (Ingold, 1999, p. 407). The ego is small and the self is large (Taylor, 2010). Selves grow in a supportive web of relations, developing action capacities and perceptual capabilities where personal autonomy "unfolds in purposed action within the web of nurture" (Ingold, 1999, p. 407). Moreover, although conflicts do arise, a person usually does not act against others but *with* them. An individual's intentions and actions originate from and seek realization in and through "the community of nurture to which they all belong" (Ingold, 1999, p. 407). The SBGH orientation to individual-group relations is a good match for Aristotle's rhetoric about virtue and virtue development (Urmson, 1999). Virtue is cultivated within a community and implemented or fulfilled in that community (Narvaez, 2006). And the community envelops not only the humans but all known entities. SBGH spend their lives in what would be called a "higher consciousness," aware of connection and interrelationships with the natural world and cosmos (Taylor, 2010).

Anarchy prevails among SBGH. That is, there is no central authority and no formal leaders. Adults have the freedom to roam and do what they want (Hewlett & Lamb, 2005; Konner, 2010). Children, too, are considered free beings, reincarnations of relatives or gods, not to be coerced (Sahlins, 2008). Among the Semai, for example, coercion is assumed to harm the spirit (*punan*; Dentan, 1968). More experienced persons, such as elders, can *persuade* others to follow their suggestions but no force can be used. Among the Semai, even parents have no authority to coerce children to do something (Dentan, 1968). Yet this does not mean that power is not appreciated. Instead of power as coercion of others, as Westerners often understand it, power is found in a person's skill or wisdom that garners community attention (Ingold, 1999). Relationships are founded on trust—which entails acting "with the person in mind, in the hope and expectation that they will do likewise" toward you, without compulsion or obligation (Ingold, 1999, p. 407). In fact, any move toward domination over another can break a relationship.

SBGH do not countenance inequality in resources or status (Ingold, 1999). They are fiercely egalitarian, an ancient universal (Boehm, 2001). Although individuals may want to lord it over others at times, SBGH have ways to keep this from happening. All over the world in SBGH communities, anthropologists have noted 'rough good humor,' also known as leveling or humility-enforcing after success (Lee, 1988, p. 264). For example, among the Ju/'hoansi or !Kung, when a hunter is successful, ritual insulting of the game takes place. The larger the animal, the greater the teasing. Here is sample dialogue after a successful hunt provided by frequent onlooker Richard Lee (1988, pp. 265–266):

> Hunting group member: "It's so small, it's hardly worth our while; why don't we just leave it? It's still early; we could actually go and hunt something good."

> To which the hunter replies: "You know, you're right. It's nothing. Why don't we just leave it, and go off and hunt something else. Even a porcupine, a rabbit—anything would be better than this."

After a good laugh, they prepare the meat to take home. When asked why they talk like this, one man said: "If somebody gets a big head and thinks a lot of himself, he'll get arrogant; and an arrogant person might hurt someone, he might even kill someone. So we belittle his meat to cool his heart and make him gentle" (Lee, 1988, p. 266). In fact, when someone tries to hoard something for himself, the Ju/'hoansi call that person "far-hearted" (stingy or mean; Lee, 1988). Such social egalitarian practices prevent the individual ego from becoming too large and self-focused.

The United States presents a stark contrast. The individualism of the United States today is a strange and aberrant form of social relations that is a recent historical phenomenon (Sahlins, 2008). Big, selfish egos are assumed to be normal, especially among males and the powerful. Inequality is condoned, with the wealthiest and most powerful controlling the vast majority of resources with its harmful effects on mental and physical health as well as social well-being among the non-powerful (Wilkinson & Pickett, 2009). H-EP tends to assume incorrectly that the current state of affairs, with inequality and hierarchy, was typical of the ancestral SBGH past. On the contrary, political hierarchy (and organized violence) began in the last 1 percent of human genus existence, among societies that cultivated crops, domesticated animals, or stopped roaming and settled down (see Fry, 2006; Wells, 2011).

Group Collectivism

Although there is a greater individualism and individual autonomy among SBGH, there is also a deep collectivism and group identity that focuses on the contemporaneous membership in the group, a membership that fluctuates with the interests of individual members. SBGH members often assume that individuals would not want to be alone, accompanying another into the forest even for pit stops. No one expects or desires to be alone. Social cohesion and communal living is normative. For example, anthropologist Robert Dentan (1968) describes how he and his wife at first tried to tie shut their hut door to keep out Semai community members in order to get more sleep in the morning. But the Semai easily figured out how to untie the door and entered to converse before dawn. The cultural assumption was that the Dentans would *want* to see and talk with them—there was no conception that they would not—and that they would be up before dawn like the rest of the community.

Westerners, in contrast, are trained up to expect aloneness—children are isolated in their own cribs, rooms, and activities, even in early childhood when mammalian development is optimized by constant physical contact and intersubjective social interaction (Schore, 1994, 2001, 2003a, 2003b). Social isolation even briefly after birth in animal studies shows long-term detrimental effects on sociality (e.g., Henry, Richard-Yris, Tordjman, & Hausberger, 2009). Perhaps there is a link between the common experience of early childhood isolation and the epidemic of loneliness among adults in the United States (Cacioppo & Patrick, 2008) and the facts that single adults comprise 50 percent of the adult population and single-adult households outnumber every other type of household (Klinenberg, 2012).

Economics, Pleasure, and Desire

It is clear from ethnographies that SBGH do not fit the Western stereotype—that human nature is full of unlimited wants in a world of limited means, resulting in scarcity. *Homo economicus* (economic man) "is naturally acquisitive, competitive, rational, calculating, and forever looking for ways to improve his material well-being" (Gowdy, 1999, p. 391). As noted in the beginning of the chapter, such a person in a SBGH society would have been deemed immoral or mad. In SBGH societies, pleasure does not come from material wealth—there are few possessions and there is a careless attitude toward them since anything that is needed can be constructed anew. Instead of displaying runaway, materialistic desires presumably inherent in human nature (a notion promulgated by economic science), SBGH members demonstrate few material desires and live sustainably: "Assumptions about human behavior that members of market societies believe to be universal, that humans are naturally competitive and acquisitive, and that social stratification is natural, do not apply to many hunter-gatherer peoples". (Gowdy, 1999, p. 391).

Instead, SBGH individuals find pleasure primarily in social activities. Documented enjoyments include social playing, dancing, singing, joking, laughing, and even sitting close together (e.g., Everett, 2009; Gowdy, 1999; Ingold, 1999). SBGH has no expectation of drudgery. Necessary activities like gathering and hunting are pleasant social activities where no one is coerced to participate, and some never do but still receive a share (Woodburn, 1982).

Recent research demonstrates that pleasant social activities are the kinds of activities that keep a person and their hormones in what I would call a "moral mood"—more generous, compassionate, and easygoing (Batson, Coke, Chard, Smith, & Taliaferro, 1979; Frederickson, 2003). We know that human happiness comes from social play and social activities where a person can "lose himself" in flow with others (Brown, 2009). In contrast, focusing on possessions and money, materialism tends to make one unhappy (Kasser, 2002).

Cooperation Inside and Outside the Group

Contrary to contemporary discourse emphasizing competition in nature, the natural world is characterized primarily by mutualism and symbiosis (Kropotkin, 1902; see Ryan, 2002, for a review). Competition and aggression characterize a relatively small proportion of relations among naturally ordered systems. Humans, too, are prepared to be cooperative from birth (Trevarthen, 2005).

Nevertheless, H-EP assumes that humans are naturally selfish, a viewpoint rampant in USA culture (creating a society to match, according to Schwartz, 1986). H-EP assumes that our ancestors were naturally detached, territorial, aggressive and possession-driven, much like us today (e.g., Buss, 2005). This is also mistaken. Among SBGH, generosity and sharing are group mores (Ingold, 1999). SBGH have an immediate-return economy, in which food is used immediately rather than being stored (Woodburn, 1982). They demonstrate "lack of foresight" about food and resources, sharing them with others today rather than hoarding them for tomorrow. Sahlins (2008, p. 51) notes: "Natural self interest? For the greater part of humanity, self-interest as we know it is unnatural in the normative sense; it is considered madness, witchcraft or some such grounds for ostracism, execution, or at least therapy. Rather than expressing a pre-social human nature, such avarice is generally taken for a loss of humanity."

H-EP assumes competition and coalitionary violence among our SBGH ancestors (e.g., Pinker, 2011). But the data do not support this view. Cooperation was common among groups that often held relatives (Fry, 2006; Ingold, 1999). Groups were permeable and fluid. Yet H-EP assumes strict ingroup/outgroup relations and rivalry between groups instead of cooperation (the "pervasive intergroup hostility model," Fry, 2006; for examples, see Buss, 1999; Ghiglieri, 1999; Wrangham & Petersen, 1996). Most SBGH do not engage in war and are generally unwarlike in their cultural orientations, living "without centralized authority, standing armies, or bureaucratic systems. Yet the evidence indicates that they have lived together surprisingly well, solving their problems among themselves largely without recourse to authority figures and without a particular propensity for violence" (Lee & Daly, 1999, p. 1). There is little to be competitive about since there are no possessions, women have their own autonomy, and childrearing is communal. Wiessner (1981) documents how relations are carefully maintained with distant groups whose good will was assumed when food supplies were limited during times of stress.

Of course, aggressive tendencies are inherent in nature if one counts survival mechanisms that are triggered under perceived threat—true for all organisms. However, dispositional aggression and selfish human personality result from experience during periods sensitive to epigenetic and plastic effects (Narvaez & Gleason, 2012), or else an adopted cultural worldview (Narvaez, 2008; 2009; in preparation). Using Western personality as a baseline for describing human nature generally represents an ethnocentric and ignorant viewpoint that misrepresents the data (for reviews, see Fry, 2006; Ingold, Riches, & Woodburn, 1988a, 1988b; Lee & Daly, 1999).

Sustainable Lifestyle

Because the members of most of SBGH societies have everything they need and spend their time primarily in leisure and interpersonal enjoyment, without "social classes and arguably no discrimination based on gender" (Gowdy, 1999, p. 391), Sahlins (1972) calls the lifestyle the "original affluent society." They live "in equilibrium with their environment, without destroying the resources upon which their economies were based" (Sahlins, 1972). They have no agriculture or industry, and few possessions, challenging our notion of what a good life requires.

Some argue that because SBGH are mobile, they are unable to want too much, focused forever on the present (Sahlins, 1972). Although this may be true, they also have a greater intelligence and deep regard for natural resources—for example, making substitutions when a resource seems overstressed (Woodburn, 1980). They make decisions communally, focused on the long-term welfare of the group with a sense of relational commitment to everything in the natural world.

Human Nature, Virtue, and Natural Morality

In *The Human Cycle*, Colin Turnbull (1984) contrasts the life-course of the Mbuti gatherer-hunters of formerly Zaire (now Democratic Republic of the Congo) with that of Westerners, particularly his own upbringing in Britain (having nannies, going to boarding and exclusive schools). I find his comparisons most apt to illustrate how we have come to be such different peoples with different brains, minds, and worldviews.

The Mbuti mother and child had an "intense, continuous, and consistent physical proximity" during the first three years of life, sharing in mutual reciprocity (Turnbull, 1984, p. 75). Turnbull's own experience of "caring" was vastly different, with an emphasis on "a possessiveness that divided the family and an insistence that the child, unable to care for itself, had to have goodness, or what was deemed good for the child, imposed on the helpless creature." Because of the missing grounding of mutuality, "The cooperation that emerges later in life—and in our modern society cooperation is every bit as necessary as it is in all societies—is mechanical, rather than organic, because it was learned by imposition rather than felt through reciprocation" (Turnbull, 1984, p. 75). Whereas the Mbuti have an inner drive to cooperate, the Westerner, even through adulthood, must sometimes be coerced to behave in a social manner. He described Mbuti children on the verge of adolescence as having had all their capacities "explored and developed to the limit; not just their bodies, but their senses of sight, smell, touch, and hearing have all been nurtured as instruments of learning and communication" (Turnbull, 1984, p. 73). Turnbull contrasts his own preparation for adolescence, in which he experienced coercion toward manly violence. For example, he was roundly criticized for his failure to do well in competitive sports with hints that he was a coward because he was assumed to be afraid to use his body for violence.

SBGH didn't need a commandment to "love your neighbor" because one does so when one is raised with kindness and compassion, with early needs fully met, when secure attachment is formed along with a resilient brain and psyche (Sills, 2009). Ancestral parenting practices and social conditions foster a natural morality that follows Piaget's (1932/1965) notion that "morality is the logic of action." In the ancestral context, this is a truism. Virtue and survival go hand in hand. Cooperation is essential for life.

Contrasting Cultures: The Abandonment of Natural Virtue Development in the West

The human genus spent 99 percent of its existence in a lifestyle that is egalitarian, emphasizing individual autonomy, immersed in nearly constant, pleasurable social activity—whether gathering, hunting, social leisure, or sleeping, attending primarily to the here and now with minimal possessions or planning for the distant future. So different from the modern Western context, it is not surprising that the two environments foster different moral personalities (Narvaez, 2008; in preparation). Among SBGH, the majority of moral functioning is focused on social *engagement*—relational presence, a moral mindset that treats others as equals through social play and friendship. In fact at birth, babies appear to expect this type of *companionship* attachment as well as a caring attachment (Trevarthen, 2005) and they receive this in SBGH. Occasionally in SBGH environments, self-protection (*safety ethic*) becomes a primary mindset, mostly in reaction to predators but rarely in reaction to other people. Abstracting capabilities typically would include the community as the grounding for thought—*communal imagination*. In contrast, the US environment fosters moral functioning as mostly social self-protection—social withdrawal—or gaining control, dominance, and status. Imaginative capabilities emphasize personal gain that is emotionally detached instead of emotionally present (see Figure 17.1). The ancestral context and the modern US context foster a distinctive set of moral mindsets and capabilities. How did this happen?

Shift to Fixedness and Materialism and Away from Autonomy and Presence

What has become plain to me, from reading anthropological accounts like Turnbull's, analyzing our own childrearing practices, and comparing outcomes, is that Western culture has extirpated the evolved grounding of moral rationality and moral development (Narvaez, 2012). This has been happening for some time but may be reaching its nadir (Taylor, 2005). Historically in delayed-return societies (in contrast to SBGH immediate-return), an ideology of sacralized leadership and centralized authority emerged, with its accompanying control of women and young men by older men (Barnard & Woodburn, 1988). Those with power (older men) fostered an ideology that established fixed relations among humans (e.g., institutionalized marriage). Fixed relations were given power over individual autonomy. Further, the possessions that accumulated with power were themselves imbued with mystical power over human autonomy (e.g., private property). The pinnacle of this

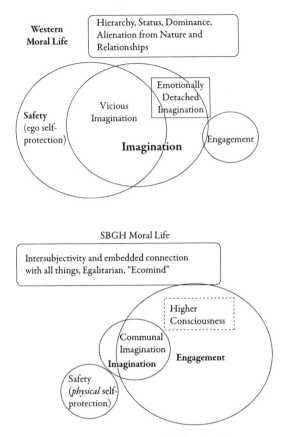

FIGURE 17.1 Contrasting moral lives: Western versus small-band gatherer-hunter.

mythology is a corporate capitalist system so powerful, pervasive, and destructive that it "shall not be named" and is taken as a baseline for how reality works so any questioning of its assumptions (e.g., competitiveness, self-interest, "free" markets) is considered absurd. Through an emphasis on consumption and materialism, US cultural narratives and societal practices have denigrated close maternal, familial, and community care, as well as true individual autonomy and the self-development necessary for a confident social being. What do I mean more specifically?

Violations of Evolved Mammalian Parenting Practices

Trauma and undercare of children may be a primary cause of our differences (Narvaez, in preparation). Undercare refers to the absence of ancestral caregiving practices in early life. Ancestral caregiving among humans represent slight variations to social mammalian parenting that emerged more than 30 million years ago: responsiveness to the needs of the child, constant touch, breastfeeding for at least two years, multiple adult caregivers, extensive positive social support for mother and child, free play in nature (Hewlett & Lamb, 2005), as well as natural childbirth. These practices are related to optimal functioning physiologically, psychologically, and morally (Narvaez & Gleason, in press). All these practices have diminished over the twentieth century in the United States (Narvaez, Panksepp, Schore, & Gleason, 2012). Widespread lack of social support for optimal early caregiving may be undermining all the rest of the practices, as this lack leads to distracted and less responsive caregiving (Crockenberg, 1981; Garmezy, 1983) that worsens by generation.

Coercion is Normative

Although humanity may have become less warlike in recent millennia and looks comparatively less *physically* violent (Pinker, 2011), today there is a great deal of violence built into a child's life from childbirth on. According to the U.S. National Center for Health Statistics, more and more children in the United States are coerced into the world with labor induction and cesareans. Hospital childbirth practices are detrimental to child well-being (e.g., Henry, Richard-Yris, Tordjman, & Hausberger, 2009). Commonly used maternal drugs during childbirth numb the fetus, and extensive interference during and after birth thwarts the newborn's energy to reach for the mother's breast (Mercer, Erickson-Owens, Graves, & Haley, 2007). Separation from mother at birth at all is traumatic and can have long-term effects but it happens routinely in the United States (Bystrova et al., 2009). Isolating children throughout childhood from close contact (i.e., in their own rooms, cribs, carriers, playpens, strollers) has become the norm, which is the equivalent of punishing young children for the mammalian desire to be physically in touch with caregivers. The trauma of early life experience for many children leads them to a self-protective orientation to social and moral life (Narvaez, 2008; in preparation).

Violation of Children's Birth Rights

Children are born ready for a companionship culture (Trevarthen, 2005). They begin to communicate, expecting a response, from the first day of a natural birth. They are ready for embeddedness in social life, which fosters not only strong emotional attachment but cognitive and emotional intelligence (Greenspan & Shanker, 2004). Denying children companionship not only leads to the multiple poor outcomes mentioned previously, but thwarts children's flourishing. In light of the decline of all ancestral early life caregiving practices, perhaps a declaration for the rights of the baby is needed.[5]

Long-Term Effects of Undercare

Children who are undercared for are more likely to have decrements on multiple levels (Narvaez, in preparation). Neurotransmitters are faulty, leading to memory problems (autobiographical, working memory); the immune system is poorly developed, leading to increased illness and "sickness behavior" that is comparable to depression; the neuroendocrine and stress response systems are poorly established, leading for example to stress reactivity (Meaney, 2001). Undercare does not foster prosocial emotions adequately, leading to faulty attachment replaced with addictions or hoarding, but also to underdeveloped moral systems.

My research collaborators and I (Narvaez, Gleason, Brooks, Wang, Lefever, Cheng, & Centers for the Prevention of Child Neglect, 2012, Narvaez, Gleason, Cheng, Wang, & Brooks, 2012; Narvaez, Wang, Gleason, Cheng, Lefever, & Deng, 2012) have been examining ancestral parenting practices, suspecting that these matter for becoming a good and useful human being of the ancestral sort. In our studies we are finding that children with longer breastfeeding, more positive touch, or more play had better self-regulation and higher empathy than those with less of each of these parenting practices. Children whose mothers had positive attitudes about all ancestral parenting practices display more joy, consideration, empathy, imagination, and social attunement. A cross-cultural comparison of our US and China samples indicates that ancestral parenting practices affected three-year-olds' moral and social functioning in both the US and China, with different patterns for each country.

Contrasting Moral Universes.

Figure 17.1 illustrates postulated differences between the typical Western mind (at least for the United States) and the SBGH mind. The sizes of the circles indicate the amount of time generally spent in each mindset. Current parenting, schooling, and culture in the United States cultivate the safety ethic (mostly as *social* self-protection rather than from an other-species predator) and detached imagination but little engagement. Maternal and familial distraction and intergenerational trauma foster little right-brain development, leaving in charge either the left-brain, detached imagination or the reptilian survival (fight, flight, or freeze) mechanisms (safety ethic). Individuals flip between apathy (especially toward nature) and fear/rage toward change/ difference/the Other. Schooling that only emphasizes conscious, explicit understanding, reasoning, logic, linearity, and representations (rather than actual experience, emotion, connection, awareness) can leave children spiritless.

Undermining the evolutionarily-evolved principles of childrearing, as the West has done, leaves the child with no internal moral compass. Instead, morality must be imposed externally—through rules, sanctions, or constructed incentives. And each group or subgroup has its ideology that clashes with another's. Beliefs become all important because there is lack of shared *experiential* knowledge and intuitions that come from intersubjective experience with one another and the natural world. This contrasts with the vast experience of regular intersubjective relational presence in the SBGH context, with imagination used for communal ends.

Could and Should We Shift Our Baselines
Back to The 99 Percent?

How did the United States in particular bring about so much truly self-centered behavior, visible in all ages and nearly all walks of life (Callahan, 2004)? The United States seems to have particularly virulent strains of Western ideologies including "human-nature-as-evil," "body-as-disgusting," "body-as-machine," "nature-as-separate," and the illusions of extreme individualism. Cultural expectations and encouragement of selfishness struck the United States hard, particularly in the twentieth century (see Ayn Rand's influence on political figures, Levine, 2011). Popular culture escalates the ongoing sense of threat and insecurity that results in a self-protective mindset. Worst of all, popular culture and some religious leaders encourage parents to violate many of the evolved basic principles of early life care, an especially sensitive period. More than ever, culture has extirpated the moral foundations for our sociality and our relationship with nature.

Some might argue that we cannot go back to earlier lifestyles, and besides—who wants to live outside with bugs and predators? The purpose of using evolutionary baselines is not to romanticize the past (or romanticize the present like H-EP seems to do). A proper evolutionary baseline can help us understand whether today's human behavior and health outcomes are normative for human beings—part of their natural nature, or maladaptations that emerge from a mismatch between evolved needs and current environments. Sometimes researchers find a mismatch and assume there is nothing that can be done (e.g., overexposure to strangers in modern cities). The point here is that there truly is something that we can do to shift current baselines for human development in a way that fosters greater well-being, not only in humans but also for the natural world.

What can we do? First, we must remember that we are mammals and mammals require particular circumstances for flourishing. We do not thrive in isolation, without autonomy or positive social support. We should not blame children for their misbehavior if they have been raised without one or more of these basic needs. Instead, we should ensure that all persons receive what they evolved to need, especially in the first years of life when brain and body systems are being established. Second, we need to remember that much of human nature and well-being is malleable but as a dynamic system, whose initial conditions are magnified and built upon for all later developments. Great care should be taken about preparing for pregnancy, childbirth, and postnatal care—by the whole community. Third, we need to reestablish ancestral parenting practices to the degree possible, to ensure that long-term well-being is fostered by a good beginning. We can change the environment for young children to match up with their human mammalian needs. Here are a few examples of what can be done. We can establish means of milk sharing among women, as occurs under ancestral conditions (Hrdy, 2009). We can establish workplaces where babies can be kept in close contact with caregivers, encourage safe bed-sharing, encourage extensive support systems for families, design child raising with free play in mind, and practice natural childbirth for most births. Some countries have been moving in these directions, such as those who have adopted the World Health Organization's "baby-friendly" hospital initiative (only 4 percent of US hospitals are "baby-friendly" according to a 2011 report by the Centers for Disease Control). Finally, promoting intersubjectivity from the beginning of life, inclusive of other creatures and life-forms as among SBGH, can help promote ecological mindedness, instead of the detached orientation to the natural world that has become so prevalent and damaging to our habitat, the earth.

Conclusion

Some argue that humanity is starting to (re-)tame the ego and reintegrate the psyche of our forebears, shown by an increased sense of empathy for the less fortunate, animals, and a deeper connection with indigenous cultures and the natural world in recent generations (Taylor, 2005). Part of this change requires a move toward a sense of Spirit (in Turnbull's term), which is a right-brain holistic orientation (see McGilchrist, 2009) that allows us to discern the ultimate unity of all living things, as we know they are at the quantum level. This higher consciousness imbues everyday experience for SBGH who have an "awareness of Spirit that enables them to accept differences of manner, custom, speech, behavior, even of belief, while still feeling an underlying unity. It is awareness of Spirit that enables them to avoid the conflict and hostility that arise so easily from such differences" (Turnbull, 1984, p. 75). Such an awareness leads to a deep respect and affection for the non-human natural world but also for children. Treating children and their needs with generosity may be required for a shift toward our full human capacities. With a greater awareness of the good life we could be living, we can reengineer our social structures and expectations away from fostering destructive and harmful lives and toward nurturing sensible, good, and useful lives.

Notes

1. The Yahgan see the goal of life to become "a good and useful human being" (Gusinde, 1937).
2. Gatherer-hunters is a more accurate term than hunter-gatherers because in these types of societies generally, the vast majority of foods sources are gathered.
3. There is some evidence of collector societies some 40,000 years ago, but this was a minority (See Vanhaeren & d'Errico, 2005).
4. For more information on immediate versus delayed-return societies, see Kelly (2007), Lee and Daly (1999).
5. See blog post on this for initial ideas for a declaration for the rights of the baby: http://www.psychologyto-day.com/blog/moral-landscapes/201111/do-we-need-declaration-the-rights-the-baby

References

Barnard, A., & Woodburn, J. (1988). Introduction. In T. Ingold, D. Riches, & J. Woodburn (Eds.), *Hunters and gatherers, Vol. 2, Property, power and ideology* (pp. 4–32). Oxford, England: Berg.
Batson, C. D., Coke, J. S., Chard, F., Smith, D., & Taliaferro, A. (1979). Generality of the "Glow of Goodwill": Effects of Mood on Helping and Information Acquisition, *Social Psychology Quarterly, 42*(2), 176–179.
Bird-David, N. (1994). Sociality and immediacy or past and present conversations on bands. *Man, 29,* 583–603.
Boehm, C. (2001). *Hierarchy in the forest.* Cambridge, MA: Harvard University Press.
Bowlby, J. (1951). *Maternal care and mental health.* New York: Schocken.
Brown, S. (2009). *Play: How it shapes the brain, opens the imagination, and invigorates the soul.* New York: Avery.
Buss, D. M. (2005). *The murderer next door: Why the mind is designed to kill.* New York: Penguin Press.

Buss, D. M. (1999). *Evolutionary psychology: The new science of the mind.* Boston: Allyn & Bacon.

Bystrova, K., Ivanova, V., Edhborg, M., Matthiesen, A. S., Ransjö-Arvidson, A. B., Mukhamedrakhimov, R., Uvnäs-Moberg, K., Widström, A. M. (2009). Early contact versus separation: Effects on mother-infant interaction one year later. *Birth, 36*(2), 97–109.

Caccioppo, J. T., & Patrick, W. (2008). *Loneliness: Human nature and the need for social connection.* New York: Norton.

Callahan, D. (2004). *The cheating culture: Why more Americans are doing wrong to get ahead.* New York, NY: Harcourt Harvest.

Campbell, J. (1959–1968). *The masks of God.* New York: Viking Press.

Coontz, S. (1992). *The way we never were: American families and the nostalgia trap.* New York: Basic Books.

Crockenberg, S. B. (1981). Infant irritability, mother responsiveness, and social support influences on the security of infant-mother attachment. *Child Development, 52*(3), 857–865.

Dentan, R. K. (1968). *The Semai: A nonviolent people of Malaya.* New York, NY: Harcourt Brace College Publishers.

Everett, D. (2009). *Don't sleep, there are snakes.* New York, NY: Pantheon.

Fredrickson, B. L. (2003). The value of positive emotions. *American Scientist, 91,* 330–335.

Fry, D. P. (2006). *The human potential for peace.* New York: Oxford University Press.

Garmezy, N. (1983). Stressors of childhood. In N. Garmezy & M. Rutter (Eds.), *Stress, coping, and development in children* (pp. 43–84). New York: McGraw-Hill.

Ghiglieri, M. P. (1999). *The dark side of man: Tracing the origins of male violence.* Reading, MA: Perseus.

Gibson, T. (1985). The sharing of substance versus the sharing of activity among the Buid. *Man, 20,* 391–441.

Gowdy, J. (1999). Gatherer-hunters and the mythology of the market. In R. B. Lee & R. Daly (Eds.), *The Cambridge encyclopedia of hunters and gatherers* (pp. 391–398). New York: Cambridge University Press.

Gusinde, M. (1937). *The Yahgan: The life and thought of the water nomads of Cape Horn,* (F. Schütze, Trans.). In the electronic Human Relations Area Files, Yahgan, Doc. 1. New Haven, CT: HRAF, 2003.

Henry S., Richard-Yris M.-A., Tordjman S., & Hausberger M. (2009) Neonatal Handling Affects Durably Bonding and Social Development. *PLoS ONE 4*(4): e5216. doi:10.1371/journal.pone.0005216

Hewlett, B. S., & Lamb, M. E. (2005). *Hunter-gatherer childhoods: Evolutionary, developmental and cultural perspectives.* New Brunswick, NJ: Aldine.

Hobbes, T. (2010). *Leviathan- Revised* Edition, A. P. Martinich & B. Battiste (Eds.). Peterborough, ON: Broadview Press.

Hrdy, S. (2009). *Mothers and others: The evolutionary origins of mutual understanding.* Cambridge, MA: Belknap Press.

Ingold, T. (1999). On the social relations of the hunter-gatherer band. In R. B. Lee & R. Daly (Eds.), *The Cambridge encyclopedia of hunters and gatherers* (pp. 399–410). New York: Cambridge University Press.

Ingold, T., Riches, D., & Woodburn, J. (1988a). *Hunters and gatherers, Vol. 1: History, evolution and social change.* Oxford, England: Berg.

Ingold, T., Riches, D., & Woodburn, J. (1988b). *Hunters and gatherers, Vol. 2: Property, power and ideology.* Oxford, England: Berg.

Kasser, T. (2002). *The high price of materialism.* Cambridge, MA: MIT Press.

Kelly, R. L. (2007). *The foraging spectrum: Diversity in hunter-gatherer lifeways.* Clinton Corners, NY: Eliot Werner Publications.

Klinenberg, E. (2012). *Going solo: The extraordinary rise and surprising appeal of living alone.* New York: Penguin Press.

Konner, M. (2010). *The evolution of childhood.* New York: Oxford University Press.

Kropotkin, P. (1902). *Mutual aid: A factor of evolution.* London: Dodo Press.

Lee, R. B. (1979). *The !Kung San: Men, women, and work in a foraging community.* Cambridge: Cambridge University Press.

Lee, R. B., & Daly, R. (Eds.) (1999). *The Cambridge encyclopedia of hunters and gatherers.* New York: Cambridge University Press.

Levine, B. E. (2011). *How Ayn Rand seduced generations of young men and helped make the U.S. into a selfish, greedy nation.* New York: Chelsea Green.

Marshall, L. (1976). *The !Kung of Nyae Nyae.* Cambridge: Harvard University Press.

McGilchrist, I. (2009). *The master and the emissary: The divided brain and the making of the Western world*. New Haven, CT: Yale University Press.

Meaney, M. J. (2001). Maternal care, gene expression, and the transmission of individual differences in stress reactivity across generations. *Annual Review of Neuroscience, 24*, 1161–1192.

Mercer, J. S., Erickson-Owens, D.A., Graves, B., Haley, M. M. (2007). Evidence-based practices for the fetal to newborn transition. *Journal of Midwifery and Women's Health, 52*(3), 262–72.

Narvaez, D. (2006). Integrative Ethical Education. In M. Killen & J. Smetana (Eds.), *Handbook of Moral Development* (pp. 703–733). Mahwah, NJ: Erlbaum.

Narvaez, D. (2008). Triune ethics: The neurobiological roots of our multiple moralities. *New Ideas in Psychology, 26*, 95–119.

Narvaez, D. (2009). Triune ethics theory and moral personality. In D. Narvaez & D. K. Lapsley (Eds.), *Personality, identity and character: Explorations in moral psychology* (pp. 136–158). New York: Cambridge University Press.

Narvaez, D. (2012). Moral rationality. *Tradition and Discovery, XXXVIII* (2), 25–33.

Narvaez, D. (in preparation). *The neurobiology and development of human morality*. New York: Norton.

Narvaez, D., & Gleason, T. (2012). Developmental optimization. In D. Narvaez, J., Panksepp, A. Schore, & T. Gleason (Eds.), *Evolution, early experience and human development: From research to practice and policy* (pp. xx-xx). New York: Oxford University Press.

Narvaez, D., Gleason, T., Brooks, J. Wang, L., Lefever, J., Cheng, A., & Centers for the Prevention of Child Neglect (2012). *Longitudinal effects of ancestral parenting practices on early childhood outcomes*. Manuscript submitted for publication.

Narvaez, D., Gleason, T., Cheng, A., Wang, L., & Brooks, J., (2012). *Nurturing parenting attitudes influence moral development in three-year-olds*. Manuscript submitted for publication.

Narvaez, D., Wang, L., Gleason, T., Cheng, A., Lefever, J., & Deng, L. (2012). *Ancestral parenting practices and child outcomes in Chinese three-year-olds*. Manuscript submitted for publication.

Narvaez, D., Panksepp, J., Schore, A., & Gleason, T. (Eds.) (2012). *Evolution, early experience and human development: From research to practice and policy*. New York: Oxford University Press.

Narvaez, D., Panksepp, J., Schore, A., & Gleason, T. (2012). The value of the environment of evolutionary adaptedness for gauging children's well-being. In D. Narvaez, J. Panksepp, A. Schore, & T. Gleason (Eds.), *Evolution, early experience and human development: From research to practice and policy* (pp. xx-xx). New York: Oxford University Press.

Piaget, J. (1932/1965). *The moral judgment of the child* (M. Gabain, Trans.). New York: Free Press.

Pinker, S. (2011). *The better angels of our nature*. New York: Viking.

Ryan, F. (2002). *Darwin's blind spot: Evolution beyond natural selection*. New York: Houghton Mifflin Harcourt.

Sahlins, M. (1972). *Stone-age economics*. Chicago: Aldine.

Sahlins, M. (2008). *The Western Illusion of Human Nature*. Chicago: Prickly Paradigm Press.

Schore, A. N. (1994). *Affect regulation*. Hillsdale, NJ: Erlbaum.

Schore, A. N. (2001). The effects of early relational trauma on right brain development, affect regulation, and infant mental health. *Infant Mental Health Journal, 22*, 201–269.

Schore, A. N. (2003a). *Affect regulation and the repair of the self*. New York: Norton.

Schore, A. N. (2003b). *Affect dysregulation and disorders of the self*. New York: Norton.

Schwartz, B. (1986). *The battle for human nature*. New York: Norton.

Shostak, M. (1981). *Nisa: The life and words of !Kung woman*. New York: Vintage Books.

Sills, F. (2009). *Being and becoming: Psychodynamics, Buddhism, and the origins of selfhood*. Berkeley, CA: North Atlantic Books.

Taylor, S. (2005). *The fall: The insanity of the ego in human history and the dawning of a new era*. New York: O-Books.

Taylor, S. (2010). *Waking from sleep: Why awakening experiences occur and how to make them permanent*. Carlsbad, CA: Hayhouse.

Thomas, E. M. (1989). *The harmless people* (rev. ed.). New York: Vintage.

Trevarthen, C. (2005). "Stepping away from the mirror: Pride and shame in adventures of companionship"—Reflections on the nature and emotional needs of infant intersubjectivity. In C. S. Carter, K. E., Grossmann, S. B., Hrdy, M. E. Lamb, S. W. Porges, & N. Sachser (Eds.), *Attachment and bonding: A new synthesis*. Cambridge, MA: MIT Press.

Turnbull, C. (1984). *The human cycle*. New York: Simon & Schuster.

Urmson, J.O. (1988). *Aristotle's ethics*. Oxford: Blackwell.

Vanhaeren, M., & d'Errico, F. (2005). Grave goods from the Saint-Germain-la-Rivère burial: Evidence for social inequality in the Upper Paleolithic. *Journal of Anthropological Archaeology, 24*, 117–34.

Wiessner, P. (1981). Measuring the impact of social ties on nutritional status among the !Kung San. *Social Science Information, 20*, 641–678.

Wells, S. (2011). *Pandora's seed: The unforeseen cost of civilization*. New York: Random House.

Wilkinson, R. & Pickett, K. (2009). *The spirit level: Why equality is better for everyone*. London: Penguin.

Wilson, P. J. (1988). *The domestication of the human species*. New Haven: Yale University Press.

Woodburn, J. (1980). Hunter-gatherers today and reconstruction of the past. In E. Gellner (Ed.), *Soviet and Western anthropology* (pp. 95–117). London: Duckworth.

Woodburn, J. (1982). Egalitarian societies. *Man, 17*, 431–451.

Wrangham, R., & Petersen, D. (1996). *Demonic males: Apes and the origin of human violence*. Boston: Houghton Mifflin.

PART FOUR

The Primatological Context of Human Nature

18

Chimpanzees, Warfare, and the Invention of Peace

Michael L. Wilson

Many features of human societies are clearly inventions, such as agriculture (Bocquet-Appel, 2011), the domestication of cattle (Zeder, 2011), and writing (Woods, 2010). Other human traits are genetic adaptations and thus the products of evolution by natural selection, such as malaria resistance (Hedrick, 2011), lactase persistence (Leonardi, Gerbault, Thomas, & Burger, 2012), and, arguably, language (Pinker & Bloom, 1990). Anthropologists have long debated whether warfare is an invention (Gabriel, 1990; Haas, 2001; Kelly, 2000; Mead, 1940; Montagu, 1976) or an adaptation (Alexander, 1979; Gat, 2006; Tooby & Cosmides, 1988; Wrangham & Peterson 1996; van der Dennen, 1995). This debate largely follows the intellectual traditions established by Hobbes and Rousseau (Otterbein, 1999; Gat, 2006). Hobbes (1651/1997) considered "Warre" to be the natural state of humans, with strong institutions (the "Leviathan") being necessary to keep in check natural tendencies toward selfishness, theft, and violence. In contrast, Rousseau (1754/1964) argued that people were basically peaceful and cooperative, until corrupted by institutions such as property ownership. Hobbes and Rousseau illustrated their arguments with imagined states of nature, based mainly on their own intuitions and experiences, combined with travelers' tales of "savages" in the Americas and elsewhere, and, for Rousseau, early descriptions of the behavior of African apes (Rousseau, 1754/1964).

While rooted in competing philosophical traditions, the question of whether warfare is an invention or an adaptation is ultimately an empirical one, which can be answered (at least in principle) by evidence from archaeology, ethnography, and other sources, including animal behavior. Field studies of our evolutionary cousins, chimpanzees, have played an important role in this debate (Boehm, 1992; Bowles, 2009; Eibl-Eibesfelt, 1979; Kelly, 2005; Otterbein, 2004; Sussman, 1999; Wrangham & Peterson, 1996). Here I review the evidence for warlike behavior in chimpanzees and discuss what these findings can tell us about human warfare. I begin with a review of the behavioral ecology of aggression, continue with an overview of the behavioral ecology of intergroup aggression in chimpanzees, and conclude with discussion of the implications for understanding the origins of war and prospects for peace in humans.

Behavioral Ecology of Aggression

A widespread impression is that biological explanations lead to models of human behavior that are simplistic and inflexible, and as a result, pessimistic about the possibilities for improving the human condition. For example, Thorpe (2003) rejects the view that warfare could be an adaptation because he infers that "universal theories" such as evolutionary psychology "imply uniformity." However, identifying a process as biological by no means implies that it occurs uniformly. Sweating, for example, is clearly a biological adaptation designed to cool the body by evaporation, but sweating does not occur uniformly: it occurs when people are hot. Moreover, some people sweat more than others, depending on their physiology and degree of experience with a particular environment.

Equating "biological" with "uniform" applies to an outmoded view of biology. For several decades, behavioral ecologists have argued differently: that animals are designed by evolution to respond appropriately to the various contexts in which they are likely to find themselves. Behavioral ecology is a branch of animal behavior studies that focuses on the ecological and evolutionary basis of the behavior of animals, including humans (Krebs & Davies, 1993). It broadly shares conceptual foundations with its intellectual offshoot, evolutionary psychology (White, Dill, & Crawford, 2007), but retains a greater emphasis on how behavior responds to specific contexts.

The central working hypothesis of behavioral ecology is that organisms are designed by natural selection to solve one basic problem: making more copies of their genes, or in more technical terms, maximizing their inclusive fitness (Dawkins, 1976/1989). Natural selection designs organisms to respond to features of their environment adaptively—that is, in ways that increase the probability that they will survive and reproduce. Some features are invariant or predictable, such as gravity or daily light cycles, while other features recur regularly, but are difficult to predict, such as the location of key food sources, the relative quality of different food sources, or the behavior of potential predators, prey, mates, and rivals. Simple rules may provide adaptive outcomes for invariant or predictable features, but organisms whose lives depend on suitable interactions with less predictable features of the environment have evolved complex sensory and nervous systems to evaluate and respond appropriately to the current state of their environment.

For animals, the most important features of their environment and yet most difficult to predict are often members of their own species (conspecifics). Animals that reproduce sexually typically need other conspecifics in order to reproduce, and they therefore may court and/or coerce potential mates. They may care for their offspring, cooperate with allies, and threaten and fight their rivals. Aggressive behavior thus constitutes only one of many dimensions of social behavior. Sussman and colleagues (2005) have argued that researchers have paid excessive attention to aggression, as it constitutes only a small proportion of the activity budget of most primate species. However, the amount of time that animals spend doing something is at best an incomplete measure of the importance of that activity in evolutionary terms. Mating, for example, occupies a tiny proportion of the activity budget for most species. For example, female ringtailed lemurs are sexually active for only 6 to 24 hours per year (Sauther, Sussman, & Gould, 1999). Nonetheless, without mating, lemurs would have no reproductive success. Likewise, being preyed upon, or being killed by a conspecific, takes up very little of an animal's activity budget, but prevents future reproduction entirely.

Natural selection involves competition, and competition is frequently lethal (Darwin 1859/2003). Predators kill their prey, as do seed predators that kill the embryos of unborn plants. Parasites consume the flesh and blood of their living hosts. Parasitoid wasps lay their eggs in living hosts, which will be eaten alive from within by the growing larvae. Animals fight other members of their species over access to key resources, and under some circumstances, fighting may be fatal.

Behavioral ecologists view aggression as a strategy that animals use when assessment indicates that the benefits will outweigh the costs, with costs and benefits measured in terms of inclusive fitness (Parker, 1974; Maynard Smith & Parker, 1976). Individuals may benefit by behaving aggressively by displacing rivals from key resources, such as mates, food, or shelter. Costs of aggression include time and energy that could be spent on other activities, as well as the risk of injury or death. Because aggression generally involves costs, animals usually avoid getting into direct fights if they can (Fry & Szala, chapter 23). Instead, they threaten and display at their rivals. If they do get into a direct fight, animals usually seem content to chase rivals off, rather than pursuing, capturing, and killing them. Fatal fights may occur, however, when the value of the resource is particularly high, or when the fighters do not expect to live long, or when the cost of killing their opponent is low (Enquist & Leimar, 1990). In some species of spider, for example, females are scattered widely across the landscape. Because males can only travel slowly and face high risks of predation, males may expect to mate with at most one female during their life. If two males happen to encounter the same female, they often fight to the death for her. This tendency is explicable given that this may be their only lifetime mating opportunity (Enquist & Leimar, 1990).

Thus, rather than following a simple strategy of always behaving aggressively, animals instead appear designed to employ aggression selectively, escalating to damaging fights only when the stakes are high, and/or assessment indicates they have a reasonable chance of winning (Keil & Watson, 2011). Animals must therefore assess likely benefits, such as the value of a particular mate or food resource, as well as their chances of winning, should a fight occur. In cases of fights, several factors influence the outcome. Most important is the relative competitive ability of opponents. Larger individuals, as well as those better equipped with weapons such as canine teeth, tusks, or horns, are generally more likely to win (Parker, 1974). In fights between groups, the larger group usually has an advantage, which can be expected to increase with increasing disparity in numbers. Motivation also plays a role, in that individuals may fight harder to defend something they already have, or if their life depends on the outcome. For example, in a series of playback experiments conducted in Serengeti National Park, Tanzania, female lions (*Panthera leo*) were more likely to approach simulated intruders the more they outnumbered them (McComb et al., 1994). Male lions, however, whose entire lifetime reproductive success depends on maintaining control of a pride of females, approached simulated intruders even when outnumbered (Grinnell, Packer, & Pusey, 1995).

In summary, behavioral ecologists view aggression as a strategic option to be used in circumstances under which, over evolutionary time, such aggression has tended to pay off. In the next section, I review what has been learned about the behavioral ecology of intergroup aggression in chimpanzees.

Intergroup Aggression in Chimpanzees

Since 1960, when Jane Goodall began the first long-term field study of chimpanzees at what is now Gombe National Park, Tanzania, field researchers have learned much about the lives of chimpanzees. Chimpanzees have been studied at over 50 sites across Africa (Wrangham, McGrew, de Waal, & Heltne, 1994). The longest-term studies include Gombe (1960–present; Goodall, 1986) and Mahale (1965–present; Nishida, 1990) in Tanzania, Kanyawara (1987–present; Wrangham, Chapman, Clark-Arcadi, & Isabirye-Basuta, 1996), Budongo (1990–present; Reynolds, 2005) and Ngogo (1995–present; Watts, 2012) in Uganda, Bossou (1976–present; Matsuzawa, Humle, & Sugiyama, 2011) in Guinea, and Taï (1979–present; Boesch & Boesch-Achermann, 2000) in Côte d'Ivoire. More recently, other study sites have reached or exceeded 10 years of detailed observation, including Kalinzu (1997–present; Hashimoto & Furuichi, 2006) in Uganda, Goualougo (2000–present; Sanz, Call, & Morgan, 2009) in Republic of Congo, and Fongoli (2001–present; Pruetz & Bertolani, 2007) in Senegal. Together, these studies have documented aspects of chimpanzee social behavior that are common among sites, such as basic patterns of social behavior (Mitani, 2009), as well as aspects that vary considerably, such as patterns of tool use and other local traditions (Whiten et al., 1999).

In the following sections, I review what we have learned from these studies about intergroup aggression in chimpanzees, including (i) patterns of intergroup interaction, (ii) the frequency of intergroup killing, (iii) ultimate causes of intergroup aggression, and (iv) proximate causes, including social and ecological factors, affecting rates of intergroup aggression.

Patterns of Intergroup Interaction

Chimpanzees live in groups called communities that may number more than 150 individuals (Mitani & Watts, 2005) but usually number around 40 individuals (median = 46.3, range 10 –144, $N = 9$; Wrangham, Wilson, & Muller, 2006). Instead of traveling in a cohesive troop like many other primates, chimpanzees have a fission-fusion social organization, in which all members of a community rarely, if ever, come together at once. Instead, they travel, forage and rest in subgroups ("parties") that change in size and composition throughout the day. Parties range in size from one to dozens of individuals. For example, mean party size was 9.2 ± 7.0 independent individuals at Kanyawara ($N = 5527$; Wilson, Kahlenberg, Wells, & Wrangham, 2012) and somewhat larger at Ngogo (mean = 10.3 ± 10.2; $N = 827$; Mitani, Watts, & Lwanga, 2002), where parties of up to 44 independent individuals were observed (Wakefield, 2008). Males usually spend their entire lives in the community of their birth, whereas females usually emigrate to another community at sexual maturity, presumably to avoid inbreeding with male kin (Pusey, 1980). When sexually receptive, female chimpanzees display a large pink swelling of the ano-genital skin (Tutin & McGinnis, 1981), which in addition to other functions, may act as a "social passport" when females transfer to new communities, as males are more likely to affiliate with and protect such females when they have a fully tumescent swelling (Boesch & Boesch-Achermann, 2000).

It may take many years for researchers to learn all the members of a previously unstudied community. For example, at Gombe, it was only by about 1966 that all the individuals of the Kasekela community were habituated to observers and individually recognized (Pusey, Wilson, & Collins, 2008). Chimpanzees, however, appear to know perfectly well who belongs in their community. When chimpanzees hear, see, or encounter evidence of unfamiliar individuals, they typically respond with fear and/or hostility, unless the stranger is a sexually receptive female without dependent offspring (Boesch et al., 2008; Goodall, 1986; Williams, Oehlert, Carlis, & Pusey, 2004).

Chimpanzees occupy large home ranges, with annual ranges covering 10–30 km^2 in forest (e.g., Kanyawara: median = 16.4 km^2, range 10.8–29.5 km^2, $N = 15$ years [Wilson, Kahlenberg et al., 2012]; Ngogo: 28.76 km^2 [Mitani et al., 2010]) and more than 50 km^2 in dry habitats (Hunt & McGrew, 2002). Males are generally more social and range more widely than females (Chapman & Wrangham, 1993; Wrangham, 1979), though males and females have more similar ranging patterns at Taï (Lehmann & Boesch, 2005). At sites in East Africa, females spend more time ranging alone, and when alone, concentrate their ranging in individual core areas, which may in turn be grouped with core areas of other females in "neighborhoods" (Gombe: Williams, Pusey, Carlis, Farm, & Goodall, 2002; Kanyawara: Emery Thompson, Kahlenberg, Gilby, & Wrangham, 2007). Chimpanzees spend most of their time toward the center of their range; for example, at Kanyawara, chimpanzees spent 85 percent of observation time within the core of their range (Wilson, Hauser, & Wrangham, 2007).

Because chimpanzees live in fission-fusion communities with large ranges, early observers only gradually recognized that chimpanzees live in groups with social and territorial boundaries. Van Lawick-Goodall (1968) and Reynolds and Reynolds (1965) initially believed that chimpanzees lived in fluid communities with open membership, separated only by geographical boundaries. In contrast, Nishida realized early on that chimpanzees at Mahale lived in distinct social groups (Nishida, 1968; 1979). Researchers eventually found this to be the case at Gombe (Goodall, 1977; Goodall et al., 1979) and among chimpanzees in general (Mitani, 2009; Wilson & Wrangham, 2003).

Males may visit the periphery of their range for multiple reasons, including searching for food and/or mates, or to conduct boundary patrols, during which they appear to search for neighbors and/or signs of encroachment (Goodall et al., 1979). Boundary patrols involve distinctive patterns of behavior, during which large parties consisting mainly of adult males travel to the periphery of their range and move cautiously and quietly, often in single file (Boesch & Boesch-Acherman, 2000; Goodall et al., 1979; Goodall, 1986; Mitani & Watts, 2005; Watts & Mitani, 2001; Wrangham, 1999). When conducting boundary patrols, chimpanzees spend more time traveling and less time feeding than at other times (Amsler, 2010). They move slowly and cautiously, but travel further, because they spend less time feeding (Amsler, 2010). Patrols thus represent an investment in defense of group territories that imposes time, energy, and opportunity costs, but is likely necessary to prevent encroachment by rival communities (Amsler, 2010). Variation exists among sites in the extent to which males conduct such distinctive patrols, with patrols occurring frequently at some sites, such as Ngogo (Amsler, 2010; Mitani & Watts, 2005) and Taï (Boesch & Boesch-Achermann, 2000), but rarely at others, such as Budongo (Reynolds, 2005). However, even at sites where males rarely exhibit distinctive patrolling behavior, males visit the range periphery more often than lactating females (Chapman & Wrangham, 1993; Bates & Byrne, 2009).

Because chimpanzees live at low densities in large ranges and concentrate their range use toward the center of their ranges, encounters between members of neighboring groups occur infrequently. For example, at Kanyawara, intergroup encounters occurred on only 1.9 percent of days on which researchers followed chimpanzees (Wilson, Kahlenberg et al., 2012). Chimpanzees living in more densely populated areas might encounter neighbors more frequently. Chimpanzees at Taï and Ngogo encountered their neighbors 1–2 times per month (Boesch et al., 2008). When encounters do occur, they are usually limited to acoustic contact. At Taï, 73 percent of 485 intergroup encounters observed among three communities involved only acoustic contact (Boesch et al., 2008), as did 85 percent of 120 encounters observed at Kanyawara (Wilson, Kahleberg et al., 2012). During acoustic encounters, chimpanzees produce loud vocalizations, including pant-hoots, which are most frequently produced by high-ranking adult males, and are often given in choruses, with many individuals calling at once (Goodall, 1986). Chimpanzees use pant-hoots to communicate with other group members over long distances (Mitani & Nishida, 1993). When chimpanzees hear pant-hoots or other calls from neighboring communities, they often show signs of fear and/or excitement, such as looking intently in the direction of the calls, standing bipedally for a better view, embracing, mounting one another, and touching each other's genitalia, and may respond with chorused calls of their own (Goodall, 1986). Chimpanzees sometimes remain silent after hearing strangers calling, and may either stay still, looking toward the source of the calls, or rapidly approach or retreat from the direction of the calls (Boesch et al., 2008; Goodall, 1986; Watts et al., 2006; Wilson et al., 2004; Wilson, Kahlenberg et al., 2012).

Most intergroup interactions remain limited to shouting matches, with members of rival groups separated by hundreds or even thousands of meters. Less frequently, chimpanzees come within visual range of each other (27 percent of encounters at Taï (Boesch et al., 2008); 15 percent of encounters at Kanyawara (Wilson, Kahlenberg et al., 2012)). Whether these close-range encounters result in hostility depends on the sex and reproductive state of the individuals involved, with aggression being most likely toward males and least likely toward potential immigrants: sexually receptive females without infants (Pusey, 1980; Boesch & Boesch-Achermann, 2000). For example, during 18 years of observation of Gombe (1975–1992), observers reported a total of 97 close-range interactions between males from the Kasekela community and unfamiliar individuals of either sex (Williams et al., 2004). Interactions with unfamiliar males always involved aggression ($N = 22$), as did one case where the sex of the stranger was not determined. The percentage of interactions with unfamiliar females that involved aggression depended on the reproductive status of the unfamiliar females, being highest when they were nonswollen females with infants (71%, $N = 31$), and considerably less when they were nonswollen females without infants (40%, $N = 20$). Swollen females, in contrast, elicited aggression less frequently, with (20%, $N = 10$) or without (8%, $N = 13$) infants (Williams et al., 2004). Resident females, however, may attack and severely injure unfamiliar females, presumably because these females are potential rivals for food resources (Boesch et al., 2008; Pusey, Murray, et al., 2008; Townsend et al., 2007).

While interactions with direct physical contact represent only a small proportion of intergroup interactions, when they do occur, the outcome is often injury, and sometimes death. At Kanyawara, 17 percent of encounters within visual range resulted in serious injuries; the two intergroup killings that were inferred to have taken place at Kanyawara were not directly observed (Wilson, Kahlenberg et al., 2012). Killings occurred during two of the 485 intergroup encounters observed at Taï (0.4 percent of all encounters, or 1.5 percent of encounters with visual contact; Boesch et al., 2008). (More killings have been observed at other sites, but the proportion of encounters leading to injury or death has not yet been published.)

Detailed observations of intergroup killings have now been reported from multiple sites (Budongo: Newton-Fisher, 1999; Townsend et al., 2007; Gombe: Bygott, 1972; Goodall, 1977; Goodall et al., 1979; Goodall, 1986; Wilson, Wallauer, & Pusey, 2004; Mahale: Kutsukake & Matsusaka, 2002; Ngogo: Watts & Mitani, 2000; Watts, Mitani, & Sherrow, 2002; Watts, Muller, Amsler, Mbabazi, & Mitani, 2006; Sherrow & Amsler, 2007; Taï: Boesch et al., 2008). Additional killings have been inferred from the discovery of recently killed bodies with wounds typical of chimpanzee attack, and/or other circumstantial evidence (Kalinzu: Hashimoto & Furuichi, 2005; Loango: Boesch et al., 2007;

other cases reviewed in Wrangham et al., 2006). Killings usually occur when the attackers encounter a lone victim, or manage to isolate a victim from a larger party, such as when the others flee (Manson & Wrangham, 1991). Attackers are usually adult and adolescent males, and demonstrate a high level of excitement, with hair erected. They may produce roar-like pant-hoots, waa-barks, screams, and other loud vocalizations, and often give charge displays before and during the attack, and generally appear eager to attack and inflict damage on the victim. Males have been observed to attack males of all ages as well as adult females and infants (Boesch et al., 2008; Goodall, 1986; Watts et al., 2006; Williams et al., 2004). Adult females may participate indirectly, by giving screams and other loud vocalizations during encounters (e.g., Newton-Fisher, 1999), and in some cases adult females also participate directly in attacks, threatening (Goodall, 1977), grabbing, and/or hitting victims (Boesch et al., 2008).

If the stranger is a mother with an infant, both mother and infant may be attacked, though sometimes attackers focus on just one or the other. At Gombe, males attacked nonswollen females more often then swollen females, and such attacks were sometimes severe (Williams et al., 2004). Nine of these females had small infants, of which three were killed (Williams et al., 2004.). The attackers may take the infant from the mother, biting the infant's head, throat, or abdomen, killing it much the way they kill monkey prey (Newton-Fisher, 1999; Sherrow & Amsler, 2007; Watts & Mitani, 2000; Watts et al., 2002; Wilson et al., 2004;), and/or flailing it against the ground or branches (Boesch et al., 2008; Goodall, 1977). Sometimes the attackers begin eating the infant while it is still alive (Goodall, 1977). Attackers often partially or completely consume infant victims, treating them much like monkey prey, begging for and sharing meat (Goodall, 1977; Newton-Fisher, 1999; Sherrow & Amsler, 2007; Watts et al., 2002; Wilson et al., 2004). However, attackers sometimes discard the carcass without eating it (Boesch et al., 2008). Figures 18.1 and 18.2 show images of Andromeda, a female infant killed during an intergroup encounter between chimpanzees of the Mitumba and Kasekela communities at Gombe. Andromeda suffered canine puncture wounds to the head in addition to other injuries (Kirchhoff et al., in press).

During attacks on weaned individuals, attackers may gang up on the victim, pinning it to the ground. Severe attacks may be directed toward individuals of either sex (Goodall, 1986; Boesch & Boesch-Achermann, 2000), though documented cases of killings involve far more male than female victims (Wrangham et al., 2006; Wilson, Boesch et al., 2012). At Ngogo, up to 16 adult and 3 adolescent males have been observed surrounding a single victim (Watts et al., 2006). During the rapid course of events, especially with numerous attackers piled onto the victim, detailed observations of individual behavior may become difficult or impossible, though when attacks are videotaped some details may be determined later (Watts et al., 2006; Wilson et al., 2004). Attackers often hit the victim with their hands, kick with their feet, and bite, inflicting canine puncture wounds (Boesch et al., 2008; Goodall, 1986; Watts et al., 2006; Wilson et al., 2004). Extremities such as tips of fingers, fingernails, and genitalia may be chewed, bitten, or pulled off. In at least

FIGURE 18.1 Andromeda, an 8-month-old female infant chimpanzee from the Mitumba community, with her mother on August 10, 2005. (Photo credit: Michael L. Wilson)

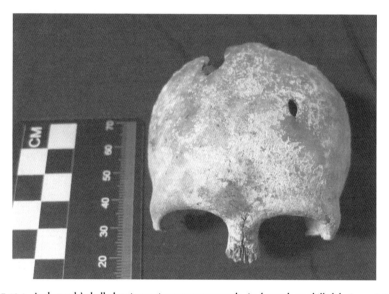

FIGURE 18.2 Andromeda's skull, showing canine puncture wounds. Andromeda was killed during an intergroup encounter between chimpanzees from the Mitumba and Kasekela communities on August 13, 2005. (Photo credit: Claire A. Kirchhoff, PhD)

one case, attackers ripped the trachea out of the victim's throat (Muller, 2002). Attackers may twist the victim's limbs around or rip strips of flesh from the victim (Goodall, 1986). Attackers sometimes continue hitting, kicking, jumping on, displaying at, and/or dragging the victim until after it is dead, but in other cases attackers leave while the victim remains alive. In some cases, the victims appear to have died from internal injuries (Watts et al., 2006). Attacks may inflict skeletal damage, including fractures and canine punctures (Terio et al., 2011).

Frequency of Intergroup Killing

As the number of chimpanzee study sites has increased across Africa, and with accumulating observations from long-term study sites, it has become clear that intraspecific aggression constitutes a pervasive risk for chimpanzees (Mitani, 2009; Wilson & Wrangham, 2003), with intraspecific killings documented for 71 percent of study communities (N = 17 communities at 10 sites; Wilson, Boesch et al., 2012). Killings occurred both within and between communities, but the majority of killings (67 percent) involved intergroup attacks (Wilson, Boesch et al., 2012). Intergroup killing thus appears to be a widespread trait of chimpanzees, rather than the result of circumstances peculiar to one or a few study sites.

Sussman (1999) and others (Hart & Sussman, 2005; Marks, 2002) have argued that intraspecific killings in chimpanzees occur infrequently, implying that they must therefore not be important. However, a proper comparison of rates must compare not just the numerator (e.g., the number of killings observed), but also the appropriate denominator, taking into account population sizes and observation time. To calculate rates of mortality from intraspecific violence for direct comparison with data from human societies, Wrangham et al. (2006) analyzed data from six chimpanzee populations with neighboring communities. The most conservative estimate yielded a median of 271 violent deaths per 100,000 individuals per year (range: 78 – 678). Of these, study communities incurred a median 69 deaths per 100,000 individuals per year from intergroup aggression (range: 0 – 417). (Some study communities, such as Ngogo, inflicted many more intergroup deaths than they incurred, but because the population sizes of the communities are not known in these cases, death rates cannot be calculated). Comparing chimpanzee data with those available for subsistence-level human societies, Wrangham et al. (2006) found that hunter-gatherers incurred a median 164 deaths per 100,000 per year from intergroup violence (range 0 – 1000, N = 12), and horticulturalists incurred a median 595 deaths per 100,000 per year (range 140 – 1450, N = 20). For comparison, the homicide rate for the entire United States during the 1970s and 1980s was 10 deaths per 100,000 individuals per year, with 45 deaths per 100,000 individuals per year in Detroit (Daly & Wilson, 1988). Thus, when population size and observation time are taken into account, chimpanzees experience a rate of intraspecific killing that is similar in magnitude to that experienced by subsistence level human societies, and much higher than that typical of industrialized democracies; indeed, six times higher than that of one of the most violent cities in the United States.

While only a small proportion of intergroup encounters result in killings, because chimpanzees are long-lived and face few other sources of mortality, intraspecific aggression can cause a significant proportion of mortality. Analysis of 47 years of demographic data from the Kasekela and Kahama communities in Gombe found that out of 86 deaths with known causes, intraspecific aggression caused 17 deaths (20 percent of all deaths; 24 percent of male deaths), second only to disease as a cause of death (Williams et al., 2008). Killings were split about evenly between intragroup killings (N = 9; 11 percent of deaths) and intergroup killings (N = 8; 9.3 percent of deaths; Williams et al., 2008).

A study focusing on a more recent sample that combined behavioral observations with post-mortem investigation of bodies recovered from the Kasekela and Mitumba communities found that intraspecific aggression caused 36 percent of deaths ($N = 4$ of 11 cases), which were evenly split between intragroup ($N = 2$) and intergroup ($N = 2$) attacks (Terio et al., 2011; one of the four killings reported here was also reported in Williams et al., 2008). Kasekela males killed at least two members of the unhabituated Kalande community (Wilson et al., 2004), constituting 13 percent of the 15 deaths with known or inferred causes for that community (Rudicell et al., 2010). Similarly, analysis of 19 years of demographic data from K-group in Mahale found that 18 of 130 deaths with known causes were caused by attack from adult male chimpanzees (16 percent of all deaths), with 5 of these cases (3.8 percent of all deaths) attributed to intergroup aggression (Nishida et al., 2003). For both Gombe and Mahale, the cause of death was uncertain for many chimpanzees (34 percent and 44 percent, respectively), and at both sites, at least some of the individuals that disappeared were thought to have been victims of intergroup aggression (Williams et al., 2008; Nishida, Hiraiwa-Hasegawa, Hasegawa, & Takahata, 1985), suggesting that these figures may underestimate the actual proportion of deaths due to intergroup violence.

Comparable data for human hunter-gatherers are sparse. Data reviewed by Gat (1999) indicate that violence among hunter-gatherers in Australia caused from 10 percent (Tiwi) to 30 percent (Murngin) of adult male deaths, and that violence caused an estimated 5 percent and 6.5 percent of all deaths in arid and well-watered areas, respectively, of Central Australia (Gat, 1999). In comparison, warfare is estimated to have caused less than 1 percent of deaths worldwide in the twentieth century (Pinker, 2011). Thus, intergroup aggression caused a similar proportion of deaths for Gombe chimpanzees and human hunter-gatherers, and a substantially higher proportion of deaths than among the global human population during a century with two world wars.

Causes of Intergroup Aggression

Following Tinbergen (1963), behavioral ecologists recognize that a full explanation of biological phenomena requires answering questions relating to multiple levels of explanation, including ultimate and proximate causes. Ultimate causes address the question: why do animals behave in such a way? Because behaviors must benefit inclusive fitness if they are to evolve by natural selection, ultimate questions can be translated into a general form: does a particular behavioral strategy increase the actor's number of direct and/or indirect descendants, and if so, how? Proximate causes address the question: how do animals behave in such a way? In particular, how do factors such as physiology and the environment influence an animal's responses?

Ultimate causes. At least two questions can be asked about intergroup aggression in chimpanzees at the level of ultimate causation. First, why do male chimpanzees aggressively defend group territories? Second, why do males sometimes kill members of rival communities, rather than merely chase them away?

The first question is in many ways the less difficult one. Intergroup aggression is widespread in group-living species, including many primates (Crofoot & Wrangham, 2010). Indeed, intergroup competition has been proposed to be a central factor in the evolution of social behavior; living in larger groups may provide individuals with a competitive advantage in obtaining scarce resources (Wrangham, 1980). Male chimpanzees may gain several different benefits from defending group territories. Possible benefits include (i) excluding outside males from mating with resident females, (ii) recruiting new females to join their community, (iii) competing for a feeding territory for self, mates, and offspring, and (iv) protecting self, mates and offspring from aggressive attack. These hypotheses are not mutually exclusive, and several or even all of them may play an important role. In support of the first hypothesis, genetic testing has found extragroup paternities to be rare (Constable, Ashley, Goodall, & Pusey, 2001; Rudicell et al., 2010; Vigilant et al., 2001; Wroblewski et al., 2009). Thus, males appear to be generally successful in excluding outside males. The second hypothesis, that males participate in intergroup aggression in order to acquire new females, has not been systematically tested. In general, however, females usually emigrate only at adolescence, at which time they appear highly motivated to leave their natal group, presumably to avoid mating with male kin (Pusey, 1980). Once females have started reproducing, they usually stay in the community where they have settled. Females do appear to prefer living in communities with multiple males, as seen by mass migration of females when K-group at Mahale and Kalande at Gombe were reduced to a single male (Nishida et al., 1985; Rudicell et al., 2010). If females have a preference to live in communities with more males, males may be able to recruit new females by advertising their community size during intergroup encounters.

Evidence is growing in support of the third hypothesis: male chimpanzees seek to defend and expand a feeding territory for themselves, their mates and offspring. Interactions occur most frequently when abundant foods are located in border areas (Wilson, Kahlenberg, et al., 2012). Chimpanzees can expand their territory by killing members of other communities (Mitani et al., 2010) or lose territory by losing intergroup contests (Wilson, Kahlenberg, et al., 2012). As territory size increases, chimpanzees have heavier body mass (Pusey, Oehlert, Williams, & Goodall, 2005), forage in larger parties (Williams et al., 2004), and have shorter interbirth intervals (Williams et al., 2004).

The fourth hypothesis, that males participate in intergroup aggression to protect themselves and their mates and offspring, is difficult to rule out, and is compatible with other hypotheses; given that intergroup aggression occurs, the best defense may well be a strong offense.

The question of why chimpanzees kill, rather than simply chase their rivals away, is a challenging one. Fatal fighting does occur in other animal species, but usually when the value of the resource being fought over is unusually high, or when a large fraction of the opponents' reproductive success is at stake (Enquist & Leimar, 1990). Among chimpanzees, the value of the resources being contested does not appear unusually large compared to other primate species, nor does a male chimpanzee's lifetime reproductive success usually depend on the outcome of a particular border squabble. The imbalance of power hypothesis, developed by Wrangham and colleagues (Manson & Wrangham, 1991; Wrangham, 1999), focuses on the costs of fighting, rather than the potential benefits. Killing a rival involves both costs and benefits. The main cost of killing is the risk of injury to the attacker, along with the time and effort expended. Benefits of killing the victim include the elimination of a genetic competitor, and a reduction in the strength of a neighboring coalition. In any species with group-level conflict, attackers could potentially benefit from killing the victim, but the costs of doing so are usually too high. But in chimpanzees, and species with similar social structures (such as humans, lions, wolves, and spotted hyenas), variation in party size creates opportunities for gang attacks, thereby reducing the costs (Wrangham, 1999).

Manson and Wrangham based their hypothesis on the observation that most of the attacks observed at Gombe in the 1970s involved gangs of males attacking individuals that were alone or became isolated after their other party members fled (Manson & Wrangham, 1991). The key factor facilitating lethal aggression thus appeared to be numerical asymmetries. When one side has such an overwhelming numerical superiority, attackers may kill an isolated victim at relatively low cost to themselves. The costs need not be zero; indeed, traveling into enemy territory is in itself a potentially costly behavior (Amsler, 2010). But once an encounter begins, participants in a gang attack can quickly subdue a rival at little risk of injury to themselves.

Observational and experimental evidence have supported multiple predictions from the imbalance of power hypothesis. Chimpanzees are more likely to conduct boundary patrols (Mitani & Watts, 2005) and visit the periphery in general (Wilson et al., 2007; Wilson, Kahlenberg et al., 2012) when they are with many males, and thus more likely to win should an intergroup encounter occur. At Kanyawara, parties visiting the periphery had on average twice as many males as parties that stayed in the core of the range (Wilson et al., 2007). Willingness to participate in intergroup encounters likewise appears to depend on numerical assessment. Intergroup encounters often begin with an exchange of vocalizations, which provides a mechanism both for advertising the size of one's own group and assessing the size of a rival group. Experimental (Herbinger, Papworth, Boesch, & Zuberbühler, 2009; Wilson, Hauser, & Wrangham, 2001) and observational (Wilson, Kahlenberg, et al., 2012) studies have found that the response to extragroup calls depends on the number of males in the listening party (Wilson et al., 2001), as well as whether the callers are neighbors or strangers (Herbinger et al., 2009). When males are alone or with only one or two other males, they usually stay silent (Wilson et al., 2001). They are less likely to move toward the calls of strangers when with few males, and if they do approach, they do so more slowly. In contrast, when males are in parties with many males, they often respond with loud choruses of counter-calls and move rapidly toward the strangers (Wilson et al., 2001). Finally, observations in recent decades have provided additional evidence that intergroup fights between large parties are rarely lethal, and that instead, killings usually involve gang attacks on greatly outnumbered individuals, in which the attackers rarely receive injuries (Boesch et al., 2008; Watts et al., 2006; Wilson et al., 2004).

The imbalance of power hypothesis has been further supported by the discovery of boundary patrols (Aureli, Schaffner, Verpooten, Slater, & Ramos-Fernandez, 2006) and lethal aggression (Campbell, 2006) in spider monkeys, which like chimpanzees have fission-fusion social societies. A challenge for this hypothesis is that capuchin monkeys, which live in stable troops, have a high rate of coalitionary killing (Gros-Louis, Perry, & Manson, 2003), suggesting that additional factors are needed to fully explain the observed distribution of coalitionary killing among species.

Proximate causes. Given the ultimate goal of optimizing inclusive fitness, evolutionary game theory predicts that animals should assess current conditions and adopt strategies likely to yield the greatest net benefits (Barash, chapter 2; Kokko, chapter 3). A male chimpanzee that always charged aggressively toward any neighbors that he detected, for example, would eventually find himself picking an unwinnable fight. Instead, animals should assess factors including their own fighting ability, the fighting ability of their opponents, and the value of resources being contested (Fry & Szala, chapter 23). In species such as chimpanzees that fight in coordinated groups, fighting ability may depend largely on the number of opponents on each side, with bigger groups beating smaller groups. The most important proximate factors affecting intergroup aggression in chimpanzees should therefore include numerical asymmetries and ecological factors, particularly the abundance and distribution of food resources. Additional proximate factors include human impacts, such as provisioning and habitat change.

Social factors. Given that intergroup killings occur most often in the context of numerical asymmetries, such asymmetries represent a critical social factor affecting the rates and severity of intergroup aggression. Numerical asymmetries affect intergroup aggression on at least two temporal scales. In the short term, party size varies frequently throughout the day. A given individual may spend part of the day alone, and part of the same day traveling in a large party. These short-term changes in party size depend intimately on ecological factors, and will therefore be discussed further in the next section. In the longer term, individuals live in communities of different size, and community size generally changes slowly as a result of birth, death and migration. While individuals in communities of all sizes spend some time traveling alone, and are thus vulnerable to intercommunity attack, communities with many males are, on average, likely to have an advantage in intergroup competition with smaller communities.

Our understanding of the effects of relative community size is limited, though, in that most studies have focused on a single study community. However, existing evidence supports the prediction that larger communities have a competitive advantage over smaller communities. At Gombe, the larger Kasekela community exterminated the smaller Kahama community (Goodall, 1986). The Kasekela community is now the largest community in Gombe, and has expanded its range greatly at the expense of the smaller neighboring communities (Rudicell et al., 2010; Wilson, 2012). At Mahale, M-group dominated the much smaller K-group during seasonal incursions into the K-group's range (Nishida, 1979). K-group's adult males gradually disappeared from unknown causes, following which M-group took over much of K-group's range (Nishida et al., 1985).

Patterns of patrolling behavior likely vary according to the level of risk posed by neighboring communities. Observers at several sites note that chimpanzees are unusually quiet when patrolling (Gombe: Goodall, 1986; Ngogo: Amsler, 2010; Mitani & Watts, 2005; Taï: Boesch & Boesch-Achermann, 2000). At both Budongo and Kanyawara, however, such silent boundary patrols appear to occur less frequently, perhaps due to lower risk of encountering neighbors at these sites (Bates & Byrne, 2009; Wilson et al., 2007). The population density at Kanyawara is about a third that of Ngogo (Wilson et al., 2007), and in most seasons, Kanyawara chimpanzees rarely encounter neighbors (Wilson, Kahlenberg et al., 2012). When visiting the periphery of their range, Kanyawara males do not consistently reduce their frequency of pant-hoot production (Wilson et al., 2007). Instead, while they call less frequently when crop-raiding, and when in some parts of their periphery, they actually increase their rate of pant-hoot production along their eastern periphery. Chimpanzees thus appear to modulate vocal production based on the costs and benefits of calling, staying quiet when the risks of detection are high (especially when crop-raiding), but advertising their presence when in parties with many males, perhaps to advertise their coalition strength and territory possession (Wilson et al., 2007).

Chimpanzees may be most likely to conduct distinct boundary patrols when they are members of a community that is sufficiently powerful to encroach on neighboring territory, and yet faced with sufficiently powerful neighbors that traveling to neighboring territory remains risky. At Gombe, the Kasekela community is now so much more powerful than neighboring communities that they face relatively little risk from border visits, and travel deep into neighboring ranges with females and infants (Gombe Stream Research Centre, unpublished data). Males in the smaller Mitumba community, however, show more signs of caution when traveling south into Kasekela territory (Mjungu, 2010).

Ecological factors. Ecology relates to intergroup aggression in chimpanzees in at least two major ways. First, food resources may attract chimpanzees from neighboring groups to the same area, causing intergroup interactions to occur (Wilson, Kahlenberg et al., 2012). Second, local differences in food availability between neighboring communities can lead to differences in foraging party size. Abundant food in one area may enable large parties to form. If scarce food in one territory forces males to forage alone or in small parties, they may become vulnerable to attack by their neighbors (Manson & Wrangham, 1991).

Intergroup encounters are most likely to occur in border areas, which chimpanzees may visit for multiple reasons. Males may conduct boundary patrols, or even raids deep into neighboring ranges, during which they may search for members of neighboring communities to attack (Goodall, 1986; Watts et al., 2006; Wilson et al., 2004). Males may search for mating opportunities, either with peripheral females of their own community, or with females from other communities. Males or females may travel to the periphery searching for food.

At Kanyawara, the abundance and distribution of food are strongly correlated with travel patterns (Wilson, Kahlenberg et al., 2012). Chimpanzees eat a variety of foods, but appear to prefer ripe fruit (Wrangham, Conklin-Brittain & Hunt, 1998). The distribution of fruit trees varies by species; some species occur more frequently in the south, others in the center, and others in the north of the range. Many of these species fruit synchronously over intervals of one, two, or even five years. When fruits located mainly in the south such as *Uvariopsis congensis* and *Psuedospondias microcarpa* are in season, Kanyawara chimpanzees spend more time in the south of their range (Wilson, Kahlenberg et al., 2012). The majority of intergroup encounters at Kanyawara occur when these southern fruits are in season, especially *Uvariopsis* (Wilson, Kahlenberg et al., 2012). These fruits thus appear to attract chimpanzees from neighboring groups to a common area, where they are more likely to meet, exchange vocalizations, display at, chase, and attack each other.

Discussions of aggression and ecology in humans often conclude that intergroup aggression is a response to resource scarcity (e.g., Read & LeBlanc, 2003). In contrast, in chimpanzees, aggression seems to be a consequence of resource abundance. For example, the Ngogo community is the largest chimpanzee community known (Mitani, 2006). The Ngogo community's range is just 12 km from Kanyawara's range, but in a more productive part of the forest (Potts, Watts, & Wrangham, 2011). The abundant food resources at Ngogo support an unusually large community, which is able to forage regularly in parties with many males. The Ngogo community is also unusually aggressive, having killed at least 18 of its neighbors in a 10-year period (Mitani et al., 2010). Having many males that are able to forage in large parties clearly gives Ngogo a competitive advantage against neighboring communities.

Aggression and Human Disturbance. When researchers at Gombe and Mahale observed intergroup aggression and killings in the 1970s, very little was known about chimpanzee behavior at other sites. Shorter-term studies at other sites reported that chimpanzees lived peacefully and did not seem to even have bounded social groups (Reynolds & Reynolds, 1965). This raised the possibility that perhaps the aggression at Gombe and Mahale was due to something unusual about those sites. Both sites are located in Tanzania, near the southeastern limits of the range for chimpanzees. Starting in the 1960s, researchers at both sites practiced provisioning, supplying chimpanzees with bananas (Gombe: 1962–2000) and sugar cane (Mahale: 1966–1987) in order to facilitate observations, photography, and filming. Feeding chimpanzees undoubtedly had multiple unintended consequences. Among them, Wrangham (1974) found that more attacks occurred on days when chimpanzees were provisioned, due both to the larger aggregations resulting from the artificial feeding, and to an increase in rate of attacks per individual.

Following up on the Wrangham's (1974) finding, Power (1991) argued that provisioning had a profound general effect on chimpanzee behavior. Power argued that provisioning caused not only intergroup killings, but also many other features of chimpanzee social behavior observed at Gombe and Mahale. Despite the wealth of new field data that have been reported since 1991, critics regularly cite Power (1991) in support of their arguments that intergroup violence in chimpanzees results from human influence, rather than being an expression of natural behavior (e.g., Ferguson, 1999, 2001a; Marks, 2002; Hart & Sussman, 2009).

Power (1991) argued that the restricted feeding of chimpanzees at Gombe and Mahale created frustration, which in turn resulted in a whole suite of behaviors: male dominance hierarchies, despotic alpha males, possessive sexual behavior, closed membership of social groups, territorial behavior, female dispersal, hunting of monkeys, and intergroup killings. Power divides research at Gombe into two periods: a "wild" period, during which only Goodall observed chimpanzees (1960–1964), and the "provisioning studies of disturbed chimpanzees" period, from 1965 on. (At Gombe and Mahale provisioning ended in 2000 and 1987, respectively.) This division is peculiar, since Goodall began feeding chimpanzees in 1962, several years before Power considered that chimpanzees were "disturbed" by provisioning, and discounts the numerous detailed studies that occurred at Gombe from the 1970s on, and likewise discounts all studies from Mahale as being from "disturbed" chimpanzees. Instead, she bases her view of "wild" chimpanzee behavior on Goodall's earliest observations at Gombe, along with reports from short-term studies of unhabituated chimpanzees (e.g., Budongo: Reynolds & Reynolds, 1965; Ngogo: Ghiglieri, 1984).

In terms of studying "wild" versus "disturbed" chimpanzee behavior, however, Power seems not to appreciate the difficulty of studying unhabituated chimpanzees, and overestimates the impact of artificial feeding on behavior away from the feeding station. Detailed studies of natural chimpanzee behavior at Gombe became possible only after the chimpanzees were habituated and when observers began following chimpanzees away from the feeding station (Goodall, 1986). During the first years of Goodall's study (1960–1962), most of the chimpanzees were unhabituated and fearful of humans, and could be observed only at a distance (Goodall, 1971). Once Goodall discovered that chimpanzees could be brought into view more easily with food, she focused her efforts on observations in and around an increasingly elaborate feeding station (Goodall, 1986). Starting around 1968, though, Goodall's team began shifting their attention back to the forest and began documenting systematically what chimpanzees did on days without banana subsidies (Goodall, 1986; Wilson, 2012). They found that chimpanzees search long and hard for food (Wrangham, 1977), they patrol the boundaries of their range (Goodall et al., 1979), and have hostile interactions with their neighbors (Bygott, 1972; Goodall, 1977; Goodall et al., 1979).

In recent decades, long-term studies of chimpanzees at sites without artificial feeding have confirmed that essentially all of the traits Power argued were the result of artificial feeding are in fact typical of wild, unprovisioned chimpanzees. Males compete with other males for rank and can be ordered in a linear dominance hierarchy (Budongo: Newton-Fisher, 1994; Kanyawara: Muller & Wrangham, 2004; Ngogo: Watts, 2000; Taï: Boesch & Boesch-Achermann, 2000). Males compete actively for matings, with higher-ranking males obtaining more paternities than lower-ranking males (Budongo: Newton-Fisher, Thompson, Reynolds, Boesch, & Vigilant, 2010; Taï: Boesch, Kohou,

Nene, & Vigilant, 2006). Females disperse from their natal communities (Budongo: Reynolds, 2005; Kanyawara: Stumpf, Emery Thompson, Muller, & Wrangham, 2009; Taï: Boesch & Boesch-Achermann, 2000). Chimpanzees hunt monkeys and other mammalian prey (Budongo: Newton-Fisher, 2007; Kanyawara: Gilby, Eberly, & Wrangham, 2008; Ngogo: Mitani & Watts, 2001; Taï: Boesch, 1994). And intergroup killings have now been reported from the majority of study sites (Wrangham et al., 2006; Boesch et al., 2008). Based on Ghiglieri's short-term study at Ngogo (but contrary to what Ghiglieri [1984] thought to be the case), Power argued that Ngogo chimpanzees exemplified her view of wild chimpanzees as peaceful egalitarians. Long-term study at Ngogo, however, has revealed that, while these chimpanzees were never provisioned, they nonetheless killed 5.7 intergroup victims per 100 adult-male years of observation, more than any other chimpanzee community that has been studied (Wrangham et al., 2006).

In seeking to understand aggression in humans and other animals, one must be careful to avoid preconceptions of what a normal society ought to be like. Such preconceptions can arise easily, and the following passage provides one of many examples, by showing that Power expected alpha males to fulfill a particular social role:

> It is the excessive, apparently unprovoked attacks on the females and young that raise the first suspicions that this aggression-based dominance hierarchy is not the normal form of organization for chimpanzees, and that the alpha Gombe animal is a despot, using his power oppressively, rather than serving the group as protective leader. (Power, p. 76)

As it turns out, chimpanzees frequently behave in ways that differ from what we might prefer them to do. Males commonly display at, chase, and hit other group members for no obvious reason (Bygott, 1979; Muller, 2002), sometimes even killing in apparently unprovoked attacks (Murray, Wroblewski, & Pusey, 2007). Males coerce females into mating with them (Muller et al., 2011). They attack, kill, and eat infant chimpanzees (Newton-Fisher, 1999; Watts & Mitani, 2000). Instead of welcoming new immigrants into their community, resident females sometimes attack and severely injure them (Pusey, Murray et al., 2008). This is not to say that chimpanzees are wicked; only that the reality of chimpanzee behavior frequently departs from common preconceptions of what benevolent forest creatures ought to do.

Apart from artificial feeding, human activities could impact rates of intergroup aggression in other ways. Widespread conversion of chimpanzee habitat to cropland may increase competition for available space (Goodall, 1977; Pusey et al., 2007). Deaths from poaching and diseases transmitted from humans can decrease the coalition size of some communities, increasing their vulnerability to intergroup attack (Goodall, 1977; Pusey et al., 2007.). However, comparing chimpanzee sites across Africa, estimates of human disturbance explain little of the variation in rates of lethal violence (Wilson, Boesch et al., 2012.).

Chimpanzees, Humans, and the Invention of Peace

Long-term data from multiple sites across Africa make clear that chimpanzees regularly live under circumstances that Hobbes would describe as Warre: "For Warre, consisteth not in Battel only, or in the act of fighting, but in a tract of time, wherein the will to contend by Battel is sufficiently known" (Hobbes, 1651/1997, p. 70). Male chimpanzees compete over access to feeding territories for themselves, their mates, and their offspring. Warlike behavior in chimpanzees thus appears to be adaptive, in that participation leads to inclusive fitness benefits: males who successfully defend and expand their group territory appear likely to sire more offspring, and likely to have more successfully reproducing kin, than males that fail to do so (Williams et al., 2004; Mitani et al., 2010).

The occurrence of warlike behavior in our evolutionary cousins is frequently cited as evidence against arguments such as Mead's (1940) that warfare is an invention (Gat, 2006; Keeley 1996; LeBlanc & Register, 2004; Van der Dennen, 1995). The antiquity of human warfare remains contentious, and cannot, of course, be settled with chimpanzee data alone. Some argue that war originated recently, within the past 12,000 years or so (Kelly, 2000; Ferguson, chapters 7 & 11; Fry & Szala, chapter 23; Haas & Piscitelli, chapter 10; Thorpe, 2003), while others argue that warlike behavior has ancient roots, perhaps dating to the common ancestor of humans and chimpanzees (Wrangham & Peterson, 1996) or perhaps evolving separately in the two lineages for similar reasons (Wilson & Wrangham 2003). A thorough review of this debate is beyond the scope of this chapter. However, warlike behavior in chimpanzees poses some provocative questions. The special features thought to be needed for humans to become warlike—weapons, agriculture, sedentary populations, ideology, states—are not present in chimpanzees, and yet chimpanzees suffer rates of intergroup killing comparable to human societies with endemic warfare (Wrangham et al., 2006). Warlike behavior in chimpanzees appears to depend on features also present in human hunter-gatherer societies: male coalitions, fission-fusion social organization, and competition with hostile neighbors (Wrangham, 1999; Wrangham & Glowacki, 2012). Moreover, many striking parallels exist between patterns of warlike behavior in chimpanzees and warfare in small-scale, non-state societies (Gat, 1999; Wilson & Wrangham, 2003). In both chimpanzees and humans, males defend group resources that are essential to their reproductive success. Conflict over land appears to be an important cause of war in hunter-gatherer societies (Wrangham & Glowacki, 2012), and similar ecological factors may affect the occurrence of intergroup conflict in humans and chimpanzees. Like in chimpanzees, where intergroup conflicts result from members of neighboring groups being attracted to seasonally available food resources (Wilson, Kahlenberg et al., 2012), on the Andaman Islands, intergroup conflict occurred most frequently during parts of the year when Jarawa and Bea hunters searched for pigs in the same areas (Kelly, 2000). If humans have lived with chronic warfare for long stretches of evolutionary time, various psychological mechanisms underlying warfare in humans are plausible candidates for adaptations (McDonald, Navarette, & Van Vugt, 2012; Tooby & Cosmides, 1988). If this view is correct, then peace, not war, is the invention—a profoundly important and good invention, but an invention all the same.

A useful analogy, perhaps, is with language and writing. Pinker and Bloom (1990) persuasively argued that the capacity for language is an adaptation. People everywhere spontaneously learn to speak, and language likely has a long history of coevolution with the human brain (Deacon, 1997). Writing, on the other hand, is undoubtedly an invention. Every society was illiterate until the invention of writing some five thousand years ago (Woods, 2010), and even now, literacy rates remain low in some parts of the world. Writing is useful and important, and nearly everyone can learn to do it, but it is not an adaptation.

Like language, war appears to be a human universal—or at least nearly so. Accounts of war from all parts of the world are depressingly similar. Whether the descriptions are from the *Iliad*, the Old Testament, history, ethnography, or the daily newspaper, during times of war people everywhere and every-when seem highly motivated to fight and kill, and often maim and torture, their enemies. Warfare appears to be endemic in tribal societies, with only a few exceptions, and these exceptions demonstrate the special circumstances required to prevent war (Gat 2006; Pinker, 2011). For example, in the 25 hunter-gatherer societies coded by Kelly (2000), "in all but a few cases one or another form of warfare occurs once every five years, or more often" (p. 51), and only in 7 of these societies (28 percent) is warfare infrequent or nonexistent. Some of the more peaceful hunter-gatherers, including the Mbuti, !Kung and Semang, have been profoundly affected by powerful neighbors with evolutionarily novel subsistence practices, including horticulture and pastoralism (Wrangham & Glowacki, 2012). Focusing on the few cases for which data are available on hunter-gatherers living with hunter-gatherer neighbors, Wrangham and Glowacki (2012) conclude that "there was a strong tendency for hostility toward members of different societies, and for killing to occur principally in asymmetric interactions."

In contrast, peace appears to be an achievement, one that may indeed have been essential for the invention of writing. Writing appeared in the early centers of civilization, including Egypt, Mesopotamia, China, and Mesoamerica, where early states and city-states provided a framework for stability, urban life, scholarship, and trade (Woods, 2010). Although many early writings document the chronic warfare that characterized the ancient world, they also include codes of law, such as the Code of Hammurabi. Indeed, writing systems, legal codes, and state formation evolved together in ancient Mesopotamia (Charpin, 2010), where following the invention of writing, disputes over, for example, ownership of land could be resolved by reference to the written deed of purchase rather than by force. Early states carried on wars with each other, but within their boundaries claimed a monopoly on violence, enabling ordinary people to carry out their business without having to assume the full responsibility for deterring theft or personal violence (Boehm, 2011; Pinker, 2011).

For most of human history, the world of peaceful relations has had strict boundaries: peace within the state, anarchy without. Only with the establishment of international organizations such as the United Nations have widespread steps been taken to achieve something like the perpetual peace that Kant (1795/1983) envisioned, and of course that goal remains elusive (Howard, 2000). Some parts of the world that formerly suffered chronic and devastating war, such as much of Europe, have achieved a remarkable degree of international peace in recent decades, but this achievement requires training, education, and the development of institutions and mores that take time and effort to acquire (Pinker, 2011). These institutions have not yet taken root in many parts of the world, with tragic consequences for those living there. But just as the ability to attain widespread literacy is within reach for all human societies, so is the ability to achieve peace.

And yet, despite this hope that global peace is a practical objective, and not just a philosopher's dream, chronic wars drag on in many parts of the world. From the perspective of behavioral ecology, we should expect rates of human warfare to vary according to social and ecological circumstances, just as rates of intergroup violence vary among chimpanzee populations. So what are some factors that should make people more or less peaceful?

As strategic inclusive fitness optimizers, people should assess the costs and benefits of participating in war. When the net costs are too high, or the net benefits too low, people should avoid fighting and choose peaceful means of resolving conflicts instead. In this view, the achievement of peace depends on arranging the costs and benefits correctly so that people adopt peaceful rather than warlike strategies to achieve their goals.

Relatively few scholars of war and peace have adopted a behavioral ecology framework (for an exception, see Mesquida & Weiner, 1996). However, researchers in international studies have independently identified many factors associated with whether nations fight wars (Doyle, 1983; Gelpi & Grieco, 2008; Mousseau, 2009; Rauchhaus 2009). Behavioral ecology provides a useful framework for interpreting these findings.

Factors that raise the costs of war include overwhelmingly powerful opponents and overwhelmingly powerful weapons. Nuclear weapons in particular appear to raise the stakes sufficiently high that nuclear powers avoid fighting one another (Rauchhaus, 2009).

The relative benefits of fighting war may also decline, particularly with the advent of trade. One of the starkest differences between humans and chimpanzees is that intergroup interactions are always a zero-sum gain for chimpanzees. Unlike humans, chimpanzees have nothing to trade with their neighbors. They stand to benefit only by excluding their neighbors from a given plot of land. In contrast, among humans, the neighbors may have key resources that would otherwise be unavailable, and may be willing to trade them: stone for tools, shells and pigments for bodily adornment, or permission to use waterholes or hunting grounds during times of scarcity. The occurrence of stone tools and other items hundreds of kilometers from their sources indicates that humans have engaged in long-distance trade at least since the Middle Stone Age in Africa (McBrearty & Brooks, 2000). Among modern nations, the more countries trade with one another, the less likely they are to fight wars (Gelpi & Grieco, 2008; Rauchhaus, 2009). If one function of war is to obtain resources, trade provides a means to obtain the benefits of war (i.e., the resources in question) at a much lower cost (i.e., the price of the goods being traded, rather than the risk of ruin and death in war). A similar process appears to apply within nations. Countries with functioning market economies have a lower incidence of civil war, presumably because people in such countries can obtain by peaceful means resources that may be unobtainable except by force in other countries (de Soysa & Fjelde, 2010).

Another prediction from behavioral ecology is that people within a society can be expected to differ in their expected payoffs from war. As Ferguson (2001b) notes, elites in general likely stand to benefit from war much more than the soldiers who are recruited or coerced into doing the actual fighting. One of the best-supported findings in international relations is the so-called liberal or democratic peace: democracies are less likely to go to war with one another than are more authoritarian governments (Doyle 1983; Gelpi & Grieco, 2008; Hobson, 2011; Mousseau, 2009). One possible mechanism for this is that democracies better align national policy with the interests of the bulk of the citizens, rather than the elites. Alternatively, citizens of societies with contract-intensive economies may be predisposed toward applying similar rules to international affairs (Mousseau, 2009).

Additional factors promoting peace may include favorable demography and reproductive leveling. Mesquida and Wiener (1996) found that countries with a relatively high proportion of young men experienced a higher rate of conflict-related deaths. The authors argue that under such demographic conditions, young men must compete more intensively for reproductive and material opportunities. Along similar lines, civil war appears to be more common in countries with widespread polygyny (Kanazawa, 2009), perhaps because when many women marry polygynously, unmarried men find their reproductive options severely constrained.

The specific factors that best promote peace continue to be debated, and are difficult to disentangle, given that the world's most peaceful countries today share multiple traits in common (Pinker, 2011). In societies with democratic elections, contract intensive market economies, and transparent laws enforced by a fair government, people can achieve their goals without resorting to violence. Stable, fair governments and the rule of law provide opportunities to benefit from one another, rather than benefit only at the expense of one another. Effective law enforcement both raises the costs of committing violence and reduces the necessity of violence. Additionally, in societies where population growth does not outstrip economic growth, and where reproductive leveling is enforced through legal restrictions on polygyny, young men are generally better off pursuing peaceful strategies.

Many critics of the hypothesis that warfare is an adaptation frame their argument in moralistic terms, as if arguing for a biological basis was equivalent to arguing that warfare is unstoppable, or perhaps even desirable (Marks, 2002; Sussman, 1999). On the contrary, though, those interested in the biology of warfare have often passionately sought ways to prevent war (Goodall & Berman, 1999; Hamburg, 2004; Wrangham, 2010). Moreover, identifying biological roots of warfare by no means implies that warfare is inevitable in humans, any more than other features that were prevalent in our evolutionary history—such as exposure to harsh weather, food scarcity, and death from infectious disease—are unavoidable in modern life. Instead, an understanding of warfare rooted in behavioral ecology seems likely to help point the way toward a better understanding of the contexts that support peaceful intergroup relations.

Acknowledgements

Many thanks to Doug Fry for the invitation to contribute this chapter, and to Doug Fry, John Ingham, Leon Kass, Claire Kirchhoff, Clarence Lehman, Anne Pusey, and Richard Wrangham for helpful comments and discussion.

References

Alexander, R. D. (1979). *Darwinism and human affairs*. Seattle: University of Washington Press.

Amsler, S. J. (2010). Energetic costs of territorial boundary patrols by wild chimpanzees. *American Journal of Primatology, 72*(2), 93–103. doi: 10.1002/ajp.20757

Aureli, F., Schaffner, C. M., Verpooten, J., Slater, K., & Ramos-Fernandez, G. (2006). Raiding parties of male spider monkeys: insights into human warfare? *American Journal of Physical Anthropology, 131*(4), 486–497.

Bates, L. A., & Byrne, R. W. (2009). Sex differences in the movement patterns of free-ranging chimpanzees (*Pan troglodytes schweinfurthii*): foraging and border checking. *Behavioral Ecology and Sociobiology, 64*(2), 247–255. doi: 10.1007/s00265-009-0841-3

Boesch, C. (1994). Chimpanzees–red colobus monkeys: a predator–prey system. *Animal Behaviour, 47*, 1135–1148.

Boesch, C., & Boesch-Achermann, H. (2000). *The chimpanzees of the Taï Forest: Behavioral ecology and evolution*. Oxford: Oxford University Press.

Boesch, C., Crockford, C., Herbinger, I., Wittig, R. M., Moebius, Y., & Normand, E. (2008). Intergroup conflicts among chimpanzees in Tai National Park: Lethal violence and the female perspective. *American Journal of Primatology, 70*, 519–532.

Boesch, C., Head, J., Tagg, N., Arandjelovic, M., Vigilant, L., & Robbins, M. M. (2007). Fatal chimpanzee attack in Loango National Park, Gabon. *International Journal of Primatology. 28*, 1025–1034.

Boesch, C., Kohou, G., Nene, H., & Vigilant, L. (2006). Male competition and paternity in wild chimpanzees of the Tai forest. *American Journal of Physical Anthropology, 130*(1), 103–115.

Boehm, C. (1992). Segmentary "warfare" and the management of conflict: comparison of East African chimpanzees and patrilineal-patrilocal humans. In A. H. Harcourt & F. B. M. de Waal (Eds.), *Coalitions and alliances in humans and other animals* (pp. 137–173). Oxford: Oxford University Press.

Boehm, C. (2011). Retaliatory violence in human prehistory. *British Journal of Criminology, 51*(3), 518–534. doi: 10.1093/bjc/azr020

Bocquet-Appel, J. (2011). The agricultural demographic transition during and after the agriculture inventions. *Current Anthropology, 52* (Supplement 4), S497–S510.

Campbell, C. J. (2006). Lethal intragroup aggression by adult male spider monkeys (*Ateles geoffroyi*). *American Journal of Primatology, 68*, 1197–1201.

Chapman, C. A., & Wrangham, R. W. (1993). Range use of the forest chimpanzees of Kibale: implications for the understanding of chimpanzee social organization. *American Journal of Primatology, 31*, 263–273.

Charpin, D. (2010). *Writing, law, and kingship in Old Babylonian Mesopotamia*. Chicago: University of Chicago Press.

Constable, J. L., Ashley, M. V., Goodall, J., & Pusey, A. E. (2001). Noninvasive paternity assignment in Gombe chimpanzees. *Molecular Ecology, 10*(5), 1279–1300.

Crofoot, M., & Wrangham, R. W. (2010). Intergroup aggression in primates and humans: The case for a unified theory. In P. M. Kappeler & J. B. Silk (Eds.), *Mind the gap* (pp. 171–196). Berlin: Springer-Verlag.

Dawkins, R. (1989). *The selfish gene* (New ed.). Oxford: Oxford University Press. (Originally published in 1976).

Daly, M., & Wilson, M. (1988). *Homicide*. Hawthorne, New York: Aldine de Gruyter.

Darwin, C. (2003). *The origin of species by means of natural selection of the preservation of favoured races in the struggle for life* (150th Anniversary Edition). New York: Signet Classics. (Originally published in 1859).

Deacon, T. W. (1997). *The Symbolic Species: The Co-evolution of Language and the Brain*. New York: Norton.

Doyle, M. W. (1983). Kant, liberal legacies, and foreign affairs, Part 1. *Philosophy and Public Affairs, 12*(3), 205–235.

Eibl-Eibesfelt, I. (1979). *The biology of war and peace*. New York: Viking.

Emery Thompson, M., Kahlenberg, S. M., Gilby, I. C., & Wrangham, R. W. (2007). Core area quality is associated with variance in reproductive success among female chimpanzees at Kibale National Park. *Animal Behaviour, 73*, 501–512.

Enquist, M., & Leimar, O. (1990). The evolution of fatal fighting. *Animal Behaviour, 39*, 1–9.

Ferguson, R. B. (2001a). Materialist, cultural and biological theories on why Yanomami make war. *Anthropological Theory, 1*(1), 99–116.

Ferguson, R. B. (2001b). 10,000 years of tribal warfare: History, science, ideology and "the state of nature". *The Journal of the International Institute, 8*(3), 1, 4–5. Permalink: http://hdl.handle.net/2027/spo.4750978.0008.301

Gabriel, R. A. (1990). *The culture of war: Invention and early development*. New York: Greenwood Press.

Gat, A. (1999). The pattern of fighting in simple, small-scale, prestate societies. *Journal of Anthropological Research, 55*, 563–583.

Gat, A. (2006). *War in human civilization*. Oxford: Oxford University Press.

Gelpi, C. F., & Grieco, J. M. (2008). Democracy, interdependence, and the sources of the liberal peace. *Journal of Peace Research, 45*(1), 17–36.

Ghiglieri, M. (1984). *The chimpanzees of Kibale Forest: A field study of ecology and social structure*. New York: Columbia University Press.

Gilby, I. C., Eberly, L. E., & Wrangham, R. W. (2008). Economic profitability of social predation among wild chimpanzees: individual variation promotes cooperation. *Animal Behaviour, 75*, 351–360.

Goodall, J. (1971). *In the shadow of man*. Boston: Houghton Mifflin Co.

Goodall, J. (1977). Infant killing and cannibalism in free-living chimpanzees. *Folia Primatologica, 22*, 259–282.

Goodall, J. (1986). *The chimpanzees of Gombe: Patterns of behavior*. Cambridge, Massachusetts: Belknap Press.

Goodall, J., Bandora, A., Bergmann, E., Busse, C., Matama, H., Mpongo, E., . . . Riss, D. (1979). Intercommunity interactions in the chimpanzee population of the Gombe National Park. In D. A. Hamburg & E. R. McCown (Eds.), *The great apes* (pp. 13–53). Menlo Park, CA: Benjamin/Cummings.

Goodall, J., & Berman, P. (1999). *Reason for hope*. New York: Warner Books, Inc.

Grinnell, J., Packer, C., & Pusey, A. E. (1995). Cooperation in male lions: kinship, reciprocity or mutualism? *Animal Behaviour, 49*, 95–105.

Gros-Louis, J., Perry, S., & Manson, J. H. (2003). Violent coalitionary attacks and intraspecific killing in wild white-faced capuchin monkeys (*Cebus capucinus*). *Primates, 44*(4), 341–346.

Haas, J. (2001). Warfare and the evolution of culture. In T. D. Price & G. Feinman (Eds.), *Archaeology at the millennium: A sourcebook* (pp. 329–350). New York: Kluwer Academic/Plenum Publishers.

Hamburg, D. A. (2004). *Learning to live together: Preventing hatred and violence in child and adolescent development*. Oxford; New York: Oxford University Press.

Hart, D., & Sussman, R. W. (2009). *Man the hunted: Primates, predators, and human evolution*. Boulder, CO: Westview Press.

Hashimoto, C., & Furuichi, T. (2005). Possible intergroup killing in chimpanzees in the Kalinzu Forest, Uganda. *Pan Africa News, 12*(1), 3–5.

Hashimoto, C., & Furuichi, T. (2006). Comparison of behavioral sequence of copulation between chimpanzees and bonobos. *Primates, 47*, 51–55.

Hedrick, P. W. (2011). Population genetics of malaria resistance in humans. *Heredity, 107*(4), 283–304. doi: 10.1038/hdy.2011.16

Herbinger, I., Papworth, S., Boesch, C., & Zuberbühler, K. (2009). Vocal, gestural and locomotor responses of wild chimpanzees to familiar and unfamiliar intruders: a playback study. *Animal Behaviour, 78*, 1389–1396.

Hobbes, T. (1997). *Leviathan*. New York: Norton. (Originally published in 1651).

Hobson, C. (2011). Towards a critical theory of democratic peace. *Review of International Studies, 37*(4), 1903–1922. doi: 10.1017/s0260210510001634

Hunt, K. D., & McGrew, W. C. (2002). Chimpanzees in the dry habitats of Assirik, Senegal and Semliki Wildlife Reserve, Uganda. In C. Boesch, G. Hohmann & L. Marchant (Eds.), *Behavioural diversity in chimpanzees and bonobos* (pp. 35–51). Cambridge: Cambridge University Press.

Kanazawa, S. (2009). Evolutionary psychological foundations of civil wars. *Journal of Politics, 71*(1), 25–34.

Kant, I. (1983). *Perpetual peace, and other essays on politics, history, and morals* (T. Humphrey, Trans.). Indianapolis: Hacket. (Originally published in 1795.)

Keil, P. L., & Watson, P. J. (2011). Assessment of self, opponent and resource during male-male contests in the sierra dome spider, *Neriene litigiosa*: Linyphiidae. *Animal Behaviour, 80*(5), 809–820.

Kelly, R. C. (2000). *Warless societies and the origin of war.* Ann Arbor, MI: University of Michigan Press.

Kelly, R. C. (2005). The evolution of lethal intergroup violence. *Proceedings of the National Academy of Sciences of the United States of America, 102*(43), 15294–15298.

Kirchhoff, C. A., Wilson, M. L., Mjungu, D. C., Raphael, J., Kamenya, S. M., & Collins, D. A. (in press). Infanticide in chimpanzees: Taphonomic case studies from Gombe. In C. A. Schmitt & C. Fellman (Eds.), *New perspectives on juvenile primates.* New York: Springer.

Krebs, J. R., & Davies, N. B. (1993). *An introduction to behavioural ecology* (3rd ed.). Oxford: Blackwell Scientific Publications Ltd.

Kutsukake, N., & Matsusaka, T. (2002). Incident of intense aggression by chimpanzees against an infant from another group in Mahale Mountains National Park, Tanzania. *American Journal of Primatology, 58*(4), 175–180.

Lehmann, J., & Boesch, C. (2005). Bisexually bonded ranging in chimpanzees (*Pan troglodytes verus*). *Behavioral Ecology and Sociobiology, 57,* 525–535.

Leonardi, M., Gerbault, P., Thomas, M. G., & Burger, J. (2012). The evolution of lactase persistence in Europe. A synthesis of archaeological and genetic evidence. *International Dairy Journal, 22*(2), 88–97. doi: 10.1016/j.idairyj.2011.10.010

Manson, J. H., & Wrangham, R. W. (1991). Intergroup aggression in chimpanzees and humans. *Current Anthropology, 32*(4), 369–390.

Marks, J. (2002). *What it means to be 98 percent chimpanzee: Apes, people, and their genes.* Berkeley: University of California Press.

Matsuzawa, T., Humle, T., & Sugiyama, Y. (Eds.). (2011). *The chimpanzees of Bossou and Nimba.* New York: Springer.

Maynard Smith, J., & Parker, G. A. (1976). The logic of asymmetric contests. *Animal Behaviour, 24,* 159–175.

Mead, M. (1940). Warfare is only an invention—not a biological necessity. *Asia, 40*(8), 402–405.

McBrearty, S., & Brooks, A. S. (2000). The revolution that wasn't: a new interpretation of the origin of modern human behavior. *Journal of Human Evolution, 39*(5), 453–563. doi: 10.1006/jhev.2000.0435

McComb, K., Packer, C., & Pusey, A. (1994). Roaring and numerical assessment in contests between groups of female lions, *Panthera leo. Animal Behaviour, 47,* 379–387.

Mesquida, C. G., & Wiener, N. I. (1996). Human collective aggression: a behavioral ecology perspective. *Ethology & Sociobiology, 17,* 247–262.

Mitani, J. C. (2006). Demographic influences on the behavior of chimpanzees. *Primates, 47*(1), 6–13.

Mitani, J. C. (2009). Cooperation and competition in chimpanzees: current understanding and future challenges. *Evolutionary Anthropology, 18,* 215–227.

Mitani, J. C., & Nishida, T. (1993). Contexts and social correlates of long-distance calling by male chimpanzees. *Animal Behaviour, 45,* 735–746.

Mitani, J. C., & Watts, D. P. (2001). Why do chimpanzees hunt and share meat? *Animal Behaviour, 61,* 915–924.

Mitani, J. C., & Watts, D. P. (2005). Correlates of territorial boundary patrol behaviour in wild chimpanzees. *Animal Behaviour, 70,* 1079–1086.

Mitani, J. C., Watts, D. P., & Amsler, S. J. (2010). Lethal intergroup aggression leads to territorial expansion in wild chimpanzees. *Current Biology, 20*(12), R507–R508.

Mitani, J. C., Watts, D. P., & Lwanga, J. S. (2002). Ecological and social correlates of chimpanzee party size and composition. In C. Boesch, G. Hohmann & L. F. Marchant (Eds.), *Behavioral diversity in chimpanzees and bonobos* (pp. 102–111). Cambridge: Cambridge University Press.

Mjungu, D. C. (2010). *Dynamics of intergroup competition in two neighboring chimpanzee communities.* (Ph.D. Thesis), University of Minnesota, St. Paul.

Montagu, A. (1976). *The nature of human aggression.* New York: Oxford University Press.

Mousseau, M. (2009). The social market roots of democratic peace. *International Security, 33*(4), 52–86.

Muller, M. N. (2002). Agonistic relations among Kanyawara chimpanzees. In C. Boesch, G. Hohmann, & L. F. Marchant (Eds.), *Behavioural Diversity in Chimpanzees and Bonobos* (pp. 112–123). Cambridge: Cambridge University Press.

Muller, M. N., & Wrangham, R. W. (2004). Dominance, aggression and testosterone in wild chimpanzees: a test of the "challenge hypothesis." *Animal Behaviour, 67*, 113–123.

Murray, C. M., Wroblewski, E., & Pusey, A. E. (2007). New case of intragroup infanticide in the chimpanzees of Gombe National Park. *International Journal of Primatology, 28*(1), 23–37.

Newton-Fisher, N. E. (1994). Hierarchy and social status in Budongo chimpanzees. *Primates, 45*, 81–87.

Newton-Fisher, N. E. (1999). Infant killers of Budongo. *Folia Primatologica, 70*, 167–169.

Newton-Fisher, N. E. (2007). Chimpanzee hunting behavior. In W. Henke & I. Tattersall (Eds.), *Handbook of Paleoanthropology* (pp. 1295–1320). New York: Springer.

Newton-Fisher, N. E., Thompson, M. E., Reynolds, V., Boesch, C., & Vigilant, L. (2010). Paternity and social rank in wild chimpanzees (*Pan troglodytes*) from the Budongo Forest, Uganda. *American Journal of Physical Anthropology, 142*(3), 417–428.

Nishida, T. (1968). The social group of wild chimpanzees in the Mahale Mountains. *Primates, 9*, 167–224.

Nishida, T. (1979). The social structure of chimpanzees of the Mahale Mountains. In D. A. Hamburg & E. R. McCown (Eds.), *The great apes* (pp. 73–121). Menlo Park, CA: Benjamin/Cummings.

Nishida, T. (Ed.). (1990). *The chimpanzees of the Mahale Mountains: Sexual and life-history strategies.* Tokyo: University of Tokyo Press.

Nishida, T., Corp, N., Hamai, M., Hasegawa, T., Hiraiwa-Hasegawa, M., Hosaka, K., . . . Zamma, K. (2003). Demography, female life history, and reproductive profiles among the chimpanzees of Mahale. *American Journal of Primatology, 59*(3), 99–121.

Nishida, T., Hirawiwa-Hasegawa, M., Hasegawa, T., & Takahata, Y. (1985). Group extinction and female transfer in wild chimpanzees in the Mahale National Park, Tanzania. *Zeitschrift für Tierpsychologie, 67*, 284–301.

Otterbein, K. F. (1999). A history of research on warfare in anthropology. *American Anthropologist, 101*(4), 794–805.

Otterbein, K. F. (2004). *How war began.* College Station: Texas A&M University Press.

Parker, G. A. (1974). Assessment strategy and the evolution of fighting behavior. *Journal of Theoretical Biology, 47*(1), 223–243.

Pinker, S. (2011). *The Better Angels of Our Nature: Why Violence Has Declined.* New York: Viking Penguin.

Pinker, S., & Bloom, P. (1990). Natural language and natural selection. *Behavioral and Brain Sciences, 13*, 707–784.

Potts, K. B., Watts, D. P., & Wrangham, R. W. (2011). Comparative feeding ecology of two communities of chimpanzees (*Pan troglodytes*) in Kibale National Park, Uganda. *International Journal of Primatology, 32*(3), 669–690. doi: 10.1007/s10764-011-9494-y

Power, M. (1991). *The egalitarians—human and chimpanzee: An anthropological view of social organization.* Cambridge: Cambridge University Press.

Pusey, A. E. (1980). Inbreeding avoidance in chimpanzees. *Animal Behaviour, 28*, 543–582.

Pusey, A. E., Murray, C., Wallauer, W. R., Wilson, M. L., Wroblewski, E., & Goodall, J. (2008). Severe aggression among female chimpanzees at Gombe National Park, Tanzania. *International Journal of Primatology, 29*(4), 949–973.

Pusey, A. E., Oehlert, G. W., Williams, J. M., & Goodall, J. (2005). The influence of ecological and social factors on body mass of wild chimpanzees. *International Journal of Primatology, 26*, 3–31.

Pusey, A. E., Pintea, L. P., Wilson, M. L., Kamenya, S., & Goodall, J. (2007). The contribution of long-term research at Gombe National Park to chimpanzee conservation. *Conservation Biology, 21*(3), 623–634.

Pusey, A. E., Wilson, M. L., & Collins, D. A. (2008). Human impacts, disease risk, and population dynamics in the chimpanzees of Gombe National Park, Tanzania. *American Journal of Primatology, 70*(8), 738–744.

Pruetz, J. D., & Bertolani, P. (2007). Savanna chimpanzees, *Pan troglodytes verus*, hunt with tools. *Current Biology, 17*, 412–417.

Rauchhaus, R. (2009). Evaluating the nuclear peace hypothesis: A quantitative approach. *Journal of Conflict Resolution, 53*(2), 258–277.

Read, D. W., & LeBlanc, S. A. (2003). Population growth, carrying capacity, and conflict. *Current Anthropology, 44*(1), 59–85.

Reynolds, V., & Reynolds, F. (1965). Chimpanzees of the Budongo Forest. In I. DeVore (Ed.), *Primate behavior: Field studies of monkeys and apes* (pp. 368–424). New York: Holt, Rinehart & Winston.

Reynolds, V. (2005). *The chimpanzees of the Budongo Forest: Ecology, behavior, and conservation.* Oxford: Oxford University Press.

Rousseau, J. (1964). *The first and second discourses* (R. D. Masters & J. R. Masters, Trans.). New York: St. Martin's Press. (Originally published in 1754.)

Rudicell, R. S., Jones, J., Wroblewski, E., Learn, G., Li, Y., Robertson, J., . . . Wilson, M. L. (2010). Impact of Simian Immunodeficiency Virus Infection on chimpanzee population dynamics. *PLoS Pathogens*, 6(9), e1001116.

Sanz, C., Call, J., & Morgan, D. (2009). Design complexity in termite-fishing tools of chimpanzees (Pan troglodytes). *Biology Letters*, 5(3), 293–296. doi: 10.1098/rsbl.2008.0786

Sauther, M. L., Sussman, R. W., & Gould, L. (1999). The socioecology of the ringtailed lemur: thirty-five years of research. *Evolutionary Anthropology*, 8, 120–132.

Sherrow, H. M., & Amsler, S. J. (2007). New intercommunity infanticides by the chimpanzees of Ngogo, Kibale National Park, Uganda. *International Journal of Primatology*, 28(1), 9–22. doi: 10.1007/s10764-006-9112-6

de Soysa, I., & Fjelde, H. (2010). Is the hidden hand an iron fist? Capitalism and civil peace, 1970–2005. *Journal of Peace Research*, 47(3), 287–298. doi: 10.1177/0022343310362167

Stumpf, R. M., Emery Thompson, M., Muller, M. N., & Wrangham, R. W. (2009). The context of female dispersal in Kanyawara chimpanzees. *Behaviour*, 146, 629–656.

Sussman, R. W. (1999). The myth of man the hunter, man the killer and the evolution of human morality (evolutionary and religious perspectives on morality). *Zygon*, 34(3), 453–472.

Sussman, R. W., Garber, P. A., & Cheverud, J. M. (2005). Importance of cooperation and affiliation in the evolution of primate sociality. *American Journal of Physical Anthropology*, 128, 84–97.

Terio, K. A., Kinsel, M. J., Raphael, J., Mlengeya, T., Lipende, I., Kirchhoff, C., . . . Lonsdorf, E. V. (2011). Pathological lesions in chimpanzees (*Pan troglodytes schweinfurthii*) from Gombe National Park, Tanzania, 2004–2010. *Journal of Zoo and Wildlife Medicine*, 42(4), 597–607.

Thorpe, I. J. N. (2003). Anthropology, archaeology, and the origin of warfare. *World Archaeology*, 35(1), 145–165.

Tinbergen, N. (1963). On aims and methods of Ethology. *Zeitschrift fur Tierpyschologie*, 20, 410–433.

Tooby, J., & Cosmides, L. (1988). The evolution of war and its cognitive foundations. Institute for Evolutionary Studies Technical Report 88-1. Retrieved from http://www.psych.ucsb.edu/research/cep/publist.htm

Tutin, C. E. G., & McGinnis, P. R. (1981). Chimpanzee reproduction in the wild. In C. E. Graham (Ed.), *Reproductive biology of the great apes* (pp. 239–264). New York: Academic Press.

van der Dennen, J. M. G. (1995). *The origin of war: The evolution of a male-coalitional reproductive strategy*. Groningen, Netherlands: Origin Press.

van Lawick-Goodall, J. (1968). Behaviour of free-living chimpanzees of the Gombe Stream area. *Animal Behaviour Monographs*, 1, 163–311.

Vigilant, L., Hofreiter, M., Siedel, H., & Boesch, C. (2001). Paternity and relatedness in wild chimpanzee communities. *Proceedings of the National Academy of Sciences*, 98(23), 12890–12895.

Wakefield, M. L. (2008). Grouping patterns and competition among female *Pan troglodytes schweinfurthii* at Ngogo, Kibale National Park, Uganda. *International Journal of Primatology*, 29(4), 907–929.

Watts, D. P. (2000). Grooming between male chimpanzees at Ngogo, Kibale National Park. II. Influence of male rank and possible competition for partners. *International Journal of Primatology*, 21(2), 211–238. doi: 10.1023/a:1005421419749

Watts, D. P. (2012). Long-term research on chimpanzee behavioral ecology in Kibale National Park, Uganda. In P. M. Kappeler & D. P. Watts (Eds.), *Long-term field studies of primates* (pp. 313–338). Heidelberg: Springer-Verlag.

Watts, D. P., & Mitani, J. C. (2000). Infanticide and cannibalism by male chimpanzees at Ngogo, Kibale National Park, Uganda. *Primates*, 41(4), 357–365.

Watts, D. P., & Mitani, J. C. (2001). Boundary patrols and intergroup encounters in wild chimpanzees. *Behaviour*, 138(3), 299–327.

Watts, D. P., Mitani, J. C., & Sherrow, H. M. (2002). New cases of inter-community infanticide by male chimpanzees at Ngogo, Kibale National Park, Uganda. *Primates*, 43(4), 263–270.

Watts, D. P., Muller, M., Amsler, S. J., Mbabazi, G., & Mitani, J. C. (2006). Lethal intergroup aggression by chimpanzees in Kibale National Park, Uganda. *American Journal of Primatology*, 68(2), 161–180.

White, D. W., Dill, L. M., & Crawford, C. B. (2007). A common, conceptual framework for behavioral ecology and evolutionary psychology. *Evolutionary Psychology*, 5(2), 275–288.

Whiten, A., Goodall, J., McGrew, W. C., Toshisada, N., Reynolds, V., Sugiyama, Y., . . . Boesch, C. (1999). Chimpanzee cultures. *Nature*, 399, 682–685.

Williams, J. M., Lonsdorf, E. V., Wilson, M. L., Schumacher-Stankey, J., Goodall, J., & Pusey, A. E. (2008). Causes of death in the Kasekela chimpanzees of Gombe National Park, Tanzania. *American Journal of Primatology*, 70(8), 766–777.

Williams, J. M., Oehlert, G., Carlis, J., & Pusey, A. E. (2004). Why do male chimpanzees defend a group range? Reassessing male territoriality. *Animal Behaviour, 68*(3), 523–532.

Williams, J. M., Pusey, A. E., Carlis, J. V., Farm, B. P., & Goodall, J. (2002). Female competition and male territorial behavior influence female chimpanzees' ranging patterns. *Animal Behaviour, 63*(2), 347–360.

Wilson, M. L. (2012). Long-term studies of the Gombe chimpanzees. In P. Kappeler & D. P. Watts (Eds.), *Long-term Field Studies of Primates* (pp. 357–384). Heidelberg: Springer-Verlag.

Wilson, M. L., Boesch, C., Gilby, I. C., Hashimoto, C., Hohmann, G., Itoh, N., ... Wrangham, R. W. (2012, April 11–14). Rates of lethal aggression in chimpanzees depend on the number of adult males rather than measures of human disturbance. Paper presented at the 81st Annual Meeting of the American Association of Physical Anthropologists, Portland, Oregon.

Wilson, M. L., Hauser, M. D., & Wrangham, R. W. (2001). Does participation in intergroup conflict depend on numerical assessment, range location, or rank for wild chimpanzees? *Animal Behaviour, 61*(6), 1203–1216.

Wilson, M. L., Hauser, M. D., & Wrangham, R. W. (2007). Chimpanzees (*Pan troglodytes*) modify grouping and vocal behaviour in response to location-specific risk. *Behaviour, 144*(12), 1621–1653.

Wilson, M. L., Kahlenberg, S. M., Wells, M. T., & Wrangham, R. W. (2012). Ecological and social factors affect the occurrence and outcomes of intergroup encounters in chimpanzees. *Animal Behaviour, 83*(1), 277–291.

Wilson, M. L., Wallauer, W., & Pusey, A. E. (2004). New cases of intergroup violence among chimpanzees in Gombe National Park, Tanzania. *International Journal of Primatology, 25*(3), 523–549.

Wilson, M. L., & Wrangham, R. W. (2003). Intergroup relations in chimpanzees. *Annual Review of Anthropology, 32*, 363–392.

Woods, C. (Ed.). (2010). *Visible language: Inventions of writing in the ancient Middle East and beyond.* Chicago: Oriental Institute of the University of Chicago, Museum Publications.

Wrangham, R. W. (1974). Artificial feeding of chimpanzees and baboons in their natural habitat. *Animal Behaviour, 22*, 83–93.

Wrangham, R. W. (1977). Feeding behaviour of chimpanzees in Gombe National Park, Tanzania. In T. H. Clutton-Brock (Ed.), *Primate ecology* (pp. 503–538). New York: Academic Press.

Wrangham, R. W. (1979). Sex differences in chimpanzee dispersion. In D. A. Hamburg & E. R. McCown (Eds.), *The great apes* (pp. 481–489). Menlo Park, CA: Benjamin/Cummings.

Wrangham, R. W. (1980). An ecological model of female-bonded primate groups. *Behaviour, 75*, 262–300.

Wrangham, R. W. (1999). Evolution of coalitionary killing. *Yearbook of Physical Anthropology, 42*, 1–30.

Wrangham, R. W. (2010). Chimpanzee violence is a serious topic. A response to Sussman and Marshack's critique of *Demonic males: Apes and the origins of human violence. Global Nonkilling Working Papers, 1*, 29–50.

Wrangham, R. W., Chapman, C. A., Clark-Arcadi, A. P., & Isabirye-Basuta, G. (1996). Socio-ecology of Kanyawara chimpanzees: implications for understanding the costs of great ape groups. In W. C. McGrew, L. F. Marchant & T. Nishida (Eds.), *Great ape societies* (pp. 45–57). Cambridge: Cambridge University Press.

Wrangham, R. W., Conklin-Brittain, N. L., & Hunt, K. D. (1998). Dietary response of chimpanzees and cercopithecines to seasonal variation in fruit abundance. I. Antifeedants. *International Journal of Primatology, 19*, 949–970.

Wrangham, R. W., & Glowacki, L. (2012). Intergroup aggression in chimpanzees and war in nomadic hunter-gatherers: Evaluating the chimpanzee model. *Human Nature, in press.* doi: 10.1007/s12110-012-9132-1

Wrangham, R. W., McGrew, W. C., de Waal, F. B. M., & Heltne, P. G. (Eds.). (1994). *Chimpanzee cultures.* Cambridge, MA: Harvard University Press.

Wrangham, R. W., & Peterson, D. (1996). *Demonic males: Apes and the origins of human violence.* Boston: Houghton Mifflin.

Wrangham, R. W., Wilson, M. L., & Muller, M. N. (2006). Comparative rates of violence in chimpanzees and humans. *Primates, 47*(1), 14–26.

Wroblewski, E. E., Murray, C. M., Keele, B. F., Schumacher-Stankey, J., Hahn, B. H., & Pusey, A. E. (2009). Male dominance rank and reproductive success in chimpanzees, *Pan troglodytes schweinfurthii. Animal Behaviour, 77*(4), 873–885.

Zeder, M. A. (2011). The origins of agriculture in the Near East. *Current Anthropology, 52*, S221-S235. doi: 10.1086/659307

19

Evolution of Primate Peace

Frances J. White, Michel T. Waller, and Klaree J. Boose

In environments where resources are limited, as is often the case for wild nonhuman primates, success in competition with conspecifics is of major evolutionary significance. Behaviors that increase competitive abilities to gain limited resources will be selected for if their benefits, in terms of differential survival and lifetime reproductive success, outweigh their costs. Nonhuman primates competing for reproductive success are typically limited by access to resources. More specifically, male reproductive success is limited by access to females while females, with the higher costs associated with gestation and lactation, are more typically limited by access to food. Wrangham's (1980) ecological model of female bonding and competition proposes that the distribution of food affects female social structures as there is a strong link between the defendability of food, the costs of female bonding, and the corresponding dispersal of females. In species that eat food that is defendable such as fruit, groups of related females were predicted to cooperatively defend food sources from outside females within a hierarchical frame. In species that depend on nondefendable foods such as leaves, competition should be reduced and females would not experience the same level of bonding and cooperation. Subsequently, their relationships would be loosely defined. Since then, primatologists have incorporated patch size (Janson, 1988), intra and intergroup contest and scramble competition (Isbell, 1991), and dispersal, tolerance, hierarchies, and kin dimensions (Sterck, Watts, & van Schaik, 1997) that have further refined models of primate sociality based on varying degrees of female competition for food.

Although food is also important for males, the success of male mammals is often more impacted by their competitive ability to gain access to reproductive females. This is especially apparent in species with little or no paternal care. As paternal care becomes more and more important for infant survival and success, male and female limiting factors become more similar and individual strategies focus on competitive skills that help successfully rear offspring. Studies of the evolution of primate social systems often approach this subject by considering the competition, distribution, and social strategies of females relative to the food distribution, and secondarily, examining the way the distribution of females influences the competition strategies of males.

Competition over resources is categorized into two general types: contest and scramble (Nicholson, 1954). Scramble competition and contest competition have different consequences for the evolution of both aggressive and cooperative strategies in primates, and operate at two main levels: within and between social groups. Scramble competition (colloquially known as "first-come, first-served") exists when individuals or groups are unable to exclude others when resources may be too plentiful or spaced too far apart. It also may exist if population density is too large. As a result of these conditions, individuals gain resources by reaching them before others and there is little advantage to disputing ownership. The resource is either used up, such as in a small food item that is eaten or a mating that is completed, or there are other opportunities elsewhere that render disputes too costly with little reward. In contest competition, however, the resource is monopolizable so that disputes over ownership can easily happen, especially if that resource is limited and relatively hard to find elsewhere.

The relative importance of scramble and contest competition has broad impacts on primates' spatial distribution and behavioral strategies as they compete over food, mates, helpers, and shelter both within and among groups. Scramble competitors adjust their distribution in relation to habitat quality so that each individual or group acquires resources at a similar rate. This spatial partitioning is known as the "ideal free" distribution (Fretwell & Lucas, 1972) and can be characterized by a lack of territorial behavior, while reproductive success reaches equilibrium due to crowding in the better habitats and fewer individuals in the poorer. Spatial contest competition arises when limited resources are economically defended through exclusion or direct displacement, leading to increased reproductive success for those individuals or groups capable of defending key resources (Brown, 1964). Where contest competition is employed, individuals or groups are spatially arranged in a "despotic free" distribution, meaning that the dominant individuals or groups have differential access to preferred resources. Consequently, in cases where there is an estimable amount of contest competition, definitive dominance hierarchies both within and between groups are expected. It is also possible that individuals can experience one type of competition while groups can experience another.

While these two distribution models may represent ends of a spectrum of spatial arrangements, they are accompanied by competitive behavioral strategies that illuminate the relationship between the distribution of individuals within and among groups and the socio-ecologic drivers of the distribution pattern. These include habitat quality, dominance hierarchies, and ranging behaviors. More specifically, where spatial behavior resembles the ideal free distribution (1) scramble competition should be observed, (2) dominance hierarchies should be weak or nonexistent, (3) reproductive success should reach equilibrium as (4) higher quality habitats (or patches) should support more individuals while lower quality habitats should support fewer. Furthermore, (5) interactions should be nonantagonistic and (6) territoriality is less likely. Conversely, when individuals or groups live in a despotic free distribution, there should be a (A) strong dominance asymmetry that results in those groups or individuals capable of excluding others enjoying (B) higher reproductive success and (C) preferential access to resources. Additionally, (D) interactions should be aggressive and (E) territoriality, behavior involved in actively preventing others from entering into an area, should be observable.

From an individual perspective, a scramble contest often gives no advantage to high rank, so that this type of competition in primates does not typically result in strong hierarchies within a group. When contest completion for monopolizable resources happens, however, disputes can be fierce at the individual level. Female primates who scramble for insects or leaves rarely show dominance hierarchies, whereas those fighting over small fruit clusters have a clearly defined and much defended ranking system. When these types of competition operate above the individual level, however, cooperation and alliances can become critical to success. The ability of two or more individuals to work together to defend a resource, whether food or females, can greatly increase the evolutionary success of both. The level of contest, however, may have been changed so that now individuals may benefit from cooperation with each other, but fighting with other groups is now significant in gaining access to large monopolizable resources.

In primates, therefore, the presence of fighting or aggression-based strategies can reflect the importance of monopolizable resources. More importantly, the absence of fighting does not reflect the absence of such resources, but rather that cooperation or peaceful strategies that are based on affiliative instead of aggressive interactions are more beneficial either at the individual level, or even potentially at the group level. By exploring the relative advantages of different competitive strategies we can examine the specific behaviors associated with intergroup behaviors in our closest relatives with the specific goal of better understanding the context in which aggression or tolerance would evolve.

Evolutionary considerations of human aggressive or affiliative individual or group behavior typically draw from studies of our closest nonhuman primate relatives: the chimpanzee and the bonobo. Until recently, scientists have focused on the violent nature of male chimpanzees, the lack of close association among female chimpanzees, and inferred parallels with early human societies (Boehm, 1992; Wrangham, 1999; Wrangham & Peterson, 1996). Conspecific coalitionary violence between animals is rare, with only a few species known to form aggressive coalitions of more than four individuals (van der Dennen, 1995). While lions, hyenas, and cheetahs occasionally employ coalitional killing of conspecifics at rates that are currently unknown (Wrangham, 1999), wolves, chimpanzees, and humans are the only species known to regularly kill adult members of other groups during territorial disputes (Mech, Adams, Meier, Burch, & Dale, 1998; Wrangham, 1999). Additionally, chimpanzees are well-known for their aggressive territorial behavior. Encounters between groups are typically hostile and, in extreme cases, can result in the death of one or more individuals or even entire communities (Goodall, 1986; Mitani, Watts, & Muller, 2002; Wrangham, 1999). Aggression between neighboring groups of chimpanzees has now been observed at several study sites including Gombe and Mahale, Tanzania (Goodall et al., 1979; Nishida, Hiraiwa-Hasegawa, Hasegawa, & Takahata, 1985), Taï National Park, Côte d'Ivoire (Boesch & Boesch-Achermann, 2000), Kibale National Park, Uganda (Watts & Mitani, 2001), and Budongo Forest Reserve, Uganda (Newton-Fisher, 1999). These attacks occur during "lethal raids" (Wrangham, 1999).

Humans, however, have an equally close relative in the bonobo. Bonobo societies are based on peaceful cooperation and strong social bonds both between males and females and among females. Studies of bonobos in their natural habitat in the 1980s and early 1990s (Kano, 1992; White 1996a,b) found that, unlike chimpanzees, bonobo communities are based on strong social ties among unrelated females and long-term bonding between individual males and females, especially adult sons and their mothers. Bonobo communities are also able to associate peacefully (Kano, 1992; White, 1996b). Male bonobos do not form the tight bands that are associated with the male cooperative killing behavior of chimpanzees. Instead, bonobo aggression is mild. Disputes and social tensions among bonobos are often diffused through sexual behavior (White, 1996b).

These two species not only represent our closest relatives but also encompass a wide spectrum of possible human behaviors. By understanding the circumstances under which an aggressive or an affiliative social system evolved, we can bring greater understanding to the importance of war and peace during human evolution and development.

Chimpanzees

While the majority of his research focused on captive chimpanzees, Henry Nissen is thought to have been the first person to set out in an effort to study chimpanzees in their native habitat. Backed by Robert Yerkes, Nissen spent nine weeks in what is today the country of Guinea studying basic behavior and published his remarks of his field study (Nissan, 1931). At the time, methods for studying wild apes were not developed and Nissen had few direct observations of chimpanzee behavior. Nonetheless, he pioneered a research approach that would illuminate chimpanzee behavior (Peterson 1998) and set the stage for Jane Goodall and Toshisada Nishida.

Beginning in 1960, the research conducted in Tanzania by Goodall at the Gombe Reserve and Nishida in the Mahale Mountains showed that the traits shared by humans and chimpanzees were not an artifact of chimpanzees having been raised in captivity. Their observations on social organization (Nishida, 1968), social aggression (Goodall et al., 1979; Nishida et al., 1985), cooperative hunting (Goodall, 1963), and the making and using of tools (Goodall, 1964) have changed the way in which humans think about our early ancestors and have overturned speculation that one or the other of these traits are unique to humans. Furthermore, the results spurred dozens of long-term field sites across equatorial Africa. What has emerged is a portrait of a species that behaves in a number of ways useful in constructing early hominin behavior (Wrangham & Pilbeam, 2001).

All chimpanzees live in multi-male/multi-female communities, or "unit-groups," where parties within the communities fluctuate in size and composition (Nishida, 1968) based on factors such as food availability (Chapman, White, & Wrangham, 1994; Goodall, 1968; Itani & Suzuki, 1967; Mitani, Watts, & Lwanga, 2002; Wrangham, 1986), predation pressure (Boesch, 1991), the presence of females in estrus (Boesch & Boesch-Achermann, 2000; Goodall, 1986; Hashimoto, Furuichi, & Tashiro, 2001; Matsumoto-Oda, 2002; Mitani, Watts, & Lwanga, 2002) and intergroup aggression (Watts & Mitani, 2001; Wrangham, 1999). Their daily lives are dictated by a rudimentary form of culture (McGrew, 1992) that varies between groups and appears centered on obtaining food.

Chimpanzees are primarily fruit eaters (Conklin-Brittain, Wrangham, & Hunt, 1998; Pruetz, 2006) although they will supplement their diet with bark, flowers, insects, eggs (Nishida & Uehara, 1983; Stumpf, 2007), and vertebrates hunted opportunistically or in a coordinated fashion (Stanford, 1996). Still, the distribution of preferred fruits play the biggest role in their social organization (Boesch, 2002; Wrangham, 1980). Seasonality (Doran, 1996), population density (Mitani, 2006), habitat structure (Pruetz, 2006), and interspecies competition levels (Waller, 2005) have all been found to vary the amount of fruit available for each community. Areas with good food sources are highly coveted, as access to more food can lead to higher reproductive success (Pusey, Williams, & Goodall, 1997; Williams, Liu, & Pusey, 2002; but see Riedel, Franz, & Boesch, 2011). As a result of the food distribution, individual females contest access to food (Doran, 1996; Nishida & Kawanaka, 1972; Pusey, 1979; Wrangham & Smuts, 1980; but see Newton-Fisher, 2006; Wakefield, 2008). Chimpanzee females, therefore, cannot afford to be very social, but spend a considerable amount of time alone with their dependent offspring.

Male chimpanzees, on the other hand, are highly social with each other. Males are philopatric and constantly struggle for status within their community (N. Newton-Fisher, 2002). From an evolutionary fitness perspective, highest-ranking males benefit from contest competition to gain preferred access to females and food (Sugiyama & Koman, 1979; Tutin, 1979). Males stay within their natal community for their entire life and interact often (Goodall, 1986). They make and break alliances frequently, which results in a fluid social hierarchy (de Waal, 1992). Despite the potential for fierce within-group contest competition, the scattered distribution of less-than-social females provides an increased benefit to male cooperation. One male cannot gain continual access to many females, but a group of males can maintain access to an area containing many females through contest competition with neighboring males.

Additional benefits to cooperation within the group come from the fact that all the males within a community are related. Relatedness increases the benefit of within-group male-male cooperative behaviors resulting in strong male bonds (Watts, 2002; but see Mitani, Watts, & Muller, 2002; Langergraber, Mitani, & Vigilant, 2007) that benefit self and kin. These bonds are beneficial, directly or indirectly (via kin selection), in that they enable male community members to coordinate hunts (Stanford, 1998; Watts & Mitani,

2001), patrol territories (Watts & Mitani, 2001), and lethally raid neighboring communities (Boesch & Boesch-Achermann, 2000; Goodall et al., 1979; Manson & Wrangham, 1991; Newton-Fisher, 1999; Nishida et al., 1985; Watts & Mitani, 2001). These behaviors result in increased access to both food and mating resources for the related males in a community (Boesch et al., 2008; Goodall, 1986; Nishida et al., 1985; Williams, Oehlert, Carlis, & Pusey, 2004). Simply stated, individual male chimpanzees benefit from grouping while the cost of grouping for individual females is prohibitively higher.

Bonobos

Equidistant to humans phylogenetically, bonobos (*Pan paniscus*) were the last of the four nonhuman great apes to be classified (Coolidge, 1933). Endemic to the Democratic Republic of the Congo (DRC) they are found primarily in the dense rainforests of the Congo River basin, but also in more open, mosaic environments in the southern portion of their geographic range (Thompson, 2001, 2002). Based on genetic and paleo-environmental analysis, bonobos were isolated from chimpanzees sometime between 800,000 and 2.5 MYA when the Congo River grew to such a size that crossing the river was impossible for forest-dwelling mammals, resulting in chimpanzees inhabiting the forests and other habitats north of the river and bonobos those to the south (Myers Thompson, 2003).

Like chimpanzees, bonobos live in communities or unit-groups (Kano, 1992; White, 1996b). Within these communities, party membership is fluid but predictable with sociality based on sets of cohesive, allied, unrelated females, particularly those with infants, that we call "cliques" (Waller, 2010). The females in cliques regularly associate in parties with each other but there is greater variability in party membership by males and females without infants (Waller, 2010; White, 1986, 1989a, 1989b; White & Burgman, 1990). Consequently, male-female interactions are more numerous in larger parties while smaller groups reflect the bonds maintained through female-female affiliation among these regular female alliances (White, 1992).

The female-female bonds are sustained through a homosexual behavior known as genito-genital (GG) rubbing (White, 1996) as well as through food-sharing behaviors not seen in female chimpanzees (White, 1994). Well known for their promiscuity, non-reproductive sex is not limited to females. Bonobos engage in sexual behavior across age categories and within and between sexes (Kano, 1992) to build alliances (de Waal, 1987; White & Lanjouw, 1992), and diffuse rising tensions (Furuichi, 1987, 1992; Kano, 1992). The number of copulations may be increased in captivity or with provisioning (Kano, 1992) and has been associated with feeding contexts suggesting that bonds are most important during feeding events. These bonds may help in creating relatively stable alliances of females that benefit by cooperatively defending food patches from others (White, 1986) and mutual protection from infanticidal males (White & Waller, 2008).

Males join parties when food availability is higher (White, 1988) and may be most closely associated with their mothers when parties are very large. Mothers can facilitate mating opportunities, as they have close social bonds with unrelated younger females (Furuichi, 1997; Ihobe, 1992; Surbeck, Mundry, & Hohmann, 2010). Males are also more likely to be found ranging alone when compared with females (Kano, 1992; White, 1992). Compared to chimpanzees, there is much less male-male bonding among bonobos (Kano, 1992; White, 1996b; White & Chapman, 1994) and the dominance hierarchy is not as clear (Furuichi, 1997; White & Wood, 2007).

Three hypotheses based on these models have attempted to explain the social differences of females between bonobos and chimpanzees, all of which center on the assumption that the female-bonded social structure reported in bonobos is a species-specific trait allowed by high food availability and the subsequent low levels of feeding competition (White, 1996a), regardless of the fact that females are unrelated. These hypotheses place different emphasis on the role of both within and between group scramble and contest competition for food.

The first hypothesis suggested that bonobo feeding competition is relatively low due to greater access to terrestrial herbaceous vegetation (THV), an abundant and ubiquitous food source (Badrian & Malenky, 1984; Wrangham, 1986). THV is eaten regularly by bonobos (Malenky & Stiles, 1991) and chimpanzees eat THV far less frequently perhaps due to the presence of sympatric gorillas (Wrangham, 1986). For example, THV accounts for 33 percent of the overall food intake for bonobos at the Wamba site and only 7 percent of overall food intake for chimpanzees at Gombe (Wrangham, 1986). This hypothesis provides an ability to be social by reducing the cost, but does not include a direct selective to female sociality. Female sociality is presumed to be advantageous for other reasons, including the ability of groups of females to mitigate the effects of male aggression. Research has shown, however, that party size is smaller when bonobos are feeding on THV compared with other foods, suggesting that THV is not a driver of sociality (White, 1996a). Furthermore, Malenky and Stiles (1991) found that although THV at Lomako was abundantly distributed, bonobos preferred particular plants (namely *Haumania liebrechtsiana*) to others, greatly reducing the otherwise seemingly ubiquitous distribution of THV patches. Consequently, Malenky and Stiles (1991) argue that it is unlikely that THV is responsible for the evolution of the bonobo social structure.

The second hypothesis, presented by Malenky (1990), suggested that the tree fruits eaten by bonobos in the Lomako region are consistently available year-round as a result of decreased seasonality and high amounts of rainfall (1853 mm at Lomako vs. 750–1250 mm at Gombe). While rainfall is undoubtedly an important factor affecting the distribution of primate foods, several chimpanzee sites receive as much or more. Additionally, research challenging Malenky's assumption that Lomako experiences less seasonality (described as the total number of months above or below 150 mm of rain) found that the Lomako Forest experiences two dry and two wet seasons and that there is no correlation between rainfall and total fruit abundance (White, 1998). Additionally, this hypothesis also focuses on the reduced cost of sociality, but does not propose selective advantages of female sociality.

The third hypothesis proposed that food patch size is ultimately responsible for both reducing the amount of feeding competition and providing the advantage to larger party sizes of bonobos (White, 1986). According to White and Wrangham (1988), more bonobos spend more time within a patch at Lomako, whereas chimpanzee feeding parties at Gombe were smaller and remained within a patch for less time, suggesting that patches at Lomako are bigger and allow for more sociality. Additional studies compared patches at Lomako and Kibale, a site that is ecologically more similar to Lomako than is Gombe, and found that patch size varied less at Lomako (Chapman et al., 1994). Bonobo females, therefore, are not prohibited from being social by fluctuating patch sizes (White, 1998). In addition to allowing sociality, large food patches create the opportunity for contest competition between groups of female allies or cliques (White, 1986). Interestingly, the frequency of the female-female affiliative behaviors such as GG rubbing and presumed alliance formation also reflect the size of food patches (White & Lanjouw, 1992).

· Given the social and cohesive nature of bonobo females, the relative costs and benefits of male competitive strategies (White, 1986; White & Wood, 2007) are different for bonobo males. Unlike chimpanzee males, bonobo females are not restricted to core areas distributed throughout the community range. Instead, both males and females range throughout the whole area (Waller, 2011). This removes the benefit to males of cooperating to defend an area containing independent female areas as is seen in chimpanzees. The cohesion of several females into predictable parties within the community instead can be seen as representing a monopolizable resource that can be defended through contest competition by a single male. Males can also use individual aggressive strategies with each other to gain preferential mating within these cohesive females. Male-male aggression among Lomako bonobos typically occurs away from females and is associated with disputes over the control of access routes into a feeding tree (White & Wood, 2007). These male-male aggressive bouts result in a single dominant male controlling the access route in to a feeding tree, and this single winning male then mates with the later arriving females. As mentioned previously, the entry into feeding trees is an important time for mating.

The social bonding among females not only impacts the relative importance of individual bonobo male strategies, it can also have direct effects on the expression of male aggression. Although male bonobos are socially dominant to females in dyadic interactions, female coalitions facilitate greater female power expressed in features such as female feeding priority and control of prized food resources such as meat within the society (White & Wood, 2007; White, 1994). The presence of female alliances in bonobos does not appear able to prevent aggression among males. For example, the rate of aggression both against females and among males increases with the number of females in a party (White & Waller, 2008), as there are more females to fight over, but this aggression among males typically happens somewhat removed from the females. In captivity, high-ranking females regularly intervened impartially into conflicts between males, terminating the conflict and preventing escalation of aggression (Boose et al., submitted).

Reduced within-group competition for food allows, but does not select for, greater female bonding in bonobos compared to chimpanzees. Rather, females bond in order to benefit from alliances that enable them to cooperatively defend food patches. Greater female bonding, however, increases within-group contest among males for access to females. As a result, males benefit from individual competitive strategies while the advantages of male-male cooperation among bonobos is reduced compared to chimpanzees. These factors also impact the costs and benefits to aggressive or affiliative interactions at the community level.

Intergroup Interactions

As noted previously, chimpanzees live in communities where related males are highly bonded. When different groups of males meet along the borders of their territories, the interactions can be lethal. According to Wrangham (1999), chimpanzee lethal raiding occurs when coordinated border patrols infiltrate a neighboring community; find one or more vulnerable individuals; assess the probability of a successful attack; bite, kick and hit, leaving the target dead or dying; and return to their own territory. Although seen at several long-term study sites, this behavior has been most dramatically described at Gombe. In the mid 1970s, two communities of chimpanzees, the Kahama and Kasekala, were the focus of researchers studying chimpanzee behavior and ecology at Gombe National Park in Tanzania (Goodall, 1986). Each group had made incursions into the other's territory, encountered lone opposing party members, and called wildly, forcing the smaller of the parties to retreat (Wrangham & Peterson, 1996). This type of territorial defense is relatively common among animals. What is not common, however, is the behavior of the Kasekala community. They were not waiting for their rivals to encroach on their territory. Groups of at least six males and sometimes a couple of females would quietly move through border zones into Kahama turf and systematically kill lone males caught unaware. One by one, the six males and four adult females that once comprised the Kahama group were beaten and disappeared while the youngest females were integrated into the Kasekala group. By the end of 1977, the Kahama group was gone and the Kasekala group ranged over their area (Wrangham & Peterson, 1996).

Of course, this is only one dramatic example of chimpanzee intercommunity interactions. The degree to which neighboring groups respond with aggression ranges from displays and shows of strength to full lethal raids. Originally described by Goodall (1986) and developed more fully by Wrangham (1999), the Imbalance of Power hypothesis proposes that the evolutionary function of unprovoked lethal raiding by chimpanzees is intercommunity dominance over the opposing party, which has the potential to increase the fitness of the aggressors through increased access to resources such as foraging areas and females. Two conditions were originally deemed necessary in order for coalitional killing to occur in chimpanzees: the first was hostility between two communities and the second was a significant power difference between the two groups such that one community can attack the other with relative ease or at a low cost (Wrangham, 1999). Males that successfully take over a portion of a neighboring territory are thought to benefit in a number of possible ways, although there is little consensus as to which potential benefit is the prime driver of coalitional killing. Early observations from Gombe and Mahale suggested that males gained access to additional mates by expanding their territory and enveloping the smaller core ranges of the neighboring females (Nishida et al. 1985; Goodall, 1986). This model has been criticized for its emphasis on the male-only community structure, as recent studies have shown that encroaching males can be aggressive to resident females who in turn contract their core areas away from changing boundaries and remain in their original communities even if some resident males are killed or disappear (Boesch & Boesch-Achermann, 2000; Boesch et al., 2008; Williams et al., 2002, 2004). More recent data from Gombe (Williams et al., 2002) and Kibale (Watts et al., 2006) suggest that males benefit by expanding their territory, which in turn allows the resident females and their offspring within the invading community increased access to food. This "food defense" hypothesis is currently more favored although data are still scant. Finally, a third potential benefit has been posited based on research at Tai. Boesch et al. (2008) suggest that lethal attacks may be male signals aimed at attracting female immigrants and that small communities will attack larger ones and take large risks to improve their reproductive success. In general, studies suggest that the social, ecological, and demographic conditions of the various communities can be important determinants affecting the level and frequency of lethal aggression (Boesch & Boesch-Achermann, 2000; Mitani et al., 2002; Williams et al., 2004).

Bonobo intergroup interactions are different. Lethal raids have never been observed. And while there may be hostility between neighboring groups during an encounter, they are just as likely to get together and act peacefully (Kano, 1992). At Wamba, the ranges of several groups overlap (Furuichi et al., 2008). The most detailed reports on intergroup interactions comes from Idani (1990), who observed 32 cases where members of neighboring communities engaged one another. The results of these encounters could be classified into one of three categories.

a) Groups bark and display at each other, but no direct interaction occurs.
b) Antagonistic interactions occur. This includes barks, screams, chases, and direct physical contact.
c) The two groups stay together for a while, interacting peacefully, with females engaging in affiliative sexual behavior (GG rubbing) before moving away.

The type "a" encounter was observed three times at Wamba. Type "b" interactions are even rarer, with only one observed. The majority of intergroup interactions fell under the type "c" category, with 28 observations.

During these intergroup encounters, individual spacing differed based on sex and group membership. Members of the same group were usually closer together, while male–female and female–female proximity was common. Females often GG rubbed, especially during the first 30 minutes of an encounter, with frequencies decreasing significantly after that. Males from each group tended to stay farther away from each other (Idani, 1990). Similar observations have been recorded at Lomako (Badrian & Badrian, 1984), although less often, and group ranges do overlap significantly (Waller, 2011).

Perhaps most telling when considering bonobo group encounters, males may change groups as adults. During war and political instability in the DRC during the 1990s, bonobo research at Wamba and Lomako was halted. When researchers returned to Wamba in 2002, they noticed that the number of males in their "E1 unit-group" was greater than would be expected based on the number of adults and juveniles in the group prior to the cessation of research. This means that at least some adult males joined the group from another, suggesting that bonobos males may tolerate unrelated males in certain circumstances.

Patrol Groups

Territorial boundary patrols in chimpanzees consist of the movement of several individuals, primarily males, toward the periphery of their community range (Goodall, 1986; Boesch & Boesch-Achermann, 2000; Watts & Mitani, 2001; Mitani & Watts, 2005). This behavior is often a precursor to lethal raiding. Movement is silent and intracommunity competitiveness is temporarily suppressed (Boehm, 1992) as the patrollers search for signs of members of neighboring communities (Mitani & Watts, 2005). When neighbors are detected, patrol groups may retreat, respond with loud calls and charging displays (Mitani & Watts, 2005), or launch coalitionary attacks against neighboring individuals that can be lethal (Boesch et al., 2008; Goodall, 1986; Manson & Wrangham, 1991; Watts, Muller, Amsler, Mbabazi, & Mitani, 2006; Wrangham, 1999).

At Lomako, we tested whether bonobo males patrolled the edges of their range. During the summers of 2007 and 2009, a map of the trails and transects at Lomako was created using a Garmin handheld GPS (global positioning system). The map was then imported into ArcGIS, a geographic information system software program that has become instrumental in spatial analysis. Next, the sightings and movements of parties from two communities (Eyengo and Bakumba) observed intermittently between 1985 and 1995 were plotted onto the map. Once the sightings were placed on the map, a 100 percent minimum convex polygon was generated to estimate the home range and boundary of each group. Once the boundary was established, the parties' distance from the edge was measured and a series of regressions were calculated based on the overall party size, number of males, number of females, number of subadults, and number of infants (Table 19.1).

There was a significant relationship between the number of infants and the border but it is the opposite of what one would expect according to the Imbalance of Power Hypothesis. In the Bakumba range, the number of infants, a proxy measurement for the number of females with infants, increased significantly closer to the border range. These results show that bonobo males do not behave in the same territorial manner as is observed

TABLE 19.1 **Significance of Regressions of Party Size, Number of Males, Number of Females, Number of Subadults, and Number of Infants**

Clique	Males	Females	Subadults	Infants
Bakumba	$p = .67$	$p = .24$	$p = .29$	$* p = .004$
	$F = .19$	$F = 1.42$	$F = 1.11$	$F = 9.66$
Eyengo	$p = .10$	$p = .08$	$p = .14$	$p = .07$
	$F = 2.75$	$F = 3.23$	$F = 2.24$	$F = 3.63$

* statistically significant

in chimpanzees. Additionally, female bonobos do not avoid the boundaries of their ranges. Female chimpanzees do avoid the boundaries (Boesch & Boesch-Achermann, 2000; Boesch et al. 2008; Williams et al., 2002; 2004), as these places are where strange males are more likely to be present, increasing the risk of infanticide.

Conclusion

Competition is a central tenet of Darwin's mechanism of evolution and plays a major role in the manner in which animals move and place themselves within their social and physical environment. Chimpanzees appear to employ a despotic free distribution spatial arrangement both within and between communities resulting in differential access to resources, unequal reproductive success, and inter- and intra-group aggression at times resulting in what can only be called intercommunity warfare. The study of chimpanzees has and will continue to offer unique insight into our own warring behavior.

The bonobos at Lomako and Wamba, however, do not show any of the components involved in lethal raiding. This is not to say that they are not territorial as there is evidence that suggests that groups may avoid community overlap areas (Waller, 2011), but they certainly do not take territoriality to the same level as chimpanzees. In this regard one might say that the spatial arrangement of bonobos more closely resembles that of an ideal free distribution. As a result, there is little evidence of inter- or intra-group dominance hierarchies and interactions are typically amicable.

It seems almost too easy to say that well-fed individuals are less likely to engage in aggressive behavior. Throw in the promiscuous nature of bonobos, where sex acts in part as a mechanism for diffusing tensions, and it should not be much of a surprise that violent acts are rarer when compared with chimpanzees. In primates in general, the presence of fighting or aggression-based strategies can reflect the importance of monopolizable resources. More importantly, the absence of fighting does not reflect the absence of such resources, but rather that cooperation or peaceful strategies that are based on affiliative instead of aggressive interactions are more beneficial to individuals than disputes.

Group living in primates presents particular problems when competition for access to resources can lead to damaging conflict. Aggression disrupts the stability of the group and individuals are threatened by both physical injury and injury to social relationships (de Waal & Aureli, 2000). When aggression spreads to include multiple individuals there can be significant cost at the group level (Boehm & Flack, 2010). Destabilization of the social resource network decreases group stability and efficiency and lowers the average fitness benefit derived from cooperation. When group stability is important for individual advantage, selection will favor active peacemaking and cooperation in our closest relatives and ourselves.

References

Badrian, A. J., & Badrian, N. L. (1984). Group composition and social structure of *Pan paniscus* in the Lomako Forest. In R. W. Susman (Ed.), *The pygmy chimpanzee; Evolutionary biology and behavior* (pp. 325–346). New York: Plenum.

Badrian, N.L., & Malenky, R. K. 1984. Feeding ecology of *Pan paniscus* in the Lomako Forest, Zaire. In: Susman RL, editor. *The pygmy chimpanzee; evolutionary biology and behavior.* (pp. 275–299). New York: Plenum Press.

Boehm, C. (1992). *Segmentary "warfare" and the management of conflict: Comparison of East African chimpanzees and patrilineal-patrilocal humans.* New York: Oxford University Press.

Boehm, C., & Flack, J. (2010). The emergence of simple and complex power structures through social niche construction. In A. Guinote (Ed.), *The social psychology of power.* London: Guilford.

Boesch, C. (1991). The effects of leopard predation on grouping patterns in forest chimpanzees. *Behaviour, 117,* 220–242.

Boesch, C. (2002). Behavioural diversity in *Pan*. In L. Marchant, C. Boesch, & G. Hohmann (Eds.), *Behavioral diversity in chimpanzees and bonobos* (pp. 1–8). Cambridge: Cambridge University Press.

Boesch, C., & Boesch-Achermann, H. (2000). *The chimpanzees of the Tai Forest: Behavioural ecology and evolution.* New York: Oxford University Press.

Boesch, C., Crockford, C., Herbinger, I., Wittig, R., Moebius, Y., & Normand, E. (2008). Intergroup conflicts among chimpanzees in Taï National Park: Lethal violence and the female perspective. *American Journal of Primatology, 70*(6), 519–532.

Brown, J. L. (1964). The evolution of diversity in anian territorial systems. *Wilson Bulletin, 76,* 160–169.

Chapman, C., White, F. J., & Wrangham, R. W. (1994). Party size in chimpanzees and bonobos: A reevaluation of theory based on two similarly forested sites. In R. W. Wrangham, W. C. McGrew, F. B. M. de Waal & P. G. Heltne (Eds.), *Chimpanzee cultures* (pp. 41–57). Cambridge: Harvard University Press.

Conklin-Brittain, N. L., Wrangham, R. W., & Hunt, K. D. (1998). Dietary response of chimpanzees and cercopithecines to seasonal variation in fruit abundance. II. Macronutrients. *International Journal of Primatology, 19*(6), 971–998.

Coolidge, H. J., Jr. (1933). Pan paniscus pygmy chimpanzee from south of the Congo River. *American Journal of Physical Anthropology, 18,* 1–59.

de Waal, F. B. M. (1987). Tension regulation and nonreproductive functions of sex in captive bonobos (*Pan paniscus*). *National Geographic Research, 3,* 318–335.

de Waal, F. B. M. (1992). Coalitions as part of reciprocal relations in the Arnhem chimpanzee colony. In A. H. Harcourt & F. de Waal (Eds.), *Coalitions and alliances in humans and other animals* (pp. 233–257). New York: Oxford University Press.

de Waal, F. B. M., & Aureli, F. (2000). Conflict resolution in primates. In D. Baltimore, R. Dulbecco, F. Jacob, R. Levi-Montalcini (Eds.), *Frontiers of life, volume 4: The world of the living* (pp. 327–335). San Diego: Academic.

Doran, D. (1996a). Influence of seasonality on activity patterns, feeding behavior, ranging, and grouping patterns in Taï chimpanzees. *International Journal of Primatology, 18*(2), 183–206.

Doran, D. (1996b). Comparative positional behavior of the African apes. In W. McGrew (Ed.), Great ape societies (pp. 213–224). Cambridge: Cambridge University Press.

Fretwell, S. D., & Lucas, H. L. (1972). On territorial behavior and other factors influencing habitat distributions of birds. *Acta Biotheoretica, 19,* 16–36.

Furuichi, T. (1987). Sexual swelling, receptivity, and grouping of wild pygmy chimpanzee females at Wamba, Zaire. *Primates, 28*(3), 309–318.

Furuichi, T. (1992). The prolonged estrus of females and factors influencing mating in a wild group of bonobos (*Pan paniscus*) in Wamba, Zaire. In N. Itoigawa, Y. Sugiyama, G. P. Sackett & R. K. R. Thompson (Eds.), *Topics in primatology, volume 2: Behavior, ecology and conservation.* (pp. 179–190). Tokyo: University of Tokyo Press.

Furuichi, T. (1997). Agonistic interactions and matrifocal dominance rank of wild bonobos (*Pan paniscus*) at Wamba. *International Journal of Primatology 18*(6), 855–875.

Furuichi, T., Mulavwa, M., Yangozene, K., Yamba-Yamba, M., Motema-Salo, B., Idani, G., & Mwanza, N. (2008). Relationships among fruit abundance, ranging rate, and party size and composition of bonobos at Wamba. In T. Furuichi & J. Thompson (Eds.), *The Bonobos* (pp. 135–149). New York: Springer.

Goodall, J. (1963). Feeding behavoiur of wild chimpanzees: A preliminary report. *Symposia of the Zoological Society of London, 10*, 39–47.

Goodall, J. (1964). Tool-using and aimed throwing in a community of free living chimpanzees. *Nature, 201*, 1264–1266.

Goodall, J. (1968). The behaviour of free-living chimpanzees in the Gombe Stream Reserve. *Animal Behavior Monographs, 1*, 161–331.

Goodall, J. (1986). *The chimpanzees of Gombe: patterns of behavior.* Cambridge: Harvard University Press.

Goodall, J., Bandora, A., Bergman, E., Busse, C., Matama, H., Mpongo, E., . . . Riss, D. (1979). Intercommunity interactions in the chimpanzee population of Gombe National Park. In D. A. Hamburg & E. McCown (Eds.), *The great apes* (pp. 13–53). Palo Alto: Benjamin Cummings.

Hashimoto, C., Furuichi, T., & Tashiro, Y. (2001). What factors affect the size of chimpanzee parties in the Kalinzu Forest, Uganda? Examination of fruit abundance and number of estrous females. *International Journal of Primatology, 22*(6), 947–959.

Idani, G. (1990). Relations between unit-groups of bonobos at Wamba, Zaire: encounters and temporary fusions. *African Study Monographs, 11*(3), 153–186.

Ihobe, H. (1992). Male-male relationships among wild bonobos (*Pan paniscus*) at Wamba, Republic of Zaire. *Primates, 33*(2), 163–179.

Isbell, L. A. (1991). Contest and scramble competition: Patterns of female aggression and ranging behavior among primates. *Behavioral Ecology, 2*, 143–155.

Itani, J., & Suzuki, A. (1967). The social unit of chimpanzees. *Primates, 8*(4), 355–381.

Janson, C. H. (1988). Intra-specific food competition and primate social structure: a synthesis. *Behaviour, 105* (1–2), 1–17.

Kano, T. (1992). *The last ape: Pygmy chimpanzee behavior and ecology.* Stanford: Stanford University Press.

Langergraber, K. E., Mitani, J. C., & Vigilant, L. (2007). The limited impact of kinship on cooperation in wild chimpanzees. *Proceedings of the National Academy of Sciences, 104*(19), 7786–7790.

Malenky, R. K. (1990). *Ecological factors affecting food choice and social organization in* Pan paniscus. Ph.D., State University of New York at Stony Brook.

Malenky, R. W., & Stiles, E. W. (1991). Distribution of terrestrial herbaceous vegetation and its consumption by *Pan paniscus* in the Lomako Forest, Zaire. *American Journal of Primatology, 23*, 153–169.

Manson, J., & Wrangham, R. W. (1991). Intergroup aggression in chimpanzees and humans. *Current Anthropology, 32*, 369–390.

Matsumoto-Oda, A. (2002). Social relationships between cycling females and adult males in Mahale chimpanzees. In L. Marchant, C. Boesch, & G. Hohmann (Eds.), Behavioral diversity in chimpanzees and bonobos (pp. 168–180). Cambridge: Cambridge University Press.

McGrew, W. C. (1992). *Chimpanzee material culture.* Cambridge: Cambridge University Press.

Mech, L. D., Adams, L. G., Meier, T. J., Burch, J. W., & Dale, B. W. (1998). *The wolves of Denali.* Minneapolis: University of Minnesota Press.

Mitani, J. (2006). Demographic influences on the behavior of chimpanzees. *Primates, 47*(1), 6–13.

Mitani J. C., and Watts, D. P. (2005). Correlates of territorial boundary patrol behaviour in wild chimpanzees. *Animal Behaviour, 70*, (5):1079–1086.

Mitani, J. C., Watts, D. P., & Lwanga, J. S. (2002). Ecological and social correlates of chimpanzee party size and composition In L. Marchant, C. Boesch, & G. Hohmann (Eds.), Behavioral diversity in chimpanzees and bonobos (pp. 102–111). Cambridge: Cambridge University Press.

Mitani, J. C., Watts, D. P., & Muller, M., N. (2002). Recent Developments in the Study of Wild Chimpanzee Behavior. *Evolutionary Anthropology, 11*, 9–25.

Mitani, J. C., Watts, D. P., & Muller, M. N. (2002). Recent developments in the study of wild chimpanzee behavior. *Evolutionary Anthropology, 11*(1), 9–25.

Myers Thompson, J. A. (2003). A model of the biogeographical journey from Proto-*Pan* to *Pan paniscus*. *Primates, 44* (2), 191–197.

Newton-Fisher, N. (2002). Ranging patterns of male chimpanzees in the Budongo Forest, Uganda: range structure and individual differences. In C. Harcourt & B. Sherwood (Eds.), *New Perspectives in Primate Evolution and Behaviour* (pp. 287–308). Otley, West Yorkshire: Westbury Academic & Scientific Publishing.

Newton-Fisher, N. E. (1999). Infant killers of Budongo. *Folia Primatologica, 70*(3), 167–169.

Newton-Fisher, N. E. (2006). Female coalitions against male aggression in wild chimpanzees of the Budongo Forest. *International Journal of Primatology, 27*(6), 1589–1599.

Nicholson, A. J. (1954). An outline of the dynamics of animal populations. *Australian Journal of Zoology, 2*, 9–65.

Nishida, T. (1968). The social group of wild chimpanzees in the Mahale Mountains. *Primates, 9*, 167–224.

Nishida, T., Hiraiwa-Hasegawa, H., Hasegawa, T., & Takahata, Y. (1985). Group extinction and female transfer in wild chimpanzees in the Mahale National Park, Tanzania. *Zeitschrift für Tierpsychologie, 67*, 284.

Nishida, T., & Kawanaka, K. (1972). Inter-unit-group relationships among wild chimpanzees of the Mahale Mountains. *African Studies, 7*, 73–122.

Nishida, T., & Uehara, S. (1983). Natural diet of chimpanzees (*Pan troglodytes schweinfurthi*): long-term records from the Mahale Mountains, Tanzania. *African Studies Monographs, 3*, 109–130.

Nissan, H. W. (1931). A field study of the chimpanzee: Observations of chimpanzee behavior and environment in Western French Guinea. *Comparative Psychology Monographs, 8*, 1–122.

Pruetz, J. D. (2006). Feeding ecology of savanna chimpanzees (*Pan troglodytes verus*) at Fongoli, Senegal. In C. Boesch, G. Hohmann & M. Robbins (Eds.), *Feeding ecology in apes and other primates*: Cambridge: Cambridge University Press.

Pusey, A. E. (1979). Inter-community transfer of chimpanzees in the Gombe National Park. In D. A. Hamburg & E. R. McCown (Eds.), *The great apes* (pp. 465–479). Palo Alto: Benjamin Cummings.

Pusey, A. E., Williams, J., & Goodall, J. (1997). The influence of dominance rank on the reproductive success of female chimpanzees. *Science, 277*(5327), 828–831.

Riedel, J., Franz, M., & Boesch, C. (2011). How feeding competition determines female chimpanzee gregariousness and ranging in the Taï National Park, Côte d'Ivoire *American Journal of Primatology, 73*(4), 305–313.

Stanford, C. B. (1996). The hunting ecology of wild chimpanzees: Implications for the evolutionary ecology of Pliocene hominids. *American Anthropologist, 98*(1), 96–113.

Stanford, C. B. (1998). Predation and male bonds in primate societies. *Behaviour, 135*(4), 513–533.

Sterck, E. H. M., Watts, D. P., & van Schaik, C, P. (1997). The evolution of female social relationships in nonhuman primates. *Behavioral Ecology and Sociobiology, 41*(5), 291–309.

Stumpf, R. (2007). Chimpanzees and bonobos: Diversity within and between species. In Campbell, C., Fuentes, A., MacKinnon, K., Panger, M., & Bearder, S. *Primates in perspective* (321–344). New York: Oxford University Press.

Sugiyama, Y., & Koman, J. (1979). Social structure and dynamics of wild chimpanzees at Bossou, Guinea. *Primates, 20*, 323–339.

Surbeck, M., Mundry, R., & Hohmann, G. (2010). Mothers matter! Maternal support, dominance status and mating success in male bonobos (*Pan paniscus*). *Proceedings of the Royal Society: Biological Sciences, 278*(1705), 590–598.

Thompson, J. A. (2001). The status of bonobos in their southernmost geographic range. In B. M. F. Galdikas, N. E. Briggs, L. K. Sheeran, G. L. Shapiro & J. Goodall (Eds.), *All apes great and small volume 1: Chimpanzees, bonobos, and gorillas* (pp. 75–81). New York, NY: Plenum / Kluwer Publication.

Thompson, J. A. (2002). Bonobos of the Lukuru Wildlife Research Project. In L. Marchant, C. Boesch, & G. Hohmann (Eds.), *Behavioral diversity in chimpanzees and bonobos* (pp. 138–150). Cambridge: Cambridge University Press.

Tutin, C. E. G. (1979). Mating patterns and reproductive strategies in a community of wild chimpanzees (*Pan troglodytes schweinfurthii*). *Behavioral Ecology and Sociobiology, 6*, 29–38.

van der Dennen, J. M. G. (1995). *The origin of war: The evolution of a male-coalitional reproductive strategy.* Groningen: Origin Press.

Wakefield, M. L. (2008). Grouping patterns and competition among female chimpanzees (*Pan troglodytes schweinfurthii*) at Ngogo, Kibale National Park. *International Journal of Primatology, 29*, 907–929.

Waller, M. T. (2005). *Competition between chimpanzees and humans over fruit of Saba senegalensis in southeastern Senegal.* MS, Iowa State University.

Waller, M. T. (2011). *The ranging behavior of bonobos in the Lomako Forest.* PhD, University of Oregon, Eugene, Oregon.

Watts, D. P. (2002). Reciprocity and interchange in the social relationships of wild male chimpanzees. *Behaviour, 139*, 343–370.

Watts, D. P., & Mitani, J. C. (2001). Boundary patrols and intergroup encounters in wild chimpanzees. *Behaviour, 138*(3), 299–327.

Watts, D. P., Muller, M., Amsler, S. J., Mbabazi, G., & Mitani, J. C. (2006). Lethal intergroup aggression by chimpanzees in Kibale National Park, Uganda. *American journal of primatology, 68*(2), 161–180.

White, F. J., & Wrangham, R. W. (1988). Feeding competition and patch size in the chimpanzee species *Pan paniscus* and *Pan troglodytes. Behaviour, 105*, 148–163.

White, F. J. (1986). *Behavioral ecology of the pygmy chimpanzee.* Ph.D. dIssertation, State University of New York at Stony Brook.

White, F. J. (1988). Party composition and dynamics in *Pan paniscus. International Journal of Primatology 9*, 179–193.

White, F. J. (1989a). Ecological correlates of pygmy chimpanzee social structure. In V. Standen & R. A. Foley (Eds.), *Comparative socioecology; The behavioural ecology of humans and other mammals* (pp. 151–164). Oxford: Blackwell Scientific Publications.

White, F. J. (1989b). Social organization of pygmy chimpanzees. In P. G. Heltne & L. A. Marquardt (Eds.), *Understanding chimpanzees* (pp. 194–207). Cambridge, MA: Harvard University Press.

White, F. J. (1992). Pygmy chimpanzee social organization: variation with party size and between study sites. *American Journal of Primatology, 26*, 203–214.

White, F. J. (1994). Food sharing in wild pygmy chimpanzees. In J. R. Anderson, N. Herrenschmidt, J. J. Roeder & B. Thierry (Eds.), *Current Primatology Volume II Social Development, Learning and Behavior (Proceedings of the 14th International Primatological Society Congress)* (vol. 2, pp. 1–10). Strasbourg, France: Universite Louis Pasteur.

White, F. J. (1996a). Comparative socioecology of *Pan paniscus.* In W. C. McGrew, T. T. Nishida & L. Marchant (Eds.), *Great ape societies* (pp. 29–41). Cambridge: Cambridge University Press.

White, F. J. (1996b). *Pan paniscus* 1973 to 1996: Twenty-three years of field research. *Evolutionary Anthropology, 5*, 161–167.

White, F. J. (1998). Seasonality and socioecology: The importance of variation in fruit abundance to bonobo sociality. *International Journal of Primatology, 19*(6), 1013–1027.

White, F. J. & Colin A. Chapman. (1994). Contrasting chimpanzees and bonobos: Nearest neighbor distances and choices. *Folia Primatologica, 63*, 181–191.

White, F. J., & Burgman, M. A. (1990). Social organization of the pygmy chimpanzee (*Pan paniscus*): Multivariate analysis of intracommunity associations. *American Journal of Physical Anthropology, 83*, 193–201.

White, F. J., & Lanjouw, A. (1992). Feeding competition in Lomako pygmy chimpanzees: variation in social organization with party size. In T. Nishida, W. C. McGrew, P. Marler, M. Pickford & F. B. M. de Waal (Eds.), *Proceedings of the Symposia of XIII Congress of the International Primatological Society* (pp. 67–79). Tokyo: Tokyo University Press.

White, F. J., & Waller, M. T. (2008). Importance of female-female affiliation in mitigating male aggression in bonobos (*Pan paniscus*). *American Journal of Primatology, 71*, 103.

White, F. J., & Wood, K. D. (2007). Female feeding priority in bonobos, *Pan paniscus,* and the question of female dominance. *American Journal of Primatology, 69*, 837–850.

Williams, J. M., Liu, H. Y., & Pusey, A. E. (2002). Costs and benefits of grouping for female chimpanzees at Gombe. In L. Marchant, C. Boesch, & G. Hohmann (Eds.), *Behavioral diversity in chimpanzees and bonobos* (pp. 192–203). New York: Cambridge University Press.

Williams, J. M., Oehlert, G. W., Carlis, J. V., & Pusey, A. E. (2004). Why do male chimpanzees defend a group range? *Animal Behaviour, 68*(3), 523–532.

Wrangham, R. W. (1980). An ecological model of female-bonded primate groups. *Behaviour, 75,* 262–300.

Wrangham, R. W. (1986). Ecology and social relationships in two species of chimpanzee. In D. I. Rubenstein & R. W. Wrangahm (Eds.), *Ecological aspects of social evolution: Birds and mammals.* (pp. 352–378). Princeton: Princeton University Press.

Wrangham, R. W. (1999). Evolution of coalitionary killing. *Yearbook of Physical Anthropology, 42,* 1–30.

Wrangham, R. W., & Peterson, D. (1996). *Demonic males: Apes and the origins of human violence.* Boston: Houghton Mifflin.

Wrangham, R. W., & Pilbeam, D. (2001). Apes as time machines. *All apes great and small: African apes.* New York: Plenum/Kluwer, 5–18.

Wrangham, R. W., & Smuts, B. B. (1980). Sex differences in the behavioral ecology of chimpanzees in the Gombe National Park, Tanzania. *Journal of Reproduction and Fertility, 28* (supplement), 13–31.

20

Conflicts in Cooperative Social Interactions in Nonhuman Primates

SARAH F. BROSNAN

All things considered, social interactions in animals are remarkably peaceful. At the most basic level, individuals of all species are in competition for mates and food sources. For social species, this list expands to include, at minimum, social partners and rank, and in most species, there are far more things over which conflicts may emerge. In particular, individuals who cooperate have to navigate a minefield of potential problems in order to successfully achieve mutual ends. Given the ubiquity of both social interactions and cooperation, it is clear that the selective benefits of such interactions outweigh the costs, and further that individuals are likely to have evolved specific mechanisms to handle the conflicts that are inherent in both.

How, then, does cooperation succeed despite this conflict? Some situations, such as reciprocity, involve outcomes that differ in time, and thus in the short term are unequal. Depending on the ultimate outcome, this may lead to direct conflict. However, even situations in which rewards co-occur may also be fraught with conflict. For instance, what happens when one partner leaves the bulk of the effort to their partner, or takes the majority of the rewards? There are two ways to address this. First one can consider the cognitive underpinnings that allow individuals to make assessments and arrive at the best outcome (that is, the one for which the benefits are the greatest per unit cost). Second, one can consider what social and ecological pressures selected species to cooperate *despite* the conflict. In this latter case, if these behaviors were sufficiently beneficial, they may have been selected without a large cognitive requirement. Thus a question of interest becomes which species show certain behaviors, and how do these species' social structures and ecological niches vary from those of species that do not show these behaviors? In this way, we can hope to uncover the situations that led to selection for coordination and cooperation despite the inherent conflict.

These questions are important for a variety of species, but one of my interests is to understand how they work in humans. To gain a comparative perspective on humans, I study nonhuman primates, who belong to the same phylogenetic Order as do humans (e.g., the Order Primates) and in some cases have even closer relationships (e.g., all great apes, including humans, are in the Family Hominidae). Thus I can look at the patterns of behavior across the primates to understand which factors were important in the evolution of successful cooperation, even in situations that include conflicting interests. However, this question is widely applicable across nonprimate taxa, so despite my focus on this Order, in some cases I expand this work beyond the primates. Taken together, these results help us to broadly understand how social interactions and ecological factors shaped the evolution of successful cooperation.

The Evolution of Behavior

A technique that I emphasize throughout this chapter is phylogenetic comparison, in which the same trait is investigated, using techniques that are as similar as possible given species-specific requirements, across as many species as possible. The technique I specifi-cally employ is behavioral phylogeny, in which the traits in question are behaviors (Boehm, 1999; Brosnan, Newton-Fisher, & van Vugt, 2009; Gosling, 2001; Wrangham & Peterson, 1996). There are two basic approaches; the first is to investigate species that are close phy-logenetically, but are disparate in social structure or ecology, to see whether differences in behavior emerge and, if they do, which of these social or ecological differences may have been the selective pressure that led to the change in behavior. The second approach is to investigate species that are quite distant phylogenetically but share similar behaviors, to see whether they share in common any social or ecological factors relevant to the behavior in question. This allows us to speculate on which of these factors led to selective pressure for the same behavior despite phylogenetic distance.

In combination, this is a powerful approach for determining the underlying causes for selection. That is, a comparison between species allows us to uncover which factors are related to the behavior from an evolutionary perspective, which then allows us to deter-mine why the behavior might have evolved, often called the ultimate cause or the evolu-tionary function. Of course, this technique is not perfect. One immediate challenge is figuring out which of a myriad of related social and ecological pressures are relevant. A second, more practical, challenge is finding paradigms that work across species, particu-larly if the species in question are anatomically quite distinct, resulting in little common ground in terms of what they can physically do. If a task is far more difficult for one species to complete than the other, results will vary, but because of how the behavior manifests in a specific situation, not for reasons related to selective pressures on the behavior. Thus there is a middle ground in which tasks and paradigms are as similar as possible between spe-cies, but also appropriate for the species in question. Examples of this problem will recur throughout this chapter.

Returning to the idea of the underlying cognitive mechanisms of a behavior, while I spend little time discussing them, mechanisms are also critical. For instance, in the cooperation literature, there is a debate about the necessary cognitive mechanisms for a species to successfully cooperate (Stevens & Hauser, 2004) and, while these are far less studied, we should also consider hormonal (Kosfeld, Heinrichs, Zak, Fischbacher, & Fehr, 2005; Soares et al., 2010; Soares et al., 2010) and neural (Knoch, Pascual-Leone, Meyer, Treyer, & Fehr, 2006; Sanfey, Rilling, Aronson, Nystrom, & Cohen, 2003) factors. Moreover, mechanisms can differ despite similar functions. Evolution works with the raw material at hand, so two species may be selected to solve a very similar problem, but find solutions that involve very different mechanisms. Although at some points my work sheds light on potential cognitive mechanisms involved, my focus is primarily on understanding how social and ecological contexts affect which behaviors are selected and using this information to infer the evolutionary function of the behavior.

The Simplest of Them All? Coordination Decisions in Primates

Although many forms of cooperation are quite complex, at the simplest level cooperation may merely imply coordination of actions by two or more individuals. In these cases, individuals match their behavior with each other, and as a result, benefit. In the very simplest cases, all benefit equally and thus there is, in principle, no conflict among them. However, even in this seemingly straightforward case, coordination may be quite challenging and the subjects may not always succeed.

For the past several years, my colleagues Michael Beran, Bart Wilson, and I have been investigating coordination across four species of primates, capuchin monkeys (*Cebus apella*), rhesus monkeys (*Macaca mulatta*), chimpanzees (*Pan troglodytes*), and humans (*Homo sapiens*). We used methods derived from experimental economics to develop a paradigm that could be used across multiple species to investigate whether and under what circumstances individuals coordinate their actions. Our work utilizes the Assurance Game, or Stag Hunt game, a well-known model of social interactions (Skyrms, 2003) in which two individuals must coordinate their actions in order to receive the best payoff, known as the payoff dominant outcome. The reward structure was such that mutual *Stag* play was the most beneficial (4 units), mutual *Hare* resulted in a low payoff (1 unit each), and the uncoordinated payoff of playing *Stag* when one's partner played *Hare* was unrewarded, while the individual who played *Hare* received 1 unit. Thus, the best outcome (the payoff dominant outcome) is for both to play *Stag* (indicated as *Stag, Stag*), which maximizes the benefit to both individuals. However, the worst outcome is to play *Stag* when your partner plays *Hare*. Thus, a second mutual outcome that occurs when partners are not sure of the other's choice is *Hare, Hare*, in which both individuals do less well, but no one receives the worst outcome.

This game is interesting to economists because strategic uncertainty plays a key role in the selection of the equilibrium, yet the players' objectives are aligned (for a summary see Ochs, 1995). In other words, the objectives may be the same (*Stag, Stag*), but the question of strategic interest is how sure a given player is that the other player will play *Stag* when he or she plays *Stag*. Although subjects should have every incentive to coordinate, as there are no possible higher payoffs (a feature that is dissimilar to many other economic games, such as the well-known Prisoner's Dilemma), this is not always the outcome (Cooper, DeJong, Forsythe, & Ross, 1990; van Huyck, Battalio, & Beil, 1990). Prior to our experiments, it was unknown how species other than humans would respond.

We have utilized two different methodologies to address this question. Researchers typically use computerized interaction for human decision-making research, but interaction with experimenters for primate decision-making research. To guarantee that each species had the chance to use their most advantageous methodology, we did both. Moreover, the computerized methodology was more amenable to subtle changes in procedure that might elicit different outcomes, allowing us to investigate the role of cues in affecting decision-making outcomes. In both cases, subjects of each species were paired with a partner of their species with whom they could interact and communicate to the extent of their species' abilities (e.g., humans could talk to each other). Each member of the pair was offered a choice between two options, and both individuals' options were identical. One represented Stag and the other Hare. Payoffs were the same in both games, according to the option chosen by each individual.

For the original test, we utilized an experimenter-based methodology in which subjects were given two tokens and had to choose which to return to the experimenter (Brosnan, Parrish, et al., 2011). In all cases, subjects could have chosen to look at their partners' choices (note that in the case of humans, this would have required "looking on" to their partners' half of the experimental table, and video analysis showed that no individual did so). We kept all aspects of the methodology as similar as possible across species, including recruiting humans with previous experience in the economics lab (excluding those with experience directly related to the Assurance, or Stag Hunt, game), sitting participants of all species directly adjacent to one another, and providing no instruction to any species, including humans, thus requiring them to learn the payoffs during the game itself. We were able to do this study with three species: humans, chimpanzees, and capuchin monkeys.

We found three notable results. First, at least one pair of each of the three species found the payoff dominant outcome, which indicated that the task was solvable by all of these primates. Second, more human pairs solved the task than did pairs of any other species, although only about a quarter of the human pairs managed the payoff dominant outcome. Some humans never found any strategy that was statistically distinguishable from random choices, indicating that even in this simplest of scenarios, in which there were no conflicts between individuals, coordination was still difficult to achieve. Finally, we found evidence in the chimpanzees that experience was critical in developing the behavior. Four of our subjects came from a group of chimpanzees that has had extensive cognitive enrichment, including symbol language training, since birth. The other twenty subjects were also group-housed in large, indoor-outdoor enclosures, giving them a remarkably enriched life. However, despite finding a coordinated outcome (many pairs matched their partners' play), these chimpanzees did not find the payoff dominant outcome found by the chimpanzees with specific cognitive enrichments. Thus, we argue that experience specific to cognitive decision-making interacts with evolved mechanisms to promote coordination in primates.

A second study was designed to further explore this paradigm using a computerized task in which subjects had to make a choice between two icons on a computer screen using a joystick (Brosnan, Wilson, & Beran, 2011). An advantage to this paradigm was that we could control whether or not the subjects saw their partner's choices as they were made, allowing us to utilize both a functionally simultaneous game, in which subjects made their choice without knowledge of their partner's choice, and an asynchronous game, in which the second mover could see the first mover's decision (we did not constrain the order or timing of choices). Subjects were seated next to one another, thus again they could choose to interact other than through the game interface. Again, the methodology was as similar as possible across species, including all of the parameters discussed above. In this case, we were able to test capuchin and rhesus monkeys and humans.

We found, first, that while all species could solve the task in the asynchronous version, only humans and rhesus did so in the functionally simultaneous version. Even after additional testing in which they played (successfully) with a partner in the asynchronous version, capuchin monkeys were unable to coordinate on payoff dominant outcomes (*Stag, Stag*) in the simultaneous game. Second, humans utilized a strategy unavailable to the other primates; during the simultaneous game, they talked to one another about their decisions. More specifically, while all pairs talked to one another (they were sitting right next to each other, sharing a computer screen), only those humans who spoke about the game found the payoff dominant outcome. To see whether humans could only solve the game using language, we ran both the simultaneous and asynchronous games using a traditional normal form game methodology in which subjects were physically separated and playing an anonymous partner (they were playing another person in the room, but they did not know which other person was their partner). In this case, humans still performed better on the asynchronous game, but were able to solve the simultaneous game, too. We are currently running control studies with the rhesus monkeys and humans to try to determine whether these similar outcomes are being achieved with similar cognitive mechanisms, or whether the mechanisms differ.

Thus, even when the incentives of both partners are aligned due to equally beneficial outcomes, coordination is still a challenge. This is true even for humans, who, thanks to language and relatively more developed cognitive sophistication, have a number of strategies available to achieve coordination. On the other hand, despite the challenges, coordination is an outcome that we see across the primate taxon. Thus, we next consider an even more challenging social situation, that in which rewards differ, leading to differing incentives and potential conflicts between social partners.

That's Not Fair! Conflict Resulting from Unequal Outcomes in Cooperative Species

If coordination is challenging when incentives are perfectly aligned, imagine the issues if they are not. Individuals must routinely work together for outcomes that may not be equal. If outcomes are not equal over the long term, the resultant interaction should be straightforward: do not cooperate with individuals with whom outcomes are typically asymmetrical. However, this can also be more nuanced; some interactions lead to outcomes that are unequal in the short-term, but equalize over a number of interactions. In this case, too strong of an intolerance to inequity actually inhibits what can be very beneficial long-term interactions, because associative learning based on the short-term interactions will work against long-term benefits (Brosnan, Salwiczek, & Bshary, 2010).

Individuals of some nonhuman primate species respond negatively to receiving a less preferred outcome than a partner (for reviews, see Brosnan, 2006, 2011). In the typical experimental test, individuals from the same social group are paired. The experimenter then alternates completing some task (e.g., an exchange) with each individual and giving him or her a food reward for doing so. In the inequity condition, one individual gets a more preferred reward for completing the task than does the other. Subjects typically respond by refusing to participate in the task or, if they complete the task, refusing to accept the food rewards that are offered. Control conditions included those (a) to establish a baseline response (e.g., both individuals get the same reward), (b) to establish how subjects respond to individual contrast (e.g., both individuals are shown a more preferred reward prior to receiving the less preferred one, so rewards differ from the expected, but not from the partner's reward), and (c) to establish the role of effort (e.g., both individuals get their rewards for "free," without completing the task).

A number of species show negative responses to inequity, including capuchin monkeys (Brosnan & de Waal, 2003; Fletcher, 2008; Takimoto, Kuroshima, & Fujita, 2009; van Wolkenten, Brosnan, & de Waal, 2007; but see also Silberberg, Crescimbene, Addessi, Anderson, & Visalberghi, 2009), chimpanzees (Brosnan, Schiff, & de Waal, 2005; Brosnan, Talbot, Ahlgren, Lambeth, & Schapiro, 2010; but see also Bräuer, Call, & Tomasello, 2009), and domestic dogs (*Canus domesticus*; Range, Horn, Viranyi, & Huber, 2008). On the other hand, many other primates do not, including orangutans (*Pongo spp.*), squirrel monkeys (*Saimiri spp.*), common marmosets (*Callithrix jaccus*), and owl monkeys (*Aotus spp.*), whereas results for cotton-top tamarins (*Saguinus oedipus*) and bonobos (*Pan paniscus*) are equivocal (Bräuer et al., 2009; Brosnan, Flemming, Talbot, Mayo, & Stoinski, 2011; Neiworth, Johnson, Whillock, Greenberg, & Brown, 2009; Talbot, Freeman, Williams, & Brosnan, 2011; Freeman, Sullivan, Hopper, Holmes, Schultz-Darken, Williams, & Brosnan, in review). So why is there this variation? One feature separates those species that do respond to inequity from those that do not: the degree to which the species socially cooperates with non-kin outside of the family group. Capuchins, chimpanzees, and domestic dogs are known for their cooperative tendencies, both in lab experiments and in the wild (Boesch, 1994; Brosnan, 2010; Creel & Creel, 1995; de Waal & Berger, 2000; Fragaszy, Visalberghi, & Fedigan, 2004; Melis, Hare, & Tomasello, 2006b; Rose, 1997). Individuals of these species cooperate in tasks ranging from food acquisition to territorial defense, and routinely form coalitions and alliances. Although all of the other species are also social to greater or lesser degrees, none show similarly high levels of cooperation with non-kin outside of the family group. Marmosets, tamarins, and owl monkeys cooperate extensively in offspring care, but this is a common goal within the family group. Thus, these individuals have different costs and benefits, despite high levels of cooperation (see below for more discussion of the implications of interdependence).

Why, then, would species that cooperate respond more negatively to inequity than those that do not? For these species, it may be critically important for individuals to compare their outcomes to those of their social partners to maximize their fitness (Brosnan, 2011). If they do less well than a partner, then they should go find a new partner with whom to cooperate. Individuals who fail to do so may still receive absolute gains, but will do relatively less well than their partners, a critical distinction in the context of natural selection, where relatively better is the only currency that counts. Additional support for this interpretation comes from the finding that capuchin, chimpanzee, and domestic dog subjects do *not* respond negatively to inequity in control conditions in which rewards are simply handed out for free. Thus, something about joint action seems to trigger this response. Thus, these data imply that inequity is used by species that cooperate as a partner evaluation mechanism.

Further evidence in support of this hypothesis comes from data on how individuals respond when they must interact with each other for rewards that may differ. In other words, does inequity really affect either the decision to cooperate or partner selection in an explicitly cooperative context? One of the earliest studies along these lines investigated whether capuchin monkeys would help their partners acquire rewards (de Waal & Berger, 2000). The monkeys could help a partner pull in a heavily counterweighted tray that brought food to their partner, but not to them. They found that the monkey who needed help shared more food with their partner in this condition than in control conditions in which the subject did not need help or in which both monkeys got food. Moreover, the more this monkey shared, the more their partner helped on subsequent trials. Thus, it seems as if the monkeys were willing to cooperate as long as food was distributed between them. Food-sharing may not be the only way to accomplish this, either; capuchins will also cooperate if rewards alternate, and will take turns helping each other to get food (Hattori, Kuroshima, & Fujita, 2005).

However, reward distribution may not always work so smoothly. In another study, de Waal and Davis (2002) examined how capuchins responded if they worked together to pull in rewards, using the same bar pull apparatus, but then had to decide how to divide the rewards after the fact. Rewards were either easy to monopolize (either clumped in to the center or dispersed so that both monkeys had to travel to reach them) or very difficult to monopolize (placed directly in front of each monkey). From the very first trial, subjects were far less likely to coordinate when the rewards were monopolizable than when they were not (de Waal & Davis, 2002). Moreover, while in each condition subjects were more likely to coordinate with kin than nonkin, the same pattern applied to both types of relationships. Thus in this context, rather than solve the conflict by dividing the rewards, the monkeys apparently preferred to avoid the conflict altogether, which served to halt cooperation.

The same pattern was found in a study in which rewards were explicitly unequally distributed between the monkeys (Brosnan, Freeman, & de Waal, 2006). Rewards were placed in front of each pulling station, and the monkeys could freely choose who would pull for the better reward (the monkeys always got the reward in front of them). Although based on the previous study we anticipated lower cooperation when reward values differed, we got an unexpected result: monkeys were equally likely to coordinate whether rewards were equal or not. What varied was the level of coordination. Some partnerships achieved very high levels of coordination while others coordinated less than one-third as often, even when outcomes were equal. It turned out that in situations in which one monkey consistently refused to pull except for the better reward, their partners quit working with them and cooperation collapsed, even in those conditions in which rewards would have been equal. Thus conflict may arise not just because of the quality or distribution of rewards, but also because of the partner's behavior. Moreover, reactions against the partner's behavior appear to carry over to future interactions; even when incentives were equal, monkeys with an unfair partner declined to cooperate.

Primates may also actively work to choose partners with whom they have less conflict for cooperation tasks. Alicia Melis and her colleagues did an elegant series of experiments in which they evaluated the role of the partner in cooperation decisions in chimpanzees. They found, first, that chimpanzees cooperated best when paired with partners with whom they were most tolerant, as measured by the ease with which the pair shared a monopolizable clump of food in a separate session (Melis et al., 2006b). Moreover, when given a choice between partners who could help with a task, chimpanzees chose the individual with whom they most tolerantly shared food (Melis, Hare, & Tomasello, 2006a). Although this may seem rather obvious, it was the first study demonstrating that a nonhuman primate could choose the best collaborator. This is a positive note for coordination, of course; individuals may overcome conflict and work to create the best ends. Nonetheless, more recent evidence indicates that, given the choice, chimpanzees prefer to work on their own rather than collaborate with a partner, at least until the rewards of collaboration exceed the rewards of individual effort (Bullinger, Melis, & Tomasello, 2011).

But what about taking it too far? In humans, beneficial interactions can be halted because of spite, or the willingness of individuals to negatively impact one another.

One study has tested this with nonhuman primates (Jensen, Call, & Tomasello, 2007). Chimpanzees were given a table of food. In one condition, another chimpanzee came in and took the food for him or herself, and in a second condition a human experimenter came in and moved the food to the other chimpanzee (in a third control, the other chimpanzee had the food all along). The original recipient could choose to pull a string that would collapse the table so that no one got any food. They did this more often when their partner took the food from them than in the situations in which they lost the food for other reasons. This indicates that chimpanzees, at least, are not spiteful.

Thus, coordination may be extremely difficult to achieve when outcomes are unequal, but it is possible. Primates dislike inequity, and tend not to cooperate in situations in which inequity exists. Moreover, they may prefer individual action to joint action, all other things being equal. However, cooperation nonetheless occurs. First, subjects choose to cooperate with tolerant partners. Moreover, a single instance of inequity is not the death knell of cooperation; primates can extrapolate across multiple trials, leaving open the possibility of success in situations in which inequity exists in the short term, on an interaction-by-interaction basis, but not in the long term (e.g., reciprocity). Finally, while primates are affected by their partners' previous behaviors even when outcomes are otherwise equal, they do not seem to be spiteful, punishing another individual who did not cause them harm. Thus, it seems that primates for whom cooperation is beneficial have been under strong selective pressure for behaviors that minimize conflict and maximize opportunities to succeed in cooperation.

Outside Influences: The Impact of Social Structure and Ecology on Conflict and Social Interaction

The Importance of Social Structure on Conflict and Cooperation

Of course, cooperation and conflict do not exist in a vacuum. These elements are inherently intertwined with a species' social structure, and the relationships between individuals may have a strong impact on their behavior and outcomes. For instance, kin should have more aligned goals than do individuals in other relationships, due to the logic of inclusive fitness (Hamilton, 1964). Taking this a step further, kin are not the only relationships with special status. Individuals who rely on one another for support, protection, or other resources may also have kin-like relationships. This may be particularly true in the case of cooperative breeders. Cooperative breeding describes the situation in which both the male and the female, and sometimes their older offspring, cooperatively take care of the young offspring. In many cases, neither the mother nor the father can raise the offspring individually, a situation that results in heavily aligned incentives to cooperate because without the care provided by both parents, the offspring will not survive. Therefore, the pair-bonded male and female are more interdependent than in most non-kin relationships. While this (presumably) emerged primarily in the context of infant care, the effects of this interdependence may extend to other behaviors.

First, prosocial behavior within family groups seems to be more common in cooperative breeders than in other primate species (Hrdy, 2009; van Schaik & Burkart, 2010). Moreover, prosocial behavior in cooperative breeders tends to be active more frequently than in other species; that is, the donor is the one who initiates the prosocial act, rather than the recipient, while among other species, it is more often the recipient of a prosocial act who initiates it (note here that "prosocial" refers to the *outcome* of the interaction, not the motivations of either of the participants). For example, cooperative breeders are unusually likely to share food, and when they do, food-sharing is far more likely to be active in nature than among other food-sharing species (Jaeggi, Burkart, & van Schaik, 2010). Moreover, in experimental tests in which actors can choose whether or not to bring food to their partners, cooperative breeders tend to behave prosocially (Burkart, Fehr, Efferson, & van Schaik, 2007; Cronin, Schroeder, & Snowdon, 2010, although see Cronin, Schroeder, Rothwell, Silk, & Snowdon, 2009; Stevens, 2010a). Despite not being classified as cooperative breeders, capuchins, too, seem to be very consistently prosocial (Brosnan, Houser, et al., 2010; de Waal, Leimgruber, & Greenberg, 2008; Lakshminarayanan & Santos, 2008). This has been attributed to capuchins' convergence on a number of traits common to cooperative breeders (Jaeggi et al., 2010), such as allomaternal behavior (Fragaszy et al., 2004), further supporting the hypothesis.

Moreover, unlike many other cooperative species, cooperative breeders and other species with bi-parental care do not necessarily respond negatively to inequitable outcomes (Freeman, et al., under review; Neiworth et al., 2009). Members of these species continue to accept rewards that are of lesser value than those received by partners derived from their family groups. Thus, not only are they more likely to behave prosocially, but also they seem to be less likely to react negatively to a potential source of conflict—unequal outcomes. Consequently, interdependent species seem to have evolved strategies to help them avoid reactions to potential conflict that would result in the dissolution of the relationship. This makes sense, as the cost of dissolution is so high. A cooperative breeder who leaves a partner must find a new empty territory (males) and mate (males and females), resulting in a period of time without a home range and family group for protection. They may lose breeding time as they seek a new mate, as well as their investment in current offspring if the remaining parent is unable to keep the babies alive. It will finally be interesting to see whether behavior varies with the life history stage of an individual, for instance with individuals showing far more sensitivity to inequity during courting, when such information would be particularly advantageous, than after pair bond formation (Brosnan, 2011).

A Big Brain Is Not Enough: The Importance of Ecology in the Evolution of Conflict and Cooperation

Ecology is a major factor influencing behavior, for the obvious reason that a species' behavior is selected to maximize outcomes in the environment in which the species has evolved. So it is not just important to consider how the current environment might affect outcomes, but also how past environments might have shaped behavior. For instance, behaviors such as risk preferences (Heilbronner, Rosati, Stevens, Hare, & Hauser, 2008) and willingness to delay gratification (Stevens, Hallinan, & Hauser, 2005) have been strongly influenced by species' ecology. Species in areas with more variable resources develop more tolerance for risk, and species that must wait long periods of time for their food to emerge (e.g., primates that eat tree gum) develop a greater tolerance for delayed rewards than those who do not. This ecological approach helps us to understand how behaviors evolved and has been particularly influential in explaining human behaviors that do not on the surface appear to maximize fitness (Gigerenzer, Todd, & Group, 1999; Jones, 2001; Stevens, 2010b).

Of course, feeding behaviors are not the only patterns affected by ecology; complex social cognition may be as well. One unfortunate yet common implicit assumption in the literature is that cooperation and complex social cognition manifest primarily in big-brained species. In fact, some of the best examples of cooperation are in smaller-brained species (Brosnan, Salwiczek, et al., 2010). One well-studied system is the cleaner wrasse (*Labroides dimidiatus*), which eats parasites off of client fish that inhabit the reef. Cleaners prefer to eat bites of the clients' mucus to parasites, yet this is not in the best interests of the clients (it hurts, and may lead to infection). Clients who can punish do so by chasing (or eating) the cleaners, but those who cannot instead react by jolting, which alerts other clients to the cleaner wrasses' bad behavior. Not only do clients prefer to associate with "cooperative" wrasse, which are known not to bite their clients, over cleaners with unknown reputations, but cleaners also bite less often in experimental conditions that mimic the presence of an audience (Bshary & Grutter, 2006). Cleaners also sometimes work in pairs. Although in most cooperative situations the payoffs are such that there is an incentive to cheat before one's partner does, wrasse cleaning with a partner are actually *less* likely to bite the client than are individually-cleaning wrasse. This cooperative approach between the partners increases the payoff to both (Bshary, Grutter, Willener, & Leimar, 2008), primarily due to an increase in cooperative behavior by the (smaller) female, who is punished by the male for biting the client (Raihani, Grutter, & Bshary, 2010). Although this behavior benefits the male, it also benefits the client, and thus may provide insight in to how third-party punishment has evolved.

In fact, we have begun to test some of these assumptions about the importance of ecology by testing primates and cleaners on tests that are ecologically appropriate for one species, but not the another (Salwiczek, et al., in revision). In our initial work, we tested cleaner fish adults and juveniles and three species of primates (capuchin monkeys, chimpanzees, and orangutans) on a task designed for cleaner fish. Cleaner fish clients come in two forms, residents and visitors. Residents do not leave the reef, and thus are forced to wait for the wrasse to clean them. Visitors have home ranges that encompass the territories of multiple cleaners and so can leave for another cleaner if they do not receive prompt service. Cleaner fish thus clean the visitors first, followed by the residents. This can be mimicked rather easily in the lab using two distinct plates, one of which is a "resident" plate that waits for the subject while the other is a "visitor" plate that leaves if not fed upon immediately (Bshary & Grutter, 2002).

In our tests, adult cleaners easily learned to eat from the visiting plate first, while primates and juvenile cleaners did not without extensive experience. In fact, this makes sense. Basic associative learning mechanisms favor a preference for the resident plate; subjects are rewarded each trial for the resident plate, but for the visitor plate only if they choose it first. This may make the payoffs difficult to learn without specific cognitive adaptations. Selective pressure for this learning mechanism is presumably absent in primates, who do not face a similar situation in their natural environments. We are currently extending this work to look at conflicts between the cleaners as they interact with the clients. Such studies help us to understand the nuances of selective pressure in different environments, and hence how solutions to different forms of conflict may have evolved.

Conclusions

Coordination and cooperation are extremely difficult to achieve, even when incentives appear to be aligned, as when rewards are equal for both parties. Once incentives are no longer aligned, as is the case when rewards are unequal or one individual does not behave appropriately, conflict emerges, making the task more challenging. However by studying the reactions of different species, we can learn how to overcome these challenges. For instance, the primates show us that even when incentives are aligned, if the partner's previous behavior was unfair, then coordination remains out of reach. On the other hand, even when incentives are not aligned, subjects can alternate being the benefitted partner, creating equity over the long term, or share the rewards, creating equity in the short term. Both of these options allow individuals to solve the conflict stemming from dissimilar rewards and to achieve cooperative outcomes.

At the core, humans are similar to other species of primate. However, as the cleaner fish show us, our large brains do not make primates inherently better at cooperation than species in other taxa. In fact, being able to consider the contingencies may, in some cases, make cooperation in large brained species such as humans more difficult than in species that are following an evolved strategy, as we may too often overly discount or place too much emphasis on inappropriate foci, inadvertently working against our own best interests (Brosnan, Salwiczek, et al., 2010). Further research comparing species with different ecologies and different social systems using identical paradigms (or those that are as identical as possible, given the constraints of the species' physical abilities) will help us to better understand those factors that allow individuals to avoid the minefield of potential conflicts encountered on the road to successful cooperation.

References

Boehm, C. (1999). *Hierarchy in the forest: The evolution of egalitarian behavior.* Cambridge, MA: Harvard University Press.

Boesch, C. (1994). Cooperative hunting in wild chimpanzees. *Animal Behaviour, 48,* 653–667.

Bräuer, J., Call, J., & Tomasello, M. (2009). Are apes inequity averse? New data on the token-exchange paradigm. *American Journal of Primatology, 7,* 175–181.

Brosnan, S. F. (2006). Nonhuman species' reactions to inequity and their implications for fairness. *Social Justice Research, 19,* 153–185.

Brosnan, S. F. (2010). What do capuchin monkeys tell us about cooperation? In D. R. Forsyth & C. L. Hoyt (Eds.), *For the greater good of all: Perspectives on individualism, society, and leadership* (Vol. Jepson Studies in Leadership Series, pp. 11–28). New York: Palgrave Macmillan Publishers.

Brosnan, S. F. (2011). A hypothesis of the co-evolution of inequity and cooperation. *Frontiers in Decision Neuroscience, 5,* 1–12.

Brosnan, S. F., & de Waal, F. B. M. (2003). Monkeys reject unequal pay. *Nature, 425,* 297–299.

Brosnan, S. F., Flemming, T. E., Talbot, C., Mayo, L., & Stoinski, T. S. (2011). Responses to inequity in orangutans. *Folia Primatologica, 82,* 56–70.

Brosnan, S. F., Freeman, C., & de Waal, F. B. M. (2006). Partner's behavior, not reward distribution, determines success in an unequal cooperative task in capuchin monkeys. *American Journal of Primatology, 68,* 713–724.

Brosnan, S. F., Houser, D., Leimgruber, K., Xiao, E., Chen, T., & de Waal, F. B. M. (2010). Competing Demands of Prosociality and Equity in Monkeys. *Evolution & Human Behavior, 31*(4), 279–288.

Brosnan, S. F., Newton-Fisher, N. E., & van Vugt, M. (2009). A melding of the minds: When primatology meets social psychology. *Personality and Social Psychology Review, 13*(2), 129–147.

Brosnan, S. F., Parrish, A. R., Beran, M. J., Flemming, T. E., Heimbauer, L., Talbot, C. F., et al. (2011). Responses to the Assurance game in monkeys, apes, and humans using equivalent procedures. *Proceedings of the National Academy of Science, 279,* 1522–1530. *doi:10.1073/pnas.1016269108*

Brosnan, S. F., Salwiczek, L., & Bshary, R. (2010). The interplay of cognition and cooperation. *Philosophical Transactions of the Royal Society, Series B, 365,* 2699–2710.

Brosnan, S. F., Schiff, H. C., & de Waal, F. B. M. (2005). Tolerance for inequity may increase with social closeness in chimpanzees. *Proceedings of the Royal Society of London, B, 1560,* 253–258.

Brosnan, S. F., Talbot, C., Ahlgren, M., Lambeth, S. P., & Schapiro, S. J. (2010). Mechanisms underlying the response to inequity in chimpanzees, *Pan troglodytes. Animal Behaviour, 79,* 1229–1237.

Brosnan, S. F., Wilson, B. J., & Beran, M. J. (2011). Old World monkeys are more similar to humans than New World monkeys when playing a coordination game *Proceedings of the Royal Society, London B, 279,* 1522–1530.

Bshary, R., & Grutter, A. S. (2002). Experimental evidence that partner choice is a driving force in the payoff distribution among cooperators or mutualists: the cleaner fish case. *Ecology Letters, 5,* 130–136.

Bshary, R., & Grutter, A. S. (2006). Image scoring and cooperation in cleaner fish mutualism. *Nature, 441,* 975–978.

Bshary, R., Grutter, A. S., Willener, A. S. T., & Leimar, O. (2008). Pairs of cooperating cleaner fish provide better service quality than singletons. *Nature, 455,* 964–967.

Bullinger, A. F., Melis, A. P., & Tomasello, M. (2011). Chimpanzees, *Pan troglodytes,* prefer individual over collaborative strategies towards goals. *Animal Behaviour, 82,* 1135–1141.

Burkart, J., Fehr, E., Efferson, C., & van Schaik, C. P. (2007). Other-regarding preferences in a non-human primate: Common marmosets provision food altruistically. *Proceedings of the National Academy of Sciences, 104*(50), 19762–19766.

Cooper, R., DeJong, D., Forsythe, R., & Ross, T. (1990). Selection criteria in a coordination game: Some experimental results. *American Economic Review, 80,* 218–233.

Creel, S., & Creel, N. M. (1995). Communal hunting and pack size in African wild dogs, *Lycaon pictus. Animal Behaviour, 50,* 1325–1339.

Cronin, K. A., Schroeder, K. K. E., Rothwell, E. S., Silk, J. B., & Snowdon, C. (2009). Cooperatively breeding cottontop tamarins (*Saguinus oedipus*) do not donate rewards to their long-term mates. *Journal of Comparative Psychology, 123,* 231–241.

Cronin, K. A., Schroeder, K. K. E., & Snowdon, C. (2010). Prosocial behaviour emerges independent of reciprocity in cottontop tamarins. *Proceedings of the Royal Society of London. B, 277,* 3845–3851.

de Waal, F. B. M., & Berger, M. L. (2000). Payment for labour in monkeys. *Nature, 404,* 563.

de Waal, F. B. M., & Davis, J. M. (2002). Capuchin cognitive ecology: Cooperation based on projected returns. *Neuropsychologia, 1492,* 1–8.

de Waal, F. B. M., Leimgruber, K., & Greenberg, A. (2008). Giving is self-rewarding for monkeys. *Proceedings of the National Academy of Sciences, 105,* 13685–13689.

Fletcher, G. E. (2008). Attending to the outcome of others: Disadvantageous inequity aversion in male capuchin monkeys (*Cebus apella*). *American Journal of Primatology, 70,* 901–905.

Fragaszy, D. M., Visalberghi, E., & Fedigan, L. M. (2004). *The Complete Capuchin: The biology of the genus Cebus.* Cambridge: Cambridge University Press.

Freeman, H. D., Sullivan, S., Hopper, L. M., Holmes, A., Schultz-Darken, N., Williams, L. E., & Brosnan, S. F. (under review). All in the family: cooperative breeders do not respond negatively to inequity when paired with a member of their family group. *Journal of Comparative Psychology.*

Gigerenzer, G., Todd, P. M., & Group, T. A. R. (1999). *Simple heuristics that make us smart.* New York: Oxford University Press.

Gosling, S. D. (2001). From mice to men: What can we learn about personality from animal research? *Psychological Bulletin, 127,* 45–86.

Hamilton, W. D. (1964). The genetical evolution of social behaviour. *Journal of Theoretical Biology, 7,* 1–52.

Hattori, Y., Kuroshima, H., & Fujita, K. (2005). Cooperative problem solving by tufted capuchin monkeys (*Cebus apella*): Spontaneous division of labor, communication, and reciprocal altruism. *Journal of Comparative Psychology, 119,* 335–342.

Heilbronner, S. R., Rosati, A. G., Stevens, J. R., Hare, B., & Hauser, M. D. (2008). A fruit in the hand or two in the bush? Divergent risk preferences in chimpanzees and bonobos. *Biology Letters, 4,* 246–249.

Hrdy, S. B. (2009). *Mothers and others: The evolutionary origins of mutual understanding.* Cambridge, MA: Harvard University Press.

Jaeggi, A. V., Burkart, J. M., & Van Schaik, C. P. (2010). On the psychology of cooperation in humans and other primates: Combining the natural history and experimental evidence of prosociality. *Philosophical Transactions of the Royal Society of London. B, 365,* 2723–2735.

Jensen, K., Call, J., & Tomasello, M. (2007). Chimpanzees are vengeful but not spiteful. *Proceedings of the National Academy of Sciences, 104,* 13046–13050.

Jones, O. D. (2001). Time-shifted rationality and the Law of Law's Leverage: Behavioral economics meets behavioral biology. *Northwestern University Law Review, 95*(4), 1141–1206.

Knoch, D., Pascual-Leone, A., Meyer, K., Treyer, V., & Fehr, E. (2006). Diminishing reciprocal fairness by disrupting the right prefrontal cortex. *Science, 314,* 829–832.

Kosfeld, M., Heinrichs, M., Zak, P. J., Fischbacher, U., & Fehr, E. (2005). Oxytocin increases trust in humans. *Nature, 435,* 673–676.

Lakshminarayanan, V., & Santos, L. R. (2008). Capuchin monkeys are sensitive to others' welfare. *Current Biology,* R999–R1000.

Melis, A. P., Hare, B., & Tomasello, M. (2006a). Chimpanzees recruit the best collaborators. *Science, 311,* 1297–1300.

Melis, A. P., Hare, B., & Tomasello, M. (2006b). Engineering cooperation in chimpanzees: Tolerance constraints on cooperation. *Animal Behaviour, 72,* 275–286.

Neiworth, J. J., Johnson, E. T., Whillock, K., Greenberg, J., & Brown, V. (2009). Is a sense of inequity an ancestral primate trait? Testing social inequity in cotton top tamarins (*Saguinus oedipus*). *Journal of Comparative Psychology, 123*(1), 10–17.

Ochs, J. (1995). Coordinate problems. In J. Kagel & A. E. Roth (Eds.), *The handbook of experimental economics,* (pp. 195–252). Princeton, NJ: Princeton University Press.

Raihani, N. J., Grutter, A. S., & Bshary, R. (2010). Punishers benefit from third-party punishment in fish. *Science, 327,* 171.

Range, F., Horn, L., Viranyi, Z., & Huber, L. (2008). The absence of reward induces inequity aversion in dogs. *Proceedings of the National Academy of Sciences, 106*(1), 340–345.

Rose, L. M. (1997). Vertebrate predation and food-sharing in *Cebus* and *Pan*. *International Journal of Primatology, 18*(5), 727–765.

Salwiczek, L., Prétôt, L., Demarta, L., Proctor, D., Essler, J., Pinto, A. I., et al. (in revision). Adult cleaner wrasse outperform capuchin monkeys, chimpanzees, and orangutans in a complex foraging task derived from cleaner-client reef fish cooperation. *PLoS ONE.*

Sanfey, A. G., Rilling, J. K., Aronson, J. A., Nystrom, L. E., & Cohen, J. D. (2003). The neural basis of economic decision-making in the Ultimatum game. *Science*, *300*, 1755–1758.

Silberberg, A., Crescimbene, L., Addessi, E., Anderson, J. R., & Visalberghi, E. (2009). Does inequity aversion depend on a frustration effect? A test with capuchin monkeys (*Cebus apella*). *Animal Cognition*, *12*(3), 505–509.

Skyrms, B. (2003). *The stag hunt and the evolution of social structure*. Cambridge: Cambridge University Press.

Soares, M. C., Bshary, R., Fusani, L., Goymann, W., Hau, M., Hirschenhauser, K., et al. (2010). Hormonal mechanisms of cooperative behaviour. *Philosophical Transactions of the. Royal Society of London B*, *365*, 2737–2750.

Stevens, J. R. (2010a). Donor payoffs and other-regarding preferences in cotton-top tamarins (*Saguinus oedipus*). *Animal Cognition*, *13*, 663–670.

Stevens, J. R. (2010b). Rational decision making in primates: The bounded and the ecological. In M. L. Platt & A. A. Ghazanfar (Eds.), *Primate neuroethology* (pp. 97–115). Oxford: Oxford University Press.

Stevens, J. R., Hallinan, E. V., & Hauser, M. D. (2005). The ecology and evolution of patience in two New World monkeys. *Biology Letters*, *1*, 223–226.

Stevens, J. R., & Hauser, M. D. (2004). Why be nice? Psychological constraints on the evolution of cooperation. *Trends in Cognitive Sciences*, *8*, 60–65.

Takimoto, A., Kuroshima, H., & Fujita, K. (2009). Capuchin monkeys (*Cebus apella*) are sensitive to others' reward: an experimental analysis of food-choice for conspecifics. *Animal Cognition*, *13*(2), pp. 249–261.

Talbot, C., Freeman, H. D., Williams, L. E., & Brosnan, S. F. (2011). Squirrel monkeys' response to inequitable outcomes indicates evolutionary convergence within the primates. *Biology Letters*, DOI: 10.1098/rsbl.2011.0211

van Huyck, J., Battalio, R., & Beil, R. (1990). Tacit coordination games, strategic uncertainty, and coordination failure. *American Economic Review*, *80*, 234–248.

Van Schaik, C. P., & Burkart, J. (2010). Mind the gap: Cooperative breeding and the evolution of our unique features. In P. M. Kappeler & J. B. Silk (Eds.), *Mind the gap: Tracing the origins of human universals* (pp. 477–497). Heidelberg, Germany: Springer.

van Wolkenten, M., Brosnan, S. F., & de Waal, F. B. M. (2007). Inequity responses in monkeys modified by effort. *Proceedings of the National Academy of Sciences*, *104*(47), 18854–18859.

Wrangham, R., & Peterson, D. (1996). *Demonic males*. Boston: Houghton Mifflin Company.

21

Rousseau with a Tail

Maintaining a Tradition of Peace Among Baboons

ROBERT M. SAPOLSKY

Western thought has often been filled with debates about highly dichotomous views about the nature and proclivities of humans—body versus mind, thought versus emotion, Coke versus Pepsi. One of the most fundamental dichotomies concerns the supposed nature of humans as a social primate—at our primordial core, are we noble savages or short, nasty, and brutish?

The fulcrum of attribution has tilted back and forth between Rousseau and Hobbes. And despite Darwin's famous quote, "He who understands baboons would do more towards metaphysics than Locke," few of the savants who have debated this issue have considered that the behavior of animals can offer important insights into this question about human nature.

Darwin's prescient insight did not bear fruit until well into the twentieth century, with the emergence of primatology and its emphasis on the behavior of primates in the wild, in their natural habitats. The primatology literature grew, anchored by extraordinary longitudinal studies of the same animals, spanning decades. And as it did, nonhuman primate metaphysics has roiled with the same debate—is the nonhuman primate a poster child for Rousseau or Hobbes?

The debate is an empty one, given that there is no archetypal "nonhuman primate" with its archetypal sociality. Instead, among the more than 150 primate species, there is enormous variability, with social groupings ranging from solitary existence to stable groups of more than a hundred individuals. Moreover, the nature of such groupings has shown as much variability. With that, the debate has become more focused, asking the same question about individual primate species. Some of the largest amounts of data and insight have accumulated concerning the baboon, a species that I have studied in Kenya for more than thirty years.

Why the baboon? To begin, by this I mean the "savanna baboon," which typically means two species and their naturally occurring hybrids (the olive baboon, *Papio anubis*, and the yellow baboon, *Papio cynocephalus*). Such baboons should be contrasted with the closely related forest-dwelling mandrill (*Mandrillus sphinx*), desert and mountain-dwelling hamadryas (*Papio hamadryas*), and gelada *(Theropithecus gelada)* baboons.

So why the savanna baboon? One answer is ecological: because they live in the open woodland/grassland savanna, a field biologist can *see* them and thus collect more behavioral data in a day than in a year of observation of some species of monkey living in the trees in a dense rain forest. Another answer is geopolitical, in that the bulk of the studies have been carried out in some of the more stable corners of Africa, namely Kenya, Tanzania, and Botswana. But most fundamentally, because the savanna baboon seems familiar, seems to be some sort of prototype for our Robert Ardrey-esque ancestral hominid who lived in stable bands of grassland hunter-gatherers for hundreds of thousands of years. Insofar as anthropologists cannot travel in time, the savanna baboon has typically been seen as a handy contemporary stand-in for our ancestors.

A distinctly Hobbesian view of baboons has permeated the field for many decades. Baboons are classic "tournament" species, where males are considerably larger than females, come replete with secondary sexual characteristics such as enormous canines, and have high rates of male-male aggression. In some troops, the aggression can be the leading cause of male mortality (either as a direct result of the fighting, because an injury becomes septic, or because an animal hobbled by an injury is more likely to be predated). These high rates of aggression have long fascinated researchers. This is perhaps best summarized by Irven DeVore, one of the most influential of primatologists, who wrote in the early 1960s that baboons "have acquired an aggressive temperament as a defense against predators, and aggressiveness cannot be turned on and off like a faucet. It is an integral part of the monkeys' personalities, so deeply rooted that it makes them potential aggressors in every situation" (DeVore & Washburn, 1961).

This sort of view brings up two key points. The first is that humans are not baboons, and other primate species, with extremely different social systems, have equal (and tenuous) claims to being a good model for our hominid ancestors. The inevitability of baboon aggression tells us virtually nothing about the extent to which human aggression is inevitable.

The second key point is that the inevitability of baboon aggression is not all that inevitable. In this chapter, I review the study of one particular baboon troop that demonstrates that the social world of these primates can be unexpectedly malleable.

Sociality in the Typical Baboon Troop

In order to appreciate the uniqueness of the particular baboon troop, an overview of the social behaviors of a "normal" baboon troop is in order (cf. Ransom, 1981; Strum, 2001). Such troops have memberships of a few dozen to more than a hundred. Troops consist of roughly equal adult sex ratios, with matrilocality, in which females spend their lives in the same troop, while males leave their natal troops around puberty and join another one.

A central fact of baboons' lives is their dominance rank, as it shapes the quality of virtually every facet of their existence. The two sexes have separate and very different dominance systems (where all but the low-ranking males will dominate all but the highest-ranking females when there is, for example, some desirable food item that is being contested).

The Female Dominance System

Because females remain in their natal group, they spend their lives surrounded by female relatives. Female dominance rank is inherited, where the alpha female will be an elderly animal, her oldest daughter will have position #2 in the hierarchy, the next oldest daughter will be #3, and so on. Thus, female dominance is less about the rank of an individual than of a lineage (Seyfarth, 1976; Altmann, 2001). There is little evidence that the inheritance of rank reflects genetics, in that there are instances in which an entire high-ranking lineage will be toppled and replaced by another. Instead, infants learn their rank at extraordinarily young ages. As an example, the infant of a high-ranking female can venture out on her own, explore further, and initiate more social interactions than can a low-ranking infant before being anxiously retrieved by her mother (Altmann, 2001).

Other than during periods of severe ecological stress (e.g., a major drought), there are few differences in survival or reproductive success among different lineages. Instead, the advantages of dominance play out more subtly, in that dominant individuals can monopolize preferred foods or desirable resting places (for example, in the shade mid-day), and are groomed more.

The Male Dominance System

Since males leave their natal troops at puberty, adult ranking is fluid, rather than hereditary. A newly transferred adolescent will typically be extremely low-ranking and peripheral (Strum, 1982). Over the course of years, the adolescent male will then slowly work his way up the hierarchy as he physically matures and gains confidence and fighting skills. Rank typically peaks around prime-age (when the male is likely to be in the top quartile of the hierarchy) and declines thereafter; this can be either gradual or precipitous (for example, after a serious injury). Adult males often change troops opportunistically; for example, an ex-alpha male may move to a different troop to try his luck there (Packer, 1979; Sapolsky, 1996).

The advantages of male dominance are numerous, ranging from preferential access to contested resources such as a kill, and from preferential access to being socially groomed. And in the textbook picture of baboon social behavior, the reproductive success of males is determined solely by rank, with the linear dominance hierarchy determining access to estrus females.

Thus, baboons live in aggressive social groups with permeating ranking systems and male dominance over females. Two facts typify the Hobbesian morass in which baboons live:

- An ecosystem like the Serengeti (where I have conducted my studies) is an ideal habitat for a baboon, with minimal infant mortality and few threats from predators (because of large troop sizes). Most baboons spend roughly three hours a day in order to acquire the day's calories. And critically, this means that baboons have roughly nine hours of free time each day to devote to their social complexities, and such complexities involve enormous amounts of psychosocial stress. Baboons are almost never stressed by lions or by food shortages. Instead, if a baboon in the Serengeti is miserable, it is because another baboon has brought that state about.
- Roughly half of baboon aggression is displacement aggression, where an individual who is frustrated for some reason attacks a lower-ranking innocent bystander. Thus, over the course of a minute, a relatively high-ranking male who has lost a fight will chase a subordinate who will then bite a female, and who will then lunge at a nearby infant (Strum, 1982; Smuts & Watanabe, 1990). Thus, for all but the highest ranking, a baboon's social world is filled with lack of control and predictability, the hallmarks of psychological stress (Sapolsky 1983, 1993).

Some Prosocial Features of Life in a Typical Baboon Troop

Despite the seeming nasty brutishness of baboon behavior, there are prosocial elements that are relevant when considering the behavior of the unique baboon troop to be discussed below. Pro-social behaviors include:

Nepotism

Because of female matrilocality, the core of pro-social behavior among females is about nepotism. Females will support their nearest relatives in dominance interactions, and in driving off a male who is displacing aggression in a particularly egregious manner; grooming and sharing of resources occur preferentially within families; the younger sister of a female with an infant will often help her with child care, perhaps holding the infant while the mother forages. Such "aunting" behavior benefits the younger sister, giving her practice with infants, improving her eventual maternal competence and increasing the odds of her own offspring surviving (Altmann, 2001; Seyfarth, 1976; Silk et al., 2006, 2009); nevertheless, this is also helpful to the older sister. Thus, cooperation and mutual defense among females are organized around nepotism, in ways that lessen the inevitability of aggression. However, because males change troops, often traveling tens of miles before picking their adult troop, they are unlikely to have a brother in that troop, making prosocial nepotism of minimal importance to male behavior.

Ritualistic Threats of Aggression

Despite the frequency of florid aggression, it is far more common for threats of aggression to occur. Males have an array of ritualistic gestures that, in effect, advertise their fighting prowess—for example, a conspicuous "threat yawn" directed at an adversary, displaying one's canines, or a distinctive type of forward lunge that ritualizes the first piece of actual aggression (Strum, 1982).

Maintaining Versus Attaining High Rank

Rising in the male hierarchy to the alpha position involves considerable amounts of aggression, and advantages accrue to individuals who are big, muscular, and have sharp canines and polished fighting skills. But once an alpha position is attained, maintaining it rarely involves these attributes. Instead, it involves ritualistic threats of aggression and psychological intimidation far more than aggression itself, skill in displacing aggression only onto individuals who are unlikely to return as a vengeful threat, and impulse control and emotional regulation in knowing which provocations to walk away from (Strum, 2001). In this system of "if you have to use it, you're teetering towards losing it," high-ranking males do not have either the highest rates of aggression or levels of testosterone. Instead, it is sub-adult males who show this profile, often provoking fights that they can't finish (Sapolsky, 1991). Thus, among male baboons, attaining high rank is about force; maintaining it is about social intelligence (or, as has been termed, "Machiavellian intelligence" [Byrne & Whiten, 1988]).

A recent study supports this in a striking manner (Sallet et al., 2011). In it, the authors studied groups of captive macaque monkeys. After characterizing dominance ranks, the authors carried out neuroimaging on each monkey, examining the sizes of different brain regions. After controlling for factors like the age and weight of the males, out popped a correlation where the higher a male's rank, the larger the average size of a particular brain region called the rostral prefrontal cortex. And its function? Making inferences based on information about what other individuals can see, what they know, what they think (something that psychologists call "theory of mind"). In humans, people with more gray matter in that region are better at doing multiple layers of mind reading (for example, the virtually impossible task of keeping track of who, in *Midsummer Night's Dream*, is in love with who, who thinks they know who is in love with who, and so on). This is a brain region that is all about social intelligence.

Alternative Male Strategies and Female–Male "Friendships"

In the early years of research on baboons, the relationship between male rank and male reproductive success was thought to be simple—the higher the rank, the more passing on copies of genes. In this "linear access model," if there was a single female in estrus in the troop, the alpha male would be the one to form a consortship with her; if there were two females in estrus, it would be the alpha and beta males forming the consortships, and so on.

But as more research accrued, it became clear that the linear access model was not correct; this was shown in ways ranging from examining patterns of mating (and as a function of the likelihood of a female ovulating at that time) to documenting paternity (Bercovitch, 1991; Seyfarth, 1978; Smuts, 1999; Strum, 2001).

Instead, it became clear that there is "female choice." At half the size of males, a female is not typically able to drive off a male with whom she does not want a consortship. Instead, a typical action might be for her to repeatedly walk near the rival of the unwelcome consorting male, generating tensions between the two males; while the males are preoccupied, the female might have a rapid, covert mating with a male that she does desire (Bercovitch, 1991; Strum, 2001).

Naturally, this raises the question of what sort of male a female would prefer to be with. This turns out to a male who has a stable, affiliative relationship with the female; in a way that is not at all anthropomorphic, these have been termed "friendships" (Smuts, 1999). Such friendships involve an array of behaviors, including high rates of grooming, low rates of displacement aggression by the male on to the female, the male coming to the aid of the female when threatened by another male, and occasional assistance with child care. Typically, these are males who are less preoccupied with male-male competitive interactions.

A small but consistent subset of males shows these behaviors. When first identified, these friendships were thought to be Platonic "just-friends" relationship. Instead, there is often covert mating between such pairs. When combined with the fact that avoiding overt male-male competition means fewer injuries, this "alternative male strategy" is one that can raise a male's Darwinian fitness.

Reconciliation

As first described by Frans de Waal and colleagues (de Waal & van Roosmalen, 1979; de Waal & Yoshihara, 1983) many species show reconciliative behavior. Specifically, this occurs when two individuals, after having tension in their relationship, have increased rates of prosocial behaviors with each other (such as grooming among baboons, or greeting gestures and kissing among chimps). Such behaviors are effective, decreasing the likelihood of subsequent tensions.

Reconciliation following tension is neither automatic nor indiscriminate. Not surprisingly, it is frequent among relatives. A number of circumstances favor postaggression reconciliation among nonrelatives (Thierry et al., 2008): a) if there is a high likelihood of the loser counterattacking; b) if affiliation based on kinship plays only a small role in a group; c) if reconciliation involves physical contact; d) if the individuals involved have a "valuable" relationship, with a history of cooperation and a likelihood of the further opportunities. In one study of pairs of captive macaque monkeys, food could be obtained either individually or through cooperation of the pair. Those pairs that developed the capacity to cooperate had higher rates of reconciliation after induced aggression than noncooperators (Cords & Thurnheer, 1993). In other words, tension-reducing reconciliation is most frequent among animals who already cooperate and have an incentive to keep doing so.

Thus, reconciliation can be an effective means reducing social tensions and the incidence of aggression. Among baboons, while it is common among females (particular relatives), it is rare among males (Cheney et al., 1995; Strum, 2001).

Male Coalitions

Most fighting by baboons occurs among individual males. However, coalitions can emerge. Most often, these are short-lived, where two males are about to fight and one will elicit the support of a third; these are most often along the lines of "the enemy of my enemy is my friend." However, stable coalitions lasting many days can occur. These typically happen among males with long histories of minimal tension and shared goals. However, "stable" is a relative term, in that when a fight actually occurs, a coalitional partner often fails to aid his partner and, in some instances, will even opportunistically switch sides (Noe, 1994). When stable, a coalition of two males will defeat virtually any single male. As such, coalitions are effective threats and can reduce the incidence of aggression.

The extent to which there are individual differences in the quality and quantity of every aspect of baboon social behavior (prosocial or otherwise) should be appreciated. And importantly, many of these differences are stable over time (even over the lifetime of an individual). This phenomenon, and the fact that it occurs among all the primates, ushers in concepts of "personality" and "temperament" into primatology (Freeman & Gosling, 2010). Among the male baboons that I have studied, there are stable personality differences in styles of male-male competition (for example, as to whether a male readily distinguishes between threatening and neutral interactions with a rival, whether he tends to be the one to initiate an inevitable fight, and so on), in sexual behavior, and in male-female affiliative behaviors (Ray & Sapolsky, 1992; Sapolsky & Ray, 1989; Virgin & Sapolsky, 1997).

Thus, amid the aggression and psychological stress in a troop of baboons, especially for the have-nots in dominance hierarchies, there are numerous realms of prosocial behavior that diminish the impact of those social stressors, provide alternatives to aggression, and reward those alternatives. All of these lessen the supposed inevitability of aggression among individuals. And as I review now, these pro-social behaviors and strong personality differences among individual baboons, when coupled with some rather unique circumstances, can lessen the supposed inevitability of aggression throughout an entire troop.

A Baboon Troop of Low Aggression and High Affiliation
Its Emergence

This case involved the "Forest Troop," a group of baboons that I had been studying continuously since the mid-1970s (Sapolsky & Share, 2004). In the early-1980s, Forest Troop slept in trees one kilometer from a tourist lodge. The lodge was in the home range of the adjacent troop, and during this period, an open garbage pit was expanded by the lodge. This neighboring "Garbage Dump" troop soon shifted its sleeping site to near the pit, and foraged almost exclusively from the food refuse in the pit (and, as it turned out, garbage dump baboons like these develop health problems of many Westernized humans, including elevated circulating levels of insulin and triglycerides, and the starts of metabolic syndrome [Kemnitz et al., 2002; Banks, Altmann, Sapolsky, Phillips-Conroy, & Morely, 2003]). During this period when the Garbage Dump troop shifted to living near the dump, approximately half of the Forest Troop males developed the habit of going most mornings to the garbage pit for food as well; these forays probably began with the lead of a male who had grown up in Garbage Dump troop. These were not males of particular ranks; instead, they were among the most aggressive individuals, and the least socially affiliative. This was the case because such garbage "raiding" required these males a) to compete with the larger number of Garbage Dump males for access to refuse and b) to forgo early morning socializing in their troop (the time of day with, for example, high rates of female-male grooming).

In 1983, a tuberculosis outbreak occurred, originating from infected meat in the dump. Over the next two years, this killed most Garbage Dump animals, and all refuse-eating Forest Troop males (amid no other Forest Troop animals dying) (Tarara, Suleman, Sapolsky, Wabomba, & Else, 1985; Sapolsky & Else, 1987).

This had two critical implications. First, the death of nearly half the males approximately doubled the usual 1:1 female to male ratio. Second, the surviving males were atypically unaggressive and socially affiliated. This produced a distinctive social atmosphere. Some of the changes concerned the male dominance hierarchy. While a hierarchy continued to exist, there was less displacement of aggression by dominant males onto subordinates and females, and more tolerance by dominant males of occasional dominance reversals by subordinates. In addition to this more "relaxed" system, there was more grooming and closer proximity among animals.

Thus, the combination of individual variation in male social behavior and selective killing of animals based on that variation produced a distinctive social milieu in Forest Troop. It should be noted that the creation of this atmosphere of low levels of aggression and high levels of social affiliation did not involve the creation of any novel behaviors or the elimination of any preexisting ones. Rather, it simply involved changes in the frequency of preexisting behaviors.

This shift in the social atmosphere of Forest Troop had health benefits for its members. The focus of my research on baboons over the years and with a number of different troops had been examining the effects of dominance rank, personality, and patterns of social behavior on patterns of stress-related disease. This work demonstrated that in a typical baboon troop with a stable male hierarchy, it is low-ranking males who are the least healthy. Their maladies include chronically elevated levels of the stress hormone cortisol, less "good" cholesterol, lower circulating levels of an endocrine growth factor, hypertension, immune suppression, vulnerability of the testicular system to stress-induced suppression, and neurochemical indices of chronic anxiety (Sapolsky, 1993, 2005). In contrast, low-ranking males in Forest Troop were spared some stress-related health stigmata, in that they no longer had elevated levels of cortisol nor the neurochemical indices of anxiety. In other words, the less aggressive and more affiliative atmosphere of Forest Troop was able to "get under the skin" of its members (Sapolsky & Share, 2004).

The Cultural Transmission of Forest Troop Sociality

Shortly after the period of tuberculosis deaths, research on Forest Troop was halted, and did not resume until 1993. Observations indicated that the distinctive features of the troop still continued. This was remarkable. As noted, because males leave their natal troop around puberty, subadult and adult males in a troop all grew up elsewhere. By 1993, no adult males remained from 1986; all adults had joined the troop following that time. In other words, males raised in typical baboon troops were able to adapt the distinctive patterns of behavior of Forest Troop. Arguably, this constitutes a case of nonhuman cultural transmission. "Culture" can mean many things, ranging from the very precise "the transmission of habits and information by social [rather than genetic] means" (de Waal, 2001) to the imprecise but intuitively satisfying "the way we do things" (McGrew, 1998, 2004). Within that range of definitions, is not solely a human phenomenon (a point of frequent contention between primatologists and many cultural anthropologists) (Boesch, 2003; Galef, 1990; Laland & Hoppitt, 2003).

Nonhuman primate culture has been most thoroughly documented in chimpanzees. In a landmark paper pooling decades of data from six different field sites in Africa (Whiten, Horner, Marshall-Pescini, 1999), 39 different features of culture were documented. Best known is the construction of "termite sticks" in some chimpanzee populations, where sticks are modified in a stereotypical way that allows animals to extract termites from mounds for eating. Other features of chimpanzee culture include techniques for breaking nuts with rock hammers, molding of leaves for sponging water from inaccessible crevices, and styles of grooming. These behaviors are restricted to particular chimp populations and are transmitted both horizontally within generations and vertically, typically between mother and child. Some behaviors occur in gradients of variation among the chimpanzee populations of a region, implying invention and diffusion (Whiten et al., 2003), while other behaviors were invented independently in widely separated populations. In some cases, different populations solve the same task in different ways, whereas in others, the same gesture or vocalization has different meanings in different populations (Nishida, 1980).

Elements of culture such as these have now been documented in orangutans, gorillas, macaques, whales, songbirds, crows, and elephants. Broadly, types of culture have fallen into four overlapping categories: a) material (e.g., the termite sticks of chimpanzees), b) food-related (e.g., a technique for separating sand from grains of rice found in one group of Japanese macaques), c) communication (e.g., regional dialects of bird song), and

d) social (e.g., distinctive styles of grooming in different chimp populations) (Cambefort, 1981; Kawai, 1965; Noad, Cato, Bryden, Jenner, & Jenner, 2000; Rendell & Whitehead, 2001; van Schaik et al., 2003; Whiten et al., 1999).

Amid these findings, the culture of low aggression and high affiliation among Forest Troop baboons is rather unique. As noted, it did not involve the invention of new behaviors (for example, using feet instead of hands to groom someone). Instead, what was novel was the frequency and context of preexisting behaviors (for example, in the case of grooming, the occasional occurrence of something virtually unheard of in a typical baboon troop, namely adult males grooming each other). More subtly, the frequencies of some of these behaviors are not unique. For example, there have been other troops studied with the high rates of grooming, or others with the low rates of displacement aggression. Instead, it was the combination of these traits that was unique to Forest Troop. Thus, this was the transmission of an assemblage of behaviors, of a social system. (And it should be noted that amid the sophistication of this, Forest Troop culture is not organized around an idea—the "isms" of human culture, such as nationalism, pacifism, or socialism).

The example in Forest Troop is reminiscent of findings in two other primate studies. The first was striking because of its natural setting. Both anubis and hamadryas baboons are found in Ethiopia. These species differ dramatically in social structure. Anubis live as typical savanna baboons, whereas Hamadryas, typically found in more arid desert regions, have a fission-fusion social system. The fusion state involves hundreds of baboons sharing a rare resource (a watering hole or cliffs used for sleeping), while the fission state consists of small dispersed groups in which a male herds young females into his group, forcibly retaining them in a stable "harem."

In one experiment, a young female from each species was transplanted into a group of the other species. Remarkably, the females adopted the novel social system within hours. In the case of the anubis female transplanted into the hamadryas group, assimilation was readily explained, in that she was quickly subject to forceful herding behavior by a (far larger) hamadryas male. In the reverse situation, after initially attempting to attach herself to an anubis male, the hamadryas female shifted to the more open anubis system (Kummer, 1971).

Another demonstration of transmission of a social milieu utilized captive rhesus macaques and stumptail macaques (de Waal & Johanowicz, 1993). Rhesus social life is characterized by rigid "despotic" dominance hierarchies, high rates of aggression, and infrequent reconciliation. Stumptail macaques, in contrast, have "egalitarian" hierarchies with frequent reversals of dominance, minimal aggression, and frequent reconciliation. In this study, groups of rhesus and of stumptail juveniles of both sexes were merged into a single group for five months. During that time, rhesus juveniles took on the behavioral style of stumptails, ultimately developing equal reconciliation rates; moreover, this acquired social style persisted after the rhesus were returned to larger, all-rhesus groups. As a number of features of this fascinating study: a) it was rhesus, rather than stumptails, who changed their behavior, despite being in the majority; b) the new social style among rhesus was not readily ascribed to their directly experiencing the more "relaxed" style of stumptails, as most social interactions were within, rather than between species; c) rhesus did not merely assimilate the concrete features of stumptail behavior, as the two species have different gestures and vocalizations for reconciliation post-fights, and the increased reconciliation rate among rhesus involved increased rates of gestures typical of their species; d) the more relaxed and affiliative behavior among rhesus was not likely to represent "solidarity" in the face of another species, as these individuals did not preferentially interact with each other when returned to the all-rhesus groups. The authors suggested that the novel rhesus social style was an emergent byproduct of living in the more relaxed, less tense and aggressive social milieu of stumptails (de Waal & Johanowicz, 1993).

The Mechanism of Cultural Transmission of Forest Troop Sociality

Thus, variation in temperament and personality among a group of baboons, coupled with the deaths of a selective subset of males, produced a distinctive social atmosphere. Moreover, this atmosphere was transmitted to new troop members, continuing these behaviors past the founder generation. This raises a question pertinent to any species with culture—what were the mechanisms by which culture was transmitted?

A first possibility is that there was, in fact, no transmission, and the perpetuation of the social atmosphere in Forest Troop was due to *self-selection*. Young males do not automatically transfer into the neighboring troop, and may sample a few of them during the transfer period (Pusey & Packer, 1986). This raises the possibility that adolescent males who joined Forest Troop already had that behavioral style. This is unlikely to be the case; during their first few months of residency in Forest Troop, transfer males had the same rates of displacement aggression as new transfers in other more "traditional" troops. Instead, following transfer into Forest Troop, it would take 3–6 months for a new male to take on the group social style. This strongly suggests that there was indeed transmission, rather than self-selection.

A possibility obviously pertinent to human cultural transmission would be *active instruction*. To use chimpanzee transmission of tool-making knowledge as an example, this might consist of a mother actively molding the hands of her offspring in the latter's tool-making attempt, something that has been both reported and debated (Boesch, 1991; de Waal, 2001). In the case of Forest Troop, there was no evidence for this occurring and, in fact, it is not clear how such instruction could be detected (since it would require something along the lines of active instruction by resident individuals as to how, for example, to resist displacing aggression onto a smaller individual when frustrated about something).

A softer form of instruction would involve *contingent shaping*, where behavior is acquired through reward and punishment. As a striking example of that, when young male cowbirds learn to produce their local song, they initially produce an undifferentiated song repertoire, and females react to the production of appropriate dialect with copulation solicitation displays, thus providing positive reinforcement (Smith et al., 2000). In the case of Forest Troop, this might have taken the form of a transfer male being less likely to be groomed in the aftermath of his displacing aggression (and where such shaping does not require conscious intent on the part of resident individuals). However, while female baboons are capable of such contingent behavior (Cheney et al., 2010), there was no evidence of this in the patterns of grooming of transfer males in Forest Troop.

More plausible and straightforward are *observational models*, where individuals acquire new skills or behaviors simply by the examples around them—that is, primates see, primates do. This is a frequent feature of primate sociality (Boesch, 2003; Fragaszy & Visalberghi, 2004; Visalberghi & Fragaszy, 1990; Whiten, 1998; Whiten et al., 2003), and has been clearly demonstrated in experimental studies. One elegant example involved two groups of captive chimpanzees. In each, the alpha female was removed and put into a space where she encountered a large puzzle box containing a desirable food item. The box could be opened in two different ways, and each female eventually hit upon and mastered one method. At that point, the females were returned to their groups, accompanied by the puzzle box. In each case, the specific technique spread within the group by observation alone (Whiten et al., 2005). A similar phenomenon has since been shown in capuchin monkeys (Dindo et al., 2009) (as well as in rats [Galef & Whiskin, 2008]).

As a truly fascinating finding, both primate studies demonstrated the existence of social conformity. As noted, each alpha female's specific solution to the puzzle spread throughout her group. However, many individuals, in the process of learning the technique, would stumble upon the alternative solution and readily master it (81 percent of the capuchins). However, in all such cases, this individual ceased marching to a different drummer, abandoning the other approach, joining the rest of the group more than 95 percent of the time (Whiten et al., 2005; Dindo et al., 2009). Something similar has been observed in capuchins in the wild, where there might be more than one way to acquire a particular food type (for example, breaking open seeds by pounding them versus scrubbing them). Despite individuals having knowledge of both techniques, they are more likely to conform to the foraging preferences of their closest social partners (Perry, 2009).

Closely related to observational models is one of *facilitation by proximity*, especially in cases of transmission of material culture from mother to offspring. For example, in the case of chimpanzees using rock hammers for breaking nuts, the tendency of a young chimp to be near her mother and the latter's hammers increases the likelihood of the former experimenting with hammers and deriving the skill herself (Boesch, 2003); there is some evidence for the occurrence of this, leading to the notion that primates do not so much learn from each other as with each other (Fragaszy & Visalberghi, 2004). Despite such interesting evidence, it is not clear how facilitation would occur in cases of transmission of nonmaterial culture (e.g., the use of a particular vocalization), particularly one of an entire social style, as in Forest Troop.

Thus, it was unlikely that the cultural transmission arose from active instruction, contingent shaping, facilitation, and/or self-selection. By process of elimination, this leaves pure observation as the most likely explanation.

However, it is possible that something else was going on; the data suggest to me a scenario in which what occurred in Forest Troop did not actually constitute cultural transmission. Instead, it may have resembled what occurred when rhesus and stumptail macaques lived in the same group (de Waal & Johanowicz, 1993). A key feature of Forest Troop was the fact that newly transferred males were treated in a more affiliative fashion by resident females than is the case for transfer males in typical baboon troops. In the latter case, it takes an average of two–three months before resident females first groom a new male or give him a ritualized "presentation" greeting. In contrast, in Forest Troop, it took less than three weeks. In a typical baboon troop, once females do begin interacting with new males, they do so at relatively low rates. In contrast, once interactions began, females in Forest Troop sat in proximity to transfer males at twice the rate and groomed them at five times the rate as in other troops. Thus, new males in Forest Troop were treated in an affiliative manner by females sooner and more often.

This suggests social facilitation in a very different sense than used with respect to material culture. As discussed, in a typical baboon troop, females are subject to high rates of displacement aggression at the hands and canines of males frustrated for unrelated reasons. Being exposed to uncontrollable threats in an unpredictable manner is the epitome of psychological stress (Levine et al., 1989); in one study, the more often females in a troop were attacked by a particularly aggressive, displacing male (aptly named Hobbes), the fewer the circulating white blood cells, a classic marker of the effects of chronic stress on the immune system (Alberts, Altmann, & Sapolsky, 1992). As one of the clearest manifestations of the distinctive social atmosphere of Forest Troop in the aftermath of the tuberculosis deaths, females were subject to less displacement aggression (both because of the smaller number of adult males, and because of their temperaments). In the absence of a major source of psychological stress, these females would be more relaxed and less anxious (as implied by the changes in the neurochemistry of anxiety among subordinates in Forest Troop [Sapolsky & Share, 2004]), and thus perhaps more willing to make noncontingent affiliative gestures toward new, unknown males. And critically, when an adolescent male is treated "better," in a more affiliative manner, he may then gradually become less affiliative.

This default scenario is as parsimonious with the data as is one of observational learning (and they need not be mutually exclusive). It involves a cascade: when females are less stressed by the random aggression of males, they are more likely to be spontaneously affiliative to new males; when new males are treated in this more affiliative manner, they gradually become more affiliative themselves. This is not cultural transmission where males *acquire* a new behavioral style; instead, the social atmosphere of the troop, most proximally mediated by the behavior of females, facilitates the *emergence* of these behaviors from males. Within the limits of baboon sociality, in the absence of Hobbesian treatment, a young male reverts to his inner Rousseau.

Is a Forest Troop Culture Stable? Is It Transmissible?

This cascade described—more affiliative males resulting in less-stressed females who are more likely to act prosocially toward new males, resulting in new males becoming more affiliative—is self-perpetuating. Despite that, there are at least two circumstances that could terminate a Forest Troop culture:

- If a sufficiently large number of new males transferred in around the same time. As noted, in ruling out the self-selection model, males transferring into Forest Troop were initially no different from those transferring into other troops, which is to say that they had the usual high rates of aggression and displacement seen in adolescent males. Thus, if enough "unassimilated" males were present at the same time, they might be sufficiently aggressive and disruptive to make females more stressed and anxious and less prosocial, breaking the self-perpetuation.
- In game theory terms, groups with high stable rates of cooperation are vulnerable to wolves in sheep's clothing, to invasion by free riders who successfully exploit the cooperation (Nowak, 2011). And even if such individuals join the troop only intermittently, as enough of them accumulate, the cascade of self-perpetuation will be broken.
- The discussion has focused on males who transferred into Forest Troop; what happened to males who grew up in Forest Troop when they transferred elsewhere at adolescence? Unfortunately, resources precluded knowing the answer, as it required monitoring an array of troops scattered across large distances. There are at least three possible outcomes, however:
  - If a single Forest Troop male transferred into a "typical" troop and continued the behavioral style typical of his natal troop, he would likely be at a distinct competitive disadvantage. This would be the classic problem of jump-starting cooperation in a population made up solely of competitive defectors (Axelrod & Hamilton, 1981).
  - That outcome would occur in a population where being a competitive defector is the only viable strategy. However, as discussed, concentration on female-male affiliative "friendships," rather than male-male competition is a viable alternative for male baboons, and these individuals are not only healthier and longer-lived, but have ample reproductive success. A Forest Troop adolescent, transferring into a typical troop, might actually have thrived (in physiological, psychological, and Darwinian ways) with this alternative behavioral style.
  - If multiple Forest Troop adolescents transferred into the same troop simultaneously, they would form a cooperative unit. Both theoretical and empirical work in game

theory show that a stable cooperative unit out-competes surrounding noncooperators, either driving them to extinction or forcing them to become cooperative (Nowak, 2011). In other words, the troop that these adolescents would have joined would have become more like Forest Troop; thus, on a quasi-metaphorical level, a baboon culture of low aggression and high affiliation can be a transmissible trait between troops.

Post-Scripts to These Speculations
The Fate of Males Transferring from Forest Troop

Because of the small size of the troop, there was an average of only one adolescent male leaving per year, typically transferring into one of three neighboring troops. Thus, there was never the opportunity for multiple Forest Troop adolescents to transfer the culture into another troop. Moreover, because of limited resources, it was not possible to know how those single transfer males fared in their new troops.

The Fate of Forest Troop Itself

Unfortunately, it is not possible to find out whether the troop culture would be destabilized by invasive free riders. During the last decade, Forest Troop expanded its range to include the tourist lodge, sharing the niche with the remnants of the Garbage Dump troop. This has involved the troop spending some amount of time at the dump. However, for most of each day, individual animals roam the lodge grounds, foraging for food from dining room verandas, houses of staffers and garbage cans. This has also lead to the shooting of a number of troop members by game park rangers, as animals have become more aggressive in their interactions with humans. As a result, the troop has essentially fragmented and no longer functions as a cohesive social unit.

Conclusions

The main point of the events in Forest Troop is, of course, the social malleability that is implied. This raises a number of issues:

- The fact that the novel culture did not require the invention of new behaviors, but instead a change in the frequency and contexts of preexisting ones. This suggests the important idea that substantial, radical change in social behavior does not require changes in the building blocks of social behavior. This is akin to a truism in molecular evolution—while evolution can be driven by alterations in the structure of genes (i.e., changes in DNA sequence in gene coding regions), it is driven far more by alterations in the contexts in which genes are expressed (i.e., changes in DNA sequences in regulatory regions of the genome).

- While the Forest Troop was unique, it was not an unrecognizably different utopia. There was still a dominance hierarchy, and males of adjacent ranks would still compete fiercely between themselves; amid there being lesser amounts of displacement aggression, it had by no means disappeared from the social landscape; amid higher rates of reconciliative behaviors, it must be remembered that reconciliation can occur only if there are social tensions that need to be reconciled. All of this suggests the obvious fact that there are not infinite amounts of social plasticity in a primate social system. What is not obvious is whether Forest Troop constitutes the limits of which baboons are capable.

- At first glance, the circumstances that brought about the Forest Troop culture are artificial and rare, requiring a unique set of occurrences built around interactions with humans and their detritus. However, the evolutionary record is replete with cases of "selective bottlenecks." This is where there is a shift from a fairly stable environment that allows balanced selection for a number of coexisting phenotypes to an extreme circumstance that strongly culls all but one. Such bottlenecks are usually thought of as involving selection at the levels of physiology (for example, a severe drought and famine sparing only those individuals with a certain renal capacity for water retention) or morphometry (for example, a severe drought and famine sparing only small-bodied individuals with fewer caloric demands). Such bottlenecks can readily select at the level of social behavior as well. There are naturalistic circumstances that would select for the sole survival of males with low levels of aggression and high levels of social affiliation.

- There were no top-down, global instructions for how the Forest Troop culture was perpetuated. Instead, the transmission was an emergent property of local "rules" (for example, the rule that when females are less stressed and anxious because of the aggressive of males, they are more likely to reach out in an affiliative manner to new males). The emergence of Forest Troop did not require a blueprint.

As emphasized early in this chapter, baboons are not convenient substitutes for our hominid ancestors. Therefore, the point of Forest Troop is not that our darkly stained Hobbesian baboon roots contain more Rousseau than 1960s textbooks might have suggested. It is that if the social system of another primate is so malleable and free from assumed inevitabilities, we must be vastly skeptical about the existence of constraints regarding human social change.

References

Alberts, S., Altmann, J., & Sapolsky, R. (1992). Behavioral, endocrine and immunological correlates of immigration by an aggressive male into a natural primate group. *Hormones and Behavior, 26,* 167–178.

Altmann, J. (2001). *Baboon mothers and infants.* Chicago: University of Chicago Press.

Axelrod, R., & Hamilton, W. (1981). The evolution of cooperation. *Science, 211,* 1390–1396.

Banks, W., Altmann J., Sapolsky R., Phillips-Conroy J., & Morley J. (2003). Serum leptin levels as a marker for a Syndrome X-like condition in wild baboons. *Journal of Clinical Endocrinology and Metabolism, 88,* 1234–1240.

Bercovitch, F. (1991). Mate selection, consortship formation, and reproductive tactics in adult female savanna baboons. *Primates*, *32*, 437–452.

Boesch, C. (1991). Teaching in wild chimpanzees. *Animal Behaviour*, *41*, 530–532.

Boesch, C. (2003). Is culture a golden barrier between human and chimpanzee? *Evolutionary Anthropology*, *12*, 82–91.

Byrne, R., & Whiten, A. (1988). *Machiavellian intelligence*. Oxford: Oxford University Press.

Cambefort, J. (1981). A comparative study of culturally transmitted patterns of feeding habits in the chacma baboon *Papio ursinus* and the vervet monkey *Cercopithecus aethiops*. *Folia Primatologica*, *36*, 243–263.

Cheney, D., Moscovicea, L., Heesenc, M., Mundry, R., Seyfarth, R. (2010). Contingent cooperation between wild female baboons. *Proceedings National Academy of Sciences USA 107*, 9562–9566.

Cords, M. & Thurnheer, S. (1993). Reconciling with valuable partners by long-tailed macaques. *Ethology*, *93*, 315–325.

de Waal, F. (2001). *The ape and the sushi master: Cultural reflections of a primatologist*. New York: Basic Books.

de Waal, F., Johanowicz, D. (1993). Modification of reconciliation behavior through social experience: An experiment with two macaque species. *Child Development*, *64*, 897–908.

de Waal, F., & van Roosmalen, A. (1979). Reconciliation and consolidation among chimpanzees. *Behavioral Ecology and Sociobiology*, *5*, 55–66.

de Waal, F., & Yoshihara D. (1983). Reconciliation and redirected affection in rhesus monkeys. *Behaviour*, *85*, 224–241.

DeVore, I., & Washburn, S. (1961). The social life of baboons. *Scientific American*, *204*, 62–72.

Dindo, M., Whiten, A., & de Waal, F. (2009). In-group conformity sustains different foraging traditions in Capuchin moneys (*Cebus apella*). *Public Library of Science ONE*, *4*, e7858.

Fragaszy, D., & Visalberghi, E. (2004). Socially biased learning in monkeys. *Learning and Behavior*, *32*, 24–35.

Freeman, H., & Gosling, S. (2010). Personality in nonhuman primates: a review and evaluation of past research. *American Journal of Primatology*, *72*, 653–671.

Galef, B. (1990). The question of animal culture. *Human Nature*, *3*, 157–178.

Galef, B., & Whiskin, E. (2008). "Conformity" in Norway rats? *Animal Behaviour*, *75*, 2035–2039.

Kawai, M. (1965). Newly acquired precultural behavior of the natural troop of Japanese Monkeys on Kishima Islet. *Primates*, *6*, 1–30.

Kemnitz, J., Sapolsky, R., Altmann, J., Muruthi, P., Mott, G ., & Stefanick, M. (2002). Effects of food availability on insulin and lipid levels in free-ranging baboons. *American Journal of Primatology*, *57*, 13–19.

Kummer, H. (1971). *Primate societies: Group techniques of ecological adaptation*. Wheeling, IL: Harlan Davidson.

Laland, K., & Hoppitt, W. (2003). Do animals have culture? *Evolutionary Anthropology*, *12*, 150–159.

Levine, S., Wiener, S., & Coe, C. (1989). The psychoneuroendocrinology of stress: A psychobiological perspective. In S. Levine, & F. Brush (Eds.), *Psychoendocrinology* (pp. 341–377). San Diego: Academic Press.

McGrew, W. (1998). Culture in non-human primates? *Annual Review of Anthropology*, *27*, 301–328.

McGrew, W. (2004). Primatology: Advanced ape technology. *Current Biology*, *14*, 1046–1047.

Nishida, T. (1980).The leaf-clipping display: A newly discovered expression gesture in wild chimpanzees. *Journal of Human Evolution*, *9*, 117–128.

Noad, M., Cato, D., Bryden, M., Jenner, M., & Jenner, K. (2000). Cultural revolution in whale songs. *Nature*, *408*, 537.

Noe, R. (1994). A model of coalition formation among male baboons with fighting ability as the crucial parameter. *Animal Behaviour*, *47*, 211–213.

Nowak, M. (2011). *SuperCooperators: Altruism, evolution and why we need each other to succeed*. (With R. Highfield). New York: Free Press.

Packer, C. (1979). Inter-troop transfer and inbreeding avoidance in *Papio anubis*. *Animal Behaviour*, *27*, 1–36.

Perry, S. (2009). Conformism in the food processing techniques of white-faced capuchin monkeys. *Animal Cognition*, *12*, 705–716.

Pusey, A., & Packer, C. (1986). Dispersal and philopatry. In B. Smuts, D. Cheney, R. Seyfarth, R. Wrangham, & T. Struhsaker (Eds.), *Primate societies* (pp. 250–266). Chicago: University of Chicago Press.

Ransom, T. (1981). *Beach troop of the Gombe*. East Brunswick, NJ: Associated University Press.

Ray, J., & Sapolsky, R. (1992). Styles of male social behavior and their endocrine correlates among high-ranking baboons. *American Journal of Primatology*, *28*, 231–250.

Rendell, L., & Whitehead, H. (2001). Culture in whales and dolphins. *Brain and Behavioral Sciences*, 24, 309.

Sallet, J., Mars, R., Noonan, M., Andersson J., O'Reilly J., Jbabdi, . . . Ruschworth, M. (2011). Social network size affects neural circuits in macaques. *Science*, 334, 697–700.

Sapolsky, R. (1983). Endocrine aspects of social instability in the olive baboon (*Papio anubis*). *American Journal of Primatology*, 5, 365–379.

Sapolsky, R. (1991). Testicular function, social rank and personality among wild baboons. *Psychoneuroendocrinology*, 16, 281–293.

Sapolsky, R. (1993). Endocrinology alfresco: Psychoendocrine studies of wild baboons. *Recent Progress in Hormone Research*, 48, 437–468.

Sapolsky, R. (1996). Why should an aged male baboon transfer troops? *American Journal of Primatology*, 39, 149–157.

Sapolsky, R. (2005). The influence of social hierarchy on primate health. *Science*, 308, 648–652.

Sapolsky, R., & Else, J. (1987). Bovine tuberculosis in a wild baboon population: Epidemiological aspects. *Journal of Medical Primatology*, 16, 229–235.

Sapolsky, R., & Ray, J. (1989). Styles of dominance and their endocrine correlates among wild olive baboons (*Papio anubis*). *American Journal of Primatology*, 18, 1–13.

Sapolsky. R., & Share, L. (2004). A pacific culture among wild baboons: Its emergence and transmission. *Public Library of Science Biology*, 2, e106.

Seyfarth, R. (1978). Social relationships among adult male and female baboons. II. Behaviour throughout the female reproductive cycle. *Behaviour*, 64, 227–247.

Seyfarth, R. (1976). Social relationships among adult female baboons. *Animal Behaviour* 24, 917–938.

Silk, J., Altmann, J., & Alberts, S. (2006). Social relationships among adult female baboons (*Papio cynocephalus*) I. Variation in the strength of social bonds. *Behavioral Ecology and Sociobiology*, 61, 183–195.

Silk, J., Beehner, J., Bergman, T., Crockford, C., Engh, A., Moscovice, L., Wittig, R., Seyfarth, R., & Dheney, D. (2009). The benefits of social capital: Close social bonds among female baboons enhance offspring survival. *Proceedings of the Royal Society, B* 276, 3099–3104.

Smith, V., King, A., & West, J. (2000). A role of her own: Female cowbirds, *Molothrus ater*, influence the development and outcome of song learning. *Animal Behaviour*, 60, 599–609.

Smuts, B. (1999). *Sex and friendship in baboons* (2nd ed.). Cambridge: Harvard University Press.

Smuts, B., & Watanabe, J. (1990). Social relationships and ritualized greetings in adult male baboons (*Papio cynocephalus anubis*). *International Journal of Primatology*, 11, 147–172.

Strum, S. (1982). Agonistic dominance in male baboons: An alternative view. *International Journal of Primatology*, 3, 175–202.

Strum, S. (2001). *Almost human: A journey into the world of baboons*. Chicago: University of Chicago Press.

Tarara, R., Suleman, M., Sapolsky, R., Wabomba, M., & Else, J. (1985). Tuberculosis in wild olive baboons, *Papio cynocephalus anubis* (Lesson), in Kenya. *Journal of Wildlife Diseases*, 21, 137–140.

Thierry, B., Aureli, F., Nunn, C., Petit, O., Abegg, C., & de Waal, F. (2008). A comparative study of conflict resolution in macaques: Insights into the nature of trait covariation. *Animal Behaviour*, 75, 847–860.

van Schaik, C., Ancrenaz, M., Borgen, G., Galdikas, B., Knott, C. (2003). Orangutan cultures and the evolution of material culture. *Science*, 299, 102–105.

Virgin, C., & Sapolsky, R. (1997). Styles of male social behavior and their endocrine correlates among low-ranking baboons. *American Journal of Primatology*, 42, 25–39.

Visalberghi, E., & Fragaszy, D. (1990). Food-washing behaviour in tufted capuchin monkeys, *Cebus apella*, and crab-eating macaques, *Macaca fascicularis*. *Animal Behaviour*, 40, 829–836.

Whiten, A. (1998). Imitation of the sequential structure of actions by chimpanzees (*Pan troglodytes*) *Journal of Comparative Psychology*, 112, 270–281.

Whiten, A., Goodall, J., McGrew, W., Nishida, T., & Reynolds, V. (1999). Culture in chimpanzees. *Nature*, 399, 682–685.

Whiten, A., Horner, V., de Waal, F. (2005). Conformity to cultural norms of tool use in chimpanzees. *Nature*, 437, 737–740.

Whiten, A., Horner, V., & Marshall-Pescini, S. (2003). Cultural panthropology. *Evolutionary Anthropology*, 12, 92–105.

22

Conflict Resolution in Nonhuman Primates and Human Children

Maaike Kempes, Liesbeth Sterck,
and Bram Orobio de Castro

Aggressive behavior in childhood poses a threat to society, since aggression tends to be quite stable in childhood, and aggressive children often become violent adults (Tremblay, 2000). Aggression has various negative effects, that is, apart from eventual wounds and damaged property, it results in postconflict stress and harms relationships. Aggression is especially harmful when it escalates. Therefore, most studies focus on the initiation and prevention of aggression in conflicts between children. This is remarkable, since conflicts of interest and the resulting aggression are integral parts of adaptive human functioning and are inevitable as individuals protect their interests. Consequently, rather than only pursuing the prevention of aggression, it may also be important to study how prosocial skills reduce the negative effects of aggressive conflicts and prevent further escalation. One important prosocial mechanism to reduce the negative impact of aggression is reconciliation, which can be defined as friendly behavior between former opponents shortly after a conflict.

This chapter stresses the importance of adequate reconciliation in keeping conflicts manageable and functional. Understanding the factors that influence reconciliation is essential to improve conflict management in children with and without disruptive behavior problems. Much knowledge on conflict management comes from animal studies (Aureli & de Waal, 2000). Therefore, we first mention the key results derived from animal studies before considering what is known about reconciliation both in typically developing children and in those with aggressive behavior problems. Second, we highlight the importance of the social environment for the development of reconciliatory skills in both nonhuman primates and human children. Third, we discuss factors that may contribute to the ability to develop and effectively execute reconciliatory skills.

Aggression and Reconciliation

Animal studies on conflict management show that reconciliation is a prominent way to repair damage caused by aggressive conflicts (Aureli & de Waal, 2000). In the short term, reconciliation may serve to reduce postconflict stress and prevent renewed aggression (Aureli, Cords & van Schaik, 2002; Aureli & van Schaik, 1991). The long-term function is to restore relationships that have been disturbed by aggression. In nonhuman primates this is expressed in a higher reconciliation tendency directed toward valuable partners (friends and kin) compared to less valuable partners (nonfriends and non-kin) (Aureli, 1997; Call, 1999; Call, Judge & de Waal, 1996; Castles, Aureli & de Waal, 1996; Cords & Turnheer, 1993; Koski, De Vries, Van Den Tweel & Sterck, 2007).

Although the body of research in children is less extensive, several studies in typically developing children demonstrated reconciliatory skills as early as three years of age (Butovskaya & Kozintsev, 1999; Fujisawa, Kutsukake & Hasegawa, 2005; Ljungberg, Horowitz, Jansson, Westlund & Clarke, 2005). In line with evidence in animals, reconciliation in children diminished renewed attacks (Ljungberg, Westlund & Forsberg, 1999) and decreased the frequency of redirected aggression (Butovskaya & Kozintsev, 1999). Furthermore, after an aggressive act stress-related behaviors were elevated, but these were reduced after subsequent reconciliation (Fujisawa et al., 2005). Moreover, reconciliation promoted tolerance between former opponents (Butovskaya & Kozintsev, 1999; Fujisawa et al., 2005; Ljungberg et al., 2005). These findings stress the importance of reconciliation to reduce the negative consequences of aggression in children in general. Surprisingly, little attention has been paid to reconciliatory behavior of children for whom reconciliation may be most important, that is, children with disruptive behavior problems.

Traditionally, psychologists, social scientists, and welfare biologists have presented aggression as an antisocial behavior. However, aggressive behavior, defined as behavior aimed at causing physical injury or threat displays that warn of impending actions (Aureli & de Waal, 2000), can actually be a useful component in the behavioral repertoire of a given species, including among developing human children. Individuals that live in a social group need to communicate their relative positions and find solutions for potential conflicts to successfully cooperate in action or exchange services and favours. Aggression, and specifically the threat of aggression, can be a powerful tool in the bargaining process between partners. Nonetheless, a child's antisocial behaviors sometimes form a pattern that goes beyond the bounds of normal aggression and becomes deviant. When aggressive behavior is disproportionately severe, frequent, and has obvious unfavorable effects on a child's functioning at home and at school, the child is diagnosed with a disruptive behavior disorder (American Psychological Association, 2000). To give these children the most adequate treatment it is necessary to better understand not only aggression but also its mechanism of control.

Most researchers studying children with aggressive behavior problems concentrate on deviances in the aggressive behavior itself or on the factors that may elicit aggressive behavior. However, studies that observe the behavior of children with aggressive behavior problems in conflict situations report either no differences (Kempes, Orobio de Castro, & Sterck, 2008; Matthys, de Vries et al., 1995) or relatively small (Kempes, de Vries, Matthys, van Engeland, & van Hooff, 2008; Matthys, de Vries et al., 1995) differences in the rate of aggressive behavior compared to typically developing children. Yet, it was found that among children with aggressive behavior problems, aggressive conflicts started earlier, lasted longer, and escalated more often in impermissibly severe aggression (Kempes, Orobio de Castro, & Sterck, 2008). This suggests that not the incidence of aggression itself, but the incidence of excessive or escalated aggression forms the crucial determinant in their aggressive behavior problems. The maladaptive nature of conflicts of these children may thus in part result from an inability to limit the negative consequences of their aggression. In line with this notion, it was found that children with disruptive behavior problems find it difficult to neutralize incipient conflicts (Matthys, de Vries, et al., 1995) and to recognize benign behavior when they are frustrated (Orobio de Castro, Bosch, Veerman, & Koops, 2003). These findings may point to deficiencies in understanding and interpreting the prosocial behavior of the peer and generating prosocial behavior in an aggressive context, capacities that may be prerequisites of reconciliation. In addition, children with disruptive behavior problems are often unsuccessful in establishing friendships with non-aggressive peers (Coie, Dodge, Terry, & Wright, 1991). This has been attributed to their higher frequency of inappropriate behaviors such as aggression and teasing (Hektner, August, & Realmuto, 2000). Since reconciliation plays an important role in restoring the relationships after a conflict in typically developing children (Fujisawa et al., 2005), it is also possible that children with disruptive behavior problems lack the ability to reconcile their conflicts and consequently have difficulty maintaining prosocial relationships. Findings of a study we recently performed corroborate the prediction that children with aggressive behavior problems are unable to reconcile. More specifically, we showed that the absence of reconciliation in these children was not due to a lack of initiation of postconflict affiliation, but because postconflict affiliative offers from peers were rejected. In addition, we found that postconflict affiliative offers from peers did not prevent the renewal of aggression (Kempes, Orobio de Castro, et al., 2008). This suggests that the ability to mitigate the effects of aggression is crucial for appropriate social functioning.

The Learning Environment

In humans the social environment has a powerful influence on the development of social behavior, and an adverse early environment may cause psychopathology, such as aggressive behavior problems. The above-described results raise questions about the development of aggressive behavior and reconciliatory skills. As noted earlier, children are already able to reconcile at the age of three. As they grow older they resolve their conflicts more frequently (e.g., Fujisawa, Kutsukake, & Hasegawa, 2006; Laursen & Hartup, 1989; Verbeek & de Waal, 2001), and around the age of five they steeply increase their tendency to reconcile

(Fujisawa et al., 2006). Several theories have been formulated concerning the way children acquire conflict resolution skills. Some attribute the early development of conflict resolution to socialization processes, whereby adults use facilitative strategies to intervene on children's peer conflicts and model constructive means of resolution (Bayer, Whaley, & May, 1995; De Vries & Zan, 1994; Katz & McClellan, 1997; Perlman & Ross, 1997). Others suggest that children's conflict resolution abilities may also emerge naturally out of children's interactions with others, especially with peers (Killen & de Waal, 2000; Killen & Smetana, 2006; Piaget, 1932). Since rearing conditions are variable in humans, some additional insights can be gleaned from the controlled studies of nonhuman primates. Rhesus monkeys (*Macaca mullata*), like humans, grow up in an environment consisting of complex social networks and often have served as a model for the effects of rearing conditions on social behavior.

Since reconciliation is thought to be a social skill that primates acquire during their relatively long period of infancy and juvenescence (de Waal & Johanowicz, 1993), it has been suggested that social learning during ontogeny is of crucial importance for the development of adequate reconciliation (Ljungberg & Westlund, 2000). How social learning processes can positively influence reconciliatory tendencies was shown in an experiment by de Waal and Johanowicz (1993), wherein juvenile rhesus macaques were placed together with juvenile stumptailed macaques (*Macaca arctoides)*. Previously, stumptailed macaques had been found to reconcile a much larger proportion of their conflicts than rhesus monkeys. In the de Waal and Johanowicz experiment, compared to their baseline level of reconciliation, the juvenile rhesus monkeys showed a threefold increase in the proportion of reconciled conflicts after being exposed to greater reconciliatory tendencies of stumptailed macaques over a five-month period. These findings stress the importance of the social environment in the development of reconciliatory tendencies, especially since a similar group of juvenile rhesus monkeys, cohoused with other rhesus monkeys for a similar period of time, did not show any sign of an increase in reconciliatory behaviors.

In the de Waal and Johanowicz (1993) experiment, the environment of the rhesus monkeys was "enriched" with stumptailed tutors that were experienced in reconciliation. While this situation seems to enhance social competence, social deprivation during the juvenile period has been linked not only to several social inadequacies in peer interactions (Harlow & Harlow, 1962), infant-mother interactions (Hinde, 1966), maternal behavior (Suomi, 1978), and sexual behavior (e.g., Harlow & Harlow, 1962; Mason, 1960), but also to aggressive behavior (Kraemer, 1992; Mineka & Suomi, 1978; Mitchell, Raymond, Ruppenthal, & Harlow, 1966). Concerning aggressive behavior, it was shown that early peer deprivation did not affect the rate of aggressive behavior (Kempes, Gulickx, van Daalen, Louwerse & Sterck, 2008). However, it does affect the intensity of the aggressive behavior. It was found that early peer-deprived rhesus monkeys compared to socially-reared rhesus monkeys showed higher rates of conflicts with high intensity aggression, but not higher rates of low intensity aggression (Figure 22.1). Moreover, whereas socially-reared rhesus

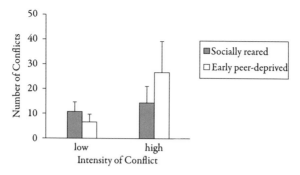

FIGURE 22.1 Low-intensity (threat) versus high-intensity (attack) agonistic conflicts in socially reared (SR) and early peer-deprived (EPD) rhesus monkeys.

monkeys show equal amounts of low- and high-intensity aggression, early peer-deprived rhesus monkeys show significantly more high-intensity aggression.

Moreover, aggression in groups of socially-deprived monkeys could escalate to the point that animals were seriously wounded or killed, necessitating repeated regroupings and movements of animals between groups (Kempes, Gulickx, et al., 2008; Ljungberg & Westlund, 2000). The aggressive behavior of early peer-deprived rhesus monkeys, therefore, seems to show a resemblance to the aggressive behavior of children with aggressive behavior problems. This raises the question whether social deprivation in rhesus monkeys also hampers reconciliatory skills.

In concordance with this hypothesis, it was found that socially-deprived rhesus monkeys do not show reconciliation behavior with their opponent after a conflict (Kempes, Den Heijer, Korteweg, Louwerse, & Sterck, 2009; Ljungberg & Westlund, 2000). In addition, in correspondence with the findings for children with aggressive behavior problems, it was found that the lack of reconciliation was not due to an inability to show postconflict reconciliatory attempts, but due to rejection of reconciliatory attempts by the former opponent (Kempes et al., 2009). In sum, these results suggest that the environment plays an important role in the development of both reconciliatory skills and functional aggressive behavior.

Capacities for Reconciliation

The foregoing results emphasize the importance of contact with group members early in life for the development of adequate reconciliation. It is hypothesized that attachment relationships may play an important role in the development of reconciliation (Weaver & de Waal, 2003). In human and nonhuman primates, early attachment experiences strongly affect the development of skills and the nature of relationships with others (Ainsworth, Blehar, & Waters, 1978; Bowlby 1969). According to the attachment theory of Bowlby, infants become attached to adults who are sensitive and responsive in social interactions with them, and begin to use such caretakers as a secure base from which to explore the immediate environment. At first, parental responses lead to the development of patterns of attachment. These, in turn, lead to internal working models which will guide the individual's perceptions, emotions, thoughts, and expectations in later relationships (Bowlby, 1969). Since children with poor early attachment relationships with their mother are more likely to show aggressive behavior patterns when they are of school age (Lyons-Ruth, 1996), it may be that reconciliation is also affected by the nature of attachment between the mother and infant.

Previous research in captive brown capuchins (*Cebus apella*) showed that the quality of relationship between the mother and offspring affected the behavior that was involved in reconciliations of their offspring (Weaver & de Waal, 2003). Weaver and de Waal (2003) hypothesize that consistent amiability within mother–offspring relationships provides secure youngsters with a better developed neurobiological (Kraemer, 1992) and psychological (Bowlby, 1969) makeup. However, although the relationship between mother and infant is important, our research with rhesus monkeys shows that the influence of contact with peers on the development of reconciliatory behavior must not be neglected.

In naturalistic settings rhesus monkeys spend their first month in intimate physical contact with their biological mother, in which an enduring attachment bond is established. However, already in their second month rhesus infants begin to explore their immediate physical and social environment, using the mother as a secure base. Throughout the rest of their childhood most juveniles spend several hours each day in active social play with peers. During the course of peer play most social behavior necessary for normal adult functioning is developed and practiced (Suomi, 2005). Recall that rhesus monkeys that were deprived of peer interaction in the first year of life did not engage in reconciliation. Therefore, the presence of peers seems to be as important as the presence of the mother for the development of reconciliation and social skills.

With respect to the influence peers may have on the development of reconciliation, we tested three hypotheses (Kempes et. al., 2009). The first hypothesis was that the absence of peers early in life may have prevented rhesus monkeys from forming valuable relationships. These monkeys may have lacked valuable relationships that needed to be restored after a conflict. However, this hypothesis was rejected since early peer-deprived rhesus monkeys did show higher affiliation rates toward friends compared to non-friends, which indicates that they actually do have valuable social relationships with other monkeys.

Secondly, we hypothesized that early peer-deprived rhesus monkeys may not have been exposed to conflict management strategies while immature. This may have resulted in an inability to invite reconciliation, shift from aggressive to affiliative behavior (Aureli et al., 2002) or interpret reconciliatory behavior correctly (Kempes, Orobio, et. al., 2008). Our results (Kempes, Gulickx, et al., 2008) show that the lack of reconciliation was not due to a lack of initiation of reconciliation, and additionally, since early peer-deprived rhesus monkeys did show third-party affiliation, we concluded that they were able to shift from aggressive to affiliative behavior. However, we found some evidence that these peer-deprived monkeys had trouble interpreting social signals of other monkeys. Kempes,

Gulickx, et al. (2008) showed that early peer-deprived monkeys react with aggression to social submission signals, that is, bare teeth, from peers. Socially-reared animals, on the other hand, react to bare teeth with inhibition of aggressive behavior. This suggests that early peer-deprived monkeys neglect or misinterpreted positive facial cues, which might explain why they did not accept reconciliatory gestures of a peer.

The third hypothesis was related to attachment theory. We hypothesized that the absence of peers in early life may have not provided rhesus monkeys with the opportunity to socially interact with others while using their mother as a secure base. This would result in anxious behavior that may have prevented them from accepting reconciliatory behavior. In accordance with this hypothesis, we found that early peer-deprived monkeys avoided their peers more often than socially-reared monkeys in both the post-conflict period and a matched control period 24 hours later (Kempes et al., 2009). In addition, it was found that early peer-deprived victims rejected reconciliatory offers from their rivals. Finally, the third hypothesis gains support from the finding that early peer-deprived monkeys in general have high anxiety levels (Kempes, Gulickx, et al., 2008). These results indicate that approaches are considered threatening and rejection of reconciliatory offers is caused by a high anxiety level in the peer group resulting in the absence of reconciliation.

In sum, the absence of peers in early life seems to have resulted in a higher anxiety level and a greater focus on negative social cues than occurs in socially-reared monkeys. This absence of peer contact in early life subsequently may result in both the rejection of reconciliatory offers and the presence of deviant aggressive behavior observed in the peer-deprived rhesus monkeys. The ability to socially interact with peers from the secure base of the mother—in other words, the normal social pattern among a group-living species of primate such as rhesus monkeys—seems to reduce anxiety levels and allow the recognition of the social signals necessary for adequate reconciliation and species-typical, aggressive behavior.

Conclusion

Altogether, reconciliation, friendly behavior between former opponents, is an important way to reduce the negative impact of an aggressive event and functions to maintain good social relationships in nonhuman primates and human children alike. Children with aggressive behavior problems show escalated aggression and fail to reconcile. This leads to our proposal that not only the initiation and rate of aggression, but also their failure to control escalation and to show reconciliation are crucial components of their aggressive behavior problems. This interpretation is strengthened by the finding that rhesus monkeys who show deviant aggressive behavior also fail to reconcile.

With respect to the learning of reconciliatory skills we conclude that the presence of peers in early life is essential for the development of functional aggressive behavior and adequate reconciliation behavior. We propose that the ability to socially interact with peers from the secure base of the mother is essential for learning how to regulate anxiety levels and for recognizing reconciliatory social signals from other monkeys. In this way socially-reared monkeys naturally learn how to employ restrained aggression, which results in less serious injuries than does higher intensity fighting, and they also learn how to resume normal interactions with their peers following an aggressive episode.

References

Ainsworth, M. D. S., Blehar, M., Waters, E., & Wall, S. (1978). *Patterns of attachment*. Hillsdale, NJ: Erlbaum.

American Psychological Association (2000). *Diagnostic and statistical manual of mental disorder (DSM-IV-TR)*. Washington DC: American Psychiatric Association.

Aureli, F. (1997). Post-conflict anxiety in nonhuman primates: The mediating role of emotion in conflict resolution. *Aggressive Behavior, 23*, 315–328.

Aureli, F., Cords, M. & van Schaik, C. P. (2002). Conflict resolution following aggression in gregarious animals: a predictive framework. *Animal Behaviour, 64*, 325–343.

Aureli, F. & de Waal, F. B. M. (2000). *Natural conflict resolution*. Berkeley: University of California Press.

Aureli, F. & van Schaik, C. P. (1991). Post-conflict behaviour in long-tailed macaques (*Macaca fascicularis*): II. Coping with uncertainty. *Ethology, 89*, 101–104.

Bayer, C., Whaley, K., & May, S. (1995). Strategic assistance in toddler disputes: sequences and patterns of teacher message strategies. *Early Education and Development, 6*, 405–432.

Bowlby, J. (1969). *Attachment and loss* (Vol. 1). New York: Basic Books.

Butovskaya, M., & Kozintsev, A. (1999). Aggression, friendship, and reconciliation in Russian primary schoolchildren. *Aggressive Behavior, 25*, 125–139.

Call, J. (1999). The effect of inter-opponent distance on the occurrence of reconciliation in Stumptail (*Macaca arctoides*) and Rhesus Macaques (*Macaca mulatta*). *Primates, 40*, 515–523.

Call, J., Judge, P. G. & de Waal, F. B. M. (1996). Influence of kinship and spatial density on reconciliation and grooming in rhesus monkeys. *American Journal of Primatology, 39*, 35–45.

Castles, D. L., Aureli, F., & de Waal, F. B. M. (1996). Variation in conciliatory tendency and relationship quality across groups of pigtail macaques. *Animal behaviour, 52*, 389–403.

Coie, J. D., Dodge K. A., Terry, R., & Wright, V. (1991) Peer status and aggression in boys' groups: Developmental and contextual analyses. *Child Development, 61*, 1289–1309.

Cords, M., & Thurnheer, S. (1993). Reconciling with valuable partners by long-tailed macaques. *Ethology, 93*, 315–325.

de Waal, F. B. M., & Johanowicz, D. L (1993). Modification of reconciliation behavior through social experience: An experiment with two macaque species. *Child Development, 64*, 897–908.

Fujisawa, K. K., Kutsukake, N. & Hasegawa, T. (2005). Reconciliation pattern after aggression among Japanese preschool children. *Aggressive Behavior, 31*, 138–152.

Fujisawa, K. K., Kutsukake, N. & Hasegawa, T. (2006) Peacemaking and consolation in Japanese preschoolers witnessing peer aggression. *Journal of Comparative Psychology, 120*, 48–57.

Harlow, H. F., & Harlow M. K. (1962). The effect of rearing conditions on behavior. *Bulletin of the Menninger Clinic, 26*, 213–224.

Hektner, J. M., August, G. J., & Realmuto, G. M. (2000). Patterns and temporal changes in peer affiliation among aggressive and nonaggressive children participating in a summer school program. *Journal Clinical Child and Adolescence Psychology, 29*, 603–614.

Hinde, R. A. (1966) *Animal behavior*. New York: Mc-Graw-Hill.

Katz, L., & McClellan, D. E. (1997). *Fostering children's social competence: The role of the teacher*. Washington, DC: National Association for the Education of Young Children.

Kempes, M., de Vries, H., Matthys, W., van Engeland, H., & van Hooff, J. (2008). Differences in cortisol response affect the distinction of observed reactive and proactive aggression in children with aggressive behaviour disorders. *Journal of Neural Transmission, 115*, 139–147.

Kempes, M. M., Orobio de Castro, B., & Sterck, E. H. M. (2008) Conflict management in 6–8-year-old aggressive Dutch boys: Do they reconcile? *Behaviour, 145*, 1701–1722.

Kempes, M. M., Gulickx, M. M. C. van Daalen, H. J. C., Louwerse, A. L. & Sterck, E. H. M. (2008). Social competence is reduced in socially deprived monkeys. *Journal of Comparative Psychology, 78,* 271–277.

Kempes, M. M., Den Heijer, D., Korteweg L., Louwerse, A. L. & Sterck, E. H. M. (2009). Socially deprived rhesus macaques fail to reconcile: Do they not attempt or not accept reconciliation? *Animal Behavior, 122,* 62–67.

Killen, M., & de Waal, F. B. M. (2000). The evolution and development of morality. In F. Aureli & F. B. M. de Waal (Eds.), *Natural conflict resolution* (pp. 352–372). Berkeley: University of California Press.

Killen, M., & Smetana, J. (2006). (Eds.). *Handbook of moral development.* Erlbaum, Mahwah, NJ.

Koski, S.E., De Vries, H., Van Den Tweel, S.W., & Sterck, E.H.M. (2007). What to do after a fight? The determinants and inter-dependency of post-conflict interactions in chimpanzees. *Behaviour, 144,* 529–555.

Kraemer, G. W. (1992). A psychological theory of attachment. *Behavioral and Brain Sciences, 15,* 493–541.

Laursen, B., & Hartup, W. W. (1989). The dynamics of preschool children's conflicts. *Merrill-Palmer Quarterly, 35,* 281–297.

Ljungberg, T., Horowitz, L., Jansson, L., Westlund, K., & Clarke, C. (2005). Communicative factors, conflict progression, and use of reconciliatory strategies in pre-school boys a series of random events or a sequential process? *Aggressive Behavior, 31,* 303–323.

Ljungberg, T., & Westlund, K. (2000). Impaired reconciliation in rhesus macaques with a history of early weaning and disturbed socialization. *Primates, 41,* 79–88.

Ljungberg, T., Westlund, K., & Forsberg, A. J. L. (1999). Conflict resolution in 5-year-old boys: Does post-conflict affiliative behaviour have a reconciliatory role? *Animal Behaviour, 58,* 1007–1016.

Lyons-Ruth, K., 1996. Attachment relationships among children with aggressive behavior problems: The role of disorganized early attachment patterns. *Journal of Consulting and Clinical Psychology, 64,* 64–73.

Mason W.A. (1960). The effects of social restriction on the behavior of rhesus monkeys 1: Free social behavior. *Journal of Comparative and Physiological Psychology, 53,* 582–589.

Matthys, W., de Vries, H., Hectors, A., Veerbeek, M., Heidemann, W., Goud, M., Van Hooff, J. A., & Van Engeland, H. (1995). Differences between conduct disordered and typically developing children in their tendencies to escalate or neutralize conflicts when interacting with normal peers. *Child Psychiatry and Human Development, 26,* 29–41.

Mineka, S., & Suomi, S. J. (1978). Social separation in monkeys. *Psychological Bulletin, 85,* 1376–1400.

Mitchell, G. D., Raymond E. J., Ruppenthal, G. C., & Harlow, H. F. (1966). Long term effects of total social isolation upon behavior of rhesus monkeys. *Psychological Reports, 18,* 567–580.

Orobio de Castro, B., Bosch J. D., Veerman, J.W., & Koops, W. (2003) Negative feelings exacerbate negative feelings in highly aggressive boys. *Journal of Clinical Child and Adolescent Psychology, 32,* 56–65.

Perlman, M., & Ross, H. S. (1997). The benefits of parent intervention in children's disputes: An examination of concurrent changes in children's fighting styles. *Child Development, 68,* 690–700.

Piaget, J. (1932). *The moral judgment of the child.* New York: Free Press.

Suomi, S. J. (1978). Maternal behavior by socially incompetent monkeys: Neglect and abuse of offspring. *Journal of Pediatric Psychology, 3,* 28–34.

Suomi, S. J. (2005). Mother-infant attachment, peer relationships, and the development of social networks in rhesus monkeys. *Human Development, 48,* 67–79.

Tremblay, R. E. (2000). The development of aggressive behaviour during childhood: What have we learned in the past century? *International Journal of Behavioral Development, 24,* 129–141.

Verbeek, P., & de Waal, F. B. M. (2001). Peacemaking among preschool children. *Journal of Peace Psychology, 7,* 5–28.

Weaver, A., & de Waal, F. B. M. (2003). The mother-offspring relationship as a template in social development: Reconciliation in captive brown capuchins (*Cebus apella*). *Journal of Comparative Psychology, 117,* 101–110.

PART FIVE

Taking Restraint against Killing Seriously

23

The Evolution of Agonism

The Triumph of Restraint in Nonhuman and Human Primates

Douglas P. Fry and Anna Szala

As murders, rapes, genocide, riots, rebellions, and wars regularly make the headlines around the world, not surprisingly there is a wide-reaching presumption in both academia and on Main Street that evolution has molded human agonism toward killing and warring. Konner (2006, p. 1) reflects this view when he opines, "There is in human nature a natural tendency to violence and, additionally, to war." Evolutionary writings on aggression have consumed considerable ink discussing killing and warring as presumed adaptations (e.g., Buss, 1999, 2005; McDonald, Navarrete, & Van Vugt, 2012; Potts & Hayden, 2008; Pinker, 1997; Wrangham & Peterson, 1996). The famous proposition that "killers have more kids" (Chagnon, 1988) reflects the idea that killing has paid fitness dividends in the evolutionary past and consequently that lethal predilections have proliferated in the human gene pool.

In this chapter, we adopt an evolutionary perspective. We place human aggression in a phylogenetic context by considering the patterns of agonism not only in humans (focusing primarily on nomadic band societies) but also in other species, especially nonhuman primates. A cross-species perspective shows that intraspecific aggression among mammals in general and in nonhuman primates in particular is *not* characterized by lethal mayhem. We suggest that despite the obvious human *capacity* to make war, intraspecific agonism in humans actually reflects similar selection pressures as in other species—which might be expected given the consistency across mammalian orders of nonlethality as the pattern. In short, we argue that the standard story line about war and violence being evolutionary adaptations is wrong for a number of reasons. Such a view makes very little evolutionary sense (1) when considered in phylogenetic perspective, (2) when the patterns of agonism in an ancestral context are reconstructed using nomadic forager analogy, and (3) when, for a long-lived species, fitness costs and benefits of extreme or lethal aggression are considered vis-à-vis those of restrained agonism. We conclude that, as in other mammalian species, the key principle in the evolution of human aggression is, in a word, *restraint*. The species-typical pattern of agonism in humans IS the use of restraint, not an evolved proclivity toward homicide or warfare.

Natural and Artificial Environments

Natural selection acts upon traits (behavioral, anatomical, and physiological) in relationship to environmental conditions. Traits that are adaptive in one environment may not be adaptive in another. For example, a thick fur coat may be adaptive for a species living in a cold climate but maladaptive in a tropical setting. The environmental conditions under which a species has evolved and adapted via natural selection can be dubbed the *natural environment* (also called the *Environment of Evolutionary Adaptedness*, or EEA for short) in contrast to markedly variant environmental circumstances, which can be labeled *unnatural environments* (Symons, 1979). For ancestral humankind, a subsistence mode based on nomadic foraging was keyed to the natural environment that included, for example, numerous predators (Sussman, chapter 6). Given the truism that any phenotypic trait is a product of the complex and multifaceted interaction of genotype and environment over the development and life of an individual, then the species-typical behavioral traits should most regularly result within environmental conditions *natural* to that species, whereas behaviors witnessed in unnatural environments—again, conditions that differ markedly from those to which the species has adapted—*may* (or may not) vary from those regularly expressed in the natural environment (Bjorklund & Pellegrini, 2002; Symons, 1979).

As we examine human behavior, we should keep in mind, first, that *Homo sapiens* exhibits a great deal of behavioral flexibility, second, that most environmental conditions under which the species now lives are markedly different from the natural environment, or EEA, of the species, and therefore, third, that behaviors manifested in twenty-first century unnatural environments of various sorts may or may not reflect the behavioral adaptations that have evolved over many millennia in the natural EEA.

If a behavioral pattern tends to recur universally across human cultural and ecological environments, for example the use of language to communicate, a case can be made for the species-typicality of the behavior, or to use another way to express this, that such behavior is a relatively obligate or fixed adaptation (Fry, 2006; Williams, 1966). However, just because a behavior (for instance, watching television or going off to war) is widespread in the twenty-first century should not lead automatically to the claim that the behavior per se reflects an evolved adaptation (Fry, 2006; Williams, 1966). It is also necessary to consider whether televisions, computers, newspapers, *Durex*, or war—the latter even in its simplest forms—actually existed in the EEA, rather than *assuming* that behaviors often observed in a current unnatural environment, such as watching *NCIS*, surfing the Internet, reading this book, using condoms, or attempting to kill enemy combatants (not necessarily all at once) are in-and-of-themselves adaptations or simply manifestations of fortuitous effects in a behaviorally flexible species with a great capacity for learning, which now lives almost exclusively in evolutionary unnatural environments (Fry, 2006). Thus we must also take into consideration both the natural environment (the EEA) and an evolutionary evaluation of fitness costs and benefits of particular behaviors, rather than simply assuming that the prevalence of a trait in unnatural environments means that it is an evolutionary adaptation.

A careful study of nomadic foragers can provide insights into species-typical behavior under natural or near-natural environmental conditions (Bicchieri, 1972; Boehm, chapter 16, 1999; Fry, 2006, 2011; Marlowe, 2005, 2010). As Marlowe (2005, p. 65) points out, "Contemporary foragers are not living fossils, but because they are pre-agricultural they are the most relevant analogs for at least Late Pleistocene humans." Therefore, as we examine human agonism within the larger frameworks of nonhuman primate agonism and mammalian agonism, we will give weight to human data from nomadic forager societies—as a source of special insight into species-typical behavior within the natural environment—in comparison to behavioral data from societies and circumstances that are clearly unnatural (Narvaez, chapter 17). However, when the same behaviors observed among nomadic foragers in near-natural environmental settings also are widespread across more unnatural environments—e.g., reciprocal exchange, expressions of empathy, cooperation, reliance on language, and, we will argue, *restrained agonism*—then, in conjunction with a careful consideration of fitness consequences, an argument can be made that we are witnessing behavioral traits that have been *strongly selected* over the evolution of the species since they recur across not only natural but also a variety of unnatural environments.

Aggression as Merely One Kind of Agonism

The agonism concept encapsulates not only physical acts of aggression, but also a variety of competitive behaviors such as dominance and territorial displays, threats, and acts of spatial displacement. The observation that agonistic behavior is widespread in the animal kingdom suggests that it has evolved to fulfill survival and reproductive functions time and again. As Sussman (chapter 6) points out, predation and intraspecific aggression are distinct behavioral systems and involve different neurophysiology. Intraspecific agonism, including physical aggression, tends to be much less bloody than predatory aggression, and is rarely lethal in mammals. There are exceptions to this generalization, such as the special case of infanticide, documented in various mammalian species, but for the most part conspecific mammals do not attempt to kill one another (Enquist & Leimar, 1990; Fry, 1980; Fuentes, chapter 5; Hrdy, 1977; Kokko, chapter 3; Popp & DeVore, 1979). Occasionally, fatalities occur due to accidents (Huntingford & Turner, 1987, pp. 46; Nagel & Kummer, 1974, p. 161).

It is well documented that curtailed or limited aggression has been favored by natural selection in many different species (Fry, Schober & Björkqvist, 2010; Kokko, chapter 3; Maynard Smith, 1974; Maynard Smith & Price, 1973). There are, as we shall see, more

continuities than discontinuities between human agonism and typical mammalian agonistic patterns. In making this evolutionary argument, we develop a comparative model
of agonistic behavior based on restraint: *In nonhuman and human primates, as well as in
mammals generally, natural selection clearly has favored judiciously employed aggression over
escalated, severe forms of violence.*

Agonistic behaviors can be classified into categories of increasing severity: avoid-
ant responses, non-contact display-oriented behavior, restrained physical aggression, and
unrestrained physical aggression (Figure 23.1). Consideration of intraspecific competition
across species reveals a variety of ways that individuals minimize the risks of injury and
other costs of aggression (Fry et al., 2010). Animals practice avoidance and hence eliminate even the possibility of confrontations. Lions (*Panthera leo massaicus*), for example,
avoid interacting with members of other prides (Schaller, 1972), and chimpanzees (*Pan
troglodytes*) avoid periphery areas of their ranges (Stumpf, 2007; Wilson, Chapter 18).
Non-contact displays are employed in substitution for physical fighting between conspecific rivals. Among northern elephant seals (*Mirounga angustirostris*), threats out-number
physical aggression by about *sixty-to-one* (Le Boeuf, 1971). When physical altercations do
occur they usually consist of restrained "ritualized" aggression. For instance, competing
giraffes (*Giraffa camelopardalis*) batter each other with their necks and heads until one
gives up (Alcock, 2005).

As we shall see, unrestrained aggression (the last category in Figure 23.1) is exceedingly rare among mammals. An important implication of this fact is that any claim that
escalated, unrestrained fighting is species-typical in humans must be strongly justified,
rather than simply assumed a priori, as such a claim flies in the face of a well-documented
mammalian pattern of restrained agonism. The burden of scientific proof reasonably rests
with any claimants that human agonism in this regard constitutes an exception to a widespread mammalian pattern. The logical default proposition would be that human aggression fits within the typical mammalian framework of limited and controlled agonism,

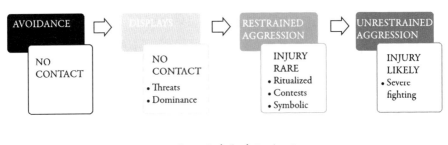

FIGURE 23.1 A model of increasing intraspecific agonism. Avoidance and Displays involve no physical contact
and hence no chance of injury. Restrained Aggression is the most typical form of physical contact aggression and
rarely results in injuries. Unrestrained Aggression (e.g., escalated fighting, severe fighting) occurs very rarely and
can result in severe injuries and death.

rather than constitutes a reversal of selection pressures to favor homicide or war. Humans, after all, are mammals, so in an evolutionary context, let's begin with the presumption that our agonism is typically mammalian—unless proven otherwise.

Evolutionary Costs and Benefits of Agonism

Aggression has both evolutionary costs and benefits. Fitness costs include physical injuries, mortality, harming one's own kin if they are opponents, losing friends and supporters through damaged relationships, draining time and energy away from other necessary pursuits such as obtaining food, finding mates, or being vigilant for predators, and being ostracized from the social group as a troublemaker (Arnold & Aureli, 2007; Archer & Huntingford, 1994, p. 10; Bernstein, 2007, 2008; Boehm, 1999; Hamilton, 1971; Jakobsson, Brick & Kullberg 1995; Riechert, 1998, p. 82). Although most intraspecific aggression in vertebrates is nonlethal (Alcock, 2005; Enquist & Leimar 1990; Hinde, 1974, p. 268; Kokko, 2008; Maynard Smith & Price, 1973), nonetheless, on occasion injuries sustained during a fight can result in death. Lethal conspecific aggression has been documented among such mammals as chimpanzees, white-faced capuchin monkeys (*Cebes capucinus*), spider monkeys (*Ateles geoffroyi yucatanensis*), hyenas (*Crocuta crocuta*), wolves (*Canis lupis*), and lions (Alcock, 2005; Huntingford & Turner, 1987; Gros-Louis, Perry, & Manson, 2003; Schaller, 1972; Valero, Schaffner, Vick, Aureli, & Ramos-Fernandez, 2006; White, Waller & Boose, chapter 19; Wilson, 1975, p. 246; Wilson, chapter 18; Wilson & Wrangham, 2003).

On the other hand, evolutionary benefits of aggression include obtaining resources such as food, territory, and mates, safeguarding one's offspring and oneself from attack, and achieving or maintaining dominance in a social hierarchy, which in turn correlates with access to resources or mates (Alcock, 2005; Archer, 1988; Jolly, 1985; Wilson, 1975, pp. 242–243). Aggression serves a variety of evolutionary functions that vary from species to species (Alcock, 2005; de Waal, 1989; Wilson, 1975). The overall conclusion is that aggression can be costly but it also can be beneficial to individual fitness (Fry, Schober, & Björkqvist, 2010).

Natural selection can be seen as shaping the aggressive behavior of a species over many generations to maximize benefits and minimize costs to fitness. Natural selection has performed these cost-benefit analyses and restraint seems to be the standard outcome. Out of 1,314 agonistic interactions between pairs of male caribou (*Rangifer tarandus*), 1,308 were ritualized sparring matches between animals who followed the rules compared to a mere six bouts of escalated fighting (Alcock, 2005). This is a ratio of one escalated fight to every 218 restrained ritualized contests. As other illustrations, Enquist and Leimar (1990) note that of 107 observed fights among red deer stags (*Cervus elaphus*) only two resulted in injury, and of 305 fights in antelopes called white-eared kobs (*Kobus kob leucotis*), only four resulted in serious injuries as the opponent's horns penetrated an opponent flanks or abdomen. The risks of injury in intraspecific aggression vary depending on the mammalian species in question, but serious injuries are the exceptions, not the rule, in conspecific physical fighting. And of course not every injury results in death.

Aside from injury risk, energy expenditure, and other costs, engaging in severe aggression also holds the potential for damaging valuable relationships. Some species of nonhuman primates value long-term relationships; having partners can help an individual to attain needed resources or deal with social situations (Preuschoft, Wang, Aureli, & de Waal, 2002; Silk, Alberts, & Altmann, 2009; Sussman, chapter 6). The valuable relationship hypothesis holds that taking care of others occurs if the relationship is beneficial (Arnold & Aureli, 2007; van Schaik & Aureli, 2000; Watts, 2006). Chimpanzees from Gombe National Park in Tanzania, for instance, form groups that hunt red colobus monkeys (*Colobus badius tephrosceles*), a valuable source of nutrition (Stanford, Jallis, Matama, & Goodall, 1994). Being in good relations also helps in forming alliances against rivals that could not be defeated or scared away on one's own; female chimpanzees from Budongo Forest form coalitions with one another if there is need for retaliating against male aggression (Newton-Fisher, 2006), and coalitions of female bonobos (*Pan paniscus*) keep the males in check (White, Waller, & Boose, chapter 19; see Figure 23.2).

A valuable relationship is worth caring for, not only in terms of restoring a damaged bond, but also for maintaining an existing one. Japanese macaques (*Macaca fuscata yakui*) groom mostly with their friends, so we may conclude that maintaining these relationships is useful (Majolo & Koyama, 2006). Relatedly, in order to restore a strained relationship, individuals sometimes reconcile. Reconciliation reduces the cost of aggression by repairing a strained relationship (Fraser, Stahl, & Aureli, 2010), and occurs more often when a

FIGURE 23.2   An example of social grooming in bonobos. Physical closeness, relaxed poses, and facial expressions indicate the lack of tension. (D. P. Fry photo collection).

relationship is valuable (Brosnan, chapter 20; Preuschoft, Wang, Aureli, & de Waal, 2002; Verbeek, chapter 4).

Evolutionary Mechanisms of Restraint

Certain mechanisms have evolved to promote the least costly yet effective forms of agonism in mammals and more generally in vertebrates. These mechanisms include (1) territorialism, (2) assessment prior to physical contact, (3) dominance relations, and (4) behavioral proclivities to "follow the rules" of restraint (such as not attempting to bite or gouge vulnerable parts of an opponent's body or ceasing an attack once an opponent signals submission or attempts to flee). These evolved mechanisms of restrained competition prevent individuals from expending unnecessary energy, taking foolhardy risks, or damaging valuable relationships when interacting agonistically with their peers.

In territorial species, once boundaries have been established, threats and fights markedly decrease among neighbors (Bernstein, 2007; Kokko, chapter 3, 2008). Additionally, in lieu of actually fighting, territories can be marked and defended via safe and efficient methods such as calls, songs, barks, scents, movements, and gestures. Some but not all nonhuman primate species are territorial (Fashing, 2007; Jolly, 1985). Humans living in nomadic foraging bands typically have home ranges rather than defended territorial boundaries, and social mechanisms exist that grant permission for resource use to neighbors, which suggests that territorial defense per se is not species-typical (Birdsell, 1971; Cashdan, 1983; Holmberg, 1969; Kelly, 1995; Marlowe, 2005, 2010, p. 267; Tonkinson, 2004; Wolf, 2001). For example, Siriono bands interact peacefully and do not claim exclusive territories. If hunters see signs that a different band is camped in the area, they abstain from hunting, thus respecting the rights of the first band to the game in the vicinity (Holmberg, 1969). Obviously, humans *can* be territorial, as reflected since the advent of the agricultural revolution in a plethora of historical examples, including the current-day partitioning of the globe into nation-states (an example of an unnatural environment very different from the EEA).

A second way of avoiding unnecessary fighting is by assessing one's own size, strength, health, age, weapon quality, number of allies, and any other relevant features relative to those of an opponent (Bernstein, 2007; Wilson, chapter 18). If pertinent, the outcome of past fights or dominance rank within an existing hierarchy also can be taken into consideration before engaging in combat (Kitchen, Cheney, & Seyfarth, 2005). The ability to accurately predict probable defeat or victory would seem to be favored by natural selection (Symons, 1978); Kokko (chapter 3) notes that animals tend to avoid a fight "when the likely outcome is clear from the start." Humans certainly have the same ability to predict an outcome and generally avoid taking on a notably larger or stronger opponent. Of the nomadic foraging Yahgan of Tierra del Fuego, Gusinde (1937, p. 887) describes: "A person will literally foam with rage. . . . Nevertheless, he can muster astonishing self-control when he realizes that he is too weak to stand against his opponent." However, nomadic band ethnographies suggest that supporters, the element of surprise, and weapons (such as poison-tipped arrows) can sometimes neutralize size and strength differences, so assessment of opponents within the natural environment of the EEA undoubtedly would have involved variables beyond simply size and strength comparisons (e.g., Balikci, 1970; Lee, 1979).

A third mechanism for reducing the costs of physical altercations is dominance. Dominance hierarchies within social groups greatly reduce fighting on a daily basis, as each individual knows its place relative to the other group members (Bernstein, 2007; Kokko, 2008; Preuschoft & van Schaik, 2000). Boehm (1999) proposes that nomadic foragers developed a reverse dominance hierarchy wherein the group as a whole banded together to control any rising bully (see also Narvaez, chapter 17).

Fourth, with rare exceptions, mammals tend to follow the rules of restraint rather than escalating to more risky types of fighting. Maynard Smith and Price (1973, p.15) describe how mule deer (*Odocoileus hemionus*) "fight furiously but harmlessly by crashing or pushing antlers against antlers, while they refrain from attacking when an opponent turns away, exposing the unprotected side of its body." Generally speaking, once an opponent submits or tries to flee, prolonging a struggle serves no useful purpose to the victor; to the contrary, failing to respect a loser's submission signals may lead to escalation, a greater chance of injury, and wasted time and energy for both contestants (Bernstein, 2007; Bernstein & Gordon, 1974; Popp & DeVore, 1979; Roscoe, 2007).

In social species, there are sets of rules prohibiting certain kinds of behavior and promoting other kinds, and this fosters social coexistence. Violating rules can lead to punishments, paybacks, or ostracism. Punishment helps in maintaining dominance relationships and ensures that an individual will be less likely to violate the rules in the future (Bekoff & Pierce, 2009). Bekoff (2011, p. 115) illustrates the importance of following the rules within the context of play, which would similarly apply to respecting the rituals of ritualized aggression: "When animals play, they are constantly working to understand and follow the rules and to communicate their intentions to play fairly. . . . Coyotes [*Canis latrans*] who do not play fair often leave their pack because they do not form strong social bonds. Such loners suffer higher mortality than those who remain with others." Shortly, we will consider some examples of human rule-following when discussing ritualized aggression.

The Triumph of Restraint in Nonhuman and Human Primates

The Overall Pattern

Sussman and Garber (2007) scoured primate field studies on nearly 60 different species in order to gain an idea of how prevalent agonistic behaviors actually are. They included as agonism "mild spats, displacements, threats, stares, and fighting"—hence noncontact as well as contact behavior (Sussman & Garber, 2007, p. 640). For four subgroups—diurnal prosimians, New World monkeys, Old World monkeys, and apes—the vast majority of all social interactions were affiliative and cooperative (e.g., food sharing, huddling together, and grooming), whereas agonism accounted for *less than one percent of all interactions*. When they calculated average rates of agonism per adult, the Old World monkeys averaged less than one act of agonism per day, New World monkeys averaged about half that amount, and apes (and prosimians) *less than one agonistic act per month*. The highest rate of agonism was attained by male yellow baboons (*Papio cynocephalus*), being about 11 times per week per individual. It would appear that the chest-beating, building-smashing, airplane-swatting, blonde-kidnapping King Kong (*Gorilla* spp.) provides about as accurate a picture of primate nature as Batman portrays bats, Mr. Ed speaks for horses, or Brian from *Family Guy* reflects actual canines. Nearly everyone has seen the nature documentaries or book passages and magazine articles about "warring" chimpanzees that have been observed in commando raids, attacking a lone individual from a neighboring group (Sussman, chapter 6; Verbeek, chapter 4; Wilson, chapter 18). But as Jane Goodall points out, "It is easy to get the impression that chimpanzees are more aggressive than they really are. In actuality, peaceful interactions are far more frequent that aggressive ones; mild threatening gestures are more common than vigorous ones; threats *per se* occur much more often than fights; and serious wounding fights are very rare compared to brief, relatively mild ones" (Goodall, 1986 quoted in Bekoff & Pierce, 2009, p. 4).

If we pause to consider how the human primate fits into this cross-species comparison of our taxonomic order, obviously there are individual and cultural differences across human societies, but, such variation aside, as among other primate species the vast majority of human social interactions are positive, not agonistic, and *years* can pass for many persons without them receiving or delivering a single act of physical aggression. Consider that the most serious form of intragroup agonism, homicide, is routinely counted in numbers of annual killings, not per 100, not per 1,000, not even per 10,000, but per 100,000 persons in a population. For Batek foragers, Semai horticulturalists, the Japanese, and the Danes, the homicide rate is likely less than 1 or 2 killing per 100,000, and it is for the nomadic Hadza foragers 6.6, for Poles around 3.5, for Finns about 5.0, for El Salvadorans or Guatemalans about 50, and as an extreme comparison, for Europe during World War II an estimated rate for all types of violent deaths is between 455 and 600 per 100,000 per year (Butovskaya, chapter 14; Endicott, chapter 12; Fry, 2006; Knauft, 2011; Malby, 2010; see also Kelly, chapter 9). Currently, an overall worldwide homicide rate for *Homo sapiens*, averaged across countries, is estimated at 7.6 per annum (Malby, 2010). The upshot is that homicide in *Homo sapiens* hardly could be considered a typical behavior, let alone a frequent one. Even during the World War II high for Europe that included all war-related killings along with domestic homicides, the annual rate was only about one-half of 1 percent of the population (Knauft, 2011; Sussman, chapter 6).

Looking across the Order Primates from baboons to gorillas or from lemurs to humans, rates of agonism are dwarfed by rates of affiliative, prosocial types of social interaction. Furthermore, agonism is not always physical. The key point is that across the primate species—human and nonhuman—agonism reflects self-restraint as a central principle; agonism is limited in a number of ways as furry and not-so-furry members of our Order demonstrate in daily life that "discretion *is* the better part of valor," that it *is* best to "live and let live," "let bygones be bygones," and if fighting to "play by the rules."

There are many methods for reducing the possibility of having a dangerous encounter with a member of the same species. We will now consider how the types of restraint depicted in the first three categories of Figure 23.1 are reflected in nonhuman and human primates. Then we will consider how the fourth category, escalated aggression, is the rare exception.

Avoidance

The first effective and commonly used strategy by primates is simply to avoid contact with others. Especially in situations where the fitness risks of social interaction are likely to be greater than gains, then avoidance is a viable course of action (Enquist & Leimar, 1983; Kitchen et al., 2005). Gorillas (*Gorilla gorilla gorilla*), to avoid meeting their fellows, may move out of the path taken by other gorillas (Cordoni & Palagi, 2007). Some species also use territorialism, which helps to prevent possibly harmful encounters. One way to communicate a territorial boundary is through scent marking, as used for example by white sifakas (*Propithecus verreauxi*), ring-tailed lemurs (*Lemur catta*), or capuchin monkeys (*Cebus capucinus*) (Jolly, 1985; Palagi & Dapporto, 2007). Alternatively, some species use spacing calls to achieve the same effect. The song of the Indri (*Indri indri*) is energy-efficient and allows them exclusive foraging use of nearly all their territory: "they merely sit and sing, and hardly ever have to do anything else" (Jolly, 1985, p. 143). Wilson (chapter 18) explains how the majority of intergroup interactions among chimpanzees consists of acoustic contacts only. When groups of black howler monkeys (*Alouatta caraya*) meet on the edges of their ranges, fighting occurs only 3 percent of the time and, more typically, encounters merely involve keeping an eye on the competition (56 percent) or engaging in howling contests (41 percent) (Garber & Kowalewski, 2011). Scent marking and vocalizations facilitate avoidance and hence any risk of physical aggression by sending a clear message to "Keep Out!"

Avoidance reflects restraint (Fry, 2006). To begin with nomadic band societies, foragers are famous for "voting with their feet" in response to conflict (e.g., Balikci, 1970, on the Netsilik; Endicott, chapter 12, on the Batek; Gardner, chapter 15, on South Indian foragers; Marlowe, 2010, on the Hadza and generally). For a sample of 21 nomadic forager societies in the Standard Cross-Cultural Sample (SCCS), Fry (2011) notes ethnographic evidence for intragroup *or* intergroup avoidance in 16 (76 percent) of the societies, and Boehm (chapter 16), who does not tally within group avoidance, reports 35 percent intergroup avoidance for his sample of 49 nomadic forager societies.

More generally, Fry (2006, pp. 23–26) points out that interpersonal avoidance and intergroup avoidance are widespread cross-culturally and probably occur in all societies, can be short-term or long-term, and in some societies involve a specific cultural term or concept. Some interesting cases of avoidance by enemy troops are noted by Hughbank and Grossman (chapter 25), wherein both sides showed restraint by ignoring each other's presence rather than engaging in a firefight: "small groups of American and German soldiers knowingly passed within a few feet of each other, yet never fired their weapons." During the Vietnam War, a small group of American Green Berets, alerted to the presence of enemy soldiers, jumped into the foliage along the side of a trail. As the Viet Cong soldiers passed by, one stopped to urinate and found himself eye-to-eye with a hiding American soldier. He gestured in fear so as to convey "let's pretend this didn't happen," and then quietly went on this way without a shot being fired by either side (James Welch, personal communication, March 17, 2012).

Noncontact Displays

Displays, a second type of agonism, reduce the risk of injury to nil because they involve no physical contact between adversaries. As a general rule, across species, noncontact threats and other noncontact displays (e.g., barking, howling, jumping wildly, chasing) vastly out number actual contact events (e.g., Nagel & Kummer, 1974; Poirier, 1974). Figure 23.3 shows a back-and-forth chase-retreat episode between Barbary macaques (*Macaca sylvanus*)

FIGURE 23.3 An example of noncontact agonism in Barbary macaques. Still photos extracted from this filmed episode of noncontact agonism between two captive-living Barbary macaques illustrate noncontact agonism. Back-and-forth, the two monkeys take turns advancing and retreating, often quite rapidly, without ever making physical contact. (D. P. Fry photo collection)

in which physical contact is never actually made. Furthermore, not all contact episodes involve actual fighting.

Out of more than 15,000 agonistic events (noncontact threats and chases plus unidirectional attacks and bidirectional fights) recorded for rhesus monkeys (*Macaca mulatta*), a trifling four-tenths of one percent consisted of mutual fighting (Symons, 1978, p. 166 reporting data collected by Southwick). For a variety of Old World monkey species, Nagel and Kummer (1974) summarize reported findings on noncontact versus contact agonism. The ratios of noncontact-to-contact agonism paint a fairly consistent picture: Noncontact agonism prevails and actual wounding is very rare. Here are four more examples (Nagel & Kummer, 1974: Table 1).

Rhesus monkeys: between-group episode ratio, 26 noncontact : 0 contact (zero wounds).

Chacma baboons (*Papio ursinus*): between-group episode ratio, 4 noncontact : 0 contact (zero wounds) and within-group episode ratio, 114 noncontact : 53 contact (including 20 biting; zero wounds).

Patas monkey (*Erythrocebus patas*): between-group episode ratio, 2 noncontact : 0 contact (zero wounds) and within-group episode ratio, 39 noncontact : 10 contact (including 2 biting; zero wounds).

Silver leaf-monkey (*Presbytis cristatus*): between-group episode ratio, 90 noncontact : 27 noncontact *or* contact (i.e., "chasing *or* fighting," including zero biting; zero wounds) and within-group episode ratio, 83 noncontact : 93 contact (including 2 biting; zero wounds).

Nonhuman primates show impressive variation in noncontact display behavior. Among hanuman langurs (*Semnopithecus entellus*, formally *Presbytis entellus*) intertroop aggression is usually based on facial threats, staring, and ground slapping (Hrdy, 1977). Orangutans (*Pongo pygmaeus*) engage in many different types of displays: lip-smacking, grunting, belching, tree-shaking, branch-breaking, vine-rattling, and howling (Rodman, 1979), and gorillas display with fixated stares, through postures and locomotion such as a rigid quadrupedal stance or walk, gestures such as chest beating, a tight-lipped facial expression, and vocalizations such as grunts, roars, and screams (Cordoni & Palagi, 2007; Palagi, Chiarugi, & Cordoni, 2008; Pitcairn, 1974).

Displays of dominance or submission—reflecting an individual's place on a social ladder—are another important device of peacekeeping and managing conflict (Thierry, 2000). Dominance can be displayed through an erect, stiff-legged posture, piloerection, staring at a subordinate, or charging at an opponent (Bernstein, 2007; Jolly, 1985; Rodman, 1979). Just as such nonviolent displays point out which individual is dominant, there also are special displays of submission. In the case of rhesus macaques and Japanese macaques (*Macaca fuscata*), subordinates retract their lips and expose their teeth in deference to individuals of high rank (Thierry, 2000). Facial expression, body posture, vocalization, physical withdrawal, and other indicators depending on species are used to communicate submission (Bernstein, 2007). Observations show that individuals with similar rank in a dominance hierarchy are more likely to display toward or fight with each other (Kitchen et al., 2005), whereas larger rank differentials usually result in submission or flight by the subordinate (Stevens & de Vries, 2007). Thus agonism tends to be minimal between individuals of markedly different ranks.

Clearly, developmental experience is crucial for learning how to get along in a hierarchical society, for as Bernstein (2008, p. 60; see also Kempes, Sterck, & Orobio de Castro, chapter 22) notes, monkeys that have been experimentally deprived of opportunities to interact with other members of their species, rather than exhibiting the typical restraint of monkeys reared under normal social conditions, "launch suicidal attacks against opponents who are clearly physically superior to them or, alternatively, may mount murderous attacks on opponents who are signaling submission and attempting to withdraw from the site of a contest." Verbeek (chapter 4) calls such uncommon agonistic behavior *species-atypical*. This severely aggressive, species-atypical behavior stems from these monkeys having been raised in a very unnatural environment—one without other monkeys!

Tonkinson (chapter 13) points out how much agonism among the nomadic foraging Mardu involved noncontact displays rather than actual acts of aggression. Ideally, disputes should be vented verbally as "protagonists broadcast their grievances and accusations publically, at high volume and with maximum menace, and satisfaction is gained from the drama of the confrontation." Fry (2006) observes that the human capacity for speech allows such verbal threat displays such as those described for the Mardu. Rivals among nomadic Yahgan foragers sometimes engage in "talk contests" as each attempts to outdo the other in a verbal repartee (Gusinde, 1937). The Netsilik and other Inuit groups of the Central Canadian Arctic are renowned for song contests as an alternative to fighting (e.g., Balikci, 1970).

Displays are not just for nomadic foragers. Noncontact agonistic display mechanisms are often used in other human societies. As illustrated by Evans Pim (chapter 26), song duels, for instance, are a widely employed yet much neglected restraint mechanism against physical fighting. And Roscoe (chapter 24) examines how social signals among the Yangoru Boiken of Papua New Guinea are analogous to threat displays and ritualized contests that are widespread among mammals. Roscoe (chapter 24) concludes that Yangoru Boiken "are able to evaluate who would win a fight to the death in the event of conflict without any individual or community having to incur the costs of an actual fight to the death." Hence displays allow disputants to achieve their ends, such as resource defense, without the risks inherent in physical confrontations.

Restrained Physical Aggression

Reflecting the broader mammalian pattern, restrained aggression among primates is the norm and reduces chances of injury or death, damage to valuable relationships, wasted time and energy, and other costs compared to unrestrained aggression (Bernstein, 2007; Poirier, 1974). Restrained aggression may occur after an assessment period (Bernstein,

2007). Gorillas engage in ritualized chasing and fleeing as one animal pursues a rapidly withdrawing peer (Cordoni & Palagi, 2007). Olive baboons (*Papio anubis*) generally adhere to "rules" about which parts of the body should and should not be bitten. They direct bites at areas covered by fur, which are locations less likely to be seriously harmed, compared to the abdomen or genitalia (Owens, 1975).

As among nonhuman primates, restrained human aggression can allow for the establishment of dominance or for access to resources with substantially less risk than through escalated fighting (Fry, 2005, 2006; Fry et al., 2010). Many but not all nomadic band societies have contests or duels wherein certain rules of restraint apply. For example, among the Netsilik Inuit, two competitors take turns hitting each other on the forehead or shoulders until one man gives up—and in this way the dispute is put to rest. The Waramanga of Australia have a fire ritual for settling disputes between two men; accompanied by several supporters, the opponents rush at each other with flaming torches, trying simultaneously to strike their adversaries and to ward off blows (Berndt, 1965). After a fire ritual, the dispute is considered resolved. Grievances between Siriono men of South America are often settled through wrestling matches (Holmberg, 1969). Rules do not allow punching or hitting, and opponents typically adhere to the rules. Homicide is almost unknown among the Siriono, suggesting that aggression rarely escalates beyond the restrained pattern of the wrestling matches (Holmberg, 1969). If a married Ingalik woman ran away with another man, her lover and her husband might wrestle for possession of the woman (Osgood, 1958). As reflected in the foregoing examples and other cases listed in Table 23.1, duels and contests can be viewed as conflict resolution mechanisms that reduce the chance of serious injuries (Hoebel, 1967, p. 92).

Before considering a couple of examples of restraint in evolutionary unnatural environments, it would be useful to highlight what nomadic forager analogy suggests about salient features of agonism within the natural environment of the EEA. First, most disputes are handled in nonviolent ways, for example, by simply separating, through verbal

TABLE 23.1 **Examples of Restrained Physical Fighting Events (e.g., Duels, Wrestling Contests, Ritualized Spear-Throwing/Dodging) Within Nomadic Forager Societies**

Society & Continent	Restrained Event	References
Netsilik Inuit, North American Arctic	Reciprocal blow-striking to head and shoulders	Balikci, 1970
Slavey, North America	Wrestling	Helm, 1956
Dogrib, North America	Wrestling	Helm, 1956
Ingalik, North America	Wrestling	Osgood, 1958, p. 204
Siriono, South America	Wrestling	Holmberg, 1969
Ona, South America	Wrestling	Gusinde, 1931
Yahgan, South America	Wrestling and mock group fighting	Gusinde, 1937
Ache, South America	Club fighting	Hill & Hurtado, 1996
Tiwi, Australia	Spear throwing and dodging	Goodale, 1971
Murngin, Australia	*Makarata* peacemaking duel	Warner, 1969
Waramanga, Australia	Fire Ritual: Fighting with firebrands	Berndt, 1965, pp. 181–182

harangues or song/talk contests, through discussion, or through group mediation, as in the Mardu's Big Meeting (Boehm, chapter 16; Fry, 2006, 2011; Gardner, chapter 15; Tonkinson, chapter 13). As we have just seen, some nomadic forager societies have ritualized contests or duels that may involve physical aggression but whose aim is to reduce the chance of serious injury or homicide. Second, most disputes originate between two individuals, not between groups, and most typically involve sexuality in some form or the seeking of revenge for a misdeed (Butovskaya, chapter 14; Fry, chapter 1; Fry, 2011; Hill, Hurtado, & Walker, 2007; Tonkinson, chapter 13).

Third, nomadic forager society is typically unwarlike (Fry, chapter 1, 2006, 2011). And in those cases where war is reported to take place, the nomadic forager involvement tends not to reflect conditions in the EEA but often involves pastoralists, farmers, ranchers, colonial powers, and so forth either directly or through the disruptive effects brought about by such populations, such as encroachment upon nomadic forager lands (see Birdsell, 1971; Hill et al., 2007; Haas & Piscetelli, chapter 10). Despite often repeated claims to the contrary (e.g., Bowles & Gintis, 2011; Ember, 1978; Pinker, 2011; Potts & Hayden, 2008; Wrangham & Peterson, 1996), numerous factors in nomadic band society actually dictate *against* the practice of war: Individuals have close relatives and friends in neighboring bands (whose membership changes from month-to-month through ongoing fission-and-fusion dynamics); residence is ambilocal or multilocal, meaning that male relatives will be spread across different groups rather than being concentrated in a single patrilocal group; lethal disputes, as mentioned, generally have very personal causes (e.g., sexual jealousies), not political ones, so, consequently, it is difficult to get others involved in dangerous situations over matters that do not involve them; there are no caches of stored food or other goods to plunder; no one possesses the authority to command other band members to fight; and population densities tend to be very low with adequate resources spread over wide areas (Fry 2006, 2011; Meggitt, 1965; Marlowe, 2005, 2010; Service, 1966). Given all these variables, it should not be surprising that the majority of nomadic forager societies in the SCCS (62 percent) lack warfare (Fry, 2006, chapter 1; see also Kelly, chapter 9). Marlowe (2010, p. 264) also concludes for a large sample of foragers that warfare was not very prevalent. Unfortunately for the current purpose, Boehm (chapter 16) combines homicide, feud, raid, and war under the combined category Intergroup Conflict, so we must await future analyses of his data to learn for his sample the relative proportions of these subtypes of lethal aggression (see Fry, chapter 1, for a discussion of the term "raid"). The overall conclusion, however, is clear: nomadic foragers as a whole are not very warlike and this suggests that warfare was rare in the EEA. This ethnographically derived reconstruction of a mostly warless EEA is backed up by archaeology that shows warfare to have originated repeatedly in different world regions *within the last 10,000 years*, that is, after the beginning of the agricultural revolution (Dye, chapter 8; Ferguson, chapters 7 & 11; Haas, 1996; Haas & Piscitelli, chapter 10; Keeley, 1996; Kelly, 2000). In sum, a consideration of extant nomadic forager societies corresponds with the worldwide archaeological evidence in suggesting a paucity of warring in the ancestral past older than 10,000 years ago.

Compared to the natural environment where warfare was an anomaly, if it occurred at all, nation states with their professional militaries, from the evolutionary point of view, constitute unnatural environments. The purpose of modern warfare is to kill the enemy. Obviously, humans as members of a flexible species are able to engage in military campaigns, fight battles, and slaughter their opponents in vast numbers. But is this actually species-atypical behavior manifested in unnatural environments that are extremely different from the conditions of the EEA? There is a difference between a behavioral capacity (for instance, doing a handstand) and an adaptation (walking bipedally). Assuming that war is an adaptation may be analogous in error to assuming that doing a handstand is a behavioral adaptation.

Interestingly, there is considerable evidence that the typical soldier must overcome a resistance to killing. We suggest that this restraint against killing other human beings is the result of strong selection pressures since it clearly manifests itself even under environmental conditions designed to encourage, promote, and reward killing during times of war. Hughbank and Grossman (chapter 25) consider this topic, so here we will only mention a couple of examples briefly.

One of the most intriguing bodies of evidence that even soldiers on the battlefield show restraint against killing other human beings despite their training and pressure to do so comes from an analysis of 27,574 Civil War muskets recovered from the battlefield at Gettysburg, Pennsylvania. Nearly 90 percent of the muskets were loaded. Additionally, about 12,000 (44 percent) of the weapons were loaded more than once with some 6,000 having between three-to-ten rounds packed into the unfired musket. Grossman (1995) observes that if soldiers were firing their weapons as soon as they had loaded them, only some 5 percent of the guns, not nearly 90 percent, would have been loaded, and certainly not loaded multiple times. Clearly, a huge number of soldiers were spending their time on the battlefield loading and reloading their guns rather than firing at enemy soldiers.

Research into weapon-firing rates was conducted during World War II by US Army historian Brigadier General S. L. A. Marshall. On the basis of extensive postcombat interviews with soldiers, Marshall concluded that only 15 to 25 percent of the men in battle fired their weapons at enemy soldiers (Marshall, 2000). The restraint phenomenon also is reflected in "dog fights" of World War II: less than 1 percent of US fighter pilots accounted for 30 to 40 percent of the enemy aircraft shot down, whereas the majority of combat pilots did not shoot down a single enemy plane (Grossman, 1995). General Marshall wrote that "the average and healthy individual . . . has such an inner and usually unrealized resistance towards killing a fellow man that he will not of his own volition take a life if it is possible to turn away from that responsibility" (Marshall, 2000, p. 79). As noted by de Waal in the Foreword to this volume, the resistance toward killing also is reflected in significant rates of PTSD and also depression, suicide, domestic violence, and other problems faced by war veterans, which suggests that participating in killing can be psychologically very costly and traumatic.

Unrestrained Physical Aggression

Only rarely does nonhuman primate agonism result in death. For example, Nagel and Kummer (1974) conclude, "Inflicting damage (wounds) or even killing is so rare in Old World monkeys under natural conditions that it may be regarded as an accident." During fighting, the most vulnerable parts of the body are injured less frequently, again suggesting the overall pattern of restrained aggression (Bernstein, 2007). And across species of primates, restrained aggression outnumbers unrestrained aggression many times over.

Excluding for the moment primate infanticide, only humans and chimpanzees appear to premeditatedly kill conspecifics. In neither species is lethal aggression frequent, nor does unrestrained aggression predominate, but periodic lethal aggression does occur. Fry et al. (2010) have argued that in the EEA of humans, lethal aggression would have been selected against for three reasons. Besides the overall principle (with overwhelming evidence to support it) that natural selection favors restrained intraspecific aggression in mammalian species, a second selection pressure that has suppressed unrestrained aggression may be that humans in nomadic forager societies interact a great deal with relatives, and killing a relative is not generally fitness enhancing (Hamilton, 1964). Finally, Fry et al. (2010) hypothesize that a third selection pressure against unrestrained aggression may be uniquely human (see Fuentes, chapter 5). In many nomadic forager societies, there exists a tendency for a close family member of a homicide victim to avenge the death of their relative by disposing of the killer:

> We find no such cases of revenge homicide among other animals. This means that killers in nomadic forager society often sign their own death warrant by committing a homicide, and given that the nomadic band social organization is the social type under which humans evolved, the fitness ramifications favoring nonkilling may be significant. In other words, the tendency for family members to avenge killings may constitute a powerful supplementary evolutionary selective force against intraspecific killing in humans in addition to the two previously discussed factors. (Fry et al., 2010, p. 119)

As a Ju/'hoansi forager pointed out, "hunting men is what gets you killed" (Lee, 1979, p. 391). The execution of killers and especially recidivist killers is widely reported in the ethnographic literature on nomadic foragers (Boehm, 1999; Fry, 2006; 2011; Fry et al., 2010; Hoebel, 1967). Turning to chimpanzees as another exception to the principle of restraint against lethal aggression, chimpanzees have been observed to kill in captivity and in the wild (Verbeek, chapter 4; White et al., chapter 19; Wilson, chapter 18; Wrangham & Peterson, 1996). The jury is still out as to whether intergroup killings in the wild represent species-typical or species-atypical aggression. Some researchers such as Wilson (chapter 18) propose that intergroup patrols, raids, and killings represent adaptations for gaining access to more territory and reproductive females. By contrast, Ferguson (2011) and Sussman (chapter 6) argue that killing in chimpanzees can be traced to human influences broadly conceived to include not only food provisioning by researchers, which is known to increase aggression, but also the effects of habitat loss, tourism, poaching, epidemics, and so on.

Infanticide occurs in some mammalian species including primates, and as an exception to the restraint principle deserves comment (Angst & Thommen, 1977; Fry, 1980; Huntingford & Turner, 1987; Hrdy, 1977). Conditions under which infanticide in primates has been practiced include when a new male takes over a harem of females or when a new male becomes dominant in a multi-male group. In an evolutionary cost/benefit analysis, infants can be killed by a male with relatively low risk of injury but with high fitness dividends because females return to estrus and can bear the killer's offspring sooner than had they continued to nurse infants fathered by a previous male. Hence, infanticide by males in some species can be seen as a special case where restraint against killing conspecifics has been countermanded by a different type of selection pressure (Fry, 1980; Hrdy, 1977).

Finally, in contrast to mammals, some arthropod females mate only once or just a few times in a lifetime. Two males may fight to the bitter end for this all-or-nothing opportunity to pass along their genes to the next generation (Enquist & Leimar, 1990; Kokko, chapter 3). But such all-or-nothing or "desperado" strategies are rare among mammals. With their longer reproductive life spans that present multiple opportunities for mating and reproduction, mammals generally adopt a restrained "live to fight another day" approach to competition, as we have discussed. These aforementioned cases are exceptions to the predominate pattern of restraint (Barash, chapter 2; Kokko, chapter 3).

Conclusion

In summary, research shows that when it comes down to contact agonism between conspecifics, *restrained, non-lethal* aggression, in contrast to more risky escalated combat, has evolved as the predominant pattern in mammals and many other species (Alcock, 2005; Archer & Huntingford, 1994; Bernstein, 2007; Bernstein & Gordon, 1974; Fry et al., 2010; Hinde, 1974, p. 269; Kokko, 2008, p. 49; Riechert, 1998, p. 65). Natural selection favors non-lethality among conspecifics. "If aggression is elicited, then it must be limited, controlled, and regulated in such a way that it terminates with minimal risk of injuries," explains Bernstein (2008, p. 59). The prevalence across mammalian species of displays instead of contact aggression and ritualized tournaments instead of "total war" suggest that restraint is a more successful evolutionary strategy than engaging in unbridled aggression.

Our approach in this chapter has been both *evolutionary*, as we considered fitness costs and benefits, and *novel*, as we argued that restraint is a guiding principle in humans. The usual focus when considering humans has been on how killing and warring have presumably evolved as adaptations (Konner, 2006; McDonald et al., 2012; Pinker, 1997; Wilson, chapter 18). We propose instead that conspecific killing in humans is species-atypical behavior, the exception not the rule, and that neither an evolutionary cost/benefit analysis nor an examination of the data support the assertion that intergroup killing, per se, is an adaptation (Fry, chapter 1, 2006; Fry et al., 2010).

We have contextualized human agonism in four ways: (1) within the broader mammalian realm, (2) within the Order Primates more specifically (3) with data on nomadic forager societies (and a few other cultural contexts as well), and (4) with reference to the worldwide archaeological record. The first two contexts clearly show that lethal fighting constitutes an exception to the normal expression of agonism, suggesting that natural selection, as an overarching pattern, tends *not* to favor lethal aggression between conspecifics. The key human nature question is: To what extent does *Homo sapiens* also reflect this widespread principle of restraint? The picture that emerges from a careful consideration of extant nomadic forager data (see also Fry, chapter 1) is that contrary to widespread presumptions, there are numerous recurring features of nomadic forager society that (1) correspond with the principle of restraint, and (2) are not conducive to warfare in this natural or near-natural environment. Correspondingly, there is a paucity of archaeological evidence for warfare in the Pleistocene, and there are a number of well-documented sequences that show the beginning of warfare from previous warless conditions, within the time frame of the last 10,000 years (see Part II). The fact that warfare occurs periodically in very recent millennia and today—that is, in unnatural evolutionary environments—is not evidence in and of itself for an adaptation; the behavior in question must also have been present in the EEA to be considered for adaptation status (for further discussion see Fry, chapter 1; Fry, 2006, pp. 217–241).

As in other species, most agonism in humans occurs without any physical contact. With language available, a plethora of possibilities has been devised to deal with conflicts and competition that minimize risks to life and limb. For example, humans regularly just walk away or bite their tongues; verbally reprimand, insult, threaten or argue; negotiate, mediate, arbitrate or go to court; punch, wrestle, or duel; and only very occasionally kill. In other words, the percentage of grievances, disputes, and rivalries that actually end with one or more corpses is miniscule. Restraint generally prevails. In humans, the fact that even the highest recorded homicide rates are still some fraction of one percent of the population shows that killing in humans is the rare exception, not the rule.

Restrained physical aggression in humans, as among mammals in general, results in less risk to the rivals than all-out fighting. Thus restrained aggression in humans is less risky for the participants than unbridled aggression with its many costs including energy expenditure, potential damage to valuable relationships, chance of injury, expulsion from the social group, susceptibility to predation, distraction from mating or securing food, and so forth, activities which may include, ultimately, a lowering of fitness (Fry 2006). Fry et al. (2010) go one step further to propose the operation in the EEA of an additional uniquely human selection pressure against lethal aggression: The tendency in the natural environment of the nomadic forager band is for the family members of a homicide victim to seek lethal retribution against the killer of their loved one. "Hunting men is what gets you killed" (Lee, 1979, p. 391). An evolutionary model that gives restraint a central place accords better with observed facts and evidence than does a model that presumes a priori that killing and warfare are adaptations.

Acknowledgments

Some of the data reported in this chapter were collected as part of a research project funded by the National Science Foundation (NSF grant number 03-13670) to Douglas P. Fry, and this support from NSF is gratefully acknowledged. Anna Szala expresses her gratitude to Kaj Björkqvist, Åbo Akademi University, and to the Max Planck Institute for Evolutionary Anthropology.

References

Angst, W., & Thommen, D. (1977). New data and discussion of infant killing in Old World monkeys and apes. *Folia Primatologia, 27*, 198–129.

Alcock, J. (2005). *Animal behavior: An evolutionary approach* (8th ed.). Sunderland, MA: Sinauer.

Archer, J. (1988). *The behavioural biology of aggression*. Cambridge: Cambridge University Press.

Archer, J., & Huntingford, F. (1994). Game theory models and escalation of animal fighting. In M. Potegal & J. Knutson (Eds.), *The dynamics of aggression: Biological and social processes in dyads and groups* (pp. 3–31). Hillsdale, NJ: Erlbaum.

Arnold, K., & Aureli, F. (2007). Conflict reconciliation. In Campbell, C., Fuentes, A., MacKinnon, K. C., Panger, M., & Bearder, S. (Eds.), *Primates in perspective* (pp. 592–608). New York: Oxford University Press.

Balikci, Asen (1970) *The Netsilik Eskimo*. Garden City, NY: The Natural History Press.

Berndt, R. (1965). Law and order in Aboriginal Australia. In R. M. Berndt & C. H. Berndt (Eds.), *Aboriginal man in Australia: Essays in honour of Emeritus Professor A. P. Elkin* (pp. 167–206). London: Angus & Robertson.

Bernstein, Irwin (2007). Social mechanisms in the control of primate aggression. In C. Campbell, A. Fuentes, K. MacKinnon, M. Panger, and S. Bearder (Eds.), *Primates in Perspective* (pp. 562–571). New York: Oxford University Press.

Bekoff, M. (2011). Cooperation and the evolution of social living: Moving beyond the constraints and implications of misleading dogma. In R. W. Sussman & C. R. Cloninger (Eds.), *Origins of altruism and cooperation* (pp. 111–119). New York: Springer.

Bekoff, M., & Pierce, J. (2009). *Wild justice: The moral lives of animals*. Chicago, IL: University of Chicago Press.

Berndt, R. (1965). Law and order in Aboriginal Australia. In R. M. Berndt & C. H. Berndt (Eds.), *Aboriginal man in Australia: Essays in honour of Emeritus Professor A. P. Elkin* (pp. 167–206). London: Angus & Robertson.

Bernstein, I. S. (2007). Social mechanisms in the control of primate aggression. In C. Campbell, Fuentes, K. MacKinnon, M. Panger, & S. Beader (Eds.), *Primates in perspective* (pp. 562–571). New York: Oxford University Press.

Bernstein, I. S. (2008). Animal behavioral studies: Primates. In L. Kurtz (Ed.-in-Chief), *Encyclopedia of violence, peace, and conflict, vol. 1* (2nd ed.) (pp. 56–63). New York: Elsevier/Academic Press.

Bernstein, I., & Gordon, T. (1974). The function of aggression in primate societies. *American Scientist, 62*, 304–311.

Bicchieri, M. (Ed.) (1972). *Hunters and gatherers today*. Prospect Heights, IL: Waveland.

Birdsell, J. (1971). Australia: Ecology, spacing mechanisms and adaptive behaviour in aboriginal land tenure. In R. Crocombe (Ed.) *Land tenure in the Pacific* (pp. 334–361). New York: Oxford University Press.

Bjorklund, D., & Pellegrini, A. (2002). *The origin of human nature: Evolutionary developmental psychology.* Washington DC: American Psychological Association.

Boehm, C. (1999). *Hierarchy in the forest: The evolution of egalitarian behavior.* Cambridge: Harvard University Press.

Bowles, S., & Gintis, H. (2011). *A cooperative species: Human reciprocity and its evolution.* Princeton: Princeton University Press.

Buss, D. (1999). *Evolutionary psychology: The new science of the mind.* Boston: Allyn & Bacon.

Buss, D. (2005). *The murderer next door: Why the mind is designed to kill.* New York: Penguin.

Cashdan, E. (1983). Territoriality among human foragers: Ecological models and an application to four Bushman groups. *Current Anthropology, 24,* 47–66.

Chagnon, N. (1988). Life histories, blood revenge, and warfare in a tribal population. *Science, 239,* 985–992.

Cordoni, G., & Palagi, E. (2007). Response of captive lowland gorillas (*Gorilla gorilla gorilla*) to different housing conditions: Testing the aggression-density and coping models. *Journal of Comparative Psychology, 121*(2), 171–180.

de Waal, F. (1989). *Peacemaking among primates.* Cambridge: Harvard University Press.

Ember, C. (1978). Myths about hunter-gatherers. *Ethnology, 17,* 439–448.

Enquist, M., & Leimar, O. (1983). Evolution of fighting behaviour: Decision rules and assessment of relative strength. *Journal of Theoretical Biology, 102,* 387–410.

Enquist, M., & Leimar, O. (1990). The evolution of fatal fighting. *Animal Behaviour, 39,* 1–9.

Fashing, P. (2007). African colobine monkeys: Patterns of between-group interaction. In Campbell, C., Fuentes, A., MacKinnon, K. C., Panger, M., & Bearder, S. (Eds.), *Primates in perspective* (pp. 201–224). New York: Oxford University Press.

Ferguson, R. B. (2011). Born to live: Challenging killer myths. In R. W. Sussman & C. R. Cloninger (Eds.), *Origins of altruism and cooperation* (pp. 249–270). New York: Springer.

Fraser, O. N., Stahl, D., & Aureli, F. (2010). The function and determinants of reconciliation in *Pan troglodytes. International Journal of Primatology, 31,* 39–57.

Fry, D. P. (1980). The evolution of aggression and the level of selection controversy. *Aggressive Behavior, 6,* 69–89.

Fry, D. P. (2005). Rough-and-tumble social play in children. In A. Pellegrini & P. K. Smith (Eds.), *The nature of play: Great apes and humans.* New York: Guilford.

Fry, D. P. (2006). *The human potential for peace: An anthropological challenge to assumptions about war and violence.* New York: Oxford University Press.

Fry, D. P. (2011). Human nature: The nomadic forager model. In R. W. Sussman & C. R. Cloninger (Eds.), *Origins of altruism and cooperation* (pp. 227–247). New York: Springer.

Fry, D. P., Schober, G., & Björkqvist, K. (2010). Nonkilling as an evolutionary adaptation. In J. Evans Pim (Ed.), *Nonkilling societies* (pp. 101–128). Honolulu: Center for Global Nonkilling.

Garber, P. A., & Kowalewski, M. (2011). Collective action and male affiliation in howler monkeys. In R. W. Sussman & C. R. Cloninger (Eds.), *Origins of altruism and cooperation* (pp. 145–165). New York: Springer.

Goodale, J. (1971). *Tiwi wives: A study of the women of Melville Island, North Australia.* Prospect Heights, IL: Waveland.

Gros-Louis, J., Perry, S., & Manson, J. (2003). Violent coalitionary attacks and intraspecies killing in wild white-faced capuchin monkeys (*Cebus Capucinus*). *Primates, 44,* 341–346.

Grossman, D. (1995). *On killing: The psychological cost of learning to kill in war and society.* Boston: Little Brown.

Gusinde, M. (1931). *The Fireland Indians, volume 1: The Selk'nam, on the life and thought of a hunting people of the Great Island of Tierra del Fuego.* In the electronic Human Relations Area Files, Ona, Doc. 1. New Haven, CT: HRAF.

Gusinde, M. (1937). *The Yahgan: The life and thought of the water nomads of Cape Horn* (F. Schütze, trans.). In the electronic Human Relations Area Files, Yahgan, Doc. 1. New Haven, CT: HRAF.

Haas, J. (1996). War. In D. Levinson & M. Ember (Eds.), *Encyclopedia of cultural anthropology, volume 4,* (pp. 1357–1361). New York: Henry Holt.

Hamilton, W. D. (1964). The genetical evolution of social behaviour, II. *Journal of Theoretical Biology, 7,* 17–52.

Hamilton, W. D. (1971). Selection of selfish and altruistic behavior in some extreme models. In J. F. Eisenberg & W. S. Dillon (Eds.), *Man and beast: Comparative social behavior*. Washington, DC: Smithsonian.

Helm, J. (1956). Leadership among the Northeastern Athabascans. *Anthropologica, 2,* 131–163.

Hill, K., & Hurtado, A. M. (1996). *Ache life history: The ecology and demography of a foraging people*. New York: Aldine de Gruyter.

Hill, K., Hurtado, A. M., & Walker, R. S. (2007). High adult mortality among Hiwi hunter-gatherers: Implications for human evolution. *Journal of Human Evolution, 52,* 443–454.

Hinde, R. (1974). *Biological bases of human social behaviour*. New York: McGraw-Hill.

Hoebel, E. A. (1967). *The law of primitive man: A study in comparative legal dynamics*. Cambridge: Harvard University Press.

Holmberg, A. (1969) *Nomads of the long bow: The Siriono of Eastern Bolivia*. New York: American Museum of Natural History. Originally published in 1950.

Hrdy, S. B. (1977). *The langurs of Abu: Female and male strategies of reproduction*. Cambridge: Harvard University Press.

Huntingford, F., & Turner, A. (1987). *Animal conflict*. London: Chapman and Hall.

Jakobsson, S., Brick, O., Kullberg, C. (1995). Escalated fighting behaviour incurs increased predation risk. *Animal Behaviour, 49,* 235–239.

Jolly, A. (1985). *The evolution of primate behavior*. New York: Macmillan Publishing.

Keeley, L. (1996). *War before civilization: The myth of the peaceful savage*. New York: Oxford University Press.

Kelly, R. C. (2000). *Warless societies and the origin of war*. Ann Arbor: University of Michigan Press.

Kelly, R. L. (1995). *The foraging spectrum: Diversity in hunter-gatherer lifeways*. Washington, DC: Smithsonian.

Kitchen, D. M., Cheney, D. L., & Seyfarth, R. M. (2005). Contextual factors mediating contests between male chacma baboons in Botswana: Effects of food, friends and females. *International Journal of Primatology, 26*(1), 105–125.

Knauft, B. (2011). Violence reduction among the Gebusi of Papua New Guinea—And across humanity. In R. W. Sussman & C. R. Cloninger (Eds.), *Origins of altruism and cooperation* (pp. 203–225). New York: Springer.

Kokko, H. (2008). Animal behavioral studies: Non-primates. In L. Kurtz (Ed.-in-Chief), *Encyclopedia of violence, peace, and conflict, vol. 1* (2nd ed.) (pp. 47–56). New York: Elsevier/Academic Press.

Konner, M. (2006). Human nature, ethnic violence, and war. In M. Fitzduff & C. E. Stout (Eds.), *The psychology of resolving global conflicts: From war to peace, volume 1: Nature versus Nurture* (pp. 1–39). Westport, CT: Praeger Security International.

Le Boeuf, B. J. (1971). The aggression of the breeding bulls. *Natural History, 80,* 83–94.

Lee, R. B. (1979). *The !Kung San: Men, women, and work in a foraging community*. Cambridge: Cambridge University Press.

McDonald, M., Navarrete, C., & Van Vugt, M. (2012). Evolution and the psychology of intergroup conflict: The male warrior hypothesis. *Philosophical Transactions of the Royal Society, B, 367,* 670–679.

Majolo, B., & Koyama, N. (2006). Seasonal effects on reconciliation in *Macaca fuscata yakui*. *International Journal of Primatology, 27*(5), 1383–1397.

Malby, S. (2010). Homicide. In S. Harrendorf, M. Heiskanen, & S. Malby (Eds.), *International statistics on crime and justice*, HEUNI Publication Series No. 64. (pp. 7–19). Helsinki: European Institute for Crime Prevention and Control.

Marlowe, F. (2005). Hunter-gatherers and human evolution. *Evolutionary Anthropology, 14,* 54–67.

Marlowe, F. (2010). *The Hadza hunter-gatherers of Tanzania*. Berkeley: University of California Press.

Marshall, S. L. A. (2000). *Men against fire: The problem of battle command*. Norman: University of Oklahoma Press. Originally published in 1947.

Maynard Smith, J. (1974). The theory of games and the evolution of animal conflicts. *Journal of Theoretical Biology, 47,* 209–221.

Maynard Smith, J., & Price, G. R. (1973). The logic of animal conflict. *Nature, 246,* 15–18.

Meggitt, M. (1965). *Desert people: A study of the Walbiri Aborigines of Central Australia*. Chicago: University of Chicago Press.

Nagel, U., & Kummer, H. (1974). Variation in Cercopithecoid aggressive behavior. In R. Holloway (Ed.), *Primate aggression, territoriality, and xenophobia: A comparative perspective* (pp. 159–184).

Newton-Fisher, N. E. (2006). Female coalitions against male aggression in wild chimpanzees of the Budongo Forest. *International Journal of Primatology, 27*(6), 1589–1599.

Osgood, C. (1958) Ingalik social culture. *Yale University Publications in Anthropology, 53*, 1–289.

Owens, N. W. (1975). A comparison of aggressive play and aggression in free-living baboons, *Papio Anubis. Animal Behaviour, 23*, 757–765.

Palagi, E., Chiarugi, E., & Cordoni, G. (2008). Peaceful post-conflict interactions between aggressors and bystanders in captive lowland gorillas (*Gorilla gorilla gorilla*). *American Journal of Primatology, 70*, 949–955.

Palagi, E., & Dapporto, L. (2007). Females do it better: Individual recognition experiments reveal sexual dimorphism in *Lemut catta* (Linnaeus 1758) olfactory motivation and territorial defence. *Journal of Experimental Biology, 210*, 2700–2705.

Pinker, Steven (1997). *How the mind works*. New York: Norton.

Pinker, Steven (2011). *The better angels of our nature*. New York: Viking.

Poirier, F. E. (1974). Colobine aggression: A review. In Holloway, R. L. (Ed.), *Primate aggression, territoriality, and xenophobia* (pp. 123–157). New York: Academic Press.

Popp, J., & DeVore, I. (1979). Aggressive competition and social dominance theory: Synopsis. In D. Hamburg & E. McCown (Eds.), *The great apes* (pp. 316–338). Menlo Park, CA: The Benjamin/Cummings.

Potts, M., & Hayden, T. (2008). *Sex and war: How biology explains warfare and terrorism and offers a path to a safer world*. Dallas, TX: Ben Bella.

Preuschoft, S., & van Schaik, C. (2000). Dominance and communication: Conflict management in various social settings. In F. Aureli & F. de Waal (Eds.), *Natural conflict resolution* (pp. 77–105). Berkeley: University of California Press.

Preuschoft, A., Wang, X., Aureli, F., & de Waal, F. B. M. (2002). Reconciliation in captive chimpanzees: A reevaluation with controlled methods. *International Journal of Primatology, 23*(1), 29–50.

Riechert, S. (1998). Game theory and animal contests. In L. Dugatkin & H. Reeve (Eds.), *Game theory and animal behavior* (pp. 64–93). New York: Oxford University Press.

Rodman, P. (1979). Individual activity patterns and the solitary nature of orangutans. In D. Hamburg & E. McCown (Eds.), *The great apes* (pp. 235–255). Menlo Park, CA: Benjamin/Cummings.

Roscoe, P. (2007) Intelligence, coalitional killing, and the antecedents of war. *American Anthropologist, 109*, 485–495.

Schaller, G. (1972). *The Serengeti lion*. Chicago: University of Chicago Press.

Service, E. R. (1966). *The hunters*. Englewood Cliffs, NJ: Prentice-Hall.

Silk, J., Beehner, J., Bergman, T., Crockford, C., Engh, A., Moscovice, L., ... Cheney, D. (2009). The benefits of social capital: Close social bonds among female baboons enhance offspring survival. *Proceedings of the Royal Society B, 276*, 3099–3104.

Stanford, C. B., Jallis, J., Matama, H., & Goodall, J. (1994). Patterns of predation by chimpanzees on red colobus monkeys in gombe national park. *American Journal of Physical Anthropology, 94*(2), 213–228.

Stevens, J. M. G., & de Vries, H. (2007). Sex differences in the steepness of dominance hierarchies in captive bonobo group. *International Journal of Primatology, 28*, 1417–1430.

Stumpf, R. (2007). Chimpanzees and bonobos: Diversity within and between species. In Campbell, C., Fuentes, A., MacKinnon, K. C., Panger, M., & Bearder, S. (Eds.), *Primates in perspective* (pp. 321–344). New York: Oxford University Press.

Sussman, R. W., & Garber, P. (2007). Cooperation and competition in primate social interaction. In Campbell, C., Fuentes, A., MacKinnon, K. C., Panger, M., & Bearder, S. (Eds.), *Primates in perspective* (pp.636–651). New York: Oxford University Press.

Symons, D. (1978). *Play and aggression: A study of rhesus monkeys*. New York: Columbia University Press.

Symons, D. (1979) *The Evolution of Human Sexuality*. New York: Oxford University Press.

Thierry, B. (2000). Covariation of conflict management patterns across macaque species. In Aureli, F., & de Waal, F. B. M. (Eds.), *Natural conflict resolution* (pp. 106–128). Berkeley: University of California Press.

Tonkinson, R. (2004). Resolving conflict within the law: The Mardu Aborigines of Australia. In G. Kemp and D. P. Fry (Eds.), *Keeping the peace: Conflict resolution and peaceful societies around the world* (pp. 89–104). New York: Routledge.

Valero, A., Schaffner, C., Vick, L., Aureli, F., & Ramos-Fernandez, G. (2006). Intragroup lethal aggression in wild spider monkeys. *American Journal of Primatology, 68*, 732–737.

van Schaik, C. P., & Aureli, F. (2000). The natural history of valuable relationships in primates. In F. Aureli & F. B. M. de Waal (Eds.), *Natural conflict resolution* (pp. 307–333). Berkeley: University of California Press.

Warner, W. L. (1969). *A black civilization: A social study of an Australian tribe*. Gloucester, MA: Peter Smith. Originally published in 1937.

Watts, D. P. (2006). Conflict resolution in chimpanzees and the valuable-relationships hypothesis. *International Journal of Primatology, 27*(5), 1337–1364.

Williams, G. (1966). *Adaptation and natural selection: A critique of some current evolutionary thought.* Princeton: Princeton University Press.

Wilson, E. O. (1975) *Sociobiology: The new synthesis.* Cambridge: Harvard University Press.

Wilson, M., & Wrangham, R. (2003). Intergroup relations in chimpanzees. *Annual Review of Anthropology, 32,* 363–392.

Wolf, E. (2001). Cycles of violence: The anthropology of war and peace. In D. Barash (Ed.) *Understanding violence* (pp. 192–199). Boston: Allyn and Bacon.

Wrangham, R., & Peterson, D. (1996). *Demonic males: Apes and the origin of human violence.* Boston: Houghton Mifflin.

24

Social Signaling, Conflict Management, and the Construction of Peace

PAUL ROSCOE

Introduction

There are some singular oddities about the way anthropology approaches war and peace. For one thing, we phrase the issue in binary terms, as though communities are either at war or at peace—either "on" or "off." This is really not the case: even when they are at war, communities are also always at peace. What I mean by this rather cryptic statement is that political communities, the units that wage war, are spheres of peace, units whose members somehow or another contrive to remain more or less at peace with one another on an ongoing basis. War can and does periodically break out between political communities— different spheres of peace—but even at war, they remain internally peaceful; indeed, their internal unity typically increases, peace being aggressively asserted in service of the common defense. Commonly, moreover, this "sphere of peace" extends to neighboring polities: most polities maintain "alliances"—relations of peace—with other nearby polities, albeit that these relations are more fragile and contingent than those within a polity. And yet, when we come to study peace, we usually focus on where it potentially can or does break down—in the interstices between these spheres of peace, the frontiers across which states of war (or cold war) prevail. Certainly, this is an important realm of analysis, but we should perhaps divert more attention to understanding these spheres of peace—polities and alliances of polities—where humans have manifestly succeeded in constructing it.

A second imbalance in the anthropological approach to peace is to focus on its *culture*, in the narrow sense of this term. We look to peace as the product of a mentalist state—a system of "values, attitudes, socialization practices, and conflict resolution procedures that emphasize nonviolent approaches to social tension" (Fry, 2006, p. 57; see also Bonta 1996, p. 405; Sponsel, 1996, p. 98). Again, there is nothing at all wrong with this approach, but as the foregoing paragraph implies, peace is also a political product, a function of whatever collective interests motivate the construction of polities and alliances of polities. Even for the small-scale communities that existed at the beginning of the Holocene, these spheres of enduring (or more evanescent) peace were a triumph of social construction. Nowadays, when nation-states cover large swathes of the globe, embracing millions upon millions of people, their existence is little short of remarkable: if anything underscores the human potential for peace (Fry, 2006), it is surely these "imagined communities" (Anderson, 1991). If we are to further an understanding of peace, it would be useful to understand its political production.

In this paper, I will address the political dimensions of peace. What are the processes that generate and maintain the peace within every political community? And what are the processes—economic, diplomatic/political, cultural, ideological—that maintain peace between allied communities (or even, for that matter, between communities linked in cold war relations)? These questions are far too broad to address adequately in a short chapter, so my principal focus will be on small-scale societies. My aim is to document in ethnographic detail the working of a "social signaling" system, a mechanism for managing internal conflict within and among allied political communities that I have elsewhere outlined only in general (Roscoe, 2009a). My ethnographic reference is to the Yangoru Boiken of Papua New Guinea, among whom I have conducted some two years' fieldwork. My specific focus will be the role that competitive pig-exchange played in transforming potentially lethal conflicts over land-tenure into nonviolent, symbolic conflicts, thereby maintaining the peace and integrity of political communities and alliances of these communities.

Spheres of Peace: Motives and Mechanisms

Even in the social sciences, polities qua polities are greatly under-analyzed, a curious state of affairs when one considers how fundamental they are to human existence. To be sure, the properties and workings of their parts have received close and extensive attention, but as entities in themselves political communities tend to be taken as primordial facts, their existence simply assumed a priori rather than as objects of analysis. What, then, is the basis for the conception of "a deep horizontal comradeship" (Anderson, 1991, p. 7) that underlies not just the internal peace of nation-states but of all polities?

I suggest we must consider both motive(s) and mechanisms: the chances of peace are better ensured among people who have both motive and social mechanisms to maintain it. Elsewhere, I have argued that polities are first and foremost entities dedicated to mutual defense, perhaps against nonhuman predators early in our hominid prehistory, though against human predators at some later point (Roscoe, 2009a, 2013). Empirical evidence strongly supports the proposition for small-scale societies like those of New Guinea (Roscoe, 1996, 2009a, pp. 80–88). But the case is also plausible as the basis for the nation-state (Roscoe, 2013). After all, defense "from the invasion of foreigners" was the principal function that Hobbes granted the Leviathan in addition to its role in preventing individuals from "the injuries of one another" (Hobbes, 1660, Chapter 17).

If polities are communities dedicated to mutual defense, then their motives for maintaining internal peace become self-evident. If they are to function effectively as a defensive force against external violence, polity members must be committed to, and capable of, acting *as* a defensive unit, of submerging their individual agency, when required, into that of the community. Violence is antithetical to these demands. In the extreme, if violence rises to the level of sustained lethality, the political community disintegrates. Rather than a collectivity united in defense against external violence, its membership erodes into smaller collectivities warring among themselves. If a community is to maintain its efficacy as a defensive organization, in other words, the potential for internal physical violence has to be suppressed.

We do not have to accept that collective defense was the *ur*-motive for polity formation, however, to recognize that violence—lethal violence in particular—endangers polity survival whatever collective end it serves. To exist, therefore, a polity has to maintain some semblance of internal peace. It is obliged to implement ethics that abhor the use of force: beliefs, norms, and values exhorting peace are the product of collective interest, not the necessary precursor for peace. And it must institute nonviolent means for managing internal conflicts, including institutions for detecting, adjudicating, and/or sanctioning infractions.

In the case of the nation-state, these ethics and mechanisms are seemingly obvious. Conflicts of interest are managed through elaborate and supposedly "objective" systems of governmental control: legislative bodies that define legitimate interests and prescribe sanctions for infringing upon them; police systems that monitor and detect infringements; court systems that mediate, adjudicate, and resolve conflicts of interest; and penal systems that enforce court decisions and attempt to deter future infractions. Even in the case of the state, where the ethics and mechanisms guaranteeing the peace seem so obvious, however, there are a number of less visible mechanisms—for example, moral codes of amity that usually are accepted without question and yet profoundly influence behavior; and what Foucault (1991) has called the apparatus of "governmentality"—the institutions, procedures, analyses and reflections that allow power to be tacitly exercised via the medium of politico-economic knowledge.

When we consider small-scale politically uncentralized communities, mechanisms maintaining the peace within and among allied entities are even less visible. As in nation-states, to be sure, codes of morality and "legal" codes of behavior enjoin nonviolence, the former bolstered by conscience and both sanctioned by gossip, moots, and ostracism. Passionate ethics esteem the internal harmony of the political community, abjure intragroup violence, and exalt the use of peaceful rather than violent means of advancing the former over the latter (for New Guinea, see Roscoe, 2009a, pp. 93–94). They also have rudimentary judicial systems: headmen, priests, or gatherings of peers, for example, before whom complaints can be brought for mediation, arbitration, or adjudication. Should preemption, conciliation, and adjudication fail and physical violence break out, further-more, strenuous attempts are commonly made to blunt its mortal consequences. Rather than take up deadly arms, members of a community resort rather to scuffles with bare fists, sticks, or balks of timber, and should things escalate and more deadly weapons be snatched up, these are usually wielded in comparatively harmless ways. War clubs are used to stun rather than to kill an opponent. Arrows are shot in the air rather than at an antagonist. If they are aimed at a human target, they may be targeted on limbs or buttocks rather than on heads or torsos, and so on (for New Guinea, Roscoe, 2009a, pp. 93–94; for small-scale communities elsewhere, Fry, 2006, pp.14–40).

In comparison to a nation-state's centralized organs of detection, mediation, adju-dication, and sanction, however, the judicial mechanisms of small-scale society were extremely limited in relation to the conflict they had to manage and the free-riders they had to deter. The New Guinea evidence strongly indicates, however, that they were but-tressed by a hitherto largely unnoticed system, "social-signaling," a form of "threat system" that replaced the deployment of physical violence with the display and evaluation of fight-ing strength (Roscoe, 2009a).

Social Signaling

How do individuals and subgroups in small-scale societies ensure that conflicting inter-ests within their community do not result in the kind of lethal fighting that would not only destroy lives but also the community and the collective interests it serves? Essentially, they institute a system analogous to the threat displays or "ritualized" fights commonly found among numerous nonhuman species. In these confrontations, conflicts over mates, resources, sanctuaries, and so on are decided not by dangerous fighting but by honest sig-nals of fighting strength such as threat displays (e.g., charging, roaring) or trials of strength (e.g., head butting, tail biting, or pushing contests). These contests, in essence, are a low-cost means by which individual competitors of approximately equal fighting strength can assess which of them would win a fight to the death without either of them having to incur the catastrophic risks involved in an actual fight to the death (e.g., Archer and Huntingford, 1994; Clutton-Brock, Albon, Gibson, & Guinness, 1979; Enquist & Leimar, 1990; Jakobsson, Radesäter, & Järvi, 1979; Maynard Smith & Price, 1973; Parker, 1974).

Small-scale societies, I have argued elsewhere (Roscoe, 2009a), adopt a system with a similar logic. It has been widely reported that small-scale systems in places such as New Guinea, Africa, and South America devote an enormous amount of ceremonial labor to competitive feasting, distributions of material valuables, performances of singing and dancing, and other conspicuous, cooperative activities. These ceremonial displays, I argue, are a means of reliably signaling the military strength of the individuals, subgroups, and/or communities that sponsor them. Through these displays, the individuals and subgroups within a political community and the political communities that make up an alliance of communities are able to establish in a nonlethal way who would win a fight to the death over some conflict of interest without any individual or group having to risk an actual fight to the death. Those who consistently demonstrate superior military strength through competitive ceremonial displays show that they have the military strength to prevail in lethal conflict, and their interests therefore tend to prevail when internal conflicts arise within a community or alliance. Those who fall short in their displays demonstrate inferior fighting capacity; when their interests are thwarted, they are therefore wise to yield. The system works to everyone's advantage, even those who mount inferior displays, because: a) they avoid the potentially catastrophic costs of physical violence, and b) they maintain the integrity of the community (and/or alliance of communities) and the collective benefits it provides.

In New Guinea, the most authentic means of signaling military strength was to deploy it successfully against enemies, those who lay beyond the community and its allied communities. A multitude of reasons motivated New Guineans to launch assaults against their foes, but success in an attack also served vividly to demonstrate military strength. An important target for these signals, of course was their enemies: by military successes against one enemy, an individual, subgroup, or community communicated its dangerous potency to the rest. But military achievement also signaled military strength to audiences closer to home—to others within the political community and in allied communities. Individuals, subgroups, and communities that proved themselves in warfare abroad encouraged deference from their counterparts at home.

Where the home audience was concerned, however, military strength was signaled as much if not more by nonviolent displays than by military actions. In New Guinea, the most widespread of these demonstrations involved conspicuous distribution, the competitive exchange of food and other material commodities. Conspicuous exhibition—large, coordinated performances of singing and dancing—was a second mode, especially common in the highlands. And conspicuous construction—the erection of gigantic spirit houses—was a third, limited mostly to the lowlands of the island.

Although individual military skill and bravery might be knowable only through action on the battlefield, these ceremonial displays provided authentic signals of every other component of a group's military strength. The quantities of food, pigs, and other valuables mustered in a material distribution; the scale, intricacy, synchronization, and duration of a conspicuous performance; and the sheer size and rococo artistry of a cult house signaled the size and commitment of its sponsoring group, the number of kin and allies willing to support its projects, the individual commitments and abilities of the individuals belonging to these groups, and their capacity to suppress their individual interests in order to work together and organize large-scale action *as* a group. A subgroup or political community that could overwhelm its competitors with gifts of food or other valuables, that could continue to deafen an audience with its singing and dancing long after its competitors had sagged with weariness, or that could construct and ornament a large and exquisite spirit house was one that was also likely to prevail against all-comers on a battlefield.

The Yangoru Boiken

Just such a system characterized the Yangoru Boiken of the East Sepik Province of Papua New Guinea. Speakers of the Yangoru dialect of the Boiken language, the Yangoru Boiken are slash-and-burn horticulturalists who reside around Yangoru Government Station in the rugged southern foothills of the coastal Prince Alexander Mountains (Roscoe, 1991). Their subsistence staples are yam, taro, and sago, supplemented by small-scale hunting and gathering, the domestication of pigs, and in modern times trade-store foods.

At contact, the Yangoru Boiken were grouped into village communities that contained between about 100 and 300 people. The inhabitants of a village were divided among several clans, and they occupied a score or so of small hamlets clustered together on hilltop and ridgetop complexes (Figure 24.1). The village of Sima, for example, had about 200-or-so residents around 1930, when Australian pacification began to take effect; these residents were divided into eight clans; and they lived in some 30 hamlets on a pinwheel of ridges about 400 m. above sea level. Political organization was typical of the Melanesian Big-man model, involving intense competition among individuals, their clans, and their village communities, the political reputations of clans and villages resting on the concerted actions and reputations of their members, and the status of all three dependent on their performance in war and competitive display.

The Yangoru Boiken engaged in conspicuous exhibitions of singing and dancing, as well as the conspicuous construction of spirit houses as modes of display (Roscoe, 1995). Conspicuous material distribution, however, was their principal mode of demonstrating individual and group "strength" (*halinya*). A good amount of this distribution took the form of shell-wealth transactions between kinfolk and revolved around rights in persons:

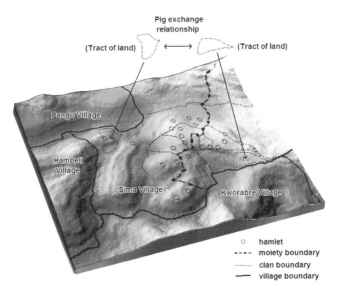

FIGURE 24.1 The clans and pig-exchange system of Sima Village, Yangoru, at contact. (Illustration credit: P. Roscoe)

bride-wealth was transferred at marriage; child-wealth was required at birth; and payments to maternal kin were demanded throughout a male's life and, for a female, until her marriage. The conspicuous distribution of pigs, however, was the more elaborate mode of display. It revolved around rights in land, and it is the mode that I focus on here.

War and the Control of Land

In Yangoru, clan control of land was rooted in the capacity of clan members to defend one another from enemy attacks as they lived on, moved around, or worked their land. The importance of military capacity to land-tenure is a frequent theme of clan settlement histories. Autochthonous clans—clans whose ancestors originated beneath village territory—are commonly said to have welcomed immigrants as reinforcements to village strength, providing them with land and saying: "Now this is your land. Now you will fight with [name of enemy village]." In Sima village, several instances were routinely recalled of clans that failed to defend their territory and therefore had to surrender it in whole or part. Perhaps the best known instance involved the small Pramra clan. Pramra had suffered a series of ambushes from Ambukanja. The final straw was a daylight attack on the Pramra hamlet of Yekimbu, which killed Tretatak, a young lass who had been the only person at home that day. Tretatak's Pramra kinfolk returned at dusk to find her body dumped unceremoniously down the southern slope of Yekimbu, and later that evening they buried her.

> That night, they heard a bird crying out, "Kudjakeyik! Kudjakeyik!" "Oh dear," they said, "I think the enemy are coming to attack again." [The calls of disturbed birds may signal the approach of an enemy.] So during the night, some fled, while the rest left at dawn. The Sima clan came and said, "Alright, I don't think you are able to fight this enemy. I had better take this hamlet over." So they did. The Pramra men said, "Alright, this is your ground, this is your bush, this is your water—and these are your enemies now. We are leaving them to you."

Accordingly, Pramra surrendered Yekimbu, along with a tract of land on the border with Ambukanja, to the more numerous Sima clan.

The importance of military defense to land title also surfaces from time to time in land disputes. In late 1980, Tibatua of the Mandazima subclan took advantage of the absence in Rabaul of Walandua, of the Kela-Howi subclan, to try and evict Walandua's wife, Pabuningai, from a patch of Mandazima land that her natal subclan had for many years called its own (all personal names fictitious). She tearfully protested Tibatua's infamy, claiming that her Pangu-village ancestors had assisted Mandazima in the battles that wrested the land from Ambukanja village and that therefore her brothers had title to it. Tibatua rebuffed these protests, claiming that Pabuningai's ancestors had not shed blood for the land and that therefore they had no claim. This was a concocted rationale that impressed no one. Tibatua tried another tack, protesting rather lamely that war was a thing of the past—that is, military assistance could no longer be invoked in these postcolonial days to justify access to material resources. This, too, went nowhere: the fact that Pabuningai's ancestors had defended the land in question with the spear was decisive.

The Land Tenure and Pig-Exchange Systems

Although land and the material resources upon it were really partitioned and defended by the clan, they were subdivided and exploited by subclans, of which there were usually two to four. Concomitantly, land passed down within a subclan, and ideologically at least it was supposed to go from father to son. In practice, however, subclans and clans were small; population growth combined with demographic fluctuation commonly created imbalances between owners and available resources; and it was consequently commonplace for sons from a subclan with too little land to end up with insufficient resources to support a family. Their option then was to search out and negotiate membership in a subclan with surplus land to give. This could be (in rough order of frequency) a mother's brother's subclan, another subclan of the natal clan, or a subclan of a completely different clan. Whatever the source and however they were contracted, two conditions were critical if a man were to maintain his membership in a subclan and his access to its land: he had to assist the subclan and the clan of which he was part in defending their lands with the spear; and he had to sustain the pig-exchange relationship with which his particular grant of land was associated.

The connection between pig-exchange and land-tenure worked like this. At contact, every Yangoru Boiken village community was divided into two pig-exchanging moieties, and the parcel of subclan land that a young man inherited on reaching adulthood was associated with a particular exchange partner in the opposite moiety (Figure 24.1). (In principal, therefore, the sons of exchange partners themselves became exchange partners.) If he was to retain control of the land he had inherited, the young man had to give pigs on a regular basis—in practice, once every year or two—to this exchange-partner. So long as he maintained his obligations, his rights to the land were assured; if he was delinquent, though, they were jeopardized—opened to challenge. If the delinquent was an immigrant "son," I was told, he might well end up evicted from the land. If he was a "true" son of the previous holder, it was unlikely he would be evicted entirely, though a subclan or clan brother who was obliged to step in and help him with his obligations would likely appropriate at least a portion of the land at issue.

What was true at the level of the individual was true also at higher structural levels. A subclan or clan with a solid history of maintaining its pig-exchange obligations to partners in the opposite moiety validated its land rights, while those of a subclan or clan with a miserable pig-exchange history were jeopardized. Just as a history of defending land with the spear was crucial to land ownership in the face of encroachment by external enemies, in other words, so a history of giving pigs to exchange-partners associated with parcels of land was crucial to possession in the face of encroachment by competitors from within a village or alliance of villages.

But why should pig-exchange be associated with land tenure in the first place? There is nothing intrinsic to pigs or to their exchange that obviously suits them to land regulation, and vice versa. The answer, to which we now turn, lies not in what pigs and pig-giving intrinsically are but in what they symbolize. Both explicitly and implicitly, pig-exchange was a symbolic form of war, and just as individuals and subgroups had to defend their land with the spear against enemy encroachment so, in the symbolic "war" of pig-exchange, they had to "defend" their land with gifts of pigs against encroachments by those against whom they could not use the spear—other members of their political community and their allies.

The Yangoru Pig-Exchange System

At contact, pig-exchange in Yangoru took two principal forms. Most conferrals were made individually, on relatively informal, small-scale occasions known as *polyawavi* ("pig and yam [gifts]") (Figure 24.2). A donor invited his pig-exchange partner to his hamlet, and with loud—and patently insincere—declarations of how ashamed he was at the miserable size of his gift, conferred the pig on the partner before a small audience of their relatives. In a somewhat more elaborate and prestigious version of this exchange, the *polya pak* ("baked pig"), the donor cooked the pig for his partner and feasted him and his relatives with vegetable foods. In a yet more prestigious version, the *polya chugweyi* ("pig soup"), he not only

FIGURE 24.2 *Polyawavi*, Sima Village, 1980. (Photo credit: P. Roscoe)

conferred a pig but also feasted the 20 to 30 members of his partner's moiety with a pork soup and the first fruits of his gardens.

Notwithstanding their semi-private nature, everyone knew when one of these exchanges was taking place. Quite apart from the gossip that ensured every significant village event was common knowledge well before it happened, the donor would announce the impending exchange by pounding his slit-drums—ostensibly to summon his exchange partner and his relatives, in actuality to let everyone within two miles or more know of his ambitions. Once the pig had been handed over, the achievement was again announced on the slit-drums; and for several days afterwards there would be yet other gatherings, as the recipient butchered the pig and distributed the pork among his relatives.

In addition to these small-scale exchanges, the men of one moiety also joined together every two to five years or so to confer pigs, pig soup, and other foods on members of the other moiety in a large, elaborate ceremony that drew an audience not just from within the sponsoring village but from allied and even some enemy communities as well. These ceremonies alternated, one moiety giving pigs to the other, the other then later reciprocating, and they took one of two forms. The *nimba gur* ("beard cutting") was mounted to terminate the mortuary sequence: it "finished (i.e., honored) the names" of those from the sponsoring moiety who had recently died, releasing male mourners from various taboos. The other ceremonial form, the *walahlia* ("call/song to the *wala* spirit") could also be pressed into service as a terminal mourning ceremony, but its principal purpose was to rejuvenate the earth.

The *walahlia* was more elaborate than the *nimba gur*. Both, however, climaxed in a large, communal pig lining, followed by two nights of celebratory singing and dancing. Pig linings got underway toward midmorning. To the pounding of slit-drums and triumphant

FIGURE 24.3 Members of the Lebuging moiety enter to receive their pigs, Kworabre Village, 1979. (Photo credit: P. Roscoe)

singing, the pigs were born into the festival hamlet trussed to poles and then lined up across its ceremonial piazza (Figure 24.3). In the normal course of events, some 20 to 30 pigs would be lined up, and the array would be organized and marked off in such a way that everyone knew how many pigs were being presented by which subclan and clan.

The tally of pigs was formally counted off on the slit-drums, the donors celebrated the count with loud whooping, and the men of the receiving moiety, followed by their wives, then entered the hamlet to receive the pigs. Several masked, befronded, and decorated figures representing the *wala* spirits of the donor clans would first appear and dance in a courtly fashion around the line of pigs. The hogs were then formally conferred on their recipients by the leaders of the donor clans, each pig being whisked away in turn until just one giant "head pig" remained. Ideally, this animal was the largest on display and so heavy that it had to be bound to a litter so that four men could carry it. After briefly withdrawing to arm themselves with spears and palm-wood war-swords, the receivers would return and, after a fury of insults back and forth, suddenly descend on the remaining pig, hoist it to their shoulders and, with members of the donor moiety dogging their steps with mock spear thrusts, try to rush it off the piazza without dropping it.

Pig-Exchange as Symbolic Warfare

The notion that competitive exchange is a kind of "fighting with food" or "fighting with property" is widespread in small-scale societies both within and beyond New Guinea (e.g., Codere, 1950, pp. 118–129; Kaberry, 1941/42, p. 344; Tuzin, 1972; Young, 1971, p.223). Even to a naïve observer, it is obvious that Yangoru's pig-exchange ceremonies had similarly aggressive connotations, and local exegesis reveals that the entire complex was, in fact, an elaborate symbolic war (Roscoe, 2009b). The symbolism begins with the pig, which, depending on the context, stands as both a spear and a human being. As a *gift*—a commodity in the process of transaction—it is said to be a symbolic spear. "Pigs are our spears!" one young man declared proudly to me as he surveyed the hogs being carried into a *walahlia*. "A small pig, that is just a small spear," another man commented. "But if I give a big pig, then I have truly speared." Yet another man, whose pig had just been conferred on its recipient yelled in triumph to the crowd: "I have speared a man . . . now he feels pain!"

This pig = spear symbolism is made explicit in other ways as well. A celebrated ancestor of Hambeli village was said to have "a two-headed spear" because he gave pigs to partners in two different villages: "One way, he threw it [the spear] at Sima; the other, he flung it at Kworabre." The term for exchange partner, *gurli*, is a cognate of the verb *gurlu*, "to spear": thus, *gurli*, the person to whom a pig is given, can be translated as, "One who is speared." A man who encounters difficulty persuading his relatives to help him reciprocate his partner's pig will complain to them: "This man's spear is in me!"

At the same time as they are "spears," pigs are also symbolic humans. Members of one's own village, for instance, are referred to as "village pigs" or "pigs without tails" (a reference to the Yangoru practice of docking the tails of domestic piglets in the belief that this will prevent them from going wild). Conversely, people from other villages are "pigs with tails" or "wild pigs," creatures that dwell in the surrounding bush. If someone dreams of being chased and bitten by a pig, it is an omen that an enemy or rival is plotting his or her death—an enemy armed with a spear if the pig has a tail, a real or classificatory consanguine using sorcery if it has none. Likewise, if a man dreams of his exchange-partner receiving a pig, it means the partner is doomed soon to die.

This equivalence of pigs and humans also features in *hwabu*, the little stories that are told around the evening fire, primarily as bedtime tales for the children. In *The Story of Why Men Exchange Pigs*, for example, it is said that long ago pigs used to truss men to poles and give them to their exchange partners. Forewarned of their impending fate by a *mogrumbwino* lizard, however, the men one day jumped up, grabbed the pigs, and bound them to poles. Pigs replaced humans, in other words, and this is why nowadays men exchange pigs rather than pigs exchanging men. *The Story of the Women Who Were Pigs* tells of two women/pigs who could pass back and forth between the realm of the humans and that of the pigs, taking off their pig skins to become women, and vice versa.

This dual symbolism—the pig as spear and the pig as human—mapped onto the symbolism of war in several ways, but the dominant mode was by direct equation: pig exchange was war, exchange partners were warriors, and pigs were spears (in the act of being given to the exchange partner) or fallen warriors (once they had been given over and were lying on the ground like dead warriors). The military imagery begins with the two moieties, which were named after the two great war confederacies—Lebuging ("white or light-colored pig") and Samawung ("black or dark-colored pig"). Pig-exchange itself was explicitly referred to as a "fight" against the "enemy." Time and again, I would ask the identity of a man's exchange partner, only to be told: "I fight with [so-and-so]." "*Wunera gurliwa, nana waliau mungera polyera*," it was said: "My exchange partner and I, we fight with pigs and yams."

The kind of "fighting" in which these partners engaged differed with the nature of the exchange. The small informal exchanges that took place in the donor's hamlet were said to be "pretend ambushes," while the great, communal *nimba gur* and *walahlia* ceremonies were likened to "pretend open battles." The latter symbolism came to special prominence at the climax of the pig-lining, described above, when the receiving moiety harassed by the donor moiety attempted to hustle the large, litter-bound "head pig" off the ceremonial piazza without dropping it. This theatrical vignette was an explicit reenactment of the climactic moment in open battle, when a spear or spear-thrower dart brought down an enemy warrior. The victorious side would immediately attempt to ensure a kill by launching a "heavy rain" of spears and darts at the other side to cover the advance of a death squad, which would attempt to surround the fallen warrior and smash his skull with a heavy palm-wood club. At the same time, the victim's comrades would have dispatched a rescue squad to try and drag him away from the front to safety. It was this contest between death squad and rescue party that was enacted at a pig-lining, the pig-receivers trying to hustle the "fallen" body of their "comrade" off the "field" while their "enemy" chased after them, trying to make them drop him. "If they trip and drop the pig, we [the pig donors] laugh. We say, 'You're not up to it! You lose! You die!'"

The metaphor of battle was also echoed in the songs of "victory" with which pig-givers celebrated the success of their pig-lining:

> I flung my spear into you [the exchange partner],
> And you are laid low.
> I pluck it out, and you are made tall again!
> I speared a frightened man!
> I killed a frightened man!

On the evening following a pig-lining, the donors would proudly proclaim on their slit-drums the number of pigs they had conferred on their exchange partners, just as they would announce the number of enemies they had slaughtered in battle. The *lumohlia* festivals that celebrated "victory" in a pig-lining were likewise those that celebrated kills in battle. And woe betide any clan that had fallen short in its gifts of pigs: the opposite moiety would ridicule them mercilessly in song. Or, as the Yangoru Boiken put it, *Gira tung gurluk*: "They [the singers] shoot [their exchange partners] with spears."

Pig-exchange, in sum, was a symbolic form of war: symbolic "enemies" threw symbolic "spears" that symbolically "killed" one another. The point of this metaphoric mayhem was not who got "killed." Indeed, the exchange-partner is viewed as a partner, not an opponent: he is a "friend" or "wife" whose actions support one's political fortunes. The point, rather, was to be seen to be *"throwing"* symbolic "spears," for in so doing one symbolically "defended" the land upon which one resided and subsisted. With a vigorous symbolic defense of the land, one retained rights to it; by defaulting on this symbolic defense, one was likely to lose control of it—just as one would in failing to defend it against real enemies.

Pig-Exchange and Conflicts over Land

Land conflicts in Yangoru were of two sorts. First, there were boundary disputes, which were most likely to occur in the transition from the wet to the dry season, when people set about clearing new gardens for the coming year. Then there were quarrels, not over boundaries but over ownership of the tract of land enclosed by those boundaries. Given the web of ownership claims generated by demographic vicissitude and population growth in Yangoru, these latter were the greater source of land-tenure conflict. With no written records of land inheritance, with political entrepreneurs promising different things to different people, and with subclans (and even occasionally clans) small enough that their male membership could go extinct, conflicting claims to the same piece of land were common.

The symbolic war that pig-exchange created regulated these conflicts in two ways. Border disputes were usually resolved with reference to the overall social-signaling system, decided by the comparative reputations for military strength that the two parties had built up through ceremonial display. Along with their performance in conspicuous exhibitions, conspicuous construction, and shell-wealth distributions, the number and size of the pigs that individuals, subclans, and clans conferred on their exchange partners demonstrated their "strength" (*halinya)*. Those individuals and subclans who had proved themselves through display to be the "stronger" of the claimants in a border dispute were those who were more likely to get their way. It was not that the "strong" could blatantly fudge boundary lines to extend their land-holdings at the expense of the "weak": they had to provide some plausible narrative that supported their claims. But to the extent they were able to muddy the waters about the location of a boundary line, their superior "strength" was recognized in the court of public opinion, and their claims were likely to prevail over those of "weaker" opponents.

Land ownership disputes, however, were directly regulated by the pig-exchange system, ownership essentially going to the contestant who had given (or helped to give) the most pigs to the pig-exchange partner associated with the land in question. In symbolic terms, those who had "thrown" the most "spears" against symbolic "enemies" to defend the land at issue were those who gained ownership of it. Most of these conflicts, it seems, were resolved informally. Sometimes, a potential challenger might give way without even mounting a claim: it would be obvious both to him and everyone else that his rival had given a far greater number of pigs on behalf of the land, and he would give up without a "fight," so to speak. Sometimes, the two competitors would meet, outline their claims and the history of pigs they or their subclan had presented on behalf of the land at issue, and the matter would be resolved informally. The two contenders' comparative reputations for "strength" were no doubt a factor in the resolution, but in so far as there was an "objective" record of pig-exchange against which to judge the competing claims, the verdict was decided on the merits of the case. Commonly, this record was a tally in the form of sticks prominently displayed on the food-houses of parties to the dispute. But, in Yangoru, pigs and pig prestations were as popular a subject of male discussion as baseball or soccer in the West, and it was no easy matter to contradict a record of past exchanges kept alive for a couple of generations in the collective memory.

Occasionally, however, circumstances conspired to create conflicts over land ownership that were not as readily or peacefully resolved, and on these occasions the system's operation burst into the open. One such incident occurred in Sima Village in late September, 1980. Two young Sima-village men, Hamahwazi from the Mandazima subclan of Sima clan and Kwiandua of the Pramra clan, fell to blows over ownership of a tract of Ambukanja-village land that lay on the border between Sima and Ambukanja (all personal names fictitious). The land in question had lain fallow for many years and, after a rather tortured inheritance history, had come into the possession of an Ambukanja man, Sengirama, who had no use for it himself. The background to the brawl was counterclaims that had been made to the land by Hamahwazi and Kwiandua. Hamahwazi and his father, Yegihamba, had laid claim to it on the basis that, in the past, their subclan had married the sister of an earlier owner and had helped him in giving a total of 12 pigs to the exchange partner associated with it. Kwiandua and his father, Yukramiamba, however, disputed these pretensions, contending that in the past their subclan had treated the previous owner as a classificatory wife's brother and had helped to give four pigs to the land's exchange partner. The fight broke out when Yukramiamba publically questioned Hamahwazi and Yegihamba's claim that their subclan had given 12 pigs on behalf of the land.

The fight was not considered serious in terms of injuries sustained. In terms of the social breach involved, however, it was far graver, and a large moot was subsequently convened to resolve matters. At this gathering, the case revolved around who had done more to help "defend" the land with pigs, and several older Ambukanja men were present to testify in Hamahwazi and Yegihamba's support. Yukramiamba and Kwiandua remained skeptical, but they had little choice other than to accept the general opinion that Hamahwazi and Yegihamba were entitled to the land. Shortly thereafter, a small peace-making ceremony was held at which a couple of older men delivered stock homilies about the virtues of peace within the village; Hamahwazi and Kwiandua shook hands to signify that their anger had "cooled"; and the pair exchanged ten-kina banknotes to compensate the injuries each had caused the other in the fight.

Conclusion: Community and Alliance

In this chapter, I have used competitive pig exchange among the Yangoru Boiken of New Guinea to show in close ethnographic detail the operation of a social signaling system, one of the most important ways with which small-scale societies surmount conflicts of interest over mates, resources, and other rewards in order to maintain peace within a political community and among allied communities. The system rests on a set of competitive displays that serve as honest signals of individual and collective military strength. Thereby, participants are able to evaluate who would win a fight to the death in the event of conflict without any individual or community having to incur the costs of an actual fight to the death. Yangoru Boiken pig exchange is exceptionally well-suited to illustrating how such a system worked and what it achieved because not only was it a central component in their social signaling system, but its military symbolism also rendered its operation dramatically visible. Simply put, competitive pig exchange maintained peace within and among allied village communities by substituting symbolic warfare for real warfare. Other elements of the Yangoru Boiken social signaling system—distributions of shell valuables, feasts, spirit-house construction (and these days exchanges of beer and liquor)—trafficked in a similar military symbolism (Roscoe, 1982, pp. 251–254, 1995, 2009a, pp. 100–101), though the metaphors were less explicit than those associated with pig exchange.

There is strong evidence that social signaling was the foundation of peaceful relations within and among allied communities throughout New Guinea (Roscoe, 2009a), and so it is plausible that it had emerged among small-scale societies elsewhere in the world. To take just one example of how it can help us understand the emergence of peace, consider the remarkable "peace system" that had developed among the four village-tribes of the Upper Xingu in the Amazon (Fry, 2006, pp. 13–20; Gregor, 1985, 1996). Although these groups practiced occasional witch killing across tribal lines and customarily defended themselves against attacks by outsiders, there was no tradition of violence among the communities themselves. How did they achieve this? There were several pillars to the "peace system," but one very significant element, which operated to maintain peace both within and among the communities, was activities that patently had martial overtones. In *yawari* ceremonial, for instance, pairs of relatives from different tribes would hurl (and attempt to dodge) wax-tipped arrows at one another in turn (Gregor, 1994), performances that Fry characterizes as "a controlled expression of antagonism that ends with a reaffirmation of friendly, nonhostile intentions" (2006, p. 16).

The most prominent male activity, however, was wrestling. Like Yangoru Boiken pig-exchange, wrestling preoccupied adult male life and discussion, and like pig-exchange it was the measure of a man.

> A powerful wrestler, say the villagers, is frightening. . . . Likened to the anaconda in the quickness of his holds and the way he "ties up" his opponents, he commands fear and respect. To the women, he is "beautiful" . . . in demand as a paramour and husband. Triumphant in politics as well as in love, the champion wrestler embodies the highest qualities of manliness. Not so fortunate the vanquished! A chronic loser, no matter what his virtues, is regarded as a fool. (Gregor, 1985, pp. 96)

Wrestling took place both among the members of a village men's house and between the men's houses of different villages. Combat within the village was an everyday occurrence: three o'clock in the afternoon was "wrestling time." But in the drier parts of the year, matches were also organized against other villages in the peace system.

Fry (2006, p. 18) and Gregor (Gregor & Robarchek, 1996, p. 180) interpret these activities—Xingu wrestling and the *yawari* ritual—as expressive if not cathartic activities, and there is little doubt that they were. But it is difficult to avoid a conclusion that even more so were they elements of a social signaling system, that wrestling and *yawari* ritual also kept the peace by substituting nonlethal displays of fighting strength for lethal deployments of it. Indeed, where wrestling is concerned, there can be few activities more suited to the honest, nonlethal display of individual and collective military strength. Individually, wrestlers directly demonstrated their fighting capacity in the acuity, agility, and physical strength they displayed in these fights. At the same time, intertribal bouts put collective—village—fighting strength on display:

the numbers a village could muster to a fight, the fighting capacity of the individuals making up these numbers, and their commitment to their village and to propagating its collective strength.

Further, as we might expect if wrestling, like pig-exchange among the Yangoru Boiken, was indeed an activity dedicated to displaying fighting strength, it was spoken of in martial metaphors that could have been stolen from the Yangoru Boiken:

> At the great intertribal bouts, "the masters of wrestling" ... fight first, followed by the lesser wrestlers. The man who is constantly at the end of the line must cope with a tremendous loss of self-esteem, which is reflected in the terminology of victory and loss. The winner is said to *ukutene* his opponent, a word that literally means "shoot with an arrow" but more generally means to kill or maim seriously. A passive form of this verb ... is applied to the loser; he has been "killed" by the victor. (Gregor, 1985, p. 98)

In conclusion, we might ask, does this analysis scale? If social signaling generates sociality in small-scale societies, does it persist in more complex societies such as the nation-states of the contemporary world? It is useful here to consider the internal and external relations of political communities separately. In nation states, social signaling has clearly declined dramatically as a mechanism regulating internal relations. As noted earlier, these are entities characterized by enormously powerful, centralized institutions that include legislative bodies, police forces, and penal systems, which play a much greater role than any social signaling mechanism in managing internal conflicts of interest. The dynamics of this decline are not easy to fathom. It is not obvious whether, as political systems developed greater complexity, these centralized institutions expanded to displace social signaling, whether social signaling became increasingly unworkable, or both, though the enormous scale of the typical nation-state does cast serious doubt on whether displays that signal military strength could ever be a practical means of regulating internal conflict among its members and component parts.

There is some evidence, even so, that within the interstices of the state social signaling does persist in attenuated forms. Perhaps the most obvious instances in western states concern the management of conflict between individuals—especially males, and in particular those in subpopulations such as prisons or contexts such as barrooms. In these cases, direct assessments of fighting capacity (e.g., relative height and weight, number of allies) and indirect assessments (e.g., reputations for fighting capacity) have been shown to play an important role in mediating interpersonal and intergroup conflict (Archer, 2007; Archer & Benson, 2008; Nisbett & Cohen, 1996), much as did performance on a New Guinea battlefield (see earlier).

Less common in the nation-state than in small-scale societies, it seems, is the deployment of nonsomatic signals to manage conflict such as the conspicuous distribution, performance, and construction enlisted in New Guinea. It is not that such activities are absent from mainstream culture in the nation-state, but they assume different forms and play different roles. Conspicuous distribution and conspicuous construction become conspicuous consumption and rather than communicating fighting capacity they create, maintain, and signal social status. Nonetheless, the members of some nation-state entities such as urban gangs and organized crime families do seem to deploy rampant conspicuous consumption (and even distribution) as signals of fighting strength. For these individuals and groups, lavish personal ornamentation, the ownership of luxury cars and mansions (and plenty of them), and ostentatious local philanthropy can plausibly be viewed as signals not just of status but also of fighting strength. Significantly, these are also individuals and groups that operate beyond the effective range of state judicial sanction and, by the nature of their activities, neither can nor usually want to appeal to state judicial protection. (It is probably also relevant that they commonly adhere to comparatively elaborate codes of "honor," "respect," and "deference" not unlike those emphasized in small-scale communities like those of New Guinea.)

In the contemporary world of nation-states, social signaling seems to play a more prominent role in the external relations rather than the internal organization of the political community. In this sphere, it is more plausible to view the nation-state as a small-scale community writ large. Like the latter, the former exists in a social universe of allies, cold-war antagonists, and (from time to time) real-world enemies, and no effective super-ordinate structure of control exists to regulate relations among these entities. As we might expect, therefore, social signaling—displays of fighting capacity—appears to play a significant role in managing interstate conflict. Colonial history had its gunboat diplomacy and such bizarre (and ultimately tragic) episodes as the wildly expensive naval arms race in which Britain and Germany engaged between 1890 and 1914. More recently, social signaling has been starkly apparent in the May-day armament parades of the Soviet Union (and nowadays, their counterparts in North Korea), the military "exercises" that nations periodically mount even today, and the "new gunboat diplomacy" sparked by a contemporary struggle for submarine resources such as those beneath the melting ice cap at the North Pole (Landler, 2011).

Nor is social signaling limited to the realm of military ostentation: it can be seen, too, in the patently symbolic warfare of international sports. The Olympics still rivet the attention of the world's nations, as they aspire through competitive displays of strength and agility to eclipse one another in the medal counts they can pile up. Likewise, the quadrennial soccer World Cup and the more localized European Cup, which alternates with it every two years, is almost as effective as a neutron bomb in sweeping traffic from the streets of many world cities, and the euphoria and dejection accompanying victory and defeat, respectively, is a wonder of the modern world. Trivial in their intrinsic value, the trophies at stake nonetheless signal the quality of human capital on which a nation can draw, communicating the message "Don't mess with us!" and reaping through nonviolent means priceless returns in "national honor," international stature, and even global dominance.

Acknowledgments

For comments on earlier versions of this chapter, I am most grateful to Douglas Fry and Terry Hays.

References

Archer, J. (2007). Physical aggression as a function of perceived fighting ability among male and female prisoners. *Aggressive Behavior, 33*, 563–573.

Archer, J., & Benson, D. A. (2008). Physical aggression as a function of perceived fighting ability and provocation: An experimental investigation. *Aggressive Behavior, 34*, 9–24.

Archer, J., & Huntingford, F. (1994). Game theory models and escalation of animal fights. In M. Potegal & J. F. Knutson (Eds.), *The dynamics of human aggression: Biological and social processes in dyads and groups* (pp. 3–31). Hillsdale, NJ: Erlbaum.

Anderson, B. (1991). *Imagined Communities: Reflections on the Origin and Spread of Nationalism.* London: Verso.

Bonta, B.D. (1996). Conflict resolution among peaceful societies: The culture of peacefulness. *Journal of Peace Research, 33*, 403–420.

Clutton-Brock, T.H., Albon, S.D., Gibson, R.M., & Guinness, F.E. (1979). The logical stag: Adaptive aspects of fighting in Red Deer (*Cervus alaphus* L.). *Animal Behavior, 27*, 211–225.

Codere, H. (1950) *Fighting with property: A study of Kwakiutl potlatching and warfare, 1792–1930.* New York: J. J. Augustin.

Enquist, M., & Leimar, O. (1990). *The evolution off fatal fighting. Animal Behavior, 39*, 1–9.

Foucault, M. (1991). Governmentality. In G. Burchell, C. Gordon, & P. Miller (Eds.), *The Foucault effect: Studies in governmentality* (pp. 87–104). Chicago: University of Chicago Press.

Fry, D. P. (2006). *The human potential for peace: An anthropological challenge to assumptions about war and violence.* New York: Oxford University Press.

Gregor, T. (1985) *Anxious pleasures: The sexual lives of an Amazonian people.* Chicago: University of Chicago Press.

Gregor, T. (1994) Symbols and rituals of peace in Brazil's Upper Xingu. In L. E. Sponsel & T. Gregor (Eds.), *The anthropology of peace and nonviolence* (pp. 241–257). Boulder, CO: Lynne Rienner.

Gregor, T., & Robarchek, C. A. (1996). Two paths to peace: Semai and Mehinaku nonviolence. In T. Gregor, (Ed.), *A natural history of peace* (pp.159–188). Nashville, TN: Vanderbilt University Press.

Hobbes, T. (1660) *The Leviathan.* Retrieved from http://oregonstate.edu/instruct/phl302/texts/hobbes/leviathan-contents.html

Jakobsson, S., Radesäter, T. & Järvi, T. (1979). On the fighting behavior of Nannacara anomala (Pisces, Cichlidae) males. *Zeitschrift für Tierpsychologie, 49*, 210–220.

Kaberry, P. M. (1941/42). Law and political organization in the Abelam tribe, New Guinea. *Oceania, 12*, 79–95, 209–225, 331–363.

Landler, M. (2011, November 13). A new era of gunboat diplomacy. *New York Times: Sunday Review*, p. 4.

Maynard Smith, J., & Price, G.R. (1973). The logic of animal conflict. *Nature, 246*, 15–18.

Nisbett R.E, & Cohen D. (1996) *Culture of honor: The psychology of violence in the South.* Boulder, CO: Westview Press.

Parker, G.A. (1974). Assessment strategy and the evolution of fighting behavior. *Journal of Theoretical Biology, 47*, 223–243.

Roscoe, P. (1982) Alcohol use in the Yangoru Subdistrict, East Sepik Province. In M. Marshall (Ed.), *Through a glass darkly: Beer and modernization in Papua New Guinea* (pp. 245–256). Boroko, Papua New Guinea: Institute of Applied Social and Economic Research.

Roscoe, P. B. (1991). Yangoru Boiken. In T. E. Hays (Ed.), *Oceania: Encyclopedia of world cultures*, vol. 2 (pp. 388–391). Boston: G.K. Hall & Co.

Roscoe, P. B. (1995). Of power and menace: Sepik art as an affecting presence. *Journal of the Royal Anthropological Institute, 1*, 1–22.

Roscoe, P. B. (1996). War and society in Sepik New Guinea. *Journal of the Royal Anthropological Institute, 2,* 645–666.

Roscoe, P. (2009a). Social signaling and the organization of small-scale society: The case of contact-era New Guinea. *Journal of Archaeological Method and Theory, 16,* 69–116.

Roscoe, P. (2009b). Symbolic violence and ceremonial peace. In M. Dickhardt, E. Hermann, and K. Klenke (Eds.), Form, Macht, Differenz: Festschrift für Brigitta Hauser-Schäublin (pp. 207–214). Göttingen: Universitätsverlag Göttingen.

Roscoe, P. (2013). War, collective action, and the "evolution" of human polities. In D. Carballo (Ed.), *Cooperation and Collective Action: Archaeological Perspectives* (pp. 57–82). Boulder, CO: The University Press of Colorado.

Sponsel, L. (1996). The natural history of peace: a positive view of human nature and its potential. In T. Gregor (Ed.), *A natural history of peace* (pp. 95–125). Nashville, TN: Vanderbilt University Press.

Tuzin, D.F. (1972). Yam symbolism in the Sepik: An interpretative account. *Southwestern Journal of Anthropology, 28,* 230–254.

Young, M. W. (1971). *Fighting with food.* Cambridge: Cambridge University Press.

25

The Challenge of Getting Men to Kill

A View from Military Science

RICHARD J. HUGHBANK AND DAVE GROSSMAN

Introduction

The history of violence and conflict can be seen as the evolution of a series of ever more efficient devices to enable humans to kill and dominate their fellow human beings. The concept of an "evolution" of combat is appropriate since the battlefield is the ultimate realm of Darwinian natural selection. With few exceptions, any weapon or system that survives for any time does so because of its utility, not because of superstition. Anything that is effective is copied and perpetuated, and anything ineffective results in its death, defeat, and extinction. There are fads and remnants (the military equivalents of the human appendix that serves no useful function), but over the long run only the systems and weapons that result in survival and victory in combat persist. Ultimately, the limitations of our bodies *and* our minds determine the nature of our weapons.

The physical needs for force, mobility, distance, and protection interact with each other in the evolution of weapons, but psychological limitations are even more influential in this process. Lord Moran (1945, p. 154) the great military physician of World War I and World War II, called Napoleon "the greatest psychologist of all time." Napoleon said that, "In war the moral is to the physical as three to one," meaning that the psychological advantage or leverage is three times more important than the physical (Chandler, 1966, p. 155). Modern studies support Napoleon's contention (Table 25.1).

In preparation for combat, the need for emotional "training" is as important as any other aspect within a military training cycle. During times of combat, psychological issues have traumatic affect due to physical exhaustion, a continuous state of high mental alertness, fear of failing your fellow warriors, and fear of dying. These emotional states can only be overcome by constant and strenuous physical training and a collective sense of camaraderie by all who are involved in combat actions. Once enabling factors have crept into

TABLE 25.1 **Landmarks in the Evolution of Combat**

Date	Event
-c.1700BC:	Chariots provide key form of mobility advantage in ancient warfare
-c.400BC:	Greek phalanx
-c.100BC:	Roman system (pilum, swords, training, professional leadership)
-c.900AD:	Mounted knight (stirrup greatly enhances utility of mounted warfare)
-c.1300:	Gunpowder (cannon) in warfare
-c.1300:	Wide-scale application of long bow defeats mounted knights
-c.1600:	Gunpowder (small arms) in warfare, defeats all body armor
-c.1800:	Shrapnel (exploding artillery shells), ultimately creates renewed need for helmets,-c.1850:
c.1850:	Percussion caps permit all-weather use of small arms
*c.1870:	Breech-loading, cartridge-firing rifles and pistols
-c.1915:	Machine gun
-c.1915:	Gas warfare
-c.1915:	Tanks
-c.1915:	Aircraft
*c.1915:	Self-loading (automatic) rifles and pistols
-c.1940:	Strategic bombing of population centers
-c.1945:	Nuclear weapons
-c.1960:	Large-scale introduction of operant conditioning in training to enable killing
*c.1960:	Large-scale introduction of media violence begins to enable domestic violent crime
-c.1965:	Large-scale introduction of helicopters in battle
-c.1970:	Introduction of precision-guided munitions in warfare
-c.1980:	Kevlar body armor provides first individual armor to defeat state-of-the-art small arms in 300+ years
*c.1990:	Large-scale introduction of operant conditioning through violent video games begins to enable mass murders in domestic violent crime
-c.1990:	First extensive use of precision guided munitions in warfare (approximately 10 percent of all bombs dropped), by US forces in the Gulf War
-c.1990:	Large-scale use of combat stress inoculation in law enforcement, with the introduction of paint bullet training
-c.2000:	Approximately 70 percent of all bombs used by US forces in conquest of Afghanistan and Iraq are precision-guided munitions
-c.2000:	Large-scale use of combat stress inoculation in US military forces, with the introduction of paint bullet combat simulation training

Note: Dates generally represent century or decade of first major, large-scale introduction.
* Represents developments that also influence domestic violent crime.

the minds of combatants, morale drops, and commanders face a slippery slope in future mission success.

Another critical aspect leading to psychological issues in combatants is dealing with death. Military combatants are trained to defend through superior military action. This is accomplished through the use of force, and the ultimate use of force involves killing. By our vary nature, humans are not wired to take the life of another. It is this contradictory nature that all military personnel must overcome. Accordingly, the necessity to kill in combat becomes an extraordinary psychological barrier to overcome within each individual as they prepare for combat.

The Resistance to Killing

At the heart of the psychological processes on the battlefield is the resistance to killing one's own species—a resistance that exists in every healthy member of virtually every species (Grossman, 1995). To understand the nature of this resistance, we must first recognize that most participants in close combat are literally "frightened out of their wits," as the saying goes. Once the arrows or bullets start flying, combatants stop thinking with the forebrain (that part of the brain which makes us human). Instead, their thought processes localize in the midbrain, or mammalian brain, that primitive part of the brain generally indistinguishable from that of an animal. At this point, the trust in one's training, equipment, and fellow warrior become the essence of how a person acts in the chaos known a combat.

In conflict situations, this primitive, midbrain processing can be observed in a consistent trend toward resisting and avoiding killing one's own species. During territorial and mating competition, animals with antlers and horns slam together in a relatively harmless head-to-head fashion, rattlesnakes wrestle each other, and piranhas fight their own kind with flicks of their tails. However, against any other species these creatures unleash their horns, fangs, and teeth without restraint. This is an essential survival mechanism that prevents a species from destroying itself during territorial and mating rituals.

This resistance can be seen in other places besides mating and territorial contests. Why is it that the biggest kitten in every litter does not smother and kill all the other kittens? Why is it that in most bird species the first chick out of the egg does not shove the other eggs out of the nest? That chick's personal survival would be greatly enhanced if it did. Now, there are a few species of birds such as the cuckoo that lays its egg in another bird species' nest, and when the invader's egg hatches the chick shoves the other bird's eggs out, but those are eggs from a different species. With rare exceptions, creatures of the same species tend not to kill their conspecifics. Why is it that you can leave your three-year-old child with your six-month-old infant for a few minutes and the older one does not leap on the little one and smother or somehow kill it? Again, most healthy members of most species appear to have a hardwired resistance against killing their own kind. Any species that did not have this restraint would cease to exist.

Yes, once every couple of years we may hear of some horrendous incident in which a three- or four-year-old, who has been negatively influenced in some way, murders an infant child, but this is extremely rare. When it does happen, it shocks us down to our core because it is a horrible abnormality.

One major, modern revelation in the field of military psychology is the observation that this resistance to killing one's own species is also a key factor in human combat. Brigadier General S. L. A. Marshall first observed this phenomenon during his work as the Chief Historian of the European Theater of Operations in World War II. Based on his new, innovative technique of postcombat interviews, Marshall (1978) concluded in his landmark book *Men Against Fire*, that only 15 to 20 percent of the individual riflemen in World War II fired their weapons at an exposed enemy soldier.

Marshall's findings have been somewhat controversial, but every available, parallel, scholarly study validates his basic findings: the translations by Freely and Cotton (2005) of Ardant du Picq's surveys of French officers in the 1860s and his observations on ancient battles; Keegan and Holmes' (1985) numerous accounts of ineffectual firing throughout history; Paddy Griffith's (1989, 1990) data on the extraordinarily low killing rate among Napoleonic and American Civil War regiments; Stouffer's (1949) extensive World War II and postwar research; Richard Holmes' (1985) assessment of Argentine firing rates in the Falklands War; the British Army's (Fink, 2010) laser reenactments of historical battles; the FBI's (Fink, 2010) studies of nonfiring rates among law enforcement officers in the 1950s and 1960s, and countless other individual and anecdotal observations, all confirm Marshall's fundamental conclusion that man is not, by nature, a close-range interpersonal killer.

Somewhere inside our midbrain, at least in the brains of healthy members of the human race, we appear to have a powerful resistance to killing our own kind. While this is true, the question begs to be asked: why then have we been so good at filling up our military cemeteries across the years?

The existence of this resistance can be observed in its marked absence in sociopaths who, by definition, do not feel either empathy or remorse for their fellow human beings. Pit bull dogs have been selectively bred for sociopathy, that is, bred for the absence of the resistance to killing their own kind, to ensure that they will perform the unnatural act of killing another dog.

Breeding to overcome this limitation in humans is impractical, but humans are adept at finding *mechanical* means to overcome natural limitations. Humans were born without the ability to fly, so they found mechanisms that overcame this limitation and enabled flight. Humans were also born with constraints on their ability to kill fellow humans, so throughout history they have devoted great effort to finding ways to overcome this resistance which is further motivated by the fight or flight syndrome. In terms of weapons evolution, the history of warfare can be viewed as a series of successively more effective tactical and mechanical mechanisms to enable or force combatants to overcome their resistance to killing.

Posturing as a Psychological Weapon

Posturing is an interesting sociological and psychological concept, especially when physical contact is imminent. This action-reaction-counteraction scenario begins with a person, or persons, (A) establishing a firm position either verbally or physically. Their opponent (B) now has the option to either back away or establish their own posturing position. Should opponent (B) establish their own posturing position, then opponent (A) has to reconsider their initial position. Opponent (A) must now determine if opponent (B) is representing a valid position of strength and superiority or a false sense of bravado. It is at this point that opponent (A) must either back down in his show of force or maintain his position. This leaves opponent (B) with one last decision in the posturing equation. He must reevaluate his strength and position and either stand his ground or choose to stand down to opponent (A). At this juncture of the exchange, final decisions have been made leading to the potential for combat.

The resistance to killing can be overcome, or at least bypassed, by a variety of techniques. One way is to cause the enemy to flee (often by getting in their flank or rear, which almost always causes a rout). It is widely understood that most killing happens after the battle, in the pursuit phase—Clausewitz (1984) and Ardant du Picq (Freely & Cotton, 2005) both commented on this—which is apparently due to two factors. First, the fleeing victim has his back turned. It appears to be much easier to deny his humanity if you can stab or shoot him in the back and not look into his eyes as you kill him. Secondly, psychologically, the opponent apparently changes from a fellow male engaged in a primitive, simplistic, ritualistic, head-to-head, territorial, or mating battle, to a prey who must be pursued, pulled down, and killed. Anyone who has ever worked with dogs understands this process: you are generally safe if you face a dog down in a threatening situation. When you have to move, always back away from a dog (actually, almost any animal). If you turn and run, you are in danger of being pursued and viciously attacked. The same is true of soldiers in combat.

The battlefield is psychological in nature. In this realm, the individual who puffs himself up the biggest or makes the loudest noise is likely to win. From one perspective, the actual battle is a process of posturing until one side or another turns and runs, and then the real killing begins. Thus posturing is critical to warfare and the side that does it best will gain a significant advantage on the battlefield.

Bagpipes, bugles, drums, shiny armor, tall hats, chariots, elephants, and cavalry have all been factors in successful posturing (convincing oneself of prowess, while daunting ones enemy). But ultimately, gunpowder proved to be the ultimate posturing tool. For example, the longbow and the crossbow were significantly more accurate, with a far greater rate of fire and a much greater accuracy range than the muzzle-loading muskets used up to the early part of the American Civil War. Furthermore, the longbow did not need the industrial base (iron and gunpowder) that muskets required. Also, training the long bowman was easy.

Mechanically speaking, there are few reasons why there should not have been regiments of longbows and crossbows at Waterloo and Bull Run, cutting vast swathes through the enemy. Similarly, there were highly efficient, air-pressure-powered weapons available as early as the Napoleonic era (similar to modern paintball guns) which had a far higher firing rate than the muskets of that era, but they were never used. We must keep in mind Napoleon's maxim that in war the mental factors are three times more important than the mechanical factors. The reality is that if you go *doink, doink,* on the battlefield, and the enemy goes *BANG! BANG!*, they gain a powerful psychological advantage that ultimately may mean that you, the "doinkers," lose.

In his book *War on the Mind*, Peter Watson (1980, p. 155) has noted that one universal finding of weapons research is that the amount of noise a weapon makes is a key factor in that weapon's effectiveness on the battlefield: "... noise of many kinds, usually incredibly loud, often painfully so—small arms, shells, bombs and aircraft during an attack. This can be prepared for, but the first time in real battle is always different."

This phenomenon helps explain the effectiveness of high-noise-producing weapons ranging from Gustavus Adolphus's small, mobile cannons assigned to infantry units, to the US Army's M-60 machine gun in Vietnam that fired large and very loud 7.62mm ammunition at a slow rate, versus the M-16's smaller and comparatively less noisy 5.56mm ammunition that fired at a rapid rate. It is important to note that both the machine gun and the cannon are also crew-served weapons, which, as we will consider also, enables killing.

Mobility and Distance as Psychological Weapons

Once it is understood that the destruction and defeat of an enemy happens in the pursuit, the utility of those weapons that provide a mobility advantage becomes clear. First, a mobility advantage often permits a force to get at the enemy's flank or rear. Combatants seem to have an intuitive understanding of their psychological and physical vulnerability when an opponent attacks from their rear, a tactic that almost always results in a mass panic. Secondly, it is during the pursuit that a mobility advantage is needed if a pursuing force is to kill the enemy. An opponent who has cast aside his weapons and armor can generally outrun an armed pursuer, but a man on foot cannot outrun chariots or cavalry. These mobile forces have their greatest utility stabbing and shooting helpless, terrified men in the back.

Distance as a Psychological Weapon

The utility of weapons that kill from afar cannot be understood without understanding the psychological enabling aspect of distance. Simply stated, the farther away you are the easier it is to kill. Thus, dropping bombs from 20,000 feet or firing artillery (commonly referred to as indirect fire) from two miles away is, psychologically speaking, not at all difficult (and there is no indication of any noncompliance in these situations). However, firing a rifle from 20 feet away is difficult (with a high incidence of nonfirers) and there is great psychological resistance to stabbing an opponent at close range in hand-to-hand combat.

John Keegan's (1983) landmark book *The Face of Battle* made a comparative study of Agincourt (1415), Waterloo (1815), and the Somme (1916). In his analysis of these three battles spanning more than 500 years, Keegan repeatedly noted the absence of stab wounds incurred during the massed bayonet attacks at Waterloo and the Somme. Keegan (1983, p. 201) stated that after Waterloo: "There were numbers of sword and lance wounds to be treated and some bayonet wounds, though these had usually been inflicted after the man had already been disabled, there being no evidence of the armies having crossed bayonets at Waterloo."

By World War I, edged-weapon combat had almost disappeared. Keegan (1983, p. 269) noted: "Edged-weapon wounds were a fraction of one per cent of all wounds inflicted in the First World War."

Indeed, evidence uniformly indicates that ancient battles were not much more than great shoving matches until one side or the other fled. This can be observed in Alexander the Great who, according to Ardant du Picq's (Freely & Cotton, 2005) studies of ancient records, lost only 700 men "to the sword" in all his battles put together. This is because Alexander the Great always won, and nearly all the killing happened to the losers, *after* the battle in the pursuit phase.

The only thing greater than the emotional resistance to killing at close range is the resistance to *being* killed at close range. Close range interpersonal aggression is the universal human phobia, which is why the initiation of midbrain processing is so powerful and intense in these situations. Thus, one drawback to killing at long range is that greater distance has a reduced psychological effect on the enemy. This manifests itself in a constant thwarting of each new generation of air power advocates and other adherents of sterile, long-range, high-tech warfare, since it is close-range, interpersonal aggression that frightens the enemy and modifies their behavior.

Peter Maass (2004, p. 38) captured this paradox of the failure of firepower as it applies to counterterrorism warfare.

> At the outset of the Vietnam War, Col. John Paul Vann, who would emerge as one of the most thoughtful and ultimately tragic officers in the war, recognized the paradox and realized his firepower-loving commanders had not. In 1962, he warned David Halberstam, then a young reporter for *The New York Times*, that the wrong strategy had been adopted. "This is a political war, and it calls for the utmost discrimination in killing," he told Halberstam, as recounted in William Prochnau's *Once Upon a Distant War*. "The best weapon for killing is a knife, but I'm afraid we can't do it that way. The next best is a rifle. The worst is an airplane, and after that the worst is artillery. You have to know who you are killing."

Watson (1980) noted in *War on the Mind* that weapons research has concluded that the weapons that pose a direct threat to the individual are more psychologically effective than "area" weapons. Thus, the sniper is more effective than a hail of machine-gun fire, and the precision-guided bomb is more effective than the artillery barrage. The more accurate the weapon, the greater the fear it inspires. As Watson (1983, p. 167) opined, "Fear equals accuracy, noise, rapidity of fire—noise being the only truly nonlethal characteristic that is feared."

According to Bob Woodward's (2003) book *Bush at War*, the US armed forces gained control in Afghanistan in 2001 with less than 500 Americans on the ground. It should be noted that these 500 Americans were well-assisted by elite troops from the British, Australian, and New Zealand SAS, and the Canadian JTF 2. The Americans were mostly

US Special Forces (Green Berets) and CIA operatives (with the proverbial "suitcase full of money"), who were funding, supplying, guiding, and controlling the forces of the Afghani warlords on the ground. Whenever possible, each Green Beret A-Team was supported by a team of US Air Force Combat Controllers (CCTs) who called in the precision airstrikes, which were pivotal to winning that war.

In the Gulf War, just a decade prior, approximately 10 percent of the bombs dropped on the enemy were precision guided. In Afghanistan in 2001 and Iraq in 2003, approximately 70 percent of the bombs were precision-guided munitions that were dropped on the enemy with pinpoint accuracy. In two months, the US-led coalition did what the Russians could not do in 10 years. Barely a year later, they repeated the performance in Iraq, conquering an entire nation in three weeks. This could not have happened without a vast stockpile of modern, precision-guided munitions. However, it also would not have been possible without those elite troops on the ground directing and exploiting the air strikes, and working with indigenous forces to provide the universal human phobia, that personal face of death and destruction that is so effective at modifying human behavior.

Leaders as Psychological Weapons

In the great debate of nature versus nurture, leadership usually takes a front seat among professionals and scholars alike. As former military leaders, we argue that leaders are not born but created through various academic and professional venues. In his research and writings on leadership, Day (2001, p. 583) has postulated that training ". . . development is thought to occur primarily through training individual, primarily intrapersonal, skills and abilities." Historical military leaders from the United States such as Generals Robert E. Lee, Ulysses S. Grant, George S. Patton, and David Petraeus all began their careers after graduating from the United State Military Academy where they learned fundamental leadership traits. Upon commissioning in the military, they continued their professional leadership development through various schools, practical experiences, and, eventually, in the chaos of combat.

We discussed earlier that in World War II only 15 to 20 percent of front-line soldiers would fire (Marshall, 1978). However, almost everyone participated when there were leaders present ordering them to shoot. Lest you think that a leader cannot possibly be that omnipotent, recall the classic study of obedience conducted by Milgram (1963).

In 1963, Stanley Milgram of Yale University conducted a series of experiments looking at obedience to authority. He instructed his subjects to administer electric shocks to people, who were actually secret confederates of the doctor, whenever they erred on questions given on a test. Milgram found that the subjects followed his orders even when they believed they had actually killed the people they were shocking.

If a subject in the experiment asked permission to stop, the leader, a scientist wearing a lab coat and holding a clipboard simply said, "The experiment requires that you continue." Many subjects in the experiment continued because the man in the position of authority, wearing the lab coat, directed them to. How many people do you think were willing to shock a fellow human being to death just because someone with a white lab coat told them to? The incredible answer is that 65 percent were willing to do so!

This study has been replicated using only women applying the "electric shocks" and it has been duplicated in other cultures and nations, always with a similar, incredibly high percentage of willingness to obey orders from a person of authority. Now, if a man with a white lab coat can make 65 percent of all human beings kill another person as long as they do not have to personally see it happen, what can people with real trappings of authority do? What can a military commander do?

On March 16, 1968, the enraged and frustrated troops of Charlie Company, 11th Brigade, 23rd Infantry Division (The American Division), under the command of Lt. William Calley, entered the little village of My Lai, Vietnam, nestled in the middle of a densely mined Vietcong entrenchment. Several men in Charlie Company had recently been maimed or killed in the surrounding area, so they were flustered and angry, and more than ready for a fight with the Vietcong. They were on a "search and destroy" mission.

Calley ordered his men to enter the village firing, although they had not received information of enemy fire coming from it. As the mission unfolded, it quickly deteriorated into a slaughter of over 300 apparently unarmed civilians, including women, children, and the elderly. Eyewitnesses later said that numerous elderly men were bayoneted, praying women and children were executed in the back of their heads, one girl, possibly more, raped and then killed. Calley, according to reports, ordered a group of villagers into a ditch and then gunned them down with his weapon on full automatic.

Months later, Calley would be charged with murder. At the trial, he argued that he was just following orders from his captain to kill everyone in the village.

So a captain can order a lieutenant to kill, and the lieutenant can order his troops to kill—and they do it. The modern concept of a combat leader usually envisions a hardened veteran moving behind a battle line of his men, exhorting, encouraging, punishing, rebuking, correcting, and rewarding them. However, combat leadership has not always been like this. Armies have always had leaders, but the Romans were the first to take proven warriors and systematically develop them into professional leaders starting at the lowest levels. Prior to this, leaders were usually expected to get into the battle and lead from the front, but the Romans were the first to place leaders behind their men in an open order of battle.

The influence of this kind of leadership was one of the primary factors in the success of the Roman way of war. The process of a respected, proven, small-unit leader behind his men who demands killing from them has continued to be paramount in effective combat in the centuries to follow. (The fact that he does not necessarily have to *personally* kill the enemy provides a diffusion of responsibility, which also enables the killing.) This kind of leadership largely disappeared along with the Roman Empire, but it appeared again in the firing lines of the English long bowmen. Then again as a systematically applied factor in the firing lines of the successful armies of the gunpowder era. It has continued to the present.

Groups as Psychological Weapons

Although only 15 to 20 percent of riflemen would fire in World War II, it was learned that when there was a crew-served weapon, that is, a gunner and an assistant gunner, the crew almost always fired. This was a result of mutual support, accountability, and diffusion of responsibility. As Marshall (1978, p. 42) wrote in *Men against Fire*: "I hold it to be the one of the simplest truths of war that the thing which enables an infantry solider to keep going with his weapons is the near presence or presumed presence of a comrade."

A soldier can make the decision in his own heart not to pull the trigger, but when he is part of a team, such as a crew-served weapon, he would have to talk to the other soldier about it, and they would have to agree not to shoot. That rarely happens.

Crew-served weapons have generally been responsible for the majority of killing throughout the history of warfare, beginning with the earliest crew-served weapon, the chariot. The chariot often employed a driver and a "passenger" who generally fired a bow (which added the factor of distance in the killing-enabling equation), which was most effective in pursuit. The powerful group dynamics of the chariot (along with its mobility) were to show up again, over two millennia later, in the tanks of the twentieth century.

The Greek phalanx was a mass of spearmen in tight ranks, carrying spears approximately four meters long and protecting themselves with overlapping shields. They were highly trained to move in a formation organized in depth (i.e., moving and fighting "in column," as opposed to "in line") and trained to strike the enemy as a coherent mass. This was a form of crew-served weapon in which newer members were placed in the front under direct observation and accountability of veteran warriors behind them. The phalanx was of such utility that it has shown up repeatedly throughout history and around the world.

The military first used gunpowder in their cannons, which immediately dominated the battlefield. Unlike early muskets, cannons were effective killers from the beginning, as not only did they provide the best form of posturing (i.e., noisemaking) to be seen on the battlefield, they were also a highly effective crew-served weapon, being generally manned by numerous individuals and directly commanded by an officer or a sergeant.

Rarely did the crew show hesitation or mercy in killing the enemy. At close range, the cannon fired "grape shot" into tightly-packed enemy formations, thus becoming, in effect, a huge shotgun capable of killing hundreds of men with a single shot. Napoleon, that "great psychologist," demonstrated his understanding of the true killing utility of cannon (and the comparative ineffectiveness of infantry) by ensuring that his armies always had a higher percentage of cannon than his enemies, and by massing those cannon at key points in the battle.

In the twentieth century, the cannon became an "indirect fire" system (i.e., firing over the heads of friendly combatants from a great distance away), and the machine gun (with its gunner and assistant gunner or loader) came to replace the cannon in the crew-served, "direct fire" role on the battlefield. In World War I, the machine gun was called the "concentrated essence of infantry" (Keegan, 1983, p. 232), but it was actually just a continuation of the cannon in its old, crew-served, mass killing role.

The crew-served machine gun is still the key killer on the close-range battlefield, while the evolution of group-enabling processes continues in tanks and armored personnel carriers. At sea, the dynamics of the crew-served weapon have been in play since the beginning of the gunpowder era, along with the enablers of distance and the influence of leaders.

Conditioning and Stress Inoculation as Psychological Weapons

By 1946, the US Army had completely accepted Marshall's findings of an extremely low firing rate among American riflemen. As a direct result of his work, the Human Resources Research Office of the US Army pioneered a revolution in combat training that replaced the old method of firing at bull's eye targets. The new method involved deeply ingrained conditioning using realistic, man-shaped pop-up targets that fall when hit. Psychologists know that this type of powerful operant conditioning is the only technique that will reliably influence the primitive, midbrain processing of a frightened human being. Just as fire drills condition terrified school children to respond properly during a fire, and repetitious, "stimulus-response" conditioning in flight simulators enables frightened pilots to respond reflexively to emergency situations, frightened soldiers can also be conditioned to shoot reflexively.

Throughout history the ingredients of posturing, mobility, distance, leaders, and groups have been manipulated to enable and force combatants to kill, but the introduction of conditioning in modern training was a true revolution. The application and perfection of these basic techniques appear to have increased the rate of fire from the very low percentage reported for World War II to approximately 55 percent in Korea and around 95 percent in Vietnam. Similar high rates of fire resulting from modern conditioning techniques can be seen in FBI data on law enforcement firing rates since the nationwide introduction of modern conditioning techniques in the late 1960s.

One of the most dramatic examples of the value and power of this modern, psychological revolution in training can be seen in Richard Holmes' (1985) observations of the 1982 Falklands War. Lt. Col. Grossman is a graduate of the British Army Staff College in Camberley, where they conducted in-depth studies of the Falklands war. The superbly trained (i.e., conditioned) British forces in the Falklands were without air or artillery superiority and were consistently outnumbered three-to-one while attacking the poorly trained but well-equipped and carefully dug-in Argentine defenders. Superior British firing rates, which Richard Holmes (1985) estimated to be well over 90 percent as a result of modern training techniques, have been credited as a key factor in the series of British victories in that brief but bloody war.

The British forces' achievement of repeated, successful attacks against a well-prepared enemy that outnumbered them by a ratio of three-to-one flies in the face of all military theory. Some would claim that the British success was because the Argentine forces were draftees or conscript troops. However, the US Army draftees in Vietnam were trained in the new style and they had a firing rate of around 95 percent. They were generally credited with never losing a major ground engagement in that war.

Others point to the M-16 rifle and the close ranges of jungle warfare in Vietnam to explain the high firing rate. Yet the Sten, the M-1 carbine, and the Thompson submachine gun in jungle warfare in World War II did not have any significant advantage in firing rates as opposed to any other individual weapon. However, key weapons (such as the BAR and flame-thrower) and crew-served weapons (such as machine guns) *did* have a significant advantage in firing rates in World War II because of group and leadership influences.

There are *still* nonfirers. One of them was Drew Brown, a Knight Rider reporter with the 1st Ranger Battalion in the invasion of Panama. Brown, in correspondence with Grossman (2004, p. 139) said:

> I was particularly intrigued when I read how studies show that many soldiers find that they cannot pull the trigger when the moment comes. Despite all of our training, I saw it happen to fellow Rangers in Panama. It happened to me. There were a number of times after our parachute assault on Tocumen Airport when I could have shot what I knew were enemy soldiers. But I just didn't feel the need to. I've rationalized it over the years by telling myself that I was alone and outnumbered at the time, and that since they weren't shooting at me, I wasn't going to shoot at them. Sort of a live and let live attitude. I came across an anecdote a few years ago in Stephen Ambrose's book on D-Day, in which he described how small groups of American and German soldiers knowingly passed within a few feet of each other, yet never fired their weapons. I felt sort of justified then. While I can understand how the average Joe might not pull the trigger, it's always seemed odd to me that the same thing might happen, even in elite, well-trained units. Do you explain it simply by accepting the proposition that most people, even soldiers have a natural aversion to killing?

There are a host of factors, such as groups, leadership, relationship to the target and training, that influence the decision to kill, and almost all of them were working together to reduce the probability that Brown would fire in this situation. Brown (Grossman, 2004, p. 139) finished his observation with this question: "While out watching an urban warfare exercise a few weeks ago, one of the battalion commanders explained that what they were trying to teach these soldiers was 'reflexive shooting.' Is the Army's answer training soldiers how to overcome that aversion?"

Yes, that *is* the best answer we have. It seems to work and it appears that this is a revolutionary step forward. There are still nonshooters, but the problem has been significantly reduced.

During the preparation of his combat military police company for their deployment in support of Operation "IRAQI FREEDOM," Major Hughbank realized that a high percentage of his machine gunners were extremely young and had never deployed into a combat situation. His concern for their ability and willingness to fire their weapon systems in an urban environment with a controlled rate of fire led him to use a unique training tool. Major Hughbank, along with his junior leaders, opted to set up a group of red and blue balloons at the training range—red represented the enemy and blue the friendly forces on the battlefield. On command, his gunners fired a 3–5 round burst into the collective balloons aiming for the red balloons. After completing the firing exercise, each gunner gained a greater understanding of their ability to control rates of fire and that the killing of innocents, while extremely unfortunate, was a byproduct of war.

We will never achieve perfection on the battlefield, but there can be no doubt that future armies that attempt to go into battle without the kind of psychological preparation provided to the British forces in the Falklands is likely to meet a fate similar to that of the Argentines. The difference between an estimated 15 to 20 percent firing rate and a 90 percent firing rate represents a four-and-a-half to six-fold increase in combat effectiveness, which was repeatedly and consistently sufficient to overcome the Argentine's three-fold advantage in raw numbers of troops on the ground.

One additional new development is the use of combat stress inoculation through force-on-force paint-bullet training (realistic training exercises in which trainees might be hit with low-impact bullets that sting and leave a paint mark). There is tentative evidence that this type of stress inoculation has reduced the fear-induced spray-and-pray response (an adrenaline-charged incident in which a police officer or soldier fires multiple rounds in hopes that one or two will hit the threat) and increased law enforcement hit rates (as opposed to firing rates) from around 20 percent to approximately 90 percent. This is an additional four-fold increase in combat effectiveness through training, which combines with the up to six-fold increase in firing rates.

Lt. Col. Grossman has trained numerous combat units associated with the US Army, Navy, and Marines as they prepared for the invasion of Iraq in 2003. All of these troops had incorporated the use of paint bullets in their training to inoculate themselves against combat stress. Additionally, the US armed forces and their allies have integrated state-of-the-art video firearms simulators and laser engagement simulators into unit training.

This systematic integration of simulations technology has made it possible to achieve combat performances such as this:

> During the invasion phase of the Iraq War, Captain Zan Hornbuckle, a 29-year-old Army officer from Georgia, found himself and his 80 men surrounded by 300 Iraqi and Syrian fighters. Unable to obtain air or artillery support, Captain Hornbuckle and his unit—*who were never before in combat*—fought for eight hours. When the smoke cleared, 200 of the enemy were dead . . . not a single American was killed. (Veith, 2003, emphasis added)

Thus modern training has made it hypothetically possible to increase the firing rate of the individual warrior approximately six-fold, and each of these individuals may well be four times more likely to hit their targets. This is a combined effect that represents a potential for a 24-fold increase in the effectiveness of the individual warrior! Now, that hypothetical potential is based on crude estimates and might never be completely achieved since a variety of factors will always get in the way. There can be no doubt, however, that these new forms of training have provided a startling new revolution in combat effectiveness on the modern battlefield. In the end, it is not about the hardware, it is about the "software." Amateurs talk about hardware (equipment), and professionals talk about software (training and mental readiness).

It is quite possible that future generations will come to think of the beginning of the twenty-first century as a "warrior renaissance," a period of remarkable progress in which the full potential of the human factor in combat began to be realized. It is entirely possible that elite warriors in the future will be able to selectively control responses to combat stress, such as auditory exclusion and slow motion time. If they do achieve this capability, they will look back on these years as the era in which we began to discover this untapped human potential.

The Mind is the Final Frontier in Combat Evolution

John Keegan (1983, p. 311) in his book, *The Face of Battle*, described "an atmosphere of high lethality":

> By the beginning of the First World War, soldiers possessed the means to maintain a lethal environment over wide areas for sustained periods ... where one layer of the air on which they depended for life was charged with lethal metallic particles ... It was as if the arms-manufacturers had succeeded in introducing a new element into the atmosphere, compounded of fire and steel.

An atmosphere of high lethality has existed since World War I, and in the realm of individual, small arms engagements, it has not changed significantly. The pump-action 12-guage shotgun in police cars across America is still the most effective weapon for inflicting massive trauma at close range. It is a weapon that has been available and basically unchanged for over 120 years. Transportation and long-range killing technology (missiles, aircraft, and armored vehicles) have all evolved at quantum rates, and their availability to the soldier on the ground gives them great power. The ability of one soldier to call in a 500-pound bomb to land with pinpoint precision makes the individual deadly, while the weapon he holds in his hand has not improved by any comparable quantum leap.

It is useful to think of evolution in combat in the twentieth century and extending into the beginning of the twenty-first century as having moved through "solid," "fluid," and "gaseous" phases as the "energy" in the individual "atoms" or "molecules" (i.e., the soldiers) increased.

- Solid Phase: The solid phase lasted from the ancient phalanx up to World War I, with compact, crystalline masses of humanity grinding into each other. In the end, whoever had their structure—their formation—shattered first, lost.
- Fluid phase: Late in World War I, desperate Germans introduced fluid warfare with Storm Troopers, or Von Hutier tactics, consisting of small units with heavy firepower, commanded by leaders authorized to conduct independent actions. Their objective, as high-energy particles, was to infiltrate through the hard outer shell, into soft, vulnerable units and key terrain in the rear, like water coming through a small gap in a dam, gaining momentum, and forming what was called an "expanding torrent."
- This was refined in World War II into "blitzkrieg" using high-energy "armor" molecules with closely integrated air and artillery support. Today, this is called "maneuver warfare" (as opposed to attrition warfare), and it is a key doctrinal foundation for US and British tactics.
- Gaseous phase: As individual atoms and molecules (soldiers and systems) gain more and more energy (more powerful systems), the result is greater dispersal and a tendency to move upward, into the third dimension. Today, helicopters make whole divisions "air mobile" and "air assault" capable, with transport, attack, recon, and "command and control" from the air. Transports, fighters, bombers, and recon aircraft can saturate the areal dimension of combat space. Satellites complete the equation to form a comprehensive, three-dimensional battlefield, which the US has incorporated as a war-fighting doctrine.

Just as weapons evolution has driven combat from solid, to fluid, to gaseous states, so too has the increased "energy" of the battlefield increased the area "heated" or affected by combat. The result is an ever-expanding battlefield across time and space, which has progressed, for example, from Agincourt in 1415, a battle that was only hours long and covered an area not much deeper than the range of a longbow, to Gettysburg in 1863, a battle that lasted three days (but stopped at night), covering an area as deep as cannon direct fire (about a mile) to World War I, 1914–1918, when combat lasted for months on end, day and night, and indirect artillery fire extended the depth of the battlefield for many miles. Today, we live in a world in which no place or time is safe in war. Although the soldier on this modern battlefield is like some ancient demigod calling in thunderbolts from above, the basic technology of close-range weapons carried by the soldiers, weapons that kill by simply transferring kinetic energy from bullet to body, have reached an evolutionary dead end; in the twentieth and twenty-first centuries these weapons have not changed fundamentally in nearly a hundred years. However, there has been a new, evolutionary leap in the conditioning of the mind that uses that weapon to kill at close range. The development of psychological conditioning processes to enable a person to overcome the average, healthy individual's deep-rooted aversion to close-range killing of one's own species is a true revolution.

Acquired Violence Immune Deficiency Syndrome (AVIDS)

There are two filters that a human mind must pass through to kill at close range (Grossman, 1995; Grossman & Siddle, 2010). The first is the forebrain. A hundred things can convince the forebrain to take a gun in hand: poverty, drugs, gangs, leaders, radical politics, and the social learning of violence in the media—magnified when the armed person is a child from a broken home and searching for a role model. Traditionally, all of these influences slam into the resistance that a frightened, angry person confronts in the midbrain. With the exception of sociopaths (who by definition do not have this resistance) the vast majority of circumstances are not sufficient to overcome this midbrain safety net. However, when a person has been conditioned to overcome these midbrain inhibitions, they become a walking time bomb, a pseudo-sociopath just waiting for the random factors of social interaction and forebrain rationalization to put them at the wrong place at the wrong time.

Consider this analogy. HIV/AIDS does not kill people. Rather, the virus destroys the immune system and makes the victim vulnerable to death by other factors. The "violence immune system" exists in the midbrain. Conditioning via the media—violent movies, television, and video games—creates an "acquired deficiency" in this system, resulting in "Acquired Violence Immune Deficiency Syndrome" or AVIDS. As a result of this weakened immune system, the victim becomes more vulnerable to violence-enabling factors, such as poverty, discrimination, drugs, gangs, radical politics, and the availability of guns.

In weapons technology terms, this indiscriminate use of combat conditioning techniques on children is the moral equivalent of giving an assault weapon to every child in every industrialized nation in the world. If this were done, the vast majority of children would almost certainly not kill with their assault rifles. However, if only a small percentage did, the results would prove tragic and unacceptable. But it is increasingly clear that this is not a hypothetical situation. Indiscriminate civilian application of combat conditioning techniques as entertainment has increasingly been identified as a key factor in sky-rocketing violent crime rates. Thus, the influences of weapons technology can increasingly be observed on the streets of nations in many parts of the world.

Conclusion

Once diplomacy has stalled or completely failed, wars are fought by one group of humans to force another group to submit to their will. Weapons are tools that help humans overcome their physical and psychological limitations in order to inflict their will upon others. Democratic nations seldom, if ever, go to war against each other (Lynn-Jones, 1998). Instead, they choose less destructive methods of influence.

With the coming of the age of democracies, there can be hope that the time of wars may be on the distant horizon, and thus the passing of war may also mark the passing of some of its instruments. An argument can be made that the early twenty-first-century conflicts in Iraq and Afghanistan and concerns about nuclear arms in Iran and North Korea are actually problems of "democracy deficits," as remaining pockets of totalitarian nations are slowly and painfully confronted. Perhaps this is too optimistic a view, but precedence for an end to war can be found in weapons evolution.

It has become increasingly obvious that each act of violence breeds ever-greater levels of violence, and at some point, the genie must be put back in the bottle. The study of killing in combat teaches us that soldiers who have had friends or relatives injured or killed in combat are much more likely to kill and commit war crimes.

Contrary to Steven Pinker's (2011) argument that violence has decreased, the world is just now recovering from the most violent and bloody century in human history and the streets of the western, industrialized nations are the scenes of a level of violence that is unprecedented in human history. Each individual injured or killed by violence provides a point of departure for further violence on the part of their friends and family. Every destructive act gnaws away at the restraint of human beings. Each act of violence eats away at the fabric of our society like a cancer, spreading and reproducing itself in ever-expanding cycles of horror and destruction. The genie of violence cannot really ever be stuffed completely back into the bottle. It can only be cut off here and now before the slow process of healing and resensitization can begin.

It can be done; it has been done in the past. As Richard Heckler (1989) has observed, there is a precedent for limiting violence-enabling technology. It started with the classical Greeks, who for four centuries refused to implement the bow and arrow even after being introduced to it in a most unpleasant way by Persian archers.

In *Giving Up The Gun*, Noel Perrin (1988) explained how the Japanese banned firearms after their introduction by the Portuguese in the 1500s. The Japanese quickly recognized that the military use of gunpowder threatened the very fabric of their society and culture. So they moved aggressively to defend their way of life. The feuding Japanese warlords destroyed all existing weapons and made the production or import of any new guns punishable by death. Three centuries later, when Commodore Perry forced the Japanese to open their ports, the Japanese did not even have the technology to make firearms. Similarly, the Chinese invented gunpowder but elected not to use it in warfare.

But the most encouraging examples of restraining killing technology have occurred in the last hundred years. After the tragic experience of using poisonous gases in World War I, the world has generally rejected its use ever since. The atmospheric nuclear test ban treaty continues after three decades, the ban on the deployment of antisatellite weapons is still going strong after two decades, the nuclear weapons arsenals of the United States and former USSR have been steadily reduced over the past twenty-some years, and we have seen a Nobel Peace Prize awarded to a new movement to eliminate land mines. As we have deescalated instruments of indiscriminate mass destruction, so too can we deescalate instruments of indiscriminate mass desensitization as entertainment in the media.

Firearms probably will not go away anytime soon. However, their abuse will almost definitely be influenced by technology that will make guns "keyed" so that they can only be fired by a designated individual. Similarly, violence in the media will not go away as long as there is a market for it. We can hope that there will be movement away from the indiscriminate violence-enabling of children through violent video games and violence in the media, while still permitting their availability to adults. This can be done just as alcohol, tobacco, prescription drugs, pornography, and guns are kept away from children.

Heckler (1989, p. 287) pointed out that there has been "an almost unnoticed series of precedents for reducing military technology on moral grounds," precedents that show the way to understanding that we do have a choice about how we think about war, about killing, and about the value of human life. In recent years, we have exercised the choice to move ourselves back from the brink of nuclear destruction. In the same way, our society can also take the evolutionary steps away from the technology that psychologically enables killing in children. Education and understanding is the first step. The end result may be for weapons evolution to take a considered step backward and for our civilization to come through the dark years of the twentieth century and enter into a healthier, more self-aware society in the current century.

References

Chandler, D. (1966). *The campaigns of Napoleon*, vol. 1, New York: Simon & Schuster.

Clausewitz, C. V. (1984). *On war*. Princeton: Princeton University Press

Day, D. V. (2001). Leadership development: A review in context. *Leadership Quarterly, 11*(4), 581–613. Retrieved from: http://www.profjayrfigueiredo.com.br/LID_AC_04.pdf

Fink, G. (2010). *Stress of war, conflict, and disaster*. Oxford: Academic Press.

Freely, J. N., & Cotton, R. C. (2005). *Battle studies: Ardant du Picq, Charles Jean Jacques Joseph, 1821–1870.* Retrieved from ardant-du-picq-charles-jean-jacques-joseph-1821–1870_battle-studies.pdf

Griffith, P. (1989). *Battle tactics of the civil war*. New Haven: Yale University Press.

Griffith, P. (1990). *Forward into battle*. Novato, CA: Presidio Press.

Grossman, D. (1995). *On killing: The psychological cost of learning to kill in war and society*. New York: Little, Brown.

Grossman, D. (2004), *On combat: The psychology and physiology of deadly conflict, in war and in peace*. Millstadt, IL: Warrior Science Publications.

Grossman, D., & Siddle, B. K. (2010). Psychological effects of combat. In G. Fink (Ed.), *Stress of war, conflict, and disaster* (pp. 440–455). Oxford: Academic Press.

Heckler, R. (1989). *In search of the warrior spirit*. Berkeley, CA: North American Books.

Holmes, R. (1985). *Acts of war: The behavior of men in battle*. New York: The Free Press.

Keegan, J. (1983). *The face of battle: A study of Agincourt, Waterloo, and the Somme*. New York: Penguin.

Keegan, J., & Holmes, R. (1985). *Soldiers*. London: Hamish Hamilton.

Lynn-Jones, S. (1998). *Why the United States should spread democracy*. Discussion Paper 98–07, Center for Science and International Affairs, Harvard University. Retrieved from http://belfercenter.ksg.harvard.edu/publication/2830/why_the_united_states_should_spread_democracy.html

Maass, P. (2004, January 11). Professor Nagl's war. *New York Times Magazine*. Retrieved from: http://www.nytimes.com/2004/01/11/magazine/professor-nagl-s-war.html?pagewanted=all &src=pm

Marshall, S. L. A. (1978). *Men against fire*. Gloucester, MA: Peter Smith.

Milgram, S. (1963). Behavioral study of obedience. *The Journal of Abnormal and Social Psychology*, 67, 371–378.

Moran, L., (1945), *The anatomy of courage*. New York: Avery.

Perrin, N. (1988). *Giving up the gun: Japan's reversion to the sword, 1543–1879*. Boston: David R. Godine.

Pinker, S. (2011). *The better angels of our nature: Why violence has declined*. New York: Viking.

Stouffer, S. (1949). *The American soldier: Combat and its aftermath*. Princeton, NJ: Princeton.

Veith, G. (2003) Sentimentality has replaced both martial virtues and clear thinking. Archived Nov. 29, 2003. Vol. 18(46). Retrieved from http://worldmag.com

Watson, P. (1980). *War on the mind: Military uses and abuses of psychology*. New York: Penguin.

Woodward, B. (2003). *Bush at war*. New York: Simon & Schuster.

26

Man the Singer

Song Duels as an Aggression Restraint Mechanism for Nonkilling Conflict Management

JOÁM EVANS PIM

Introduction

Darwin argued in *The Descent of Man* (1871) that singing would have constituted a "musical protolanguage" that shaped the evolution of human communication as a means for sexual selection. But, curiously, this protolanguage did not vanish with the emergence of complex natural languages, remaining as a "living fossil," of which this study will reveal some interesting examples. While Darwin expressed the view that sexual selection was the primary driver for the development of musical and linguistic skills, here we will argue that ritualization, restraint, and avoidance strategies to prevent or minimize potentially lethal physical aggression are a driving evolutionary selection pressure that favored the development of communicative abilities in humans. Using Darwin's "living fossil" metaphor this study will focus on song duels, a widespread practice among human societies with formal and functional counterparts among nonhuman animals.

The title of this essay brings about yet another critical reformulation of the "Man-the-Hunter"/"Man-the-Warrior" themes, recurrent in anthropological literature on human aggressiveness as part of long-held assumptions on the warlike killing-prone behavior of our species (see Fry, 2007, chapter 8). Hart and Sussman (2008, p. 30) and again Sussman and Marshack (2010, p. 11) suggested tongue-in-cheek that an alternative to "Man-the-Hunter" could be "Man-the-Dancer," arguing that "the first battle may not have involved killing at all but a battle of the bands" (Sussman, 2000, p. 93). Evidence such as a recently found 35,000-year-old bone-flute (Ghosh, 2009; also see Kunej & Turk, 2001, and "lithoacoustic" experiments by Zubrow, Cross, & Cowan, 2001) actually suggest that our ancestors may have been more busy singing and making music than killing each other. In fact, representations of intrahuman violence are absent in Palaeolithic art and only start to appear in the late Neolithic (Giorgi, 2009, pp. 115–116; Haas & Piscitelli, chapter 10; see also Giorgi & Anati, 2004). Huizinga (2002 [1949]) also made a similar strong argument for playfulness as a transcendent human element in his *Homo Ludens*. In this essay the idea of singing as a universal phenomenon among humans (versus the clearly nonuniversal and much less frequent practice of killing) is entertained, focusing on the widely spread institution of song duels as a mechanism for preventing potentially lethal physical aggression through the nonkilling management and resolution of conflicts. Similar arguments have been proposed for laughter (Mithren, 2005), dance (Ehrenreich, 2007), and music (see Urbain, 2008).

Fry, Schober and Björkqvist (2010) consider ritualization and restraint mechanisms among human and nonhuman animals during intraspecific aggressive interactions as a result of natural selection pressures that favor nonkilling behavior. As intraspecific killing is rare across species, a wide range of alternatives that exclude or minimize physical aggression and agonistic situations are present. These include strategies such as noncontact displays, forms of ritualized aggression, definition of boundaries, dominance hierarchies, and avoidance, all of which reduce the expense of energy and greatly reduce the risk of injury (Fry et al., 2010, pp. 103–104). Ritualized contests include displays where no physical contact is involved (such as song duels) and tournaments where ritualized fighting is set by a series of rules that reduce the possibilities for serious injury (this is the case of ungulate head butting or human wrestling). Following this approach, human song duels are considered in the wider framework of evolutionary ritualized restraint mechanisms.

Canonical anthropological literature on song duels provided considerable attention to a small set of particular cases—such as the Inuit or the Tiv—but the difficulty of documenting improvised music—which has frequently been neglected and marginalized due to its ephemeral character—is still a significant burden. Hoebel (1941) described the song duels of the Inuit (also studied by Rasmussen, 1929) as a juridical instrument to "settle disputes and restore normal relations between estranged members of the community" (Hoebel, 1941, p. 681). The main goal would not be restitution but rather psychological satisfaction and relief (Hoebel, 1941, pp. 678, 682) through a form that privileges the means of a pleasurable public competition. Hoebel continued to discuss this issue in his 1954 essay *The Law of Primitive Man: A Study in Comparative Legal Dynamics*, explaining the nature of the "song-duel complex" as a "substitute for violence to close issues of dispute without recourse to steps that may lead to feud" (1954, p. 329).

Following Hoebel, Gluckman (2009 [1965]) also considered song duels in his *Politics, Law and Ritual in Tribal Society* (see also Gluckman 1954, 1963). Bohannan (1957, 1967) widened the picture by tackling the case of the Tiv of Nigeria, where contests between an offended person or group of persons and his/their opponents could last for weeks. (For a more recent account see Keil, 1979.) All these approaches (and others such as Mayer, 1951; Herndon & McLeod, 1972; Brenneis & Padarath, 1975; Ingham, 1986; Frank, 1989) defended the interpretation of song duels as a mechanism for nonkilling conflict and dispute management and resolution, which has been recurrent in manuals and other literature (i.e., Galtung, 1965, p. 369) and that will also be adopted in this work.

This chapter starts out with a form of Galizan song duel from Europe's southwestern Atlantic coast, but many other forms of song duelling and similar performances can easily be found throughout the world. Table 26.1 presents an exploratory inventory and certainly an examination of additional literature would offer further cases from other locations around the world.

TABLE 26.1 **Song Duels and Related Practices Around the World**

EUROPE

Iberia	Andalusia (Campo Tejedor, 2006), Catalonia, Valencia, and the Balearic Islands (Ayats, 2007), the Basque Country (Frank, 1989; Aulestia, 1995; Díaz-Pimienta, 1998; Garzia Garmendia, Sarasúa and Egaña, 2001; Bertsozale Elkartea, n.d,), Portugal, (Câmara, 1984, pp. 70–71; Avery, 1984; Castro, 1983).
Balkans	Lockwood (1983: 31), Sugarman (1988, p. 36), Foley (1991).
Germany	Horak and Horak (1986), Eibl-Eibesfeldt (1986, p. 80).
Italy	Pagliai and Bocast (2005), Pagliai (2009, 2010).
Malta	McLeod and Herndon (1975), Herndon and McLeod (1972).
Greece	Herzfeld (1988, Ch. 4).

AFRICA AND THE MIDDLE EAST

Turkey	Erdener (1995), Reinhard and Pinto (1989), Hickman (1979), Glazer (1976), Dundes, Leach and Özök (1970).
Lebanon	Haydar (1989).
Palestine	Yaqub (2007), Sbait (1993).
Yemen	Caton (1990).
Tuareg Berbers	Aulestia (1995).
Somalia	Andrzejawski and Galaal (1963), Andrzejawski and Galaal (1964), Luling (1996).
Ethiopia	Shack (1974, p. 34).
Tanzania	Hill (2000, pp. 369–370, 375), Topp-Fargion (2000, pp. 43, 48), Gunderson (2001).
Nigeria	Ojaide (2001), Bohannan (1957), Keil (1979).

AMERICA[1]

Inuit-Aleut	Rasmussen (1976 [1929]), Hoebel (1941), Eckert & Newmark (1980), Laughlin (1980, p. 53), Briggs (2000), etc.
Caribbean	Posada (2003).
Brazil	Bastide (1959); Crook (2005, pp. 98–106), Travassos (2000).
Guyana	Edwards (1979).
Quechua	Turino (1993), Solomon (1994, 2000).
Trio	Urban (1986), Rivière (1971), Carlin and Boven (2002, pp. 28–29).
Kuna	Sherzer (1987), Urban (1986).
Mapuche	Titiev (1985 [1949]).
Chamula Maya	Gossen (1971).
Otomí	Boilès (1978).
Kalapalo	Basso (1985, p. 246).
Saramaka	Price & Price (1991, p. 5).
United States	Abrahams (1962, 1968), Labov (1972), Lefever (1981).

ASIA/PACIFIC

Central Asia	Kirghis, Kazakhians, Turkomans, Azerbaijanis, Telengites, Shor, Yakut, Tajik, etc. (Emsheimer, 1956).
Malay	Daniels (2005, p. 226).
New Guinea	Chodkiewicz (1982), Kulick (1993).

Continued

TABLE 26.1 *Continued*

Indonesia	Bowen (1989, p. 25).
Lepcha	Foning (1987, pp. 175–176).
The Philippines	McKenna (1997, p. 63).
India	Gumperz (1964), Osella and Osella (1998, p. 195).
Fiji	Indian communities in Fiji (Padarath, 1975).

Note 1. There is a limited volume of literature in English on this region. For Latin America see *Argus: Oral Improvisation in the World* at http://www.argodat.com/ and the website of the Cuban *Centro Iberoamericano de la Décima y el Verso Improvisado* at http://www.diversarima.cult.cu/.

The personal connection with Galizan song duelling,[1] the practically nonexistent literature in English on this specific case, and the richness of the example—which moves away from the usual reliance upon hunter-gatherer societies as main ethnographic sources—are the major reasons for considering *regueifa* as a point of departure in this essay. *Regueifa* is probably the oldest and most genuine form of Galizan song duels (Suárez, 1982), integrating in a complex ritual a wide array of elements such as song, dance, gifts and redistribution, praise and blessing, critique, insult, recognition and forgiveness, eating and drinking, and mainly the reinforcement of coexistence of opinions and beliefs in the wider setting of societal and interpersonal relations (Blanco, 2009, p. 16). In fact, this resonates with common features of song duels in other places where an interplay takes place between "individualistic and community needs, creative urges with societal controls, conflict with cooperation and festivity with hostility" in an ambiguous setting where friends or kin are also adversaries, singing but arguing, joking but attacking (Eckert & Newmark, 1980, pp. 208–209).

Galizan Song Duels and Related Practices

Galizan song duels have been presented as a mechanism for "the regulation of individual and collective aggressiveness," transforming "violence and dissatisfaction into words, humour, verbal inventiveness and entertainment" (Blanco, 2009, p. 20). The improvised *regueifa* verses are passionate accounts of "rights, obligations, loyalties, virtues, immorality, ideas and feelings," poeticizing experience and presenting facts from moral grounds seeking to emotionally persuade individuals and communities to "honour their duties, behaviour, order and synchrony" (Lisón Tolosana, 2004, p. 47). As a ritual, *regueifa* brought together the community in a controlled setting in a way crucial not only to monitor and prevent the development of physical aggression and mitigate the extent of verbal attacks but also to sanction the outcome (Prego Vázquez, 2000, pp. 107–114). All these patterns are closely related to similar mechanisms throughout the world, of which an exploratory overview is sketched in the next section.

Several variations and denominations for Galizan song duels coexist.[2] One of the most widely known forms is the *regueifa*. Probably derived from the Arabic word *ragif* (رغيف, pl. ارغفة, *argifat*), meaning "cake" (Steingass, 1882, p. 49), the term has three interwoven connotations within Galizan culture.[3] In a first semantic level it refers to a large bread roll made of wheat, eggs, sugar, butter, and sometimes other ingredients such as cinnamon or grated lemon rind, which after being baked in a wood burning oven is decorated with colored ribbons, chocolates, caramelized fruits, and other sweets and garlands (Ledo Cabido, 2002; Casal Vila, 2003). There are records of its manufacture since the fourteenth century and also of its high value, especially for rural communities where it was considered an extraordinary culinary delicacy. Nevertheless, the *regueifa* is no ordinary cake, as it is prepared exclusively for weddings or, in some accounts, for other exceptional celebrations such as christenings (Hartley, 1912, p. 226).

Usually provided as a gift to the bride by the *madrinha* (roughly equivalent to the "matron of honour" in weddings or to the "godmother" in christenings), the *regueifa* roll used to be displayed in a prominent position, and all other wedding gifts should be placed around it (Risco, 1962, p. 565). The *regueifa* ultimately becomes the prize—to be collectively redistributed—of a traditional practice that is referred to by the same name. In this second semantic level the *regueifa* refers to a complex ritual that begins when the *madrinha* (or in some instances the bride herself) walks out of the dwelling where the celebration is taking place while carrying the *regueifa* bread roll on her head. There, all the young men and women from the village (sometimes from other villages of the same parish and even other parishes) would be waiting, at times in very large numbers, even if they had not been formally invited as wedding guests—who would also join in the ritual (Suárez, 1979, p. 40; 1982, pp. 12–13).[4] What follows is possibly the most playful and festive ritual that integrated Galizan wedding ceremonies (Álvarez Lombariñas, 2009, p. 171), where the *regueifa* expresses a third semantic level indicating a display contest of dance and song.

As a dance, the *regueifa* has two distinctive moves. Firstly, a very slow dance is performed by the *madrinha* or bride while holding the *regueifa* roll on her head.[5] Secondly, a dancing duel is performed by two or more masculine participants, executing the most complex set of moves (*pontos*) they are able to carry out, usually following *moinheira*—a fast dance in 6/8 time, similar to the Irish jig and often played with the bagpipe (Ledo Cabido, 2002, p. 351). In this display, being able to carry out extremely complex steps with agile movements and fast turns while maintaining rhythmic gracefulness was the most valued aspect of the performance. Though usually limited to men (Taboada Chivite, 1972, p. 193; Prego Vázquez, 2000; Casal Vila, 2003, p. 60), variations on this custom coexisted in different locations. Risco (1962, pp. 546, 566) explains how in some areas *regueifa* dance duels were performed only by married or older men or women, while song duels were the domain of younger villagers.

After this initial dancing display a song duel contest was initiated, which also receives the name of *regueifa*, as does the genre it represents. This form of improvised oral versified contest (also referred to as *retesia* or *porfia*) follows a conversational logic—where gesticulation also has a great importance—confronting two, and in some cases more than two, adversaries. The formal structure is characterized by that of the *cuarteta*, a poetic form composed of four octosyllabic verses (exceptionally three-verse stanzas were used) where even verses rhyme (assonant or consonant) while uneven verses remain free, although the first verse of each stanza must rhyme with the last verse of the previous one, in other words following the pattern "abcd" but also "abab" (Álvarez Lombariñas, 2009, p. 174; Blanco, 2008, p. 104; Blanco, 2009, p. 14). The formal complexity and the absence of any instrumental interludes require great ability, spontaneity, and fast thinking, making improvisation extremely difficult, although the slow, repetitive, monotonic melody—which is particular to this genre—somewhat eases the task.

The genre is characterized by a humorous, cheeky attitude dominated by *retranca*—a distinctive crafty blend of irony and hidden or ambiguous meanings. A degree of verbal aggressiveness is expected, but keeping sufficient moderation so that the contest does not overflow into physical aggression (Blanco, 2009, pp. 12–13). Each time a singer would put out a stanza he would receive a reply from one or more opponents, to which he should also answer back with speed and cleverness. The verbal *porfia* should move along in an unstable equilibrium, where "the ability to act under pressure, submitted to constant attack and required to answer and refute in just seconds" (Blanco, 2009, pp. 21–22) were necessary to avoid public embarrassment. *Regueifas* could last for hours, thus demanding the singer's physical and mental resistance, along with the appropriate doses of humor and respectfulness, so as to avoid excessively offending adversaries or audience.

A progression exists from the humorous critique of those who are close relatives to the more hostile lambasting of non-kin. This kind of framing is common in song duels across cultures as it helps to isolate the special setting of the duel from everyday life (Eckert & Newmark, 1980, p. 199; Brenneis & Padarath, 1975; Bowen, 1989). The first stanzas would usually consist of a salutation to those present, followed by a critique of the *regueifa* roll itself (size, ornamentation, and so on). The next stanzas would be directed at the bride and groom (or the parents in a christening), aiming at such issues as prenuptial sexual behavior, reasons for marriage (especially economic), physical appearance and dress of the bride, appropriateness of the age of bride and bridegroom, and so forth. Usually one singer would be praising the couple while his adversary would make pejorative remarks (Suárez, 1982).

The couple's families, godparents, and wedding guests would be targeted next, moving along to neighbors, fellow villagers, and people from nearby villages or parishes who were attending the contest (Ledo Cabido, 2002, p. 351). Typically, *regueifas* would critique real or perceived infractions of the local moral order, especially arrogance; vanity or selfishness; adultery; neglect of obligations, such as those owed to illegitimate sons; theft; womanizing; or just plain wickedness (Lisón Tolosana, 1978, 2004, pp. 40–41). Eventually, factions would spring up along age lines, gender roles, territorial membership (one village or parish against another), and social class distinctions (everybody against the *caciques*— the local political elites), representing a public form of debate across generational, gender, territorial, and class-based factions (Suárez, 1982, p. 23). This process allowed for the open critique of individuals, families, communities and institutions, where a normative degree of well-articulated humorous aggressiveness and offensiveness were allowed. This critique,

rather than seeking to humiliate a specific adversary, intended to publicly expose and cen-
sor actions, events, and behaviors considered reprehensible in the community's normative
terms (Blanco, 2009, pp. 19–20).

The contest would end when after a long confrontation one of the adversaries failed
to answer back, either due to inability to find the appropriate verses or arguments or due
to plain exhaustion. At this point, the duel would either be over or someone else could join
in and take on the argument—or bring in a new one—from where the previous participant had left off. In some instances, it was up to the crowd to decide who had distinguished
himself more for his humor, style, or *retranca* (Álvarez Lombariñas, 2009). As a prize, the
winner had the honor of distributing the *regueifa* roll among all those attending the ritual,
but the main incentive was the possibility to overtly solve—or at least expose—existing
disputes, being able to gain increased consideration by the community through the victory
of one set of arguments, "facts" or opinions.[6]

Song duels were extremely popular—and to some extent still are—in Galizan *festas
menores* (minor celebrations), where resources were usually scarce and musicians could not
be hired, unless they were part of the community. Therefore, improvisation was a viable
alternative, even if not exclusive to this kind of festivities (Blanco, 2009, p. 12). Besides
weddings, christenings, or village religious patrons, song duels would mark the conclusion
of the building of new dwellings or communal works, such as *fias* (spinning), *espadeladas*
(flax cleaning), *panilhadas* or *palilhadas* (lace making), and *albaroques* (field clearing),
where helpers were rewarded with a feast following the completion of the task, even if no
regueifa roll would be offered (Lisón Tolosana, 2004, pp. 27–28; Blanco, 2009, pp. 14–15,
17). Song duels would start after the dinner offered by the beneficiary to co-helpers dis-
pensing some of the more ritualistic aspects of *regueifa*. In these nocturnal gatherings following a day of communal solidarity, people "insult each other alluding to things they
said or did, or should not have said or done, namely omissions in neighborly issues such
as diverting water from an irrigation channel or taking a cow to graze in somebody else's
pasture" (Lisón Tolosana, 2004, p. 39). If things got touchy, the other dinner guests would
act as moderators.

The disappearance of traditional *regueifa* rituals as described above is probably linked
to the shifting of song duels from these traditional settings to more intentional scenarios,
together with the emergence of semiprofessional *regueifeiro* figures that would be hired to
perform in organized contests. In some places, the bride and bridegroom each started to
hire their own renowned *regueifeiro* to praise their own virtues while criticizing the other's
defects (Álvarez Lombariñas, 2009, p. 174), but this custom eventually disappeared and
today the *regueifa* has vanished from Galizan weddings. *Regueifa* display tournaments also
moved gradually from community celebrations to taverns (especially at the end of market days), local parish festivities, and processions and secular celebrations such as *entroido*
(Blanco, 2009, p. 16). In some areas such as the Bergantinhos region this led to a climax
in the popularity and public visibility of *regueifa* from the mid-twentieth century to the
1970s, where public competitions were organized and an informal "league" of competing

regueifeiros arose and the *regueifa* roll as an honor was replaced by a monetary prize. (See Lisón Tolosana, 2004, pp. 31–33; Blanco, 2009; Calvo Gómez, 2007; González Muíño, 2008.) However, in most regions traditional *regueifa* fell into a relentless decline and eventually disappeared, even if some practitioners are still active, namely in the Bergantinhos region and the Caurel Eastern mountain ranges (Alonso Piñeiro, 2005, p. 4). Other forms of song duels have remained popular and even the older genres are currently being reintroduced and reshaped through contemporary influences.

Beyond the obvious explanation of rural decline—eroding most traditions, and especially those linked to orality—Suárez (1982, pp. 37–39) places the end of traditional *regueifa*, at least in the Noia region, at the end of the Spanish Civil War (1936–1939). These years were marked by famine, social tension, and extreme poverty in the disadvantaged rural areas where traditional oral practices such as *regueifa* had their stronghold. Social tension and violence ended up "making *regueifas* an increasingly dangerous and unpleasant feast due to the numerous fights" and eventually *regueifeiros* and those demanding the customary ritual were expelled with stones thrown by the wedding guests at their arrival (1982, pp. 37, 38). Lisón Tolosana (2004, p. 31) explains how the *regueifa* was abandoned, as it was increasingly used as a pretext to randomly insult and start fights. Ironically, in this context of great unrest, the *regueifa* appeared to be unable to continue to function as a social mechanism for the dissipation of interpersonal conflict and the avoidance of physical aggression, actually becoming in some instances a source for the exacerbation and escalation of violence. It could be argued that the disintegrating rural societies surpassed the maximum threshold of conflict manageable by song duel contests or that it is the disintegration of these traditional societies that disabled the functionality of song duels.[7]

In spite of their displacement from traditional settings and rituals, song duels as such never disappeared from Galizan society and actually have regained some dynamism since the mid-1990s. The unlikely source of this revival came from contemporary music genres such as rap and hip-hop (Álvarez Lombariñas, 2009, p. 176), leading to a cultural blend sometimes referred to as "agro-rap," which claims the *regueifa* tradition as its own. Singers such as Pinto d'Herbom and Luís Caruncho were instrumental in the restoration of this genre in the public sphere and in cultivating new practitioners within urban areas (Tarela, 2003, p. 18). In addition to individual singers, larger efforts are being developed to introduce improvised song duels in schools, fostering consideration for the genre in the wider society through workshops, organized contests, gatherings, and the like. ORAL, a nonprofit organization established in 1997,[8] has been extremely active in promoting events such as the International Oral Improvisation Tournament—now in its eleventh year and bringing together participants from all over the world—and generally fostering the presence of improvised song duels in schools and local celebrations (Barros, 2002). This has been especially important in urban areas, where Galizan culture and language are in greater danger of disappearance and also where conflict resolution techniques have proven extremely valuable. *Regueifas* have been considered a way of simultaneously promoting Galiza's language and culture while linking them with contemporary forms of musical expression such as hip-hop that are popular among younger people.

Several nonmutually exclusive interpretations of the origins and significance of the *regueifa* can be found among the scarce literature that tackles this practice. Carré Aldao (see Taboada Chivite, 1972, p. 36) and other authors have considered *regueifa* song duels as reminiscent of pre-Roman epithalamium chants—public songs praising the bride and bridegroom—which continued through medieval minstrel practices. The medieval Occitan *tenso* or *tençon* (and related genres as the *partimen* and the *cobla* exchange) has indeed a very similar logic, where two troubadors debate in turns on a certain issue, sometimes including a third participant (*contension*) who would judge the outcome. Risco (1962) preferred to interpret the complex ceremonies that surround Galizan traditional weddings as rites of passage, marked by their agonistic or competitive exchange character,[9] and Suárez (1979, p. 40; 1982, p. 36) explained the *regueifa* as a forgiveness ceremony, considering that the union of bride and groom would constitute "a lack of solidarity with the rest of the village"—both would no longer have the same status and would cease or alter their participation in social events where unmarried couples had particular roles. Also related to this is Lisón Tolosana's (2004, pp. 39–40) structuralist approach, that considers *regueifa* a way of "reaffirming the group at a point of momentary excision or exclusion," as both guests and uninvited *regueifeiros* are two parts of one ceremony—some are physically and symbolically outside while others are inside—simultaneously disapproving and ratifying the existence of units and segments within the community.

More interesting are Lisón Tolosana's (2004, p. 46) views on the atmosphere, which allows for verbal aggressiveness, defining *regueifa* as a control mechanism. Song duels usually take place after the affirmation of group solidarity, whether through reciprocal collective works or through a wedding or similar celebration to which guests—sometimes everyone in the village—contribute. This is certainly the case for variations on the *regueifa* such as *loia* or *brindes*, where song duels begin after the coworkers have become house guests and have received a plentiful dinner following a long day marked by cooperation, comradeship, and festivity. This is the context in which the discharge of aggressiveness is allowed, representing the local norms of coexistence from an individual perspective: "all accumulated aggressiveness must be kept to be released not privately but publicly, and not arbitrarily but under a set of rules and conditions." It is this ceremonial release "that tames individual aggressiveness or at least conditions its eruption to controlled circumstances which prevent dangerous blazes" (Tolosana, 2004, p. 46). Tolosana further describes this mechanism in the following terms:

> Your aggressiveness can be unlimited, there are no barriers to expressing it as
> long as it is exteriorized after dinner, publicly and singing in verse. You may show
> your irritation to whomever you choose and as much as you want, but singing.
> You can be stubbornly aggressive, but in verses. Is it the case that the amount

of concentration required for versification and singing shifts the attention that would be focused exclusively on emotional charge toward the creation of beautiful complexities? This is the Galizan aesthetics of aggression or the Galizan aesthetic aggression.

Song Duels: A Cross-Cultural Comparison

The description of Galizan song duels will certainly resonate with similar practices throughout the world. To initiate a comparative approach this chapter will move away from the "canonical" studies and explore some lesser-known examples. This will of course remain an exploratory approach, as only a small fraction of the vast existing literature is being considered. As the Galizan *regueifa* was customarily set up in the ritualized context of weddings, some similar practices will be explored, even though other settings, with significant commonalities, are frequent. Nevertheless, the fact that weddings are usually a delicate moment for inter- or intra-group relations suggests the strategic importance of placing this practice in such a setting. To some extent, airing grievances and past transgressions at the time of the wedding is reminiscent of the "Speak now or forever hold your peace" from the Christian marriage liturgy.

Song duels in Northern India have been described by Gumperz (1964), and Brenneis and Padarath (1975) discuss similar "challenge singing" among the Bhatgaon, a Fiji Indian village where Muslims and different sects of Hindus coexist. Communal and religious rivalry was significant until the 1970s, when song duelling started to decay. Song duels would usually take place at weddings or other social events in which large numbers of people congregate, "create[ing] an artificial environment in which issues of great importance and sensitivity can be publicly aired" (1975, pp. 283, 285). Those involved abided by set rules wherein overtly taking offense was deemed to be a sign of weakness and lowered one's prestige (Brenneis & Padarath, 1975, p. 290).

Religion is used as a means to catalyze personal quarrels, even if attacks and insults gradually shift to personal accusations regarding immorality or misbehavior that would in other contexts "provoke physical assault or other overt conflict" (Brenneis & Padarath, 1975, p. 283). Defeat comes when singers are embarrassed, unable to respond, or call for an end to the duel. This occurs when they "cannot continue to produce novel insults within the rules, or when they respond to insults as real accusations and become angry" (Brenneis & Padarath, 1975, p. 290).

Gayan (song) usually consists of a set framework of unrhymed couplets ending in a repeated tag phrase that is sung by a chorus.[10] Generally, *Gayan* begins exhorting the qualities of one's faith, then moves to challenge aspects of the other's faith, and finally sets out to deal with more sensitive and personal issues, referring to "commonly known incidents from the public biographies of individual targets" (Brenneis & Padarath, 1975, pp. 286, 287). Breaches of traditional practices and morality (sexual morality, male prestige, theft, malicious mischief, among other topics) are challenged through song, stressing "not only what values and ways of behaving are important to the community, but also how men should uphold them and deal with their violation" (Brenneis & Padarath, 1975, p. 290).

Bowen (1989) brings forward an extremely interesting study on how the practices of song duelling have been transformed and restructured as a society shifts from a traditional organization based on "equality and exchange" to a new form "increasingly organized in terms of hierarchy and rivalry" through the influence of the modern state (1989, p. 25). Bowen analyzed the poetic duels of the Gayo of northern Sumatra in Indonesia in light of the deep political changes that have occurred since the turn of the twentieth century and especially from the 1940s onwards: "Poetic duels, once structured around the complementary and transformative exchange of words, have been reshaped by these political shifts, and increasingly highlight combat and control in nontransformative displays" (Bowen, 1989, p. 26).

Precolonial Gayo poetic duels (*didong* or *didong ngerjë*) were performed in the context of "exchange of persons and goods at a wedding" (Bowen, 1989, p. 27). Performers (*céh*) carried out their displays outside the house where the wedding took place, representing particular villages or subvillages. Each singer would imitate the movements of his opponent, culminating in an exchange of riddles related to the wedding, reaching resolution when one opponent is unable to reply and acknowledges defeat (Bowen, 1989, p. 28). The duel follows a fixed structure of two-line parallel proverbs, where the "origins of the event," usually the wedding but sometimes other ceremonies, are explained, followed by a number of queries and objections and finalizing with an agreement on what the outcome should be (Bowen, 1989, p. 30). This performance was crucial to the necessary negotiations between Gayo autonomous political units, whose relations "were made public, concrete, and perceptible in the resolution of disputes and in marriages" (Bowen, 1989, p. 27).

A new form of poetic duelling (referred to as *didong klub*) emerged in the late 1940s involving two teams of 10 to 30 men who represented their villages in organized contests sponsored by the Indonesian government and other political or religious organizations as a form of fundraising and propaganda. *Céh* started to write songs on demand supporting the ruling ideologies, and by the 1960s this became the predominant type of duelling in detriment to traditional practices linked to wedding ceremonies and dispute resolution, which eventually disappeared in the 1980s:

> It is structured around the performance of previously composed (indeed, often written) songs by two teams of 10 to 20 men and boys, each led by 2 to 4 *céh*, taking strictly timed half-hour turns from about nine in the evening until dawn. The contest does not resolve or culminate; it simply ends when the appropriate number of rounds has been completed (Bowen, 1989, p. 31).

While traditional duels were carried out with the expected outcome of preventing and managing conflicts and reaching agreements and compromises that would guarantee the continuation of relations and exchanges among different villages and groups, the new forms of duel exacerbated a static irresolvable rivalry between political or religious factions, following the dominant logic of the Indonesian state (Bowen, 1989, p. 27).

Yaqub's (2007) essay on song duels at Palestinian weddings (*sahrah*) and their wider Arab context also provides an account on how traditional duelling practices suffered radical transformations under changing political and economical contexts. Typical performances associated with weddings and other public celebrations would feature two or more singers who would compete following an established set of rules regarding rhyme, meter, form, and musical melody (Yaqub, 2007, p. 8). Duels take place at the groom's celebration on the eve of the wedding (*sahrah*) and on the wedding day as part of the procession (*zaffah*). As in other song duels performed throughout the Arab world, namely the *munāfarah*, some recurrent topics in these disputes were sexual rivalry, grazing rights, ancestry, appearance, and tribal affiliation (Yaqub, 2007, pp. 38, 39), while a set of traditional values (for instance, generosity, nobility, piety, courage, fidelity) are repeatedly praised (Yaqub, 2007, p. 161). Yaqub explains how the *munāfarah* is effective in reducing violence in various forms:

> It directs conflict that could have exploded on the physical plane to the verbal, and circumscribes the potential of the verbal conflict through the use of poetic rather than referential language. Furthermore, it not only diffuses the violence through this redirection but actually transforms the potentially divisive conflict into a community-building act of co-creation that draws together not just the two quarrelling men, but their respective families and communities as well (Yaqub, 2007, p. 38).

Comparing traditional and contemporary forms of song duelling in Palestine, Yaqub observed how the exchange of insults and boasts had been displaced. Yaqub interprets wedding eve celebrations as a liminal event where the established social hierarchies and norms were disrupted to allow a more open dialogue. But in the current context of cultural and political threat from the Israeli state these celebrations have been transformed into an occasion to reaffirm those hierarchies and social norms: "Rather than creating *communitas* in which a sense of connection between individuals unfettered by the stratifying rules of social interaction is created, the poetry duel celebrates and reaffirms those Palestinian structures which continue to exist" (2007, p. 161).[11]

Singing duels are also integrated as a permanent feature of wedding rituals in many central Asian peoples, such as Kirghis, Kazakhians, and Turkomans (Emsheimer, 1956), or the Himalayan Lepcha (Foning, 1987). There are also accounts of wedding song duels among central Ethiopian peoples such as the Amhara and Tigrina, where "the groom's party is met at the entrance to the bride's father's house by a group of young girls who, while drumming, engage the boys in a vituperative song duel" (Shack, 1974, p. 34), which is also the case for the Yemeni *bālah* and *zāmil*, performed both at weddings and other festive occasion with the intent of resolving latent conflicts (Caton, 1990, p. 113). In the Philippines the *dayunday* song duels are also most often associated with wedding celebrations (McKenna, 1997, p. 63).

Discussion: Song Duels in an Evolutionary Perspective

Singing is present among many nonhuman species, from birds and gibbons to marine mammals such as whales, seals, and dolphins. Research findings have shown important parallels between bird songs and human communication (Marler, 1970; Geissmann, 2000) and have highlighted the capacity of certain nonhuman species to compose and improvise (Payne, 2000) and the relevance of ritualization in human and nonhuman species (Cullen, 1966; Erikson, 1966). The importance of singing and music for human sexual selection was stressed by Darwin and further developed by Miller (2000), while the original "musical protolanguage" that would have shaped vocal control through sexual selection still persists as a living fossil (see Wallin, Merker, & Brown, 2000). Jordania (2006, 2009) suggested singing displays have a defensive function, preventing aggression through intimidation but also serving as a form of reinforcing group cohesion through trance.

Dissanayake (2006, pp. 31–32) defended the idea that music is "a behaviour that evolved in ancestral humans because it contributed to their survival and reproductive success," describing important similarities between evolutionary ritualization in nonhuman animal communication and the ritual use of musical behavior in human ceremonies. Culturally created human music would, to some extent, draw from biologically evolved skills, especially those related to kinesic-vocal-facial ritualized behaviors of mother-infant interactions such as formalization, regularization, stereotypy, repetition, exaggeration, and elaboration (Dissanayake, 2006, pp. 38, 40).[12]

Song duels among birds are very much related to territoriality, especially during the breeding season when fighting and chasing frequently occur along boundary lines. These confrontations are mediated through song on a relatively frequent basis, where "birds may move a short distance apart and conduct a song duel" (Falls, 1978, p. 71). This vocal behavior is set in turns and is also known as "countersinging," common among species such as Northern Cardinals, Tufted Titmice, and Wood Thrushes. The Marsh Wren engages in a related behavior called "song-matching," where "participants in a countersinging bout match each other's song types" (Elliott & Read, 1988, p. 20). Kroodsma (1979, p. 514) actually noted the formal and functional similarities between Marsh Wrens' song duelling and human verbal duels such as those of the Inuit, the West Indies calypso, or Turkish boys insult exchanges, "serving as an intragroup competitive strategy that is an alternative to actual fighting" (Kroodsma, 1979, p. 514). Kroodsma suggests song duelling displays could be a form to express dominance and subordination, comparable to practices of other species such as frog choruses. As natural selection does not tend to favor intraspecific aggression that can lead to killing, nonlethal restrained display contests are actually a common pattern in many species, including examples such as push-ups among side-blotched lizards, aerial displays among male tarantula hawk wasps, or roaring bouts among red dear (Fry et al., 2010; Fry & Szala, chapter 23).

The most common form among humans is the verbal display of anger and hostility in an open argument, either sung or spoken, even if the distinction between these is sometimes blurred. Other forms include contests related to specific skills such as hunting or wealth contests, settled through the accumulation, destruction, and/or distribution of goods.[13] Rather than physical aggression that can result in killing or serious injury, disputes are settled through ritualized mechanisms wherein participants display "their most clever lyrics, haranguing endurance, hunting prowess, sorcery skills, and wealth amassment abilities" in a defined and controlled context with rules that promote restraint and an audience that guarantees their enforcement (Fry et al., 2010, pp. 108, 110). Interestingly, Lorenz (1966, p. 124) noted how restraint mechanisms have a greater relevance among those species where lethal capabilities are strongest, thus reducing the probabilities of intraspecific killing.

As men tend to be more frequently involved in severe physical aggression than women, Fry et al. (2010, p. 115) also suggest that "[n]atural selection has led to the evolution of greater *restraint* among human males regarding physical aggression because they have the capacity to more readily inflict serious injury and death than do human females." This would be a reasonable explanation to the fact that in many societies it is men alone or predominantly men who are involved in song duels. If men are overwhelmingly responsible for intraspecific killing, it makes sense for men to also be the main actors of restraint mechanisms such as song duels. In addition, and taking into consideration the case of *regueifa* where song duels are usually limited to men but sometimes also restricted to or at least more common among the younger and unmarried males, it could be argued that restraint mechanisms are more common among age groups that are more likely to engage in lethal physical aggression. The links between how duels serve as a way to prove masculinity (Hulan, 2003, p. 92), the fact that duels are more frequent among age groups where males are actively seeking to engage women, and the frequency of sexual behavior and more-or-less explicit sexual content as themes must be further explored.

Song duels are also more common among relatively egalitarian societies where institutionalized agents for dispute settlement are not present or play a small role.[14] Where interdependence and kinship links are the norm, conflicts can pose a significant threat over the whole community. Among the Inuit for example, in some instances the only alternative to song duels was the elimination of the conflicting individual(s) through murder, suicide, or withdrawal. Offenses (usually related to hostility, greed, jealously, laziness, thievery, pretentiousness, immodesty and sexual access) "could make existence within the community impossible" as "the accused would find his position [impossible] as the known committer of a serious offense, and the rest of the community would find intolerable their position as implicit accusers and witnesses to his guilt" (Eckert & Newmark, 1980, p. 198). Conflict resolution through song duels aims at keeping both the accused and the accuser within the community. It would be interesting to look at what kind of roles, if any, these mechanisms would play in societies where killing and violence are rare or absent and also if these practices are also valid for intergroup relations.

In most cases, song duels appear to operate as a mechanism for intragroup conflict management, but there are also examples of the use of duels at the intergroup level. This is especially interesting when the ethos of groups is considerably divergent. Fortier (2002) explores the *git* (songs) of the Rāute, a Tibeto-Burman-speaking hunter-gatherer society. Rāute recur to *git* during the sometimes tense barter negotiations with surrounding Indo-Nepalese Hindu agriculturalists. Interestingly, Rāute do not practice song duels among themselves but only when interacting with other societies, serving to "smooth intercultural relations" and to "create a space of common ground" (2002, pp. 236, 246).[15] Also among the Trio of the Brazil-Surinam border, ceremonial ritualized dialogues were most likely to take place with the arrival of strangers to a village and in the context of exchanges of goods and marital agreements. Apparently, "the more socially distant the person, the more 'chanting' the dialogues became." (Personal communication with Jimmy Mans on November 26, 2010; see also Rivière, 1971; Urban, 1986; Carlin & Boven, 2002, pp. 28–29). It is still to be determined if the intragroup usage of song duels will tend to be absent in societies where there is little or no risk of potentially lethal physical aggression or if they will act as an instrumental element in keeping these societies free from killing. The possible relationship between levels of physical aggression and social tension and presence/absence of more complex restraint mechanisms has to be studied.

Of course, as the cases of the Galizan *regueifa*, Gayo *didong*, Palestinian *sahrah*, and Inuit song duels show, the disintegration of traditional societies within the larger modern state apparatus also brought a shift in the uses and settings of song duel practices, sometimes replaced by other institutional frameworks for dispute resolution such as the state judicial system, but also surviving in new forms and contexts. Rather than being relegated to inevitable disappearance within the current context of globalized cultural shifts, song duels are persistently reinventing themselves, redrawing the contexts for their occurrence and the formal aspects of performances themselves. We have seen how contemporary musical styles such as rap or hip-hop—actually historically rooted in duel practices as "sounding" or "playing the dozens"—have facilitated the revival of traditional practices in such cases as the Galizan *regueifa*. The use of song duels as a useful strategy for managing conflict has also been successfully tested in new contexts such as schools, as mentioned earlier with the ORAL school projects in Galiza and elsewhere (Casals Ibáñez, 2004, 2009; Casals, Vilar, & Ayats, 2008). Briggs (2000) argues that Inuit radio talk-shows have become a new medium that recreates the settings of traditional song duelling, having many common characteristics such as publicity, ambiguity, and a key role of the audience, allowing "people to confront without confronting and to respond without responding" (Briggs, 2000, p. 121). As in song duels, talk shows embed and isolate conflict in a formal, ritualized context of referential ambiguity, where an audience is "giving (imagined) support; providing (imagined) sanctions; creating safe distance between potential opponents; and, through all of the above, controlling antagonism and preventing actual conflict" (Briggs, 2000, p. 121).

Briggs (2000, p. 113) suggested that mechanisms such as song duels would only work well in the interdependent context of small homogeneous communities, where people know each other and share a common set of values so that "people can agree on the issues of social life, without having to make them explicit and thus open to argument." Nevertheless, it is not that difficult to see the commonalities, as Hoebel (1954) did, between traditional mechanisms such as song duels and modern judicial settings and bodies for dispute resolution. It is also clear that song duels continue to operate in complex societies up to this day, as they still offer an unmatched setting for solving certain issues that are or remain beyond the margins of institutionalized conflict management. And why not consider, in the light of evolutionary adaptation, the many settings designed for our globalized world such as the United Nations, the modern Olympic games, or even the Eurovision Song Contest as mechanisms for restraint of physical aggression among nation-states?

In *The Beginnings of Diplomacy* Numelin (1950) actually places the origins of diplomatic relations much further back in time than most scholars tend to do. Not only does he refer to song duels (p. 218) but also links formal features of modern diplomacy, such as the inviolability of those designated to talk or carry a message (p. 62), the establishment of certain times and spaces specially arranged for the invocation of peace (usually festivals or rituals such as those of song duels), where traditional practices also related to ritualization and restraint. These features have strong parallels both with the liminal and dialogical settings in which song duels are carried out and with the inherent immunity of those involved, topics that are deserving of closer attention.

Huizinga, in his *Homo Ludens* (2002 [1949]), which also deals with song duels (Huizinga, 2002 [1949], p. 86), traces the play-element among a wide array of human activities. Play is defined as a "make-believe" experience placed outside everyday life, circumscribed in time and space and carried out in accordance to a set of rules, and fostering group relationships sometimes beyond those of ordinary experience. Even if it may appear to be below the level of seriousness, play can also make it to the sublime level of the beautiful and sacred (Huizinga, 2002 [1949], p. 19). In such a way, it generates a fiction or autonomous world that can be ruled by, and can operate with, different conventions, derived from *poièsis* or the play space of the mind. Song duels are certainly both serious and playful, involving the physical dimension of competition (Blanchard, 1995, p. 28) but also a related metacommunicative context that makes them "serious yet not dangerous," as the possibilities for injury are excluded or greatly minimized, while only status and esteem are at stake (Fry et al., 2010, p. 110). As Brenneis (1978, p. 281, emphasis added) puts it: "Play and purpose are inextricably linked in verbal duelling. Only the gamelike and playful definition of the duel makes it possible; *insult unrestrained by traditional practice could be deadly serious.*" In fact, in some traditional societies, physical aggression actually degrades and humiliates the aggressor and not the victim. As Herzfeld (1988, p. 143) explains in relation to Cretan *mandinadha*: "Often, a clever verse riposte serves to restrain physical violence. To respond with a knife or fist would demean the assailant by suggesting that he was incapable of responding with some witty line of his own."

This ritualized atmosphere of control is, according to Abrahams (1962), the primary tool for the duel rhetoric, as the constraints imposed by rules and context allow for a space of liminality where issues that could easily lead to potentially lethal physical aggression are dealt with in a playful manner. Following Yaqub (2007), these liminal and dialogic spaces are key for the emergence of periods of *cummunitas*, when "relations among people are no longer defined by the separateness and hierarchy that mark the structures of society, but rather by an intense feeling of unity and equality among members of the participating group" (Yaqub, 2007, p. 160). This context of general ambiguity, where the boundaries of play and seriousness, praise and insult, humor and seriousness are blurred, is where critique of deviant behaviors and social structures is permitted and encouraged. This is especially evident both in Bohannan's accounts on the Tiv song duels, where truth and fantasy coexisted in an ambiguous equilibrium, and among the Inuit, where "participants are constrained at all times to behave as if all statements in the duel are ironic," since if guilt and accusation were to be publicly declared the community would no longer be able to continue to function after the duel (Eckert & Newmark, 1980, p. 202). Demonstration of anger—acting as if insults were not ironic—would simply give oneself away leading to three transgressions:

> (1) acknowledging the possible truth of the insult, (2) bringing the event into the real world and thus precipitating overt conflict and (3) not performing properly in the speech event and thus declaring oneself a poor participant and an outsider to the community (Eckert & Newmark, 1980, pp. 204–205).

Reframed from the perspective of Bakhtinian dialogism, Yaqub (2007, p. 153) considers song duels as a deeply transformative event, affecting "the nature of relationships and social structures" in a framework where the agonistic character of disputes is not exclusively conflict-oriented and competitive but also consensual and cooperative. As Briggs (2000, p. 113) explains, "since people were not singled out as 'bad people' in the social drama, they were neither isolated nor humiliated by being made the focus of critical attention but rather were kept integrated in the community." This is the reason why duels mainly take place at liminal times such as weddings or among liminal groups—this is the case of the duels among African American and Turkish male adolescents, where insult duels offer a form of sanctuary in which participants "are freed from personal responsibility for the acts [they] are engaged in" (Labov, 1972, p. 168). This place of liminality was achieved through isolation of song duels, framed in a safe temporary context characterized by ambiguity that secludes overt conflict from everyday life (Eckert & Newmark, 1980).

Brenneis (1978, p. 282) further highlights the importance of the audience not only evaluating the quality of songs but most importantly enforcing restraint: "[t]he audience is an authoritative witness to performers' conduct and self-control; it also can stop the contest if [a]fight seems imminent." In societies that are essentially egalitarian, where internal legal agents or institutions do not exist or have little effectiveness, the audience serves as a third-party control to monitor the appropriate resolution of conflict without turning to physical aggression. Regarding this point, Brenneis (1978, p. 282) makes a distinction among adolescent performances—that tend to offer a window for social ranking and leadership realignment—and adult song duel rituals, that tend to "result in the public rebalancing of individuals' interests and reputations and help to ensure their good relations in the future." In evolutionary terms, this distinction could also be linked to the importance of restraint in different age groups where lethal physical aggression is more likely to occur.

Song duels deal with two dimensions of transgressive behavior: on the one hand they tackle contraventions of social norms and on the other they serve as a barrier for blocking or greatly reducing the possibilities of lethal aggression—which is by itself transgressive, as it disrupts the normal existence of a society. This resonates with what Lorenz (1959 in Schechner, 2003, p. 279) described as "displacement activities," where two mutually inhibiting motivations bring about an equilibrium that forces both of them into a stall:

> What happens then is that another movement, which is usually inhibited by both of them, becomes disinhibited because the other two neutralize each other. So, if a bird wants to attack and is afraid in more or less perfect equilibrium of these two motivations, he may start to preen or to scratch, or to perform other activities which are inhibited both by attack and escape, attack and escape being at the moment mutually inhibited.

It is also important to consider the therapeutic value of song duels. As Eckert and Newmark (1980) and Lisón Tolosana (2004) pointed out, duel versification is an intellectual effort that requires a great amount of concentration on the formal and semantic contents of the verses, shifting attention from anger toward the multitasking creative process. The Inuit are a great example of this, as the "singer had to unify his dance movements, the beating of the drum, and the recitation of his *piseq* (lyrics), his eyes closed, concentrating on the inner source of his song" (Eckert & Newmark, 1980, p. 192). This also relates to the functional link between singing displays and group cohesion through trance (McNeill, 1995; Benzon, 2001; Jordania, 2006, 2009; Malloch & Trevarthen, 2009). And, of course, in many traditional cultures trance is induced through music (López Vinader, 2008, p. 154).

Final Remarks

To sum up, the evidence brought forward suggests the possibility that evolutionary selection has favored mechanisms for rule-based ritualized restraint that allows competition to openly take place without the threat of lethal physical aggression. It seems that recurrence to these mechanisms is more common among those segments of human population that are more likely to be engaged in lethal aggression, even if the sometimes incomplete ethnographical data does not allow for firm conclusions. Males—who are more frequently responsible for cases of intraspecific killing—and, among them, younger unmarried men, are usually the main participants in duels across cultures.

It is also worth exploring the characteristics of restraint mechanisms along the continuum that stretches from simple hunter-gatherer societies where intergroup killing is rare or absent to modern nation-states engaged in large-scale warfare. A proportional relation between levels of aggressiveness and complexity of restraint mechanisms could be indicative of evolutionary patterns, ranging from simple nonconfrontational verbal arguments in egalitarian societies to large international organizations for dispute-resolution such as the United Nations in the complex contemporary "society of nations."

Considering that intraspecific killing can easily jeopardize the existence of small interdependent communities, shifting them toward extinction (the case of the Inuit is worth considering closely), extended communicative abilities and related cultural practices such as song duels significantly mitigate the pressure of lethal potentiality. This allows for individual survival and group continuity, while explaining the evolutionary trend of diversification and complexification of communication mechanisms. Talking (or singing) oneself out of potentially lethal aggression offers greater chances of survival.

The increasing complexity of hominid societies would have also led to the increasing complexity of restraint mechanisms. Thus, it could be argued that the basic forms of hominid singing protolanguages would have become more and more complex as selection pressures favored behaviors reducing human nonkilling potentiality while enhancing nonkilling propensity. This accounts not only for the emergence of complex natural human language but also for political institutions designed for the nonkilling resolution of conflicts and prevention of potential physical aggression, from incipient legal systems to contemporary international institutions.

This proposal has further implications, considering the blurred limits between singing and speaking. (See the "musilanguage model" proposed by Brown, 2000). Authors such as Tomasello (2008) have defended a continuity model for the emergence of complex human language that builds upon the study of animal communication. As identified by zoosemiotics, the main functions of communication, besides courtship and food-related signals, are directly related to mechanisms that prevent or minimize lethal aggression, such as display contents, recognition of boundaries, threat warning signals, and metacommunicative signals distinguishing play or mock aggression from serious engagements. On the other hand, displays themselves are mainly linked to disputes over food, territory, dominance, or sexual access to mates. This provides further grounds for many of the views expressed in this chapter (including those of Dissanayake, 2006) and provides a basis for new perspectives.

Acknowledgements

I am extremely grateful to Professor Douglas P. Fry for his kind invitation to participate in the "Aggression and Peacemaking in an Evolutionary Context" workshop, Lorentz Center, Leiden University, The Netherlands, and for his editorial comments. A first draft of this chapter served as the basis for a plenary speech delivered on the final day of the workshop. I thankfully acknowledge the kind comments and recommendations of other workshop participants, namely Professor Brian Ferguson and Professor Agustín Fuentes. For comments on a later draft I am indebted to Bruce Bonta, Robert K. Dentan, Charles Keil, and Olivier Urbain. I also acknowledge the precious references and ideas provided by Jimmy Mans, Celso Alvarez Cáccamo, José Luis do Pico Orjais, and Ramom Pinheiro Almuinha. The many shortcomings still present remain my own responsibility.

Notes

1. As a teen, I had been regularly involved in song dueling in my Galizan hometown of Rianxo. This was a relatively common activity during the local end-of-summer festivities, usually performed at dawn after nightly partying. The fond memories of this experience reemerged when, as an undergraduate student of Anthropology, I read Gluckman's *Politics, Law and Ritual in Tribal Society* (1965), where an account of the Inuit and Tiv song dueling performances was provided in terms of a conflict resolution social mechanism. The unexpected connection between Galizan and other forms of song duels was scribbled on the side of Gluckman's book and stayed there for years.

2. While *regueifa* is more common in Galiza's Western coastline (still alive in the Bergantinhos region), in the Eastern mountain ranges a similar form is called *loia* (Lisón Tolosana, 2004, pp. 28–30), *brinde* or *brindo* (Amigo González, 2005; Foxo Ribas, 2011). Other close forms are the *enchoiada* (song duel with men against women or with two men competing for one woman, using the *alalá* arrhythmic chant), *parrafeo* (usually memorized male vs. female duels; Vázquez Osorio, 1991), *desafío* (Lisón Tolosana, 2004, p. 43), the *atrancos* or *atranques* of the Ulha region (common in the *entroido* or carnival celebrations) and the *quites* of Terra de Caldelas (Álvarez Lombariñas, 2009, pp. 175–176).

3. Blanco (2009, pp. 16–17) believes that this semantic overlay is due to the exceptionality of the *regueifa* roll in the Galizan agriculturalist diet. The roll, which is only an aspect, would give its name to the whole ritual and to its other key elements. The term *regueifa* itself, having an Arabic origin, probably emerged at a much later date than the ritual that took its name.

4. If the *regueifa* was not offered to the community or if it was too small, this could lead to a boycott of the celebration, usually referred to as *cencerralada*, where the villagers would surround the house of the "transgressors," singing offensive songs and making loud noises with horns, pans, and irons until dawn (Suárez, 1982, p. 34).

5. Suárez (1982, pp. 13, 33) explains how in the twentieth century—especially after the 1936–1939 Civil War—the levels of social violence forced a shift in this practice so that the person carrying the *regueifa* (also called *levador*, meaning "taker" or "carrier") into the crowd was no longer the *madrinha* or bride but the strongest among the guests attending the wedding, accompanied by assistants that would escort him to prevent anyone from taking it from him. It would be this *levador* who would initiate the *regueifa* dance, inviting all to participate in the ritual.

6. The bride would hand over the *regueifa* to the winner, but he would only distribute it after the main dance was over, sometimes at dawn. After a night of dancing, at the sound of *gaitas* (bagpipes) and *pandeiretas* (tambourines), the roll was shared among the crowd, especially among young people—who were usually the main participants of song duels and were also more likely to make it to such hours—and the participants made sure no unmarried woman did not get her portion (Casal Vila, 2003, p. 60). Even though the *regueifa* would usually be considered over once the main dance started, in some places it would be

534   TAKING RESTRAINT AGAINST KILLING SERIOUSLY

common to interrupt the dancing from time to time allow new competitions over new issues to spring up (Suárez, 1982, p. 23).

7. An important issue Eckett and Newmark (1980) brought forward in their study of Inuit song duels is the actual success of this mechanism in reducing killings. Even though cooperation was indispensable for survival, there was, the authors describe, a relatively high level of physical aggression among the Inuit, including behaviors such as suicide, senilicide, homicide, and female infanticide. It is hard to determine if this was the dominant pattern in precontact times or if it is related to historical disruptions linked to more recent trade contacts. In fact, the decay of song duels among the Inuit has been directly related to the changing cultural environment, with larger settlements of individuals from diverse origins (Briggs, 2000 p. 113). The cases brought forward by Bowen (1989) and Yaqub (2007) also remind us of the need for caution when studying song duels in the context of disintegrating traditional cultures and the need for relating such practices and their mutations with their specific historical context.

8. Visit http://www.regueifa.org.

9. Solomon (2000) also noted how Huizinga (2002 [1949]) and Emsheimer (1956) had also explained the Eurasian dueling complex as an expression of an agonistic cultural ethos that would characterize nomadic peoples. Eating, drinking, but mainly spending excessively was—and to a great extent still is—an essential part of Galizan wedding feasts and other ceremonies in which song duels usually exercised a significant role: christenings, house inaugurations, completion of collective works, etc. (Risco, 1962, p. 564). Significantly, prohibitions and limitations on the degree of expenditure and number of guests allowed were established and enforced as early as the 1493. In many ways these rites of redistribution and reciprocity of wealth are reminiscent of other cultural practices such as those of the *potlatch*. Curiously, these "excesses" were condemned and prohibited by the Catholic Monarchs (Queen Isabella I of Castile and King Ferdinand II of Aragon) in their *Pragmática* issued in Barcelona on October 14, 1483 (González González, 1985, pp. 124–125), using very similar terms as those applied when the *potlatch* practices were prohibited in 1885 in Canada in an amendment of the 1880 *Indian Act*, also under the argument that it was an uncivilized wasteful practice. (See Cole, 1990.)

10. For example: "*aur ane wala kon hei ... aur bacane wala kon hei ...*," meaning "and who else is coming... and who else will save you ..." (Brenneis & Padarath, 1975, p. 286). This chorus is actually very similar to those performed in contemporary Galizan song duels: ("*e zumba-lhe ao boneco / e o boneco zumba / e zumba-lhe ao boneco / e o boneco zumba, zumba*" meaning "and beat the puppet / and the puppet beats back / and beat the puppet / and the puppet beats and beats.")

11. A similar phenomenon could be described among migrant Galizan communities in South America, where *regueifas* reinforced the reproduction of communities far away from home (Villar, 1998, p. 145, n. 11; p. 159).

12. Dissanayake (2006, p. 43–49) depicts six social functions of ritual music: display of resources, control and channelling of individual aggression, facilitation of courtship, establishment and maintenance of social identity, relief from anxiety and psychological pain, and promotion of group cooperation and prosperity.

13. The well-known *potlatch* festivals of the North American Northwest Coast Indians and the Melanesian yam and pig displays are good examples of ritualized restraint from physical aggression, where the influence, prestige, and political power of chiefs and "big men" were determined by means other than physical aggression, as described in the canonical works of Marcel Maus (*The Gift*) and Marshal Sahlins ("Poor Man, Rich Man, Big Man, Chief: Political types in Melanesia and Polynesia").

14. Mathias's (1976) work on Sardinian song duels is a good example. Considering the small-scale Sardinian village societies and the mistrust for governmental agents, mechanisms for social control stay mainly in the informal arena, emphasizing values and qualities stressed in the traditional code of behavior such as honor, virility, strength, honesty, truthfulness, hard work, intelligence, village-allegiance, and opposition to state and power agents and institutions (the *Padrone*, the *Carabiniere*, ...). *La Gara Poetica* becomes a restatement of pastoral social norms and ideas "accomplished through symbolic interaction, which inhibits eruption into open hostility" and contains aggression (the *Padrone*, the *Carabiniere*, p. 504). Beyond personal and village disputes, "*La Gara Poetica* provides a medium of expression through which the shepherd may rail against authority figures and against bad treatment and social injustice" (the *Padrone*, the *Carabiniere*, p. 502). Duels would take place rather spontaneously after work or in the village's celebrations and "will continue for as long as the two contestants are willing to sing and can think up arguments" (the *Padrone*, the *Carabiniere*, p. 492). Those who did not participate as duellers would be engaged in the chorus, in such

a form that "no member of the group is excluded from participating in the performance in some way" (the *Padrone*, the *Carabiniere*, p. 491).

15. Fortier (2002, p. 250) provides an interesting example: "For example, Gogane Raute, a decent negotiator, could not get Nandakali, a village woman, to fix a fair barter for her grain. In anger, she dashed his wooden bowl on the courtyard floor. Those of us watching were frightened by this outburst. Rather than react violently, however, Gogane simply said, '*manche herda ramro bydbahar herda camro*' (She appeared to be a good woman. But perhaps she's just a selfish woman). In his backhanded flattery, Gogane adroitly managed to be diplomatic, even when arguing with an angry farm woman. Nandakali had to smile and compose herself and the transaction of grain for woodenware eventually occurred."

References

Abrahams, R. D. (1962). Playing the Dozens. *Journal of American Folklore*, 75, 209–220.

Abrahams, R. D. (1968). Introductory remarks to a rhetorical theory of folklore. *Journal of American Folklore*, 81, 143–158.

Alonso Piñeiro, C. (2005). Improvisación oral en verso. *Revista das Letras*, November, 17, 4–5.

Álvarez Lobariñas, X. B. (2009). Breve aproximación ao feito cultural da regueifa. In X. A. Fidalgo Santamariña, X. M. Cid Fernández, M. Fernández Senra, & X. Fernández Senra, Xulio (Eds.), *Patrimonio Etnográfico Galego II* (pp. 173–177). Coruña: Deputación Provincial da Coruña.

Amigo González, A. (2005). Os brindos. *Galicia encantada*, 1. Retrieved October, 2010, from http://www.galiciaencantada.com/dentro.asp?c=34&id=525

Andrzejawski, B. W., & Galaal, Musa H. I. (1963). A Somali Poetic Combat. *Journal of African Languages*, 2 (1, 2, 3), 15–28; 93–100; 190–205.

Andrzejewski, B. W., & Lewis, I. M. (1964). *Somali poetry: An introduction*. Oxford: Clarendon Press.

Bertsozale Elkartea (n.d). *Argus: Oral improvisation in the world*. Donostia: Bertsozale Elkartea. Retrieved October, 2010, from http://www.argodat.com/english/index.htm

Aulestia, G. (1995). *Improvisational poetry from the Basque country*. Reno: University of Nevada Press.

Avery, T. L. (1984). *Structure and strategy in Azorean-Canadian song duels* (Unpublished Ph.D. dissertation). Bloomington: Indiana University.

Ayats, J. (2007). *Les chants traditionnels des Pays Catalans*. Tolouse: Centre Occitan des Musiques et Danses Traditionelles.

Barros, M. (2002). Regueifa, o hip-hop galego. *A Nosa Terra*, 1057(25), 33.

Basso, E. B. (1985). *A musical view of the universe: Kalapalo myth and ritual performances*. Philadelphia: University of Pennsylvania Press.

Bastide, R. (1959). *Sociologia do folclore brasileiro*. São Paulo: Anhambi.

Benzon, W. (2001). *Beethoven's anvil: Music in mind and cultures*. New York: Basic Books.

Blanchard, K. (1995). *The anthropology of sport: An introduction*. Westport: Greenwood.

Blanco, D. (2008). A literatura de transmisión oral. In E. Fernández Rei, & X. L. Regueira Fernández (Eds.), *Perspectivas sobre a oralidade* (pp. 95–118). Santiago de Compostela: Conselho da Cultura Galega.

Blanco, D. (2009). *A regueifa en Cabana de Bergantiños*. A Carvalha: Concello de Cabana de Bergantiños.

Bohannan, P. (1957). *Justice and judgement among the Tiv*. Oxford: Oxford University Press.

Bohannan, P. (Ed.). (1967). *Law and warfare: Studies in the anthropology of conflict*. Garden City: Natural History Press.

Boilès, C. L. (1978). *Man, magic and musical occasions*. Columbus: Collegiate Publishing.

Bowen, J. R. (1989). Poetic duels and political change in the Gayo Highlands of Sumatra. *American Anthropologist*, 91(1), 25–40.

Brenneis, D., & Padarath, R. (1975). "About those scoundrels I'll let everyone know": Challenge singing in a Fiji Indian community. *The Journal of American Folklore*, 88(349), 283–291.

Brenneis, D. (1978). Fighting words. *New Scientist*, 78(1101), 280–282.

Briggs, J. L. (2000). Conflict Management in a modern Inuit Community. In P. Schweitzer, M. Biesele, & R. K. Hitchcock (Eds.), *Hunters and gatherers in the modern world: Conflict, resistance, and self-determination* (pp. 111–124). Oxford: Berghahn Books.

Brown, S. (2000). The "Musilanguage" model of music evolution. In N. L. Wallin, B. Merker, & S. Brown (Ed.), *The origins of music* (pp. 271–300). Cambridge: MIT Press.

Calvo Gómez, F. (2007). *Recordos dun regueifeiro*. A Carvalha: Concello de Cabana de Bergantiños.

Câmara, J. M. B. da (1984). *Para a sociologia da música tradicional Açoriana*. Lisboa: Instituto de Cultura e Língua Portuguesa.

Campo Tejedor, A. del (2006). *Trovadores de repente: Una etnografía de la tradición burlesca en los improvisadores de la Alpujarra*. Salamanca: Centro de Cultura Tradicional Ángel Carril.

Carlin, E. B., & Boven, K. M. (2002). The native population. Migrations and identities. In E. Carlin, & J. Arends (Eds.), *Atlas of the languages of Suriname* (pp. 11–46). Leiden: KITLV Press.

Casal Vila, B. (Dir.). (2003). Regueifa. In *Gran enciclopédia Galega Silverio Cañada*, Vol. 38 (pp. 60–61). Lugo: El Progreso.

Casals Ibáñez, A. (2004). Etnicitat I cançó tradicional a l'escola (Unpublished master's thesis). Universitat Autònoma de Barcelona, Barcelona.

Casals Ibáñez, A. (2009). *La cançó amb text improvisat: Disseny i experimentació d'una proposta interdisciplinària per a Primària* (Unpublished Ph.D. dissertation). Universitat Autònoma de Barcelona, Barcelona.

Casals, A., Vilar, M., & Ayats, J. (2008). La investigación-acción colaborativa: reflexiones metodológicas a partir de su aplicación en un proyecto de música y lengua. *Revista Electrónica Complutense de Investigación en Educación Musical*, 5(4). Retrieved October, 2010, from http://www.ucm.es/info/reciem/v5n4.pdf

Castro, A. B. de (1983). *Cantigas ao desafio*. Porto: Edição do autor.

Caton, S. C. (1990). *"Peaks of Yemen I Summon": Poetry as cultural practice in a North Yemeni Tribe*. Berkeley: University of California.

Chodkiewicz, J.-L. (1982). Song contests in New Guinea. *Newsletter of the Association for Political and Legal Anthropology*, 6(1), 5–9.

Crook, L. (2005). *Brazilian music: Northeastern traditions and the heartbeat of a modern nation*, volume 1. Santa Barbara: ABC-CLIO.

Cullen, J. M. (1966). Reduction of ambiguity through ritualization. *Philosophical Transactions of the Royal Society of London*, 251(772), 363–374.

Daniels, T. P. (2005). *Building cultural nationalism in Malaysia: Identity, representation, and citizenship*. New York: Routledge.

Díaz-Pimienta, A. (1998). *Teoría de la improvisación: primeras páginas para el estudio del repentismo*. Oiartzun: Sendoa.

Dissanayake, E. (2006). Ritual and ritualization: Musical means of conveying and shaping emotion in humans and other animals. In S. Brown, & U. Volgsten (Ed.), *Music and manipulation: On the social uses and social control of music* (pp. 31–56). New York: Berghahn Books.

Dundes, A., Leach, J. W., & Özök, B. (1970). The strategy of Turkish boys' verbal dueling rhymes. *Journal of American Folklore*, 83, 325–349.

Eckert, P., & Newmark, R. (1980). Central Eskimo song duels: A contextual analysis of ritual ambiguity. *Ethnology*, 19(2), 191–211.

Edwards, W. F. (1979). Speech acts in Guyana: Communicating ritual and personal insults. *Journal of Black Studies*, 10(1), 20–39.

Ehrenreich, B. (2007). *Dancing in the streets: A history of collective joy*. New York: Metropolitan Books.

Eibl-Eibesfeldt, I. (1986). *Love and hate: The natural history of behavior patterns*. Munich: Aldine Transaction.

Elliott, L., & Read, M. (1998). *Common birds and their songs*. New York: Houghton Mifflin Harcourt.

Emsheimer, E. (1956). Singing contests in Central Asia. *Journal of the International Folk Music Council, 8*, 26–29.

Erdener, Y. (1995). *The song contests of Turkish minstrels: Improvised poetry sung to traditional music*. New York: Garland.

Erikson, E. H. (1966). Ontogeny of ritualization in man. *Philosophical Transactions of the Royal Society of London*, 251(772), 337–349.

Falls, J. B. (1978). Bird song and territorial behaviour. In L. Krames, P. Pliner, & T. Alloway (Ed.), *Aggression, dominance, and individual spacing* (pp. 61–89). London: Plenum Press.

Foley, J. M. (1991). *Traditional oral epic: The Odyssey, Beowulf, and the Serbo-Croatian Return Song*. Berkeley: University of California Press.

Foning, A. R. (1987). *Lepcha: My vanishing tribe*. New Delhi: Sterling Publishers.

Fortier, J. (2002). The Arts of Deception: Verbal Performances by the Rāute of Nepal. *The Journal of the Royal Anthropological Institute, 8*(2), 233–257.

Foxo Ribas, X. L. (2011). *Os últimos brindeiros de Forgas*. Madrid: Mundimusica.

Frank, R. M. (1989). Singing duels and social solidarity: The case of the Basque Charivari. In W. A. Douglass, (Ed.), *Essays in Basque social anthropology and history* (pp. 43–80). Reno: University of Nevada.

Fry, D. P. (2007). *Beyond war: The human potential for peace*. New York: Oxford University Press.

Fry, D. P., Schober, G., & Björkqvist, K. (2010). Nonkilling as an evolutionary adaptation. In J. Evans Pim (Ed.), *Nonkilling societies* (pp. 101–128). Honolulu: Center for Global Nonkilling.

Galtung, J. (1965). Institutionalized conflict resolution: A theoretical paradigm. *Journal of Peace Research, 2*(4), 348–397.

Garzia Garmendia, J.; Sarasúa, J., & Egaña, A. (2001). *The art of Bertsolaritza: Improvised Basque verse singing*. Donostia: Bertsozale Elkartea; Andoain: Bertsoari Liburuak. Retrieved October, 2010, from http://www.bertsozale.com/liburua/ingelesa/sarrera/sarrera1.htm

Geissmann, T. (2000). Gibbon songs and human music from an evolutionary perspective. In N. L. Wallin, B. Merker, & S. Brown (Ed.), *The origins of music* (pp. 103–124). Cambridge: MIT Press.

Ghosh, P. (2009). "Oldest musical instrument" found. *BBC News*, June, 25, 2009. Retrieved October, 2010, from http://news.bbc.co.uk/2/hi/8117915.stml

Giorgi, P. P., & Anati, E. (2004). Violence and its evidence in prehistoric art: A comparison of ideas. In E. Anati (Ed.), *Prehistoric and tribal art: New discoveries, interpretations and methods* (pp. 263–269). Capo di Ponte: Edizioni del Centro.

Giorgi, P. P. (2009). Nonkilling human biology. In J. Evans Pim (Ed.), *Toward a nonkilling paradigm* (pp. 95–122). Honolulu: Center for Global Nonkilling.

Glazer, M. (1976). On verbal dueling among Turkish boys. *The Journal of American Folklore, 89*(351), 87–89.

Gluckman, M. (1954). *Rituals of rebellion in South-East Africa*. Manchester: Manchester University Press.

Gluckman, M. (1963). *Order and rebellion in tribal Africa*. London: Cohen & West.

Gluckman, M. (2009 [1965]). *Politics, law and ritual in tribal society*. New Brunswick: Transaction Publishers.

González Muíño, J. (2008). *Regueifa dunha vida*. A Carvalha: Concello de Cabana de Bergantinhos.

Gossen, G. H. (1971). Chamula Genres of Verbal Behavior. *Journal of American Folklore, 84*, 145–67.

Gumperz, J. J. (1964). Religion and social communication in village north India. *Journal of Asian Studies, 23*, 89–97.

Gunderson, F. (2001). "Dancing with porcupines" to "Twirling a hoe": Musical labor transformed in Sukumaland, Tanzania. *Africa Today, 48*(4), 3–25.

Hart, D., & Sussman, R. W. (2008). *Man the hunted: Primates, predators, and human evolution*. Boulder: Westview Press.

Hartley, C. G. (1912). *The story of Santiago de Compostela*. New York: E. P. Dutton.

Haydar, A. (1989). The development of Lebanese Zajal: Genre, meter, and verbal duel. *Oral Tradition, 4*, 189–212.

Herndon, M., & McLeod, N. (1972). The use of nicknames as evaluators of personal competence in Malta. *Texas Working Papers in Sociolinguistics, 14*, p.xxx–p.yyy

Herzfeld, M. (1988). *The poetics of manhood: Contest and identity in a Cretan mountain village*. Princeton: Princeton University Press.

Hickman, W. C. (1979). More on Turkish boys' verbal dueling. *The Journal of American Folklore, 92*(365), 334–335.

Hill, S. (2000). Mchezo umelala [The dance has slept]: Competition, modernity, and economics in Umatengo, Tanzania. In F. Gunderson, & G. Barz (Ed.), *Mashindano! Competitive music performance in East Africa* (pp. 367–378). Dar es Salaam: Mkuki na nyota Publishers.

Hoebel, E. A. (1941). Law-ways of the primitive Eskimos. *Journal of Criminal Law and Criminology, 31*(6), 663–83.

Hoebel, E. A. (1954). *The law of primitive man: A study in comparative legal dynamics*. Cambridge: Harvard University Press.

Horak, G., & Horak, K. (1986). *Tiroler kinderleben in reim und spiel* (vol. 1). Innsbruck: Institut fur Tiroler Musikforschung.

Huizinga, J. (2002 [1949]). *Homo ludens*. London: Routledge.

Hulan, R. (2003). *Northern experience and the myths of Canadian culture*. Montreal: McGill-Queen's University Press.

Ingham, J. M. (1986). *Mary, Michael, and Lucifer: Folk Catholicism in Central Mexico*. Austin: University of Texas Press.

Jordania, J. (2006). *Who asked the first question? The origins of human choral singing, intelligence, language and speech*. Tbilisi: Logos.

Jordania, J. (2009). Times to fight and times to relax: Singing and humming at the beginning of Human evolutionary history. *Kadmos, 1*, 272–277

Keil, C. (1979). *Tiv song*. Chicago: University of Chicago Press.

Kroodsma, D. E. (1979). Vocal dueling among male marsh wrens: Evidence for ritualized expressions of dominance/subordinance. *The Auk, 96*(3), 506–515.

Kulick, D. (1993). Speaking as a woman: Structure and gender in domestic arguments in a New Guinea village. *Cultural Anthropology, 8*(4), 510–41.

Kunej, D., & Turk, I. (2001). New perspectives on the beginnings of music: Archeological and musicological analysis of a middle Paleolithic bone "Flute." In N. L. Wallin, B. Merker, & S. Brown (Eds.), *The origins of music* (pp. 235–268). Cambridge: MIT Press.

Labov, W. (1972). *Language in the inner city: Studies in Black English vernacular*. Philadelphia: University of Pennsylvania Press.

Laughlin, W. S. (1980). *Aleuts: Survivors of the Bering land bridge*. New York: Holt, Rinehart, and Winston.

Ledo Cabido, B. (Ed.). (2002). Regueifa. In *Enciclopedia Galega universal* (Vol. 14, p. 351). Vigo: Ir Indo.

Lefever, H. G. (1981). "Playing the dozens": A mechanism for social control. *Phylon, 42*(1), 73–85.

Lisón Tolosana, C. (1978). Verbal art in modern rural Galicia. In R. M. Dorson (Ed.), *Folklore in the modern world* (pp. 281–300). The Hague: Mouton.

Lisón Tolosana, C. (2004). *Perfiles simbólico-morales de la cultura gallega*. Madrid: Akal.

Lockwood, Y. R. (1983). *Text and context: Folksong in a Bosnian Muslim village*. Columbus: Slavica Publishers.

López Vinader, M. E. (2008). Music therapy: Healing, growth, creating a culture of peace. In O. Urbain (Ed.), *Music and conflict transformation: Harmonies and dissonances in geopolitics* (pp. 147–171). London: I. B. Tauris.

Lorenz, K. (1966). *On aggression*. New York: Bentam.

Luling, V. (1996). "The law then was not this law": Past and present in extemporized verse at a southern Somali festival. *African Languages and Cultures, 3*, 213–28.

Malloch, S., & Trevarthen, C. (Eds.). (2009). *Communicative musicality exploring the basis of human companionship*. Oxford: Oxford University Press.

Marler, P. (1970). Birdsong and speech development: Could there be parallels? *American Scientist, 58*, 669–673.

Mathias, E. (1976). La Gara Poetica: Sardinian shepherds' verbal dueling and the expression of male values in an agro-pastoral society. *Ethos, 4*(4), 483–507.

Mayer, P. (1951). The joking of "pals" in Gusii age-sets. *African Studies, 10*(1), 27–41.

McKenna, T. M. (1997). Appreciating Islam in the Muslim Philippines. In R. W. Hefner, & P. Horvatich (Eds.), *Islam in an era of nation-states: Politics and religious renewal in Muslim Southeast Asia* (pp. 43–74). Honolulu: University of Hawai'i Press.

McLeod, N., & Herndon, M. (1975). The Bormliza: Maltese folksong style and women. *Journal of American Folklore, 88*, 81–100.

McNeill, W. H. (1995). *Keeping together in time: Dance and drill in human history*. Cambridge: Harvard University Press.

Miller, G. (2000). Evolution of human music through sexual selection. In N. L. Wallin, B. Merker, & S. Brown (Eds.), *The origins of music* (pp. 389–410). Cambridge: MIT Press.

Mithren, S. (2005). *Singing Neanderthals: The origins of music, language, mind, and body*. London: Weidenfeld and Nicolson.

Numelin, R. (1950). *The beginnings of diplomacy: A sociological study of intertribal and international relations*. London: Oxford University Press.

Ojaide, T. (2001). Poetry, performance, and art: "Udje" dance songs of Nigeria's Urhobo people. *Research in African Literatures, 32*(2), 44–75.

Osella, C., & Osella, F. (1998). Friendship and flirting: Micro-politics in Kerala, South India. *Journal of the Royal Anthropological Institute, 4*(2), 189–206.

Pagliai, V. (2009). The art of dueling with words: Toward a new understanding of verbal duels across the world. *Oral Tradition, 24*(1), 61–88.

Pagliai, V. (2010). Conflict, cooperation, and facework in contrasto verbal duels. *Journal of Linguistic Anthropology, 20*(1), 87–100.

Pagliai, V., & Bocast, B. (2005). Singing gender: Contested discourses of womanhood in Tuscan-Italian verbal art. *Pragmatics Journal, 15*(4), 437–58.

Payne, K. (2000). The progressively changing songs of humpback whales: A window on the creative process in a wild animal. In N. L. Wallin, B. Merker, & S. Brown (Eds.), *The origins of music* (pp. 135–150). Cambridge: MIT Press.

Posada, C. (2003). La décima cantada en el Caribe y la fuerza de los procesos de identidad. *Revista de Literatura Populares, 3*(2), 141–154.

Prego Vázquez, G. (2000). *Prácticas discursivas, redes sociales e identidades en Bergantiños (Galicia): La interacción comunicativa en una situación de cambio sociolingüístico* (Unpublished doctoral dissertation). Universidade da Corunha, Crunha.

Price, R. & Price, S. (1991). *Two evenings in Saramaka*. Chicago: University of Chicago Press.

Rasmussen, K. (1976 [1929]). *Intellectual culture of the Copper Eskimos* (Vol. 9). New York: AMS Press.

Reinhard, U., & Pinto, T. de O. (1989). *Anger und Poeten mit der Laute: Tarkische Aqik und Ozan*. Berlin: Dietrich Reimer Verlag.

Risco, V. (1962). Etnografía. Cultura espiritual. In R. Otero Pedrayo (Ed.), *Historia de Galiza* (pp. 255–777). Buenos Aires: Editorial Nós.

Rivière, P. (1971). The political structure of the Trio Indians as manifested in a system of ceremonial dialogue. In T. O. Beideman (Ed.), *The translation of culture* (pp. 293–311). London: Tavistock.

Sbait, D. H. (1993). Debate in the improvised-sung poetry of the Palestinians. *Asian Folklore Studies, 52*(1), 93–117.

Schechner, R. (2003). *Performance theory* (Vol. 10). New York: Routledge.

Shack, W. A. (1974). *The Central Ethiopians Amhara, Tigrina and related peoples*. London: International African Institute.

Sherzer, J. (1987). Poetic structuring of Kuna discourse: The line. In J. Sherzer, & A. C. Woodbury (Eds.), *Native American discourse: Poetics and rhetoric* (pp. 103–139). Cambridge: Cambridge University Press.

Solomon, T. (1994). Coplas de Todos Santos in Cochabamba: Language, music, and performance in Bolivian Quechua song dueling. *The Journal of American Folklore, 107*(425), 378–414.

Solomon, T. (2000). Dueling landscapes: Singing places and identities in highland Bolivia. *Ethnomusicology, 44*(2), 257–280.

Steingass, F. J. (1882). *English-Arabic dictionary*. London: W. H. Allen.

Suárez, A. (1979). *Luaña: mitos, costumes e crencias dunha parroquia galega*. Vigo: Galaxia.

Suárez, A. (1982). *A regueifa*. Vigo: Edicións Castrelos.

Sugarman, J. C. (1988). Making *muabet*: The social basis of singing among Prespa Albanian men, *Selected Reports in Ethnomusicology, 7*, ppxxx–ppyyy.

Sussman, R. W. (2000). Piltdown man: The father of American field primatology. In S. C. Strum, & L. M. Fedigan (Eds.), *Primate encounters: Models of science, gender, and society* (pp. 85–103). Chicago: University of Chicago Press.

Sussman, R. W., & Marshack, J. L. (2010). Are humans inherently killers? *Global Nonkilling Working Papers, 1*, 7–28.

Taboada Chivite, X. (1972). *Etnografía Galega (Cultura Espiritual)*. Vigo: Galaxia.

Tarela, S. (2003). Da regueifa ó estilo libre: novas tendências musicais galegas que chegan "caghando duro." *Interea, 1*, 18–20.

Titiev, M. (1985 [1949]). Social singing among the Mapuche. In P. J. Lyon (Ed.), *Native South Americans: Ethnology of the least known continent* (pp. 208–220). Prospect Heights: Waveland Press.

Tomasello, M. (2008). *Origins of human communication*. Cambridge: MIT Press.

Topp-Fargion, J. (2000). "Hot kabisa!" The Mpasho phenomenon and Taarab in Zanzibar. In F. Gunderson, & G. Barz (Ed.), *Mashindano! Competitive music performance in East Africa* (pp. 39–53). Dar es Salaam: Mkuki na nyota Publishers.

Travassos, E. (2000). Ethics in the sung duels of North-Eastern Brazil: Collective memory and contemporary. *British Journal of Ethnomusicology, 9*(1), 61–94.

Turino, T. (1993). *Moving away from silence: Music of the Peruvian Altiplano and the experiment of urban migration*. Chicago: University of Chicago Press.

Urbain, O. (Ed.). (2008). *Music and conflict transformation: Harmonies and dissonances in geopolitics*. London: I. B. Tauris.

Urban, G. (1986). Ceremonial dialogues in South America. *American Anthropologist, 88*(2), 371–386.

Vázquez Osorio, J. M. (1991). Parrafeos e cantigas das terras de Bande. *Larouco, 1*, 209–211.

Villar, M. (1998). Xervasio Paz Lestón (1898–1977), un poeta galego na emigración arxentina. *Estudos migratorios, 5*, 139–176.

Wallin, N. L., Merker, B., & Brown, S. (Eds.). (2000). *The origins of music*. Cambridge: MIT Press.

Yaqub, N. G. (2007). *Pens, swords, and the springs of art: The oral poetry dueling of Palestinian weddings in Galilee*. Leiden: Brill.

Zubrow, E., Cross, I., & Cowan, F. (2001). Musical behaviour and the archaeology of the mind. *Archaeologia Polona, 39*, 111–126.

PART VI

Conclusions

27

Cooperation for Survival

Creating a Global Peace System

DOUGLAS P. FRY

The radio talk show host begins with a grand tour question.

INTERVIEWER: What is the main conclusion to draw from *War, Peace, and Human Nature*?

Fry: Well, there are several main conclusions and they interconnect with each other. If we consider war first, there is ample and definitive evidence that war is not ancient. First, archaeology shows this. Second, by analogy from existing nomadic forager societies, the ancestral type of nomadic band social organization simply is not conducive to warfare for a number of reasons. Third, and I must start with the caveat that data on humans is more relevant to understanding humans than are data from bonobos and chimpanzees, but, that said, clearly among our closest living primate relatives, we can see that one cousin, the chimpanzee, sometimes "wars" and that the other cousin, the bonobo, does not, preferring instead to eat, groom, and have sex. So the primate analogs in-and-of themselves simply cannot logically be used to peddle a view of human nature as either warlike of nonwarring. Humans are not bonobos and we are not chimps either. It is interesting that among three different closely related species of apes—if we count humans as honorary apes—that we see this variation in agonistic behavior. Finally, regarding warfare, this book goes back to the basics, back to "Evolutionary Principles 101" so to speak, by exploring the widespread restraint against killing that exists both in humans and other mammals: ethology, game theory, and cost/benefit analyses of fitness show the triumph of restraint as an overall biological principle in contrast to an often-heard assertion that humans have evolved a predisposition for killing. The grand conclusion, therefore, from archaeology, nomadic forager studies, primatology, and evolutionary theory, as applied afresh to aggression, is that in humans, war is recent, not ancient, and war is a capacity, not an evolved adaptation. In short, war was rare to nonexistent under the conditions in which our species evolved but obviously prevalent in more recent times that are dramatically different ecological and cultural circumstances.

Interviewer: OK, but what about peace? I don't think you've mentioned the word once so far.

Fry: You are absolutely right. And that is a typical bias among scholars, politicians, and in society generally—to pay much more attention to war than to peace. In my own defense, I was going to talk about peace next. One reason for this is that I think we take peace for granted as the default. War and violence shatter the expected calm and grab the headlines. The main message about peace that I glean from the chapters in this book is that it is the norm, the typical, the behavioral default. In my view, peace is not just an absence of war, but also people getting along prosocially with each other: the cooperation, sharing, and kindness that we see every day in any society. Peace is positive reciprocity: I show you a kindness and you do me a favor in return, multiplied throughout the social world a million times over. This book can be seen as reflecting a broader change in thinking that acknowledges the huge part that cooperation, kindness, fairness, conflict resolution, and peace have played over the course of evolution and continue to play on a daily basis in humans and other social species. For instance, in the evolutionary sciences, we are seeing the outbreak of a cooperation and conflict resolution "epidemic." Consider these recent book titles: *Nonkilling Psychology, Origins of Altruism and Cooperation, SuperCooperators, Wild Justice, Natural Conflict Resolution, The Age of Empathy, Beyond Revenge*, and my own books *The Human Potential for Peace* and *Keeping the Peace* [Aureli & de Waal, 2000; Bekoff & Pierce, 2009; de Waal, 2009; Evans Pim, 2012; Fry, 2006; Kemp & Fry, 2004; McCullough, 2008; Nowak, 2011; Sussman & Cloninger, 2011]. The traditional emphasis has been on the presumed naturalness of competition over cooperation, violence over conflict resolution, revenge over forgiveness, and, of course, war over peace. I think now we are seeing a dramatic shift away from "nature, red in tooth and claw," to quote Alfred Tennyson's famous line, to recognize also the importance of prosociality, social reciprocity, a sense of equity, and conflict resolution as reflected in "nature, read in truth and law." Lord Tennyson also has written, and this is a real quote, not a play on the famous poet's words: "The old order changeth, yielding place to new." Taken as a whole, *War, Peace, and Human Nature* presents a new view. The book challenges the "old order" that humanity is warlike by nature and contributes to the growing body of evidence and exposition that if we are talking about *by nature*, then the mounting evidence for humanity being peaceful *by nature* has much more going for it than the traditional Hobbesian view that has taken on the look in recent years of a dogma, not a science, resting on faith not fact. *War, Peace, and Human Nature* is filled with data that support a new view of a kinder, less violent, more prosocial human nature.

Interviewer: Many people will think this type of heretical talk is pure fantasy: Just look at all the violence in the world! What would you say to them?

Fry: Well, I could go in many directions. The first is to rely on data. Looking at the evidence, we see actual case studies within the book of some non-warring, non-feuding societies: Living without war is possible [see Kemp & Fry, 2004]. And several chapters absolutely demonstrate, beyond a shadow of a doubt, with archeological data, that warfare is not ancient. These are facts, not fantasies. My second thought is epistemological. We all "know" certain things, and I put "know" in quotes because such so-called knowledge is not based on objective data but instead is simply a set of beliefs we have taken on uncritically as part of growing up and living within a particular culture, whatever culture, including the subculture of academia. Stepping back to gain a little distance can help us see the phenomenon that I'm talking about. If we are La Paz Zapotec, we just "know" that a witch's spell can enter the body through the holes in a woman's pierced ears and cause sickness, and therefore it is very important to always wear earrings to "fill the holes." Everybody just knows that! It doesn't matter that proof is lacking [Fry, 2004]. If we are Batek, a nonwarring culture described in the book by Kirk Endicott [chapter 12], we "know," again in quotes, that Gobar, the god of thunder, sends wild fruit for people to eat but also can send fierce thunder storms to punish humans for misdeeds. My point is that much of what we ostensibly know, in any culture, stems from cultural beliefs that we just take for granted, not scientific facts. In Western civilization one such belief is that human beings are naturally warlike—and this belief seeps into academia too. Some people, as you implied in your question, won't quite know what to make of a book that challenges the beliefs about human nature they have heard their whole lives. So my first suggestion is to become aware of the powerful, largely unconscious grip that cultural beliefs about human nature, war, and peace hold on all of us, whether we are citizens, scientists, or scholars.

Here is a personal story. In 1996, I read a just-published chapter by my colleague Leslie Sponsel, who concluded that before the agricultural revolution the prehistoric world population was basically living in peace [Sponsel, 1996]. My first reaction: I thought Les Sponsel had really gone off the deep end! In reflecting with some sadness on the seeming mental collapse of Sponsel, I somehow got the thought over subsequent days: What if Les actually could be right? Once that heretical idea occurred to me, there was no turning back. I then asked myself: "How do you actually *know* that there has always been war?" My answer to myself was fluffy stuff like, "Well of course there has always been war," and "How could there not have been war?" and "Wars have raged over history, so why would it have been different in the Pleistocene?" Once I finally got around to looking at the evidence— and now some seventeen years later there is even more evidence in this book—I realized that I had just swallowed hook, line, and sinker, like Barak Obama in his Nobel prize acceptance speech, the presumption that "war . . . appeared with the first man." So, to wrap this answer up, my main advice to those whose first reaction is "this can't be true" is to go take a careful look at the facts. Look at the data. The evidence shows war is not ancient. Peaceful, nonwarring societies do exist. Most men must undergo extensive military training to kill in combat. In societies around the world, most disputes are resolved without any violence at all. So my suggestion is that rather than dismissing a new idea as nonsense, it is better to keep an open mind and to separate data and fact from assumptions and presumptions. Charles Darwin [1957/1887] pointed out in his autobiography that facts that don't fit are more easily dismissed and forgotten than pieces of evidence that reaffirm one's previous convictions. We all could learn from Darwin on this point. I think an open-minded reader will find the evidence presented in *War, Peace, and Human Nature* quite convincing that a new "take" on human nature is warranted. It is now time to upgrade our cerebral software about the nature of human nature.

Interviewer: I'm afraid we are nearly out of time. As a final question, do you have any ideas about how to bring about a more peaceful world?

Fry: The last chapter of *War, Peace, and Human Nature* presents some ideas about approaching peace and security within a new global cooperative paradigm. The central ideas are, first, to have *vision* that conflicts can be solved without war, second, to recognize the role of global *interdependence* as a key to promoting *global cooperation*, and third, to focus on creating multiple *identities* ranging from the local community to the global community. I like to play with the "Us versus Them" concept and say in this interdependent world of the twenty-first century that we need to "Expand the Us to include the Them." These ideas receive attention in the closing chapter of the book.

The Closing Chapter

The current world system is composed of nation-states, but it is important to recognize that nation-states are not very old. The birth of nations is generally attributed to 1648 and the Treaty of Westphalia. An implication of this observation is that there is nothing sacred about a world system based on nation-states; alternative systems of governance can be visualized. In this chapter, I will explore the possibilities of adding one or more levels of governance above that of the nation-state to facilitate peace and cooperative global problem solving. We will start with a consideration of how higher levels of governance can bring about peace among previously disparate or hostile social entities.

Stepping back from the current nation-state system and surveying the types of human societies that exist, we can note that some societies are politically acephalous whereas others are not (Reyna, 1994). Humanity has spent the overwhelming majority of its tenure on the planet living in nomadic forager bands that are noted for their lack of political leadership. The lack of authority and, to the contrary, the emphasis on egalitarianism and individual autonomy are consistent hallmarks of this original form of human socio-political organization (Boehm, 1999; Butovskaya, chapter 14; Endicott, chapter 12; Fry, 2006; Gardner, chapter 15; Narvaez, chapter 17). Likewise, tribal peoples lack much central leadership. But with the, archaeologically-speaking, recent rise of chiefdoms, within the last 12,000 years or so, humanity made a socio-political shift toward centralized leadership and authority (Fry, 2006). And with the subsequent development of the first ancient civilizations, a mere 5,000 to 6,000 years ago, we see the birth of the state as a new form of social organization. Chiefdoms, ancient civilizations, kingdoms, and modern nation-states have social hierarchies with rulers at the top who hold positions of authority and leadership (Reyna, 1994).

Two points are worth emphasizing. First, despite the fact that in the twenty-first century a global system of nation-states is taken as a fact of life, the first states, appearing in the form of ancient civilizations, are only several millennia old, whereas the modern version of the state, the nation-state, is only a few hundred years old. Second, politically-speaking, it has not always been this way and it does not always have to be this way. In other words, there is nothing inherently natural or normal about a global system based on nation-states. New forms of governance—for instance, with supranational layers—can be conceptualized as alternatives to the nation-state model. In fact, as we shall consider shortly, supranational governance already does coexist with nation-states in today's world.

An anthropological perspective, which surveys social systems over time and geographical distance, broadens the view. In this chapter, I will adopt this type of cross-cultural view of human societies and governance to see what lessons may be deduced about peace and security. One principle of central importance is that the unification of disparate social units reduces hostilities among them. This principle has been demonstrated repeatedly in human social development (Ferguson, 1984; Fry, 2006). Unification can be voluntary on the part of the constituent social units or it can be imposed, top down, from a central authority. Empires impose peace by outlawing fighting among the peoples they conquer, as illustrated by the Pax Romana and Pax Britannica.

Anthropologist Nadel (1947) provides a glimpse into the socio-political transition process from an acephalous to a cephalous form of governance for the Otoro Nuba of Africa. The Otoro Nuba engaged in feuding until one rising leader announced that no longer would this type of self-redress be allowed. Nadel (1947, p. 163) explains: "The first aims of the chieftainship which arose in Otoro were to eliminate this open test of strength between the component segments of the group. It attempted to establish a unity that would supersede the segmentary structure. It assumed the prerogative of using force as a means of maintaining internal peace. . . ." Disputes were henceforth to be handled in court with justice being dispensed by the chief and his administrators. In the new system, the self-redress violence of individual against individual, or of one kin group against another, was to be superseded by the chief's law as the people began to bring their grievances to court for resolution. This shift in Otto Nuba society reduced violence between individuals and among kin-groups, thus illustrating how the imposition of a higher authority over social units can reduce aggression among them. Basically, the Otoro Nuba underwent a shift from weak governance, which allowed violent self-redress, toward a more centralized form of governance, a chiefdom, which brought peace among the corporate groups in Otoro Nuba society.

A different example of the pacifying potential of higher-level socio-political authority, this time more democratic in nature, involves the formation of the Iroquois confederacy in fifteenth-century North America. The Iroquois confederation consisted initially of the Cayuga, Mohawk, Oneida, Onondaga, and Seneca and was subsequently expanded to include the Tuscarora. Dennis (1993, p. 77) writes: "Initiating new rituals and practices, and inventing new social and political institutions, the prophet Deganawidah and those who followed his teachings found ways to assure domestic concord, to extend the harmony within longhouses, lineages, and clans to wider domains, and to confront the ever-present threats to stability, reason, and peace." Through the development of their confederacy, these indigenous nations put an end to the feuding and warfare among them (Wallace, 1994). Peace and security were the driving objectives, with the remarkable result that the Iroquois created new levels of governance and social identity. Former enemies were transformed into relatives and neighbors "who found shelter, security, and strength under the branches of the Great Tree of Peace" (Dennis, 1993, p. 109).

Current-day international relations are similar to those of the Iroquoian peoples before they unified to create peace within their confederacy. Like the Iroquois, twenty-first century people do not feel secure on a planet that takes the waging of war for granted. The challenge of the peoples of Earth in the twenty-first century is remarkably similar to that faced by the Iroquoian peoples of the fifteenth century: how can the war and the threat of war be eliminated? How can a social system where bloodshed and mass destruction remain an ever-present danger be replaced by a social universe in which peace and security are not merely dreams for the future but become the new social and political realities of the present?

Anthropology provides an avenue for exploring these questions. Peace systems consisting of neighboring societies that do not make war on each other, and sometimes not with outsiders either, have been described in various parts of the globe. In addition to the Iroquois confederacy, ethnographic examples of peace systems include the tribes of the Upper Xingu River basin in Brazil, the societies of the Nilgiri Hills and Plateau in India, the indigenous peoples of Peninsular Malaysia, and the Western Desert Aborigines of Australia, and, as we shall soon see, the European Union, or EU (Fry, 2006, 2007, 2009, 2012; Miklikowska & Fry, 2010).

The ten tribes of the Upper Xingu River peace system, for instance, representing four different language groups, have converted divisive Us-Them perceptions of each other into a unified vision of their broader social system by "Expanding the Us" to a new level (Fry, 2006, 2009, 2012). These peoples still have their own tribal identities, but they also see their tribes as belonging to something greater. Shared rituals, frequent intermarriage, and trade partnerships that crisscross tribal lines reinforce the perception that each person, from whatever tribe, is also a member of a larger, peaceful social system. It is significant that the tribes specialize in the production of particular trade goods—such as pottery, hardwood bows, or salt—and this type of economic specialization creates multiple economic interdependencies among these tribes.

Likewise, the peoples of the vast Australian Western Desert region are interlinked by overlapping networks, which, like the groups comprising the Upper Xingu peace system, transcend local band membership and language dialect (Myers, 1986; Tonkinson, chapter 13). The Western Desert peoples view themselves as "one country," for they see the land as boundaryless, as reflected by the fact that they include all inhabitants of this region within the same kinship system (Myers, 1986; Tonkinson, 2004). As among the Xingu peace system, the inclusion of the Them within the Us, as members of one moral universe, prevents the development of the Us-Them mentality that can contribute to violence.

Some non-warring peace systems could be termed acephalous in the sense that they consist of neighboring groups who do not make war with each other but which lack a clearly formed overarching authority. The peoples of aboriginal Malaysia, referred to collectively as Orang Asli, illustrate such an acephalous peace system. In this case, a long tradition of nonviolence in belief and practice make the idea of engaging in warfare alien to peoples such as the Batek, Semai, Chewong, and Jahai (Endicott & Endicott, 2008; Endicott, chapter 12; Dentan, 2004, 2008). Howell (1988:150) notes that peaceful coexistence is an Orang Asli trademark: "None of these [societies] has any history of warfare, and overt acts of aggression are very rare." For instance, "the Jahai are known for their shyness toward outsiders, their non-violent, non-competitive attitude, and their strong focus on sharing. . . . In times of conflict, the Jahai withdraw rather than fight" (Sluys, 1999, pp. 307, 310). The peace system and nonviolence of these neighboring aboriginal societies is reflected not only in the lack of feuding and warfare of any type amongst them, but also in their lack of armed resistance even to slave raiding (Endicott, 1983, p. 238; Dentan, 2004). In short, the ethnographies on these indigenous cultures paint a consistent picture of their nonviolence. The second type of nonwarring peace system can be termed cephalous because such systems have developed unifying, identity-expanding, social and political institutions that promote and maintain the peace and security amongst the constituent social units. An excellent example of such a cephalous peace system is the Iroquois confederacy, mentioned earlier, because its formation included not only a shift in values toward peace, an elaboration of kin-relations to include members of other groups, and a creation of new inclusive rituals, ceremonies, and symbols to galvanize peaceful interaction, but also a new governing body that consisted of some fifty chiefs that met regularly as a newly created political entity. This League of Peace consisted of Leaders of Peace who shared a strong commitment to maintaining harmonious relationships within the confederacy (Dennis, 1993; Wallace, 1994). One concrete shift in Iroquois judicial philosophy was the forbearance of blood revenge in favor of the payment of compensation for any acts of violence that did occur. In this way, the Otoro Nuba and the Iroquois found the same overall principle: the law of force, as typified in blood vengeance, can be replaced by the force of law, as typified in the payment of compensation (Fry, 2006, 2007).

In the remainder of this chapter, we will consider some of the processes that appear to be important for the creation of security through peace systems. Topics of consideration will include the importance of having a visionary goal of peace, having an awareness of existing interdependence (and the deliberate augmentation of interdependence) to promote multilateral cooperation, and expanding the social identity to encompass all the members of the larger socio-political community.

The Importance of Vision

"Some people see things as they are and say *why?* I dream things that never were and say *why not?*" (Robert F. Kennedy paraphrasing from George Bernard Shaw's *Back to Methuselah*). Nobel Peace Prize Laureate Wangari Maathai (2010, p. 31) reflects on how inspiration to work for change can originate:

> Sometimes the inspiration to act arrives as a spark; sometimes it takes the form of a process. Whether one is drawn into an action through a sudden rush of inspiration, or through the slow dawning of a realization that something needs to change, I would argue that it all comes from the Source. But it's nonetheless essential to cultivate an attitude that allows you to take advantage of that awakening. This entails keeping your mind, eyes, and ears open, so that when an idea arrives you'll be ready for it.

The importance of developing an alternative vision is overlooked in many discussions of peace and security. A common assumption is that a dramatic social transformation away from war is not possible. Such an attitude easily becomes a self-fulfilling prophecy. The point of this section is rather simple, yet critically important: having a vision of a new socio-political system without war is the first step toward bringing change to a flawed existing system (Hand, 2010).

A widespread cultural belief that warfare stems ultimately from a warlike human nature contributes to the self-fulfilling prophecy that war is just "in the nature of the beast." A main message of this book is that such fatalism is simply wrong, and that in fact game theory, ethology, archaeology, nomadic forager studies, primatology, as well as lines of evidence in various other fields reveal a more hopeful assessment of human nature that balances the obvious capacity to make war with the potential to make peace (see Ferguson, chapter 11; Narvaez, chapter 17; Sussman, chapter 6). Similarly, Hand (2010, p. 46) points out "to argue that we cannot end war because we are the passive victims of culture, or that ending war is an impractical goal to embrace because doing so would take centuries, are simply not legitimate arguments." Instead, we need to begin with a vision that it could be done and work to achieve the goal.

Prior to the development of their peace system, the ancestral tribes of the Iroquois confederacy lived in constant fear of attack from each other. The evidence documents how they constructed elaborate stockades around their villages. Archaeological excavations near Elbridge, New York, for instance, show how early Onondagas had dug trenches and built a 15-foot high double or triple wall around their village (Dennis, 1993, p. 54). The

FIGURE 27.1 The Iroquois Great Tree of Peace as depicted on the flag of the Oneida Nation, one of the founding societies of the Iroquois Confederation. The Cayuga, Mohawk, Oneida, Onondaga, and Seneca (later joined by the Tuscarora) brought an end to the chronic feuding and war-making among them. They created a powerful symbol for peace in the Great Tree of Peace, under which, according to legend, they interred their war hatchets and war-clubs. An underground river then washed these weapons of war away, making them irretrievable, thus symbolically reinforcing the five nations' commitment to peace. The eagle of vigilance is shown, as are the white roots for peace, the latter symbolizing the Iroquois desire to spread peace to all the peoples of the world. The legendary prophet Deganawidah proclaimed, as the weapons of war were swept away, "We have rid the earth of these things of an Evil Mind.... Thus ... shall the Great Peace be established, and hostilities shall no longer be known between the Five Nations, but peace to the United People" (Wallace, 1994, p. 30).

development of a new social and political system, the confederacy, which also is sometimes called the Iroquois Great League of Peace, brought an end to the fear of endemic raiding. In the epic myths of the Iroquois, the visions and teaching of one man, Deganawidah the prophet, were critical in transforming a war system into a peace system. In the epic tale, Deganawidah and his followers created a Great Tree of Peace (as depicted on the flag of the Oneida Nation, shown in Figure 27.1), whose spreading roots symbolized how peace and law could eventually extend to all humanity. Dennis (1993, pp. 94–95) explains:

> Deganawidah and the chiefs then uprooted a great and lofty pine, exposed a chasm, and discarded their weapons of war. A swift current of water swept them away, they replanted the tree, and they proclaimed "Thus we bury all weapons of war out of sight, and establish the 'Great Peace.' Hostilities shall not be seen nor heard of any more among you, but 'Peace' shall be preserved among the Confederated Nations."

Deganawidah saw things the way they could be if neighboring peoples viewed each other as kinfolks, expanded their identity beyond the single village or tribe, and addressed conflicts through council meetings rather than through bloodshed. According to legend, Deganawidah spoke of a new way of thinking, a new mindset with peace at its core, changes that would abolish war and create the Iroquois Great League of Peace. The prophet also transferred his vision of peace to future generations who could continue to extend the peace system by ritually transforming enemies from outside the confederacy into kins-people.

Jean Monnet and the birth of the European Union provide another illustration of the importance of having a vision. Monnet was "A man of vision rather than a man of power." (Harryvan interview in Smith, 2011). Former German Chancellor Konrad Adenauer expressed that Monnet has been sent by God, because he provided the leaders with a visionary insight and a plan for how to avoid the next war in Europe (Harryvan interview in Smith, 2011). Part of Monnet's perception was to realize that the centuries of warfare in Europe—in his own lifetime World Wars I and II—fundamentally stemmed from a nation-state system, and therefore to abolish warfare in Europe, a new order with centralized, supranational institutions must be set up. Like Deganawidah, Monnet was a prophet with a clear image of how to create a lasting peace, and like Deganawidah, Monnet realized the need to unify different groups, not just formulate agreements and treaties among them. The key was to create a higher level of governance, a new common identity, and a new unity of purpose. EU Commissioner Jose Manuel Barroso (2006) recalls how President Kennedy once praised Monnet: "In just 20 years, Jean Monnet did more to unite Europe than a thousand years of conquerors. Monnet's vision transformed a whole continent and forged an entirely new form of political governance."

Interdependence

The EU also provides a modern-day example of how interdependence can purposefully be augmented as part of a deliberate plan to create a new level of governance. It is sometimes forgotten that a major impetus behind the multistage process of European integration was to eliminate the threat of war in the region (Bellier & Wilson, 2000, p. 15; Reid, 2004; Staab, 2008, p. 144). "Amid the misery and ruin left behind by the twentieth century's two lethal world wars, a group of Europeans set out to create a lasting peace on the continent and a shared economy. They did not aim low. Their dream was to produce, once and for all, an end to war on the continent, and an end to poverty" (Reid, 2004, p. 25).

In Zurich in 1946, Winston Churchill proposed that a pan-European peace could be forged through the creation of strong trade relations. He called for the creation of the United States of Europe (Elliott, 2005, p.20; Hill, 2010). The name did not stick, but a number of leaders such as French Foreign Minister Robert Schuman and Germany's Chancellor Konrad Adenauer adopted Churchill's and Monnet's dream of Europe as an interdependent union that would once and for all put an end to war (Reid, 2004; Smith

2011). In 1953, Monnet, in an interview on CBS television (in Smith, 2011), explained what he saw as the sentiment in Europe at the time:

> I don't think there is anyone in Europe, who has lived the last fifteen years, who at a certain moment has not realized that a great deal of the reason for the catastrophe we have experienced comes from the fact that those nations had been separated by national sovereignty; and they see in this effort of unifying the people a hope and an assurance that that is the greatest contributions to peace that can be made; and they see in it, at the same time, the creation of a big market and, therefore, prosperity *and* peace.

The approach these founding fathers took was to visualize and move toward a level of sovereignty above the level of the nation-state by increasing the interdependence among the national economies so as to make Europe progressively more and more economically integrated (Fry, 2009; Reid, 2004). They began in the early 1950s by placing coal and steel—critical resources in times of peace and war—under supranational control. This was the beginning of a series of cooperative steps toward unification that continues to this day (Staab, 2008). The architects of European integration envisioned that the augmentation of economic interdependence and unity would spill over into the social and political realms. Indeed, this is what has happened, and the significant outcome has been peace and security on the European continent. The EU is a deliberately created peace system. Reid (2004, p. 193) comments, "The EU, after all, is a cooperative community that has been an historic success at its main goals, preventing another war in Europe and giving European nations new stature on the world stage."

Using supranational institutions and the deliberate promotion of interdependence to create peace is a remarkable achievement. War between EU members has become unthinkable (Bertens, 1994; Hill, 2010; Smith, 2011). Bellier and Wilson (2000, p.16) point out that "In the EU, the emphasis has been put on the means to reduce political divergence between the nation-state governments in order to bring peace and tolerance." This shift in thinking represents a huge change from the first half of the twentieth century when World War I and World War II ravaged Europe.

Expanding the "Us": Creating Overarching Social and Political Identity

Charles Darwin (1998, pp.126–127) understood the process of social aggregation that I like to call "Expanding the Us to include the Them" when he reflected, "As man advances in civilization, and small tribes are united into larger communities, the simplest reason would tell each individual that he ought to extend his social instincts and sympathies to all the other members of the same nation, though personally unknown to him. This point being once reached, there is only an artificial barrier to prevent his sympathies extending to the men of all nations and races." The ten tribes of the Upper Xingu River basin, the Iroquois, the Aborigine bands of the Western Desert, and other such cases unequivocally demonstrate that clusters of neighboring societies can Expand the Us and get along peacefully as members of a larger peace system (Fry, 2009, 2012; Miklikowska & Fry, 2010).

Anthropological and psychological research suggests that there are many ways to Expand the Us to develop higher-level social identity. First, cross-cutting ties can be created among groups, for example, through exchange relationships, intermarriage, cross-group friendships, and participation in common rituals and ceremonies (Rubin, Pruitt, & Kin, 1994; M. Sherif, Harvey, White, Hood, & C. Sherif, 1961; Coleman & Deutsch, 2012). Members of each Xingu tribe form trade relationships with members of other groups, a practice that helps to Expand the Us identification across all the ten tribes (Gregor, 1990). The role that intermarriage can play in "Expanding the Us" is reflected as a Xingu man gestured, so as to mark from head-to-toe the midline of his body, and said, "This side . . . Mehinaku. That side is Waurá" (Gregor & Robarchek, 1996, p. 173). Second, working together on superordinate goals can contribute to a higher-level social identity (Sherif et al., 1961). Psychological studies demonstrate that engaging in cooperative activities among groups can enhance trust, friendship, positive relations, and a common identity (Aronson, Blaney, Sikes, & Snapp, 1978; Deutsch, 2006a, 2006b; Sherif et al., 1961). Some additional methods that may also facilitate Expanding the Us include empathy training, socialization for caring for people beyond one's own immediate group, and the teaching of nonviolent conflict resolution strategies (Deutsch, 2006a, 2006b; Miklikowska & Fry, 2010; Staub, 1996).

Returning to the EU, a new higher level European identity is gradually emerging, not to replace national identities, but rather as an additional level of social identity (Hill, 2010). Signs of the emerging European identity include the issuance of EU passports, the Euro as a common currency (now adopted by most member countries), EU car license plates, the opening of borders to the free movement of people, democratic elections for EU Parliamentarians, an EU flag, and so forth (Fry, 2009; Bellier & Wilson, 2000; Reid, 2004). In short, the continuing trend is toward the development of a new pan-European identity that parallels how the Western Dessert Aborigines, the Upper Xingu peoples, and the Iroquois developed an additional social identity as members of an overarching peaceful social system.

Conclusion

With by far the largest military on the planet, some US politicians still seem to think that safety and security can be achieved through the barrel of a gun. But such thinking does not take into consideration the current realities of global interdependence. Competitive military-based strategies are no longer effective in an interdependent world facing common challenges such as the urgent need to halt global warming (Fry, 2006, 2007). No nation on its own can successfully deal with the threat of climate change; international cooperation is mandatory in this "sink or swim together" world.

International cooperation is possible. One example that proves this point is the successful protection of the Earth's ozone layer. In the late 1980s, the countries of the world negotiated and implemented the Montreal Protocol on Substances that Deplete the Ozone Layer and subsequently have worked together to phase out ozone destructive chemicals such as CFCs worldwide (Ostrow, 1990; United Nations Environmental Program, 2000). Since the elimination of global CFCs and other ozone-depleting substances, the Earth's protective ozone layer has been mending. Through multilateral international cooperation among virtually all countries on the planet, "the world quickly, indeed almost painlessly, headed off a major man-made threat" (Sachs, 2008, p. 113). International cooperation, even at the global level, is possible. In a similar fashion, the peoples and nations of this interdependent planet now need to effectively address climate change and other common threats to human survival.

There will always be naysayers—those that ask the question "why?" instead of the more visionary "why not?" In the twenty-first century, humanity can naysay itself into oblivion or, alternatively, engage in visionary thinking followed by determined cooperative action. Why not actively create a global peace system and abolish war from the planet? After all, the people of the earth today face some of the same challenges that Europeans successfully addressed following World War II. First, the world's people, like the citizens of postwar Europe, face the challenge of how to create peace and prosperity. Additionally, the people of today must figure out how to solve shared challenges like global warming, oceanic pollution, and ecosystem degradation that threaten not merely some regions of the planet but endanger human survival overall. Can we glean some inspiration from visionaries like Deganawidah and Monnet?

The fact that people in different places and times have created and maintained non-warring peace systems proves that alternatives to the current-day war system are possible. Ethnographic examples of peace systems including the EU can stimulate our imagination and provide insight for how to create a global peace system. There are several take-home messages in this chapter. First, creating an overarching level of governance can contribute substantially to peace within the constituent social units. This principle is well-established (e.g., Dennis, 1993; Ferguson, 1984; Fry, 2006, 2007; Nadel, 1947; Smith, 2011). Second, there must be the vision followed by concrete steps to transform the inspiration into a new reality. Third, understanding that interdependence exists (and can be augmented further) is critically important. Interdependence can provide the rationale for why cooperation and new supranational institutions of governance are necessary to address common threats such as global warming and climate change. Safety and security in an interdependent world require joint action among all the parties. This principle of interdependence clearly applied in the creation of the EU and continues to maintain other peace systems as well (Fry, 2009, 2012; Fry, Bonta, & Baszarkiewicz, 2009). The concerted cooperative effort to save the Earth's common ozone layer via the Montreal Protocol also illustrates that an understanding of interdependence can lead to cooperation (Fry, 2006; Rubin, Pruitt, & Kim, 1994; Sherif et al., 1961). The success of the Montreal Protocol shows that the nations of the world are capable of working effectively together when they realize that their fates are interlinked and that it is in their common interests to cooperate. Finally, as we think about our social identities, we must Expand the Us to include a common identity of humanity as a whole. The Iroquois turned enemies into kin, created unifying rituals and ceremonies, and created myths and symbolism to reinforce the values of peace. They Expanded the Us. The EU seems headed in the same direction within Europe. It may take some time but adding one more level of social identity to include all human beings on a shared planet is both possible and necessary for the long term safety, security, and survival of the species as a whole.

Human survival requires that nation-states give up the institution of war and replace it with a cooperatively-functioning global peace system—for the well-being and security of all people everywhere. Constructing a peace system for the entire planet involves many synergistic elements, including the transformative vision that a new peace-based global system is possible, the creation of new effective political institutions at a supranational level, the understanding that interdependence and common challenges require cooperation, an expanded perception of social identity along the lines that Darwin (1998) envisioned, and finally, the development of values, symbolism, expressive culture, and ceremonies that reinforce peace (Fry, 2012). The Great Peace of the Iroquois illustrates how peace is an active process that must be created and re-created. Could a global peace system really be created? I suspect that the Xinganos, Iroquois, and founders of the EU would say "yes" for they have already created their own peace systems. German philosopher Arthur Schopenhauer (1788–1860) is credited with saying: "All truth passes through three stages. First, it is ridiculed. Second, it is violently opposed. Third, it is accepted as being self-evident."

References

Aronson, E., Blaney, N., Stephan, C., Sikes, J., & Snapp, M. (1978). *The jigsaw classroom*. Beverly Hills: Sage.

Aureli, F., & de Waal, F. (2000). *Natural conflict resolution*. Berkeley: University of California Press.

Barroso, J. M. (2006). Jean Monnet. Retrieved from http://www.time.com/time/magazine/article/0,9171, 1552584,00.html

Bekoff, M., & Pierce, J. (2009). *Wild justice: The moral lives of animals*. Chicago: University of Chicago Press.

Bellier, I., & Wilson, T (2000). Building, imagining, and experiencing Europe: Institutions and identities in the European Union. In I. Bellier & T. Wilson (Eds.), *An anthropology of the European Union* (pp. 1–27). Oxford: Berg.

Bertens, J.-W. (1994). The European movement: Dreams and realities. Paper presented at the seminar *The EC after 1992: The United States of Europe?* Maastricht, The Netherlands, January.

Boehm, C. (1999). *Hierarchy in the forest*. Cambridge: Harvard University Press.

Darwin, C. (1957). *The autobiography of Charles Darwin, 1809–1882*. New York: Norton. (Originally published in 1887).

Darwin, C. (1998). *The descent of man*. New York: Prometheus Books. (Originally published in 1871).

de Waal, F. (2009). *The age of empathy: Nature's lessons for a kinder society*. New York: Harmony Books.

Dennis, Matthew (1993). *Cultivating a landscape of peace*. Ithaca: Cornell University Press.

Dentan, R. K. (2004). Cautious, alert, polite, and elusive: Semai of Central Peninsular Malaysia. In G. Kemp and D.P. Fry (eds.) *Keeping the Peace: Conflict Resolution and Peaceful Societies around the World* (pp. 167–184). New York: Routledge.

Dentan, R. K. (2008). *Overwhelming terror: Love, fear, peace, and violence among Semai of Malaysia*. Lanham, MD: Rowman & Littlefield.

Deutsch, M. (2006a). Cooperation and competition. In M. Deutsch, P. Coleman, & E. Marcus (Eds.), *The handbook of conflict resolution* (pp.23–42). San Francisco: Jossey-Bass.

Deutsch, M. (2006b). Justice and conflict. In M. Deutsch, P. Coleman, & E. Marcus (Eds.), *The handbook of conflict resolution* (pp.43–68). San Francisco: Jossey-Bass.

Deutsch, M., & Coleman, P. (2012). Psychological components of sustainable peace: An introduction. In M. Deutsch & P. Coleman (Eds.), *The psychological components of sustainable peace* (pp. 1–14). New York: Springer.

Elliott, M (2005). The decline and fall of Rome. *Time*, European Edition. 165 (24) 20–21.

Endicott, K. M. (1983). The effects of slave raiding on the Aborigines of the Malay Peninsula. In Reid (Ed.), *Slavery, bondage and dependency in Southeast Asia* (pp. 216–245). New York: St. Martin's Press.

Endicott, K. M. & Endicott, K. L. (2008). *The headman was a woman: The gender egalitarian Batek of Malaysia*. Long Grove, IL: Waveland.

Evans Pim, J. (2012). *Nonkilling psychology*. Honolulu: Center for Global Nonkilling.

Ferguson, R. Brian (1984). Introduction: Studying war. In R. B. Ferguson (Ed.), *Warfare, culture, and environment* (pp. 1–81). Orlando: Academic Press.

Fry, D. P. (2004). *Multiple paths to peace: The "La Paz" Zapotec of Mexico*. In G. Kemp & D. P. Fry (Eds.), Keeping the peace: Conflict resolution and peaceful societies around the world (pp. 73–87). New York: Routledge.

Fry, D. P. (2006). *The human potential for peace: An anthropological challenge to assumptions about war and violence*. New York: Oxford University Press.

Fry, D. P. (2007). *Beyond war: The human potential for peace*. New York: Oxford University Press.

Fry, D. P. (2009). Anthropological insights for creating non-warring social systems. *Journal of aggression, conflict and peace research*, *1*(2), 4–15.

Fry, D. P. (2012). Life without war. *Science, 336*, 879–884

Fry, D. P., Bonta, B. D., & Baszarkiewicz, K. (2009). Learning from extant cultures of peace. In J. De Rivera (Ed.), *Handbook on building cultures of peace* (pp. 11–26). New York: Springer.

Gregor, T. (1990). Uneasy peace: Intertribal relations in Brazil's Upper Xingu. In J. Haas (Ed.), *The Anthropology of War* (pp. 105–124). Cambridge: Cambridge University Press.

Gregor, T. & Robarchek, C. A. (1996). Two paths to peace: Semai and Mehinaku onviolence. In T. Gregor (Ed.), *A natural history of peace* (pp. 159–188). Nashville: Vanderbilt University Press.

Hand, J. (2010). To abolish war. *Journal of Aggression, Conflict, and Peace Research, 2*, 44–56.

Hill, S. (2010). Europe's promise: Why the European way is the best hope in an insecure age. Berkeley: University of California Press.

Howell, S. (1988). From child to human: Chewong concepts of self. In G. Jahoda & I. M. Lewis (Eds.), *Acquiring culture: Cross cultural studies in child development* (pp. 147–168). London: Croom Helm.

Kemp, G., & Fry, D. P. (Eds.) (2004). *Keeping the peace: Conflict resolution and peaceful societies around the world*. New York: Routledge.

Kennedy, R. F. "Some people see things . . . ." Retrieved from http://en.wikiquote.org/wiki/Robert_F._Kennedy

Maathai, W. (2010). *Replenishing the earth: Spiritual values for healing ourselves and the world*. New York: Doubleday.

McCullough, M. E. (2008). *Beyond revenge: The evolution of the forgiveness instinct*. San Francisco: Jossey-Bass.

Miklikowska, M. & Fry, D. P. (2010). Values for peace. *Beliefs and Values, 2*, 124–137.

Myers, F. R. (1986). *Pintupi country, Pintupi self. Sentiment, place and politics among Western Desert Aborigines*. Berkeley: University of California Press.

Nadel, S. F. (1947). *The Nuba*. London: Oxford University Press.

Nowak, M. (2011). *SuperCooperators: Altruism, evolution, and why we need each other to succeed* (with R. Highfield). New York: Free Press.

Ostrow, M. (1990). *Race to save the planet: Now or never* (episode 10). Annenberg, PBS series.

Reid, T. R. (2004). *The United States of Europe: The new superpower and the end of American supremacy*. New York: Penguin.

Reyna, S.P. (1994). A mode of domination approach to organized violence. In S. P. Reyna & R. E. Downs (Eds.), *Studying war: Anthropological perspectives* (pp. 29–65). The Netherlands: Gordon & Breach.

Rubin, J., Pruitt, D., & Kim, S. (1994). *Social conflict: Escalation, stalemate, and settlement.* New York: McGraw-Hill.

Sachs, J. (2008). *Common wealth: Economics for a crowded planet.* New York: Penguin Press.

Sherif, M., Harvey, O., White, B., Hood, W., & Sherif, C. (1961). *Intergroup conflict and cooperation: The Robbers Cave experiment.* Norman: University of Oklahoma Press.

Sluys, C. M. I. van der (1999) Jahai. In R. B. Lee and R. Daly (Eds.), *The Cambridge encyclopedia of hunters and gatherers* (pp. 307–311). Cambridge: Cambridge University Press.

Smith, Donald C. (2011). *Jean Monnet: The father of Europe* [documentary film]. Retrieved from http://www.law. du.edu/index.php/jean-monnet-father-of-europe/documentary. Accessed August 28, 2011.

Sponsel, L. E. (1996). The natural history of peace: A positive view of human nature and its potential. In T. Gregor (Ed.), *A natural history of peace.* Nashville, TN: Vanderbilt University Press.

Staab, A. (2008). *The European Union explained: Institutions, actors, global impact.* Bloomington: Indiana University Press.

Staub, E. (1996). The psychological and cultural roots of group violence and creation of caring societies and peaceful group relations. In T. Gregor (Ed.), *A natural history of peace* (pp. 29–155). Nashville: Vanderbilt University Press.

Sussman, R. W., & Cloninger, C. R. (2011). *Origins of altruism and cooperation.* New York: Springer.

Tonkinson, B. (2004). Resolving conflict within the law: The Mardu Aborigines of Australia. In G. Kemp & D.P. Fry (Eds.), *Keeping the peace* (pp. 98–105). New York: Routledge.

United Nations Environmental Program (2000). *The Montreal Protocol on Substances that Deplete the Ozone Layer.* Retrieved from http://www.unep.org/ozone/pdfs/montreal-protocol2000.pdf. Retrieved from http://www. unep.org/themes/ozone/?page=home

Wallace, P. (1994). *White roots of peace; The Iroquois book of life.* Santa Fe, NM: Clear Light. (Originally published in 1946).

Index